W9-BVE-608

B 15186

B 1672

745

10,14

SOCIAL PSYCHOLOGY

SOCIAL PSYCHOLOGY

Roger Brown

NEW YORK *The Free Press*
LONDON *Collier-Macmillan Limited*

Copyright © 1965 by The Free Press, A Division of the Macmillan Company. *Printed in the United States of America.* All rights reserved. No part of this book may be reproduced or utilized in any form or by any means, electronic or mechanical, including photocopying, recording or by any information storage and retrieval system, without permission in writing from the Publisher. Collier-Macmillan Canada, Ltd., Toronto, Ontario. Library of Congress Catalog Card Number: 65–11321.

Seventh printing December 1967

This book is dedicated to the memory of my mother, *Muriel L. Brown* and of my father, *Frank H. Brown*

Preface

There are more topics discussed in this book than I have ever managed to include in a single semester of social psychology. At one time or another I have taught each one but never the lot in a single course. The chapters are independent enough so that an instructor can freely assign the ones he wants and omit the others. He can also put assigned chapters in a new order without causing the student serious difficulty.

I have had great pleasure from the writing of this book over the past three-and-one-half years; partly because I enjoyed the work but also because the Boston FM stations provided a sustaining flow of Bellini, Verdi, Puccini and Wagner. My first acknowledgment of help is to them.

Professors James L. Bruning and George R. Klare of Ohio University each read one-half of the manuscript and I am grateful for their encouragement and criticisms. I am grateful too to Mr. Robert Frager, a graduate student in social psychology at Harvard, who commented on the entire manuscript and checked the first collection of references. My colleague Professor Thomas Pettigrew very generously allowed me to read the galleys of his book *A Profile of the Negro American* (D. Van Nostrand, 1964). I have cited the book in many places and have benefited greatly from the use of its bibliography.

I want to thank Miss Ellen Anderson for typing some of the early chapters that were written when I was at M.I.T., Mrs. Elizabeth Burnham for helping later on at Harvard, and Miss Carmela Ciampa for doing the illustrations. My greatest debt is to my secretary, Miss Esther Sorocka, who has done a prodigious amount of skilled work on the manuscript and has been a real partner in its preparation.

R. B.

ACKNOWLEDGMENTS

Chapter 2

The Massachusetts Institute of Technology Press for permission to reproduce Figures 2-2 and 2-3 and to adapt certain text material from "The Pronouns of Power and Solidarity" by Roger Brown and Albert Gilman, which appeared in *Style in Language*, edited by Thomas Sebeok, in 1960.

Chapter 3

John Wiley & Sons, Inc., for permission to adapt Table 3-1 from *Elmtown's Youth* by August B. Hollingshead, published in 1949; to the National Opinion Research Center of the University of Chicago for permission to adapt Table 3-2 from the September 1, 1947, issue of *Opinion News;* to the International Sociological Association for permission to reprint Table 3-3 from *Transactions of the Second World Congress of Sociology*, Volume II, published in 1954.

Chapter 5

Basic Books, Inc., for permission to reproduce Figure 5-1 from *The Growth of Logical Thinking* by Bärbel Inhelder and Jean Piaget, published in 1958.

Chapter 6

The American Psychological Association and Alvin M. Liberman for permission to use Figure 6-2 from "The Role of Consonant-Vowel Transitions in the Perception of the Stop and Nasal Consonants" by Professor Liberman, P. C. De Lattre, F. S. Cooper, and L. J. Gerstman, which appeared in *Psychological Monographs: General and Applied*, Volume 68 (1954), Whole No. 379, and to reproduce Figure 6-3 and to adapt Figure 6-4 from "The Discrimination of Speech Sounds Within and Across Phoneme Boundaries" by Professor Liberman, Katherine S. Harris, H. S. Hoffman, and B. C. Griffith, which appeared in *Journal of Experimental Psychology*, 54 (1957), 358–368; to Johnson Reprint Corporation and Jean Berko Gleason for permission to reprint Figure 6-12 from Dr. Gleason's "The Child's Learning of English Morphology," which appeared in *Word*, 14 (1958), 150–177; to *Harvard Educational Review* for permission to reprint Figure 6-13, Tables 6-2, 6-3, 6-4, 6-5, 6-6, and 6-7, and certain text material from "Three Processes in the Child's Acquisition of Syntax" by Roger Brown and Ursula Bellugi, which appeared in the Spring, 1964, issue of that journal; to Dr. Gloria Cooper of the Center for Cognitive Studies of Harvard University for permission to use Table 6-1.

Chapter 7

The Journal Press for permission to reproduce Figure 7-2 from "The Attainment of Concepts: I. Terminology and Methodology" by Edna Heidbreder, which was published in *Journal of General Psychology*, 35 (1946), 173–189; to Holt, Rinehart & Winston, Inc., for permission to use Figure 7-3 from *An Introduction to Descriptive Linguistics* by H. A. Gleason, Jr., Revised Edition published in 1961; to Basic Books, Inc., and George G. Harrap & Co. Ltd for permission to use Table 7-1 from *How Children Learn To Speak* by M. M. Lewis, published in this country in 1959.

Chapter 8

The Hogarth Press Ltd for permission to reproduce portions from "Analysis of a Phobia in a Five-Year-Old Boy," which appears in the Standard Edition of Sigmund Freud's *Complete Psychological Works*, revised and edited by James Strachey; to Harper & Row, Publishers, Incorporated, for permission to quote from *Patterns of Child Rearing* by R. R. Sears, Eleanor E. Maccoby, and H. Levin, published in 1957; to William McCord for permission to quote from *Psychopathy and Delinquency* by Professor McCord and Joan McCord, published in 1956, reprinted by permission of Grune & Stratton, Inc.

Chapter 9

David C. McClelland for permission to reproduce with slight alterations Figure 9-1 from *The Achievement Motive* by Dr. McClelland, John W. Atkinson, Russell A.

Clark, and Edgar L. Lowell, published by Appleton-Century-Crofts in 1953; to D. Van Nostrand Company, Inc., for permission to reproduce Figure 9-2 and text material from J. W. Atkinson's *Motives in Fantasy, Action and Society*, copyright 1958 D. Van Nostrand Company, Inc., Princeton, N.J., and Figure 9-3, Tables 9-2, 9-3, and 9-4, and text based on David C. McClelland's *The Achieving Society*, copyright 1961, D. Van Nostrand Company, Inc., Princeton, N.J.

Chapter 10

Routledge & Kegan Paul Ltd for permission to reproduce Figure 10-1, slightly altered, from *The Psychology of Politics* by H. J. Eysenck, published in 1954; to The Free Press for permission to reproduce Table 10-3 from " 'The Authoritarian Personality'—A Methodological Critique" by H. H. Hyman and P. B. Sheatsley, which appeared in *Studies in the Scope and Method of "The Authoritarian Personality,"* edited by R. Christie and Marie Jahoda and published in 1954; to the American Psychological Association and Milton Rokeach for permission to reprint Table 10-4 from "Eysenck's Tender-Mindedness Dimension: A Critique" by Dr. Rokeach and C. Hanley, which appeared in *Psychological Bulletin*, 53 (1956), 169–82 to Harper & Row, Publishers, Incorporated, for permission to use text selections from *The Authoritarian Personality*, by T. W. Adorns, et al., Copyright 1950 by the American Jewish Committee, reprinted with the permission of Harper & Row, Publishers, Incorporated.

Chapter 11

Holt, Rinehart & Winston, Inc., for permission to reproduce Figures 11-1, 11-2, 11-3, 11-7, and 11-8 and to rework text material from my article "Models of Attitude Change," which appeared in *New Directions in Psychology* by Roger Brown, E. Galanter, E. Hess, and G. Mandler, published in 1962.

Chapter 12

The American Psychological Association and Solomon Asch for permission to reprint Table 12-1 from Professor Asch's paper "Forming Impressions of Personality," which appeared in *Journal of Abnormal and Social Psychology*, 41 (1946), 258–290.

Chapter 13

Addison-Wesley Publishing Company, Inc., and Robert F. Bales for permission to reproduce Figure 13-4 from Professor Bales's *Interaction Process Analysis*, published in 1950; and to *Behavioral Science* for permission to reproduce Tables 13-1 and 13-2 from "The General Inquirer: A Computer System for Content Analysis and Retrieval Based on the Sentence as a Unit of Information" by P. J. Stone, R. F. Bales, J. Z. Namenwirth, and D. M. Ogilvie, which appeared in that journal, 7 (1962), 484–498.

Contents

LIST OF TABLES

LIST OF FIGURES

Introduction

"Shall we clap into't roundly, without hawking or spitting or saying we are hoarse, which are the only prologues to a bad voice?"

As You Like It V. iii

In teaching social psychology I never begin by trying to define the field or describing course objectives but simply begin with the first topic. Preliminary statements of intention are so often belied by subsequent action that one prefers to let intention be discovered in what is done. However, now that the course is put down on paper I find that I have, after all, some hawking and spitting to do to explain why it takes the form it does.

Social psychology is not a system of psychology in the sense that psychoanalytic theory and reinforcement theory are such systems. Neither is social psychology a simple "extrapolation to the social level" of principles developed in general experimental psychology. Furthermore, while social psychology utilizes data and concepts from the social sciences, especially sociology, it cannot be considered a grand synthesis of psychological and sociological knowledge. Social psychology in 1964 is a set of topics that have exceeded the grasp of a non-social psychology but which are being effectively investigated by a psychology that draws upon the social sciences.

A rather authoritative list of the topics that constitute social psychology in 1964 can be made from the chapter headings used in the most recent edition of *Readings in Social Psychology* prepared by the Society for the Psychological Study of Social Issues (Maccoby, Newcomb, and Hartley, 1958). This is the list: 1. Language and Stereotypes; 2. Perception, Memory, and Motivation; 3. Perception of Persons; 4. Communication and Opinion Change; 5. Interpersonal Influence; 6. Reference Groups; 7. Behavior under Situational Stress; 8. The Socialization of the Child; 9. Social Stratification; 10. Role and Role Conflict; 11. Leadership; 12. Group Structure and Process; 13. Intergroup Tension, Prejudice. Where the *Readings* volume says "Opinion Change" some of us would say "Attitude Change"; where it says "Group Process" some would say "Group Dynamics"; and the book's "Behavior under Situational Stress" is in part "Crowd Behavior." I would add "The Social Behavior of Animals" to the list and someone also might add "Personality and Politics," but the list as it stands is a representative one and can reasonably be said to define the range of social psychology at the present time.

Can one abstract from the list of topics that are being successfully studied in a social-psychological manner the logical class of topics that should be studied in this manner and so identify the proper domain of social psychology and foresee its future development? I myself cannot find any single attribute or any combination of attributes that will clearly distinguish the topics of social psychology from topics that remain within general experimental psychology or sociology or anthropology or linguistics. Roughly speaking, of course, social psychology is concerned with the mental processes (or behavior) of persons insofar as these are determined by past or present interaction with other persons, but this *is* rough and it is not a definition that excludes very much.

The fact that the domain of social psychology cannot be sharply defined is no cause for embarrassment. Social psychology is a field of study, an historical development, not a theoretical construct. The boundaries of formal studies are seldom sharply defined. It is not perfectly clear by what principle one separates chemistry from physics and both of these from biology and the lot of them from bio-chemistry, bio-physics, and a multitude of others. It is also not perfectly clear what principles separate the study of literature from linguistics and both of these from the study of languages and the lot of them from psycholinguistics, ordinary-language analysis in philosophy and a multitude of others. Distinctions among fields that are not simply descriptions of a contemporary division of labor but which correspond to profound aspects of subject matter are probably nearer to being the last, than they are to being the first, achievement of formal study. Biology did not begin with a good definition of life nor linguistics with a good definition of language.

The topics of social psychology have had different starting points and have developed in comparative independence. The methods and concepts that figure in one research tradition are sometimes not utilized in any other. The theories that exist are, for the most part, miniature theories; theories for a certain problem or a small class of problems. The traditions are sending out shoots toward one another and a few have made contact but, for the most part, they remain independent.

This textbook has not integrated the traditions. The fourteen chapters of the book discuss fourteen research traditions and each chapter invokes the concepts and theories that have developed in the tradition discussed. The range is wide: it includes ecology and ethology, balance theory, role theory, Piagetian theory, psycholinguistics, psychoanalytic theory, learning theory, dissonance theory, and game theory. No attempt is made to "translate" these theories into a common language.

The chapters of the book are as independent of one another as are the research traditions they discuss—but not more so. Where real conceptual and theoretical ties exist they are utilized. The theory of cognitive balance, for example, is employed in four of the chapters: Chapter 2 which is on the dimensions of inter-personal relationship; Chapter 11 which is on attitude change; Chapter 12 on the perception of persons; and Chapter 13 on group dynamics. Some propositions concerning status and solidarity that are developed at length in Chapter 2 are also invoked in Chapters 1 and 3. And there are other partial integrations across chapters, but they are all partial.

Of course I do not consider that fourteen largely independent chapters make the best *Social Psychology* imaginable. A theoretically integrated book would be very much better, but since the discipline itself has not achieved integration the author of the textbook would have to achieve it. That was more than I could do.

It might have been possible to conceal the independence of our fourteen topics by the use of a "unifying" terminology. However it is not a service to social psychology to pretend that a trivial verbal integration is the same thing as a genuine theoretical integration. The translation of incommensurable concepts into a common language blurs the original meanings and loosens the intellectual connections within each tradition. It seemed better to maintain the integrity of the traditions and allow the discontinuities that exist to appear.

A *Social Psychology* relieved of the obligation to integrate its topics gains freedom to attempt other things. I take seriously the view that it is the purpose of short-term formal education to initiate lifelong informal education. A process of continuing education in social psychology seems more likely to result from participation in the process of creating social psychology than from simple acquaintance with its results. It is more fun and more worthwhile to learn to play the game than to learn to keep the score.

The game of social psychology begins with some sort of living inter-action and moves by abstraction to the creation of data and then concepts, from which it moves to the manipulation of conceptual systems, the generation of hypotheses and back to data again. In playing this game I think it is important to be concrete before one attempts to be abstract and so the reader of this book is sometimes asked to take the role of sub-ject and write a TAT story or to form an impression of a personality from a description of behavior. He is also sometimes asked to read data that others have produced: a group discussion of a problem involving financial risk; the conversations between five-year-old Hans and his father which served Freud as data for a psychoanalysis-in-absentia.

In order to stimulate participation a *Social Psychology* must describe some experiments in enough detail so that the reader can criticize them. Some lines of argument must be reproduced in enough detail so that the reader can think with the book and ahead of it. If a conceptual model is to be taken seriously the book must give the reader the opportunity to build facility in operating it and must provide enough examples from familiar experience to start a flow of personal insight. These are the uses this book makes of the space and time gained by giving up an attempt at overall integration.

The 14 chapters are grouped into five sections. The first section in-cludes only Chapter 1, "The Social Behavior of Animals," which provides a comparative baseline for the rest of the book. Part Two is called "Prob-lems of Psychology and Social Structure" and includes three chapters: Chapter 2, "The Basic Dimensions of Inter-Personal Relationship"; Chap-ter 3, "Social Stratification"; Chapter 4, "Roles and Stereotypes." Among the problems discussed in Part Two the following are included: Why is it that increases of intimacy between persons of unequal status are almost always initiated by the superior? Is social class in the United States a psy-chological reality for ordinary citizens? Does the distribution of innate temperaments justify the view that males are naturally more aggressive than females, or is this view simply an arbitrary feature of sex roles in our society?

Part Three is called "The Socialization of the Child" and it includes Chapters 5, 6, 7, and 8. The first of these chapters is called "The De-velopment of Intelligence." It is an exposition of the discoveries of Jean Piaget and the Genevan school of psychology. The major tension in the chapter derives from the question: Are the Genevan stages of development a universal biological sequence or do they describe an order of learning about physical and social reality which is usual in Europe and the United States?" Chapters 6 and 7 deal with "Language, The System and Its Acquisition." They describe the systems of phonology, grammar, and semantics and what is known of their acquisition by children. Chapter 8, "The Development of Morality," begins with an instructional exercise. The chapter offers for interpretation a dream and a symptom from Freud's famous case "A Phobia in a Five-Year-Old Boy" together with facts and conversations, extracted from the case report, that are directly relevant to the interpretation of the dream and symptom. The intention is to give the reader an opportunity to try his hand at clinical inference. Chapter 8 goes on to discuss Freud's theories of identification and of the development of the superego and to give an account of the experimental work these theories have inspired. Finally it adds a dimension of morality that Freud neglected, the intellectual dimension.

Part Four is called "Personality and Society," and it comprises two chapters: Chapter 9, "The Achievement Motive," and Chapter 10, "The Authoritarian Personality and the Structure of Attitudes." The studies of the Achievement Motive and the Authoritarian Personality have the range and significance we should hope to find more often in social psychology. Both stories start with the invention of a measure. The measures in question, the Achievement Motive scoring for TAT stories and the F-Scale of Anti-Democratic Trends, have been two of the most popular in social psychology and so there are substantial research traditions to describe.

Part Five is called "Social-Psychological Processes" and it includes four chapters: Chapter 11, "The Principle of Consistency in Attitude Change"; Chapter 12, "Impressions of Personality, Including One's Own"; Chapter 13, "Group Dynamics"; Chapter 14, "Collective Behavior and the Psychology of the Crowd." The consistency principle discussed at length in Chapter 11 and applied there to attitude change is applied in Chapter 12 to problems of impression formation and in Chapter 13 to problems in group conformity. The chapter on group dynamics is organized around a recent discovery that goes counter to popular belief and has proved difficult to explain: The decisions made by people in groups are riskier than the decisions the same people make when they are in isolation from one another. The chapter goes in quest of an explanation in the literatures on conformity, leadership, and group problem-solving. The final chapter on crowd psychology explores the possibility of describing crowd behavior in terms of the theory of games; it is distinctly speculative.

In the chinks between the large questions there are small ones which are more fun. "Why," for instance, "should contestants in the Miss America contest, which is, after all, a beauty contest, be expected to demonstrate some accomplishment, to recite something or cook something or sing something? What must a hen know in order to play her part in a pecking order? Why did the native African in French Africa find it galling to be addressed by the white man with the affectionate pronoun *tu?* Puzzling over these small problems helps to unlock the large ones.

Part One

A COMPARATIVE

BASELINE

*T*HE first chapter begins by asking why social systems exist in the animal world and goes on to ask what internal mechanisms govern the social behavior of the individual animal. In answering these questions we incidentally start many themes that are developed later in the book. It may be useful to list a few of them.

In Chapter 1 two ubiquitous patterns of animal social life are described, the patterns of territoriality and dominance. Chapter 2 deals with two ubiquitous patterns of human social life, solidarity and status. The parallels between the animal and human patterns are manifold. An animal species manifesting territoriality is divided into local groups which live intimately and cooperatively within themselves but are aggressive to intruders. Solidarity among humans similarly involves proximity and cooperation and usually an opposition to out-groups. When an animal group is organized into a dominance order each superior enjoys rights of precedence over his inferiors, precedence of access to food, mates, and space. Precedence is also a prerogative of high status humans. The parallels are impressive but, as we should expect, solidarity and status involve symbols, sentiments, and ideas that do not appear in connection with territoriality and dominance.

Chapter 1 inquires about the cognitive demands placed on individual animals by various kinds of social structure. A dominance order, for example, seems to require that each animal be able to recognize all of his inferiors and distinguish them from his superiors. Perhaps there are cognitive limits on the ability of a species to make such identifications which limit the size of a group that can be organized as a dominance order. In Chapter 3 a rather similar question is raised in connection with human social structure. Is it possible that human societies are organized as social classes rather than as finely graded status orders because half-a-dozen or so status identifications are as many as human cognition can manage?

There are other connections that I will only mention. The division of labor in animal groups on lines of sex and maturity is a primitive system of roles related to systems described in Chapter 4. Communication occurs in all species of animals that are social but communication, we shall see in Chapters 6 and 7, is not the same as the human technology that is called language. In connection with the study of imprinting among birds we first become acquainted with the idea that there are "critical periods" in development when certain kinds of learning can occur that cannot occur at a later age. Critical periods are invoked again in connection with Piaget's stages of intellectual development (Chapter 5) and in connection with the acquisition of language (Chapters 6 and 7) and in connection with Freud's theory of identification (Chapter 8). Some ethologists have found it necessary to posit the existence in animals of "action-specific energies" which "drive" social responses. The properties of behavior which lead to the postulation of drives in the animal case are, some of them, the same as the properties which lead us to postulate the existence of social motives in humans in Chapter 9. In these various ways Chapter 1 is introductory to all the other chapters.

The Social Behavior of Animals

Since we have even less sympathy with animals than with one another it is possible to impose experimental conditions on them that we are unwilling to impose on humans. Because we are a self-centered species and at present a powerful one (the smart money is on the insects for the longer run), these experimental studies are usually designed to illuminate problems of interest to humans rather than to the species doing the work. For example, man is extremely interested in the determinants of comparative individual intelligence but quite unwilling to submit to the experiments that would separate out the contributions of heredity and environment. So we have made use of rats and dogs and other enslaved creatures.

In one study learning ability was first tested in a large number of laboratory rats by compelling them to run mazes. Those who learned with fewer errors were mated together and the duller ones likewise. The next generation was also tested for learning ability and also selectively bred for intelligence. By the seventh generation or so there was little or no overlap in the scores of the bright and dull groups. It has been possible to produce rat strains with different amounts of hereditary learning ability, and so perhaps individual differences of intelligence in humans also are determined by heredity.

3

Another experiment equated heredity in two groups of animals by the "split-litter" method: half of the members of a litter received one kind of experimental treatment and half received another kind. Members of one group were reared in very restricted environments, each animal isolated in its own cage, the cage containing no objects and offering no opportunity to solve problems and the animal unable to see out. The members of the other group were reared in a much more stimulating environment, a sort of "amusement park for rats," Hebb (1958) has called it, with a variety of objects and barriers and pathways. The two groups were tested at maturity for problem-solving ability and the group that had grown up in the richer environment showed a lasting superiority. A similar study has been done with dogs with similar results and so it is possible that individual differences of intelligence in humans also are determined by environment.

The outcomes of these two sorts of study are not contradictory. In the experiment where heredity proved to be an important determinant of ability, environment was held constant; all the rats were brought up in identical cages. In the experiment where environment proved to be important, heredity was held constant by the "split-litter" method. Both factors are determinants of intelligence but either can be eliminated by experimental control. Of course it is possible that the results of such studies are true only for the species studied and not true for humans at all.

Studies using animals as subjects but directed at problems in human psychology do not constitute an intellectually unified topic. There is no point in bringing them together; it is better to describe each one in connection with the issue that inspired it. There are animal studies of another kind, however, that do make a unified topic. These are the studies of animal life in its natural state, of animal life outside the laboratory.

When studying a species living in its natural state we are often concerned with behavior peculiar to that species or to some few closely related species. When this is so the question is certain to be asked: "Why bother about behavior that is not produced by human beings?" The best answer is: "Because our intellectual life is not completely anthropocentric and nothing compels us to make it so." We do not have to answer to an appropriations committee in these matters. We can study animal social behavior because it is intrinsically interesting. There is always also the possibility that a genuinely comparative social psychology will give more insight into human nature than will a relentlessly anthropocentric approach to animal behavior (Beach, 1960). Man is an animal, though a distinctive one, and it is likely that the theories we make about the societies of other animals and the psychology of other animals will have implications for the human animal.

Students of animal behavior in its natural state are sometimes primarily concerned with explaining the form of a society or a social system and sometimes primarily concerned with explaining the social behavior of the individual animal. In this chapter we will consider first the problem of explaining animal society as such and secondly the problem of explaining the individual animal in society. Finally we will provide an example of the kind of animal study which, though it begins with behavior that is peculiar to certain lower species, becomes richly suggestive for the study of man. This is the section on imprinting and the critical period.

The Animal Society

Which animal species live socially and which do not? *Homo sapiens* certainly does and so too do the social insects—the termites, wasps, and honeybees. These species live as aggregated populations throughout their life cycles. Individuals within the population perform different functions and these functions are integrated in the interest of the general welfare. In short there is a coordinated division of labor. There are also systems of communication; complex ones for both humans and honeybees. Most animal species do not live as lifelong aggregations with a high degree of interdependence among individuals and a well-developed system of communication, and so most species are somewhat less social than man and the honeybee. However, most species come together at some point in their life cycle and interact in a structured way and so almost all species are, in some degree, social.

Social manifestations in the animal world are myriad. Apes and monkeys live in nomadic, food-gathering bands. Many birds on the seacoast roost in great colonies. Certain wasps, locusts, and butterflies gather each night into dense slumber aggregations and remain together until the morning sun warms the air. Even the larvae of the barnacle prefer to attach themselves where other barnacles are.

Each form of social life has evolved as a characteristic of a species and so presumably has brought some advantage to the species. This advantage has enabled the individuals or groups having it to leave more progeny than those not having it. The advantage has functioned as a selection pressure. Many kinds of advantage have been described. Consider, for example, the advantages of sexual reproduction. This form of reproduction involves a minimal sort of social interaction and it is nearly universal in the animal world. From the evolutionary point of view, sexual reproduction is a mechanism for promoting genetic variability since it reshuffles parental gene combinations. Adaptive forms are selected from genetic variations and so a high level of genetic variability will help a species to remain continuously adapted to its environment.

The advantages of social life make a long list. An integrated division of labor like that found among the social insects permits each type of individual to do what it is best equipped to do. Communication in the beehive permits one bee to learn from another where nectar is to be found. Emperor penguins, in extreme cold, form "huddles" of as many as five or six thousand individuals. In these circumstances, experiment has shown, the expenditure of fuel reserves, as measured by the daily loss in body weight, is only about half that sustained by solitary individuals (Prévost and Bourlière, 1957).

Many particular kinds of survival value have been attributed to the many forms of social life. In 1962, however, a more general theory was proposed. This theory holds that, while the various forms of social organization may have values peculiar to themselves, they all also serve as means to a single end. The author of this theory is V. C. Wynne-Edwards, Regius Professor of Natural History at the University of Aberdeen.

The Homeostatic Theory of Social Organization

Each animal species has certain vital requirements by way of food, shelter, temperature, and the like, which, taken together, define the potential habitat of the species. All of the potential habitat will meet minimal specifications but, within this habitat, the food supply of the species is certain to vary in abundance. General observation as well as controlled study suggest that each species tends to reproduce itself in numbers sufficient to fill up the habitat but not in such numbers as to overcrowd it. In addition it appears that each species tends to disperse its numbers in such a fashion that the population is denser where food is more abundant and less dense where food is less abundant. The survival of a species would seem to be heavily dependent on its ability to regulate population size and population dispersion in just these ways. The Wynne-Edwards theory holds that all of the elementary forms of social organization have evolved because they are means of attaining ideal numbers and dispersion.

The human species meets the problems of population with a mixture of mechanisms, some cultural and some biological, some deliberate and some not. The mechanisms include birth control and the prohibition of birth control, abortion and laws against abortion, immigration and immigration quotas, warfare, and whatever it is that sometimes causes the birthrate to rise after warfare. The mixture is not always adaptive and has more than once seemed to threaten catastrophe. Wynne-Edwards argues that animals other than man, the lemmings and sticklebacks and flour beetles and a million or so others, have evolved instinctive social processes for coping with the problems of population.

POPULATION ADJUSTMENT IN A CLOSED ENVIRONMENT

We will consider first an experimental population problem that is somewhat simplified by an imposed constraint. The animal population is living within a closed small area which means that movement or migration cannot be important for achieving optimal numbers and dispersion. Controls on reproduction and mortality are therefore highlighted. The experiment to be described was done with the flour beetle (*Tribolium confusum*) but comparable results have been obtained with guppies, rats and mice, and with the fruit fly *Drosophila*.

Chapman (1928) set up a number of *Tribolium* environments consisting of different quantities of whole-wheat flour. Each environment was maintained at a fixed level; that is, the flour was continually renewed so that there was no diminution of the food supply. In these environments *Tribolium* colonies were created, starting with varying numbers of pairs. The size of each population was then repeatedly ascertained; after fifteen days, after thirty days, and so on. By the time some six months had elapsed a very striking outcome was evident. In all the colonies, whether the environment consisted of four grams of flour or 128 grams and whether there had been one pair of founding beetles or thirty-two pairs, there had come to be an almost exactly identical ratio of beetles to food. There were, in all environments, about forty-four insects per gram of flour. This meant of course that the richer environments in which food was more abundant had larger populations and the poorer environments smaller populations. The experiment has been many times repeated and there can be no doubt of the reliability of the outcome in *Tribolium* and in some other species.

How do *Tribolium* and the other species that have been studied in this way regulate their numbers so as to fill up a fixed habitat and yet not overcrowd it? Filling up the habitat is not ordinarily a serious problem, since most species are able to reproduce themselves in numbers very greatly in excess of what a closed environment can support. The main problem is one of keeping numbers down. In the *Tribolium* colonies, as the number of beetles per gram of flour went up and began to threaten nutritional insufficiency, the adult beetles reduced fertility, laid fewer eggs, and in addition turned increasingly cannibalistic, eating the eggs and larvae that were produced. Guppies and mice and rats operate in a similar fashion.

While filling up the habitat is not ordinarily a difficult problem for an animal species one can make it a problem by experimental means. The experimenter can "crop" (or kill off) large percentages of each animal generation. When this has been done with *Tribolium*, with the sheep blowfly, guppies, and various other creatures, the animal populations have increased the number of eggs laid, the number of pregnancies, the size of the litters, or the number of young that survive. These adjustments all tend to make up the loss of life and to push the population upwards until it approaches a certain ratio of animals to volume of food, the same ratio that is more usually maintained by reducing fertility and increasing cannibalism. This food ratio seems to represent some kind of an optimum that the species strives, without insight, to maintain.

The automatic regulation of population size by adjustments of fertility and mortality reminds one of the regulation of room temperature by modern thermostatic devices. Suppose that the thermostat for a room is set for 70°. That setting then functions as an optimal value, a value to be maintained, comparable to the ratio of individuals-to-food characteristic of the animal species we have discussed. Whenever the temperature of the room falls below 70° the heat turns on and the temperature goes up, very much in the way that fertility rises when the animal population falls too low. When the thermometer once again reads 70° the heat clicks off. If it should rise above 70°, as it might on a summer's day, a refrigerating or air-conditioning mechanism turns on and restores the ideal state. Refrigeration here plays the role of fertility reduction (frigidity?) and cannibalism. Population size, we noted, usually needs to be limited rather than increased and thermostatic mechanisms too are ordinarily more active in one direction than the other. In the case of room temperature, of course, the direction depends on the season. In summertime we require chiefly to refrigerate and in winter chiefly to heat. The facts on animal reproduction and its control discussed by Wynne-Edwards suggest that in this sphere it is usually mid-August.

The thermostat belongs to the general class of mechanisms called "homeostatic." "Homeostasis" means "uniform state" and homeostatic mechanisms are mechanisms for attaining and preserving some such state. The thermostat is a manufactured device, but homeostatic mechanisms occur also in nature and are probably most familiar in the context of physiology (Cannon, 1932). The living cells of our bodies exist in an internal fluid environment that is fed and drained by the circulating blood. In order to sustain life certain steady states or ideal values must be maintained in this environment with regard to temperature, oxygen concentration, blood sugar, and so on. When the environment threatens to fall away from its steady state there are intricate internal processes that automatically operate to restore the ideal. It is Professor Wynne-Edwards' thesis that elementary social processes in animal life are also homeostatic mechanisms and that the state these mechanisms tend to maintain is one of ideal population size and dispersion.

Let us refer to the steady state of social homeostasis as a constant volume (K) of food per individual available in the individual's feeding or foraging area. The value of K is presumed to be characteristic of the species and we are further presuming that it is an optimum value. It should be advantageous for a species to have no less and no more than K food per individual. In these circumstances the habitat will be filled but not over-crowded. It is Wynne-Edwards' position that the elementary social proc-esses are so many means to this end.

The only social processes we have so far considered are cannibalism and fertility reduction. There are more complicated processes to be con-sidered, though scarcely more basic ones, when we lift the experimental constraint of a closed environment. However, even the simple case of *Tribolium* casts an interesting light on certain practices of human groups. There are many societies, for instance, which impose on women a tabu on sexual intercourse for some period of time following the birth of a child, sometimes as long as two years. There are societies, India has been one, in which unwanted children, usually females, have been left exposed to the elements to die. In Japan, a very densely populated country, abortion is legal, while in the less densely populated United States it is illegal. In France, during a period of declining population, and also for a time on the American frontier, the government paid bounties for babies. All of those cultural practices accomplish biological effects comparable to the effects *Tribolium* achieves, but while *Tribolium* may be assumed to operate without insight the human operates both with and without insight.

STARVATION AS A REGULATING MECHANISM

There is one fundamental problem that must be raised in connection with the Wynne-Edwards theory. Why should it be necessary to invoke social processes to account for the regulation of populations so as to main-tain a volume (K) of food per individual? Imagine a case in which there were too many beetles for the available flour. Why should not starvation eliminate the surplus, bringing the population down to the level where each individual has his quota K? In the *Tribolium* experiments, and in other cases, we know that it was not in fact starvation that controlled the density. Cannibalism and fertility reduction did the job before starvation could occur. But the question is why should these self-regulating tech-niques have evolved? Would not starvation work just as well? There are some reasons to think that it would not.

Suppose there were six Basques on a raft with only a small supply of food. If they were chiefly concerned to make sure that some Basques sur-vived, any Basques, so that the group might endure, how ought they to divide the food? An equal part to each person? But then all might die of starvation before a ship could come. If the essential thing were to keep the

Basque strain alive then it would probably be best to push four Basques off the raft and give all the food to a remaining male and female. Or even better—cannibalize the surplus four. Some such consideration may have figured as a selection pressure in evolution so that the flour beetles do not all eat too little flour when the supply is short but some eat all the flour and the surplus beetles besides. The chances that the group will survive are, consequently, optimal.

While I have never heard of a case in which six Basques were castaways on a raft I have heard of cases in which there was an inadequate supply of food for a number of creatures and an overriding concern that at least one should survive. In these circumstances human beings generally have enough insight to realize that equal sharing of the food is not the best strategy, but they usually shrink from *Tribolium's* "ultimate solution." In the expeditions to the South Pole of Scott and of Amundsen a small amount of food was carried by a few men and dogs and the goal was to get a human being to the Pole. Amundsen and his human companions, in the end, ate almost all of the sixty dogs that had pulled their sleigh. If they had continued to share their food with the dogs they would certainly not have attained the Pole. One member of Scott's group, suffering from frostbitten feet, perceived that if the group slowed its progress to the rate he could maintain, all must perish; but if he were to surrender his claim on food and allow them to speed up, there might be enough food for some to complete the journey. He bravely committed suicide. The instinctive adjustments of population accomplished by *Tribolium* are a very dramatic feature of the natural world, but the limitations on adjustment mechanisms that arise from humane feeling are also dramatic. In England, by the way, Amundsen's solution was considered rather contemptible; but then, it was Amundsen who first reached the Pole.

The food supply of an animal species is usually, unlike the flour on which *Tribolium* feeds, another animal species or a vegetable, some living thing. For this usual case Wynne-Edwards offers an interesting theory as to why starvation should not be the means of regulating numbers. The essence of the argument is that, by the time starvation began to reduce the numbers of the predator, the numbers of the food species would have been reduced to a dangerously low level. Dangerous for the survival of the food species and so ultimately for the predator. It appears to be the case that, some time before a species is exterminated, it may be "overcropped" or "overfished" to the point where its numbers will never recover and may even go on to extinction. Wynne-Edwards starts his argument with an example in which man figures as the predator, whose dispersion is to be explained, and the whale figures as prey.

In the early years of the nineteenth century the North Atlantic whaling industry reached a peak of prosperity. Vast numbers of men and quantities of capital flowed into whaling. In New England one sees the remnants of these days in the museums of Nantucket and New Bedford. Man the predator exploited his prey to the limit. The result was very severe overfishing. The number of whales drastically declined. The density of the prey became too low for whaling to be profitable and the North Atlantic industry fell into ruins. Even today, some fifty years since whaling ceased to be profitable, the stocks of northern "right whales" remain at very small fractions of their original levels. If man had been dependent on the whale as a major food source, in the way that many animal species are dependent on a small variety of foods, man would also have declined in numbers or perhaps become extinct. The turning point for the whale population, when their numbers became doomed to severe decline, seems to have been reached long before the whalemen themselves felt any serious hardship.

For the right whales there appears to have been a critical lower limit of numbers such that reduction below that value left the species incapable of returning to its earlier and much higher population level. There may be such levels for most or even all species. Silliman and Gutsell (1958) have experimentally demonstrated the existence of such a danger level for guppies. Uniform aquaria were stocked with the fishes and with more than enough food for all. The experimenter then acted as fisherman and "cropped" or killed some fixed percentage of the fish population in each aquarium every time a new generation appeared. Up to a point the fish responded to the cropping by increasing their rate of reproduction—as the homeostatic theory requires. When the predator experimenters fished at about the 60 per cent level or higher, however, the population in that aquarium fell off to total extinction. This did not occur because of food shortage and, of course, not all the guppies had been killed by the experimenters. Exactly why extinction occurs below a critical level is not known.

It is important to note that when the turn toward extinction occurred, only 60 per cent of the fish were being cropped and real fishermen need not have been threatened with starvation at that point. Experiments with the sheep blowfly (Nicholson, 1955) show that the critical level may be very much nearer to the level of actual extinction than it was for the guppies. But for some food species, at least, if the predator had to wait for starvation to regulate his own numbers he would be in danger of destroying his food supplies. And that may be the reason why natural selection has favored the evolution of self-regulating social mechanisms that are activated long before the ultimate regulator of starvation can come into play.

MORTAL COMBAT AS A REGULATING MECHANISM

There is another mechanism that one might think could serve to regulate dispersion that has not been favored by natural selection. If food is short why should not animals fight among themselves over the scant food available and so kill enough individuals to bring the numbers of the species down to the right level? A century ago, men in the North Pacific fur-seal fishing industry seemed to be on the verge of this kind of competitive combat. Things got so bad that vessels had to mount cannon to defend themselves. International incidents and bloodshed occurred, but further deterioration was averted by the North Pacific Sealing Convention of 1911, an international treaty establishing catch limits. Species other than man do not commonly battle over food among themselves but have, rather, evolved self-regulating mechanisms that accomplish results much like those achieved by the North Pacific treaty.

Combat to the death would be a poor mechanism for controlling numbers. To mention only one difficulty, the combat would be likely to leave many individuals maimed and therefore severely handicapped in the struggle for survival. *Tribolium* eats its young but there is no combat involved and so no damage to the survivors. Direct combat over food among conspecifics is rather uncommon in the animal world. Mechanisms have evolved for achieving dispersion short of the ultimate mechanisms of mortal combat or starvation.

POPULATION ADJUSTMENT IN OPEN ENVIRONMENT

It is not only the animal population in an experimentally restricted habitat that operates to maintain a volume, K, of food per individual. Consider the extreme case of the pelagic birds, creatures that live their lives on the open seas. These birds chiefly feed on plankton, freely floating, microscopic plant and animal life. On an oceanographic expedition, Jespersen (1924, 1930) had the opportunity to sample the densities of both bird and plankton life in many locations in the North Atlantic. The correlation between the two was + .85. In short, there was a high positive relation between the density of a predator and the density of its prey. Since Jespersen found more birds where there was more plankton and fewer where there was less, it follows that the supply of food per pelagic bird approached a constant value, K, across the North Atlantic. Where food is very plentiful each individual can find its "K-ration" in a small area and so the animals will be rather densely packed into this area. Where food is scarce each animal will require a large area to attain its volume, K, and so the animals will live farther apart.

How might animals in an open environment maintain a constant volume of food for each individual? In the degree that the animal groups or populations are stationary within a given region they must control fertility and mortality in the ways we have discussed. In the degree that they are mobile they can move or migrate from regions where food is scarce to regions where it is abundant. Movement is, of course, a more rapid adjustment than control of reproduction and one might have expected it alone to be sufficient when the species members are free to move. The evidence is that most species live in groups or populations that are geographically stable. The fundamental reason for this involves technical aspects of genetics and the theory of evolution. It seems to be the case that the ideal mode of life for maintaining a continuously good adaptation, including rapid evolution when adaptive change is necessary, is one in which a species is divided into a large number of moderate-sized local breeding groups, with some cross-breeding between adjacent groups. (See Simpson, 1949, for a discussion of this point.) Consequently, while migration plays some part in adjusting the distribution of many species it is not usually the only mechanism and it is not usually perfectly free migration.

Let us consider one example of adjustive migration. Starlings (and many other flying animals) have the custom, when they are not breeding, of coming together at night to make a communal roost of some building or group of trees. Starlings have been known to roost in numbers as high as half a million. Some of their roosts have been used by many successive generations; there is one in Dublin's Phoenix Park that seems to have been used since 1845. Trafalgar Square in London contains a starling roost. In Washington, D.C. there is a government building which is, each night, completely covered by noisy, bickering starlings.

Apparently the birds sharing a communal roost forage for food in the same limited territory near that roost. Wynne-Edwards suggests that the nightly convocation has evolved primarily as a mechanism by which the starlings can assess the density of their own species in the feeding territory. All day long the bird has an opportunity to determine the abundance of food in the area. Each bird continually receives, therefore, the two items of information that are required for judging whether there is K food per bird: the abundance of food and the number of birds. The food supply fluctuates, of course, and so does the bird population. When there is less than K food per bird, migration is likely to occur down to the ideal level of population. The theory is, in short, that the birds test for K (as the thermometer tests for 70°), and if K is not attained they migrate down to the level that will restore it. Wynne-Edwards argues that many kinds of animal communal display—not only in roosts but also in breeding colonies, spawning swarms, the evening rise to the surface of freshwater fish, and even the synchronized morning song of birds—have evolved because they function in tests of density.

Any test for density requires that animals be able to recognize their own conspecifics. It is therefore an implication of the theory that each species should be distinctive in some way that can be detected by the receptors of the species. It is consistent to find, for example, that animal groups containing many highly colored species—some of the insects, bony fishes, and birds—are known to have color vision. Specific signals that could function in density tests are spectacularly various. Visual recognition need not depend on distinctive coloring or marking but may depend upon some species-specific movement such as the "pronking" of the springbuck, a stiff-legged jump seven to twelve feet into the air. Species recognition may sometimes depend on auditory signals such as the songs of birds, the strident siren of the cicada, the howls of howler monkeys. Specific signals are sometimes undetectable by human senses. Certain aquatic vertebrates, eels, and some very long fishes, have a "lateral line sense" that is responsive to low frequency vibrations of water, vibrations too slow to be detected as sound by the human ear. The electric eel, which is capable of a discharge that will fell a horse, also produces weak discharges that may function in specific recognition and dispersion. In insects, smell is often the critical signal. And one fish, the European smelt, which is aptly but accidentally named, produces a curious odor variably described as reminiscent of cucumbers and of violets.

We have had the rudiments of the Wynne-Edwards theory; the author's own full treatment fills more than six hundred pages. Now we will see what the theory has to say about two well-established and extremely ubiquitous aspects of animal social behavior—territoriality and the dominance order. These are phenomena of peculiar interest to us because both are found in all of our nearest animal relatives—the anthropoid apes—and because both are found in all known primitive or preliterate human societies. Territoriality and dominance are closely related to solidarity and status, which are, I have argued in Chapter 2, the fundamental dimensions of social relationship.

TERRITORIALITY

With the onset of the breeding season for songbirds, early spring in New England, the male birds begin to contest for territories or parcels of land. The songbird territory is typically an all-purpose family area in which mating, nesting, and food-seeking occur. The male bird resists by threat or actual attack any intrusion into the area from other male birds. Wynne-Edwards and others believe that the chorus of birdsong at dawn is not primarily a hymn to spring nor primarily an invitation to mate, but functions chiefly as a warning from one male to another. It carries the message: "This piece of land is occupied and any invasion will be resisted." These are the facts of territoriality in songbirds. What do they mean?

There is some evidence, not a lot, that the average size of territories for a given species in a given year varies with the abundance of food in the region. Kluyver and Tinbergen (1953) found that titmice lived closer together in areas well supplied with food than in areas poorly supplied with food. The Alaskan pomarine jaeger is a bird that feeds chiefly on a small rodent called the lemming. The lemming population in this climate is extremely variable. In 1952, when there were only moderate numbers of lemmings in the region near Barrow, Alaska, the jaegers nested at a density of about four pairs per square mile. In 1953, a very good year for lemmings, the jaegers averaged eighteen pairs per square mile. The average jaeger territory was much larger when food was scarce than when it was plentiful (Pitelka, Tomich, and Treichel, 1955).

The facts above suggest that territoriality is a mechanism for dispersing birds in their habitat to provide some constant (K) ideal amount of food per family. The theory is strenghtened by the observation that while male birds do not ordinarily resist invasion of their territory by males of other species, they do attempt to bar birds of closely related species having similar food requirements. Dispersion can be accomplished by mechanisms other than territoriality but division of a feeding area into private family estates brings a peculiar advantage. The parent birds need not go very far from the nest in search of food and so the young birds need not be left unprotected for long.

Territoriality in songbirds is associated with breeding; outside of the breeding season many of these birds live in large flocks. The association with breeding suggests that territoriality functions in a second way to regulate the population. A territory is a license to breed and males who fail to establish a territory do not breed. There seems always to be a non-breeding surplus. In years and regions where food is scarce the territories that are established will be large. Therefore there will be fewer territories than in richer years and regions, and fewer territories mean a larger surplus of non-breeding birds. The result would be a lower rate of reproduction, and that is the correct homeostatic adjustment for keeping the volume of food optimal.

The individual land-holding of the songbirds is not the only form of territoriality. The major alternative among birds is colonial nesting in which great numbers of birds establish their nests in close proximity. Bird colonies sometimes cover small islands or great cliffs along the seashore. Colonial nesting is believed to be characteristic of all the hundreds of species of birds that draw their food from the sea during breeding season, but which nest on the land. The sea is unsuited to the establishment of individual property rights since boundaries cannot be marked. The birds that nest in a colony appear to share fishing rights in a single large territory of the sea, a kind of communal territory. The number and dispersion of colonial birds is controlled at the nesting site. If the density gets high no additional birds will be permitted to establish themselves.

There is territoriality of one sort or another among many insects, fishes, amphibia, and land mammals. You may have noticed the belligerence of dogs when their territories are invaded. The compulsive urination of male dogs is thought to be a technique of marking the territory, something like leaving one's hat on a restaurant table to show that it is taken. The anthropoid apes—baboons, chimpanzees, gorillas, and gibbons—are nomadic creatures who travel in bands feeding as they go (Nissen, 1951). However, they do not wander without limit, but stay within a fairly fixed territory. Some species fiercely resist invasion of their territory by conspecifics. This nomadic form of life is also characteristic of the simplest human societies, those that live by hunting and gathering food.

SOCIAL DOMINANCE

To the casual observer, life in a henyard seems to involve a great deal of random aggressive pecking (Schjelderup-Ebbe, 1935). The structured nature of this behavior is not detectable until one learns to recognize each individual hen. When that occurs, it turns out that not every hen pecks every other hen but, in fact, between any two birds there is one that pecks and one that is pecked. Each social dyad in the henyard shows an asymmetry with regard to pecking. There is reason to believe that this is an asymmetry of dominance-submission, since the peck is painful and the bird that does the pecking also looks fiercely at the other and may utter threat sounds while the "henpecked" one acts submissively or runs away.

When all the structured dyads in the henyard are considered together one discovers a dominance order defining, for each hen, those that may be pecked and those from whom pecks must be suffered. Sometimes this is a true rank order (like height or weight) in which relations are transitive; i.e., if hen A pecks hen B and B pecks C then A also will peck C. It sometimes happens, however, that intransitivities occur with C pecking A. In order to understand the occurrence of both transitivity and intransitivity we must consider the determinants of a hen's position in the pecking order.

If an experimental flock is created by putting together a collection of mutually unacquainted full-grown hens, the dominance relations in each dyad are established by threatening behavior or, if neither hen yields to threat, by combat. The relation once established will last the lifetime of the birds if they are continually together. When birds are separated for a long period the relation will have to be established by a new test of strength. In general, strength and aggressiveness seem to be the determinants of the outcome and, insofar as these are stable individual characteristics, dominance ought to work out as a transitive order. Intransitivity can arise, however, because strength and aggressiveness are not perfectly constant personal characteristics. Hen A can be ill on the occasion of its encounter with hen C and healthy and energetic on the occasion of its encounter with hen B. As a result A may forever peck B and submit to pecks from C though B pecks C.

A dominance order would seem to make greater cognitive demands on a species than does either a test for population density or the establishment of a territory. In order to test for density the individual animal must be able to distinguish its own species from all others. In order to defend a territory the individual must be able to distinguish a category within its species—adult males. But in order to know whether to bow or peck in every social encounter the individual must be able to recognize individuals, to know whether each is a superior or a subordinate. Probably there is some finite "memory for faces" in most species that limits the size of the population that can be structured into a dominance order.

Human beings in a group structured by social dominance, such as a military contingent, ordinarily learn the total order. Suppose, for example, that the individual is C and the total order is: A, B, C, D, E. Person C would, by observation of who salutes whom, learn the position of each one relative to each other one. He would know that in the dyad AB, A is dominant though he himself is not a member of this dyad. As far as I know, no one has determined whether animals in a dominance order have this kind of knowledge. The fact that an animal C knows whether to peck or yield in every pairing involving itself does not guarantee knowledge of relations in pairs not involving itself. The behavior that has been reported for animals in a dominance order would result if each animal only knew its own standing *vis-à-vis* each other animal and were totally ignorant of differences among its superiors and among its subordinates. There are certain advantages in being able to learn the total order. Person C could learn how to behave with everyone from A to Z by having direct encounters with only B and D and observing the others. From his relations with B and D and their relations with others, C can infer his relations with others. The poor hen seems to have to bluff it out or fight it out with every bird in the flock.

Pecking orders have been observed in many bird species, including sparrows, finches, canaries, wrens, larks storks, crows, jackdaws, parrots, cockatoos, woodpeckers, owls, ducks, and geese, as well as chickens. In all species the very young birds do not exercise dominance over one another. Dominance behavior matures at some age that is characteristic for the species and does not need to be learned from the example of older birds; it matures equally well and early in birds prevented from observing social pecking as in birds not so prevented. The younger birds are, from the first, subordinate to the full-grown birds and this relation is generally preserved into maturity, though there may be revolt against conspicuously enfeebled old birds. In a given brood those birds in whom social pecking matures early tend to establish dominance over more slowly maturing birds. Generally, then, position in the pecking order, like position in the status hierarchies of many human societies, is correlated with age.

In many bird species (e.g., the silver pheasant, turkey, and chicken), the males are uniformly dominant over the females, though in a few species (certain sparrows) the females are dominant. In some species dominance is not predictable from sex and in some species the dominance relation shifts from one sex to another at different stages of the life cycle. It has been suggested that the size of the two sexes may be the factor determining dominance. The tendency for the male to be dominant, though not always and not in all species, is again rather like the connection between sex and status across human societies. The male is likely to have more status, though this is not quite invariably true (Schjelderup-Ebbe, 1935).

Dominance orders are not restricted to birds; they occur in all classes of vertebrates (Hebb and Thompson, 1954; Hediger, 1955). Sometimes (e.g., goats) one does not discover a stable order for every two members of the animal society. For goats there are relatively stable groups at the top and bottom of the order, but there is a large middle group where relative positions shift a great deal (Blauvelt, in Schaffner, 1955). The notion of dominance order can be applied to relations between species (where it is called biological rank) as well as to relations between individuals of the same species (Hediger, 1955). Whenever species have overlapping geographic ranges and are sufficiently similar to be in competition, an order of dominance and submission is likely to prevail such that the one species gives way without battle if a question of food or space arises. Hediger (1955) suggests, for instance, that the grizzly bear has precedence over the black bear and leopard, and these latter two dominate the cheetah.

Hediger, in a book about the behavior of animals in zoos and circuses (1955), says that the trainer of such predatory animals as lions and tigers must establish himself as the chief animal, the head of the dominance hierarchy. In the beginning a harness is put on each cat and held by the cage boys, and the cat and trainer fight it out toe to toe. A successful trainer puts on an intimidating performance by charging at the animal in a frenzy, cracking his whip, brandishing a club, whooping and snarling. Once the dominance relation has been established with each animal, the business of putting them through their act is, for the rest of their lives, a fairly routine matter.

Lions, incidentally, perform very differently from tigers. In the wild, lions live and hunt in packs (called "prides"), whereas tigers are solitary except when mated. The two species have a strong antipathy and when they are combined in a circus act, murderous fights are possible. The tigers are likely to lose these battles. When a quarrel develops, the lions charge in a gang to aid their comrade and proceed from killing the original antagonist to finishing off the rest of the tigers one by one. But while the current tiger battles all the lions, the other tigers wait their turns, gazing disinterestedly up in the air.

We have had some of the facts about dominance in animals. It remains to ask what is the function of this elementary form of social organization.

Dominance in an animal population brings two kinds of privileges. 1) The dominant animal takes precedence over the subordinate one in feeding. Individual animals have been marked for identification and their behavior observed at some group feeding place. The subordinate stands aside for his superiors. In some species a subordinate will relinquish, to a superior, food that he already holds. 2) The dominant animal takes precedence over the subordinate in mating. In some species, for example the sage grouse, the top male does almost all of the mating (Scott, 1958). Dominance is also related to territoriality and we might have listed as a third privilege the holding of a territory. However, possession of a territory is chiefly a license to feed and mate and so this third privilege is not clearly an addition to the other two. Zuckerman (1932), writing of apes and monkeys, makes a statement that summarizes the implications of dominance for all animals. For any individual "the degree of its dominance determines how far its bodily appetites will be satisfied."

If an animal is to leave any progeny it must feed and mate so it would appear that the dominant members of any animal group have a superior opportunity to leave offspring. Dominance therefore looks like a mechanism of natural selection on the individual level. Whatever the personal characteristics may be that cause one sort of animal to be dominant, those characteristics should increase in the genetic stock of the population. This makes it look as if a species ought to evolve in the direction of greater size, strength, or ferocity since these are characteristics that seem likely to produce dominance. It may be so, or it may sometimes be so, but it is far from certain.

The major difficulty with the theory that dominance is a mechanism of individual selection is summarized in the following sentences by Wynne-Edwards (1962). "Attempts have in fact been made by a number of experimenters to try to show whether dominant individuals in fowls, pigeons, budgerigars, and canaries were larger, heavier, differed in any of their internal organs, or showed greater ability in learning mazes, than the average of their group. In so far as adults are concerned, each of these attempts has drawn blank" (p. 140).

The average contest for dominance between two males is not settled by serious combat in which strength and ferocity and weaponry would be critical. The victor is ordinarily the animal who puts on the more intimidating show. Males strut or roar or show their teeth or shake their antlers or wave their pincers. They make a display of their "warpaint"— plumes, crests, neck ruffs, manes, and the like. Snakes may wrestle but seldom use their venomous fangs; horned animals may have a pushing contest but seldom gore one another. Occasionally, of course, there is a real fight, but it is usually the bark that settles the contest for dominance rather than the bite.

How has it come about that the competitive struggles within a species are ordinarily settled on a symbolic or ritualistic level? It could happen that animals in their lifetimes are conditioned to yield before a ferocious display by having the experience of punishment following such a display. Conceivably, however, there is sometimes an innate tendency to yield before certain kinds of threat. The threat is ordinarily a movement that is a preliminary to a real attack, an exposure of weapons, or a symptom of anger. If these threatening signs have long been antecedents of attack, then any individuals who had an innate tendency to give way before the signs might have a superior opportunity to survive. That tendency would therefore become characteristic of the species. The difficulty with this argument is, of course, that any animal that gave way invariably would lose its opportunity to mate. It would be best to give way only when the other animal makes a more ferocious display than the first animal itself can make. This would happen when the other animal had better-developed weapons or a more aggressive nature, and it would happen when the other animal had superior aggressive makeup (like the lion's mane) because it was a more mature specimen. In such unequal pairings, the lesser member would do well to yield food, space, or mate without a battle since that battle would be likely to go against him. The animal would not yield when it was in competition with less ferocious individuals and so its turn to feed and mate would come. An innate tendency to yield to comparative or relative threat would be adaptive and may sometimes have evolved for that reason.

Wynne-Edwards believes that the dominance order is not primarily a mechanism of selection on the individual level but that it operates chiefly to insure group survival. The dominance order is, he suggests, a "social guillotine." Whenever food begins to be in short supply the tail end of the society is cut off and required to migrate or forego mating or even to starve. There is a kind of social contract to feed and mate and occupy space in a society from the top down, and so a shortage of resources does not lead to combat but to migration or to reduced fertility or increased mortality in a foreordained segment. This is a good arrangement, not primarily because it favors individual specimens that are larger or more ferocious, but rather because it is a *peaceful convention* guaranteeing that *some* members of the group will endure. In considerable measure, of course, dominance is determined by maturity rather than by relative adult size or ferocity and so could be considered a convention requiring that, when necessary, the younger generation leave home and seek its food elsewhere or postpone breeding for a season.

Let us return to the six Basques on a raft. We have argued that preservation of the Basque culture makes it important to give all the food to a single mating pair but we did not say how that pair should be chosen. Clearly they ought not to fight it out on a fragile raft in shark-infested seas. There should be an automatic convention causing four Basques cheerfully to jump into the sea once they have assessed the situation. The view that dominance orders are a mechanism of individual selection holds that this convention should leave the stronger, larger, more intelligent pair safely on the raft. Wynne-Edwards' position seems to me to hold that the individual qualities of the two that remain are not very important. What chiefly matters is that there should be a clear convention defining the cutoff point. Any sort of intimidating display would do. If two Basques are members of the nobility with "good" accents and fine ruffles and four Basques are commoners, the four may be counted on to see their duty.

The Individual Animal in Society

Concerning animal social systems, the question has now been asked: "Why are they organized as they are—in terms, for instance, of territoriality, dominance, migration, and fertility controls?" We have looked, for an answer, to the Wynne-Edwards theory of the evolution of social structure. The question to be asked next is: "Why does the individual animal in a social system behave as he does?" The kind of answer we have in mind is a statement about the internal mechanisms and energies of the individual creature which govern its behavior. Statements of this sort, we know, often take an *as if* form; the animal acts *as if* it had a hydraulic system inside governing its sexual behavior or *as if* it had two electronic memories inside, one for short-term storage and one for long-term storage. These are attempts to describe internal mechanisms in terms of models or analogues having certain abstract properties that must also be possessed by the real internal mechanisms, whatever the substantial nature of these real mechanisms may be. Models are not intended as a literal neurophysiology. Sometimes, however, statements can be made about individual behavior that are in the terms of serious neurophysiology. This is the case, for example, for statements concerning the role of hormones in the governing of sexual behavior (Beach, 1942).

Among students of animal behavior, those who call themselves ethologists (Lorenz, Tinbergen, Thorpe, Hinde, Hess, and others) have been much concerned with the theory of the internal mechanisms of the individual organism. Ethological studies are distinguished by this concern from many of the studies cited by Wynne-Edwards, which show more concern with theory on the level of populations or social systems. Both of these sorts of study are distinguished from much of experimental animal psychology, especially work on learning in rats, by their focus on the natural behavior of a species in its natural habitat. Indeed, the ethologists (e.g., Tinbergen, 1951; Hess, 1962) recommend that a complete description of the normal behaviors of a species throughout its life cycle be made before analytic experimental inquiries are begun into the *why* of any part of this behavior. A full description of this kind is called an "ethogram." The ethological school is further characterized by a strong interest in physiology and by an emphasis upon the importance of innate behavior. Most of the facts and ideas to be covered in this section of the chapter have been contributed by ethologists.

We can begin with something we already know about, the defense of a territory in springtime by a male songbird. Let it be the English robin (Lack, 1943). When another robin comes "bob-bob-bobbin' along" the first one will begin to "threaten" it. We know what such threats are good for—in terms of the spacing of families and survival of the species—but we do not know what makes the individual male robin respond as he does with a threatening posture.

A STIMULUS-RESPONSE MODEL

The threat response of the robin is an instance of what ethologists call an "innate fixed action pattern." A fixed action pattern is a response that is more complex than a muscular reflex; it involves numerous muscles and parts of the body. A fixed action pattern is not flexible in the way that purposive behavior is; the motor elements run off in a rigid mechanical order. The pattern is not the same as a chain reflex because it is "motivated" as the reflex is not; this is a distinction that is explained later on. Finally, the fixed action pattern is innate or inborn. That means, in the first place, that it can be obtained from all normal members of the species of appropriate age and sex; it means, furthermore, that members of the species do not learn the pattern from one another or from trial and error with the objects involved. Animals reared in isolation from their own species will produce the innate fixed action patterns of the species the first time they are presented with the objects or situations involved.

The nut-burying program of the squirrel is a fixed action pattern that has been shown by careful experiment to be innate (Eibl-Eibesfeldt, 1956). When squirrels raised in isolation from other squirrels and deprived of nuts and nut-like objects were first given a nut, they ran through a complete burying pattern—even on a bare floor. They made scratching efforts to dig, tamped the nuts with their noses as if to push them into the floor, and then made covering movements in the air. All of which left the nut exposed as before.

The threatening response of the male robin is an innate fixed action pattern and so it is presumably based on an inherited specific central nervous mechanism. What causes the response to be produced on a given occasion? A first-level answer obviously is—the sight of another male robin. In our discussion of territoriality we noted in passing that the social facts require us to assume that adult males of a species can be recognized as such. How is this recognition accomplished? On what does it depend? The question can be answered by experiments providing the robin with various kinds of dummy males approximating the real animal in some respects and not in others, to see which features of the real animal are critical for producing the fixed pattern. Lack (1943) has shown that the red breast does the trick. A mere bundle of red feathers will elicit threat whereas a complete mounted robin having all the characteristics of the adult male, excepting only the red breast, will not.

Ethologists call the particular feature of the environment that elicits a fixed action pattern a "sign stimulus" or "releaser." Let us have some other examples of sign stimuli. The three-spined stickleback, a fish that has been very thoroughly studied by Tinbergen (1951), defends a territory in breeding season even as the robin does and will attack an invader. An encroaching stickleback's threatening posture involves a kind of headstand in which he shows his belly to the holder of a territory. Tinbergen made a number of stickleback models, some of them so crude as to bear little resemblance to the stickleback or indeed to any sort of fish. However, if the latter sort of crude model had what could be regarded as a red belly, it was more likely to be attacked than a model exactly like a male stickleback except for this critical feature. The red belly seems to be the sign stimulus.

Of course, sign stimuli do not always involve the color red and fixed action patterns are not always aggressive postures or actions. Certain moths and wasps are stimulated to copulation by sexual odors emanating from females (Tinbergen, 1951). Brückner (1933) has shown that a domestic hen is stimulated to come to the rescue of a chick by its distress call. Sign stimuli also release responses that are not social. On Massachusetts beaches one can see gulls take a closed clam in their beaks, fly about ten yards into the air and drop it—which often serves to crack the clam. The sign stimulus for this reaction seems, simply, to be hardness in an object of a certain size. Tinbergen (1951) offered a gull a wooden pellet in the shape of an egg and the bird twice dropped it as if to crack it.

Red bellies, distress calls, and sexual odors are somewhat unrepresentative sign stimuli because they are absolute qualities rather than relations and sign stimuli seem usually to be relational. The nestling thrush responds to the return of a parent by widely gaping. This response, once the nestling's eyes are open, is directed toward the parent's head. What identifies the head? Tests with models showed that shape was not important but size was. When two knobs of unlike size were attached to a large circular model of the parent's body the thrush aimed at the larger of the two knobs. However, it was not the absolute size of this knob that released the nestling's response but its relation to the size of the model body. When the same two knobs were attached to a smaller body it was no longer the large knob that attracted the nestling but the smaller. The smaller knob had the same proportionate relation to the small body as the large head had to the larger body. The sign stimulus for the nestling's response is a head knob which stands in a certain relation of size to the body (Tinbergen and Kuenen, 1939).

Another sort of relational stimulus has been revealed for young ducks and geese (Lorenz, 1939; Krätzig, 1940). A properly shaped silhouette, involving wings and a short protuberance at one end and a long protuberance at the other, will release in these birds the same reactions as would a flying bird of prey. But the silhouette will only work if it is sent sailing overhead, short protuberance foremost. Flying in this way the short protuberance appears in the position of a head and the total has a hawk-like appearance. Sailed in the other direction it looks more like a goose or swan and the young birds are not frightened. The sign stimulus is not an absolute body shape but a shape moving in a certain direction in relation to the two protuberances.

The relational nature of some releasers is most dramatically revealed by the existence of "supernormal" releasers. Koehler and Zagarus (1937) found that egg recognition in the ringed plover depends upon contrast between darker spots and lighter background. In the normal egg the spots are a darker brown and the background a lighter brown, but since the effective factor is a relation of contrast it was possible to heighten this relation beyond the normal. The plover was offered a white egg with black spots, an egg quite outside the normal range, and the plover preferred this supernormal egg to the usual sort. There are also cases in which birds have preferred abnormally large eggs, even eggs too large for them to sit on. It is probable that a species evolves responsiveness to a relational re-leaser, like the contrasting spots and ground of the plover's egg, because that relation serves unequivocally to distinguish the proper object from similar objects ordinarily encountered. It seems conceivable that the animal has evolved responsiveness to the relation in general rather than just to the range ordinarily encountered, and so when something outside the ordinary range, but in the preferred direction, is presented, it elicits the response.

The critical features of objects which release fixed action patterns are such that the action is usually appropriate. The red belly of the stickleback and the breast of the robin are peculiar to mature members of these spe-cies, to the male in case of the stickleback. The distress call that summons the mother hen is produced only by chicks in distress. The odor that at-tracts the male moth ordinarily comes from a receptive female moth. If the usual sort of environment is changed a bit a kind of rigidity, a sort of stupidity, is exposed as in the stickleback who attacks a painted decoy and the bird that tries to sit on an egg as large as itself. If a chick is put under a glass dome, such that it can be seen struggling but cannot be heard calling, the mother hen will remain indifferent to its distress. Wasps and moths will not only attempt to copulate with odor-producing females, but also with a piece of paper on which such a female has been squashed.

Lovemaking in humans, the rescuing of children, and the threatening of enemies are largely learned patterns not released by a few specific stimuli but by a large and expandable variety of signs. A human mother would go to the rescue of her child if she heard it call, noticed it in any sort of danger, or saw it manifest any of a great variety of expressions of distress, or if she missed the child at some appointed time or was told that the child was in trouble or read a note to that effect. In this case reaction is made to any of a large array of stimuli and the reaction is such as to be appropriate to some object or situation of which all these stimuli are signs. Under these circumstances we think of the reaction as governed by the situation "child in distress" rather than by any particular stimulus. The mother hen on the other hand does not seem to be governed by "chick in distress" but rather by certain sounds. The ethologists' term "sign stimu-lus" is actually rather misleading, because insofar as a specific stimulus rigidly "releases" an action pattern, there is no reason to suppose that the stimulus is functioning as a sign of anything. It is when many stimuli, which are related to the same object, have an equivalent potentiality for releasing behavior appropriate to that object that the stimuli may be said to function as signs.

We are ready for one of those *as if* statements about individual animal behavior. Animals act *as if* for each innate fixed reaction pattern there were a kind of lock inside the nervous system and the "sign stimulus" were the key to that lock. The lock is fitted to an appropriate and usually available key so that the response is an adaptive one. Or, to put it another way, although fixed action patterns are more complex than muscle reflexes and releasers more complex than the units of energy that stimulate reflexes, there does not seem to be a difference in mode of operation. The response is produced by a stimulus; given stimulus A, we must expect response B. Since much of animal social behavior involves fixed action patterns, especially reproductive behavior, territoriality, fighting, and migration, it seems that the theory of social behavior on the individual level for which we are searching is simply: lock and key; first A, then B.

A STIMULUS-RESPONSE-AND-DRIVE MODEL

There are additional facts about sign stimuli and fixed action patterns that have been held back until now so that we might see how conceptions of internal mechanism are shaped by facts about behavior. The stimulus-response model is not the model ethologists have constructed for instinctive behavior. The model they favor takes account of some further observations.

Fixed action patterns are not always, perhaps not even usually, responsive to only one sign stimulus. Let us go back to the fighting of the male stickleback. In the experiments with dummies which established the red belly as a sign stimulus, all the dummies were presented in the same position and so the experiments were not designed to uncover any possible effects of position. The real encroaching male takes up a kind of vertical headstand in exposing his red belly to the holder of a territory. In further experiments with dummies Tinbergen (1951) showed that a model in vertical posture evoked much more vigorous attack than did a red-bellied model in horizontal position. In short, the fighting response of the stickleback is not only released by a red belly, but also by a certain aggressive posture. There are two sign stimuli and they are more effective as a combination than in isolation.

Most fixed action patterns seem to be responsive to more than one sign stimulus and the number of sign stimuli can be greater than two. Seitz (1940) has studied the fighting response of a male cichlid fish. He found that the following sign stimuli were somewhat effective: 1) silvery blue-ness; 2) dark margin; 3) highness and broadness produced by means of fin erection; 4) parallel orientation to the opponent; 5) tail beating. All five are combined in an actual intruding male.

The revelation that there are likely to be multiple sign stimuli may seem to disprove our recent claim that human acquired responses differ from instinctive responses in terms of the number of stimuli that function as signs. Actually the new facts require us only to modify the claim. The difference is not absolute but a matter of degree. Innate fixed action patterns are ordinarily released by only a small number of signs. The number is smaller in simple animals like the wasp and the moth than in higher animals and the resultant rigidity and "stupidity" of the simpler animals is correspondingly greater. For all the well-studied fixed action patterns, however, the sign stimuli are far from including all of the characteristics of a model or situation which the reacting animal is able to detect by virtue of its sensory potential. Tinbergen (1951) puts it this way: "As a rule, an instinctive reaction responds to only very few stimuli, and the greater part of the environment has little or no influence, even though the animal may have the sensory equipment for receiving numerous details" (p. 27).

Since there is usually more than one sign stimulus we naturally wonder what happens when they are combined. The best evidence (Seitz, 1940; Weidmann and Weidmann, 1958) is that their effects are additive. The strength of responses is sometimes assessed by the frequency of a response (as in peckings of a chick), sometimes by an impression of vigor (as in the fighting of a fish), and sometimes by continuous quantitative measurement (as in extent of muscle flexion or amount of salivation). The apparently additive effects of innate sign stimuli further distinguish them from the acquired signs that govern most human response. A mother's efforts to rescue her child have an all-or-none character. If the signs of a particular trouble are convincing she makes the complete effort.

Now that we have faced the fact that sign stimuli can vary in adequacy or completeness and that innate responses can vary in frequency or intensity, we are ready for the disclosure that will transform the model. It is, simply, that a given sign stimulus does not invariably produce an innate response of a given intensity and that a response of a given intensity is not always preceded by a certain sign stimulus. We must posit some kind of internal sensitizing or driving factor that varies in strength and causes the innate response to be sometimes easily fired and sometimes difficult or impossible to fire.

What is the evidence? The effects of an optimal sign stimulus are not always the same. Some fixed action patterns show a seasonal variation in sensitivity and, in the extreme case, cannot be produced at all out of season. The male robin threatens a red breast only in springtime when it is defending a territory. There is also a variation in sensitivity to an optimal stimulus, which is a function of how recently and frequently the fixed action pattern has been performed. The same optimal stimulus will, on repeated presentation, produce less and less intense responses and eventually perhaps none at all. The white-throat, for instance, is a bird that feigns injury when a predator approaches its nest. Lorenz (1937) has shown that the same stimulus that strongly releases this response on first presentation fails to release the response at all on the third or fourth repetition. Innate responses are "exhaustible" and apparently (Tinbergen, 1951; Thorpe, 1956) it is not simply specific muscular fatigue that produces exhaustion. Neither is it a completely general sort of fatigue or exhaustion of energy, because when one response is refractory others may be highly sensitive. There is something like a finite pool of energy specific to the particular response (Lorenz, 1935–39).

Holding the response constant at some level of completeness or intensity, there is variation in the number of sign stimuli required to produce it; variation in the firing threshold. Beach (1942) has marshalled much evidence that the adequacy of the stimulus required to produce mating responses varies inversely with the sexual excitability of the animal. Males in sexual condition, but prevented from mating, become more and more ready to accept less than ideal objects. For sexual behavior it has been shown that hormones are internal determinants of excitability.

In certain cases innate responses will even "go off in a vacuum" or "explode" in the absence of any adequate sign stimulus. Lorenz (1937) observed this effect in a captive starling. The bird went through the whole fixed routine of insect hunting, from watching the prey through catching, killing, and swallowing, in the absence of any discernible stimulus.

How do observations of this kind reflect on our model of individual behavior? They show that it is wrong. It is not the case that a sign stimulus always produces a response; A does not always lead to B and B is not invariably preceded by A. A more adequate formula would be: $A + A^1$ produces B where A is a sign stimulus and A^1 is some kind of internal drive or energy factor and the frequency or intensity of B varies directly as the sum of these two. It is interesting to note, in passing, that the $+$ sign can be partially justified. A and A^1 apparently combine additively rather than multiplicatively. If it were their multiple that mattered it should not be possible to obtain B if either A or A^1 had the value of zero, since zero times any number is zero. But the fact of vacuum activity, which occurs when the stimulus (A) has the value of zero, suggests that the relation is not multiplicative.

We can keep the lock and key model, provided we recognize that it takes more than the key to open the door. There must be a pressure applied when the key is turned or the door will not open. The equivalent of vacuum activity in this analogy is a pressure on the door great enough to "explode" it open without any key at all.

What kind of internal mechanism do the ethologists suggest? They hold that behavior has two kinds of determinant: the external determinant, corresponding to "A" above, is the sign stimulus or releaser; the internal determinant is a state of drive or a charge of energy specific to the fixed action pattern and indeed produced by the mechanism of that pattern. It was Lorenz (1935–39) among the ethologists who first proposed the notion of "action-specific energy." It is not at all clear how to translate these "energies" into serious neurophysiology and some ethologists (Hinde, 1959) prefer the term "specific action potential." The idea is that there must be distinct forces pressing for the performance of distinct reaction patterns. Some of these forces may be rather continuously generated and some are probably seasonal. These forces intensify with time and their strength determines the ease of firing the action pattern. Performance of the action reduces the strength of the internal force.

If the forces for specific actions are always being produced, why does the animal not constantly perform these actions? The ethologists posit the existence of specific inhibitory blocks that ordinarily prevent discharge. The inhibitory block is removed by an "innate releasing mechanism" operated by a releaser stimulus. Only now, by the way, are we in a position to understand why sign stimuli are also called "releasers"; the stimuli release blocked energy. The elements of the ethologists' conception are: an action-specific potential or force or energy, specific inhibitory blocks, innate releasing mechanisms, and releaser stimuli.

A partial analogue for this mechanism of individual behavior is the ordinary dime-store mousetrap. I have one before me now. The first thing you do in loading the trap is force back the spring-operated loop of copper that will serve as guillotine. The spring is an action-specific force striving to fire the trap. To block the firing there is a long straight rigid bar that reaches over and across the guillotine portion. This bar is the inhibitory block. You slide it under the lip of the small doo-flingus that holds the bit of cheese. This part of the process is delicate since the bar has a hairtrigger fit. The doo-flingus into which the bar fits is, of course, the innate releasing mechanism. And the releaser? Either the mouse's nudge or that of one's own finger.

A MORE COMPLICATED MODEL

We have found a model, in ethology, that will account for a large part of animal social behavior in terms of mechanisms in the individual. There is much more to the conceptions of ethology but we cannot do more than suggest the nature of these. Ethologists have shown a lot of interest in behavior conflict. Consider the circumstance in which two males of a territory-owning species, such as the stickleback, meet one another at the common boundary of their two territories. When a male is well inside his own territory he would be stimulated to threat or attack by the entry into his territory of another male; that other male, being outside his own territory, would take flight. When both are just inside their own territories and just outside one another's, both are simultaneously inclined to retreat and to attack. This kind of ambivalence in the stickleback is likely to produce alternate attack and retreat. It has been suggested by Leyhausen (1956) that a similar conflict in the domestic cat produces its characteristic threat posture in which the front feet retreat while the back feet advance. And certainly the sketch \ /   is the essence of a frightened and angry cat.

There is another reaction to conflict, the reaction ethologists usually call "displacement activity," though Makkink's (1936) term, "sparking over," is a more apt one. From two conflicting drives at high intensity, some quite irrelevant activity is produced, activity belonging to neither drive. It is as if the energies blocked by conflict "sparked over" into a different "track." For example, two domestic cocks presumably torn between attack and retreat may suddenly peck at the ground as if they were feeding (Lorenz, 1935; Tinbergen, 1939). Scratching of the fur in mammals and preening in birds are other common displacement activities. Tinbergen (1951) reminds us that humans in conflict also show displacement activities—twisting the lip, adjusting the coiffure, scratching behind the ear, handling keys, and the like. The displacement activity is always one not ordinarily fired by either of the drives that, in conflict, do produce it. The fact that the intensity of the displaced activity is sometimes proportionate to the intensity of the blocked drives suggests that the "sparking over" idea should be taken seriously. It is rather as if a mousetrap, under great tension but prevented from firing, were suddenly to set the electric fan whirring.

This is the right point at which to make explicit some similarities between ethological theory and the theories of Sigmund Freud (see Chapter 8). Both theories are "dynamic," which is to say they are theories that make much use of the concept of drive. Both concentrate on innate drives or instincts and, indeed, Freud's emphasis on sex and aggression is nearly matched in ethology. Both deal with drives in conflict; both recognize the possibility of diverting drive energy from one channel to another. The most interesting convergence between the two, however, is on the concept of the "critical period." Ethology's discovery of the critical period lies a few paragraphs ahead.

Finally, we must acknowledge that there is more to instinctive behavior than the fixed action patterns we have been discussing. These are the most rigid species-specific component of instinctive behavior. However, the fixed action pattern often belongs to a more elaborate system of behavior organized as a hierarchy. The pattern will fall on a lower level of this hierarchy and higher levels will be characterized by more flexible behavior.

The peregrine falcon, a predatory bird, performs a series of fixed action patterns involving the killing, plucking, and eating of its prey. However, these fixed actions come last in a sequence that usually begins with relatively random roaming over the bird's hunting territory. Ethologists call this more variable behavior, which will ordinarily include some learned components and perhaps aspects of insight, "appetitive" behavior. The roaming will continue until some sort of potential prey is sighted. Let us imagine, with Tinbergen (1951), three possibilities: 1) a flock of teal executing flight maneuvers; 2) a sick gull swimming apart from its flock; 3) a running mouse. These several potential prey do not directly release the fixed actions of killing and eating. They rather release three new varieties of appetitive behavior, all of them more specific than the first random roaming over the territory. The teal release a series of sham attacks which serve to cut off one or a few individuals from all the others. The sick gull will release sham attacks of another sort, attacks which tend to force the gull to take to the air. The mouse might release a more straightforward swoop of attack. Only after the prey has been captured by one of these varieties of appetitive behavior is killing and eating released. Fixed action patterns, when they come last in a sequence in this way, are called, by ethologists, "consummatory" acts. The idea is that the final rigid act *consumes* the energy that set the whole process in motion.

How can this more complex behavior be modeled? One possibility is to imagine it as a sort of hydraulic system. The water or energy flows in on the first level—the level of random roaming—and cannot move down until one of the innate releasing mechanisms just below is opened. We have imagined three of these and three releasers: 1) the sight of teal; 2) the sight of a gull; 3) the sight of a mouse. When one of these releasers is provided the corresponding floodgate is opened and the energy flows on to activate a more specific sort of appetitive behavior. The energy must stay at this level until the new appetitive behavior results in the capture of prey. The capture then releases the fixed action pattern of killing. Only in the final stage is the energy consumed. This model preserves therefore the essential idea of an action-specific energy or drive or potential. In the present conception, however, this potential flows from level to level in a stepwise fashion until it reaches the level at which it can be used up. At every level except the last there is appetitive behavior that tends to bring the animal into contact with one or another releaser. The releaser opens a channel to a lower center and so the energy moves on.

There are some serious difficulties with a model of this kind. Thorpe (1956) has shown, for example, that the possibility of "sparking over" into displacement activities complicates matters. If an aggressive and fearful bird sometimes takes to vigorous preening or food pecking then the energy or potential at that point cannot be completely specific to fighting or retreating. It seems as though there would have to be some connections between centers at a given level.

The territorial defense behavior of the male stickleback belongs to a rather elaborate behavioral hierarchy. The sequence begins with migration from the sea into more shallow fresh water; this seems to be a general kind of appetitive behavior stimulated by the male hormone, testosterone, and also by a rise in temperature. The fish migrates until it encounters the sign stimuli for a suitable territory: shallow, warm water and appropriate vegetation. It then undertakes another sort of appetitive behavior, simply swimming about in the territory until it encounters a new releaser that will make possible a more specific activity. The new releaser might be a female to be courted, materials to be built into a nest, or a male to be threatened or attacked. If the releaser is another male the defending fish does not advance directly to such consummatory acts as threatening or biting, but engages in a more specific appetitive behavior—swimming toward the potential opponent. This behavior is likely to bring the defending fish into contact with the particular releaser from the other fish which will channel energy either into threatening or chasing or biting.

Tinbergen has attempted to make a model mechanism for all of the above and also for some details we have omitted. His model has stimulated much discussion by Thorpe (1956), Hinde (1959), Hess (1962), and others. Guidance for the design of ever more adequate models comes from new studies of behavior (e.g., Hinde, Thorpe, and Vince, 1956) and also from neurophysiology (e.g., Hess, 1956; Von Holst, 1957; Von Holst and St. Paul, 1960, 1962). In Hess's opinion (1962) the neurophysiological evidence to date has "confirmed the ethological propositions on the nature of appetitive behavior and fixed action patterns, particularly the hierarchical organization of behavior" (p. 218). The lock and key and the hydraulic system and my mousetrap are being replaced by genuine neural mechanisms.

Imprinting and the Critical Period

If social behavior is any interaction among members of the same species, then all social behavior relies upon the ability of the individual animal to recognize its own kind. Think of the many kinds of rather similar birds that can simultaneously inhabit a given region. The sorting-out problem is formidable but it must be solved if the species is to survive. If sexual approaches were made across species lines the likely outcomes would be no mating at all, no offspring, or infertile offspring. If parent birds undertook the care and feeding of the young of another species, that care and feeding would not be optimal. If the young followed after adults of another species they would often walk into danger. If mature males respected the territorial rights of all other mature males, of whatever species, there would be a serious shortage of territories. In fact, mix-ups of this kind very seldom occur.

The sorting-out problem is, in the first place, a problem of information; each species must be potentially discriminable from each other species and they are so whether by color, odor, movement, or song. Thorpe (1956) has shown, for example, that the species songs of four closely related finches are all quite distinct. Given the existence of perceptible features peculiar to a species, the sorting-out problem could be solved by building into each species a set of innate releasing mechanisms exactly fitted to these peculiar features. Let the robin be threatened by the robin's distinctive red breast and let the male wasp be attracted by the peculiar odor of the female of its own species. If the various innate "locks" were designed to fit releaser-keys that belong only to species members the sorting-out problem would be solved.

Innate releasing mechanisms are not always preformed so as to provide an exact fit for species characteristics. That fact was accidentally discovered in isolation experiments with birds. The isolation experiment, in which individuals are reared apart from their own kind, is critical for determining which behavior patterns are innate and which are learned. It has been done with many species of European songbirds (Heinroth and Heinroth, 1924–33). In one such experiment, Heinroth (1910) found that greylag geese, reared from the egg by human keepers and in complete isolation from other geese, followed after human beings, in the way that goslings ordinarily follow their parents. The following response of the greylag is an innate fixed-action pattern, but the releaser for this pattern does not seem to be fixed by heredity. Furthermore, when goslings raised in this fashion became sexually mature they directed their sexual approaches to humans rather to other greylag geese. The releaser for sexual behavior seems to have been shaped by the early acquisition of a releaser for following. Lorenz (1935) verified and extended these observations of earlier workers and showed that the social and sexual attachment of the greylag to members of another species depended upon exposure to this species at a critical period early in life. Lorenz named this phenomenon "imprinting."

The greylag gosling appears to be imprinted to the first relatively large moving object that it sees. The process seems to be confined to a very definite period of life and to require only a brief exposure. Grey-lags imprinted to Lorenz followed him about and peeped in distress when he moved away. Such a gosling placed with its own parents and in a brood that was following the parents in the normal way showed no tendency to stay with parents and brood but ran off to Lorenz or any other passing human. Lorenz's greylags accompanied him everywhere like faithful dogs, even going along on swimming tours in the Danube. In maturity the geese were indifferent to their own kin and directed their sexual behavior at humans.

Lorenz (1937) demonstrated imprinting in some other birds, for ex-ample the muscovy duck, the jackdaw, and the shell parakeet, and failed to achieve imprinting with the curlew and a few others. He showed that an imprintable species can often be imprinted to a variety of other species and sometimes to inanimate objects. A fledgling shell parakeet was reared away from its own kind in a cage in which a celluloid ball was attached so as to swing to and fro when touched. Very soon the bird would move close to the ball before settling down to rest and would make preening movements with the ball as object just as if it were preening the short plumage of another bird's head. It is particularly interesting that the bird consistently behaved as if the ball had been the head of a fellow parakeet. When the ball was attached to the bars in such a way as to leave the bird free to hold onto the bars and to take up any position it chose relative to the ball, the bird always placed itself so that its head was on a level with the ball. When Lorenz dropped the ball on the floor of the cage the parakeet reacted as this species does to to the death of a cage-mate: it fell silent and sat with feathers pressed close to its elongated body in what is called a "fright attitude" (Lorenz, 1937).

The greylag goose and the shell parakeet can be imprinted to a large variety of animals and things and in this respect represent an extreme. The opposite extreme is represented by the curlew, which can-not be imprinted at all. In this latter case it seems as though the innate releasing mechanism for the "following-mother" response must have so definite and detailed a form that nothing in nature but an adult curlew will fit. The innate mechanism in the greylag, however, seems to have a very sketchy, generic form since any large moving object will cause it to follow. Other species, if they imprint at all, always have certain perceptual requisites that must be satisfied but these are ordinarily general enough so that an experimenter can find an adequate object other than an adult of the same species.

The first adequate object encountered in a critical period in early life, the first object possessing the essential attributes which consti-tute the releaser for following, is imprinted. Imprinting seems to mean registering and becoming attached to characteristics of the adequate object beyond those constituting the innate releaser for following. Lorenz found that additional characteristics are not registered in the detail that would leave a bird attached to one particular other creature, but only in sufficient detail to leave the bird attached to the species to which the adequate object belongs. Greylag goslings who saw Lorenz before they saw any other large moving thing were imprinted—not to Lorenz, but to humans. To be sure, continued contact with one individual, over a long period of time, can cause the attachment to become quite particular, but the imprinting itself, occurring early, quickly, and permanently, is to the species.

The *sine qua non* of imprinting is an object meeting the minimal requirements of a releaser; where these are few many kinds of object can do so—always including the mother. Lorenz and a mother goose are both large moving objects but they differ in featheredness, posture, and the like and the gosling, in being imprinted, registers enough of these additional characteristics to leave it attached to one of the two species.

Our first thought about the way in which nature would have solved the sorting-out problem was that she would have equipped each species, as she seems to have equipped the curlew, with innate releasing mechanisms making a detailed perfect fit to the characteristic features of the species. Instead she seems usually to leave a margin for error. The releasing mechanisms are so generic that objects other than species members can fire them. But, of course, they would not often do so in the natural state. The first large moving object a greylag goose is going to see is its mother—except when Lorenz, or someone else, upsets the natural order by raising goslings by hand. Nature has not evolved mechanisms to deal with this contingency which is, after all, a new thing in the world. What does seem to have evolved is an innate releaser just specific enough to sort out mothers from other usual alternatives. It is as though natural selection had worked on a principle of minimal effort and had evolved only as much innate machinery as is strictly required.

The generic innate releaser alone would not suffice for the lifetime of the bird. It would not be very long before other large moving objects would appear, and these might be almost anything. The only one whose identity can be confidently foreseen is the first and that will be the mother. So the bird with the generic releaser has also evolved a period of quick and permanent learning for registering additional features of the first creature to release following. These features will be those of the species and so the sorting-out problem will be solved for life.

Lorenz (1937) listed four characteristics that seemed to him to distinguish imprinting from ordinary associative learning. 1) The process is confined to a critical period early in life and may be very brief. 2) The process, once accomplished, is totally irreversible and in this regard

especially unlike associative learning. This irreversibility is most dramatic
when the bird is attached sexually to a species with which it cannot possibly
mate and yet chooses members of this species over available members of
its own. 3) A releaser can be established by imprinting when the actions
to be released have never yet been performed and will not be performed
until a long time afterwards. This is the case when the character of future
sexual objects is fixed by imprinting the following response in very early
life. There is also reason to believe (Thorpe, 1956) that young songbirds
imprint their species song from hearing it performed by adult birds long
before they themselves are ready to sing. 4) Imprinting is not to the
particular individual but to the species, not to Lorenz but to humans. We
have discussed this above.

Lorenz's four-part description of imprinting has been somewhat qualified by later research. There is evidence showing, for example, that imprinting is not always completely irreversible (Thorpe, 1956). Later
research has also expanded our knowledge of the scope of imprinting,
showing that it occurs in many bird species, in some insects and fishes,
and in such mammals as the alpaca, sheep, and deer (Hess, 1962). The
later research has also revealed the relevance of imprinting to such behavior as singing in birds and its probable relevance to the attachment
to particular features of landscape shown by some species (Thorpe, 1956).

Controlled experimentation has revealed some of the variables governing imprinting in a particular species. Hess (1959, 1962) worked with an
apparatus that used a decoy of a male mallard duck to imprint mallard
ducklings. The decoy moved on a circular runway and produced, through
a loudspeaker, a sound that Hess renders as "Gock, gock, gock, gock,
gock." The duckling was taken from its incubator and placed on the
runway where it could follow after the decoy if it chose. At the end of
the imprinting period, which was usually less than one hour, the duckling
was restored to its incubator. For the test of imprinting the duckling
would be placed midway between two models, one the decoy to which
it had been exposed and the other a decoy of a female mallard, differing
from the male in its coloration. Degree of imprinting was indicated by the
percentage of trials on which the duckling approached the model to
which it had been exposed.

With the "gocking" apparatus Hess obtained very clear evidence of a
critical period. Some ninety-two ducklings were given a standard imprinting experience, lasting just ten minutes. The ducklings had this experience at different ages, ranging from one hour out of the egg to thirty-
two hours. The critical period in which this species was most intensely
imprinted was consistently between thirteen and sixteen hours. The imprinting experience was very much less effective for ducklings who were
either younger than thirteen hours or older than sixteen hours. Indeed,

no perfect test scores were made by birds younger than about five hours or older than twenty-one.

Hess has also been able to go a long way toward explaining the existence of a critical period. His experiments indicate that the lower bound, the younger age limit, may be dependent on the maturation of ability to walk and so to follow after the decoy. This locomotor ability rises very rapidly until about the age of thirteen to sixteen hours, when it tends to level off. Hess has good evidence that for imprinting to occur the bird must not only see the decoy, but must also exert effort which it does by walking after the gocking mallard. The upper bound to the critical period, the higher age limit, is correlated with the first emergence of fear reactions to strange objects. Birds younger than about thirteen to sixteen hours very seldom showed fear at sight of the decoy and indeed the newborn of many animal species show no fear of the unfamiliar for some period after birth. Locomotion is good from about thirteen hours on and fear does not develop until about sixteen hours. It looks very much as if the critical period were the interval when the bird can locomote well and is not yet afraid.

Since the human species also has a period after birth in which it does not show fear, about five and a half months according to some observers (Bridges, 1932; Spitz and Wolf, 1946), Hess has suggested that this period may be the time of maximum imprintability for babies. But the human baby cannot walk and so cannot follow. All the species that have thus far proved to be imprintable are species in which the young are mobile almost immediately after birth as the human species is not. And one can see why species with mobile young have had to evolve a mechanism for keeping the young with its parents. There may be nothing of the kind in humans.[1]

There are some things about the attachment of human young to a human mother that remind us of the attachments imprinted in some animals. The bond is a strong one and may even be irreversible, though it can be overlaid with various attitudes. Freud has argued that this attachment is one of the principal factors causing the human being to become socialized; to internalize the values of his society, to feel concern for others, and in maturity to select an appropriate sexual object. There is clinical evidence that impaired relations between mother and child in the critical period of infancy function as a cause of such adult disorders as withdrawal, hostility, sexual maladjustment, alcoholism, and inadequate maternal behavior (summarized by Spitz, 1945). For these various reasons there would be great interest in isolation experiments done with human

1. Scott (1963) holds that the primary socialization of the human infant in the first six months of life shows some of the basic characteristics of imprinting though not such superficial characteristics as the following response.

subjects, but such experiments cannot be done with humans. They can, however, be done with animals belonging to the same order as man, with the other primates, either anthropoid apes or monkeys. They have been done with macaque and rhesus monkeys by Harry and Margaret Harlow (1958, 1962) at the Primate Laboratory of the University of Wisconsin.

The isolation experiments began almost incidentally. The Wisconsin laboratory wanted to have a stock of sturdy and disease-free monkeys available for experimental work and so undertook to separate the young ones from their mothers a few hours after birth in order to feed them a superior formula and rear them hygienically. The monkeys so reared proved to have excellent physical health but to be seriously impaired socially and psychologically. The worst impaired were those reared for the first two years in complete isolation from all other living creatures. These monkeys were fed by remote control and observed through one-way mirrors. Some of them have now been out of isolation and among their own kind for two years. They are seriously deficient in all the social behavior of their species. They do not play with other monkeys. When they are attacked they do not defend themselves. Though sexually mature none of them has mated and it seems certain that they will leave no offspring. Other monkeys have been put in isolation for periods of less than two years and when taken out of isolation have been defective in varying degree. The Harlows believe that total social isolation during the first year of life and for a period of six months or more produces ir-reversible social and psychological damage. They suggest that this is a critical period for the monkey.

Monkeys are born somewhat more mature than human babies but, like human infants, they have a long period of dependence on their mothers. In this period the baby monkey spends most of its time clinging to its mother. It appears to be composed in her company and frightened in her absence. As the monkey grows older it begins to play with its age mates. There are wild games of arboreal tag and mock fighting and in-complete sexual posturing. In quieter moments monkey friends, like all other primates except man, groom one another—which is to say, they sit and pick over one another's fur, removing skin parasites. The monkey in total isolation is deprived of all this experience and so we cannot tell which parts of it are critical for producing his total social inadequacy. But experiment can separate out the components of normal monkey childhood and determine their several implications.

The Harlows (1958) constructed surrogate mothers for some isolated monkeys. These mothers come in two models. Both have cylindrical, armless and legless bodies, and heads that are wooden balls. There are faces painted on the wooden heads that have an uncanny, science-fiction look about them. Both models can be equipped with a nursing bottle attached to the upper thoracic region—the Harlows call it a "unibreast"—both are kept warm by internal heat lamps. Thus far they are alike. The difference is that one model is constructed of wire mesh while the other is made of sponge rubber and covered in terrycloth. They are the "wire mother" and the "cloth mother."

The surrogate mothers do not provide any social experience; they are silent and motionless. The monkeys with surrogate mothers were also deprived of the society of their peers. What they had was an opportunity to nurse—as much as they liked—and something to cling to. Some monkeys grew up with only the one mother available, some with only the other mother available. Some had both mothers available but were nursed on the wire mother only; some had both mothers available and were nursed on the cloth mother only. Some psychologists have asserted that affection for the mother develops, by conditioning, out of her caretaking function, that she becomes a rewarding and reassuring presence chiefly because she feeds the child. If this theory were correct then the monkeys ought to have clung to whichever mother fed them and also perhaps to have shown affection for that mother. The results of the Harlows' work clearly discredit this theory. The nursing function did not direct the monkeys' clinging and affection.

The Harlows had noticed that some of the monkeys they had raised in isolation cages became very attached to the gauze-covered pads that covered the bottoms of their cage. The baby monkeys clung to their pads and had tantrums when the pads were removed for reasons of sanitation. In this they were reminiscent of children who also often will not be parted from beloved blankets or cuddly toy animals. It occurred to the Harlows that primates, and perhaps other animals, have a need for comfortable contact, a need that would ordinarily be satisfied by mother. Terrycloth should be more like a monkey mother than wire mesh.

The monkeys who had access to both surrogates spent almost no time clinging to the wire mother—whether or not they fed from her. They spent upwards of twelve hours a day clinging to the cozier cloth mother and continued to do so for 165 days of testing. When the monkeys were frightened by a mechanical toy they ran over and jumped on the cloth mother. When they were put into a strange room containing many new things that might be explored, they at first clung to the cloth mother as to a haven of security. After a time they made small excursions out into the room and then ran back to soak up more courage. When the cloth mother was not in the strange room the monkeys ran about looking for her and crying with fear. One monkey, as it happened, lived for its first 180 days with a faceless cloth mother and then this mother was replaced by the usual sort with a painted face. The monkey repeatedly screwed the new mother's head around so as to restore the beloved blank. Eventually the monkeys were separated from their surrogate mothers but some two years later, when the cloth mothers were restored, the monkeys' affection was still very strong. The Harlows find that the monkey's love for its cloth mother and the security derived from her presence seem to be no less great than they are with a real mother. This appears also to be a love that can endure over two years of separation. The whole thing is apparently founded on contact comfort.

Terrycloth will release clinging and induce affection and security but it is not enough to produce a normal monkey. At three to five years of age the children of cloth mothers are all socially and sexually aberrant. None of them has mated normally. It looks as if contacts with fellow members of the species are necessary for psychological and social development, but is it necessary that these contacts be with a mother? The Harlows have raised some monkeys with a cloth mother, but also with living and lively age mates. In these circumstances the monkeys show a social and psychological development somewhat slower than the normal but ultimately indistinguishable from the normal. The opportunity to play with peers seems to be able to substitute for social stimulation from a living mother. There is even some suggestion that for monkeys, peers may be more important than mothers. The Harlows found that monkeys with their normal mothers from the start, but deprived of contact with other monkeys for a period of seven months, were seriously retarded. In fact the mothered but peer-less monkeys more closely resembled monkeys raised in total isolation than did any other group.

Self-defense, play, and mating in monkeys do not develop normally in total social isolation. A cloth mother can provide some comfort and security but is not alone enough to produce normal social development; there must be contact with other monkeys, either a mother or age mates. There is some evidence that the critical period in which social isolation is able to produce permanent damage is the first year and that six months is something like the maximum of isolation from which recovery can be expected. The evidence for a critical period is not complete.

While isolation experiments with humans are not done by scientists, their equivalent is sometimes done by mothers and by institutions. From time to time a child is discovered living in an attic or cellar under conditions of minimal social contact. The child, usually illegitimate, may see only a nurse or its mother for a few minutes each day when she comes with food. Such children are ordinarily speechless and lacking in all social responsiveness (Davis, 1940; 1947). It is, however, difficult to learn anything very definite from these sad cases because there is often some reason to suspect that the child is of congenitally subnormal intelligence and because the quantity and nature of social contact the child has had are not always known. Information about children reared in impersonal institutions has been more helpful.

Spitz (1945) made a comparison of development in children who were being raised in a foundling home with children being raised in a nursing home. Both institutions provided good food and medical care and were admirably hygienic. However, while the babies in the nursing home were all cared for by their own mothers, the babies in the foundling home, forty-five of them, had just six nurses to care for them all. As a result the children in the foundling home necessarily had very much less daily contact with another human being than did those in the nursing home. The institutions differed in another respect. In the nursing home each infant could, from its crib, watch the bustling life in the ward, could see other babies at play and watch the mothers and staff come and go. In the foundling home it was a routine practice to hang sheets on the bars of each crib in such a fashion that the baby within could see nothing on the outside. This undifferentiated stimulus field constituted a condition of comparative "sensory deprivation"—the sort of dull environment that we now know produces impaired intelligence in rats and dogs. The children in the foundling home, in short, lived in circumstances of relative social isolation and relative sensory deprivation.

In the first four months of life the children in the foundling home were superior to those in the nursing home on a number of developmental indices and so we can be sure that heredity did not favor the latter group. By the last four months of the first year the children in the foundling home had deteriorated to a level far below that of those in the nursing home and had indeed fallen into a vitiated physical and mental condition that Spitz calls "hospitalism." They had a great susceptibility to infection and a high mortality rate. In the second and third years of life, when children in the nursing home were, like family-reared children, walking and talking, only two of twenty-six foundlings were able to walk, only these same two spoke at all, and even these two said only a few words. Children in this age range would ordinarily speak hundreds of words and would also be constructing sentences. In subsequent studies Spitz (1962) discovered that children reared in institutions of this kind had not by their fourth year initiated the sort of play with their own genitals that in normal children usually appears at about the end of the first year. Spitz takes this as a bad omen and strongly suspects that children who survive conditions of isolation to reach maturity will be impaired in their sexual life even as the Harlows' rhesus monkeys have been.

These unhappy experiments that society sometimes sets up do not of course separate variables as neatly as a laboratory study can do. We cannot yet tell which aspects of isolation and deprivation are critical for the various kinds of intellectual, social, and sexual impairment that humans can suffer. But from the work of Spitz, and related work of Ribble (1944) and Bowlby (1960) and others, it is clear that social contact in infancy is crucial for normal human development.

There is one thing that human societies regularly accomplish in early childhood that animal societies do not accomplish: the internalization of moral values, the creation of the internal mechanism we call a conscience. It is a mechanism essential for the integration of human social life. Wynne-Edwards believes that natural selection has favored the evolution of man into a species with conscience, a species that can feel the force of socially transmitted values. This capacity frees man from the necessity of evolving new innate releasing mechanisms to meet every change in the world around him. He can remain continuously adapted by changing acquired values from one generation to another.

The conscience certainly will not develop in social isolation, but it can go very wrong even with ample social contact. There are psychopaths who have too little feeling for right and wrong and there are guilt-ridden persons in whom these feelings are over developed. Variations in the conditions of early social life are probably causally related to variations in the quality and strength of conscience. There is reason to think that the internalization of values is a special kind of learning, that it will fail in circumstances where the learning of purely intellectual systems will succeed. The internalization of moral values may depend, as Freud thought it certainly did, upon the development of strong affection. For this development there may be critical periods and critical persons. The acquisition of conscience has an integrating role in human life something like the "consciousness of kind" that is established in birds by imprinting. But these are matters for later chapters, chapters that concentrate on humans.

It is a pleasant incidental consequence of the study of animal behavior that we are alerted to the variety of life around us in the grass, the trees, and the ocean. It has made me into a spare-time birdwatcher and a less reluctant visitor to museums of natural history. On a recent visit to the great museum in New York City I had no time for the dinosaurs but, because of Wynne-Edwards, headed straight for the stuffed lemmings. They turned out to look a little like rats, only dustier.

The study of animal behavior also exerts a force on our conceptions of ourselves and of our species. The consequences can be startling. Mary McCarthy in her novel *The Group*, which is about eight Vassar girls, says that one of the girls, Kay, had been amazingly altered "by a course in Animal Behavior she had taken with old Miss Washburn (who had left her brain in her will to Science). . . ." From a shy, pretty girl, active in hockey and in the choir, she became a "thin, hard-driving, authoritative young woman, dressed in dungarees, sweat shirt, and sneakers." A young woman who talked airily "of oestrum and nymphomania," called her friends "by their last names loudly," counselled "premarital experiment and the scientific choice of a mate. Love, she said, was an illusion." But these too are matters for later chapters.

REFERENCES

Beach, F. A. Analysis of factors involved in the arousal, maintenance and manifestation of sexual excitement in male animals. *Psychom. Med.*, 1942, **4**, 173–198.

Beach, F. A. Experimental investigations of species-specific behavior. *Amer. Psychologist*, 1960, **15**, 1–18.

Blauvelt, Helen. Neonate-mother relationship in goat and man. In Schaffner, B. (Ed.), *Group Processes*. Transactions of the Second Conference, 1935. Josiah Macy, Jr. Foundation, 1956, 94–140.

Bowlby, J. Grief and mourning in infancy and early childhood. In *The psychoanalytic study of the child*. Vol. 15. New York: International Univer. Press, 1960.

Bridges, K. M. B. Emotional development in early infancy. *Child Developm.*, 1932, **3**, 342–351.

Brückner, G. H. Untersuchungen zur Tiersoziologie, insbesondre der Auflösung der Familie. Z. *Psychol.*, 1933, **128**, 1–120.

Cannon, W. B. *The wisdom of the body*. New York: Norton, 1932.

Chapman, R. N. The quantitative analysis of environmental factors. *Ecology*, 1928, **9**, 111–122.

Davis, K. Extreme social isolation of a child. *Amer. J. Sociol.*, 1940, **45**, 554–565.

Davis, K. Final note on a case of extreme social isolation. *Amer. J. Sociol.*, 1947, **52**, 432–437.

Eibl-Eibesfeldt, I. Angeborenes und Erworbenes in der Technik des Beutetötens (Versuche am Iltis, *Putorious putorious* L.). Z. *Säugetierkunde*, 1956, **21**, 135–137.

Harlow, H. F. The nature of love. *Amer. Psychologist*, 1958, **13**, 673–685.

Harlow, H. F., and Harlow, Margaret. Social deprivation in monkeys. *Scient. American*, 1962, **207**, No. 5, 136–146.

Hebb, D. O. *A textbook of psychology*. Philadelphia: Saunders, 1958.

Hebb, D. O., & Thompson, W. R. The social significance of animal studies. In G. Lindzey (Ed.), *Handbook of social psychology*. Vol. 1. Reading, Mass.: Addison-Wesley, 1954.

Hediger, H. *Studies of the psychology and behaviour of captive animals in zoos and circuses*. Transl. by Geoffrey Sircom. New York: Criterion, 1955.

Heinroth, O. Beitrage zur Biologie, namentlich Ethologie und Psychologie der Anatiden. *Verhl. 5 Int. Orn. Kongr.*, 1910, 589–702.

Heinroth, O., & Heinroth, M. *Die Vögel Mitteleuropas*. Berlin: Lichterfelde, 1924–1933.

Hess, E. Ethology: An approach toward the complete analysis of behavior. In R. Brown, E. Galanter, E. Hess, & G. Mandler, *New directions in psychology*. New York: Holt, Rinehart & Winston, 1962.

Hess, E. The relationship between imprinting and motivation. In M. R. Jones

(Ed.), *Nebraska symposium on motivation.* Vol. VII, 1959, Lincoln: Univer. of Nebraska Press.

Hess, W. R. *Hypothalamus and Thalamus. Experimental-dokumente.* Stuttgart: Thieme, 1956.

Hinde, R. A. Some recent trends in ethology. In S. Koch (Ed.), *Psychology: A study of a science.* Vol. II. New York: McGraw-Hill, 1959.

Hinde, R. S., Thorpe, W. H., & Vince, M. A. The following response in young coots and moorhens. *Behaviour,* 1956, **9,** 214–242.

Holst, E. v. Die Auslösung von Stimmungen bei Wirbeltieren durch "punkt-förmige" elektrische Errengung des Stammhirns. *Naturwiss.,* 1957, **44,** 549–551.

Holst, E. v., & St. Paul, U. v. Vom Wirkungsgefüge der Triebe. *Naturwiss.* 1960, **18,** 409–422.

Holst, E. v., & St. Paul, U. v. Electrically controlled behavior. *Scient. American,* 1962, *206,* No. 3, 50–59.

Jespersen, P. The frequency of birds over the high Atlantic Ocean. *Nature, London,* 1925, **114,** 281–283.

Jespersen, P. Ornithological observations in the North Atlantic Ocean. *Danish 'Dana'-Exped.* 1920–22, *Oceanogr.,* 1930, Rep. no. 7: 1–36.

Kluyver, H. N., & Tinbergen, L. Territory and the regulation of density in tit-mice. *Arch. néerl. Zool.,* 1953, **10,** 265–289.

Koehler, O., and A. Zagarus. Beiträge zum Brutverhalten des Halsbandregen-pfeifers (*Charadrius h. hiaticula L.*). *Beitr. Fortpfl. biol. Vögel,* 1937, **13,** 1–9.

Krätzig, H. Untersuchungen zur Lebensweise des Moorschneehuhns *Lagopus l. lagopus,* wahrend der Jugendentwicklung. *J. Ornithol.,* 1940, **88,** 139–166.

Lack, D. *The Life of the Robin.* (1st ed., 1943.) Revised edition. Harmonds-worth, Middlesex, England: Pelican, 1953.

Leyhausen, P. Verhaltensstudien an Katzen. Beiheft 2 zur Z. *Tierpsychol.,* 1956.

Lorenz, K. Z. Der Kumpan in der Umwelt des Vogels. *J. Ornith.,* 1935, **83,** 137–213, 289–413.

Lorenz, K. Z. Imprinting. (1st ed., 1937.) In R. C. Birney & R. C. Teevan (Eds.), *Instinct.* Princeton: D. Van Nostrand, 1961.

Lorenz, K. Z. Über die Bildung des Instinktbegriffes. *Naturwiss.,* 1937, **25,** 289–300, 307–318, 324–331.

Lorenz, K. Z. A contribution to the comparative sociology of colonial-nesting birds. *Proc. VIII Int. Orn. Congr.,* 1938, 206–218.

Lorenz, K. Vergleichende Verhaltensforschung. *Zool. Anz. Suppl.,* 1939, **12,** 69–102.

Makkink, G. F. An attempt at an ethogram of the European avocet (*Recurvi-rostra avosetta L.*) with ethological and psychological remarks. *Ardea,* 1936, **25,** 1–60.

Nicholson, A. J. Compensatory reactions of populations to stresses, and their evolutionary significance. *Aust. J. Zool.,* 1955, **2,** 1–8.

Nissen, H. W. Social behavior in primates. In C. P. Stone (Ed.), *Comparative psychology.* (3rd ed.) New York: Prentice-Hall, 1951.

Pitelka, F. A., Tomich, P. Q., & Treichel, G. W. Ecological relations of jaegers and owls as lemming predators near Barrow, Alaska. *Ecol. Monogr.,* 1955, **25,** 85–117.

Prévost, J., & Bourlière, J. Vie sociale et thermorégulation chez le manchot empereur *Aptenodytes forsteri. Alauda,* 1957, **25,** 167–173.

Ribble, Margaret A. Infantile experience in relation to personality development. In J. McV. Hunt (Ed.), *Personality and the behavior disorders*. Vol. II. New York: Ronald, 1944.

Schjelderup-Ebbe, T. Social behavior of birds. In C. Murchison (Ed.), *A handbook of social psychology*. Worcester: Clark Univer. Press, 1935.

Scott, J. P. *Animal behavior*. Chicago: Univer. of Chicago Press, 1958.

Scott, J. P. The process of primary socialization in canine and human infants. *Monogr. Soc. Res. Child Developm.*, 1963, **28**, No. 1, Serial No. 85.

Seitz, O. Die Paarbildung bei einigen Cichliden. I. Die Paarbildung bei *Astatotilapia strigigena* (Pfeffer). *Z. Tierpsychol.*, 1940, 4, 40–84.

Silliman, R. P., & Gutsell, J. S. Experimental exploitation of fish populations. *U. S. Fish and Wildlife Service Fishery Bull.*, 1958, **58**, No. 133, 214–252.

Simpson, G. G. *The meaning of evolution*. New Haven: Yale Univer. Press, 1949.

Spitz, R. A. Hospitalism: An inquiry into the genesis of psychiatric conditions in early childhood. In *The psychoanalytic study of the child*. Vol. I. (3rd ed.) New York: International Univer. Press, 1958.

Spitz, R. A. Autoerotism re-examined: The role of early sexual behavior patterns in personality formation. In *The psychoanalytic study of the child*. Vol. XVII. New York: International Univer. Press, 1962.

Spitz, R. A., and K. M. Wolf. The smiling response: a contribution to the ontogenesis of social relations. *Genet. Psychol. Monogr.*, 1946, **34**, 57–125.

Thorpe, W. H. *Learning and instinct in animals*. London: Methuen, 1956.

Tinbergen, N. On the analysis of social organization among vertebrates, with special reference to birds. *Amer. Midl. Nat.*, 1939, **21**, 210–234.

Tinbergen, N. *The study of instinct*. London: Oxford University Press, 1951.

Tinbergen, N., & Kuenen, D. J. Über der auslösenden und die richtunggebenden Reizsituationen der Sperrbewegung von jungen Drosseln (*Turdus m. merula* L. und *T. e. ericetorum* Turton). *Z. Tierpsychol.*, 1939, 3, 37–60.

Weidmann, R., & Weidmann, U. An analysis of the stimulus situation releasing food-begging in the black-headed gull. *Brit. J. Anim. Behaviour*, 1958, **6**, 114.

Wheeler, W. M. *Social life among the insects*. New York: Harcourt, Brace, 1923.

Wynne-Edwards, V. C. *Animal dispersion in relation to social behaviour*. Edinburgh and London: Oliver and Boyd, 1962.

Zuckerman, S. *The social life of monkeys and apes*. London: Kegan Paul, 1932.

Part Two

PROBLEMS OF PSYCHOLOGY

AND SOCIAL STRUCTURE

S TRUCTURE appears in the social behavior of both animals and humans. Territoriality and mating and care of the young in robin and stickleback are social structures or patterns. This is to say that the behavior involved is reliably manifested by animals of specifiable classes in specifiable circumstances, that the behavior is regular or rule-governed. In these cases it is also largely instinctive. However dominance orders in the animal world constitute structured behavior that is learned and so more like human structured behavior.

Social structure becomes actually visible in an anthill; the movements and contacts one sees are not random but patterned. We should also be able to see structure in the life of an American community if we had a sufficiently remote vantage point, a point from which persons would appear to be small moving dots. We should see these dots mobile by day and immobile for much of the night. We should see that these dots do not randomly wander over the terrain but follow fixed paths and return regularly to what appear to be family territories. We should see that these dots do not randomly approach one another, that some are usually together, some meet often, some never. The determinants of perceptual structure called "proximity" and "common fate" would group the dots for us into cohering dyads, families, and strata. The determinant of perceptual structure called "similarity" would cause us to notice that dots with trousers lift their hats to dots with skirts, that dots in blue uniforms stand in the street blowing whistles and waving their arms at dots in cars. If one could get far enough away from it human social life would become pure pattern.

The social norm is the basic concept for describing social structure. A norm is, in the first place, a regularity of learned behavior. In stating a norm one must specify the kind of behavior, the kind of situation in which the behavior occurs and the kind of person who behaves so. Motorists (class of person) driving automobiles in America (class of situation) stay on the right side of the road (class of behavior). Sometimes behavior that is easily imagined almost never occurs, and these regularities of non-occurrence can also be called norms. The non-occurrence of incest is a norm.

Because there are regularities in social behavior and because people can learn, we find that for each behavioral norm there is likely to be an expectancy norm. Not only do we ourselves drive on the right-hand side of the road, but we expect others to do the same. Very generally the expectancy is likely to be held by everyone familiar with the class of persons, class of situations, and class of behavior specified in stating the behavioral norm. Expectancies and regularities of action usually go together and one term, *social norm*, has been used for both.

Behavioral regularities and the expectancies that go with them are not all social norms. Suppose we were to move in a little closer to the community of dots and mark two of them for continued observation. We might find that one of them was often alone, the other almost always in company. The one often alone might be seen to be always reading or carrying a book; the other might have a transistor radio clapped to his ear when he was not conversing. There might, in short, be distinctive regularities in the behavior of each. Clearly such regularities can give rise to expectancies in others; perhaps we are now prepared for friendly, outgoing "extravert" behavior from one dot and seclusive "introvert" behavior from another. But these regularities and expectancies are not social norms; they concern personality and the perception of personality. Norms have to do with socially recognized classes of persons rather than with individuals.

There is one other thing to be said in separating norms from behavioral regularities in general. Consider what happens when a reliable regularity is broken, a well established expectancy disappointed. What if our introvert friend puts on a lampshade for a hat and kisses all the girls? What if our dog speaks Chinese and our cat collects stamps? We will be surprised. We will tell people the news. Probably we will be rather pleased; we have an appetite for novelty. What happens when there is less extreme departure from regularity? Our friend does not like the book we were sure he would like, or our dog does not go to the door to be let out at his usual hour. We are likely to feel some slight chagrin; especially in those cases where our wishes are violated but also where the unexpected action is agreeable enough in itself. It throws us off. We are prepared for the usual and so do not have the right behavior ready. But none of these reactions to the unexpected has the quality of a reaction to departure from a social norm.

If a man drives on the left-hand side of the street in America, he is not just surprising, he is *wrong*. If a policeman smiles happily at this idiosyncracy, then the policeman is also wrong. If a man cohabits with his daughter, then he is *really* wrong. Social norms are not just departed from, they are *violated*. There is always some feeling that the behavior is inappropriate; that it ought not to occur. Norms are prescriptions ("Love thy neighbor") and proscriptions ("Thou shalt not kill"). A norm is, in its most fundamental sense, a shared rule or guide to behavior that is appropriate or inappropriate.

Since culture is often defined as the totality of shared, transmitted guides to behavior, it follows that a norm is simply a fragment of culture. Norms are culture particularized. When we use the word "norm" without specifying either "behavioral norm" or "expectancy norm," it will be in the sense of a rule or guide to behavior, a standard for the judgment of behavior.

Culture is always partly "exosomatic," partly external to human beings, partly in the form of tools, pottery, dwellings, and writings. The exosomatic norm is the one that is written down: rules for students contained in university catalogues and also the laws of the land. The written norm is usually called "explicit" and the many norms that are not written are implicit. Implicit norms are discovered by observing regularities in human groups and by asking questions. "Do you think it is right for a student to come to class in a bathing suit?" The norm is real enough, but it is not on the books.

When we think of norms one at a time and pick examples from here and there, we are likely to conceive of their totality, culture, as a bundle of unrelated sticks. In fact, however, a culture is always systematic. Rules cannot be combined at random; there are several kinds of constraint.

In the first place the rules must be such as to satisfy certain basic requirements for the humans following them. There must be a means of subsistence adapted to a given environment, there must be provision for shelter, for the care of the young, and for the propagation of the species. In the second place the rules cannot contradict one another too often or too seriously. They must compose a set that can be learned and can be followed. If a man feels equally obligated to his mother and to his wife, he must often experience conflict. If a school of engineering teaches one kind of mathematics while the practice of engineering requires another kind, then the graduates of the school will have difficulties. A culture always does contain a certain amount of latent internal contradiction, and this is a very important dimension on which cultures vary. It provides an interesting objective basis for regarding one set of social arrangements as superior to another. Are the norms put together in such a way that most people can live relatively free of conflict?

Norms are stated in terms of classes of persons: policemen, women, fathers, friends, acquaintances, workers, etc. Persons can be classified in infinitely various ways. However certain modes of classification are particularly important for the description of social structure. These include classification by inter-personal relationship (e.g., friend, acquaintance, employer, employee), classification by socio-economic stratum (e.g., gentlefolk, workers, noblemen), and classification by role (e.g., men, women, fathers, daughters, policemen, lawyers). These modes of classification are important because very many norms are formulated in terms of them, much structured behavior turns upon them. We turn to these structural concepts now and to some problems of psychology that arise in connection with them.

CHAPTER 2

The Basic Dimensions of

Interpersonal Relationship

When one person speaks to another he has, in any language, a choice of address forms. In modern English the principal option is between the personal name and the family-name-with-title: *John* or *Mr. Jones.* In some cases a title alone is used (e.g., *Senator*) and in some cases a nickname (e.g., *Jonesy*). Most of the modern European languages present the speaker with a decision point in the use of pronouns of address as well as in the use of titles and personal names. In French a single addressee may be called either *tu* or *vous*, in German either *du* or *Sie*, in Italian *tu* or *Lei.* Modern English provides no such option; we have the omnibus *you* for addressing any sort of single person and also for addressing more than one person.

In the languages of modern India there are distinctions in the pronouns of address cognate with those of the European languages, but some Indian languages require the speakers to choose among three pronouns. Even the Indian elaboration is very modest by comparison with the address systems in various Oriental languages. Japanese, for instance, provides numerous polite suffixes (e.g., *-san, -kun*) to be added to personal names, numerous pronouns of address (e.g., *anata, kimi*) and a set

51

of prefixes for nouns and variations in verbs, all of which are governed by the relation between speaker and addressee. These Oriental forms in translation yield the kind of Pearl Buck English that goes: "This unworthy person entreats your exalted self to enter his lowly dwelling and partake of his humble food."

Forms of address always follow rules that are understood by an entire society. The most important governing condition is the relationship existing between the two persons concerned, the speaker and his addressee. A word like *larger* is also governed by a relationship though not an interpersonal relationship. It is not appropriate to call any single thing *larger* but only some single thing in relation to something else. Similarly, kinship terms of address (e.g., *dad, son, mom*) are relational and, in this case, the relation is interpersonal. It is not a property of a particular man to be always called *dad*. That term only becomes appropriate when a man is addressed by someone standing in the relevant kinship relation; the same man is appropriately called *son* by a different relation.

Kinship forms of address constitute a limited or restricted language of relationship. Most of the pairs of persons (dyads) that might be put together in a given society would not call for any kinship term. To be sure, in primitive societies whose organization is based on kinship there is often an extended kinship term for everyone who belongs to the society; each person is *little brother* or *elder sister* or something of the kind. In civilized and industrialized societies, however, where the importance of kinship is reduced, the usage of kinship terminology is correspondingly curtailed. The forms with which we will be concerned in this chapter (titles, personal names, pronouns of address) constitute a universal language of address. Every dyad that can be put together calls for one or another of these forms and so the forms serve to relate each member of a society with each other member.

All societies have rules of address. To introduce the basic dimensions of interpersonal relationship we will make a study of these rules in a variety of European languages and in several historical periods. We shall find that address forms are always governed by the same two underlying dimensions: solidarity and status. However, we shall not always find these dimensions used in the same way. There have been changes in the history of Europe and there are differences today among such nations as France, the United States, and Germany. The information we have on Indian and Japanese address shows that status and solidarity are the governing relations but they are somewhat differently conceived than in Europe (sex and age are more important) and they are more finely coded. We will not attempt here to give a full description of these non-European patterns.

The dimensions that emerge from a study of linguistic address emerge also from more orthodox kinds of sociological and psychological research. Solidarity and status appear to govern much of social life. They lie behind the great regularities of everyday behavior: the way in which similarity generates liking and interaction which in turn produce more similarity; the way in which differential status confers power and privilege. These regularities founded on solidarity and status are very general but also very obvious. They are obvious probably because we have all had to work them out in order to get along with others. In any case we will move from the language of address to these obvious regularities of everyday life and to the evidence for them in social science. In a final section we will come back to the language of address, to a rule of usage that seems to be universal, a rule that appears in all the languages we have examined. From this rule we can infer a universal law about the connection between solidarity and status.

The discussion of the language of address is largely based on work that was done by a group in Boston: Professor Albert Gilman of the Boston University English Department and myself with the help of Dr. Toshio Iritani, Dr. Donald Hildum, Miss Marguerite Ford, and Mr. Veera Rag-havan. Most of the work has been reported with full procedural detail in earlier articles (Brown and Gilman, 1960; Brown and Ford, 1961). This kind of detail cannot be given here and I have substituted a single preliminary paragraph about our sources of information.

In working out the detailed rules for past and present usage of the terms of address, we always looked first at language histories and con-temporary dictionaries and grammars. The usefulness of these sources was slight because the detail is generally insufficient. Of much greater value were those linguistic and philological monographs which con-centrate on forms of address for a single language; sometimes throughout the history of the language, sometimes for a century or so, sometimes for the works of a single famous writer such as Molière or Shakespeare. We have learned about contemporary usage from literature and films and especially from published plays. The drama is the literary form in which address occurs most often. Miss Ford and I worked out the details of American English from thirty-eight anthologized *Best American Plays* (Gassner, 1947, 1952, 1958). To make sure of certain matters we asked a group of thirty-four young business executives who were studying at M.I.T. in 1958–59 to tell us about their habits of address with four kinds of business associates: a superior, a subordinate, an equal with whom the informant was on friendly terms, an equal with whom he was on distant or formal terms. For contemporary usage in French, German, Italian, other European languages, the languages of India, and Japanese we con-ducted interviews with large numbers of native speakers. Finally, we obtained a direct life-situation check on certain aspects of American English with the help of a gentleman who is employed by a Boston drafting firm. This man took advantage of free moments at his desk to note all the instances of address he could hear between members of his organization.

The Historical Evolution of the European Pronouns of Address

In the Latin of antiquity there was *tu* for the singular (address to one person) and *vos* for the plural (address to more than one person). The use of *vos* as a form of address for one person was at first restricted to a single case; it was the appropriate way to speak to the emperor. There are several hypotheses as to how this practice came about, and these are interesting because they suggest that social relations are often understood by analogy with physical relations.

The use of the plural to the emperor began in the fourth century. By that time there were actually two emperors; the ruler of the eastern empire had his seat in Constantinople and the ruler of the west sat in Rome. Because of Diocletian's reforms the imperial office, though vested in two men, was administratively unified. Words addressed to one man were, by implication, addressed to both. The choice of *vos* as a form of address may have been a response to this implicit plurality. There is another possibility, however. Plurality would seem to be a natural metaphor for social power. An emperor, indeed any royal person, is the summation of his people and can speak as their representative. One recalls in this connection the royal *we* of British monarchs. It is quite possible that the plural *vos* was recruited for address to the emperor because it is a good metaphor for power rather than because there were two persons holding the office. The likelihood that metaphor directed the usage is increased by the fact that languages unrelated to Latin have independently developed the plural of respect; for instance some of the Indian languages of California (Kroeber, 1925).

It may be worth one paragraph of digression to report other cases in which metaphor seems to have directed the recruitment of pronouns for the expression of social differences. The German *Ihr* was the second person plural before it was adopted as the singular of reverence during the Middle Ages. However, the Germans spoiled *Ihr* for this new purpose by being too polite. Superiors said it to inferiors just to be extra nice and a new pronoun of reverence had to be selected. Choice fell on *er*, heretofore the masculine third person singular. Perhaps there is also a guiding metaphor here. One would ordinarily use *er* to speak of someone not present, someone spatially removed. Spatial distance can be a metaphor for social distance. Though a man may be face-to-face with his king he is still far removed from him. This metaphor does not specify direction; it does not indicate whether the remote person is above or below the speaker. Perhaps it was this fact that made it possible for *er* to reverse its semantic in the nineteenth century when it came to be used as a condescending form of address. In the meantime, during the eighteenth century, the Germans hit on another reverential form; it was *Sie*, the third person plural. It is difficult to see how this choice can be improved upon since it combines plurality and distance.

Eventually the Latin plural was extended from the emperor to other high-status persons. However, this semantic pattern was not unequivocally established for many centuries. There was much inexplicable fluctuation between the pronouns cognate with *tu* and *vos* in old French, Spanish, Italian, Portuguese, and in Middle English. In verse, at least, the choice seems often to have depended on assonance, rhyme, or syllable count. However, some time between the twelfth and fourteenth centuries, varying with the language, a set of rules crystallized which we call the asymmetrical status norm. In the remainder of this chapter we shall want a generic designation for familiar pronouns like *tu* and *du* and for polite pronouns like *vos*, *vous*, and *Sie*. Let us use T for the former and V for the latter.

THE STATUS NORM

In every human society there seems to be come conception of differential social value. Men everywhere understand what is meant by the question: "Who are the better people in your community and who are the lesser ones?" Social status accrues to a person in the degree that he possesses characteristics valued by his society. In this general abstract sense status has the same meaning everywhere. However, there is much latitude for cultural variation in the characteristics which are taken as the basis for status. These can be physical strength and skill, position in the kinship system, sex, lineage, occupation, wealth, roles in an organization like the army or the church. All of this is a preliminary characterization of status which will be filled out later in the chapter.

The nature of the status role for the pronouns of address can be made clear with a set of examples from various European languages. In medieval Europe, generally, the nobility said T to the common people and received V; the master of a household said T to his slave, his servant, his squire, and received V. Within the family, of whatever social level, parents gave T to children and were given V. In Italy in the fifteenth century penitents said V to the priests and were told T. Pope Gregory I, in his letters, used T to subordinates in the ecclesiastical hierarchy while they invariably used V to him. In Froissart (late fourteenth century) all celestial beings say T to man and receive V. But the angels in turn say V to God and receive T from Him. Finally, in French of the twelfth and thirteenth centuries man says T to the animals and receives V, and among the animals the greater say T and the lesser say V. This trivial fragment of medieval culture, the rules of address, reveals the whole status system of the society and also the world beyond society, which was conceived as a great chain of being with divine figures ranked higher than man and animals ranked lower.

The V of reverence entered European speech as a form of address to the principal power in the state and eventually generalized to the powers within that microcosm of the state—the nuclear family. In the history of these languages, then, parents are emperor figures. It is worthwhile to note in passing that Sigmund Freud reversed this terminology and spoke of kings, as well as generals, employers, and priests, as father figures. The propriety of Freud's designation for his psychological purposes derives from the fact that an individual learning a European language reverses the historical order of semantic generalization. The individual's first experience of subordination to power and of the reverential V comes in his relation to his parents. In later years similar asymmetrical status relations and similar norms of address develop between employer and employee, soldier and officer, subject and monarch. We can see how it might happen, as Freud believed, that the later social relationships would remind the individual of the familial prototype and would revive emotions and responses from childhood. In a man's personal history, recipients of the non-reciprocal V were parent figures.

The status norm is a non-reciprocal or asymmetrical rule; it prescribes T for one member of a dyad and V for the other. Because it is non-reciprocal, we can guess that the status norm was never the only rule governing use of the pronouns of address. If it were the only rule, then every dyad that might be formed in a society would have to consist of persons of unequal social status. Since the full set of dyads is all possible pairs of persons, it follows that the society would have to provide unique status ranks for each person. There could be no cases of tied status-rank because the non-reciprocal norm provides no rule of address for such cases. Societies as large as the medieval European societies are never so finely structured. What the medieval societies had instead was a set of social classes: large numbers of persons were held to have roughly equivalent status, but there was a vertical order among classes of equivalents.

There was always a norm for persons of equivalent status, members of a common class. Between equals pronominal address was reciprocal or symmetrical; an individual gave and received the same form. During the medieval period, and for periods beyond that vary with the language, equals of the upper classes exchanged the mutual V while equals of the lower classes exchanged T.

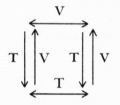

FIGURE 2-1. THE STATUS NORM

The difference in class practice derives from the fact that the reverential V was always introduced into a society at the top. In the Roman Empire only the highest-ranking persons had any occasion to address the emperor and so, at first, only they made use of V in the singular. In its later history in other parts of Europe the reverential V was usually adopted by one court in imitation of another. The practice slowly disseminated downward. In this way the use of V in the singular incidentally came to connote a speaker of high status. In later centuries Europeans became very conscious of the extensive use of V as a mark of elegance. In the drama of seventeenth-century France the nobility and bourgeoisie almost always address one another as V. This is true even of husband and wife, of lovers, and of parent and child if the child is adult. Mme. de Sévigné in her correspondence never uses T, not even to her daughter, the Comtesse de Grignan. Servants and peasantry, however, regularly used T among themselves.

The full status norm, then, prescribes non-reciprocal T-V between unequals and mutual V or T (according to absolute class placement) between equals. In Figure 2-1 this rule is diagrammed.

THE SOLIDARITY NORM

In every human society there is some conception of differential solidarity. Men everywhere understand what is meant by such a question as: "Who are the people whose welfare is of great importance to you and who are the people for whom you are less concerned?" If status is the vertical of social relationship, solidarity is the horizontal. Solidarity is often talked about in terms of being close or remote, near or far, the in-group versus the out-group. The grounds of solidarity are varied: kinship, identities of age, sex, nationality, similarities of education and occupation, a shared fate, and simply prolonged contact. Solidarity can be asymmetrical; one member of a dyad can feel a greater identification of interests than the other. Probably, however, solidarity tends to be symmetrical since it is founded on identities, similarities, and shared experiences. As in the case of status, this characterization is preliminary.

It seems probable that the solidarity norm did not become clearly established for the European pronouns until some time after the status norm. The earliest clear cases involve persons of equivalent status who would, if they followed the status norm, exchange V if they were upper class and T if they were lower class. It began to happen, however, that persons on a given class level, either high or low, made some use of Mutual V and Mutual T. Mutual V became the usual form for strangers or new acquaintances. Mutual T was for brothers and sisters, lovers, spouses, close friends, comrades in arms, schoolfellows.

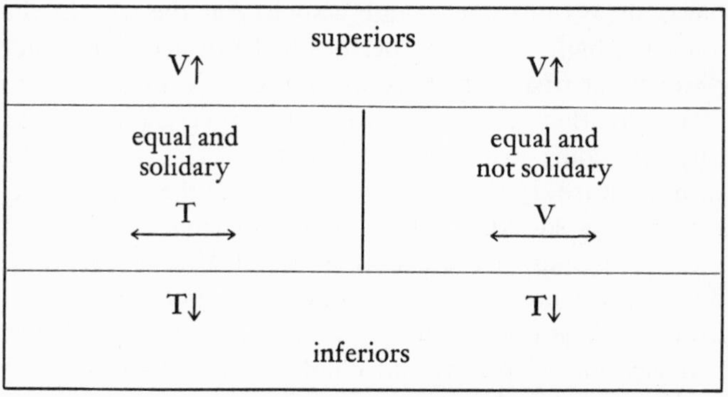

superiors	
V↑	V↑
equal and solidary T ←——→	equal and not solidary V ←——→
T↓	T↓
inferiors	

a. In equilibrium

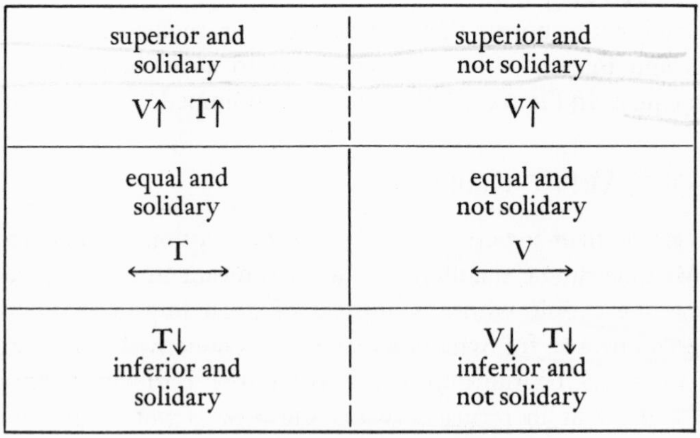

superior and solidary V↑ T↑	superior and not solidary V↑
equal and solidary T ←——→	equal and not solidary V ←——→
T↓ inferior and solidary	V↓ T↓ inferior and not solidary

b. Under tension

FIGURE 2-2. THE TWO-DIMENSIONAL NORM SYSTEM IN EQUILIBRIUM AND
UNDER TENSION

The combined solidarity norm and status norm make a neat two-dimensional system for the use of two pronouns of address. Each pronoun necessarily has two connotations: T expresses intimacy when it is reciprocal and condescension when it is non-reciprocal; V expresses formality or remoteness when it is reciprocal and deference when it is non-reciprocal. You may wonder why the connotations became linked in this particular way. Why should not intimacy go with deference and remoteness with condescension? In the history we are discussing the question is: Why was not the deferential V used in its reciprocal pattern to express intimacy and the condescending T used reciprocally for remoteness? The linkage that actually occurred in the European pronouns is, we believe, a cultural universal for all forms of address and for many other kinds of behavior. We will come back to this universal in the final section of the chapter.

CONFLICT BETWEEN THE TWO NORMS

As long as the solidarity norm was applied only in cases of status equivalence, the two kinds of norm constituted a harmonious system, a system in equilibrium (see Figure 2-2a). However, the dimension of solidarity is potentially applicable to all persons addressed. Persons of superior status may be solidary (parents, elder siblings) or not solidary (officials whom one seldom sees). Persons of inferior status, similarly, may be as solidary as the old family retainer or a younger brother and as remote as the waiter in a strange restaurant. Extension of the solidarity dimension along the broken lines of Figure 2-2b creates six categories of persons defined by their relations to a speaker. Rules of address are in conflict for persons in the upper left and lower right categories. For the upper left, status dictates V and solidarity T. For the lower right, status dictates T and solidarity V. This is an example of inconsistency or conflict within a set of norms; such an inconsistency can function as a force for cultural change.

The abstract conflict described in Figure 2-2b is particularized in Figure 2-3a with a sample of the social dyads in which the conflict would have been felt. In each case, usage in one direction would have been unequivocal (solid lines) but, in the other direction, the two norms were in opposition (broken lines). The top three dyads in Figure 2-3a involve conflict in address to inferiors who are not solidary (the lower right category of Figure 2-2b) and the bottom three dyads involve conflict in address to superiors who are solidary (the upper left category in Figure 2-2b).

Well into the nineteenth century the status semantic prevailed and waiters, common soldiers, and employees were called T while parents, masters, and elder brothers were called V. However, all of our evidence

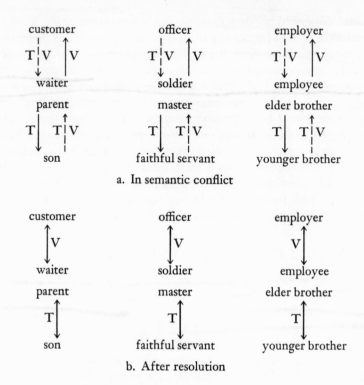

a. In semantic conflict

b. After resolution

FIGURE 2-3.   SOCIAL DYADS INVOLVING CONFLICTS OF NORMS AND THEIR
RESOLUTION

consistently indicates that in the past century the solidarity semantic has
gained supremacy. Dyads of the type shown in Figure 2-3a now reciprocate the pronoun of solidarity or the pronoun of non-solidarity. The con-
flicted address has been resolved so as to match the unequivocal address
(Figure 2-3b). The abstract result is the simple one-dimensional diagram
of Figure 2-4.

In support of our claim that solidarity has largely won out over power
we can offer a few quotations from language scholars. Littré, writing of
French usage in 1882, says: "Notre courtoisie est même si grande, que

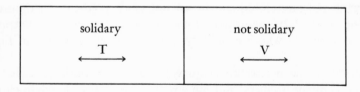

FIGURE 2-4.   THE ONE-DIMENSIONAL SOLIDARITY SEMANTIC

nous ne dédaignons pas de donner du 'vous' et du 'monsieur' à l'homme de la condition la plus vile." In 1930 Grand wrote of the Italian V: "On commence aussi à le donner aux personnes de service, à qui on disait 'tu' autrefois."

The best evidence that the change has occurred is in our interviews and notes on contemporary literature and films and, most importantly, the questionnaire results. The six social dyads of Figure 2-3 were all represented in the questionnaire. In the past our questions would have been answered in accordance with asymmetrical status. Across all six of these dyads, with French informants, results yield only 11 per cent non-reciprocal status answers, with German informants 12 per cent, Italian informants 27 per cent. In all other cases the usage is reciprocal and as indicated in Figure 2-3b. In all three of the languages, address between master and servant retains the greatest status-loading. Some of the changes toward solidarity are very recent. Only since the Second World War, for instance, the French Army has adopted a regulation requiring officers to say V to enlisted men.

The internal conflict between the two norms that governed T and V was a force for some sort of cultural change that would resolve the conflict. The particular resolution that occurred, suppression of the status norm in favor of the solidarity norm, is not the only conceivable resolution. Figure 2-2b can be put in equilibrium by suppressing the solidarity norm for persons not equal in status and so reverting to Figure 2-2a, or by suppressing the solidarity norm altogether and operating as in Figure 2-1. In terms of the dyads of Figure 2-3a, resolution by the suppression of solidarity would have meant settling on a non-reciprocal pattern in each instance and this resolution is just as simple as resolution by suppression of status. The internal contradiction in the norms motivates a simplifying change, but it does not account for the particular change that occurred. To understand the triumph of the solidarity norm, we must turn to another cause of cultural change—congruence with changes in the fundamental values of the societies in question.

IDEOLOGY AND THE NORMS OF ADDRESS

A historical and contemporary comparative study of the pronouns of address reveals a relation between the linguistic norms and a more elaborate set of norms and values. The non-reciprocal status norm is associated with a relatively static society in which power is distributed by birthright and is not subject to much redistribution. The status norm was closely tied with the feudal and manorial systems. In Italy the deferential pronoun *Lei* which has largely displaced the older *voi* was originally an abbreviation for *la vostra Signoria* (your lordship), and in Spanish *vuestra Merced* (your grace) became the deferential *usted*. The static social structure was accompanied by the Church teaching that each man had his properly appointed place and ought not to wish to rise above it. The reciprocal solidarity norm has grown with the open class society and an equalitarian ideology. The towns and cities have led the way in the semantic change as they led the way in opening society to vertical social mobility. The resolution of the internal conflict in the norms of address was accomplished by suppressing status in favor of solidarity. It seems likely that this particular resolution occurred because of its congruence with other far-reaching social changes. In addition to these rough historical correspondences, we have made a collection of lesser items of evidence favoring the thesis.

In France the non-reciprocal status semantic was dominant until the Revolution when the Committee for the Public Safety condemned the use of V as a feudal remnant and ordered a universal reciprocal T. On October 31, 1793, Malbec made a Parliamentary speech against V: "Nous distinguons trois personnes pour le singulier et trois pour le pluriel, et, au mépris de cette règle, l'esprit de fanatisme, d'orgueil et de féodalité, nous a fait contracter l'habitude de nous servir de la seconde personne du pluriel lorsque nous parlons à un seul" (quoted by Brunot, 1937, p. 691). For a time revolutionary "fraternité" transformed all address into the mutual "citoyen" and the mutual "tu." Robespierre even addressed the president of the Assembly as *tu*. In later years solidarity declined and the differences of status that always exist everywhere were expressed once more.

It must be asked why, in the case of the French Revolution, the equalitarian ideal was expressed in a universal T rather than a universal V or, as a third alternative, why was there not at this time a shift of semantic from status to solidarity with both pronouns being retained? The answer lies with the ancient upper-class preference for the use of V. There was animus against the pronoun itself. The pronoun of the "sans-culottes" was T and so this had to be the pronoun of the Revolution.

While the status semantic has largely disappeared from pronoun use in France today, native speakers are nevertheless aware of it. In part this is because it prevails in so much of the greatest French literature. Awareness of status as a potential factor in pronoun usage was revealed by our respondents' special attitude toward the saying of T to a waiter. Most of them felt that this would be shockingly bad taste in a way that other norm violations would not be. Apparently this is because there is a kind of seignorial right to say T to a waiter, an actual asymmetry of status, which the modern man's ideology requires him to deny. In French Africa, on the other hand, it was until very recently considered proper to recognize a caste difference between the African and the European and the non-reciprocal address came to life to express it. The European said T and required V from the African. This was a galling custom to the African and in 1957 Robert Lacoste, the French Minister residing in Algeria, urged his countrymen to eschew the practice.

In England, before the Norman Conquest, *ye* was the second person plural and *thou* the singular. *You* was originally the accusative of *ye* but in time it also became the nominative plural and ultimately ousted *thou* as the usual singular. The first uses of *ye* as a reverential singular occur in the thirteenth century and seem to have been copied from the French nobility. The semantic progression corresponds roughly to the general stages described in the first section of this chapter, except that the English seem always to have moved more freely from one form to another than did the continental Europeans.

In the seventeenth century *thou* and *you* became explicitly involved in social controversy. The Religious Society of Friends (or Quakers) was founded in the middle of this century by George Fox. One of the practices setting off this rebellious group from the larger society was the use of Plain Speech, and this entailed saying *thou* to everyone. George Fox explained the practice in these words:

> Moreover, when the Lord sent me forth into the world, He forbade me to put off my hat to any, high or low; and I was required to Thee and Thou all men and women, without any respect to rich or poor, great or small [quoted by Estrich and Sperber, 1946].

Fox wrote a fascinating pamphlet (1660) arguing that T to one and V to many is the natural and logical form of address in all languages. Among others he cites "Latin, Hebrew, Greek, Arabick, Syriack, Aethiopic, Egyptian, French, and Italian." Fox suggests that the Pope, "in his vanity," introduced "the corrupt and illogical practice" of saying V to one person. Farnsworth, another early Friend, wrote a somewhat similar pamphlet (1655) in which he argued that the Scriptures prove that God and Adam and God and Moses were not too proud to say and receive the singular T.

For the new convert to the Society of Friends the universal T was an especially difficult commandment. Thomas Ellwood (1714) has described the trouble that developed between himself and his father:

> But whenever I had occasion to speak to my Father, though I had no Hat now to offend him; yet my language did as much: for I durst not say YOU to him, but THOU or THEE, as the Occasion required, and then would he be sure to fall on me with his Fists.

The Friends' reasons for using the mutual T were much the same as those of the French revolutionaries but the Friends were always a minority and the larger society was antagonized by their volations of decorum.

Some Friends use *thee* today; the nominative *thou* has been dropped and *thee* is used as both the nominative and (as formerly) the accusative.

Interestingly, many Friends also use *you*. *Thee* is likely to be reserved for Friends among themselves and *you* said to outsiders. This seems to be a survival of the solidarity semantic. In English at large, of course, *thou* is no longer used. The explanation of its disappearance is by no means clear but the forces at work seem to have included a popular reaction against the radicalism of Quakers and Levelers and also a general trend in English toward simplified verbal inflection (e.g., elimination of the *wouldst* and *couldst* that went with *thou*).

The conflict in the norms that results from the convergence of two rules on two pronouns of address is a force toward simplification by suppression of one rule. In the European languages generally it is the status rule that has been suppressed and we think this is because these European societies were becoming open-class systems with an equalitarian ideology. The English language has arrived at a different resolution: the suppression of one of the two pronouns. This unique outcome eliminates the conflict in the norms by eliminating from pronominal usage any distinction of interpersonal relationship. Probably *thou* was selected for deletion instead of *ye* because it made possible a greater simplification in the inflection of verbs.

Two Other Historical Trends

The principal historical change in the semantics of T and V has been the suppression of the status norm in favor of the solidarity norm. There have been two other changes: 1) A decline in the use of the pronouns to express transient sentiments; 2) An expansion of the domain of T.

A social norm is a rule, written or unwritten, *prescribing* proper behavior and, since most behavior is proper, the norm also *describes* usual behavior. It is both right and customary for motorists in the United States to drive on the right-hand side of the road and both right and customary for parents to support their own young children. The existence of a clear norm provides always an opportunity for the expression and perception of individual personality. The motorist who keeps crossing over by a foot or so into the lane of oncoming traffic is either "careless" or "selfish" or "in a hurry." At any rate he is something more than just a motorist; his slight deviance gives him a character. If he goes all the way over into the left lane he acquires a more extreme character, that of a "drunk" or a "madman" or an "Englishman newly arrived in the States."

The two semantic rules that used to govern the European pronouns of address were, of course, social norms, and by departing from these norms speakers used to express their individuality. In French and English literature of the past, in the plays of Racine and of Shakespeare for instance, there are occasions where the choice of a pronoun clearly violates a group norm and also the customary practice of the speaker. The meaning of such a departure for other characters in a play and for audiences of the day was some attitude or emotion or trait of the speaker. The expressive meanings were derivatives of the semantic norms.

Violation of the status norm generally meant that a speaker momentarily regarded an addressee as his inferior, superior, or equal, although by usual criteria and according to the speaker's own customary usage, the addressee was not what the pronoun implied. Violations of the solidarity norm generally meant that a speaker temporarily extended sympathy and intimacy to someone from whom they were usually withheld or that he withdrew them from someone to whom they were usually given.

The oldest uses of T and V to express attitudes seem to have been the T of contempt or anger and the V of admiration or respect. Schliebitz, in his study (1886) of the French pronouns, found the first examples of these expressive uses in literature of the twelfth and thirteenth centuries, which is about the time that the status norm in address becomes clear in France, and Grand (1930) has found the same thing true for Italian. In saying T where V was usual, the speaker treated his addressee like a servant or child and assumed the right to berate him. The most common use of the expressive V in the early materials was that of a master who, feeling exceptionally pleased with a servant, elevated the servant pronominally.

Racine, in his dramas, uses the pronouns in perfect consistency with the status norm. His major figures exchange the V of upper-class equals. Lovers, brother and sister, husband and wife, none of them say T if they are of high rank. However, each high-ranking person has a subordinate confidante to whom T is said and from whom V is received. This courtly pattern is broken only in the greatest scenes of each play. Racine reserved the expressive pronoun as some composers save the cymbals. In both *Andromaque* and *Phèdre*, for instance, there are just two expressive departures from the norm and these two mark climaxes of feeling.

Jespersen (1905) believed that English "thou" and "ye" (or "you") were more often shifted to express mood than were the pronouns of the continental languages. The "thou" of contempt was so very familiar that a verbal form was created to name this expressive use. Shakespeare has Sir Toby Belch (*Twelfth Night*) use it in a speech urging Andrew Aguecheek to send a challenge to the disguised Viola: "Taunt him with the license of ink, if thou thou'st him some thrice, it shall not be amiss." In life off the stage the verb turned up in Sir Edward Coke's attack on Raleigh at the latter's trial in 1603: "All that he did, was at thy instigation, thou viper; for I thou thee, thou traitor" (Jardine, 1832–35).

The solidarity norm made it possible to express feelings of estrangement and sympathy. Shakespeare's play *Two Gentlemen from Verona*, because it concerns the Renaissance ideal of friendship, provides especially clear examples. The two gentlemen, Proteus and Valentine, initially exchange "thou," but when they touch on the subject of love, on which they disagree, their address changes to the "you" of estrangement. Molière has shown us that a man could even use the pronoun to put himself at a distance (Fay, 1920). George Dandin begins a soliloquy: "George Dandin! George Dandin! Vous avez fait une sottise. . . ."

In both French and English drama of the past, T and V were delicately expressive of approach and withdrawal. In terms of the amoeba metaphor that Freud used in theorizing about personal relations, the pronouns responded to the extension or retraction of libidinal pseudopodia. The solidarity norm continues to govern T and V today, but expressive use of these pronouns, at least in French, German, and Italian, is now very uncommon. It seems to appear last in the works of writers born in the second half of the nineteenth century. Our informants told us that the T, once it is given is, today, almost never withdrawn. To withdraw T would be to signal that a relationship had come to an end forevermore. The only modern expressive shift we have found is a rather chilling one. Silverberg (1940) reports that in Germany in 1940 a prostitute and her client said *du* when they met and while they were together, but when the libidinal tie (in the narrow sense) had been dissolved they resumed the mutual distant *Sie*. Why the expressive use of T and V should have declined in recent times is not apparent. Transient sentiments of solidarity and status continue to be expressed in speech of course. But now it is done with intonation and vocal quality and vocabulary selection rather than with the pronouns of address.

The remaining historical trend is an expansion of the domain of T. With solidarity established as the single dimension governing T and V, the number of relations considered solidary enough to merit the Mutual T is increasing and the number calling for Mutual V is correspondingly decreasing. In particular it is now common to regard the mild camaraderie that results from working on a common task or experiencing some common fate as grounds for T. We have a favorite example given to us independently by several French informants. It seems that mountaineers above a certain critical altitude shift to the Mutual T. We like to think that this is the point where their lives hang by a single thread. In general the Mutual T is advancing among fellow students, fellow workers, members of the same political group, persons who share a hobby or who take a trip together. We believe that this is the direction of current change because it summarizes what our informants tell us about the pronoun usage of "young people" as opposed to the usage of the immediately previous generation.

American English has been moving in the same direction. With the deletion from English of the pronoun *thou* the principal option of address became the choice between the first name (FN) and last name with a title (TLN). The difference between Mutual TLN (Title with Last Name) and Mutual FN (First Name) was and is a difference of solidarity or intimacy. Newly introduced adults begin, in English, with Mutual TLN even as, in the continental languages, they begin with Mutual V.

The continental languages of course have their own FN and TLN forms as well as the pronouns of address. Informants who speak English and also one of the continental languages tell us that Mutual FN in either language represents a lesser intimacy than does Mutual T. Adults speaking American English are likely to move to the FN a few minutes after being introduced. In the past, however, the FN was used more selectively by Americans. Brown and Ford (1961) compared usage in recent American plays with usage in a sample of nineteenth-century American plays (Quinn, 1917) and found that the Mutual FN in the earlier period implied a much longer acquaintance than it does today. We even have generic first names in American English for use with strangers whose first names are not known; for example the taxi driver's "Mac" and the panhandler's "Buddy."

There is some personal variation among speakers of a language in the range of acquaintances addressed intimately. In present-day Paris everyone uses T and V in accordance with the reciprocal solidarity rule but *where* a man makes the distinction in his total acquaintanceship is a matter of individual style. Brown and Gilman (1960) inquired into the detailed usage of fifty young Parisians who were studying in universities in the Boston area. The inquiry was aimed at discovering the correlates of wide and narrow use of T. There was one very strong correlate: radicalism of political and social ideology as assessed by Eysenck's (1957) Social Attitude Inventory. The more radical the ideology was, the more widely T was used.

The Eysenck Inventory is a collection of statements to be accepted or rejected concerning such matters as religion, economics, racial relations, politics, and sexual behavior. Why should "radical" opinions on such an inventory be associated with the liberal use of Mutual T? The radical on this inventory quite consistently disapproves of any sort of invidious distinction among persons on the basis of race, religion, nationality, property, or even criminality. He disapproves of any absolute line separating the solidary, the "in-group," from the non-solidary, the "out-group." The radical holds that Catholics, Negroes, and Jews are not fundamentally "different," that private property should be abolished, that a people ought not to be so nationalistic as to impede the development of a world organization. He holds that the criminal is not far enough "out" to justify capital punishment; the criminal should be re-educated and reclaimed by society.

The tendency to use a single pronoun of address, the same for everyone, would seem to be a natural expression of this ideology. While equalitarians of the past in France and England and elsewhere rebelled against the expression of deference in social relations, the equalitarian of today rebels even against the expression of difference. Of course, uniformity could be achieved by expanding the domain of Mutual V rather than by expanding T. The fact that the pattern being extended is Mutual T, the pattern used between brothers and lifelong friends, expresses the radical's intention to extend the in-group, solidary ethic to everyone.

A Residual Puzzle

The fact that the status rule has been suppressed in pronominal usage should not be thought to imply that status has been eliminated as a principle governing interaction, nor that all symbolic expressions of status have been eliminated, nor even all linguistic expressions. The same societies that no longer tolerate the non-reciprocal V and T continue to tolerate non-reciprocal address of other kinds. A French lady and her maid exchange V nowadays but the maid will say "Madame" and the lady "Yvonne." This exchange of a title for a first name also occurs within the family. In America, and in France and elsewhere, it is customary to use kinship titles to members of ascending generations (e.g., "Father," "Grandfather") and first names to members of descending generations (e.g., "Jack" and "Jill"). It is of incidental interest that, where we have some choice of titles for a certain kintype, the several options seem to express variations in the psychological quality of the relationship. Schneider and Homans (1955) have shown that the address form "Dad" for a male parent is one that almost any son feels he could comfortably use. But those sons who *usually* say "Father" would not be comfortable with a shift to "Pa" or "Papa" and vice-versa. A "Father" is pretty clearly not the same kind of a parent as a "Pa."

Brown and Ford (1961) have summarized the range of circumstances in which Americans nowadays employ the non-reciprocal first name (FN) and title with last name (TLN). Their summary is based on usage in a large collection of contemporary American plays (Gassner, 1947, 1952, 1958). A substantial difference of age seems, in the first place, to call for non-reciprocal FN and TLN: children say TLN to adults and receive FN; among adults an elder by approximately fifteen or more years receives TLN and gives FN to his junior. In the second place a difference of occupational status can activate the non-reciprocal pattern; this may be a relation of direct and enduring subordination (e.g., master-servant, employer-employee, officer-enlisted man); it may be a relation of direct but temporary subordination involving someone in a service occupation (e.g., a barber and his patron); it may be an enduring difference of occupational status that does not involve direct subordination (e.g., U.S. Senators outrank firemen). Modern European languages use titles and names in much the same way.

Brown and Ford also obtained a set of on-the-spot notations of actual usage from a man employed by a Boston drafting firm. Most of the examples of address this man recorded were Mutual FN or Mutual TLN, but there were forty different instances of non-reciprocal address. In thirty-six of these the recipient of TLN was the organizational superior and also the elder; in twenty-eight he was a member of one of the four top executive ranks, whereas the recipient of FN was a member of one of the eight lower unionized ranks. There was one instance involving a pair matched by rank but not by age, and in this case the elder received TLN. The interesting examples are the three that remain because, in these three, the two determinants of status that are usually positively associated, age and organizational rank, were negatively associated. The prototype is the thirty-year-old executive and the sixty-year-old janitor. How should they address one another? The case is interesting because it is a test of the comparative strength in our society of two sorts of status: the "ascribed" status of age, which accrues to a man willy-nilly, and the "achieved" status carried by occupation, which is based on accomplishment and effort. In other times and places, notably in Feudal Europe, in India, and in Japan, ascribed status based on lineage and sex has been important. In the United States today, of course, achievement is dominant. All three younger-men-but-executives used FN to the older-men-but-janitors and received TLN.

What is the residual puzzle? The puzzle is the survival of a status norm for titles and names in the face of its suppression for pronouns. Why should the equalitarian attack have singled out V and T? Why should the coding of differential status in pronouns be intolerable today when it is not intolerable in other forms of address?

The only idea that has occurred to us is that it may be a matter of the degree of linguistic compulsion. The use of a title or name can usually be avoided in face-to-face address, but the use of a pronoun is not so easily avoided. Even if a Frenchman does not say either *tu* or *vous*, as he would not in the imperative, one or the other will be implicit in the inflection of the verb. *Regardez* says *vous* and *regardes* says *tu*. The verb is inflected according to the pronoun spoken or intended, and so if there is a status norm governing pronouns then a continual coding of status is compulsory for speakers. By contrast, titles and names, though partially governed by status, are not compulsory forms and so it is possible to leave status unexpressed in most discourse.

When should it be desirable to leave status unexpressed? In circumstances of uncertainty or of rebellion. Uncertainty is created by changes of status or by long acquaintance between unequals. When a graduate student is awarded a doctoral degree, and thereby rather abruptly translated from student to colleague, mode of address is likely to intrude into consciousness as a problem. Among American academics it is normal, with even a small degree of acquaintance, to use the Mutual FN. But the fledgling academic after four or more years of subordination may not feel quite ready to use the FN. There is a psychic lag, a period of time in which the first name to one's former teachers still feels presumptuous. However the "tyranny of democratic manners" does not allow the young academic to continue comfortable with the polite "Dr. X." He would not wish to be thought excessively conscious of status, unprepared for faculty rank, a born lickspittle. Happily English, and any language that confines the coding of status to titles and names, allows him a respite. He can avoid any term of address whatsoever, for days, weeks, even months, staying with the uncommitted "you" until he and his seniors become accustomed to the new order of things. For this linguistic *rite de passage*, English provides a waiting-room in which to screw up courage.

Uncertainty of address also arises when there is no change of relative status in a dyad but only a long term of acquaintance between two who are not greatly different in status. A young clerk in the United States should after a time stop saying TLN to the manager if the manager is not very old and not very awesome. But when exactly? When such a relation moves into the region of uncertainty where TLN seems too formal and FN a little "fresh," speakers of American English are sometimes struck dumb—as far as names and titles are concerned. One does not use either the FN or the TLN for a time. Occasionally the more familiar term is tried out as a form of reference, rather than address, calling the boss by his first name in speaking of him in his hearing to a third party. In any case status need not be either expressed or denied so long as names and titles are the means; but with pronouns it cannot be escaped.

There is also rebellion against status. Suppose a man despises his feudal lord or his boss or even his father. If relative status is coded in pronouns he must either express a respect he is far from feeling or he must make an obviously defiant and conceivably dangerous departure from the norm. Remember what happened to the young Quaker who called his father "thou." The beauty of names and titles is that one can be a bit churlish without being held strictly accountable for it. Avoidance of the respectful title where it would often be used gratifies the rebellious impulse and communicates a message, but because the title is not really required, the speaker cannot be convicted of rebellion.

It is possible then that the expression of status differences with pronouns and verbal inflections was a more onerous custom than the expression of the same differences with titles and names because it was a more continual compulsion. As the European societies became more fluid there were more changes of status, more cases of long acquaintance between unequals, and more rebellion against claims on superiority, especially ascribed superiority. In these circumstances the rules for T and V changed but the rules for less compulsory forms did not.

Solidarity and Status as Dimensions of Relationship

Social relations between persons are very much more complicated than physical relations between objects. When you have said that one stone is the same color as another stone, that A = B with respect to color, that is the end of it. There is nothing more to say about the relationship. Similarity between stones does not give rise to sentiments. Similar stones are not disposed to seek one another's company, to cooperate with one another, to confide in one another, to call one another T. Stones do not behave. Similar stones do not create symbols to advertise their closeness; they do not wear wedding rings or call one another "dear" in public. Stones do not symbolize. People do symbolize, do behave, and do have sentiments. That is why there is more to solidarity between persons than there is to similarity between stones.

When you have said that one stone is larger than another, that A > B, there is again nothing more to be said. But when you have said that one person is "greater" than another, there is much more to be said. The greater person will enjoy a sentiment of superiority and the lesser will suffer a sentiment of inferiority. The greater will say T and exert influence and enjoy precedence; the lesser will say V and be influenced and make way. The difference between the greater and the lesser will be advertised in status symbols which they both understand and which others also understand. An inequality of status between persons is a more complicated relation than an inequality of weight between stones.

It is not clear how we ought to conceptualize the various aspects of solidarity and status. There are important regularities to be captured, regularities glimpsed in the study of address, in many kinds of behavioral science research, and in everyday life; regularities that are haunting but a little vague. What we see is a tendency for the various relations connecting one person, A, with another person, B, to cluster; for one relation to be associated with another. Two major clusters are made up of symmetrical relations: when A and B are similar each tends to like the other, each seeks to be in the company of the other, each interacts frequently with the other, each says T to the other. The opposing set of symmetrical relations

TABLE 2-1. ASPECTS OF SOLIDARITY AND STATUS

	Personal characteristics	Spatial relations	Sentiments	Behavior	Symbols
Symmetrical relations	Solidarity marked by similarities of taste, attitude, fate, age, sex, occupation, income, etc.	Solidarity marked by proximity (being near).	Solidarity marked by liking, sympathy, trust, and other pleasant sentiments.	Solidarity marked by frequent interaction, confiding in one another, beneficent actions, self-disclosure, etc.	Solidarity marked by any perceptible similarity, proximity, or intimacy.
	Nonsolidarity marked by differences.	Nonsolidarity marked by remoteness (being far).	Nonsolidarity marked by indifference or dislike which are not pleasant sentiments.	Nonsolidarity marked by infrequent interaction and little intimacy.	Nonsolidarity marked by any perceptible difference, distance, or formality.
Asymmetrical relations	Status differences marked by differences in valued characteristics such as age, sex, occupation, income, etc.	Status differences marked by being above or below, in front or behind.	Status differences marked by agreeable sentiments of superiority and by disagreeable sentiments of inferiority.	Status differences marked by influence, control, power, etc.	Status differences marked by any perceptible differences in valued characteristics, by "superior" and "inferior" spatial positions, or by influence and control.

runs: when A is unlike B, each tends not to like the other, not to seek to be in the company of the other, not to interact with the other, and each says V. In short Mutual T and Mutual V appear to belong to opposed clusters of symmetrical relations between persons. Two other major clusters consist of asymmetrical relations: when A has greater social value than B, A feels superior and B feels inferior, A exerts influence and B is influenced, A says T and B says V. The opposed cluster consists of the same relations with the roles of A and B reversed. In short the two possible dyadic combinations of V and T appear to belong to opposed clusters of asymmetrical relations.

There are many different symmetrical relations connecting A and B that can be regarded as aspects of solidarity or its absence, and there are many different asymmetrical relations between A and B that can be regarded as aspects of comparative status. The terms "solidarity" and "status" will be used in a maximally general way to characterize the two kinds of relations: symmetrical and asymmetrical. We need some scheme for classifying relations more narrowly, a scheme that will help us to see regularities and to understand them. The scheme to be used has been foreshadowed in our discussion of address forms and in the contrast above between stones and persons.

Relations between two persons may be classified into five types: relations involving personal characteristics (e.g., age, sex, nationality, education); relations in space (e.g., close, remote, above, below, before, and behind); relational sentiments (e.g., liking, dislike, superiority, and inferiority); relational behavior (e.g., cooperation, confiding in, influence); symbols of relations (e.g., wedding rings, secret handclasps, salutes, "brass"). These five types apply to relations of both the symmetrical and the asymmetrical varieties. The scheme that results appears as Table 2-1.

I would like to use the scheme of Table 2-1 to organize some remarks about solidarity and status. The remarks are grouped according to the kind of relation they chiefly concern and so there are short sections on Personal Characteristics, Spatial Relations, Sentiments, Behavior, and Symbols. For the most part we will be reporting research evidence or everyday evidence of the clustering of certain symmetrical relations and the clustering of certain asymmetrical relations.

PERSONAL CHARACTERISTICS

Any person, A, and any other person, B, in a society will have certain characteristics by virtue of which they can be compared. The relative status of A and B is calculated from their comparative possession of socially valued characteristics. Characteristics that are valued in

many societies include seniority, maleness, noble lineage, higher education, a large income, and positions of formal authority. A status order
derives from individual differences with respect to the possession of
such characteristics, but it depends also upon a general agreement as to
the characteristics to be valued and their several degrees of value. If
there were not such an agreement on standards each person might be
expected to value his own personal combination of characteristics above
all other combinations. In fact, however, members of a society agree
fairly well on one another's social value.

The dominance order found in many animal societies resembles a
human status order in that it is also composed of inequalities of privilege
and power. Dominance is like status also in its dependence upon individual
differences and especially in its dependence upon age and sex. In dominance orders the male usually outranks the female and the mature animal
the immature. This is also the usual way with human status orders. The
determinants of animal dominance beyond sex and age seem to be
strength, aggressiveness, weaponry, fearsomeness of appearance, and ability to bluff. These things are not irrelevant to human status.

The likelihood of solidarity between A and B increases as the similarity of their personal characteristics, including those valued characteristics on which status is based. It follows that equality of status makes
for solidarity. There is very extensive documentation of the link between status equality and solidary sentiments and actions. Kahl and
Davis (1955) asked 199 men in Cambridge, Massachusetts to name their
three best friends. It turned out that a man's "best friends" were usually
his status equals. Hollingshead (1949) found that cliques of high-school
students in Elmtown were largely made up of boys and girls whose families belonged either to the same socio-economic class or to adjacent
classes.

Solidarity seems to arise from characteristics that do not figure
importantly in the calculation of status as well as from those that do.
Studies of marital selection (Lapiere and Farnsworth, 1949) show that
similarity in interests and attitudes are important as well as equality
of status. At The University of Michigan in 1954 and 1955 Newcomb
(1961) was able to obtain extensive data on individual attitudes and interests from two collections of seventeen men before these men had become
acquainted. The men later lived together in a small undergraduate residence
house, seventeen of them in 1954 and seventeen in 1955. The friendships
and cliques that developed once the men came to know one another were
largely predictable from their prior similarities. One clique, for example,
was made up of five men enrolled in the liberal arts college who were
all political "liberals" with strong intellectual and aesthetic interests. Another clique was made up of three men who were all veterans and all en-

rolled in the college of engineering; these men were politically "conserva-tive" and their interests were more "practical" than "theoretical."

A common fate is also a similarity that can give rise to friendly sentiments and cooperative or altruistic behavior. Our French informants, you may recall, told us that mountaineers above a certain height begin to use the Mutual T. Solidarity in the trenches and in prison camps and among maltreated demonstrators in Birmingham, Alabama, is well known as is the solidarity that follows flood, earthquake, or fire. But solidarity can also arise from the sharing of a very trivial hardship. One day in the winter of 1960 a blizzard struck Boston and very few people went to work in the building at M.I.T. where I then had my office. Among these few there was a curious euphoria, a sense of fellowship, of the self extended. People congratulated one another on their hardihood, shared lunches, helped dig out one another's cars, and only barely re-frained from group singing. Next day the weather cleared and the mood vanished.

Not every sort of similarity between persons makes for friendship and trust and interaction. Persons of identical height or identical weight do not on that account like one another. Similarity on these dimensions does not ordinarily create like-mindedness and it seems ultimately to be like-mindedness that generates solidarity. However, persons occupying an extreme position on almost any dimension are likely to constitute a social category by virtue of their extremity and so to be like-minded. Similarity of height among dwarfs and similarity of weight among circus "fat ladies" should be grounds for solidarity.

Similarity between persons is relative. Perhaps the first psychological consequence of visiting a foreign land is the change in self-perception that results. In London an American sees the American-ness of his haircut and hears the American-ness of his speech and the new salience of these personal attributes becomes a new basis for solidarity. Americans who would have "nothing in common" in the United States greet one an-other with some warmth in Piccadilly Circus; in Shanghai they feel them-selves to be brothers. Our informants from France and Germany and India told us that they used the Mutual T with their countrymen much more readily as visitors in the United States than they would have done at home.

Let us not make things out to be simpler than they are. Similarity does not always make for liking and trust and cooperation. It does not do so when there is a conflict of interest. The similarity of occupation that can bind workingmen into a trade union can set them at one another's throats if there is a severe shortage of jobs. Insofar as students in a class share a common fate of exposure to unfair examinations, dull lectures, and dreary readings they are solidary, but if they are graded on a curve their solidarity will diminish. If conditions are created in a prison camp, as they were for Americans in North Korea, such that one prisoner can advance his own interests by sacrificing the welfare of others, there is little solidarity (Schein, 1958). Similarity makes for solidarity except where it creates payoff conditions such that A gains in the degree that B loses.

Finally we must recognize, as did Durkheim (1893), a solidarity founded on differences. Librettist and composer could not work together if both had the same talents. Husband and wife may be very close because one wants to be nurtured and the other to be nurturant. These are differences but they are complementary differences, differences which, in combination, advance goals that both persons share. And of course insofar as they share goals two persons are similar. Differences that are not subordinated to common purposes do not seem to engender liking or confidence or cooperation. Durkheim called the solidarity that arises from similarities alone "mechanical"; the solidarity that arises from complementary differences he called "organic."

The scheme of Table 2-1 proposes that similarity between persons goes with many kinds of symmetrical relation including proximity and frequent interaction, friendly sentiments, beneficent actions, and symbols of solidarity. Social psychologists who have tried to formulate the most general regularities of ordinary social behavior have usually included one or more of these correlations. Heider in *The Psychology of Interpersonal Relations* (1958), for instance, says that "*p* similar to *o* induces *p* likes *o*" where *p* is one person and *o* another. Heider also holds that "*p* likes *o* induces *p* in contact with *o*," where contact includes both proximity and interaction, and that "*p* likes *o* induces *p* benefits *o*." Heider furthermore subscribes to all of these propositions in reverse with liking inducing similarity, contact inducing liking, and benefit inducing liking. He believes, in other words, that cause and effect can work either way in these correlations. *The Psychology of Interpersonal Relations* cites a large amount of evidence that supports Heider's propositions.

From Homans' *The Human Group* (1950) comes this hypothesis: "If the frequency of interaction between two or more persons increases, the degree of their liking for one another will increase, and vice-versa" (p. 112). And also this hypothesis: "The more frequently persons interact with one another, the more alike in some respects both their activities and their sentiments tend to become" (p. 120). These propositions express in a quantitative form the association predicted by Table 2-1 between frequent interaction and liking and between frequent interaction and similarity. Homans, like Heider, believes that cause and effect can work in either direction.

Homans develops his hypotheses in connection with the close study of a real group. The real group is a collection of fourteen workers who were employees of the Western Electric Company at the company's Hawthorne Works in Chicago. These fourteen workers constituted a section responsible for wiring banks of terminals used in telephone equipment. Homans calls them the members of the Bank Wiring Room. In the years 1927–32 the Western Electric Company sponsored a famous series of studies (Roethlisberger and Dickson, 1939) designed to uncover the chief sources of satisfaction and dissatisfaction among their employees. The men in the Bank Wiring Room were among the groups studied.

The fourteen members of the wiring section were divided into two cliques that Homans designates A and B. The men themselves referred to these cliques as the "group in front" (A) and the "group in back" (B). The wiremen in Clique A worked on equipment called connector units while the wiremen in Clique B worked on selector units. The organization into cliques seems to have been produced by a spatial proximity imposed by the geography of the room and by an initial similarity of activity imposed by the work arrangements.

A clique in the Bank Wiring Room was simply a set of individuals who interacted more frequently with one another than with outsiders. Members of a clique conversed with one another, played games together, traded jobs, and helped one another with their jobs. So spatial proximity and similarity of occupation were associated with frequent interaction, some of it beneficent. The cliques were also identifiable in the pattern of personal friendships; only one strong friendship linked members of different cliques. The cliques were identifiable by their distinct styles of life. They both played games but the games were different. Both ate candy but they bought different kinds. Both turned out work but the output of A ran higher than the output of B. So the symmetrical cluster of Table 2-1 was fully realized: similarity and proximity and interaction and friendship all went together.

If similarity and proximity beget liking and interaction which in turn beget more similarity and proximity which beget additional liking and interaction, why does not human life melt down into a perfectly uniform sugar syrup? There must be something that can break up the cycle. Probably there are many things. It seems likely, for instance, that where similarity is so great that each person finds the other highly predictable, boredom may begin to drive them apart. Even if it does not, however, there is always the lure of status. What if interaction and friendship become available on a higher status level? Will not the lure of superiority-plus-solidarity pull a person out of his humbler orbit and so break the cycle?

In the Bank Wiring Room, Clique A was not only distinguishable from Clique B, it ranked above B. The members of A felt themselves to be superior to the members of B and the members of B seemed, with some resentment, to recognize this claim. The job of wiring connectors, which was carried on in A, was somewhat better paid than the job of wiring selector equipment which was carried on in B. A wireman usually started on selectors and as he gained skill and seniority moved to connectors. The connector wiremen occupied a spatial position in front of the selector wiremen and this position, with its implications of social control, suggests superiority. All the members of the Bank Wiring Room valued skill, seniority, income, and position and this agreement on standards made it possible to agree on a status order. It was possible then to break into the cycle of friendship, interaction, and similarity in B by promotion to A and probably possible to break into A with a promotion out of the department.

Life in the Bank Wiring Room was structured in terms of the two familiar dimensions: solidarity and status. Proximity in space and similarity of occupation generated interaction and liking and further similarities, all of the symmetrical relations that constitute solidarity. In addition, the members of the Bank Wiring Room all valued such characteristics as skill, seniority, and a greater income. There were differences among the workmen in these characteristics and the shared set of standards enabled them to agree on a status order. Clique A was different from B and also better than B and so asymmetrical relations held between the two.

SPATIAL RELATIONS

Near and far are symmetrical relations; if A is near B then B is near A. Nearness or proximity belongs to the cluster of solidarity and remoteness to the cluster of non-solidarity. Above and below, in front of and behind, are asymmetrical relations. If A is above B then B cannot be above A but must be below. These asymmetrical relations seem to belong to the clusters of differential status.

For Americans the spatial positions *above* and *in front of* clearly imply superiority of status. Indeed we talk about status in the language of space; persons of greater social value are "higher" and persons of lesser value are "lower." In our cities the wealthy live on Hill Street or Cleveland Heights or in Belmont. The position in front is both the position of privilege and the position of control. Officers go to the head of a line when something good is being dispensed and stand in front of their companies when giving commands. At large assemblages the "head" table is likely to be raised on a dais as well as placed in the front of the room.

I wonder how universal these implications are. Many languages other than English use their terms for spatial high and low to describe "vertical" status. An anthropologist who has travelled a great deal once told me: "Everywhere I have ever been the 'better' people live on the heights." The ancient Hindu myth of the origin of caste says that the exalted Brahman caste arose from the head of Purushu, the archetypal man, and the lowly Sudras from his feet. The implications could be universal or nearly so since they are grounded in certain natural circumstances. In personal combat the man on top, because of gravity, is likely to be in control. The dwelling or fortress on a height "commands" a view and so provides an informational advantage. If food or space is in short supply then the man in front has an advantage and is privileged. The man in front of a group that faces him can be seen by all of the group while a member in the ranks cannot be seen by all and so the man in front is in a position to control and coordinate group action.

Even in animal societies the position in front carries implications of privilege and control. Precedence of access to food, space, and mates is, we know, the chief prerogative of dominance. For animals that live as nomadic groups, including primates, the foremost member, the leader whom others follow, is, at least temporarily, in a position of social power. The implications of above and below are less clear but the animal on top in a battle is generally in control and the animal on a height has an informational advantage.

Proximity in space makes for solidarity because it is prerequisite to interaction. Nearness of dwelling unit or work position is known to favor interaction and friendship. Festinger, Schachter, and Back (1950) found that, in a housing project for married veteran students, friendships most often developed between next door neighbors. The most widely popular people in the project were those whose apartments were so located as to bring them into contact with many others; the apartments were either located centrally in a court or else they opened on stairways. Newcomb (1961), for his study of the acquaintance process in a student residence at the University of Michigan, assigned rooms arbitrarily and so was able to assess the influence of proximity upon the development of friendship. In his data as a whole proximity seems to have favored friendship, but the influence of the spatial variable was slight. The house was small and so even the most spatially remote members had ample opportunity to meet. The importance of proximity and remoteness as determinants of solidarity will of course depend upon the distances involved.

For animal species that manifest territoriality the inhabitants of a common territory live in closer proximity and in closer solidarity with one another than with outsiders. The members of a primate clan or a songbird family or an insect colony interact frequently and are similar by virtue of common heredity and shared experience. They engage in cooperative and altruistic behavior. They also seem to like one another better than they like outsiders. When two adult worker ants from the same colony meet, they touch each other's bodies with their antennae, and if one has fed recently it regurgitates a drop of honey dew which the other devours (Wheeler, 1923). Primates of the same clan, if they are on good terms, will groom one another. By turns each examines the other's skin and hair and plucks out lice, ticks, and fleas. Outsiders of the same species who approach a territory are, we know, either threatened or attacked.

The anthropologist Edward T. Hall has had some stimulating things to say about spatial relations and the quality of social interaction in his book *The Silent Language* (1959). He points out that spacing alone, in such a meeting place as an airport waiting-room, enables one to infer the approximate quality of the social relations linking the people present. Unacquainted persons, strangers, will maintain a certain distance. If there is room enough they will not sit side by side but will take alternate or more remote seats. If there are many "empties" in a line of telephone booths strangers will not choose adjoining booths. Unacquainted humans act very much like unacquainted birds on a telephone wire; they preserve their intervals.

Close contact, back to back, is more tolerable for unacquainted humans than is close contact face to face or side by side, and strangers can sit comfortably with the backs of their heads close together. In this position there is no visual contact to force interaction. In a crowded subway train, strangers are sometimes forced into face-to-face proximity but they seek to reduce their discomfort by fixing their gazes on remote advertisements. A family in the airport waiting-room can be recognized by its tendency to clot; all try to "sit together." Small children may even sit upon or in the same seats with their parents. Two lovers are distinguishable from strangers by proximity and from families by their taste for eye-to-eye contact.

In airports that have V.I.P. lounges or separate waiting-rooms for first-class passengers, differences of status can be discerned from patterns in space. The superior waiting-room in the airport is likely to be higher up than the inferior and first-class seats on planes are "up front." When food and drink are dispensed, first-class passengers are served first, of course; very much like the dominant birds in a henyard.

Hall's discussion goes beyond a simple dichotomy of solidary and non-solidary interaction to a consideration of various degrees of intimacy. It seems to him that human dyads operate with eight different intervals or zones. There is a person-to-person distance which is considered normal and appropriate for each of eight different varieties of interaction. As the distance diminishes, Hall suggests, the interaction becomes more intimate but not in a continuous way. The general quality of interaction will be uniform within a spatial zone and will change abruptly as a spatial boundary is crossed. I am a little skeptical of this thesis and once had the opportunity to express the skepticism to Dr. Hall in a face-to-face conversation. While we talked, having the sort of impersonal professional discussion that is supposed to go on at a "neutral" distance of four or five feet, Dr. Hall occasionally moved his chair forward. Whenever he did so I moved mine back. He somewhat shook my skepticism when, as we concluded our discussion, he pointed out that he had moved me a considerable distance across the room by repeatedly crossing a zone boundary.

Hall thinks that the zoning of interaction is a cultural matter and that different societies locate their zone boundaries somewhat differently. South Americans, he suggests, are accustomed to carry on polite professional conversation at closer quarters than are North Americans. In a mixed dyad Hall finds that the South American is always trying to move in closer and the North American to move back farther. The former he suggests is likely to conclude that North Americans are "stand-offish" and the North American is likely to think the South American "pushy."

What happens when animals are caused to live for prolonged periods in much closer contact than is normal for their species? Calhoun (1962) has raised populations of Norway rats in congested circumstances and he reports that interaction degenerates into a "behavioral sink." Females transporting their pups from place to place begin to drop them and leave them unretrieved. A kind of "pansexuality" develops with males mounting unreceptive females and also other males and even recently-weaned young. The male rats begin to clamp their teeth on one another's tails, not letting go until the tail is torn free or broken off. This extreme disruption of normal interaction results in a high mortality rate and so the reduction of population size (see Chapter 1).

Social stress from overcrowding can also have profound internal consequences for the victim, consequences that are quite distinct from external injuries inflicted by companions. Wynne-Edwards (1962) summarizes the evidence on pages 550–554 of his book. In rats and mice it appears that social stress can produce physiological derangements of the reproductive systems of both males and females, of the spleen, thymus, and especially of the adrenal cortex. These derangements increase mortality in the animal population and so function as a kind of population control. Most of the evidence of death from social stress has been obtained in the unnatural conditions of the laboratory. However, there are some indications that it operates in nature when large animal populations, e.g., lemmings, are prevented from migrating. It is even possible that psychological and psychosomatic disease are produced in humans

by the kind of extreme overcrowding to which the very poor are subjected in large cities.

SENTIMENTS

We learn about the sentiments of others from behavior and so it may
seem unnecessary to distinguish, as we have in Table 2-1, between sentiments and behavior. Our sense of being liked by another person or perhaps looked down upon by him generally derives from something he has
said or done. Even so a distinction can be made between behavior expressive of sentiment and behavior that is not expressive of sentiment,
between a cold disdainful glance and stepping aboard a bus. However,
in learning about psychology we are not limited to study of the other
person. Each of us has also himself. The other person can only yield
behavior but within ourselves we have states of consciousness including
sentiments of superiority and inferiority, of like and dislike. It is worthwhile to try to characterize these sentiments.

The basic sentiment in solidarity is a feeling of union with someone
else, a feeling that the self has grown beyond its skin. The contrary
sentiment of non-solidarity is perhaps simple indifference but it easily
becomes dislike. Xenophobia, the hatred of what is strange or foreign,
is common enough to have a name. Indifference may yield to dislike as
differences in personal characteristics become greater. Feelings of solidarity are extremely pleasant; they are one of the best things that life
offers. Indifference and dislike are not so pleasant. The basic sentiments
of status are superiority or inferiority; one feels that his personal value
is great or that it is slight. Superiority is the pleasanter of the two we
will all agree.

Verbal reports of liking and dislike have been much studied in social
psychology. In a typical research, members of a group, very often a
college fraternity or sorority, are asked to say which other members they
like and which they dislike. The question is not always the same. Sometimes subjects are asked to name others with whom they would be willing
to room at college or with whom they would be willing to go on a vacation trip. Subjects may be asked to report more than their own dislikes;
they may, for instance, be asked to guess how others feel about them
or about one another. This method of studying group structure is called
the sociometric method and it was developed by Moreno (1934).

Are liking and indifference or dislike symmetrical relations like the
Mutual T and the Mutual V? If A likes B, does B usually like A? We
have implied that this is the case in Table 2-1. Tagiuri (1958) has given
us an answer to this question based on his own very extensive collections
of sociometric data. In answering the question as to whether liking is

symmetrical, it is necessary to allow for the operation of chance which would alone produce many symmetrical bonds. Tagiuri finds that liking is indeed symmetrical at a level well above chance. If A likes B then B will usually like A. Dislikes, on the other hand, are not symmetrical more often than chance would permit. Some of these dislikes may, however, have involved differences of status based on differences in valued personal characteristics. I would expect symmetry to prevail between subjects who were unlike one another but not of different value. Perhaps the sentiment in these circumstances is indifference rather than dislike.

Tagiuri reports on sentiments attributed to others as well as on those reported for oneself. The question of symmetry now becomes: When A likes B, does A *think* that B likes him back? We reported above on B's actual sentiment towards A and now we will report on A's conception of B's sentiment. Sentiments are conceived to be much more symmetrical than they are. Subjects thought that both their likes and their dislikes were usually reciprocated. Their intellectual models for liking and dislike seem to have been simpler than the facts and nearer to the symmetry suggested by Table 2-1.

In social science research subjects have not often been asked to report whether they felt "superior" or "inferior" to one another. Probably this is because the two words carry an odious implication of ascribed and unalterable inequality. However subjects have often been asked to rank one another on "status" or "prestige" or "station" (see Chapter 3) and such rankings imply feelings of superiority and inferiority. These feelings, when they relate two persons, A and B, are, by definition, asymmetrical.

Liking and superiority are the two agreeable social sentiments, but because one tends to be symmetrical while the other is necessarily asymmetrical, they cannot easily be enjoyed simultaneously. Liking accompanies the recognition of similarities while feelings of superiority derive from awareness of differences. Conversations often oscillate between a solidarity game and an invidious status game. When two or more persons are introduced at a cocktail party they commonly begin by searching for points of agreement or like-mindedness. "What do you do?" "Where are you from?" "Do you know X?" and so on. If these initial explorations disclose nothing but discouraging differences the dyad is likely to break up. When there is a good initial match, however, agreeable feelings of friendliness and trust develop, feelings of being understood (at last). These are feelings that two or more players can enjoy simultaneously.

It frequently happens, however, that one or the other participant in such a conversation goes whoring after a sense of superiority and starts to disclose creditable personal characteristics which make him unlike the others. The atmosphere cools fast and the others trot out their own status claims. If one person breaks the pattern of the solidarity game in an effort to be "one up," then others will break it in order to avoid being "one down." Superiority is a sentiment not easily shared. Unless of course a set of persons similar and solidary among themselves can feel superior to another person or group. When you are caught on the bottom of this kind of a scrimmage the best thing to do is crawl out from under and leave your oppressors to vie with one another for superiority.

Sympathy is a sentiment that often seems to accompany solidarity. By sympathy I mean feeling what another feels, happy at his good fortune, sad at his bad fortune. What is it that causes sympathy to flow in human beings? It is not automatically extended to all members of the species and not always withheld from other species. A man can feel more anguish for his injured dog than for the reported suffering of a million remote Vietnamese. It does seem as if contact were one of the prerequisites. Moviemakers are expert at causing us to feel sympathy and they are able to make us feel it for any object they choose: not only little orphan girls but also murderers and narcotics addicts and slaveowners and any animal that Disney cares to draw. How is it done? The most general principle seems to be to provide a close and continued exposure to the object. We are made to dwell on the expressions of the face, the movements of the hands, the posture of the body, and the sound of the voice as if they were our own. And sympathy seems to follow. Close contact, perhaps involving the recognition of similarities between the self and the other, may be a sufficient condition for releasing sympathy.

The essential antagonism between solidarity and differential status makes for a certain amount of hypocrisy in social life. Solidary persons, good friends, tend to feel sympathy for one another and always will express sympathy. But we know in our own black hearts that we are rather easily reconciled to a friend's bad luck—if that bad luck tends to depress his status. Our own social value is inescapably relative to his and so when we feel sad at his failure there is always the comfort that his failure somewhat improves our own position. His success, for similar reasons, must inspire both happiness and chagrin.

Being in love is a particularly "heady" but precarious combination of sentiments of value and intimacy. It is sometimes sparked by little more than appearance and a few words of conversation. When two people are in this state, they are especially cautious about revealing their tastes, interests, attitudes, and past history because they recognize that maintaining their happy state depends upon maintaining a perceived close match. They monitor the disclosures they make about themselves and they try to "track" one another. Later on, if a match on fundamental interests and values has been established, the two will risk revealing some points of dissimilarity. There may come a time, as in James Joyce's relation with his wife (Ellman, 1959), where everything bad, secret, and disagreeable must be "turned out to the other's gaze" as if to test the completeness and profundity of the personal acceptance.

Romantic love is an especially unstable condition, however, because it builds on feeling valuable as well as on feeling close. One of the joys of the state is seeing in the eyes of another a very high valuation of oneself. Freud, writing at a time when he surely was not in love, called this the "overvaluation of the love object."

In the effort to preserve or to increase the ardor of the over-valuing gaze, lovers are tempted to disclose all manner of creditable things about themselves. Such disclosures are risky when the credits are not well balanced. The information that the girl one loves comes of a distinguished and wealthy family is marvelously agreeable if one's own station is not unbearably humble. Even if there is a considerable inequality it can be endured, even enjoyed, so long as the two are certainly very much in love. A strong attraction causes each to participate in the value of the other. But if (say rather when) the attraction weakens the difference becomes divisive.

BEHAVIOR

There is an experiment which shows that some kinds of interpersonal behavior have the property of symmetry, while other kinds have the property of asymmetry. The former kind seems to belong to the solidarity cluster and the latter to the status cluster. The experiment was conducted at Johns Hopkins University by De Soto (1960).

The problem set the subject resembles one of the traditional routines of experimental psychology, the learning of a list of paired verbal associates. Paired associates are usually nonsense syllables; for example, *Wug-Mib* or *Taz-Nit*. A subject would ordinarily see the first member of a pair, for example *Wug*, then try to anticipate the second member, *Mib*, being prompted or confirmed or corrected by its appearance a few seconds later. In De Soto's experiment things went a little differently. The subject saw two real words on a card; names such as *Bill———Ray*. He was to try to anticipate the missing intermediate term, the predicate of the potential sentence. In one version that predicate was always either *confides in* or *doesn't confide in*. After guessing, the subject turned over the card and read the missing term.

A subject's total task always consisted of learning the relational terms for each of twelve different pairs of men's names. The twelve pairs were all the logically possible permutations, or ordered pairs, created from the four names: *Jim, Ray, Bill,* and *Stan*. Sets of twelve pairs were created for three different relations: *confides in* or *doesn't confide in; likes* or *doesn't like; influences* or *doesn't influence.* Many different sets were created by assigning the relational terms different logical properties. Of particular interest to us is the fact that each relational term was sometimes assigned symmetrically and sometimes asymmetrically.

Consider the terms *confides in* and *doesn't confide in.* For some sets of twelve ordered pairs these relational terms were symmetrically assigned so that if one man was said to confide in another the other reciprocated and if one did not the other did not. In figure 2-5a an example of such a symmetrical structure appears: *Ray* and *Bill* are a mutually "confidential" dyad and so are *Jim* and *Stan;* the other dyads are mutually non-confidential. In Figure 2-5a these facts are represented by the assignment of terms to pairs and also by a diagram that represents the underlying structure that governs the assignment.

For other sets of twelve ordered pairs the terms *confides in* and *doesn't*

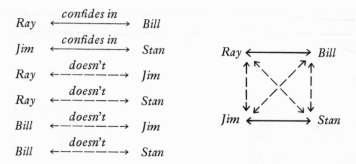

a. Symmetrical structure

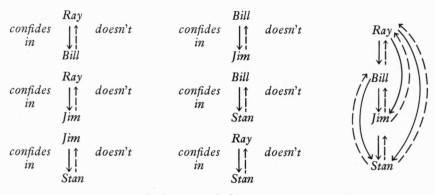

b. Asymmetrical structure

FIGURE 2-5. TWO LATENT STRUCTURES IN A VERBAL LEARNING TASK

confide in were assigned asymmetrically so that if one member of a pair does confide the other does not. In Figure 2-5b an example of such an asymmetrical structure appears in which the terms are applied so as to make a rank order of *Ray, Bill, Jim,* and *Stan.* The terms are used in this structure in the way that we would normally use such terms as *richer than* and *poorer than* or *higher than* and *lower than.*

The symmetrical structure of Figure 2-5a strikes me as a more "natural" use of the terms *confides in* and *doesn't confide in* than does the asymmetrical rank-order structure. And this seems to have been true for De Soto's subjects. Those who were given a set of twelve pairs, in which the "confiding" terms were used symmetrically, learned that set more quickly than did subjects who were given a set in which the terms were used asymmetrically. What does this difference in ease of learning mean? It may mean that new applications of a relational term are easy to learn when the term is used in a manner consistent with its usage in ordinary English and difficult to learn when the term is used in a manner not consistent with its ordinary usage. The expression *confides in* may be a term that English speakers expect to follow a symmetrical pattern. And perhaps the expression is symmetrical because the relational behavior it names is symmetrical. Two people either confide mutually or mutually do not confide.

We have to set aside another possibility. It is conceivable that symmetrical patterns are just simpler to learn than are asymmetrical patterns, regardless of the terms used. De Soto made up sets of cards using the terms *influences* and *doesn't influence* in accordance with the two structures of Figure 2-5. In this case the asymmetrical rank-order structure seems the more natural one. Influence or control or power is likely to be greater in one direction than in another. And it turned out that those subjects who had to learn sets of pairs using the "influence" relation in an asymmetrical way learned their sets very much more quickly than did subjects who had to learn sets using the relation symmetrically. This outcome is the reverse of the outcome for the confiding relation and so we can conclude that it is not the nature of the structure alone that chiefly matters but rather the appropriateness of the structure to the terms.

De Soto defined his terms for his subjects; these definitions strongly suggest that the interpersonal behavior called *influence* belongs to the asymmetrical status cluster while *confiding in* belongs to the solidarity cluster. The italics in the quotations below are mine. "To influence someone means to have some degree of *control* over what he does" (p. 419). "To confide in someone means to have complete *faith* and *confidence* in him so that you *trust* him with secrets or *rely on him for help*" (p. 419). The italicized words name actions and sentiments belonging to the two clusters.

The connection between superior status and the enjoyment of social influence or control or power is extensively documented in the next chapter. We will be content here with one silly example, selected because it shows the power of status even in situations where it has no reasonable place. In downtown Austin, Texas, one day, at several different intersections, certain pedestrians crossed the street when the traffic light said "Wait." Some of these pedestrians were shabby-looking fellows in scuffed shoes, patched trousers, and unpressed denim shirts. Others were natty in polished shoes, pressed suits, white shirts, ties, and straw hats. All of them were accomplices of psychologists (Lefkowitz, Blake, and Mouton, 1955) who wanted to see whether a pedestrian who appeared to have high status would influence more people to violate a traffic law than would a pedestrian whose status appeared to be lower. The high-status violators were imitated by many more people than were the low-status violators.

The connection between solidarity and confiding in has been illustrated in some of our work with terms of address. We made use of a Self-Disclosure Questionnaire devised by Jourard and Lasakow (1958). This questionnaire requires the respondent to indicate whether or not he has discussed with a designated other person each of sixty topics classifiable under the headings: Attitudes and Opinions, Tastes and Interests, Work (or Studies), Money, Personality, and Body. We had twenty-two French respondents and twenty-one Japanese respondents; all were males. They told us which of the topics they had discussed with various of their friends and acquaintances. For both nationalities, topics classified under the first three headings—Attitudes and Opinions, Tastes and Interests, Work (or Studies)—turned out to have been discussed more fully and with more other people than were topics in the three highly personal areas of Money, Personality, and Body. It is as if the self were an onion with three outer layers and three inner layers, the outer layers being more readily exposed than the inner. We knew how our informants were accustomed to address their various friends and acquaintances and, as we anticipated, they had confided in those with whom they exchanged the more intimate forms of address in greater degree than in those with whom they exchanged the more polite forms.

De Soto in his learning experiment used terms that name a relational sentiment as well as the terms naming relational behavior. Some subjects had to learn whether Ray *likes* Bill, or whether Ray *doesn't like* Bill. These terms, like the others, were sometimes used symmetrically and sometimes asymmetrically. Since liking is the principal sentiment of solidarity we are not surprised that those sets in which liking was symmetrical were more quickly learned than sets in which it was asymmetrical.

In another study De Soto (with Kuethe, 1959) set subjects a related but different task to perform with the word *likes*. A subject was first asked to perform the rather curious task of estimating the probability that *Al*, a person not known to him, likes *Les*, another person not known to him. All one could do, I suppose, is to answer in terms of the general probability that any one person will like another. The point of the procedure becomes clear with the second part of the inquiry. Suppose that *Les likes Al.* In these circumstances what is the probability that *Al* will like *Les?* The increment over the base probability indicates how general the subject thinks it is for liking to be symmetrical. De Soto and Kuethe found that *likes* was understood to be a symmetrical relation and so were such other terms of solidarity or nonsolidarity as *trusts, confides in*, and *dislikes.*

Notice how the data converge. Tagiuri found that liking, in his sociometric data, was in fact a symmetrical relation; dislike was not significantly symmetrical. However, Tagiuri found that perceived or attributed dislikes were symmetrical and that attributed likings were even more regularly symmetrical than were actual likings. De Soto and Kuethe found that both *like* and *dislike* were understood to be symmetrical. Finally De Soto demonstrated that the symmetrical schema we have in our heads for liking makes it easy to learn materials that fit this schema and difficult to learn materials that violate it.

SYMBOLISM

We could have dispensed with symbols in this discussion since they are always personal characteristics or spatial relations or behavior. The solidarity of two sisters might be symbolized by similarities of appearance, the fact that they live in adjoining houses, or by their frequent confidential conversations. The differential status of a lady and her maid might be symbolized by the richer dress of the former, the contrast between a front upstairs bedroom and a back bedroom off the kitchen, or by the fact that one gives orders and the other obeys. However, none of these is a symbol unless another condition is fulfilled. Someone must use the relation of appearance, spatial arrangement, or behavior as a basis for inferring solidarity or status, or someone must intend that they should be so used. In short, none of the aspects of social relationship that we have described is to be regarded as a symbol unless someone intends it as such or treats it as such.

When do we need symbols of social relations? Imagine a large evening party made up of guests who are largely unacquainted with one another. In order to behave properly we must work out the important relations among those present. Until important solidarities have been mapped we run the risk of flirting with someone's wife, of defaming someone to his best friend. Until statuses have been established we run the risk of deferring to the butler and handing an empty glass to a reigning monarch. Introductions usually convey the more critical information: "Mr. and Mrs. Smith" is the name of a unity; Sir Malcolm Smythe is the name of something formidable.

Sometimes, of course, we do not catch the introductions. Then we look at the beautiful woman's third finger left hand or try to get close enough to the party with the beard to see whether that is the ribbon of the Légion d'Honneur on his coat. In these circumstances a ring and a ribbon become symbols of, respectively, solidarity and status. They could also become symbols because someone intends us to read them as such. The beautiful woman guessing that we are about to go too far tears off her glove and flashes the ring at us.

Because both solidarity and status are associated with personal characteristics, the former with similarities and the latter with valued differences, the same characteristic or possession can function as a symbol of either relation. For two men who are owners of Mercedes-Benz automobiles the other man's car may function as a symbol of a certain likemindedness, similarities of taste and means. For a third man who drives a Chevrolet the same Mercedes can function as an intimidating symbol of status.

Novelists and popular writers on social science have made us thoroughly familiar with the notion of a status symbol. They have had a lot of fun making us conscious of the cues we use in reading status. The list must actually be endless since the lives of people on different levels of socio-economic status are unlike in almost every way. The list of potential solidarity symbols must also be endless since any similarity, intimacy, or proximity can function as one. For some reason, however, there is not as much fun to be had from solidarity symbols. Popular writers never mention them as such. Either we are less interested in solidarity or we feel less conflict about it. Probably the latter. It is, after all, something of a joke that people in an avowedly equalitarian society are so extraordinarily alert to signs of status.

SUMMARY

This has been a long string of statements about how one thing goes with another: similarity of personal characteristics with proximity, with liking, with frequent and intimate interaction, with Mutual T; differences with distance, with indifference or dislike, with infrequent and formal interaction, with Mutual V; differences that are valued with spatial positions above or below, with feelings of superiority or inferiority, with influence and power, with asymmetrical T and V. Saying that one thing goes with another is not the same thing as saying that one thing leads to another. Occasionally our discussion, or one of the authors we have quoted, has gone beyond the statement of correlations, of one thing associated with another, to claim a relation of cause and effect. Heider (1958), for instance, holds that similarity *induces* liking. There is not very much evidence that helps us identify causes and effects. Usually what we are given is only evidence that two variables are correlated: status and influence, liking and frequency of interaction, etc. What we require, to learn something about cause and effect, is, at a minimum, evidence that the values on one variable existed prior to the associated values on the other variable. Newcomb (1961) was able to separate similarity from friendship because he obtained information on the personal characters of subjects before ever they met. He was able to separate proximity from friendship because he was able to assign men to rooms on a random basis before friendships had developed.

The authors who have made cause-and-effect statements about solidarity relations—Newcomb, Heider, and Homans—all believe that the cause and effect can work either way. Heider, for instance, not only says that similarity induces liking but also that liking induces similarity. The information Homans gives on the Bank Wiring Room includes a good example of reciprocal cause and effect. Initial job assignments in the room must have been a cause of interaction and friendliness. This interaction and friendliness seem, in turn, to have caused an increase of similarity: members of a clique came to play the same games, to buy the same candy, and to turn out similar amounts of work. For the many symmetrical relations of Table 2-1 the evidence is incomplete but it is extremely likely that they are all able to induce one another.

The several kinds of asymmetrical status relations are probably also able to induce one another. Changes of occupation and income can, we know, cause changes in sentiments of superiority and inferiority, in personal power, and in seating arrangements at weekly staff meetings. This is probably the usual direction of cause and effect, from left to right in Table 2-1. However, social life sometimes takes the other direction. In small informal groups made up of persons who are all initially equal in status (Bales, 1958), a member who turns out to be highly influential is likely to start feeling superior. The others may give him a high prestige rating, may elect him leader. All of the conceivable sequences from Table 2-1 seem to occur. Can feelings of superiority cause a person to be influential? Probably so, if superiority gives self-confidence. Can a superior position in space cause the person to become influential? Probably it can if the superior position is central to a network of communication. There is not much evidence, but the best guess is that each aspect of status tends to induce the others.

A Universal Norm and
Its Interpretation

In one respect the forms of address in all the languages we have studied operate in identical fashion. There is an invariant, a universal norm in our materials. We are very far from having investigated address in all languages; among non-European languages we have worked only with Japanese and the languages of India. So there is the possibility that the pattern to be described will fall short of linguistic universality; but we think it will not.

Not many cultural universals are known; probably the incest tabu, the tabu on cohabitation between all members of the nuclear family except husband and wife, is the most famous and has been the most discussed. When all cultures, many of them historically independent, arrive at an identical norm that norm inspires great interest because it would seem to be required by something in ultimate human nature or by some requirement in all forms of human social life. In the case of the incest tabu there have been several suggested interpretations: 1) humans feel an instinctive revulsion against incest; 2) the tabu is a social necessity because sexual jealousies would disrupt the basic economic unit of the family; 3) the tabu by requiring family members to marry outsiders serves to extend the size of the solidary, economically cooperating group.

The invariant norm for forms of address first caught our attention in the following version: the linguistic form that is used to an inferior in a dyad of unequal status is, in dyads of equal status, used mutually by intimates; the form used to a superior in a dyad of unequal status is, in dyads of equal status, used mutually by strangers. Figure 2-6a provides some examples. The pronoun T, the FN, the Japanese pronoun *kimi*[1] are or were, all used to inferiors and also between intimates. The pronoun V, the TLN, the Japanese pronoun *anata* are, or were, all used to superiors and also between strangers. In abstract terms (Figure 2-6b), if form X is used to inferiors it is used between intimates, and if form Y is used to superiors it is used between strangers.

Considering just two address forms and the status and solidarity norms, there is one formal or logically possible alternative to the scheme we have invariably found. The form used to inferiors might also be used between strangers and the form used to superiors might also be used between intimates (Figure 2-6c). This is an abstract linkage between the norms of status and solidarity which we have never found. Why should the linkage always take the form it does take?

1. The forms we are calling pronouns are not exactly comparable to the pronouns of Indo-European languages and some linguists would prefer to say that there are no true pronouns in Japanese.

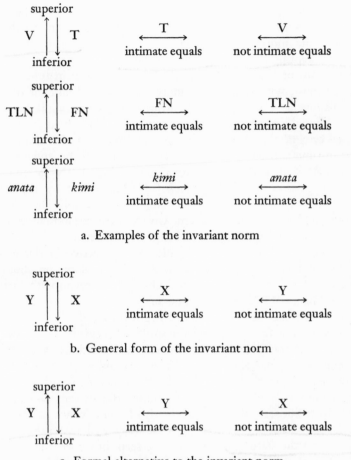

a. Examples of the invariant norm

b. General form of the invariant norm

c. Formal alternative to the invariant norm

FIGURE 2-6. THE INVARIANT NORM OF ADDRESS

A curious fact about the contemporary use of T and V provides a clue to the explanation of the invariant pattern. While the non-reciprocal norm for pronouns has generally been abandoned in Europe, inequality of status continues to affect one aspect of usage. Most dyads begin with the Mutual V and, with time, may advance to the intimacy of Mutual T. For many people the shift from V to T is an important rite of passage. The Germans even have a little informal ceremony they call the *Bruderschaft*. One waits for a congenial mood, a mellow occasion, perhaps over a glass of wine, and says: "Why don't we say *du* to one another?" The new usage is, of course, to be reciprocal. However, there is one necessarily non-reciprocal aspect of the business—someone must make the suggestion.

When there is a clear difference of status between the two the right to initiate the change unequivocally belongs to the superior—to the elder, the richer, the more distinguished of the two. The gate to linguistic solidarity is kept by the person of higher status.

The norms of English address also make a pattern in time. Members of a dyad must, with time, either increase their total amount of contact or else dissolve as a dyad. Since the Mutual TLN represents less contact than the Mutual FN, if Mutual TLN occurs at all in a dyad, it must occur at an earlier time than the Mutual FN. The place of the non-reciprocal pattern in time is between the other two and it may be understood as a step from Mutual TLN in the direction of Mutual FN—a step which, like the suggestion of the *Bruderschaft,* is taken first by the superior. Many dyads will linger for a very long time—possibly the life of the dyad—in the non-reciprocal pattern. Under these circumstances the pattern gives enduring expression to an inequality of status.

Consider a familiar sort of example. A prospective graduate student arrives at a university to meet some of the faculty of the psychology department and is interviewed by the chairman. Probably the two will initially exchange TLN. In the course of the day or, if not, shortly after the student enrolls, the chairman will begin to use the FN. He seems to extend the hand of friendship, but the student knows that it behooves him not to grasp it too quickly. The student will continue with the TLN for several years (four is probably the mode) and in this period the non-reciprocality of speech will express the inequality of status. If the chairman is neither very elderly nor very august the student will eventually feel able to reciprocate the FN and the dyad will advance to Mutual FN. Probably the interval of time that must be passed in non-reciprocality increases with the status gap. As we have seen, however, the appropriate time for the transition may not be perfectly clear and so there may be, for the person of lower status, a period of uncertainty in which terms of address will be avoided.

In Japanese, address forms are more numerous than in English but they nevertheless conform to the universal norm. Iritani asked twenty Japanese informants to describe to him some of the details of their usage of the address forms. For example, each informant was asked to think of a male fellow student, two or three years older than himself, with whom he had become quite friendly and informal. The subject was to say how he addressed his friend and how his friend addressed him when they first met (Time 1) and at present (Time 2). In addition, he was to say how they probably would address one another in the future when they should become still closer friends (Time 3).

There was a great variety of responses but with all the variety, there was the usual invariance. If the forms changed at all in time they became more intimate or solidary. Furthermore, whenever there was non-reciprocality of address the person of higher status (here just an elder by two or three years) used the more intimate form. One cannot reverse this statement and say that wherever there was a difference of status or age, as we judge it from the outside, there was non-reciprocal address. The informants sometimes judged that the difference would not have to be coded initially or would not have to be coded on very close acquaintance.

With the large set of address forms available in Japanese a dyad can advance in intimacy without necessarily arriving at mutuality. Here is an example from Iritani's data. The elder began by using LN + *kun* which is more familiar than the LN + *san* which was used by the junior. At Time 2 the elder had advanced another step in intimacy to the pronoun *kimi* while the junior continued with the deferential LN + *san*. Finally, at Time 3, the elder had advanced to the still more intimate LN with no suffix and the junior had at last also ventured an increase of familiarity, to the form FN + *san*, but the junior's form is a much less intimate one than that of the elder. This is a progression of intimacy that never ceased to code the inequality of status. In English or the European languages one cannot mark many advances of intimacy without arriving at mutuality of address.

The universal norm that we have found for pronouns, names, and titles applies to a much wider range of social behavior. It applies, for instance, to the most common greetings in American English: *Hi* and *Good morning*. Perhaps you remember that we asked a group of thirty-four young business executives, who were studying at M.I.T. in 1958–59, to tell us about their habits of address with four kinds of business associate: a superior, a subordinate, an equal with whom the informant was on intimate or friendly terms, an equal with whom he was on distant or formal terms. In addition to analyzing the greetings in terms of FN and TLN we analyzed them in terms of *Hi* and *Good Morning*. A familiar pattern appeared: *Hi* was used mutually between intimates and non-reciprocally from superior to subordinate; *Good morning* was used mutually between strangers and non-reciprocally from subordinate to superior. With respect to these common greetings, then, it is again the case that the superior initiates advances in solidarity.

The rule extends beyond linguistic rituals to every kind of dyadic behavior that marks an advance in intimacy. From whom does one feel free to borrow a pocket comb? The business executives told us they could ask for the comb of an intimate and also of a subordinate. The subordinate would presumably feel honored. But one cannot make such a request of either a stranger or a superior. We asked about many behaviors of this kind. What sort of associate can one slap on the back? Again, we found, either an intimate or subordinate but not a stranger or superior.

Consider the rules that govern invitations to dinner between an employer and an employee. If they were only very slightly acquainted, an invitation to dinner would be an advance in intimacy. The employee would not feel free to make such an invitation but the employer would be quite free to do so.

Consider the rules that govern association among workers of unequal rank. In the Bank Wiring Room that Homans has described members of the superior clique of wiremen, clique A, initiated interaction with the wiremen of B more often than B initiated for A. In addition to the wiremen there were soldermen and the soldermen in the room clearly ranked below the wiremen. Workers in the Bank Wiring Room sometimes traded jobs for a time to relieve the monotony even though the company forbade the practice. Homans found that job trading between the higher ranking wiremen and the lower ranking soldermen was always suggested by the wiremen; the soldermen apparently did not feel free to make the suggestion. Because of these other facts Homans (1950) put forward the hypothesis: "a person of higher social rank than another originates interaction for the latter more often than the latter originates interaction for him" (1950, p. 145).

It seems clear that for persons of unequal status the superior is the pacesetter in the total progression toward increasingly solidary or intimate behavior, and this may well be a cultural universal. But this is a very surprising universal for the reason that it is directly contrary to the behavior one would expect on the basis of even the most obvious analysis of the motivations involved. For surely it is the lesser member whose value will be enhanced by intimacy with a greater, the lesser who will wish to initiate such intimacy, and yet the universal norm forbids him to do so.

Let us devise a model or miniature theory of the social psychology of dyadic relations between persons of unequal status. This model is closely related to some that are presented in Chapter 11, "The Principle of Consistency in Attitude Change." Social status can be represented by a scale of values from 0 to +5. Two persons of unequal status will then be two points on such a scale (as in Figure 2-7). Increases of intimacy such as invitations to dinner, more familiar address, comb-borrowing, and the like will be represented in the model as associative bonds (curved line in Figure 2-7) linking the two members of the dyad. Finally, let us suppose that the effect of such bonds is to cause the persons so bonded to move toward one another on the status scale. An invitation to dinner between unequals will elevate the status of the lesser member and depress the status of the greater. If President Johnson appoints a presidential adviser of mediocre quality then the adviser will gain status and the president will lose. If a beautiful girl dates a homely boy, then the girl's status will fall and the

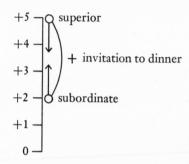

FIGURE 2-7. A MODEL OF ACTS OF INTIMACY BETWEEN UNEQUALS

boy's will rise. In general, acts of intimate association between persons of unequal status will exert forces toward the equalization of status. This means that the member of a dyad who has less status should be motivated to increase the intimacy of interaction since he stands to gain while the person of higher status should be motivated to resist such intimacy.

The model is obviously sound in a very general way. In America the large professional convention displays the rather ugly psychology of status flow in bold form because it provides occasions (e.g., "Social Hours") when persons of unequal status are expected to mix freely and where it is quite acceptable for a man of lower status to initiate conversation with a man of higher status. Professional standing is the major component of social status in America and positions on the scale are very much in everyone's mind at a convention of professionals. If we look about us at a convention of the American Medical Association or the American Psychological Association we shall see our model working. Wherever there is a conversational dyad of unbalanced status note the keen interest, the total absorption of the lesser member. The greater member is looking just past the ear of the lesser, scanning the throng for an acquaintance whose status is greater than his own from whom enhancement may be drawn. It tickles me that this rather obvious social psychology is as blatant at a meeting of the American Psychoanalytic Society as at a gathering of electrical engineers. One might have expected the analysts to be above it or "deeper" than it.

The model's prediction that a person of higher status will lose something by association with an inferior is not so obviously correct as the prediction that the inferior will gain. Does an employer really lose anything by having dinner with an employee? Probably not. Similarly, President Johnson would not lose status by inviting a person of humble station to dinner. However, if President Johnson were to invite James Hoffa to dinner the President would fall in popular esteem. When Yugoslavia's Tito visited Washington in 1963 the President was noticeably formal in his behavior as if aware that a friendly association with the Communist leader would be damaging. These observations suggest that a serious model ought to distinguish between persons who have a small amount of positive status and persons who are on the other side of zero and so have negative status or notoriety. It may only be association with notoriety that causes a superior to fall on the status scale; association with a person on the positive side of zero may leave the superior where he was.

While the model is incomplete its central notion that the person of lesser status stands to gain more by intimate association than does the person of greater status is surely correct. It is this central notion that makes the universal norm difficult to understand. Clearly, the norm is not a simple expression of the motives of the participants.

In the case of the universal tabu on incest, also, many social scientists have concluded that the norm is not a simple expression of human motives such as an instinctive revulsion against the act. Freud's argument here was very forceful. He pointed out that if there were no desire for incest, there would be no need for a tabu and especially for severe punishment —often death—for breaking the tabu. Societies do not require people to breathe or eat or copulate; norms do not have to be established for what everyone naturally wants to do. In the case of incest Freud argued that there is actually a universal strong attraction to the act. The tabu exists because the act would be disruptive of social life and so must be prevented. Perhaps the norms of dyadic interaction between status levels are similarly controls on individual motivation made necessary by social life.

An integrated division of labor, we know, greatly contributes to the survival and dominance of a society. Some notion of status, of differential social value, seems to be a necessary concomitant of a division of labor. It may be that status enhancement is a necessary incentive and reward for recruiting people to positions requiring talent, training, and long hours of work. Or perhaps the notion of status is an inevitable byproduct of the unequal distribution of power and wealth that goes with a division of labor. In any case a status order is a universal property of human societies.

A status order, though rewarding to the top levels, can impose a considerable psychological strain on the lower levels. Since self-evaluation is relative to the evaluation of others one cannot reward some with esteem without depriving others. There must then be a continuing danger from below of antagonism, or rejection of the status system and rejection of authority.

The integration of society requires some association between status levels. Those on the lower levels will be eager for such association, but if they are permitted to act out their eagerness by free initiation of intimacy in an upward direction, they will suffer many painful rebuffs. Superiors usually have little to gain and much to lose by such association and so would often reject advances from below. In terms of our little model it may be suggested that a rebuff from above, an act of dissociation, would depress the status of the rebuffed person. This painful loss of esteem could generate a great deal of antagonism.

If, however, a culture rules that initiation of intimacy must come from above, there will be few rebuffs and little antagonism. The lesser member can be assumed to be more ready for asssociation than the greater so that initiation from above will seldom be rejected. The universal norm may then represent a social arrangement that serves to minimize antagonism between status levels somewhat in the way that the permanent precedence (or pecking) order minimizes fighting among social animals.

REFERENCES

Bales, R. F. Task roles and social roles in problem-solving groups. In Eleanor E. Maccoby, T. M. Newcomb, & E. L. Hartley (Eds.), *Readings in social psychology.* (3rd ed.) New York: Holt, 1958.

Brown, R., & Ford, Marguerite. Address in American English. *J. abnorm. soc. Psychol.,* 1961, **62**, 375–385.

Brown, R., & Gilman, A. The pronouns of power and solidarity. In T. A. Sebeok (Ed.), *Style in Language.* Cambridge: Technology Press, 1960.

Brunot, F. *Histoire de la langue Française.* Paris: Librairie Armand Colin, 1937.

Calhoun, J. B. A "behavioral sink." In E. L. Bliss (Ed.), *Roots of behavior.* New York: Harper, 1962.

De Soto, C. B. Learning a social structure. *J. abnorm. soc. Psychol.,* 1960, **60**, 417–421.

De Soto, C. B., & Kuethe, J. L. Subjective probabilities of interpersonal relationships. *J. abnorm. soc. Psychol.,* 1959, **59**, 290–294.

Durkheim, E. *The division of labor in society.* (1st ed., 1893) Translated from the French by George Simpson. New York: Free Press, 1949.

Ellman, R. *James Joyce.* New York: Oxford Univer. Press, 1959.

Ellwood, T. *The history of the life of Thomas Ellwood.* London: J. Sowle, 1714.

Estrich, R. M., & Sperber, H. *Three keys to language.* New York: Rinehart, 1946.

Eysenck, H. J. *Sense and nonsense in psychology.* Baltimore: Penguin Books, 1957.

Farnsworth, R. *The pure language of the spirit of truth. . . . Or, "thee" and "thou" in its place is the proper language to any single person whatsoever.* London: 1655.

Fay, P. B. The use of "tu" and "vous" in Molière. *University of California Publications in Modern Philology,* 1920. 8, 227–286.

Festinger, L., Schachter, S., & Back, K. *Social pressures in informal groups: a study of human factors in housing.* New York: Harper, 1950.

Fox, G. *A battle-doore for teachers and professors to learn plural and singular.* London: 1660.

Gassner, J. (Ed.) *Best plays of the modern American theatre: Second series.* New York: Crown, 1947.

Gassner, J. (Ed.) *Best American plays: Third series.* New York: Crown, 1952.

100   PSYCHOLOGY AND SOCIAL STRUCTURE

Gassner, J. (Ed.) *Best American plays: Fourth series.* New York: Crown, 1958.
Grand, C. *"Tu, voi, lei"; étude des pronoms allocutoires Italiens.* Ingebohl, Switzerland: P. Theodose, 1930.
Hall, E. T. *The silent language.* Garden City: Doubleday, 1959.
Heider, F. *The psychology of interpersonal relations.* New York: Wiley, 1958.
Hollingshead, A. B. *Elmtown's youth.* (1st ed., 1949) New York: Science Ed., 1961.
Homans, G. C. *The human group.* New York: Harcourt, Brace & World, 1950.
Jardine, D. *Criminal trials.* Vols. 1–2. London, 1832–35.
Jespersen, O. *Growth and structure of the English language.* Leipzig: Teubner, 1905.
Jourard, S. M., & Lasakow, P. Some factors in self-disclosure. *J. abnorm. soc. Psychol.,* 1958, **56**, 91–98.
Kahl, J. A., & Davis, J. A. A comparison of indexes of socio-economic status. *Amer. sociol Rev.,* 1955, **20**, 317–325.
Kroeber, A. L. *Handbook of the Indians of California.* Washington: Bureau of American Ethnology, 1925, Bulletin 78.
LaPiere, T., & Farnsworth, R. *Social psychology.* (3rd ed.) New York: McGraw-Hill, 1949.
Lefkowitz, M., Blake, R. R., & Mouton, Jane Srygley. Status factors in pedestrian violation of traffic signals. *J. abnorm. soc. Psychol.,* 1955, **51**, 704–705.
Littré, É. *Dictionnaire de la langue Française.* Vol. IV. Paris: L. Hachette, 1882.
Moreno, J. L. *Who shall survive?* Washington: Nervous and Mental Disease Pub. Co., 1934.
Newcomb, T. M. *The acquaintance process.* New York: Holt, Rinehart and Winston, 1961.
Quinn, A. H. (Ed.) *Representative American plays.* New York: Century, 1917.
Roethlisberger, F. J., & Dickson, W. J. *Management and the worker.* Cambridge, Mass.: Harvard Univer. Press, 1939.
Schein, E. H. The Chinese indoctrination program for prisoners of war: A study of attempted "brainwashing." In Eleanor E. Maccoby, T. M. Newcomb, & E. L. Hartley (Eds.), *Readings in social psychology.* (3rd. ed.) New York: Holt, 1958.
Schliebitz, V. *Die Person der Anrede in der französischen Sprache.* Breslau: Jungfer, 1886.
Schneider, D. M., & Homans, G. C. Kinship terminology and the American kinship system. *Amer. Anthropologist,* 1955, **57**, 1194–1208.
Silverberg, W. V. "On the psychological significance of 'du' and 'sie.'" *Psychoanal. Quart.,* 1940, **9**, 509–525.
Tagiuri, R. Social preference and its perception. In R. Tagiuri, and L. Petrullo (Eds.), *Person perception and interpersonal behavior.* Stanford: Stanford Univer. Press, 1958.
Wheeler, W. M. *Social life among the insects.* New York: Harcourt, Brace, 1923.
Wynne-Edwards, V. C. *Animal dispersion in relation to social behaviour.* Edinburgh and London: Oliver and Boyd, 1962.

CHAPTER 3

Stratification

In a study of the social life of the howler monkeys that live on Barro Colorado Island in the Panama Canal Zone, Carpenter (1934) tells us that members of the species would sometimes occupy the same tree with a collection of cebus monkeys. The two species, feeding side by side, would not interact. The signals of one would not be directed to the other and would not be attended to by the other. And when it was time to move on, the creatures would separate out by species. In Harvard Square, in Cambridge, Massachusetts, the Harvard students and the Cambridge city boys and girls walk and chatter and feed and groom in similar perfect independence. They are two streams of primate life; not quite separate species, but separate subcultures or social strata.

Harvard Square marks the junction of several large avenues and it is the last stop on the Boston-to-Cambridge subway. The Harvard Yard is on one side of the Square and, on the other side, a block away from the Square and strung along the Charles River, are the Harvard undergraduate Houses. The Harvard student's daily routine, therefore, takes him through the Square. In the direction of Boston on Massachusetts Avenue, and not very far from the Square, begins a large area of inexpensive housing, where working-class families live. For some parts of the area Harvard Square is the nearest subway stop, the nearest bus stop, and the nearest *bright lights*. So Cambridge working-class boys and girls have also many occasions for going to the Square.

While neither group presents an absolutely uniform appearance there are very few individuals who cannot be placed on sight. If a young man has a beard or a green book bag he is from Harvard; if he is wearing an outdoor waist-length jacket, he is a city boy. Girls in dark, heavy knee-length stockings are from Radcliffe. Nobody wears a hat except the occasional politician on his way to the State House for another day of *rewarding* public service.

The two groups can also be separated out by their patterns of patronage. The Brattle Theater, which shows foreign films and those American movies that have unhappy endings, is for Harvard and Radcliffe. The King's Bar and Joe and Nemo's lunch counter are mostly for Cambridge. Everybody goes to Brigham's for ice cream, but only the city boys stand out in front—watching all the girls go by.

It sometimes happens that the unwritten segregation rules are violated. I was there the day a Cambridge boy wandered into one of the men's clothing stores that cater to the college students. The elegant cricketers who play at being salesmen there were standing about trying silk rep ties against Harris tweeds when the intruder appeared. It took them a full minute to realize that no enforceable law had been broken, that the boy was free to buy something, even to give one of them an order. It took the boy less than a minute to feel as out of place as if he had landed in the ladies' room and he bolted.

Life in Harvard Square is not uniform. Some social scientists would have it that this life and all complex social life is "stratified." In geology, strata are layers of sedimentary rock or earth lying one upon another, and the geological sense suggests the rudiments of the sociological. To say that social life is stratified is to say that it runs in streaks or bands that are relatively uniform within themselves and different one from another. It is to say also that these streaks have a vertical order, that some are higher and some lower. No one doubts that social life is always organized in terms of a vertical socio-economic status, but some of us do doubt that it is always organized as a set of discrete strata. Socio-economic status could function as a continuum of indefinitely numerous ranked positions.

Because social stratification refers to an aspect of human life there must be phenomena involved that do not appear in geology. These are chiefly patterned interaction, style of life, and stratum consciousness. Interaction involves at least two persons reacting to one another. When certain interactions (e.g., confidential talks, dining together, "dates") occur within a set of persons but not between sets, there is evidence of stratification. A style of life is manifest in occupations, possessions, recreation, manners, and the like. Behavior is involved here as it is in patterned interaction. However, when we speak of style of life, we are concerned with the form or quality of behavior; not who speaks to whom, but with what accent. Massive uniformities and discontinuities in style of life are evidence of stratification. In addition, a society's system of stratification ought to be a part of the cognitive structure of members of that society and it should enter into consciousness in certain circumstances and cause a person to talk about the stratification system in his community.

We shall use the term "stratification" as a generic term for social life that is organized either by caste or by class. The defining distinction between castes and classes is that membership in the former is fixed at birth for life, whereas membership in the latter can change in a man's lifetime. Castes are "closed" and classes are "open." What the two are supposed to have in common, the characteristic defining stratification in general, is the organization of social life into a set of categories uniform within themselves and sharply discontinuous at their boundaries. Both uniformity and discontinuity would be manifest in styles of life, patterns of interaction, and stratum consciousness. There is no doubt that societies like medieval India and medieval Europe were stratified and that the strata were castes. Modern industrialized societies are also supposed to be stratified, but into open classes rather than castes. We shall argue that contemporary life in the United States is not stratified at all; that there are no classes here.

The concept of stratification is closely linked with the concept of status and the concepts of caste and class with the opposition between "ascribed" status and "achieved" status. In the last chapter we defined status as any sort of social value. In studying stratification we shall be concerned with just one sort of social value, that which is called socio-economic. Insofar as socio-economic status is "ascribed" in a society, caste-like conditions will prevail and, insofar as it is "achieved," open classes or an open continuum will appear. Before beginning the study of socio-economic status and stratification something must be said about the other sorts of status.

Socio-economic status is largely determined by occupation and income. It accrues to total family units rather than to individuals alone and it determines the total style of life and network of interaction for the family. Other sorts of social value tend to accrue to persons rather than to families, and their consequences tend to be less profound and pervasive. Age, sex, beauty, strength, style, and talent all can produce social status that is not socio-economic. One sees the difference in the occasional pairing of an elderly, ugly, but very rich man with a young, beautiful, glittering girl. Each is the best of a class.

In most societies mature adults are accorded a kind of authority and respect that is denied to children and, in some societies, the very elderly are accorded a very special deference. The status that comes with age cannot be shared. A young boy does not gain status from the age of his father (unless the father is old enough to be a curiosity). And so it is with the status that is based on sex: a Japanese wife cannot participate in the social value that accrues to her husband in virtue of his maleness. Contrast these cases with the "spread" of occupational status: both son and wife share in the glory of a husband and father who is a Supreme Court Justice.

The ordinary run of variations in beauty, athletic prowess, or musical talent does not greatly affect a person's interaction network or style of life. Extreme values have larger effects and the effects spread a bit. The family that includes a son who is a college football star or a daughter who is a great beauty can "take pride" in the fact. They fall within the circle of light, but it does not play on all with an equal brilliance. The inter- action patterns and style of life of a family are not determined by the athletics of a son or the beauty of a daughter, unless these gifts are "out- size" enough to create occupations. If the young man is good enough at football to play professionally and the girl is beautiful enough to become a movie star, then the lives of their families are profoundly affected. But in this case the status is founded on occupation and income and so is socio-economic.

In discussions of status, whether socio-economic or not, the terms "ascribed" and "achieved" are often used. Sex, age, and lineage are usually said to be ascribed, whereas any sort of job performance is said to be achieved. India is often cited as a society in which socio-economic status is chiefly ascribed, and the United States as a society in which it is achieved. What do the terms mean?

The terms strongly suggest that the contrast is between personal characteristics that are true of one willy-nilly and personal characteristics that are attained by personal effort. One cannot by exerting will power do anything about age, sex, or lineage; this much is clear. A certain con- fusion enters with the observation that job performance and performance on examinations are affected by intelligence and talent as well as by efforts, and intelligence and talent are in considerable degree innate, un- alterable characteristics. Furthermore, in the United States, an achieve- ment society, we seem to set great value on intelligence itself.

There is another way of making the distinction, one that is closely related to willy-nilly and willed, but is possibly a little clearer. Ascribed characteristics are fixed from birth, whereas achieved characteristics can change in a lifetime. This way of putting the contrast leads very nicely to the distinction between a caste system in which there is no individual lifetime mobility and a class system in which there is much individual lifetime mobility. The problem here is the attribute of age, for age does change in a lifetime and the status that goes with age also changes. This fact does not violate the link between caste, and an ascription emphasis because the status based on age is not socio-economic status. As it happens, however, this independent attribute of age tends to be an important determinant of its own kind of status in caste societies where lineage fixes socio-economic status. But age is not, like lineage and sex, an attribute fixed for life, and so we cannot define ascribed attributes in this fashion if we want to encompass all three attributes.

The clearest distinction is, I think, the following: achieved attributes are performances or behavior; ascribed attributes are not. Age, sex, and lineage can all be determined without reference to anything a person does. The intelligence which is valued in America is actually *demonstrated intelligence*, demonstrated in jobs or academic grades or performance on some kind of intelligence test. Intelligence is an achievement in the sense that it is behavior even though it may be behavior that is partly determined by innate characteristics.

A society that pins socio-economic status to occupational achievement tends to be uncomfortable with the assignment of any sort of status on the basis of ascribed characteristics. American culture in this century seems to have been straining toward pure performance criteria for every kind of social value. The effort to eliminate prejudice and discrimination against Negroes is an effort to remove an inconsistent caste element from our system of socio-economic status. The rights-for-women movement which succeeded in winning the vote and other concessions was an effort to eliminate the ascription of differential status on the basis of sex. In our manners it is clear that age receives less respect than it formerly did. If we pit age against occupation as a claim on status, occupation generally wins. over age

Even in small matters there is a strain toward pure achievement criteria. The Miss America contest is a beauty contest and beauty is largely an ascribed characteristic. In recent years, however, the contestants have had to do more than make an appearance in a bathing suit. They are now expected to perform in some way and so the judges have to listen to highly expressive but technically uncertain renditions of Shakespeare, Beethoven, and Puccini from girls whose existence should be enough to win them honor. It may be that we feel a little uncomfortable about awarding all the status of the Miss America title on the basis of ascribed attributes alone. However absurd the pretense, Miss America must show that she has done something to earn the title.

Emphasis on achievement as the ground of status accompanies industrialization. The modern competitive production system makes it important to have the best-qualified person in each job; it is bad business to prefer the less well-qualified man because he is your nephew or to pass over the superior applicant because he is a Negro. Industrialization greatly speeds up the pace of social change and that suggests a reason why the high status accorded the aged in pre-industrial ascription societies is not accorded them in achievement societies. As long as a culture is relatively static, useful knowledge will be cumulative with the years and the oldest man will often be the wisest. Where a culture changes rapidly the information gained in youth is largely useless in maturity, and age maximizes the opportunity for negative transfer or cognitive interference. The oldest man is simply the most out of date.

Solidarity, like status, can be based on either ascribed or achieved attributes and it appears to be true that the two relationships in any given society will be based on the same kind of attribute. In caste India the status relation between two men depended chiefly on their lineage and so, too, did their solidarity relation. The Indian had bonds of ascribed solidarity with his joint family and his caste; lifelong bonds that carried obligations of mutual aid. Even today caste associations collect funds to provide scholarships for their young people and to give aid to their poor. Wealthy members of a caste may create hostels that are free to their young people and may rent houses to caste members at a low rate. In America today solidarity, like status, must be earned. Parents must "deserve" the love of their children and wives must take care to maintain the affection and concern of their husbands. It is fairly easy to withdraw solidarity by divorce and even possible to withdraw it from the closest kin.

Ascribed status frustrates the mobility striving of lower elements but there may be some compensation for the disadvantaged elements in the ascribed solidarity that goes with ascribed status, in the security of intimacies and obligations that are fixed for life. Achieved status gratifies mobility striving, but an achievement emphasis is not altogether agreeable in the sphere of solidarity. Close ties cannot be counted on but must always be earned anew. It is my impression that the literature of social protest, the literature of mobility striving, when it achieves its aim of an open (achievement) society, gives way to a literature of loneliness. Certainly we hear a great deal in the modern world about the difficulty of reaching other people, the ultimate isolation of each human being, and this may be a yearning for the fixed solidarities of an ascription society.

The first section of this chapter describes the caste pattern of life in India and in medieval Europe. In the second section I will argue that life in the United States is not stratified, that there are no classes here. At the same time, however, I will argue that life in the United States is organized by socio-economic status, organized as a continuum of positions rather than as a set of classes.

There is more movement on this socio-economic continuum, more vertical mobility, than there is in a caste system. However, it is a popular belief that mobility in the United States has declined since the early years of this century. In the third section we will present evidence that this belief is mistaken and inquire into the sources of the belief. By the time we reach the end of the third section we shall be thoroughly weary of upward striving and perhaps pleased to recollect that high status has its dark side. The last section discusses the link between high status and suicide. A long mundane chapter about superiors and inferiors and mobility and income ought not to end without a reminder of tragedy.

Caste in India and Feudalism in Europe

The oldest literary remains of any Indo-European language, older than anything in Latin or Greek, are the four Vedic hymns of India. One of these, the Rig-Veda, describes the mythic origin of caste. When Purusha, the archetypal man, was sacrificed the Brahman caste arose from his head, the Kshatriyas from his arms, the Vaisyas from his thighs, the Sudras from his feet. Here, in metaphorical form, are two major characteristics of caste. The castes, like the parts of the body, were differentiated by function: the Brahmans were the priests; the Kshatriyas were warriors; the Vaisyas were traders, cultivators, craftsmen; the Sudras did the dirty work. Castes, like the parts and functions of the body, existed in a vertical order; some were high and some were low (Edwardes, 1961).

Probably the four great castes, the Varnas, did not spring from Purusha. They may have existed in the social system of the Aryan invaders who began moving into the Indian peninsula from the north about 2000 B.C. The Aryans were a tall, fair, straight-nosed people, who described the peoples of the Indus valley civilization as short, black, and noseless. Probably the conquered indigenous population formed the lower castes.

The four classical Varnas are really supra-castes. They seem always to have been rather elaborately subdivided. The main subcastes directly below the Varnas are called *jatis*. In 1901, the last year in which the Indian census made a complete tabulation of the castes, there were 2,378 *jatis* and subdivisions of these were still more numerous. However, no subcaste is represented all over India, and most of them are very narrowly regional. In any particular village there would only be a small number of subcastes (Davis, 1951).

The classical occupational specialization of the Varnas no longer holds (Prabhu, 1963). Only a small percentage of modern Brahmans, for example, are priests. The Brahmans are differentiated into a very large number of subcastes; the variety of occupations among these is great and not all of these Brahman groups rank high today. Occupational specialization is still fairly strong on the level of the local subcaste but not on the level of the great castes (Davis, 1951).

The caste system of India probably provided less mobility than has any large society in human history. Even in India, however, there seems always to have been a little mobility (Davis, 1951). This was mostly mobility of an extended family group or of an entire subcaste. The *Pasis*, for instance, had the despised occupation of hunting and fowling. Some of the *Pasis* managed to accumulate enough money to buy a little land, and they began selling fruit and farming. Eventually they became a distinct caste, the *Phansiya*, and stopped intermarriage with the *Pasi*, who stayed behind. An upwardly mobile subcaste like the *Phansiya* worked at establishing itself in a higher position by increasing its devotion to values subscribed to by all Hindus: knowledge of the holy books, purity of diet, the seclusion of women, and celibacy of widows. The ambitious caste also may attempt to discard its caste name when that name has too many odious connotations. In recent times, provincial census officials have been selected as the persons who ought to be able to effect such changes and they have been besieged with requests.

Modern urban and industrial conditions operate to improve the position of lower castes, to open possibilities of movement for both individuals and groups, and to weaken the caste principle as a whole (Prabhu, 1963). Increased geographic mobility breaks the hold of local caste associations and urban life offers an anonymity that enables a man to break with the caste. Universal suffrage gives power to the lower castes. Hospitals, trains, modern sanitation, all make the ritual avoidances difficult. Industry creates new occupations which offer possible new individual or subcaste status.

Some of the former extreme deprivation of the lower castes, produced by a rigid social structure, was compensated by a religion that offered mobility not in a lifetime—but across lifetimes. In the period of the *Upanishads* (between 800 and 600 B.C.) the doctrine of metempsychosis, migration of the soul from body to body, came into the Hindu religion. According to this doctrine, a man's conduct, the sum of his actions (*Karma*) in a previous incarnation, is supposed to determine the position into which he will be born in the next incarnation. Men who have been wicked come back in the body of a hog, a dog, or perhaps a *Chandala*, which was the name for offspring of a *Brahman* woman and a *Sudra* man. The cycle of reincarnation continues until the individual soul is released into the World Soul (*Atma*). These religious beliefs must have helped to ease strains generated by the rigidity of the Indian social structure.

The most profound cleavage in modern India is the line between the clean castes (also called the interior castes) and the unclean castes (also called the outcastes or the Untouchables). In 1931 there were about fifty million Untouchables, which was about 27 per cent of the Hindu population. They have suffered gross social disadvantages and are probably the largest downtrodden segment in any modern state. Negroes in America, who have been in a somewhat comparable situation, are only 10 per cent of the population. In recent times, of course, efforts have been made to elevate the condition of the outcastes whom Ghandhi called the *Harijans* or "beloved people." In 1948 the Indian Constituent Assembly legally abolished "Untouchability" but this legislation, like our own Emancipation Proclamation, was not immediately realized in social practice (Davis, 1951; Prabhu, 1963).

While there have been many changes in the details of India's caste system, its basic structure persisted for three thousand years. It has been what Davis (1951) calls the most thoroughgoing attempt in human history to utilize absolute inequality as the basis for a society. India's caste reached a kind of peak of rigidity and inequality during the medieval period. During this period Europe also had a caste-like stratification system.

The European system was feudalism. It lasted with minor changes and variations from one country to another for many centuries; in France and England from the eleventh century until the eighteenth. In feudalism the landowner, a nobleman or high churchman, was supposed to hold his land as a gift from the king who, again in theory, was the owner of all land. The noble lord was the king's vassal and owed him military and financial aid, hospitality and other duties. There were often several levels of subinfeudation with each man a lord to some and a vassal to others. In general, a lord owed to his vassals the protection of their land and persons. In theory, a man's "fief" or gift of land was not hereditary but, in practice, it usually passed to the eldest son. If there were no heirs the land escheated to the lord (Easton, 1955).

On the local level feudalism was the manorial system. In some cases the resident lord of the manor was a nobleman, but great noblemen often had many manors and most of these would be supervised by bailiffs and stewards. About one-third to one-sixth of the land was the lord's own demesne and was cultivated for him by the peasants. The remainder of the land was parceled out among the peasantry, some six to thirty acres to a man, and cultivated by them for their own benefit (Easton, 1955).

There were three major strata in feudal society: the First Estate consisted of the higher clergy who were often noble; the Second Estate, who were the secular nobility and often made war their chief business; the Third Estate, who were the peasantry and craftsmen, though, in eighteenth-century France, the bourgeoisie used the term Third Estate for themselves alone.

The parallel between the Varnas of India and the Estates of medieval Europe is striking (Prabhu, 1963); in both societies the priestly role is ranked at the top, the warrior next, and the craftsman and peasant below. Like the Varnas, the Estates can be subdivided into narrower strata, though these are not so numerous and sharply marked as are the subcastes of India.

The peasantry divides into freemen, villeins who were technically free but bound to certain manorial duties not required of true freemen, and serfs, who were owned by the lord. A serf could be brought back by force if he left the land; he had to have the lord's permission to marry, and was in every way the property of the lord. The serf had a few rights: he was not supposed to be sold and if he could escape the manor and not be recaptured for a year, he became a freeman. The villeins and freemen were actually bound to the manor almost as tightly as the serf since, in general, they had nowhere else to go. There were, however, some distinctions among freemen. In medieval rural France the *sergents*, who were the household administrators of great noblemen, ranked at the top of the non-nobility. They tended to marry at their own level or even into the lower nobility (Barber, 1957).

In the average village on a manorial estate in medieval times there lived about 400 souls, perhaps 250 adults and 150 children. All of these people ordinarily lived their entire lives in that village and they saw very few people from the outside. As Coulton (1930) puts it, a peasant lived, cradle to grave, in association with about four busloads of people all known by name, all having a familiar fixed station in life.

Among the secular nobility, too, there were distinctions of degree. In eighteenth-century France before the Revolution, for example, the *noblesse d'épée* stood higher than the *noblesse de robe*. The former were descended from medieval lords who had given military service to the king. The latter were descended from lawyers, financiers, or merchants; their families had not yet given military service to the king and they lived away from the court in the provinces (Barber, 1955).

The clergy were not all members of the First Estate. The parish priest often lived on the level of the peasantry. The parish was coextensive with the manor and the priest was appointed by the lord. However, the monks and bishops and the other higher clergy owned both land and serfs; in the Middle Ages the wealth of the monks alone has been estimated as one-third of the national wealth. It is a little surprising that monks occupied this position in view of their rule of poverty, but the Middle Ages saw a great relaxation in monastic life. One amusing example concerns the eating of meat, which was originally forbidden to monks except when they were ill and in the infirmary. After a time they developed the practice of going to the infirmary when not ill for the purpose of eating meat. In some monasteries a room was built midway between the refectory and the infirmary, a room called *misericord*, "the Room of Mercy," where meat could be eaten. In 1337 Benedict XII allowed the monks to use this room on alternate days but, later on, the Benedictines even complained against the harshness of this rule. Before 1300 it had become quite exceptional for a monk to work in the fields or at any handicraft. They did not shave themselves, wash their own linen or do the kitchen work. In a large monastery there might be three servants to one monk (Coulton, 1960).

The stratification system of feudal Europe was very rigid, but there was some mobility of individuals. From *Piers Plowman*, a poem of the late Middle Ages, we learn that it was scandalous for a bondman's bairn to become a bishop and a soap-seller's son a knight. It scandalized, but evidently it happened. Pope Gregory VII we know was the son of a serf (Barber, 1957). In the three or four centuries before the Revolution in France, there were many ways in which wealthy families could elevate themselves. There were many offices for sale that carried ennobling titles: those giving immediate hereditary nobility cost the most; those that conferred hereditary nobility only if they were held for several generations cost the least. A rich dowry would enable a young woman of wealthy bourgeois family to marry into the lower nobility. It has been estimated that 20–30,000 *livres* would buy a solicitor for a husband; 75–150,000 *livres* a counselor in the *Parlement;* and 200–600,000 *livres* would buy just about anyone (Barber, 1957).

In Europe, as in India, religious beliefs were well suited to relieve tensions generated by the social system. Medieval thought was dominated by the belief that it was the chief business of every man to save his soul. Serfs had souls just as did noblemen and they could best save them by performing the duties of the station in which a "Divine Providence" had placed them. A man's social position was his testing ground. There was no doctrine of reincarnation and so no promise of mobility across lifetimes. However, since there were many mansions in Heaven to which a serf might aspire, there was a kind of mobility in the Hereafter, a mobility across existences.

The social strata called castes or Estates were clearly visible vertical streaks in the social life of their time. An outsider landing in France in the Middle Ages or in India any time during the past three millennia would have been certain to discover the stratification systems. Perhaps they were most obviously manifest in styles of life. Both the Varnas and the Estates were defined in terms of supra-occupations: the priesthood, the secular nobility, tradesmen, and laborers. There was also a finer occupational structure. In the Central Provinces of India, earlier in this century, the weaving of cloth was partitioned as follows: thread was spun by the Katias, cotton cleaned by the Mohammedan Bahmas; coarser cloths were woven by such lower castes as the Mahars, Gandas, and Koris and finer cloths by higher castes (*Encyclopedia Britannica*). In a large city of India there was a subcaste of chauffeurs and a local joke that this caste was bound to subdivide into a superior caste of men who drove Rolls-Royces and an inferior caste of men who drove Fords (Barber, 1957). Caste membership affected the style of life in many dimensions: language, proper names, attire, diet, and place of residence. In feudal Europe the styles of life of the baron, the serf, and the monk were equally distinct.

Stratification was detectable, secondly, in patterns of interaction. The evidence was of two kinds: reciprocal intimate interaction distinguished persons belonging to the same stratum from persons belonging to different strata; one-way deferential and condescending interaction distinguished higher strata from lower. Marriage is a good example of intimate interaction. India was rigidly endogamous; marriage was always within the caste. Parents selected a suitable bridegroom for a daughter when she was still a child. In feudalism, similarly, the peasantry did not intermarry with the nobility. Not only marriage but all sorts of familiar and intimate interaction occurred within a stratum more often than between strata. Indeed, in India there were extremely elaborate ritualistic avoidances prescribed even for neighboring subcastes. They might be forbidden to mix together at social festivals, to touch the same earthen pots, to smoke together, drink together, or dine together (Murphy, 1953). The number of avoidances increased with the remoteness of the castes and so their ordering could have been discovered from interaction alone.

It is possible to know the ordering of things and yet not know which is the top end of the order and which the bottom end. The top and bottom of a social system are always discoverable from the fact that intimacy downward is more welcome than intimacy upward. Brahmans had a greater range of social acceptability than other castes. In addition, the "up" and "down" of the feudal and caste societies were marked by pronouns of address, curtsies, honorific titles, and by the exercise of authority and condescension. For example, the Chamars, a lower caste of modern India, are supposed to stand up if a Brahman happens to pass by their door. They do not regularly do so nowadays and some Brahmans complain about it (Murphy, 1953).

Finally, both Indians and Europeans in the feudal period were conscious of their stratification systems and showed it by what they said. In France before the Revolution, and among university students in modern India, the best evidence of consciousness of stratification was the flood of speech and writing attacking the system. In India a man's caste was usually revealed by his name and so was likely to enter consciousness with every social introduction. There is one datum on caste-consciousness that is closely comparable with the sort of information we have about class consciousness in modern American society. The 1931 census inquiring about caste offered a "No Caste" alternative. At that time there was considerable propaganda against caste, and yet fewer than one per cent of Hindus chose to say that they had no caste (Davis, 1951). This is quite different, we shall see, from American responses in comparable circumstances.

The defining distinction between a caste system and a class system is that the vertical boundaries separating one level from another are in the former relatively rigid or impermeable, whereas the boundaries in the latter are somewhat permeable. Individuals are placed in the caste of the group into which they are born and, for the most part, must stay there throughout their lives. In a class system, individuals have the status of their families until they assume independent occupations or get married, but then their class membership can change.

Stratification in general, whether of caste or class, is manifest in uniformities of life style, patterns of interaction, and stratum-consciousness. How does the difference of rigidity or mobility work out in terms of these three manifestations? Where there is caste nearly all individuals will, throughout their lifetimes, follow one life style, conform to one pattern of interaction, and be conscious of membership in one stratum. Where there is a class system some individuals shift life style, interaction patterns, and consciousness. Stratification seen from afar is a visible pattern in the movements of millions of microscopic particles; where caste prevails each particle stays in one pattern over its life cycle and where class prevails some particles jump from one pattern to another.

The Reality of Social Class

For most social scientists class in the modern industrialized world is a reality. They see it in the life around them: in England, France, Japan, the United States, and the Soviet Union. They see it in the local community and also in the national life. There is some variation in description of "the class structure in America" or elsewhere, but one can generalize that class in the modern state means, to social scientists, some three to ten vertical strata closely linked with occupation and income.

In one sense the identification of socio-economic classes is an arbitrary decision which the social scientist is free to make as he wishes. Suppose an investigator wants to see whether the number of children that a man has varies with his annual income. The investigator probably will elect to break up the natural continuum of income into some small number of categories or classes: Under $1,000 a year; $1,000 to $2,000; $2,000 to $3,000, etc. These intervals are, in one sense, socio-economic classes. However, there may be nothing in the underlying data that tells the investigator where to draw boundaries. He is simply imposing a convenient subdivision and that is a perfectly reasonable thing to do for his purposes. It makes no sense to ask him how many classes there really are or whether he has drawn the lines in the right places. There are however many he chooses to create and the lines may be drawn where he pleases. What he has done is a little like making "cutting points" on a perfectly continuous distribution of test scores in order to assign letter grades. The grade categories do not exist in the behavior of the students who took the test; they exist in the mind of the grader. Imposed classes which do not pretend to be descriptions of an underlying social reality had best be called *categorizations*.

When we ask whether there really are social classes in the United States, and if so how many, we are not asking foolish questions because we are not asking about imposed categorizations. If classes are real for a population being studied, their boundaries will be detectable in the life of that population. Our question is: Do the variations in style-of-life, the patterns of interaction, and the talk about class in modern societies (especially the United States) justify the conclusion that stratification exists, that classes have a social and psychological reality? It is rather like asking whether a distribution of test scores shows "natural" cutting points or discontinuities.

The reality of class in a community will be undeniable in the following circumstances: (1) the population is conscious of classes, agreed on the number of classes, and on the membership of them; (2) styles of life are strikingly uniform within a stratum and there are clear contrasts between strata; (3) interaction is sharply patterned by stratum; (4) the boundaries suggested by the three kinds of data are coincident. These are conditions to which caste-structured societies approximate but the conditions are logically independent of mobility and could obtain without rigidity of boundaries. In the degree that the conditions listed are not satisfied, the reality of class becomes doubtful.

If classes are real, are truly descriptive, it can still be asked whether they are profoundly descriptive. Are the strata not only available to consciousness but, in addition, often in consciousness? Are they cognitively salient? How much interaction and what kind of interaction is structured by strata? How many aspects of a man's style of life are patterned by stratum?

CONSCIOUSNESS OF CLASS

In general one guesses at someone's consciousness from his talk or his writing. There are many kinds of talk and many ways of eliciting talk. What do they tell us about the reality and profundity of class? Perhaps the least directive or suggestive way of eliciting talk that is likely to be relevant to social class is to invite some people to tell about their community in their own words. We will look first at what happens in these circumstances.

In the early 1930's W. Lloyd Warner and his colleagues studied the stratification of a New England town they have called Yankee City. They "discovered" the class structure of Yankee City in the free talk of its inhabitants (Warner and Lunt, 1941). Warner, a social anthropologist, had recently completed a three-year study of Australian aborigines and he wanted to employ the techniques of anthropology—the prolonged flexible study of men in their total socio-cultural context—to a modern American community. He wanted a small community with a coherent tradition, and Yankee City, a town of 17,000 inhabitants with a long history in New England commerce, satisfied the requirement.

Warner began with a series of open, nondirective interviews of people in Yankee City who seemed to him to be well spread out in the community class structure. From the content of these interviews he abstracted the town's class system; there were six strata called by Warner the upper-uppers, the lower-uppers, the upper-middles, the lower-middles, the upper-lowers, and the lower-lowers. Warner's terminology is his own; Yankee City people did not talk about their community in these words. However, some of them were definitely class-conscious and spoke of strata in a local lexicon that identified the very top people as "Hill Streeters" and some lower strata people as "clam diggers" or "wool hats." Warner attributes this kind of awareness to observant and intelligent people in Yankee City—not to everyone. Using a set of elaborate procedures that are not altogether objective (called the technique of "Evaluated Participation") Warner induced the class structure from the content of the interviews. What we are interested in now, however, is the fact that some people, but by no means all, talked about classes in their own terms when asked freely to describe life in a small New England town.

In India a man's caste is an important part of his identity; he reveals it in telling his name. If an American is asked: "Who are you?" his first response will be his personal name and with us that does not reveal class. If we persisted in asking the question, pressing for information beyond the personal name, we would usually be given the name of a vocation, a religion, race, or nationality, perhaps a city of residence. It would very seldom happen that anyone would answer: "I am a member of the working class" or "I am a member of the upper-upper class" (Hyman, 1942; Kahl, 1953). Class membership does not seem to be a very salient category for self-identification.

Sargent (1953) asked a question to get at the cognitive salience of social class which is a little more clearly aimed at social class than the question, "Who are you?" Two hundred residents of Ventura, California, were asked: "What would you say are the most important *differences* found among the people of Ventura?" Asking a question about people probably is more suggestive of classes than is a question about a person (oneself). In addition, most discussions of social class stress the *differences* between levels rather than the homogeneity within a level, and so the word *differences* is likely to evoke notions of class. Nevertheless explicit mention of class or status were not common—only 17 per cent of the responses. Most of the responses were in terms of income, occupation, religion, residential area, and ethnic membership. All of these categorizations are related to social class and two of them—occupation and income—are very intimately related. Only a few categorizations completely independent of class were mentioned; one of these was "Oldtimers *vs.* Newcomers."

An inquiry about differences in a population does not often elicit talk about social class, but it does often elicit talk about occupation and income. These are distinctions thought to be determinative of social class but they are not identical with the concept of class. Income is a continuous variable, not a small number of categories; occupations are categories, but they are much more numerous than the social classes any investigator has described for America.

One can inquire into the psychological reality of social class by using a fairly direct suggestion. Rogoff (1953) finds that the question, "What word would you use to name the class you belong to?" has elicited no answer from 19.5 per cent of people sampled in France and 27.5 per cent of people sampled in the United States. Gross (1953) used the question, "What class do you belong to?" with a sample of the population of Minneapolis. Over one-third of his respondents said that there were no classes in Minneapolis, or that they themselves did not belong to any class, or that they did not know what class they were in. Compare this result with the one per cent of Hindus who reported in 1931 that they had "No caste."

When the interviewer makes his question into a multiple-choice item with a set of fixed alternatives, the percentage of people who put themselves in a class rises. A famous survey conducted by *Fortune* Magazine in 1940 asked: "What social class do you belong to?" and offered three alternatives: 1) Upper Class; 2) Middle class;)3 Lower class. About 80 per cent of the respondents placed themselves in the middle class. Centers

(1949) showed that the way the percentages fall depends on the way the classes are named. He provided the three alternatives of the *Fortune* poll plus the designation "working class" and obtained the following distribution:

Upper class	3%
Middle class	43%
Working class	51%
Lower class	1%

Although no alternative to class membership was provided, 2 per cent of the respondents said either that they did not know their class or that they did not believe in classes.

The results we have described are already pointing to a conclusion and we may as well make it explicit now so that we can keep track of it in what follows. The various kinds of inquiry that ask people to talk about social life without directly suggesting social class do not reliably elicit talk about class. "Tell me about life in Yankee City" "Who are you?" "What kinds of differences are there between people in Ventura?" Most respondents do explicitly mention things related to social evaluation—income, occupation, race, etc. It looks as if differential social value, rankings of some kind, are a profound social and psychological reality, but it does not look as if this reality were consciously structured as a small number of classes.

When the inquiry becomes more directive ("What class would you say that you belong to?") the evidence of class naturally becomes stronger. But even with such a question, as many as one-third of the respondents refuse to put themselves in a class. When the question provides fixed alternatives that do not include a response of "No class," a respondent must really violate his instructions to avoid giving evidence of class. And a few, one or two per cent, do so. Most do not. But suppose we asked people "What color are your eyes?" and provided a list of alternatives; everyone would check some alternative. But eye color is of no importance in structuring social life. It is not often in consciousness, it is unrelated to life style, and it does not govern interaction. It is simply something people will report if you ask for it.

The direct question with fixed alternatives cannot tell us whether class is real or profound or salient. It is completely insensitive to variation in these dimensions. The fact that most people in the United States will put themselves in one of a set of alternative classes does not offset the other evidence that classes are seldom in consciousness.

These first data have served to reveal what it is that is doubtful about class in modern society. It is not the notion of differential social value, of social rankings, but rather the notion that rankings are thought of as a small set of classes. Taking social ranking for granted, it is possible to collect data that will be quite directly informative about the reality of class.

Hollingshead (1949) has made a study of a small community in the American corn belt, a community he calls Elmtown. Hollingshead was particularly interested in the ways in which the social life of adolescents was affected by their class membership. He developed a completely explicit and objective technique for determining social class and his results are very instructive for our present purpose. Hollingshead's general idea was to find a set of families who were well known in Elmtown and whose stations were unequivocal and then to use these families as a kind of reference list for the placement of all other families. He worked by asking respondents to rank families in prestige without suggesting classes to them and yet leaving it open to them to describe classes.

From his initial interviews Hollingshead got the names of thirty families that were often mentioned and seemed to be well scattered in social position. The family names were put on cards and twenty-five community members were asked to put each family where it belonged in terms of its "station" or "standing." The raters all divided the cards into stacks such that families in the same stack were thought to be of equal rank; in short, they all described classes rather than unique ranks. How much agreement was there on the number of classes and the membership in them?

> 19 made 5 classes
> 3 made 3 classes
> 2 made 4 classes
> 1 made 2 classes

The amount of agreement in family placement was 77 per cent, chiefly focused on twenty of the thirty families. These twenty names were then given to twelve new informants with the instruction that all twenty be placed in their appropriate stations. The result was:

> 10 made 5 classes
> 1 made 4 classes
> 1 made 3 classes

The correlation in placements for those who used five classes with those in the previous set of informants who had used five classes was .88. Hollingshead decided that there were five classes in Elmtown and he assigned the control families values from one to five corresponding to the class positions.

The next question was: Could new families be placed by equating them with one or another family on the control list? Eight raters were used and fifty-three family names. The raters were asked to place only those of the fifty-three families with whom they were personally acquainted. They were to place a family by pairing it with the one on the control list which it most closely matched in terms of the way the families lived, income and possessions, participation in community affairs, and general prestige. Twenty-nine of the fifty-three families were placed by all eight raters and when the ratings were divided into sets at random, the composite correlation across sets was .82.

Hollingshead went on to obtain the class positions of all 535 families with which he was concerned. Each new family was assigned the mean values of the control families with which it had been equated. Class I was defined as families having means from 1.0 to 1.50; Class II as families having means from 1.51 to 2.50; Class III as families from 2.51 to 3.50; etc. A class, in the end, was a range of ratings. Before considering the implications of Hollingshead's results for the psychological reality of social class, we will look at the outcomes of two other prestige-rating studies.

Lenski (1952) worked on the stratification of Danielson, Connecticut—a town of 6,000 persons, which makes it the same size as Elmtown. Twenty-four respondents were asked to rate a sample of their townsmen. The result:

1 used 3 classes
4 used 4 classes
7 used 5 classes
8 used 6 classes
4 used 7 classes

Kaufman (Kahl, 1953, pp. 40, 50, 51), in a village of 1500 inhabitants, asked fourteen informants to rate every family they knew in the township, using *as many strata as possible*. The outcome:

2 used 4 classes
2 used 5 classes
6 used 6 classes
2 used 7 classes
1 used 9 classes
1 used 10 classes

These three studies make an instructive pattern. When people are asked to rate others on prestige they use classes rather than unique ranks, even when the instructions do not clearly direct them to do so. What is more, when the instructions press them to differentiate as finely as possible, it still happens that all subjects use classes and none uses more than ten. It does appear that for inhabitants of American small towns the local prestige dimension is conceived of as a small number of classes.

Classes may appear in the prestige-ranking task primarily because of cognitive limitations—perhaps people cannot discriminate more than ten or so degrees of prestige. The question is: How are the cutting points determined? Is there a social reality that dictates where the breaks must occur, or do they fall arbitrarily? If there is a reality behind the piles of names on cards, one would expect respondents to agree on the number of piles and the membership of them. If the piles simply result from a need to reduce complexity, then their number and membership should be more idiosyncratic.

In Elmtown, good majorities—nineteen of twenty-five raters and ten of twelve raters—agreed that the number of classes was five, but there the families rated had been picked for the unequivocality of their stations. In Danielson, a town of about the same size as Elmtown, there was not a majority for any single version of the number of classes. This was true again in Kaufman's study when informants were asked to differentiate as finely as they were able. There is doubt, then, that a particular class structure has reality in these small communities.

All of the data on consciousness of stratification indicate the profound reality of social rankings, but leave me quite unconvinced that these rankings are construed as a small number of classes on which people are agreed. Perhaps data on the structure of interaction will be more convincing.

CLASSES FROM INTERACTION

It is possible for the structure of interaction to tell us quite clearly whether there are classes, how many there are, and how important they are. We can see how this would work by contrasting a categorization of human beings that has no social-psychological significance with a categorization that has great significance. For the former, let us use blue-eyed persons and brown-eyed persons; for the latter, the categories male and female. How would interaction reveal the insignificance of one contrast and the importance of the other?

Imagine that we are concerned with a community of only six persons (A, B, C, D, E, and F), and that we are able to keep track of interaction among them over a considerable period of time. To find structure in our data we make an interaction matrix (Figure 3-1) with all persons listed twice, once at the heads of columns and once at the ends of rows. Each square is defined by the interception of two names. The squares on the diagonal line from the upper left to the lower right are the loci in which each name intercepts with itself (AA, BB, CC, etc.), and these are squares we do not need for our interaction matrix. Furthermore, each square above the diagonal duplicates one below; for example AB is above and BA is below. We need only one box for each pair of different persons, and so the squares above the diagonal are left empty in Figure 3-1.

	A	B	C	D	E	F
A						
B	baseball cokes library trees					
C	baseball cokes trees	baseball library trees				
D	cokes dance married	dance library	dance library			
E	cokes dance library	cokes dance married	cokes dance library	cokes beauty parlor shower		
F	dance library	cokes dance library	dance library married	beauty parlor shower cokes	beauty parlor library shower	

baseball = playing catch with a baseball
beauty parlor = visiting the beauty parlor
cokes = having cokes
dance = going to a dance
library = studying in the library
married = getting married
shower = going to a bridal shower
trees = felling trees

FIGURE 3-1.   AN INTERACTION MATRIX FOR SIX PERSONS

Suppose we have some way of classifying two-person (dyadic) inter-actions: playing catch with a baseball, visiting the beauty parlor, having cokes, going to a dance, studying in the library, getting married, going to a bridal shower, and felling trees. In each square we would list all the interactions in which the two persons who define the square have participated together. Frequencies of each interaction would be helpful in discovering structure but for this example we will imagine results that enable us to do without frequencies.

Into what categories do the six persons we have imagined fall? Dyads put together for *felling trees* or for *playing catch with a baseball* are always made up of two persons from the set: A, B, and C. Apparently any two from this set will serve, but no member of the set D, E, and F, is ever involved in these interactions. However, dyads put together for *visiting the beauty parlor* or for *going to a bridal shower* are always and only drawn from the set: D, E, and F. We can, therefore, distinguish two sets or categories on the basis of interaction alone.

The two categories are confirmed by the pattern we see for the interactions called *getting married* and *going to a dance*. The dyads involved are invariably composed of one member drawn from the set A, B, C, and one member drawn from the set D, E, F. It is by now apparent that A, B, and C, are males and D, E, and F, are females. Members of the same category, whichever one it is, have the same privileges of interaction; for some purposes they join with one another, for other purposes they join with members of the complementary category. Interaction in this community is regular—in terms of the categories male and female.

This method of analyzing social interaction for the purpose of discovering functional social categories is essentially the same as the method a linguist uses for discovering regularities of syntax in speech. Such parts of speech as the noun and verb are categories of words that have the same privileges of combination with other words. In certain kinds of constructions, two nouns may be combined; in other constructions, two verbs; and for other constructions one must have a noun and a verb. Both the well-formed sentence and the well-formed interaction combine members of functional categories in certain prescribed ways. It seems very likely that the same sort of intellectual mechanism would be required for learning and operating with the syntax of interaction as for learning and operating with the syntax of speech. The similarity cannot be made clear in this one paragraph, but the paragraph is introduced here so that we will remember to think of social structure when we study linguistic structure in Chapter 6.

Returning to the matrix of Figure 3-1, there are some interactions, *having cokes* and *studying in the library*, that do not pattern by sex. These interactions are formed promiscuously from two members of the male set or two of the female set, or one from each set. In terms of the sex categories, these interactions do not manifest any regularities. Of course, there are more than six persons in most communities and more functional categories than the male and female. In a larger and more varied array of persons *having cokes* and *studying in the library* might fall into a regular pattern. If, for instance, there was variation by age in the array of persons we might find that certain ones, the older ones, never do study in the library or have cokes.

The number of interactions which pattern by sex, as do *felling trees, going to a bridal shower*, and *getting married*, is an index of the importance of sex as a structuring principle. We know that the number is large in our society and that sex is an extremely important principle. Age also is an important principle. In essence there is much in our social life that hinges on sex and age.

You may object that, in Figure 3-1, the interaction pattern is drawn with unrealistic clarity. Certainly the pairs of interactions, like *baseball* and *felling trees*, which mark out same-sex groups, would not usually have identical distributions. They would simply show some degree of overlap, but that overlap would still serve to distinguish them from such others as *beauty parlor* or *getting married*. In addition, it could happen, once in a long while, that two boys would go together to a dance—as "stags"— or two girls—as "does." An infrequent departure from the pattern would not prevent us from discovering the pattern. If we went further and asked the participants who broke the pattern how they felt about such deviant interactions, we would obtain plentiful support for the importance of the usual pattern. The same-sex pairs going to a dance would feel uncomfortable and would want to explain to us how they happened to find themselves in this anomalous position.

Could we discover the categorization of persons in terms of eye color from such an interaction pattern? Clearly not. We can distribute blue and brown eyes among A, B, C, D, E, and F, in any way at all without making the interaction pattern unrealistic. Combinations of blue eyes and of brown eyes can play baseball, fell trees, dance, marry, visit the beauty parlor, or what have you. It is difficult to imagine a set of interactions that patterns by eye color; it is difficult to imagine a set that does not pattern by sex.

Would the lines of social class emerge from an interaction matrix as does the division of sex, or would they fail to emerge in the manner of eye color? I do not know of a study that makes a matrix of the kind pictured in Figure 3-1, but there are many studies showing that one or another kind of interaction is more frequent within a social class than across classes. Perhaps the data from these studies will yield the answer we are seeking.

Kahl and Davis (1955) asked 199 men living in Cambridge, Massachusetts, to name their three best friends. The investigators assigned occupational status scores to each respondent and each friend. The scores of the friends of a respondent were averaged and the resulting mean status scores of best friends were correlated with the status scores of the respondents. The tetrachoric correlation was .70 which indicates a strong relationship. Men find their friends at their own status levels.

One of the interesting things Hollingshead did in Elmtown was to chart the clique structure of the high-school students. Cliques, of course, are close, informal friendship groupings. A clique tie is any common membership between two persons. Of 1,258 clique ties in the Elmtown high school, Hollingshead found that three out of five linked students whose families belonged to the same social class, two out of five were between adolescents of adjacent class, only one in twenty-five was between classes twice removed. Dating relationships, Hollingshead found, closely paralleled the pattern of clique associations. Sixty-one per cent of daters in Elmtown belonged to the same social class; 35 per cent belonged to adjacent classes; and 4 per cent were two classes apart. In a later study in New Haven Hollingshead demonstrated that social classes are also endogamous; marriages generally united members of the same social class rather than members of different classes. In New Haven, in 1948, 83 per cent of all marriages were between persons of the same class or immediately adjacent classes.

The results we have cited certainly show that intimate interaction is conditioned by socio-economic status; they seem to show that status functions as a set of classes. Kahl and Davis found that best friends belong to the same class; Hollingshead found that dates, cliques, and marriages all tend to occur within classes. The classes in question, however, were not discovered in the patterns of interaction. Class memberships had been assigned on the basis of prestige ratings or occupation or something other than interaction. When interaction data were analyzed in terms of such independently determined class memberships, the frequency of the interaction was always greatest within a class, less between adjacent classes, and still less for more remote classes. However, a report of this kind does not tell us whether class boundaries could actually be discovered in the pattern of interaction.

All of the interaction data I have seen are compatible with either of two hypotheses about the underlying status structure: 1) There are a small number of internally homogeneous ranked classes; 2) there is a continuum of ranked persons or families. The two hypotheses predict different patterns in an interaction matrix of the imaginary kind pictured in Figure 3-1. If there are social classes we should find relatively uniform frequencies of interaction over class members with definite discontinuities at class boundaries. If there is simply a status continuum the frequency of interaction should fall off with the distance between any two persons or families, but discontinuities should not occur.

We can illustrate the point with some new imaginary matrices. Suppose we have nine persons, our familiar A, B, C, D, E, and F, plus G, H, and I. All nine are mutually acquainted and we ask each one to name two good friends from the set. In this matrix (unlike the one that appears as Figure 3-1) we need two squares for each pair of persons since A may choose B as a friend and B may choose A. Suppose now that, in truth, the nine persons belong to three socio-economic classes: A, B, and C to Class I; D, E, and F to Class II; G, H, and I to Class III, and that good friends are always chosen from class-equals. The existence of the three classes appears very clearly in Figure 3-2. Each person is linked with two members of his class. There are no bonds across classes. Disregard the circles in Figure 3-2 for the moment.

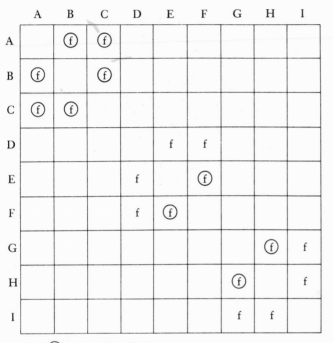

	A	B	C	D	E	F	G	H	I
A		(f)	(f)						
B	(f)		(f)						
C	(f)	(f)							
D					f	f			
E				f		(f)			
F				f	(f)				
G								(f)	f
H							(f)		f
I							f	f	

f and (f) = friendship choice

(f) = a within-class choice when it is believed that A, B, C, D = Class I; E, F, G, H = Class II; I = Class III

FIGURE 3-2. FRIENDSHIP CHOICES AMONG NINE PERSONS THAT REVEAL A CLASS STRUCTURE

Suppose, on the other hand, that the nine persons occupy unique social ranks and can be ordered as A, B, C, D, E, F, G, H, I. Each chooses as his two good friends the two persons nearest him in social rank. For B, C, D, E, F, G, and H, this means one friend on either side; for A it means two friends who are immediately below him and for I the two friends will be immediately above. The interaction matrix of Figure 3-3 reveals a rank order; there is not the discontinuity that reveals the classes in Figure 3-2. Disregard the circles in Figure 3-3 for the moment.

The studies of interaction by social class, known to me, either did not

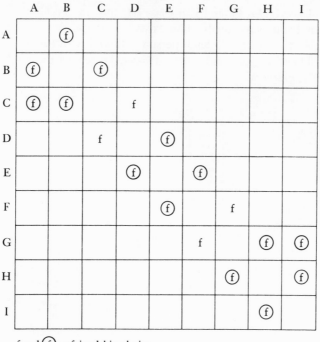

f and (f) = friendship choice

(f) = a within-class choice when it is believed that A, B, C = Class I; D, E, F = Class II; G, H, I = Class III

FIGURE 3-3. FRIENDSHIP CHOICES AMONG NINE PERSONS THAT REVEAL A STATUS CONTINUUM

obtain the full set of data required for matrices like Figures 3-2 and 3-3 or else do not report the data in this form. Hollingshead, for example, has published (1949) Table 3-1. His index of the class positions (I-V) of boys and girls in Elmtown was obtained, quite independently of the interaction data, from the ratings of families made by community members which were described in the previous section of this chapter. For our present problem of seeing whether classes can be extracted from interaction matrices, we should like to know whether the boundaries of the prestige classes corresponded with clear discontinuities in the interaction data. From Table 3-1 and from Hollingshead's other tables we cannot tell whether this was so. We can clearly see that clique relations were most frequent between persons matched by class and that they became less frequent as the class distance increased. However, a pattern of this kind could be obtained from an underlying matrix that is either like Figure 3-2 or like Figure 3-3.

TABLE 3-1.   PERCENTAGE OF CLIQUE RELATIONS OBSERVED WITHIN AND
BETWEEN CLASSES BY SEX

BOYS

Class	I and II	III	IV	V
I and II	49	38	13	0
III	11	61	27	1
IV	5	33	60	2
V	0	13	31	56

GIRLS

Class	II	III	IV	V
II	56	26	18	0
III	7	64	28	1
IV	4	21	70	5
V	0	4	36	60

Suppose the underlying reality were like Figure 3-3, i.e., a ranking rather than a class system. Suppose that our independent prestige ratings had suggested to us the class structure: A, B, C, as Class I; D, E, F as Class II; G, H, I as Class III. The circled f's in Figure 3-3 would then represent friendship choices within a social class. There are fourteen of these or 77.8 per cent. The uncircled f's would represent ties between persons of adjacent class and there are four of these or 22.2 per cent. Between classes twice removed there are no ties. This is a pattern in which within-class interaction has the highest frequency and in which the frequencies fall off with class distance. But in the realities of the interaction there are no classes.

Suppose the underlying reality were, like Figure 3-2, a class system rather than a ranking. If our independent index of class position placed the nine members exactly as does the matrix (A, B, C, as I; D, E, F as II; G, H, I as III), we would find that the within-class frequency of friendship choices equaled 100 per cent. For persons one class apart or two classes apart, the frequencies would be zero. In this case we would know that the interaction matrix perfectly corresponded with the system yielded by prestige ratings. However, the literature contains no report of such sharply discontinuous data. Even for marriages in New Haven for *same-or-adjacent* class this frequency was 83 per cent, not 100 per cent.

Is it possible that the real situation could be like Figure 3-2 when the reports always find frequencies that fall off gradually rather than abruptly with class distance? Suppose that our independent index had not yielded a class structure that exactly corresponded with the one implicit in Figure 3-2, but instead had suggested: A, B, C, D, as Class I; E, F, G, H as Class II; I as one person in Class III. In this case the within-class choices would be those circled in Figure 3-2 and they total ten or 55.6 per cent. Adjacent class choices would be the f's not encircled and they total eight or 44.4 per cent. Between classes twice removed there would be no friendship ties. Here then is a pattern of the type that is universally reported where the underlying reality is a sharply discontinuous class system.

Patterns of interaction by class of the sort reported in the literature on this subject are consistent either with an underlying socio-economic continuum or with an underlying system of classes. It follows that, while the empirical literature definitely demonstrates that social rank affects interaction, it fails to demonstrate that social ranks function as a small set of classes.

CLASSES FROM STYLE OF LIFE

For the members of a family who have an occupation, that occupation is a major part of life, and for those dependent on them the occupation is a prime determinant of the style of life. The occupations of the medieval peasantry were very unlike the occupations of the nobility and so were their residences, their clothing, food, recreation, and manners. Can we find discontinuities of life style that mark off social classes in the modern nation?

The interaction matrix and the technique of ranking persons for prestige can be used to investigate stratification in small communities, but they are of no use for working out the national stratification system in a country like the United States. Most of the people in this vast population never meet and so cannot interact. We do not know one another by name and so cannot rank one another. Occupations are roles in which many people have membership and the names of occupations can be ranked by respondents all over the country. In this indirect way we can place nearly everyone in the country on a prestige scale. The rank of a man's occupation describes his potential point of entry into many local interaction networks and also his potential position on many local scales of prestige. If a banker and a bus driver both move from Cleveland to Denver, they will enter Denver social life at different points and will assume different prestige positions in Denver minds.

The study of occupational prestige that dwarfs all others is the one made in 1947 under the direction of North and Hatt (National Opinion Research Center, 1947). A representative sample of the adult population of the United States, a total of 2,920 persons, was interviewed. Each respondent was asked to rate ninety occupations in terms of his "*own personal opinion*" of the *general standing* that such a job has on a scale from excellent (1 point) to poor (5 points).

How could classes emerge from such data? Suppose that Americans thought of one set of occupations as belonging to a single class distinct from another set which constituted a second class. The average ratings for occupations in the same class should be relatively uniform and there should be a decisive break between classes. In short, one would look for marked discontinuities in the distribution of scores, even as a teacher looks for such discontinuities in trying to find cutting points for grades.

Hatt and North combined the ratings in such a way that any occupation which was always rated "excellent" would receive a score of 100. In Table 3-2 we present the occupations that fell into the top twenty ranks with their individual rating scores. The largest "breaks" in the ratings occur between Rank 1 (U.S. Supreme Court Justice) and Rank 2 (Physician), and between Rank 5 (Diplomat in the U.S. Foreign Service) and Rank 6 (Mayor of a large city). These gaps are only very slightly larger than others and do not correspond with any common impression of class boundaries in the United States.[1]

TABLE 3-2.   PRESTIGE RATINGS FOR THE TOP TWENTY OCCUPATIONS IN THE HATT AND NORTH STUDY

Occupation	Score	Occupation	Score
1. U.S. Supreme Court Justice	96	11. Government scientist	88
2. Physician	93	12. County judge	87
3. State governor	93	13. Head of a department in a state government	87
4. Cabinet member in the federal government	92	14. Minister	87
5. Diplomat in the U.S. Foreign Service	92	15. Architect	86
6. Mayor of a large city	90	16. Chemist	86
7. College professor	89	17. Dentist	86
8. Scientist	89	18. Lawyer	86
9. United States Representative in Congress	89	19. Member of the board of directors of a large corporation	86
10. Banker	88	20. Nuclear physicist	86

A sample of the populations of six large Japanese cities rated thirty occupations in 1952 (Japan Sociological Society, 1954). In Table 3-3 these occupations and their mean ratings appear. There are slight discontinuities in these data; for example, outsize breaks appear after No. 6 and No. 12. However, the breaks are not large; they are not followed by exceptional uniformity of ratings, they do not correspond with familiar

1. The 1947 study was replicated by the National Opinion Research Center in 1963 (Hodge, Siegel, and Rossi, in press). The correlation between the 1947 scores and the 1963 scores was .99. There was no more evidence of classes in the 1963 data than in the 1947 data.

TABLE 3-3. PRESTIGE RATINGS OF OCCUPATIONS IN JAPAN

Occupation	Mean score	Occupation	Mean score
1. Prefectural governor	3.78	14. Ward-office clerk	15.38
2. University professor	4.56	15. Company-office clerk	16.13
3. Local court judge	4.69	16. Small independent	
4. Officer of large company	5.51	farmer	16.38
5. Doctor	6.97	17. Policeman	16.41
6. Section head of government office	7.19	18. Tailor	17.68
		19. Department store clerk	19.76
7. Architect	9.51	20. Insurance agent	20.18
8. Owner of medium or small factory	10.21	21. Carpenter	20.22
		22. Barber	20.46
9. Chairman of national labor union federation	10.77	23. Bus driver	20.93
		24. Latheman	21.05
10. Newspaper reporter	11.17	25. Fisherman	22.02
11. Elementary school teacher	11.73	26. Coal miner	23.70
		27. Charcoal burner	24.42
12. Priest of Buddhist temple	12.46	28. Road worker	24.80
		29. Street stall keeper	24.92
13. Owner of retail store	15.30	30. Shoe shiner	26.86

class distinctions and they might disappear if more occupations had been listed.

It is clear that populations of modern states have definite ideas of the relative prestige of occupations and in all these studies there is evidence of a high consensus on the positions of most occupations. Furthermore, Inkeles and Rossi (1956) have shown that there is high agreement in these rankings among the United States, Great Britain, New Zealand, Japan, and the U.S.S.R. However, in none of the results is there clear evidence of a class structure. The dominant impression is rather one of a continuum of occupational prestige.

Centers (1953) used the facilities of the National Opinion Research Center to ask a national sample of adults in the United States to place a number of occupations in one of four classes: upper, middle, working, and lower. Here again, as in Centers' study of self-placement in classes, the alternatives were provided. For some occupations there was substantial agreement on a single class; the largest consensus was found for big-business owners and executives who were placed by 82 per cent of respondents in the upper class. However, almost all occupations were sometimes placed in each of the four classes. Those few that did not fall in all four classes fell in three: big-business owners and executives, doctors and lawyers, and bankers were never put in the lower class; janitors, sharecroppers, and servants were never placed in the upper class. The former occupations were sometimes put in the working class and the latter sometimes in the middle class. Again, there is scant evidence that class is a social-psychological reality.

Occupation determines income and the relationship here is too familiar to warrant printing an illustrative table. Income is potentially a perfect continuum and I have seen no tables in which the actual distribution suggests a class structure. Somewhat more interesting than tables relating occupation and income is a table Warner made showing the percentage of income spent on food, shelter, and clothing in each of the six classes of Yankee City (Warner and Lunt, 1941). The results were as follows:

Upper-upper	33%
Lower-upper	35%
Upper-middle	51%
Lower-middle	59%
Upper-lower	66%
Lower-lower	75%

There is one striking discontinuity in these figures: the two top classes are almost the same and there is a difference of 16 per cent between the lower-upper and the upper-middle. If we had this kind of pattern for individuals it would be evidence of the reality of class. The data presented, however, can only suggest that the two divisions in the upper class are more alike than the lower half of this class and the top of the middle class.

The income left over after purchase of food, shelter, and clothing can be used for the purchase of possessions of every kind, and since this percentage goes up with class level, it follows that the possessions of the higher strata will be more numerous and more expensive than those of lower strata. Indeed, certain possessions have been thought sufficiently diagnostic to serve as indices of social class.

Chapin (1935) developed a Living-Room Scale for stratification studies in the United States. The living room is the most important room for advertising status, revealing attitudes and values. One part of Chapin's scale is a check list of possessions such as: a large rug, drapes, piano bench, etc. I admire Chapin's cleverness in picking piano bench rather than piano. Presumably the idea is that anyone who has a piano bench is bound to have a piano, but not vice versa. The second part of his scale concerned the state of repair of the furniture, the level of taste in the furnishings, etc.

Level of education is, of course, closely related to both occupation and income. While years of education is a continuum, the units are not all of the same size in terms of their social implications. Sixteen years of schooling is a greater social increment to fifteen years, than is fifteen to fourteen. The years that bring the degrees are disproportionately significant. Job requirements are ordinarily specified by degrees, not years, and most of us think of education in terms of such categories as: people who have not graduated from high school; high-school graduates; college graduates; people with advanced degrees. More than any other dimension of life style this one seems to be categorical. It has not been demonstrated, however, that the breaks in the educational scale are preserved in scales of occupational prestige or income. Neither has it been shown that the web of interaction breaks on lines coincident with the possession of various academic degrees.

There is very little in life that does not vary, at least probabilistically, with social standing. An infant born into a middle-class family in America today is likely to be trained in a "permissive" way; he may be breast fed and his weaning and toilet training will come late. The infant in a working-class family is not likely to be treated so permissively. The parents of the middle-class child will have higher expectations of achievement and independence than will the parents of a working-class child. The middle-class parents are more likely to discipline with "psychological" punishments and the working-class parents more likely to use physical punishments (Bronfenbrenner, 1958).

Young men with eight or fewer years of education have more premarital sexual intercourse while young men with thirteen or more years of education do more masturbating (Kinsey, Pomeroy, and Martin, 1948). Upper-class people are more likely to belong to the Episcopalian Church or the Congregational Church; lower-class people are more likely to be Baptists or Roman Catholics (Pope, 1948). High-income people are more likely to vote Republican, and low-income people, Democratic (Saenger, 1945). People who think of themselves as working-class are more likely to favor trade-unionism and government regulation of industry than are people who think of themselves as middle class (Centers, 1949). Members of the higher classes are more likely to become neurotic, while members of the lower classes are more likely to become psychotic (Hollingshead and Redlich, 1958). It appears from the Georges' study (1955) of Roman Catholic saints from the first through the nineteenth centuries that members of the upper-class have had a much better chance of being canonized than have members of the lower-class. Finally, Mayer and Hauser have shown (1953) that a member of the higher economic classes has a life expectancy greater than a member of the lower economic classes by about five to ten years.

The life style differences arborealize into the flimsiest trivia. Upper-class Americans like martinis before dinner, wine with dinner, and brandy after dinner; beer is a working-class beverage. The upper class likes a leafy green salad with oil and vinegar, while the lower class likes a chopped salad or head of lettuce with bottled dressing. If you are middle class you say *tuxedo,* where the upper class says *dinner jacket;* in England you would say *mirror* where the aristocracy says *looking-glass.* If you, like me, give your trousers a little hitch when you sit down so that they will not bag at the knee, then you are quite irredeemably middle class.

As indices of socio-economic status, especially for persons not from the same local community, the style of life variables are much handier than either interaction or class consciousness. There is no simple highly diagnostic question that can be asked about interaction and for people who are not acquainted the variable just does not apply. The difficulty with asking people what class they are in is that large numbers will say either that they do not know or that there are no classes. If you provide a limited set of alternatives you may be forcing unreal responses; the way people respond is known to depend on the names you give to classes. Style of life variables like income, occupation, education, rental value of house, and style of living room, involve objective facts which are comparable all across a nation.

In his study of Jonesville, Warner (1949) initially worked out the five local classes from interview material using the rather subjective method he calls Evaluated Participation. He also developed a more objective Index of Status Characteristics (the ISC) that was made up from ratings on six items: occupation, amount of income, source of income, house type, residential location, and amount of education (Warner, Meeker, and Eells, 1949). The six items were given different weights: occupation a weight of 4; source of income 3; residence area 2; etc. Two hundred people were assigned class positions on the basis of both Evaluated Participation and the ISC. The correlation between the two was .97. Occupation alone correlated .91. In Jonesville it was possible to use the more limited and cumbersome methods of inquiry about people known personally, their interaction and social class placements, as well as the simpler style of life inquiries. The style of life index did much the same job as the more elaborate data.

Hatt (1950) used a three-item simplification of Warner's index that proved generally applicable across the United States. He included: occupation, source of income, and rental value of house. Kahl and Davis (1955) did the instructive thing of computing scores for the same 219 men on nineteen different indices of socio-economic status. The scores were all highly intercorrelated and when they were factor analyzed, the primary factor was occupation.

In summary, the style of life of a family unit in this country depends chiefly on the occupation of the father. There seems to be nothing in the prestige ratings given occupations to suggest a class structure and there seem to be no discontinuities in style of life that are great enough to suggest such a structure.

ARE CLASSES REAL?

We have treated this as an empirical question, a question to be answered by data rather than by fiat. Because the question is empirical, it cannot be answered as it stands above. By fiat we could obtain one answer for all times and all places, but data can only answer the question for specified times and places. Classes could be real in 1964 in England and unreal in the United States; they could have been real in the United States in 1864 and yet be unreal in 1964.

The question of empirical reality is not only specific to time and geographic locale but also to region of the socio-economic distribution. It is conceivable that in one region of the distribution a genuine discontinuity or class boundary might appear with all the rest being structured as a socio-economic continuum. Landecker (1960) found evidence of such a structure in a stratification study of the metropolitan area of Detroit. He obtained rankings on four status-relevant variables: income, occupation, amount of education, and ethnic-racial membership. His method of searching for class boundaries in these data was essentially to ascertain the degree of coincidence in placement across dimensions. There was one rather distinct stratum; Landecker calls it an "elite." Members of the elite were characterized by a completed college education, occupations on a high professional or executive level, and incomes in the highest 7 per cent of the population. Below the elite Landecker found no other clearly distinct strata but rather a continuum which he designates the "mass."

Most of the data we have reviewed were obtained in the United States in recent years. They were classified under the headings: 1) class consciousness; 2) interaction; 3) style of life. If classes were real in the United States we ought to have found discontinuities in each kind of data and the discontinuities or boundaries ought to have been coincident across the kinds of data. The data are, as they always are, incomplete, but as they stand they are very far from revealing the pattern we looked for. Landecker's results do suggest the existence of one class boundary in one city, but he does not report interaction data or evidence of class consciousness. I conclude that social classes are not real in the United States.

What are real social categories like, categories that genuinely govern social life? Male and female are such categories, and so are child and adult, husband and wife, doctor and nurse and orderly. All of these are roles; sex roles, kinship roles, and occupational roles. We are conscious of them, they structure interaction, and they govern style of life. If we were to ask a man who was a doctor, "Who are you?" he would tell us, soon after he gave his name, "I'm a doctor." If we were to make an interaction matrix for a collection of persons that included doctors, nurses, and orderlies, it would be possible to recover the categories from regularities in the matrix. If we were to ask how such people spend their days, how they dress, and how much money they earn, we would discover discrete styles of life. Roles are functionally real social categories and they are the subject of the next chapter.

The castes of India and the estates of feudal Europe were also real categories that satisfied all our criteria. There is another criterion of social reality which they satisfied and which roles satisfy and which classes in the United States do not satisfy. Social norms, prescriptions for the guidance of behavior, are formulated in terms of real categories. Suppose we were to begin a statement: "A Brahman should. . . ." and use it to elicit norms from Indian informants. The list of responses would be a long one and quite different from that we would elicit with the beginning: "A Pasi should. . . ." All the caste regulations governing diet and social contact and religion and occupation should be forthcoming. In medieval Europe we could have obtained equally long lists by asking about the obligations of the clergy, the nobility, and the peasantry. In the United States today inquiries using role titles would work the same way. All of the following incomplete statements suggest numerous completions: "A man should . . ."; "A child should . . ."; "A doctor should. . . ."

Suppose we were to begin a statement: "Members of the middle class should . . ." or a statement: "Members of the working class should. . . ." They do not start a flow of completions. Norms in the United States do not seem to be organized in terms of class, but rather in terms of roles. Some of the roles fall on a continuum of socio-economic status, but behavior is prescribed in terms of the roles. This is a last reason for concluding that classes are not functionally real.

Vertical Mobility in the United States

From its beginning this nation has valued individual equality. Furthermore, it has long believed and continues still to believe that "there is more equality in this country" than anywhere else. Given the value on equality we must have the belief in the existence of equality if we are to feel that the United States is a success as a social system. Some of the people who have told pollsters that there are no classes in the United States or that they do not know what class they belong to, are probably responding in terms of what ought to be as much as in terms of what is. But while we may be "classless" we certainly are not equal. Not actual socio-economic equality, then, but something else about our social system sustains the belief that we have made great progress toward equalitarianism. What is this crucial feature of our system and how is it holding up in the modern world?

The assertion from the Declaration of Independence that "All men are created equal" is susceptible of two interpretations that would make it false. One of these is that the socio-economic condition of all men is the same; that has never been true in this nation, probably cannot be true in an industrialized society, and is not even thought desirable by most Americans. The second interpretation is that all men have identical abilities, talents, and temperaments—equal potentialities. While there is some reluctance in America to believe it, this assertion is definitely false. The third interpretation makes Jefferson's sentence more nearly true as an assertion and more generally acceptable as a goal: All men are or ought to be equal in opportunity insofar as opportunity is regulated by society. If this value were perfectly realized, then a man's socio-economic status would be entirely determined by his abilities and motives—not at all by the wealth or position of his parents. Since it is clear that abilities and temperaments are not identical for parent and child, there ought to be, in each new generation, many who fall below and many who rise above the station of their parents. The factual base of American equalitarianism or classlessness is, as Sibley (1942) has said, not equality of status or even near-equality, but a high rate of vertical mobility.

The American belief that opportunities are equal here has survived some facts that contradict it. The most blatant contradiction is the existence within our society of a caste—the Negroes. There is no doubt of the social and psychological reality of the categories white and Negro. If people in a mixed community are asked, "What are the important differences among people around here?" they will certainly mention race. If they are asked, "Who are you?" they are likely to include a racial identification. If you ask people, "What race do you belong to?" very few will reply that they do not know. There is a sharp break in the interaction pattern along the Negro-white line. In many states the discontinuity was, for a long time, codified into laws prescribing educational, recreational, and residential segregation, and into laws against intermarriage. Where the discontinuity was not enjoined by the law, it nevertheless existed in practice.

Within the Negro caste there is a scale of socio-economic status similar to that among whites. There is an incidental irony in the fact that Negroes among themselves have tended to accord higher status to their lighter, more white-like members. The underprivileged minority within itself makes some use of the very standards from which the minority as a whole suffers. This tendency can also be seen in the anti-Semitism of

Jews, some of whom disdain their "kikey" members who "make it difficult for the rest of us." Probably a minority always participates in the values of the larger society and so is tempted to participate in its own undervaluation.

The Untouchables of India are also subdivided into numerous castes which practice ritual avoidance and endogamy. There is a difference, however, in the comparative openness of the classes within the Negro caste. There are possibilities for mobility within a lifetime up to the line that separates the races. Across that line there can be no movement in a man's lifetime, but he can participate in a mobility across generations. While intermarriage between the races has been uncommon, interbreeding has been very common. It is estimated that something like 75 per cent of American Negroes have at least one white ancestor (Pettigrew, 1964). Some of the offspring of such unions will be light enough to "pass" as white and so there is an odd kind of mobility possible; where the Hindu religion allows for mobility across incarnations and the medieval Church allowed for it across existences, racial relations in America allow for it across generations.

What exactly is the Negro's present position in American society? If we attempt a diagram (Figure 3-4) we find that there are some points of uncertainty. For simplicity of diagramming we will represent white American society as if it were stratified into four classes, though, in fact, we think it is organized into a continuous scale of socio-economic status. Because there are more people at lower levels than at higher levels, we have drawn the system as a pyramid. This form would be misleading if it were taken to mean that the largest group is the lowest class; with a forced choice inquiry you remember that most Americans put themselves within the "middle class" or the "working class" rather than the "lower class." The pyramid is all right if we simply take it to mean that lower-status occupations tend to account for more people than higher-status occupations. To indicate the openness of classes, the boundaries between them are drawn as broken lines, whereas the caste separation appears as a solid line.

Probably some people would say that all Negroes in America rank below any whites and Figure 3-4a is the diagram of that view. Others would say that Negroes are not ranked at all by virtue of race. Each Negro has the status of his occupation; he is on a par with his occupational match among whites, but there are barriers to interaction. Figure 3-4b diagrams this view. But is the Negro doctor ranked as high as the white doctor? Probably many people would say that he is not. They would conceive of his total status score as having two major components, one being race and the other occupation. One score is high and the other low and so the total must be below that of the white doctor.

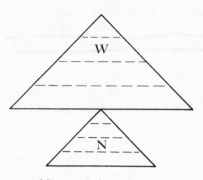

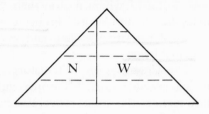

a. Negroes below all whites

b. Negroes and whites in the
same occupation equal in status

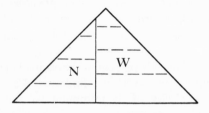

c. Negroes below whites
in the same occupation

FIGURE 3-4.   THE POSITION OF THE NEGRO IN AMERICAN SOCIETY: THREE
VIEWS

Figure 3-4c diagrams this view. We cannot decide which of these three
diagrams is the true description of the present status of the Negro in
America for the reason that this status is at issue. Each diagram has its
champions, people who believe it represents the way things are and, even
more, the way things ought to be. Social status exists in human minds
and the status of the Negro in America is controversial.

For those people who rank the Negro doctor low on race and high
on occupation, he is a difficult person with whom to interact. Does one
treat him as a Negro or as a doctor? The man himself suffers from an
extreme incongruency of status. There are two sets of expectations
applied to him and it must be very difficult to know how to react to
these. With a patient it may be very clear that the occupational role is
to the fore and so offers the best guide to proper behavior. For the Negro
doctor with white colleagues, however, the situation would be more
difficult. It has been observed that upper-class Negroes, in one southern

city, avoided all contact with upper-class whites as far as they were able to do so (King, 1953).

For Americans outside the Negro caste is there, in fact, a high rate of mobility, and is that rate increasing, steady, or decreasing? Most of us have the impression that the rate was very high in the past, especially in the nineteenth century. But total mobility rates have never been systematically computed and publicized. The impression that there was a high rate in the nineteenth century and early twentieth century derives chiefly from historical and journalistic accounts of the spectacular rises of a small number of men. "Rags to riches" has always been newsworthy and that, of course, is because it has never been the usual thing. This kind of news may have had more publicity in America than in some other countries because it is an outcome that accords with our values. In addition, the news has been bolstered by popular fiction like the stories of Horatio Alger and our impressions of mobility may not clearly distinguish wish-fulfilling fictions from actual events.

In recent years an impression has developed that the mobility rate in the United States has declined, that opportunities are not as good as they were. Certainly there have been changes in America that have acted to reduce upward mobility. Until 1925 this country took in about one million immigrants a year and this immigration created opportunities of upward mobility for the native American population. If the immigrants had been distributed *pro rata* among the American socio-economic levels, they would have had no direct effect on the amount or direction of mobility. However, a greatly disproportionate number of them were impecunious and unskilled; of the 642,724 immigrant workers admitted during the year ending June 30, 1914, 603,378 stated that they were engaged in manual occupations. This is about 100,000 more blue-collar workers than would have been found among an equivalent number of workers taken at random from the native American population. The broad occupational distribution prevailing in a country is set by the requirements of the production system at a given time. In order to maintain that distribution as it was in 1914 in the face of an influx of 100,000 excess blue-collar workers, it must have been necessary for 100,000 persons to move upward from blue-collar to white-collar jobs. Most of those who ascended will have been native Americans. If people in the higher-level occupations must constitute some definite proportion of the people in lower-level occupations, then immigration into the lower levels creates a force for upward mobility. Since 1925, immigration has been curtailed and now is a thin trickle of persons who mostly fill higher-level positions. So immigration has changed from a powerful force for upward mobility to a very slight force for downward mobility (Kahl, 1953; Sibley, 1942).

For many years the higher strata in America had a lower birth rate than the blue-collar strata. For example, a rough estimate made in 1928 of the average number of sons born to men in various occupational levels finds that for professional persons it is .87; for farm laborers, 1.52; and for other unskilled workers, 1.35. Men in higher-level occupations were not reproducing themselves, which means that positions were opening above for the excess supply of sons produced below. Since World War II, along with the great absolute rise in the birthrate, the differences of fertility between higher and lower strata have narrowed, and they may be expected to narrow still further. As a country industrializes it seems that the upper-level urban families are the first to learn about and practice effective methods of birth control. After a time the technique passes to lower levels. In Stockholm, Sweden, where birth-control information has been easily available for a long time, the fertility rates of the higher socioeconomic levels are greater than those of the lower levels; with most births "planned" the number of children has tended to become proportionate to the ability of parents to support them. If this trend is realized in the United States, fertility rates will cease to be a force for upward mobility and become a force for downward mobility (Carter, 1962; Kahl, 1953; Notestein, 1936).

Immigration and reproduction rates have changed in this century so as to reduce upward mobility. If these were the only changes we could be confident that the impression of reduced opportunities is correct. There is, however, a counterbalancing change in technological progress; between 1920 and 1960 technology has drastically reduced the proportion of the population engaged in physical labor and increased the proportion in clerical, managerial, and professional work. So positions have been opening in white-collar categories and closing in blue-collar categories.

Immigration, fertility, and technology are the three great factors determining the balance between upward and downward mobility, and the factors have changed in this century. It must be recognized, however, that the amount of mobility could change in a society without shifting the balance. At one extreme each son might succeed his father in the same occupation, which is to say there might be no mobility either upward or downward. At the other extreme there could be complete individual mobility, with each son occupying a position at a level different from his father, but for every son who moved up a given distance, there would have to be a son who moved down the same distance. The amount of individual mobility depends on the degree to which the criteria applied in job selection are affected by the parentage of job candidates. In India the criterion used to be parentage itself and so there was no individual mobility. If jobs were allocated by competitive examination to candidates with identical possibilities of preparation, there would be mobility within the limits set by the importance of heredity as a determinant of abilities and motives (Kahl, 1953).

There are very many studies of actual mobility rates in the United States but, because results of these studies converge on a single conclusion, it will suffice to describe one. Rogoff (1953) has made a careful comparison of mobility in Indianapolis for a period centering on 1910 with mobility in the same city for a period centering on 1940. Applications for a marriage license require that a man give both his own occupation and his father's occupation and so provide the essential data for determining rates of occupational mobility. Rogoff examined the applications of all white males for 1905–12 (centering on 1910) and 1938–41 (centering on 1940). The most likely outcome for both periods was occupational succession. Most of the mobility that occurred in both periods was of small degree, though there were a few dramatic large changes in both periods. The percentage of sons who changed their occupation was about the same in 1940 as in 1910. The general conclusion consistent with all studies (Barber, 1957) is that there has been no clear change during the last fifty to a hundred years in the United States either in the total amount of mobility or in the balance between upward and downward mobility.

It is my impression, nevertheless, that most Americans believe that the opportunity to rise in socio-economic status is not as great in America today as it was in the past. It is not at all clear how we come by this belief. Studies of mobility rates within the country over time indicate that there is no factual base for the impression of a decline. It is conceivable that impressions depend chiefly on the publicized cases of a rise to the highest business elite rather than on general conditions in the total population. But there are many studies of the origins of business leaders and these suggest that no great change has occurred in recent years. Warner and Abegglen (1955) found, for instance, that, in 1952, 31 per cent of big-businessmen had fathers who were also big-businessmen. We may feel that the recruitment of 69 per cent of business leaders from lower levels indicates that our society is still very "open." On the other hand, we may feel that the fact that there were 31 per cent whose fathers were at the same level indicates considerable rigidity, since, in a completely open society with a random relationship between the occupations of father and son, only 4 per cent of the present elite should come from a previous elite. In any case the percentages were about the same in 1928 as in 1952. Whether we think that the present facts about the elite do or do not represent a satisfactory realization of the equalitarian ideal, there is, at any rate, no justification for the belief that we were nearer the ideal in the past than we are today.

Impressions of the amount of mobility in a society do not simply reflect the sociologist's indices of mobility. There are several possible determinants of such impressions. Let us be concrete and think of a man who is today a civil engineer and whose father was a public-school teacher. At the present time and also in the father's day, the occupation of civil engineer had a prestige rank in America that was somewhat higher than the occupation of public-school teacher. There are neither rags nor riches in this story but a small prestige advance from one white-collar job to another. How mobile will the engineer feel that he has been? The sociological datum is clear enough; he has advanced a certain number of steps on the prestige scale. However, while the engineering occupation continues to have a high prestige rank, it has in certain ways been devalued during the last thirty years and is not quite the goal on which the man set his sights when he was a boy. The absolute number of people in this profession and those nearby on the scale has greatly increased. Even the percentage of the labor force at this level has gone up. There are many more professional people than there used to be and so the occupation does not have the distinctiveness it formerly had. It is even possible that the profession of civil engineer today stands at about the same position as did that of public-school teacher thirty years ago if we calculate position in terms of the number of people or perhaps the percentage of the labor force that ranks below a given occupation. For these reasons the engineer may not "see" himself as having moved very far.

The major force maintaining upward mobility rates in recent years has been technological progress which operates to increase the number of white-collar or higher-level positions. Upward mobility that comes about in this way may not make quite the same psychological impression as mobility that results from immigration and differential fertility. These latter two factors create openings on higher levels without increasing the percentage of the population found at these higher levels.

It is not only the higher occupations themselves that have become somewhat devalued, but also many of the experiences and possessions formerly symbolic of high status. When the civil engineer was a boy only the very rich made trips to Europe; he may be the first member of his family to do anything so grand. It must detract from this sense of "arrival" when, on his trip, he keeps running into people from his home town—perhaps a couple of girls who teach in the high school, or a retired policeman and his wife. Not only is there a larger percentage of the population in his occupation, but large numbers of people who have modest jobs are today able to afford many of the old symbols. This is because in the United States in this century the average real income (after adjustments for inflation) has greatly increased.

When a symbol becomes more generally available, it is usually somewhat changed. Opening night at the opera is an occasion that has always meant "society" in America and the civil engineer might expect some gratification from his first attendance at such an event. But let us suppose that it occurs in Boston in the early 1960's. The Boston Opera House has been torn down and the opening occurs in a motion picture theater. The marquee that reads *Don Giovanni* tonight last week read *Gidget Goes to Hawaii.* During the entr'actes the audience bravely stages a nineteenth-century promenade in the lobby, looking away from the darkened pop-corn machine. But overhead a loudspeaker booms at them: "Folks, don't forget to have your traditional glass of opera champagne." The civil engineer will begin to feel that he arrives everywhere too late; the vul-garians are always there waiting for him. Shining sign posts, glimpsed from afar in boyhood, when he draws abreast of them turn out to read "Burma Shave."

If many people have an impression that opportunities are not quite so great in the United States as formerly, most of these people probably believe that opportunity is, nevertheless, greater here than it is anywhere else in the world. This again is an impression that is not justified by mobility data. Lipset and Zetterberg (1955) have compared such data from a national sample of the United States with data for different industrialized European nations. While there are deficiencies in the data and problems of comparability, the conclusion is warranted that similarly high rates of mobility prevail in all of these countries. Probably it is the high real income in America that creates the impression of superior opportunities. Even with corrections for cost-of-living differences, most of us will find ourselves economically better off than people in comparable occupations in any other country.

Perceptions or impressions or beliefs concerning the degree of one's personal success and the amount of opportunity in a society are important to the functioning of the society and the vitality of its values. Very little has been done to work out the determinants of such impressions, but the way is open and the problems are interesting.

The Dark Side of High Status

Every good thing seems to go with high status—more income, posses-sions, and travel; less likelihood of psychosis, a longer life, and better chances of canonization. There is, however, one risk that goes with high status: something to reconcile us to a position short of the top. The probability of suicide is greater there. Durkheim wrote in 1897 in his great monograph on suicide: "the possessors of most comfort suffer most" (1958, p. 257).

Durkheim's monograph reports the first important attempt to discover the determinants of suicide from a comparative study of rates in various populations. Poverty-stricken Calabria, he noted, had almost none and there were few among the wretched peasantry of Ireland; Spain had a tenth as many as France. In the Departments of France itself, the more people there were who had independent means, the more numerous were suicides. Concerning status and suicide, Durkheim wrote: "Everything that enforces subordination attenuates the effects of this state. At least the horizon of the lower classes is limited by those above them, and for this same reason their desires are more modest. Those who have only empty space above them are almost inevitably lost in it, if no force restrains them" (1958, p. 257).

Statistical studies, of the kind Durkheim did for suicide, are sometimes called "epidemiological" studies. In an epidemiological study the rates of occurrence of some disorder, either social or somatic, are compared for various population groupings. The groupings may be made by age or sex or income or nationality or in terms of such a habit as cigarette smoking. The pathology may be lung cancer, heart disease or schizophrenia, murder, suicide or juvenile delinquency. The main purpose of such studies is to find clues to the causes, the etiology of the disorder. The discovery of a causal link between cigarette smoking and lung cancer represents a conspicuous modern success for epidemiological work. There is an older very dramatic success in the discovery that general paresis results from syphilitic infection (White, 1956).

Until Pinel in eighteenth-century France made it standard practice to keep case records for mental patients, general paresis (or *dementia paralytica*) was not separated out as a disease entity from other kinds of "madness." Case records revealed the existence of a certain symptom complex—delusions of grandeur, dementia, and progressive paralysis—that led to a fairly rapid fatal outcome. This entity proved to have a suggestive epidemiological pattern. It was about three times as frequent in men as in women; it rarely occurred before the age of thirty or after the age of fifty; it was more common in men addicted to "loose" living, men who drank heavily, men who had been soldiers or sailors, than in contrasting groups. In 1894 Fournier showed that a history of syphilis was obtained in 65 per cent of paretics as compared with 10 per cent of other mental patients. He suggested that general paresis had its origin in syphilitic infection which, even though apparently cured, had somehow invaded the tissues of the brain. It told against his hypothesis that histories of syphilis were not obtained for all cases of general paresis, but then, one knew that there would be strong reason to conceal such histories. In 1897 Krafft-Ebing performed an extremely bold experiment. Nine paretic patients who denied previous infection were inoculated with the syphilitic virus. If, in fact, they had previously been infected they would have been immune; if not they would have developed syphilis. All of them were immune and this outcome established the theory of syphilitic origin. It was then only a few years until the specific agent was identified and a cure found.

The epidemiological study of suicide has not produced a cure but it has produced a rather persuasive theory of the causes. After Durkheim's monograph, some of the notable works are Halbwach's *Les Causes du Suicide* (1930), Dublin and Bunzel's *To Be or Not to Be* (1933), and, in 1954, Henry and Short's *Suicide and Homicide*. Henry and Short drew together a large array of statistical data and from the data induced a general theory. The theory utilizes some of Durkheim's ideas, especially his ideas about egoistic and anomic suicide, but Henry and Short are more psychological than Durkheim and also more explicit. Henry and Short do not, incidentally, claim that their theory of suicide is valid for populations outside of the United States. Suicide in Japan, for example, is a different phenomenon from suicide in the United States.

It seemed to Henry and Short that the differential suicide rates in various population groups could be summarized by two generalizations. The first of these is that rates are higher for persons of higher status than they are for persons of lower status. In the United States suicide rates for men have been about three times as great as rates for women, and rates for whites have been about three times as great as for Negroes. In the United States armed forces suicide rates for commissioned officers have been higher than rates for enlisted men. Suicide has ranked higher as a cause of death, in the United States, among holders of large insurance policies than it has among holders of smaller policies and higher among small policyholders than among the general population. The data relating suicide to income or occupation are poor, but Dublin and Bunzel (1933) conclude that the weight of the evidence is that suicide rates have been highest on the highest levels of socio-economic status.[2]

The second generalization is that suicide rates are higher for those who have little close involvement with other persons than for those who have much involvement. Studies of the distribution of suicide in large American cities (for example those by Cavan, 1928, and Schmid, 1928) have all revealed extreme concentrations in the central disorganized sectors of the city. It is in these "skid row" sectors that one finds, among other things, rooming houses and cheap apartment-hotels, in which live anonymous, isolated, homeless people. Suicide rates have been greater in large

2. A report (Powell, 1958) of suicide rates for specific occupations in the city of Tulsa, Oklahoma, during the years 1937–56, shows that rates are not uniform within such large occupational groupings as "Professional-Managerial" and "Unskilled Labor." Physicians, for instance, had a higher rate than engineers, and cab drivers a higher rate than truck drivers. In the Tulsa data the two highest rates occurred at the extreme upper and lower ends of the occupational scale.

cities than in small cities or rural areas, and urban life has less continuity and stability than does rural life. Married persons have at least one meaningful and intimate relationship that the unmarried do not have and suicide rates for the married have been lower than rates for the unmarried whether single, widowed, or divorced. Finally, suicide rates rise sharply with old age, and old age increases the probability that one will have retired from employment, that parents and lifelong friends will have died, and that children will have left home. Suicide is a plague of social isolation (or, as we might prefer to say, of the absence of solidarity), as well as a plague of high status.

There is one large difficulty with epidemiological data. Any two populations that one may contrast are likely to differ in more than a single characteristic. The question about the early statistics on cigarette smoking and lung cancer was: Since smokers may differ from nonsmokers in many respects, in the kind of work they do, the state of their nerves, and the amount of industrial waste in the air they breathe, is it not possible that one of these other factors causes lung cancer? It was possible and other kinds of evidence had to be obtained to establish smoking as the cause. The same sort of difficulty arises for the data on suicide.

Consider, for instance, the differential rates of married and single persons. In raw form, with other things not held constant, the married persons' rate is *greater than* the single persons' rate. But then, suicide rates are known to be associated with age and so, of course, is marriage; a large proportion of single persons would be very young, and suicide is uncommon among the very young. With age held constant, the married persons' rate is consistently *lower than* the single persons' rate. For married and unmarried populations the statistics available to Henry and Short made it possible to control for other relevant variables, but for some populations this was not possible.

The differential rates for skid row sections of a city and for settled residential sections are especially difficult to interpret. Skid row rates are higher and Henry and Short saw, in this fact, evidence that social isolation disposes to suicide. But a skid row is a many-faceted phenomenon and isolation is just one facet. A skid row is an area of low socio-economic status, and if we attend to that fact, we have a case in which the suicide rate is negatively associated with status, which is a disconfirmation of the Henry and Short thesis that suicide rates rise with status. There are still other ways in which a skid row differs from a residential area; in many cities the nonwhite population would be large, the average age might be high, the number of persons who are migrants to the city might be large, etc. These factors cannot be disentangled in available statistics and that is true of some of the other population contrasts. Therefore, while the

Henry and Short generalizations about status and isolation are consistent with available data, they cannot be said to be proved by these data.

Henry and Short sought to increase the economy of their formulation by reducing their two empirical generalizations to a single more abstract generalization. In order to do so they had to think of some respect in which social isolation and high status were alike. What they hit on is the notion of comparative freedom from "external restraint." People who are involved in many solidary relationships must frequently act so as to meet the expectations and satisfy the wishes of other people. A married man must consider his wife and children in deciding whether to move to a new city for a better job. A man in a small rural community must have more regard for what his neighbors will think than a man living in a rooming house. The person with many ties of solidarity is subjected to a large amount of "horizontal" restraint. With status it is "vertical" restraint that varies. The low-status person, the employee, the enlisted man, the Negro, the woman, has less social power and so less freedom of action than does a higher-status counterpart. The suicide-prone groups then are characterized by a comparative absence of external restraint, both horizontal and vertical.

Why should the risk of suicide increase with the degree of personal freedom? If a man is able to act with comparative independence then it follows that he must see himself as responsible for his actions. If things go wrong, if his aims are frustrated, then he has no one to blame but himself. He will be "intropunitive" (self-blaming) rather than "extrapunitive" (other-blaming). Grinding poverty may cause misery in a poor farmer, but it does not make him contemplate suicide since he has not made his fate. A devoted family man may regret missed economic opportunities but he does not blame himself—he did it for his wife and children.

One of the common consequences of frustrating either man or animal is aggression (Dollard, et al., 1939). If you stand between a hungry dog and his food he will snap at you. If you make a distracting racket when your roommate is trying to study, he will verbally snap at you. If you interfere between a man and the woman he desperately loves, you may get killed. Frustration occurs when something happens to block the progress toward a goal of a motivated man or animal. An immediate consequence is likely to be aggression and, Henry and Short point out, aggression takes one of two major directions: it goes toward the self or toward others. Aggression will tend to be directed against others under conditions of high external restraint and toward the self when external restraints are weak. The chain of reasoning is completed when we add that suicide is an extreme form of aggression against the self.

The Henry and Short hypothesis receives some support from a second epidemiological pattern. Murder or homicide has a distribution partially complementary to that of suicide. Negroes have had higher homicide rates than whites, and homicide rates in economically depressed southern states have been higher than in richer northern states even with race held constant (Pettigrew, 1964). Homicide rates have been higher in younger age groups, whereas suicide rates have been high for people over sixty-five. Durkheim had data indicating that homicide rates were greater for married persons than for unmarried persons; Henry and Short did not have such data for the United States. They did have data suggesting that rural rates were higher than urban rates. On the other hand, male homicide rates have been higher than female rates, and homicide rates have been high on skid row, even as suicide rates have been. Henry and Short, by making certain congenial assumptions, are able to argue that the pattern generally links homicide with high external restraint. A pattern of this kind, complementary to that for suicide, is predicted by the Henry and Short theory.[3]

Suicide rates, according to the Henry and Short theory, must be dependent on two abstract variables: the degree of external restraint, and also the amount of frustration. Stable differential rates among population groups are explained by differences in the degree of external restraint. Is there some index of levels of frustration that could be checked for a relationship with suicide rates? Henry and Short argue that such levels can be inferred from the business cycle. Periods of economic depression produce declining incomes which result in high levels of frustration; periods of prosperity have the reverse effect. A number of investigators have demonstrated a high negative relationship between economic prosperity and suicide rates in the United States, England, and Wales. Henry and Short say that the relationship is so strong that about two-thirds of the variation in suicide rates over time in the United States is attributable to economic fluctuations.

Since homicide rates ought also to be affected by level of frustration, it is to be expected that they would vary with economic conditions as do suicide rates. The actual data for homicide are not quite this simple. For high-status white persons, the data show the predicted trends varying directly with suicide and so, inversely, with prosperity. For Negroes, however, homicide rates decline with economic depression and rise with prosperity. Henry and Short argue that homicide-prone Negroes are probably at the very bottom of the status hierarchy and that persons in such a position experience a *relative* gain in status in times of depression

3. Gold (1958) has used a single ratio to relate suicide rates to homicide rates and has worked out the values for various population contrasts. He develops a theory of the causes of suicide and homicide that is related to the theory of Henry and Short, but which seems to predict more accurately for the male-female contrast and also for the contrast between a skid row and a settled residential area.

and a relative loss in times of prosperity. This would be the case because, in times of depression, it is the higher-income groups that suffer the greater relative loss of income; the lowest group cannot lose much and still continue to exist. So depression brings the higher levels down nearer to the bottom, which makes people at the bottom feel somewhat less deprived than they do when prosperity raises the higher levels far above them.

Socio-economic status has been a variable in countless studies; almost always a useful one, as there is not much in human behavior that is completely independent of status. From any demonstrated covariation one can always guess at an intervening psychological explanation. For example, it seems probable that fertility has varied inversely with status, because low-status groups have been slow to learn about and practice techniques of birth control. Oftentimes a particular covariation suggests more than one hypothesis. High-status people are more prone to develop neurosis and low-status people are more prone to develop psychosis (Hollingshead and Redlich, 1958). This might be because psychoses are largely caused by hereditary factors and these factors are more common in people on lower levels, or it might be that psychosis is caused by the stressful experience of lower-class life. Or, concentrating on the other aspect of the relationship, we might guess that diagnosed neuroses are indulgences or luxuries that only the well-to-do can afford.

The peculiar excellence of the work of Henry and Short derives from the fact that their guess as to the psychological basis for the tie between status and suicide serves also to account for the tie between solidarity and suicide as well as the epidemiology of homicide and the relation of both pathologies to the business cycle. They accomplish something very gratifying: the reduction of several kinds of data to a simple systematic explanation. They may be wrong; the data are inadequate at some points and seriously unaccommodating at others. But the creation of a general theory imposes order on what is known and gives direction to future work.

REFERENCES

Barber, B. *Social stratification.* New York: Harcourt, Brace & World, 1957.

Barber, Elinor G. *The bourgeoisie in 18th-century France.* Princeton: Princeton Univer. Press, 1955.

Bronfenbrenner, U. Socialization and social class through time and space. In Eleanor E. Maccoby, T. M. Newcomb, & E. L. Hartley (Eds.), *Readings in social psychology.* (3rd ed.) New York: Holt, 1958.

Carpenter, C. R. A field study of the behavior and social relations of howling monkeys. *Comp. Psychol. Monogr.,* 1934, **10**, No. 2 (whole No. 48).

Carter, C. O. Changing patterns of differential fertility in northwest Europe and in North America. *Eugenics Rev.,* 1962, **9**, 147–150.

Cavan, Ruth S. *Suicide*. Chicago: Univer. of Chicago Press, 1928.

Centers, R. C. *The psychology of social classes*. Princeton: Princeton Univer. Press, 1949.

Centers, R. Social class, occupation, and imputed belief. *Amer. J. Sociol.*, 1953, **58**, 546–563.

Chapin, F. S. *Contemporary American institutions*. New York: Harper, 1935.

Coulton, G. C. *The medieval scene*. London: Cambridge Univer. Press, 1960.

Davis, K. *The population of India and Pakistan*. Princeton: Princeton Univer. Press, 1951.

Dollard, J., Doob, L. W., Miller, N. E., Mowrer, O. H., & Sears, R. R. *Frustration and aggression*. New Haven: Yale Univer. Press, 1939.

Dublin, L. I., & Bunzel, Bessie. *To be or not to be*. New York: Harrison Smith and Robert Haas, 1933.

Durkheim, E. *Suicide*. (1897) Transl. by J. A. Spaulding & G. Simpson. New York: Free Press, 1958.

Easton, S. C. *The heritage of the past*. New York: Rinehart, 1955.

Edwardes, M. *A history of India*. New York: Farrar, Straus & Cudahy, 1961.

George, Katherine, & George, C. H. Roman Catholic sainthood and social status: A statistical and analytical study. *J. of Religion*, 1955, **35**, 85–98.

Gibbs, J. P., & Martin, W. T. A theory of status integration and its relationship to suicide. *Amer. Sociol. Rev.*, 1958, **23**, 140–147.

Gold, M. Suicide, homicide and the socialization of aggression. *Amer. J. Sociol.*, 1958, **63**, 651–661.

Gross, N. Social class identification in the urban community. *Amer. sociol. Rev.*, 1953, **18**, 398–403.

Halbwachs, M. *Les causes du suicide*. Paris: Libraire Felix Alcan, 1930.

Hatt, P. K. Occupation and social stratification. *Amer. J. Sociol.*, 1950, **55**, 533–543.

Henry, A. F., & Short, J. F. *Suicide and homicide: Some economic, sociological, and psychological aspects of aggression*. New York: Free Press, 1954.

Hodge, R. W., Siegel, P. M., & Rossi, P. H. Occupational prestige in the United States: 1925–1963. *Amer. J. Sociol*. In press.

Hollingshead, A. B. *Elmtown's youth*. New York: Wiley, 1949.

Hollingshead, A. B., & Redlich, F. C. *Social class and mental illness*. New York: Wiley, 1958.

Hyman, H. The psychology of status. *Arch. Psychol.*, 1942, **38**, (whole No. 269).

Inkeles, A., & Rossi, P. H. National comparisons of occupational prestige. *Amer. J. Sociol.*, 1956, **61**, 329–339.

Japan Sociological Society, Research Committee. Social stratification and mobility in the six large cities of Japan. In *Transactions of the Second World Congress of Sociology*, Vol. II, 1954, 414–431.

Kahl, J. A. *The American class structure*. New York: Rinehart, 1953.

Kahl, J. A., & Davis, J. A. A comparison of indexes of socio-economic status. *Amer. sociol. Rev.*, 1955, **20**, 317–325.

King, C. E. The process of social stratification among an urban southern minority population. *Soc. Forces*, 1953, **31**, 352–355.

Kinsey, A. C., Pomeroy, W. B., & Martin, C. E. *Sexual behavior in the human male*. Philadelphia: Saunders, 1948.

Landecker, W. S. Class boundaries. *Amer. sociol. Rev.*, 1960, **25**, 868–877.

Lenski, G. E. American social classes: Statistical strata or social groups? *Amer. J. Sociol.*, 1952, **58**, 139–144.

Lipset, S. M., & Zetterberg, H. L. *A theory of social mobility*. Bureau of Applied Social Research, Columbia Univer., 1955, No. A-185.

Mayer, A. J., & Hauser, P. Class differentials in expectation of life at birth. In R. Bendix and S. M. Lipset (Eds.), *Class, status, and power*. New York: Free Press, 1953.

Murphy, G. *In the minds of men*. New York: Basic Books, 1953.

National Opinion Research Center. Jobs and occupations: A popular evaluation. *Opin. News*, 1947, **9**, 3–13.

Notestein, F. W. Class differences in fertility. *Ann. Amer. Acad. Polit. Social Sci.*, November, 1936, 1–11.

Pettigrew, T. F. *A profile of the Negro American*. Princeton: Van Nostrand, 1964.

Pope, L. Religion and the class structure. *Ann. Amer. Acad. Polit. Social Sci.*, 1948, **256**, 84–91.

Powell, E. H. Occupation, status, and suicide: Toward a redefinition of anomie. *Amer. sociol. Rev.*, 1958, **23**, 131–139.

Prabhu, P. H. *Hindu social organization*. (4th ed.) Bombay: Popular Prakashan, 1963.

Rogoff, Natalie. *Recent trends in occupational mobility*. New York: Free Press, 1953.

Saenger, G. H. Social status and political behavior. *Amer. J. Sociol.*, 1945, **51**, 103–113.

Sargent, S. S. Class and class-consciousness in a California town. *Soc. Probl.*, June, 1953, **1**.

Schmid, C. F. Suicide in Seattle, 1914–1925: An ecological and behavioristic study. *Univer. of Washington Publs. in the Social Sciences*, *V*, 1928.

Sibley, E. Some demographic clues to stratification. *Amer. sociol. Rev.*, 1942, **7**, 322–330.

Warner, W. L., et al. Democracy in Jonesville. New York: Harper, 1949.

Warner, W. L., & Abegglen, J. C. Occupational mobility in American business and industry, 1928–1952. Minneapolis: Minn. Univer. Press, 1955.

Warner, W. L., & Lunt, P. S. *The social life of a modern community*. New Haven: Yale Univer. Press, 1941.

Warner, W. L., Meeker, M., & Eells, K. *Social class in America: A manual for procedure for the measurement of social status*. Chicago: Social Science Research Associates, 1949.

White, R. W. *The abnormal personality*. New York: Ronald, 1956.

CHAPTER 4

Roles and Stereotypes

The word *role* is borrowed from the theater and there is little in its social-psychological sense that is not prefigured in its theatrical sense. A role in a play exists independently of any particular actor and a social role has also a reality that transcends the individual performer. Shakespeare's *Macbeth* has lasted for about 350 years; very many actors have passed in and out of the role and have proved shorter lived than the role. Actors are human beings; a role is a scenario prescribing certain actions and a script prescribing the lines to be spoken. Roles in society, too, are prescribed actions and words rather than persons. The role of college student was here before we came and will be here when we have gone. The roles of father and mother, of doctor and teacher will survive those who now perform them.

A role in a play permits of a certain amount of interpretation. Consider the famous interchange before the murder of Duncan in which Macbeth says: "If we should fail?" and Lady Macbeth responds: "We fail?" Lady Macbeth's line has been read as if failure were unthinkable, as if she were prepared to react to failure with resignation, and as if she were for a moment deterred by the thought of failure. The precise inflection of the line is for the actress to determine. Some actors have even deleted lines or rearranged scenes in Macbeth. Always, however, there are some aspects of a role that must be performed. Macbeth must murder Duncan; Lady Macbeth must walk in her sleep. If they refused to do these things they would be ousted from their parts.

Roles in society also permit of a certain amount of creative interpretation. A college president must meet with the trustees, supervise the administrative staff, and try to raise funds for his school, but in his public addresses he is free to stress scholarship, football, or the "whole man." A college student must take some minimal number of hours for credit and maintain some minimal grade average, but he is quite free to grow a beard, eat an unbalanced diet, or join the Young Conservatives. The parts of a role that must be performed are often set down in print. For students they are in the college catalog and in departmental pamphlets; for teachers they are in a book of Regulations for Officers of Instruction. It is not often the case that a role in society presents the aspirant with lines to be spoken, but it does happen sometimes. During the War, reserve midshipmen in Navy training schools were handed lists of "salty lingo" to get up by heart before going to sea: walls were "bulkheads" and floors were "decks" and permission to smoke was given by saying, "The smoking lamp is lighted."

There is a theory of acting which holds that the way to play a role well is to live it, to experience the emotions of the character one plays, but there is another theory which holds that a role ought to be played with deliberate technique and some emotional detachment. William James was once interested enough in these theories to ask a number of famous actors which approach they recommended; some favored one and some the other. In the playing of roles in society I think we function in both ways but in a fixed order: first with conscious technique, later living the part.

Try to remember a time when you had newly assumed some role that made a sharp break with your previous life. The first days of the freshman year in college or the first days in the Army will serve. At such times one is keenly alert to a new set of prescriptions and one tries to learn them and to satisfy them. The talk of college students or soldiers, their routines, their tastes and values are alien at first. You can still distinguish between that which is really you and that which you have undertaken to become. There is a feeling of "walking through the part," but this usually passes and one becomes a student or a soldier.

I remember being very embarrassed in my college days by the fact that everyone seemed to know facts about "composed" music (sometimes called "classical" or "serious" music) of which I was completely ignorant. With bourgeois deliberation, I set out to learn. For a time I had the radio going steadily and kept a card file of the names of all compositions heard, arranged by composer, alphabetically. It was a long time before I could tell one from another. The first pleasure in music was a side-effect of recognition. Does one like Beethoven or is one simply pleased to have identified something he wrote? In the early stages of discrimination training, liking is always confounded with recognition. Do visitors to the Louvre really like the Mona Lisa or are they simply relieved to find a familiar face?

Probably it was my plan to listen to music only until I had memorized some names and titles and trained my discrimination to the point where Mozart would not be taken for Sibelius. But the thing became autonomous, not just self-sustaining but something of a passion. I can recall quite well, however, when I felt the phoniness, the pretension in my "taste for music." It began as something pasted on, not a part of the living tissue.

Roles are units of a social system and personalities are enduring traits and motives linked to a human organism. Roles and personalities are mutually determinative. The personality one brings to a role determines the manner of its interpretation. A "strong performance" can accomplish some redefinition of the role. Just as a new and powerful reading of Macbeth may change the acting tradition, so a very original and successful President of the United States, like Franklin D. Roosevelt, can change the nature of the office.

The influence works also in the other direction. Important roles leave a residue in the personality, indeed personality is largely an integration of all the roles that have been played. It is an integration and not a simple sum. When some external prescription is, without alteration, translated into personal behavior, there may be some suspicion that it has not been truly internalized. Musical tastes, for instance, that fall too exactly into the highbrow pattern of Baroque-plus-Contemporary are likely to be assumed rather than real. It cannot often happen that one's personality will dictate a pattern of preferences in perfect accordance with an approved stereotype. Where such a pattern is professed, I suspect a deliberate conformity to expectations rather than a genuine internal processing of expectations and other data. A self is created out of social demands but it need not simply reflect them. To be oneself is not to reject all social influence—a thing that cannot be done—but to make an individual integration of influences.

Basic Concepts in Role Theory

Roles are norms that apply to categories of persons. There will be some essential characteristic that defines the membership of the category. The sex roles of male and female, the kinship roles of father, mother, son, and daughter, the age roles of infant, child, teenager, and adult are all ascribed on biological grounds.

Occupational roles, like doctor and college president and cab driver, have their membership defined by legal procedures of certification, contract, and hiring. A training role like that of college student begins with the payment of registration fees. When the defining characteristic applies to someone, then the norms of the role apply to him.

It is not customary to regard all social categories for which there are norms as social roles. For such a category as the cyclist or bicycle-rider there are a few norms peculiar to the membership: Ride on the street, not the sidewalk; with the traffic, not against it; and at night show a light. Still, most sociologists would not call the cyclist a role. There are also norms for smokers—Do not drop ashes on rugs or in other people's drinks—but the smoker is scarcely a role. The rough implicit criterion that separates smokers and cyclists from fathers and engineers seems to be the number of norms that are stated in terms of the category. A rather substantial number of norms must exist for a category if it is to be a role (Nadel, 1957).

Role norms vary in their requiredness. A college teacher must meet classes and submit grades. He definitely ought to award grades on the basis of competitive achievement rather than on grounds of personal liking, friendship with a student's family, or bribes from a student's father. It is strongly recommended that he read examinations carefully, arrive at his classes on time, and refrain from telling students how to vote in an election. If he smokes cigarettes while lecturing or wears tennis shoes to class, he violates norms that are not crucial and the sanctions applied are mild. Probably he will pick up a reputation as a "character" but not be reprimanded by the dean. It is interesting that one acquires a "character," a perceptible personality, by violating minor role norms.

Abravanel has shown (1962) that the personality perceived in behavior depends upon the role that is presumed to apply. Subjects listened to a recording of one end of a telephone conversation. Some were told that the talker-on-the-telephone was a college student and some that he was the chairman of an academic department. The listener on the other end of the line, who was never heard, was supposed to be a college instructor, either the teacher of the student or a member of the chairman's department. From the talk on the telephone one gathered that the talker was about to see the Dean and expected to be asked about the instructor's teaching. "I'm afraid your teaching hasn't been . . ." said the talker. Afterwards subjects were asked to characterize the presumed student or the presumed chairman. The characterizations varied with the presumptions. The conversationalist, to those who thought him a student, seemed "aggressive," "ambitious," and "egotistical." To those who thought him a chairman he seemed "hesitant," "compassionate," "indecisive." Apparently the words and style of the conversationalist were not "normal" for either a student or a chairman, but the significance of the deviation varied with the role.

Who holds the expectations or prescriptions that constitute a role? For some roles—father, mother, doctor, etc.—almost everyone in a society is familiar with the chief requirements. However, the expectations of some people are more important than those of other people for guaranteeing a satisfactory level of role performance. Sanctions rewarding proper performance and punishing poor performance are generally applied by the occupants of complementary roles and so it is their expectations that chiefly matter.

One role (A) is complementary to another (B) when the functions prescribed for A must be stated in terms of B and vice-versa. The role of father cannot be described without reference to the role of child; the role of husband is defined in terms of the role of wife; teacher in terms of student. Very often a role exists in an elaborate set of mutual complementarities. The role of college president necessarily involves reference to college trustees, administrative officers, faculty, alumni, and students. Each of these in turn involves the others. Together they make an organization—the American college—and the units of an organization are always roles, not persons. We can be certain of this from the fact that the by-laws and regulations of a company, a union, or a social club are written in terms of role titles; personal names do not appear in them.

Roles are sets of norms and norms are prescriptions for behavior. Disagreement of any kind among such prescriptions must create a problem for the occupant of a role. If he wishes to do what is expected or recommended, he will be in conflict if the recommendations are in conflict. Conflicts are, for the most part, a good thing to avoid and the number and character of the role conflicts in a social system provide a basis on which to evaluate the system as well designed or badly designed.

All of the possible kinds of role conflict are likely to arise for a college student and we will distinguish four different kinds with reference to someone in this position. In Figure 4-1 the personality appears as P and is given simultaneous membership in two roles: that of college freshman and that of son. We all occupy more than one role and usually more than two. Each of the roles is given two complementaries; for the son, mother and father are complementary roles and from their occupants come expectations or prescriptions which apply to him as a son. For the college student the complementary roles are college upperclassmen and faculty. These complementary roles have numerous occupants whose expectations play on P and so these roles are drawn as circles to indicate that they are categories. The mother and father roles appear as points because there is only one occupant of each whose expectations are important for P.

One possible conflict is that between the prescriptions of two different

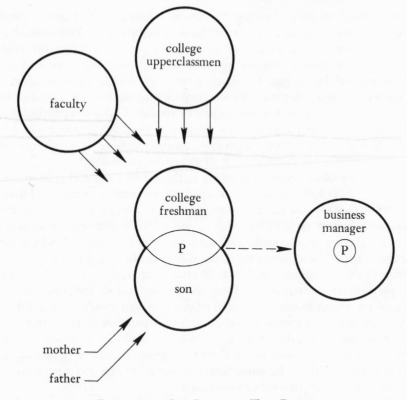

FIGURE 4-1. ONE PERSON IN TWO ROLES

roles—inter-role conflict. If P's parents expect their son to come home to visit them on weekends and the college expects its students to work in the library on weekends, then P has a problem. To cite another example, a doctor and father is presented with an inter-role conflict if a patient calls him out on the evening of his small daughter's birthday party. For this kind of conflict to arise, two conditions must be satisfied: (1) the same person must simultaneously occupy two roles; (2) the two roles must make opposed recommendations or rules about the same area of behavior. When two roles never have the same occupants (e.g., male and female), the roles can apply different rules for the same areas of behavior; but when two roles have an overlapping membership (e.g., son and college freshman), opposed rules for the same behavior are not so likely. Sometimes a potential inter-role conflict can be recognized and forestalled. It is standard practice for a college professor to advise his sons to attend a college other than the one at which their father teaches; or if the son insists on attending his father's college, he must not enroll in his father's courses. If your son is also your student you run the risk of conflict between a good father's duty to do everything he can to advance his son and a good teacher's duty to grade on the strict basis of comparative achievement. If the son is not in your courses, there is still a possible conflict for your teaching colleagues, a conflict between professional obligations and the obligations of friendship. While these conflicts would be disturbing, I think we can agree that the superior resolution in our culture would be to play the role of teacher without regard to kinship. This is a resolution that gives an achieved occupational role priority over an ascribed role and it is a resolution congruent with a general cultural emphasis. It would not be the right answer for cultures with an ascription emphasis.

There are some potential conflicts in the roles of son and college student; both roles have something to say about manners, language, and dress and what they say can be acutely contradictory. Because the two roles are ordinarily played on different stages, one at home and one on campus, their conflicting recommendations can be separately satisfied. Under these circumstances, P will have two rather different life styles; he may be unaware of the divergence until he is threatened at school with a visit from his parents. An inter-role conflict with geographical or temporal separation of the scenes in which the two roles are played should have a different effect than would such a conflict with no separation. In this latter case action would be paralyzed until the conflict could be resolved; in the former case, action could proceed on two opposed lines. A resolution of the conflict would not be immediately essential but the divergence could create problems of personality integration.

Inter-role conflict occurs only in persons who fill two or more roles; but there is also the possibility of intra-role conflict for occupants of a single role. Intra-role conflict arises from disagreement on what is proper behavior for role occupants. Because there are two ways in which such disagreement can arise there are two forms of intra-role conflict. The important expectancies for a role commonly emanate from two or more complementary positions. Disagreements on what is proper might occur within one such complementary group; among the faculty of P's college there may be little consensus on what to expect of students. Disagreement might alternatively occur between complementary groups with comparative agreement within each group. The faculty might agree among themselves and upperclassmen among themselves, but faculty and upperclassmen could be at loggerheads.

Intra-role conflicts could all be eliminated by a social consensus among and between complementaries. Inter-role conflicts could be eliminated by arranging expectancies so that they either do not disagree or do not apply to the same person on the same scene. These conflicts make no reference to the person himself. We have proceeded as if P can be counted on to do whatever is expected of him if only those expectations are made consistent.

The problem seems to be entirely one of the design of the external system. However, the person is not neutral, not empty. There is also a problem of the goodness of fit between his personality and the role. He is not infinitely malleable or at any rate he need not be.

During World War II reserve officer candidates were selected because they had college degrees of one sort or another and they were commissioned with a minimum of orientation. Peacetime officer selection starts with a population of young men who are attracted to the military role, and that presumably guarantees their possession of values that are reasonably well tuned to that role. The years at the military academy should strengthen those values and create the patterns of thought and action required of an officer. The less selective recruitment procedures of wartime brought into the role many men whose personalities were in conflict with its requirements and the few months of officer training did not suffice to establish the habits needed for the role.

Equalitarianism is a powerful American ideal and the formal expression of differential status is minimal in our manners. The military services are a deviant subculture which requires continual expression of formal status in salutes, address, precedence, and privileges. Daily practice in the recognition of rank is supposed to automatize the operation of the chain of command and make it resistant to disruption in time of crisis. But for officers and enlisted men drawn into the service without regard for their fitness for it, military manners were very disagreeable. Reserve officers during the War were forever wanting to be pals with the enlisted men, to set aside formal deference, to pitch in and work with the others. On small ships with only a couple of officers, "sirring" and saluting sometimes disappeared. On Pacific Island bases, many reserve officers literally could not exercise the privileges of their rank—for example, going to the head of a line formed outside the ship's service.

The military roles did not accord well with general American character and so the playing of them was sometimes distorted. Still, the privileges of rank were usually exercised and this exercise left a certain resentment. How great the resentment was appears in the following trivial incident.

For a short time after the War, everyone who had been mustered out took pride in wearing his service pin. One former officer wrote a letter to the Public Letter Box of a city newspaper deploring the fact that men who had been officers were given the same sort of pin as former enlisted men. It seemed to this writer that a distinction should be made. The newspaper was buried in violently abusive letters from both former enlisted men and officers.

Some roles function primarily as preparation for subsequent roles. It is the business of military academies and professional schools to transform the personalities they receive into a form that is adapted to the later occupational role. The transformation must be both intellectual and motivational. Sometimes such feeder roles lose contact with changing professional realities and supply inappropriately trained people.

M.I.T. graduates, for instance, used to function professionally as engineers who needed specific technical knowledge but today a great many of them assume non-technical managerial positions. This shift in job prospects has affected the curriculum; the role of M.I.T. student now involves study of the humanities, economics, psychology, and industrial management. In addition, the school recognizes that technology changes so rapidly nowadays that the specific knowledge that can be conveyed in school is likely to be outmoded before it can be used. As a consequence, people teaching science and engineering try to find a level of general knowledge that will prepare a man for flexible adaptation to future technologies.

We have distinguished role conflicts of the following kinds: (1) inter-role conflicts which occur in a person who occupies two roles; (2) intra-role conflicts which result from a lack of consensus among the occupants of one complementary role; (3) intra-role conflicts which result from a lack of consensus between complementary roles; (4) personality-role conflicts which result from an imperfect fit between the two. Conceptual distinctions of this kind have always something arbitrary in them. Our four varieties are not all possible varieties and are not known to be the most important varieties. Perhaps one should distinguish among intra-role conflicts in terms of the number of complementary roles involved. Perhaps inter-role conflicts should be analyzed in terms of the sorts of roles that conflict. Conceptual distinctions need not be arbitrary forever. If a distinction is worth making, something will follow from it; the cases distinguished will function differently. For example, consider the various sorts of role conflict as problems in social engineering. What needs to be corrected in each case?

Inter-role conflicts can be solved by a deliberate separation of performances in space or time. Intra-role conflicts involving the expectancies of a single complementary group might be solved by asking the members of the group to discuss their differences and arrive at some consensus. Intra-role conflicts involving disagreements between complementary groups will often stem from a conflict of economic interests. The public-school superintendent in the United States is expected by his school board to try for a minimal increase in teachers' salaries and expected by teachers to try for a maximal increase (Gross, et al., 1957). The way out may be the recognition by both groups that either selfish interest relentlessly pursued is self-defeating; there must be a reconciliation and the superintendent is the right person to make it.

The solution to personality-role conflicts lies in a very different direc-

OCT 14   5 9 6 0

$ 07.45
$ 00.45

*$ 07.9OLL

tion from any of the foregoing. If the personality requirements for a role can be created, then improved training procedures are the answer. Teach the trainees what they will need to know. If the requirements are not easily created—high levels of intelligence or "drive"—then improved selection procedures are the answer. When you cannot produce the type of person you want, you must try to find him in the available pool of talent.

The conceptual distinctions we have made among role conflicts seem to be real distinctions in the sense that they call for different kinds of social adjustment; they are distinct social problems. They may also be distinct psychological problems. A personality-role conflict may produce a different experience than does an inter-role conflict; there may be different psychic mechanisms for coping with the various kinds of conflict. We will consider the psychological and social problems involved in one kind of conflict between personality and role.

Sex and Temperament

We have all heard it said in praise of some little boy, "He's all boy!" or in praise of some little girl, "She's a real little girl!" How can a boy be less than all boy or a girl other than a real girl? It is the roles built around the biological distinction of sex that make maleness and femaleness matters of degree.

In the United States a *real* boy climbs trees, disdains girls, dirties his knees, plays with soldiers, and takes blue for his favorite color. A real girl dresses dolls, jumps rope, plays hopscotch, and takes pink for her favorite color. When they go to school, real girls like English and music and "auditorium"; real boys prefer manual training, gym, and arithmetic. In college the boys smoke pipes, drink beer, and major in engineering or physics; the girls chew Juicy Fruit gum, drink cherry Cokes, and major in fine arts. The real boy matures into a "man's man" who plays poker, goes hunting, drinks brandy, and dies in the war; the real girl becomes a "feminine" woman who loves children, embroiders handkerchiefs, drinks weak tea, and "succumbs" to consumption.

The roles fully realized are grotesque; a slightly inconsistent performance is more human. However, a persistently bad performance is punished; in childhood, by painful sobriquets. The boy who acts like a girl is a *sissy;* the girl who acts like a boy is a *tomboy.* The two terms are exact semantic parallels but they are not equally punishing. One is worse than the other. *Sissy,* you will agree, is a harsher term than *tomboy.* Why should this be so?

In spite of American distaste for ascribing status, there remains a difference of rank between male and female. Women have not always had the vote and have not yet produced a President. It is a little "better" to be male than female. A girl who acts like a boy is, therefore, doing something we find more understandable than is the boy who acts like a girl. We can think of the girl's behavior as motivated by a wish to improve her status rather than by a compulsion to act like a male. The sissy, on the other hand, is mimicking a group that ranks below himself. There is nothing in our values that will make his behavior acceptable or even comprehensible. We must suppose that he acts as he does in spite of himself, because his nature is somehow female.

In part, the roles of the two sexes seem to be necessary consequences of the defining biological differences. In simple cultures it is almost inevitable that women assume the duties of infant care, since they must, in any case, be available for nursing. Where subsistence activities involve a little light agriculture as well as hunting, it is economical for women to do the former and men the latter, since this division of labor will not take the women far from their children.

Some parts of our contemporary male and female life styles are clearly arbitrary since they are different in other cultures. In societies around the world it is about as common for females to wear trousers and for men to wear skirts as is the reverse arrangement. In modern America men are supposed to be much less interested in personal adornment than are women, but, in eighteenth-century France, male courtiers took a lively interest in curled wigs and silks and satins.

For many aspects of the sex roles it is difficult to say whether the distinctions are grounded in natural differences or are arbitrary impositions of a culture. Girls in the United States are supposed to be less good at mathematics than are boys. And in a recent representative year the average scores of high school seniors on the Scholastic Aptitude Test of the College Entrance Examination were:

	Math	Verbal
Boys	527	479
Girls	467	486

Does a difference of this kind arise because the female sex has less natural gift for mathematics, or because girls in this country learn it is not feminine to be very good at numbers? Certainly they do learn the latter lesson.

In the words of a bright college girl: "A boy advised me not to tell of my proficiency in math and not to talk of my plans to study medicine unless I know my date well" (Komarovsky, 1946, p. 188). This is not to say that girls taking the Mathematical Aptitude Test deliberately do less well than they might, but rather to suggest that the cultural identification of mathematics as a masculine domain may diminish the interest girls would otherwise have in this subject and ultimately, therefore, their knowledge of it.

Girls do less well than boys in arithmetic from the very earliest school years. If it is the sex role that accounts for the difference the role must be effective very early in life. And it could be.

During the war years, 1941–45, many American fathers were separated from their families. Kuckenberg (1963) wondered whether boys born in this period when fathers had been absent during their early years differed at maturity from boys whose fathers had been present, and she selected Scholastic Aptitude Scores as her dependent variable. If an interest in mathematics and a knowledge of mathematics develop as part of the male sex role, and if that role is learned by identification with the father, then boys whose fathers had been present should show greater mathematical aptitude in later life than boys whose fathers had been absent. If, on the other hand, mathematical interest and competence are rooted in biological masculinity, the two groups of boys should not differ. Kuckenberg had data for thirteen hundred subjects and found that the mathematical aptitude scores were higher relative to verbal aptitude scores for father-present boys than they were for father-absent boys. The mathematical aptitudes were especially low in cases where the father had left before his son's birth and was away for as long as two to three years.

The argument from Kuckenberg's data to the difference in the mathematical competence of boys and girls is fairly straightforward. If mathematical competence in boys is in some degree acquired as an aspect of a sex role, so may it be in girls. And since girls are not encouraged to identify with the male role, their mathematical scores should fall below their verbal scores, as, in fact, they do.

In addition to differences of occupation, avocation, dress, and abilities, most cultures hold that the two sexes have different temperaments. With us a boy is supposed to have a more aggressive nature and a girl a more passive, gentle nature. *Aggression* is a word with two major meanings: it signifies a readiness to fight and also an energetic, active, dominant temper. We think it ideal for a boy to manifest both kinds of aggressiveness; as men they are not expected to fight unless the provocation is extreme, but they are always supposed to be aggressive in the second sense. Girls and women should be neither fighters nor too forceful and domineering.

These imperatives for the male and female temperament have something in them that is not found in the imperatives of occupational roles. We do not apprehend them as social imperatives that could be different than they are. In fact, it seems a little strange to call them imperatives at all. Can it do any good to adjure someone to be aggressive or passive? It is, we feel, the nature of the male to be aggressive and of the female to be passive. The social roles seem to formulate biological necessities, to recommend what must be. The feeling of inevitability, of natural law, accrues more strongly to our ideas about the temperaments of the two sexes than to other parts of the male and female roles. It is startling, therefore, to find Margaret Mead (1935) concluding on the basis of her studies of sex and temperament in several primitive societies: ". . . we may say that many, if not all, of the personality traits which we have called masculine or feminine are as lightly linked to sex as are the clothing, the manners, and the form of head-dress that a society at a given period assigns to either sex" (p. 190).

Dr. Mead hit upon a very striking pattern of evidence with respect to the tie between aggressive and passive temperaments and sex. In New Guinea she found one people, the Arapesh, who thought of a gentle temperament as ideal for both sexes. She found a second people, the Mundugumor, who held an aggressive and suspicious temperament to be ideal for both sexes. And finally, in the Tchambuli, she found a people who held that an aggressive dominating temperament was right for women and an emotionally dependent, artistic, sensitive temperament for men. If to these we add the American-European case, which reverses the Tchambuli pattern, the full array of cultural variation seems to combine two sexes with two ideals of temperament in all possible ways. How, then, can we believe that the male is naturally aggressive and the female naturally passive?

The evidence is not quite so sharp as the closing sentences in the previous paragraph suggest. The actual temperamental comparisons are not identical across all four cases. Notice that the descriptive terms shift a little from one society to another: passive and gentle and dependent and artistic and "sensitive" constitute one cluster; aggressive, independent, suspicious, and dominating the other. While the Tchambuli men are supposed to be artistic and "sensitive" as men are not in our society, still it turns out that when the Tchambuli go to war it is the men who do the fighting; so we can hardly say that the male is, among the Tchambuli, the less aggressive sex. What Dr. Mead has actually put together is a set of cultural variations on the sex typing of a set of related temperamental characteristics roughly summarizable by the polarity aggressive-passive. It is possible, of course, that the clustering of these temperamental characteristics is itself specific to our own culture.

Because she thought she had found all conceivable combinations of sex and the temperamental ideals called "aggressiveness" and "passivity," Dr. Mead concluded that there was little or no innate link between sex and the dimension of temperament. Furthermore, most people in each of her societies manifested the temperament that was held to be ideal for them. And so Dr. Mead adds: ". . . human nature is almost unbelievably malleable, responding accurately and contrastingly to contrasting cultural conditions" (p. 191).

The argument thus far seems to be heading for a very stale conclusion: human nature has no content; it is simply a capacity to be conditioned by culture. Various cultures have hit upon various ideals and the prevailing local ideal determines the character of those who live there. There is one fact that is profoundly disruptive of this view. In each of her four societies Dr. Mead found some individuals of deviant temperament—an aggressive Arapesh, a gentle Mundugumor, a dependent Tchambuli woman, and a dominant Tchambuli man. We know, in addition, that there are passive American males and aggressive American females. Reflect on the significance of such deviance. If human nature were completely homogeneous raw material, lacking specific drives and characterized by no important constitutional differences between individuals, then there ought to be no individuals who display traits antithetical to the emphasis of their culture.

In rejecting the idea that temperament is innately sex-linked, Dr. Mead did not intend to reject the notion that temperament is innate. "Let us assume that there are definite temperamental differences between human beings which if not entirely hereditary, at least are established on a hereditary base very soon after birth" (p. 193). She posits congenital variations of temperament but holds that the range of variations would be about the same for male and female. The basic premises of the entire argument Dr. Mead develops concerning sex and temperament are that: 1) there are genetic variations in temperament on a dimension of aggressiveness-passivity; 2) these variations are not linked with sex; temperaments are similarly distributed in the two sexes.

It is obviously very important to know whether Dr. Mead's premises are factually correct and there is some good evidence that they are not completely correct. However, we can defer discussion of this evidence because the revisions we shall want to make in the premises will not invalidate Dr. Mead's important thesis. So please entertain the premises for a time to see what follows from them. In developing Dr. Mead's argument we will use an analogy from optics which is suggested in her book but not elaborated.

The innate variations of temperament may be imagined as so many individual light sources varying in wave length along the spectrum. The longer wave lengths, the "hot" red lights, can be thought of as the aggressive temperaments and the short wave lengths, the "cool" blue lights, as passive temperaments. There is a separate spectrum of temperament for each sex. Above the two spectrums we have drawn bell-shaped curves to indicate the numbers of human beings having each sort of innate temperament. Extremes of aggression and passivity are represented as less common than intermediate temperaments; this is a plausible assumption but it is irrele-

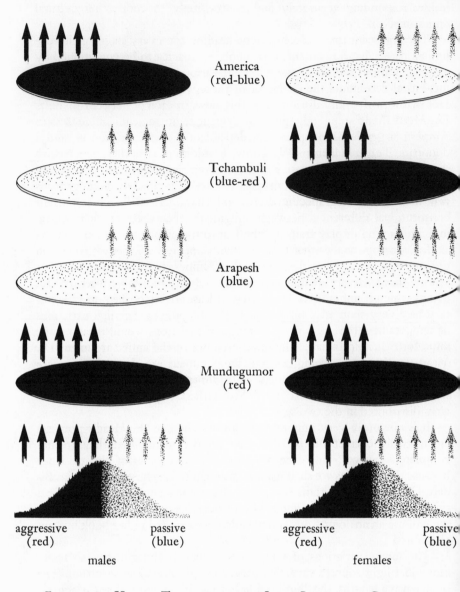

FIGURE 4-2.   HUMAN TEMPERAMENTS AS LIGHT SOURCES AND CULTURES AS
FILTERS

vant to the argument. Mead's suggestion that variations of temperament
are not sex-linked suggests that the curves for the two sexes be exactly the
same and they are drawn so in Figure 4-2.

If innate temperaments are to be light sources, cultural ideals of temperament had better be represented as filters. In optics a selective filter

transmits light from a source to which it is "tuned" but absorbs light from other sources. The basic analogy is between these optical relations and the way in which a cultural ideal provides full, easy expression for personalities naturally tuned to the ideal but suppresses personalities to which it is not tuned. The Mundugumor culture must be a red filter; it permits the transmission of longer wave lengths (the aggressive temperaments) but not of shorter wave lengths (the passive temperaments). Furthermore, among the Mundugumor, there is the same filter for both sexes; the red lights of either sex are at home here.

What about the wave lengths other than red? If they were perfectly monochromatic and the filter transmitted only reds, then the shorter wave lengths would be totally absorbed. This is not a very good analogue for what happens. Most children born to the Mundugumor manifest the ap- proved aggressive style, however congenial it may be to their innate temperaments. Presumably there is enough of an aggressive component in almost everyone so that he can act as the culture requires. We will do better, then, to conceive of each innate temperament, each light source, as a combination of all wave lengths rather than as a single wave length. The differences among them then are best thought of as differences in the relative strengths of the components. The red lights are those with pre- dominantly red wave lengths; green and yellow would be present but at low strength. It remains appropriate to range the lights along the spectrum with the difference that the position of a source does not represent a unique wave length but rather a dominant wave length. The lights at the shorter end of the spectrum contain the longer wave lengths, but these are a small part of the total. The greater part of these innate dispositions finds no expression in Mundugumor culture. If the light sources at the extreme blue end are thought of as lacking any red component, the corresponding temperaments would find no expression among the Mundugumor.

Arapesh culture will be a *Pacific* blue filter, the same for both sexes. Blue temperaments stream through without hindrance or distortion, but other kinds cannot burn so brightly. The red light that is at home among the Mundugumor must be culturally "disenfranchised" among the Ara- pesh. Both the American culture and the Tchambuli provide two filters: for the Tchambuli it is red for females and blue for males; for the Ameri- cans the pattern is reversed. The temperament that is transmitted if it emanates from a male is not transmitted if it emanates from a female. Temperament has been incorporated into sex roles.

The culture that sex-types temperament presents a profoundly differ- ent psychological situation from the culture that does not sex-type tem- perament. The deviant person among either the Arapesh or the Mundugu- mor must think of himself as different from other people, as not a proper sort of human being. The deviant person among the Tchambuli or the Americans is not simply different; he is different from his own biologically defined sex and like the opposite sex. Among the Arapesh or Mundugumor the temperamentally aberrant child will be admonished, "People don't do that" or "If you behave like that, people won't like you." Among the Tchambuli or Americans admonitions will take the form, "You're a boy, don't act like a little girl" or "Girls don't do things like that."

The sex-typing of temperament must lead, in Mead's opinion, to problems of confused sexual identity. The little girl with a "male temperament" must begin to wonder if she is not in some fundamental way truly male, if she has not been misclassified. She may feel more similar to and so more closely identified with her father who is her temperamental match than with her mother who is not. This kind of cross-sexual identification could perhaps contribute to inversion of the mature sex life, to active homosexuality. It is certainly interesting that Dr. Mead found no homosexuality among either the Arapesh[1] or Mundugumor where temperament is not sex-typed. Dr. Mead is of the opinion, however, that active homosexuals are not an etiologically uniform class; they may be produced in various ways and constitutional predisposition may sometimes be a factor. The more common and important outcome of rigid sex-typing is, she suspects, a neurotic concern with sexual identity—a feeling of not being altogether female or altogether male.

What is the evidence relevant to the premise that temperament is genetically determined and the premise that temperament is not sex-linked? The evidence of a genetic factor in aggression derives from experiments in the selective breeding of animals. We know, of course, that man has selectively bred strains of domestic animals to reduce aggressiveness. Perhaps the clearest example is that of the Norway rat which in its original wild state could only be handled with gloves or tongs, but two centuries of breeding the tamer individuals have produced the mild white rat of the laboratory. This creature can (usually) be safely handled without gloves and in a fairly rough fashion. Man has also selected in favor of the opposite pole of temperament. Breeding for aggressiveness has produced the gamecock for the sport of cockfighting and the bull terrier for the sport of dog fighting.

Different breeds of dog greatly vary in aggressiveness. Fox terriers, for instance, are better fighters than beagles, though beagles are larger. One study (James, 1951) made use of a litter of fox terriers and a litter of beagles born on the same date. The investigator shuffled them into two mixed-breed litters, half the dogs in each litter being beagles and half being fox terriers. By fifteen weeks the smallest beagle was larger than

1. Fortune (1939) does not report the existence of homosexuality among the Arapesh, but he does say that there was a definite class of effeminate men who were called, in effect, "women male." The existence of such a class does not accord well with Mead's claim that the Arapesh idealized the same temperament for both men and women.

the largest terrier. James tested the dogs in pairs for relative dominance or aggressiveness by putting a beagle and a terrier in competition for a single bone or pan of food. The terriers almost invariably won out and, in addition, they monopolized all the females and in due course sired all the puppies. Here were two breeds of animals reared together and of the same age with a clear difference of aggressiveness by breed sufficient to offset differences of size and weight.

Scott (1954) found that African Basenji dogs were more aggressive than cocker spaniels. When the two breeds were genetically crossed the first generation of offspring showed a degree of aggressiveness that was midway between the levels of the parental breeds. When the offspring were crossed back with the pure breeds the dogs of this second generation showed a reversion of temperament in the direction of the pure breed involved in the cross.

Some of the methods for determining relative aggressiveness or dominance in animal breeding studies are very clever. My favorite is one that has been used with white mice. Each of two mice is separately trained to go through a long, narrow pipe to get food at the opposite end. The two animals are then simultaneously introduced at opposite ends of the same pipe and the one who backs out the other is the dominant mouse. Only a few days after I first saw this procedure demonstrated I turned my car into one end of a narrow Cambridge street, just as someone turned his car into the same street at the other end. We came at one another like two combative mice, getting angrier as we approached, until at close quarters I recognized a colleague. We both switched to smiles and each offered to back out in favor of the other.

The animal studies are strong presumptive evidence that aggression is in part genetically determined and there is even stronger evidence that this determination is linked to sex. The human male is, to begin with, better equipped for fighting than is the female. Terman and Tyler (1954) summarizing the data on physical differences between the sexes report that males at maturity average 20 per cent heavier than females, 10 per cent taller, and by some indices, 50 per cent stronger. Differences of strength and of the ability to maintain a high output of energy (vital capacity) show up in the world's records for various track and field events in which the women's records are almost invariably inferior to the men's. Of course, greater physical strength and endurance do not guarantee greater aggressiveness; women may be as fox terriers to our beagles.

Perhaps because fighting and teasing and pushing are school disciplinary problems there are numerous comparisons of the frequencies with which boys and girls do these things. Boys are always found to be more aggressive—even as young as two years, which is the earliest age that has been studied (Scott, 1958). At older ages male juvenile delinquency rates and also rates for every kind of aggressive crime exceed the female. In our society it is clear that males behave more aggressively than females, but this could be because that is what the sex roles require rather than because of innate differences of temperament. However, the animal evidence is against Dr. Mead's role hypothesis and in favor of innate temperament.

Among the invertebrates there is a tendency for males to be more aggressive than females, but among the social insects there are some reversals of this tendency. The male bee, the drone, has no sting and does not fight; the sting is developed from the sterile female organs of the worker bee. Among vertebrates it is clearly the general rule for the male to be more aggressive and, among primates, there are no exceptions to this rule, though the various primate species greatly vary from one to another in the amount of fighting they do (Scott, 1958).

Clark and Birch (1945, 1946) tested the effect on aggressiveness of injections of the male sex hormone with two castrate male chimpanzees. Prior to the injections they created a conflict situation by putting up a cup containing a single peanut midway between the two animals. At first there was fighting but then, as a result of the outcome of these fights, a stable order of precedence or dominance. The experimenters then gave hormone injections to the subordinate male. He revolted against the other, overthrew him, and established a stable superiority. This result is typical of many studies showing that increasing the amount of male hormone for a male animal will raise his position in a dominance hierarchy. It is less clear from the research results, what effect the male hormone has on females and what effect the female hormone has on either sex (Scott, 1958).

Even the cross-cultural evidence generally favors the proposition that the male human tends to have a more aggressive temperament than the female. Scott (1958) makes the strong point that there is no society on record in which the female does the actual fighting in warfare. Even among the Tchambuli the male does this job.

We do not often have a reliability check in anthropology, but there is one for Dr. Mead's description of the Arapesh. Margaret Mead published *Sex and Temperament* in 1935. In 1939, Fortune published an independent report on the Arapesh in which he explicitly challenged the earlier description. Dr. Mead had said that the Arapesh idealized the same temperament for both men and women, a placid, gentle sort of temperament. Since Fortune found that warfare had been well developed among the Arapesh, he rejected the notion that they were an altogether peaceful people. As far as he could discover, furthermore, they did not expect the two sexes to have the same temperament. The warriors among the Arapesh were the men.

There is a persuasive convergence of evidence on a conclusion quite different from one of Dr. Mead's premises. Males in America, from a very early age, behave more aggressively than do females; the males of our species are physically stronger and warfare is everywhere the business of the male. In the animal species nearest to man, the male is invariably the more aggressive sex and, furthermore, the male hormone seems to increase aggressiveness. It appears that Dr. Mead was right in thinking that temperament is, in part, innate, but wrong in thinking that the distribution of temperaments is the same for the two sexes.

What are the consequences of our revision of Dr. Mead's premise for her thesis that the sex-typing of temperament is likely to produce confusions of sexual identity? The animal and human evidence shows that males tend to be the more aggressive sex and so compels rejection of the notion that the distributions of innate temperament are identical for the two sexes as they are pictured in Figure 4-2. However, the evidence is equally clear in showing that the distributions of temperament show some overlap (Scott, 1958). While there are more aggressive males than females there are some males who are not aggressive and some females who are. For Dr. Mead's argument it is only necessary that there be overlap of innate temperament distributions; it is not necessary that there be identity. The number of people likely to have problems of sexual identity in a culture that sex-types temperament, as does our own and that of the Tchambuli, should increase with the amount of overlap in the two distributions. The more naturally aggressive women there are, the more women there should be in America with problems of sexual identity, and the more naturally passive men the more men with such problems. The consequence, then, of shifting from a premise of identical distributions to one of overlapping distributions, is to reduce the number of people for whom sexual confusions are predicted but not to eliminate the prediction.

It is reasonable in addition to extend Dr. Mead's argument to the non-temperamental aspects of the sex roles. Many of these are certainly not founded on innate differences between the sexes. Where the sex roles are very elaborate, including occupational preferences and every sort of taste and attitude, there are likely to be many people whose personalities will not exactly fit their sex roles. There will be few who do not have something "sissified" or "tomboyish" about them and so, few who do not experience some of that personality role conflict which is called confusion of sexual identity.

Margaret Mead's thesis is interesting because it runs directly counter to popular opinion about the likely cause and best treatment of deviations from sex role. Parents of a boyish girl or girlish boy are likely to think that they have not been sufficiently insistent on behavior appropriate to biological sex. They are likely to "deal with the problem" by firming up the definition of the role. They are likely to undertake more detailed, explicit, and rigid instruction in what boys do and what girls do. Such instruction may produce a better role performance. However, Dr. Mead suggests that if the cross-sex behavior is deeply rooted a child may not be able to give it up or may give it up with a sense of denying his true identity. In such circumstances the intensified parental insistence on sex-typing may only make the child more certain of his own ambiguity. Of course, even if parents do not stress sex roles the larger society will do so and will therefore make problems for the child who deviates. So there is no clear solution short of redesigning the culture.

If we were to redesign the culture, what would we do? The difficulty lies with the fact that temperaments and tastes and attitudes are now prescribed on the basis of biological sex when they have a very imperfect natural linkage with sex. A similar difficulty often arises when roles are assigned on the basis of other ascribed attributes: not all Brahmans have a religious "vocation"; not all elderly men are wise; not all sons of kings are equipped to lead a nation. The roles that accrue to a sex, a lineage or an age group, sometimes have no strong natural connection with the ascribed characteristics that determine membership. Many of those recruited can be trained to perform reasonably well: most biological males born to the Tchambuli were able to act as the Tchambuli expected men to act; most princes can learn to do a fairly good job of ruling a nation. However, some that are recruited, either because of their innate characteristics or because of accidental experiences, are unable to do as the role requires.

The answer must be to detach leadership, aggressiveness, aestheticism, wisdom, and the like from irrelevant ascribed attributes and incorporate them in pure achievement roles. Aggressiveness of one kind or another should be manifest by soldiers, door-to-door salesmen, and business tycoons. Recruitment to these roles should be based on achievement criteria —or behavioral manifestations of aggressiveness—not on sex. This, I think, is the essence of Margaret Mead's own ideal for a culture: role assignment based on strictly relevant prior performance. In terms of the analogy from optics: a culture should consist of many filters, each with its own characteristic hue; and light sources ought not be assigned to filters on the basis of criteria unrelated to their natural hues, but should, all of them, have the free opportunity to find their congenial filters.

Stereotypes

A social role is a set of prescriptive rules, of guides to behavior, for persons of a given category. What is prescribed for the category is ordinarily performed by the category and expected from the category.

Prescription, expectancy, and performance all converge in the social role, but in the social stereotype we have categorical expectancies without prescriptions and it is a matter of controversy as to whether or not the category performs in such a way as to confirm the expectancy. Let us begin with three examples of stereotypes.

In 1958 (Wells, Goi, and Seader) one hundred subjects were asked to characterize the owners of different makes of American automobiles by selecting the appropriate adjectives from a long list. On first thought one says: "What a ridiculous task. Any make of car is driven by millions of people and they must run the gamut." Still, when you think about it, we do have notions about Cadillac owners which are different from our notions about Chevrolet owners and it turns out that many other people have the same notions. Here are some characterizations on which there was substantial agreement:

Cadillac owners	Rich, high class, famous, fancy, important, proud, superior
Buick owners	Middle class, brave, masculine, strong, modern, pleasant
Chevrolet owners	Poor, ordinary, low class, simple, practical, cheap, thin, friendly
Ford owners	Masculine, young, powerful, good-looking, rough, dangerous, single, loud, merry, active
Plymouth owners	Quiet, careful, slow, moral, fat, gentle, calm, sad, thinking, patient, honest

These stereotypes are not simply inferences as to socio-economic status from the price of the car. There were great differences in belief about owners of the low-priced three: Ford owners were virile, youthful, and adventurous; Plymouth owners were stodgy but sensible; Chevrolet owners were just plain cheap.

Harvard undergraduates at the end of their freshman year move into one of the Harvard Houses which are residences that combine features of the English college with features of the American dormitory. An undergraduate lists his preferences among the Houses but he cannot simply be given his first choice or even his second choice since some Houses are greatly oversubscribed and others are chosen by very few. Applicants for a House are often interviewed by the housemaster or by one or another resident tutor. The final decisions were, in the early 1950's made by the housemasters meeting in secret session and the procedures followed were not public knowledge and are not known to me.

In terms of physical amenities and rents the Houses were quite similar to one another. When the Houses were built, it was hoped that they would minimize the importance among Harvard undergraduates of derived socio-economic status by rendering life styles comparatively homogeneous. Student interaction ought then to be governed entirely by values, traits, and abilities rather than by parental income. Probably the House system has done something to accomplish this effect. However, the physically homogeneous Houses have not been psychologically homogeneous; there have always been widely shared stereotypes about the kinds of men who live in each House.

In the early 1950's, I used to ask the students in the undergraduate social psychology course to characterize the members of each House by selecting from a list of adjectives. In those days Lowell House was thought to be predominantly "intellectual," Adams was for artists and musicians, Winthrop for athletes. Whether there was truth in the beliefs is unknown but the reputations were widely shared. By now they have probably changed.

In 1932 Katz and Braly asked one hundred Princeton students to characterize twelve ethnic groups by selecting from a list of traits. *Ethnic* is an omnibus term that includes nationalities (English, American, etc.), races (Negro), and the Jews. Jews are not a nationality since many are not citizens of Israel. It has become well known that they are not a race but it is not always realized that they also are not a religion. Many Jews have no religion. The best definition we can make of this group is that it includes all people who now practice or whose ancestors practiced a particular religion.

Here are a few of the characterizations on which there was great agreement:

English	Sportsmanlike	Italians	Artistic
	Intelligent		Impulsive
	Conventional		Passionate
Japanese	Intelligent	Chinese	Superstitious
	Industrious		Sly
	Progressive		Conservative
Negroes	Superstitious	Turks	Cruel
	Lazy		Very religious
	Happy-go-lucky		Treacherous

Stereotypes are not roles. Expectancies about Plymouth owners, residents of Eliot House, and Turks are not prescriptions for the people in these categories. Surely we do not feel that a Plymouth owner *ought* to be "stodgy" or a Turk "treacherous." If they violate our disagreeable expectations we will be the better pleased. While this is a correct distinction between roles and stereotypes, one must not make it sharper than life. Any established expectancy exerts some force on its object to behave as anticipated. A French psychologist once told an audience that when he speaks before Anglo-Saxon colleagues he always feels as if he ought to be rather fiery and Latin in order not to disappoint expectations. Negroes have sometimes deliberately acted the lazy, happy-go-lucky role to please whites. The stereotype will have more of this role property when the expectations are not particularly unfavorable. However, the more important stereotypes are the unfavorable ones and these have little that is prescriptive about them.

The prescriptive aspect of a role is lacking from stereotypes. Is the performance aspect, the regularity within the category, also lacking? Are Negroes "lazy," Cadillac owners "proud," and Winthrop House residents "athletic"? These are questions of fact rather than reputation. There is always the possibility that a reputation is derived from the facts, but there are also other possibilities. If the people in a category really are as they are reputed to be, then the stereotype is accurate or true; if not, it is untrue. It is clear that "stereotype" is a pejorative term, a bad word. It is not a good thing to harbor stereotypes. The question is what is bad about them? One possible answer is that they are inaccurate, members of the category are not in fact as they are reputed to be.

About twenty years after the Katz and Braly study, Gilbert (1951) repeated their procedure at Princeton. Subjects in this new generation were much less willing than their predecessors to generalize about ethnic groups. Some simply rejected the task; others gave answers but insisted that they were only describing group trends to which there were numerous individual exceptions; still others who characterized the groups declared that they were simply reporting "what people said" not what they themselves believed. Something seems to have happened to ethnic stereotypes and our attitude toward them since 1932 when Katz and Braly collected their data.

In the United States we know there has been a persuasion campaign designed to eliminate ethnic stereotypes. Advertisements in the subway train, picturing an antiseptic hospital nursery, adjured us not to "infect" children with the poisonous stereotypes. Cowboy actors told us on television that just as it was simpleminded of the old western movies to put black hats on the bad guys and white hats on the good guys, so it is simpleminded in life to suppose that character can be read from the external signs of ethnicity. A magazine like *Time* is contemptuous of "stereotyped thinking" about ethnic groups. Social psychologists teach college students that belief in ethnic stereotypes is the very hallmark of a rigid "authoritarian," and potentially fascistic personality. Popular fiction in magazines or on television no longer draws all its heroes as Anglo-Saxon and its villains as Oriental or Mediterranean. Pictures of church picnics on *Saturday Evening Post* covers are nowadays ethnically balanced. There is always one dark face among the whites—just one.

This campaign has produced some results. Educated men today know that it is bad form to give blatant expression to ethnic stereotypes. Sometimes, however, such men privately believe that their own experience proves that Negroes really are lazy or Jews aggressively competitive. When they go to Europe they will not be able to resist generalizing about nationalities and Europeans themselves do not even try to resist it. It is a favorite game of tourists to compete in trying aptly or subtly to "hit off" the Americans or Italians or Germans. And, of course, discrimination itself continues. Ethnic groups still clearly emerge in America from the interaction matrix (Chapter 3).

Leaders of opinion in the United States disapprove of stereotypes and, by attacking them, have caused many people to give them up—in their explicit verbal form. It is probable that the giving up does not go very deep, that stereotypes survive in confidential conversations and in discriminatory behavior. In order to understand why the attack on stereotypes has not completely eliminated them, we will need to make a more searching inquiry into their exact nature and, in particular, must try to discover what is bad about them.

MISTAKEN LINES OF OBJECTION

One line of argument against stereotypes (Hayakawa, 1941) is completely wrong-headed. It has been said, for instance, that the trouble with a stereotype is that it treats a large number of distinguishable persons as equivalent, it is a generalization and so ignores individual differences. In the ritualistic words of the General Semantics movement: "Negro$_1$ is not Negro$_2$ is not Negro$_3$." The implication is that we ought to react to each person and event as a unique entity. This is neither possible nor desirable.

If we were to register every discriminable feature of a space-time event, it would indeed be unique. Nothing ever repeats exactly, not even the turning red of the traffic light on the corner. For each turning there is something about the quality of daylight, the array of traffic, the people in the cars, which is distinctive. If, on that account, we refused to make any generalizations about this traffic light, we should deprive ourselves of some very useful knowledge; when the facing light is red, traffic stops at the intersection. This is a generalization that ignores time of day, pattern of traffic, and the many differences between the light on the corner and the lights on other corners. Red Light$_1$ is not Red Light$_2$ is not Red Light$_3$. Except that, for purposes of traffic control, Red Light$_1$ *is* Red Light$_2$ *is* Red Light$_3$. The lights which are potentially discriminable may for the purposes of motorists and pedestrians be treated as equivalent. We ought to react to them as a category.

If we think of each occurrence of a red light as unique, we cannot anticipate the future. Red Light$_1$ being different from Red Light$_2$ would not teach us what to expect when we encounter the latter. Events or persons in all their detail do not recur but unless we can discover recurrence, we cannot project ahead, we cannot anticipate the future. To form accurate anticipations is an obvious necessity for survival and we and all the higher animals are continually forming such anticipations. It is not unique events that recur but kinds or categories of events, and so the terms of expectancies are always necessarily categories. It is a chief occupation of the human and animal mind to form categories to the end of discovering recurrence to the end of anticipating the future. We must generalize about categories and we ought to generalize about categories.

However, not all generalizations about categories are useful. The critical question is: Does the generalization correspond with the facts? It is sometimes a good thing to ignore differences of size and position among right triangles; they are all equivalent, for instance, in that they satisfy the Pythagorean Theorem. True generalizations about Plymouth owners or residents of Winthrop House or Englishmen could be valuable. The fault is not in the abstracting and generalizing that enters into a stereotype, but it may be in the accuracy of the generalization.

Do we know that the popular stereotypes are false? If we suppose them to be intended as exceptionless generalizations (e.g., *All* Winthrop men are athletes or *all* Plymouth owners are stodgy), then we know them to be false or can very easily prove them so. A single exception will do it and there are many exceptions to all of the generalizations we have described. However, it does not seem to be the case that people who believe in stereotypes believe in them as exceptionless generalizations. They frequently say that they are only reporting tendencies or trends. It is more difficult to establish the truth or falsity of a trend than of an absolute distinction.

Consider first a case in which the necessary data could be collected. Suppose we wanted to know if Winthrop House men tend to be athletic and Lowell House men intellectual. We should have to settle on indices of athleticism and of intellectuality. For the former we could use the percentage of House members who have won varsity letters, and for the latter the percentage of men whose grades put them on the Dean's List. Winthrop should be higher on the former index and Lowell on the latter. If the differences were statistically significant we could conclude that the differential reputations were grounded in fact.

Data of this kind would be more difficult to collect for owners of various makes of automobile and more difficult again for ethnic groups. There are just scattered fragments of evidence. There are data that suggest there is some truth in the characterization of Jews as "ambitious" or "hard-driving." More Jewish young people go to college generally than do other young people from families at the same socio-economic level

(Seligmann, 1950). In school a disproportionately large number of Jews are academic "over-achievers," that is, students who get better grades than would be predicted from various intelligence test scores (Clark, 1949; Terman and Oden, 1947). Follow-up studies of college graduates show that Jews tend to earn higher incomes than do Catholics and Protestants (Havemann and West, 1952). A study of a New England city (Warner and Srole, 1945) found that Jews have risen more rapidly in the class system than have other immigrants arriving about the same time and facing similar disadvantages. Here is some support for one part of a stereotype. On the other hand the belief that Jews gravitate to high finance is not supported by the number of them in the banking profession or by the number having membership on the New York Stock Exchange (Allport, 1954).

The only study I know that attempts to compare Caucasian racial types was done by Klineberg, Fjeld and Foley (1954) in New York City with students classified as Nordic, Mediterranean, or Alpine. It is agreed by biologists and anthropologists that all mankind now on earth belong to the single species *Homo Sapiens*. The criteria for species differentiation are reasonably clear, but there are not definite criteria for the establishment of finer subvarieties, such as races. Consequently there are many different versions of the races of mankind, but the Nordic, Alpine, and Mediterranean subdivisions of the white race are often accepted. Klineberg and his collaborators administered many kinds of personality tests to their subjects—the Bernreuter Inventory, the Allport-Vernon Study of Values, tests of persistence, suggestibility, and honesty.

The familiar stereotypes accrue to nationality names rather than race names and, of course, no modern nationality is racially pure. Still it is safe to say that Sweden and Italy, for example, differ racially, in that the Nordic strain is strong in the former and the Mediterranean in the latter. Consequently, the characterizations of nationalities may be inferentially extended to races and would seem to predict differences on some of the test scores Klineberg obtained. Italians, should, for example, have had strong "aesthetic" values on the Allport-Vernon measure. In fact, Klineberg found no significant differences among the racial groups. There were large differences when the same subjects were analyzed by social class or schooling. To this fact we will shortly return.

On one stereotype there has been a substantial amount of work. Katz and Braly's subjects said that Negroes were "ignorant." There are numerous studies comparing American Negro and white scores on intelligence tests or information tests. While the distributions generally overlap, there is usually a tendency for the white group to do better (Allport, 1954; Klineberg, 1954; Pettigrew, 1964). Here, as in the case of Jewish "drive," the available data seem to support the stereotype.

Suppose an employer wants to fill a job for which he knows that an IQ of at least 120 is essential. There are two applicants, one he knows to be white and the other Negro. Would it be rational of him to choose the white? It would seem to be, since a larger percentage of whites than Negroes have IQ's above his cutoff point and so his choice maximizes his chance of getting a qualified person. Irrationality enters the picture if he is so unwise as to choose between two applicants on the basis of no information other than their respective races. Race is a very poor predictor of IQ since the distribution of scores for any race is wide. A sensible man would get more facts. But remember that Katz and Braly and many other investigators of ethnic stereotypes did not give their subjects the opportunity to be sensible men. They forced decisions on the basis of one item of information—ethnic membership. May not their subjects have been making the best of such a task?

For most of the popular generalizations about ethnic groups there is no evidence with respect to validity or invalidity, nothing to tell us whether the facts confirm the expectancies. We cannot then say that the objection to ethnic stereotypes is their demonstrated falsity. While the falsity is not demonstrated, it may be that it can be assumed because the people who hold these beliefs have not had enough experience with the groups in question to develop sound generalizations. Katz and Braly found that their one hundred Princeton men who had such definite ideas about Turks were not actually acquainted with any Turks. Stereotypes are, after all, verbal behavior—talk about groups—and this behavior is probably acquired from other peoples' verbal behavior.

Staats and Staats (1958) have demonstrated that stereotypes could be picked up by a kind of verbal conditioning without conscious awareness. They worked with the names of six nationalities: *Dutch, Swedish, French, Italian, German,* and *Greek. Dutch* and *Swedish* were the critical words which were to pick up a favorable or an unfavorable reputation; the others were to be neutral. Subjects believed they were participating in an experiment on verbal learning. There was visual presentation of six nationality names, each one appearing eighteen times. Immediately following the visual presentations other words were presented aurally. Subjects were supposed to try to learn both series of words; the experimenter was supposed to be interested in the way the two kinds of presentation would interact. For one group the order of presentation was so arranged that the word *Dutch* was always followed by unfavorable words and *Swedish* by favorable words. For a second group this arrangement was reversed. The other nationality names were followed by neutral words.

At the end of the presentation, subjects were given a booklet with a single word at the top of each page and were asked to indicate whether that word had been seen or heard or neither. Because one's feelings about a word might affect learning (subjects were told), each word was also to be rated on a seven-point scale from pleasant to unpleasant. For the group that had heard favorable words in conjunction with *Swedish*, that name was rated as very pleasant and *Dutch* was unpleasant. For the other group the ratings were appropriately reversed.

The Staatses' demonstration of verbal conditioning suggests an explanation for a joke that has long puzzled me. In the brilliant revue called *Beyond the Fringe*, a man discoursing on anti-Semitism says: "Actually, I'm not a Jew, I'm Jew-ish." The audience laughs and presumably they do so because they recognize that the logically equivalent terms, *Jew* and *Jew-ish*, are not affectively equivalent; *Jew* sounds worse. In view of the Staatses' experiment, it seems probable that this is because the noun form has been accompanied by such disagreeable modifiers as *dirty*, whereas the adjective form has not. I feel the same sort of difference between *Swede* and *Swedish*, *Turk* and *Turkish*.

The fact that the actor introduced a pause in an unusual place, saying "Jew-ish" rather than "Jewish," points to the operation of an additional factor. The derivational affix, *-ish*, formerly used only to transform nouns into adjectives, has lately gone wild in English, and is being added to words that are already adjectives, as in: "His politics are pink-ish and his conversation dull-ish." In these contexts, *-ish* operates to water down the semantic context of the word to which it is attached. If *very* is an intensifier, then *-ish* is a diminisher. The word *Jewish* antedates this development but by putting a pause before the affix, the actor cleverly suggested usage as a diminisher. This has been a digression.

The Staatses' subjects acquired their feelings about the Dutch and Swedish without realizing how they had been acquired. It would seem to follow that the many sentences one hears in which something is said about an ethnic group, sentences in informal conversation, popular fiction, or films, could create the verbal stereotypes. There need be no direct acquaintance with people belonging to the groups and not even any awareness that attitudes are being formed. This is not a very critical or careful cognitive process. Does it follow that the propositions so created will be false?

Most of our beliefs are acquired from the talk and writing of others. For most of our beliefs, we do not have adequate direct evidence. How do we know that the world is round, that Columbus discovered America in 1492, that Australia exists? If it were to be required of us that we give up any belief that is not based on our own induction from our own experience, we should have to give up most of our beliefs, including many that are valid and powerful. Much of what we pick up uncritically from other people's talk is true, and so it does not discredit ethnic stereotypes to demonstrate that they have been acquired in this way. Perhaps these reputations represent the distilled wisdom of many generations.

ETHNOCENTRISM IN STEREOTYPES

Stereotypes are not objectionable because they are generalizations about categories; such generalizations are valuable when they are true. Stereotypes are not objectionable because they are generalizations that have been proven false; for the most part we do not know whether they are true or false—in their probabilistic forms. Stereotypes are not objectionable because they are generalizations acquired by hearsay rather than by direct experience; many generalizations acquired by hearsay are true and useful. What is objectionable about them? I think it is their ethnocentrism and the implication that important traits are inborn for large groups.

The statements that Winthrop House men are athletic and Lowell House men are intellectual are subject to confirmation or disconfirmation in a rather direct way. In this respect they are unlike stereotypes concerning ethnic groups. The favorable and unfavorable statements about nationalities, which were conditioned in the Staatses' experiment are pure attitudes not propositions which can be considered true or false. The attributions in the Katz and Braly study are generally mixtures of empirical content and evaluation: "The Chinese are superstitious"; "The Italians are religious"; "The Japanese are progressive." Can one even imagine data that would establish the truth or falsity of such statements?

What is the difference between the word "superstitious" which is applied to the Chinese and the word "religious" which is applied to the Italians? In both cases one is saying that a nationality subscribes to a set of supernatural beliefs, beliefs outside the province of natural science and not testable by science. Surely one set of beliefs is called "superstitious" because that set of beliefs is not accepted in our culture. The other set of beliefs is called "religious" because it is accepted and institutionalized among ourselves.

A very common thing for Americans to say about people of other nationalities is that they are "dirty." All nationalities in the Far and Middle East seem to us to be "dirty"; in Europe only the Germans, Dutch, and Scandinavians meet our exacting standards. What makes a people "dirty"? Perhaps they do not bathe often enough. One could, with difficulty, determine the average frequency of bathing in the United States and also in, for example, and with no offense intended, Italy. Let us suppose that in the United States the average is two baths a week, whereas in Italy it is one bath in two weeks ("*Pace*"). Such data would demonstrate that Italians do not bathe *as often* as Americans, but this is not the same as the statement that they do not bathe *often enough*. What is the difference?

The local norm is more than a description of common local practice. It is a statement of what ought to be; a prescription. If we take the norms of our culture as proper guides for the behavior of mankind everywhere, then departures like the Italian are not simply different, they are less good, and we label them so with a term like *dirty*, a term that names a departure from our ideals in the sphere of cleanliness.

What difference does it make that the terms in stereotypes are evaluative as well as descriptive? Insofar as the generalizations are descriptive one could conceivably check the relevant facts and the evaluation would follow from the relation between the facts and our norms. It appears then that the validity of familiar stereotypes can be examined. However, insofar as the stereotypes are evaluative, there can only be a local validity, validity for us.

Consider the Italians whom we have represented as bathing less often than the Americans. The Italian might evaluate the same facts in a reversed way. Americans bathe too much. In a more religious age, some centuries ago, bathing was thought of as primarily a pleasure or luxury. Monks and holy men bathed very seldom because abstention was a way of mortifying the flesh. If you concentrate on the pleasurable side of bathing, the agreeable business of sozzling in a warm tub, rather than on the cleansing function, it becomes clear that much bathing can be a sensual indulgence. The descriptive part of a stereotype may then have a universal validity but the evaluative part cannot have such a validity. It is not possible, therefore, to think of the familiar stereotypes as generalizations about ethnic groups of the sort that a science of social psychology might be interested in. Social psychologists from unlike cultures would not be able to agree on the generalizations. Neither is it possible for such stereotypes to figure in an international culture of the kind many of us hope to see develop. Different nationalities could not agree on them.

While our mass media attack stereotypes of the Negro and Jew and Italian and Irishman, they do not usually attack those contemporary stereotypes that are supportive of our contemporary political alliances. For a Unesco study Buchanan and Cantril (1953) obtained stereotypes from one thousand respondents in each of nine nations: Australia, Britain, France, Germany, Italy, Netherlands, Norway, Mexico, the United States. Respondents were asked about their own nationality, the United States and the Soviet Union; some were also asked about the British, French, and Chinese peoples. If we look only at the reputations of the United States and the Soviet Union, we can trace the line of the Iron Curtain of the early 1950's in the high agreement on such traits as "cruel," "domineering," "backward" for the Soviets, while the Americans were regarded as "generous," "progressive," and "peace-loving." It can be assumed that the reputations of the two countries on the other side of the Curtain would have shown a reverse evaluation.

Nationality stereotypes have proved marvelously responsive to shifting military alliances. Shortly after Pearl Harbor, studies show that the Japanese became much more "treacherous." During World War II the Germans became more "militaristic." Today both nations are reverting to their prewar "industry" and "progressiveness," to reputations dictated by certain enduring similarities between their cultures and our own. When world politics made enemies of them, our conceptions of their national characters promptly shifted so as to provide a supportive worldview.

Recognition of the evaluative aspect of ethnic stereotypes helps us to understand how these beliefs function, what they are used for. Stereotypes are a way of thinking about nationalities and religions and races other than our own with reference to our own standards. Groups having characteristics that are valued in our culture are favorably stereotyped—the "sportsmanship" of the English, the "progressiveness" of the Germans. It is even possible for us to believe that one of our own values is more fully realized by some other group than it is by us. Groups that do not realize our values are unfavorably stereotyped. And so we have a way of dividing all the peoples of the world into cowboys in white hats and cowboys in black hats: German cowboys, Italian cowboys, Indian cowboys, and Chinese cowboys.

Certainly some of the contemporary objection to stereotypes derives from their cultural absolutism. To think of the norms of one's own group as right for men everywhere is called, in social science, "ethnocentrism." It is a frame of mind directly opposed to cultural relativism. In earlier centuries unlike cultures were seldom in contact and the peoples having such cultures had no great need to cooperate. Orientals could think of us as ugly barbarian "white devils" and we could think of them as wily, superstitious "heathen." Today when Africans, Orientals, Europeans, and Americans must often meet and must somehow avoid conflict, it is recognized that ethnocentrism is an inadequate and dangerous worldview.

THE IMPLICATION OF AN INBORN GROUP CHARACTER

One of the aspects of ethnic stereotypes to which our modern temper takes exception is their ethnocentrism. The other is, I think, the implication they convey that ethnic groups have inborn and unalterable psychological characteristics. This implication is naturally stronger for supposed races than for nationalities or religions. In the Buchanan and Cantril (1953) study, respondents were asked whether their national characteristics were mainly inborn or due to the way they had been brought up. Of the West Germans, 59 per cent believed their national characteristics were mainly inborn, of the British 39 per cent believed this, and in the Netherlands 44 per cent. In the United States only 15 per cent of respondents held this belief, and in Australia, only 23 per cent. Probably these differences exist because a relatively stable nationality can more easily think of itself as genetically distinct than can a nationality created from diverse streams of immigration. Most people in the United States know that "national characters" can be transformed in a generation, but many people are not sure that the characters of such supposed races as the Jews and the Negroes can be changed in a generation. The notion that Negroes are innately inferior to whites in intelligence has been very widely held and has been used to justify the vicious institution of segregation.

In biology and anthropology a race is supposed to be a human subspecies, an isolated mating group with distinctive gene frequencies, and so it is reasonable to think the characteristics of races more likely to be inborn than the characteristics of nationalities. However, in the world today, there are no absolutely isolated mating groups, no absolutely distinctive gene pools, and so no pure races. Race is a relative concept.

American Negroes do not constitute a very isolated or uniform mating group and are remote indeed from being a pure race. The Africans who were brought to North America as slaves originated "from areas as far apart as West Africa, Angola, and Madagascar (the present-day Malagasy Republic), and represented as great a biological range as that found in Europe" (Pettigrew, 1964). After three centuries of miscegenation with whites, 75 per cent of American Negroes have at least one white forbear and some 15 per cent have a predominantly white ancestry (Herskovits, 1930; Stern, 1954). These facts make it unlikely that American Negroes have any very sharply distinctive inborn psychological characteristics.

In the popular mind, complicated genetic facts are much simplified. Children of mixed marriages know that there is nothing ambiguous or relative about the popular definition of a Negro. Any known Negro ancestry, however outweighed by white ancestry, makes one a "Negro."

In 1942, according to a survey, three out of five white Americans believed that "Negroes" were intellectually inferior to whites (Hyman and Sheatsley, 1956). Opponents of the 1954 desegregation ruling of the Supreme Court appealed to this belief. They held that Negro children are innately inferior to white children, and that integrated education would therefore drag down the standards of white education. Is the Negro American innately inferior in intelligence to the white American?

The definitive modern discussion of this problem is by Pettigrew (1964). We will here review a few of the high points of his analysis.

For the assessment of intelligence nowadays we think at once of the many so-called "intelligence tests." When such a test is administered to randomly selected white Americans and Negro Americans, the two groups will produce normally distributed scores with the mean or average performance of the whites somewhat higher than that of the Negroes. This is the basic "scientific fact" suggesting that the American Negro is innately inferior. The fact is undeniable and yet Pettigrew finds only three American psychologists who have concluded in print that the Negro is innately inferior. The majority believe that obtained differences in intelligence test scores do not demonstrate racial inferiority. Indeed three professional societies of behavioral scientists have adopted resolutions asserting that no evidence exists of innate racial differences in mental ability (Pettigrew, 1964). The three psychologists who disagree charge that the majority has fallen victim to an equalitarian dogma. One, Professor Emeritus Henry Garrett (1961), calls the notion of racial equality the "scientific hoax of the century."

Even the comparison of random racial groups turns up some facts that are not easily assimilated by a theory of Negro inferiority that is intended to justify segregated education. While the mean scores of whites and Negroes are different, the ranges are usually about the same. This means that some Negro children attain scores in the "highly-gifted" range (Jenkins, 1948; Jenkins, 1950; Theman and Witty, 1943; Witty and Jenkins, 1936). Then there is the embarrassing fact that individual variation in IQ among "Negroes" is not related to degree of white ancestry (Herskovits, 1926; Witty and Jenkins, 1936). Indeed the brightest Negro child yet described, a child with an IQ of 200, had no known white ancestry (Theman and Witty, 1943; Witty and Jenkins, 1936).

There is a fundamental difficulty with taking differential test scores as evidence of inborn racial differences. This difficulty was dramatically revealed by two analyses of scores obtained on the Army Alpha test of verbal intelligence from servicemen in World War I. The first of these (Brigham, 1923) analyzed by presumed race and it turned out that Nordic whites had scored higher than Alpine or Mediterranean whites, and that whites, in general, had scored higher than Negroes. These outcomes were in startling accord with contemporary stereotypes. However, several social scientists (Ashley Montagu, 1945; Klineberg, 1954) made finer analyses and these showed that Negroes from Ohio, Illinois, and New York had obtained higher scores than whites from Mississippi, Kentucky, and Arkansas. By the first analysis, whites were superior to Negroes, but by the second analysis, Negroes were superior to whites. The contradiction disappears, however, if we suppose that scores on intelligence tests are not primarily determined by race at all but rather by educational opportunities in the broadest sense. Such opportunities are better for whites than for Negroes in the United States at large, but also better for men from rich northern states than for men from poorer southern states, whether the men in question are white or Negro.

What evidence do we have that intelligence test scores or IQ's are affected by educational opportunities? Many studies have found moderately high positive correlations between the IQ's of children and such indices of family socio-economic status as home rentals (Maller, 1933; Robinson and Meenes, 1947), and socio-economic status would be related to the quality of formal education and to informal opportunities to learn. Children in orphanages and other kinds of institutions tend to have lower IQ's than children in normal homes and beneficial effects from early schooling have been demonstrated for such children (Wellman and Pegram, 1944). An English study (Gordon, 1923) found that children living isolated lives in canal-boat families or in gypsy families had exceptionally low IQ's, lower than are usually obtained for Negro American children. And so it goes; the evidence is plentiful. It shows that intelligence test scores are affected by experience but not, of course, that they are totally determined by experience; other studies show the effects of heredity (see Chapter 1).

There is no direct access to innate intellectual potential. Intelligence tests set problems and elicit performances, and these performances are influenced by experience as well as by potential. The comparative quality of individual performances can only be considered indicative of the comparative level of individual potential when the experiences that can affect performance are closely similar across individuals. Such experiences are grossly dissimilar for random collections of white Americans and Negro Americans, and so the obtained differences in performance do not qualify as evidence of potential. It is possible, of course, that differences of potential exist; we do not know for sure. What we do know is that great differences of experience exist and these are not favorable to the Negro.

One sort of experience that can affect performance on an intelligence test item is experience with that item, or with related items from the same content domain. It is to be expected that children from homes where certain words are used will do better on a vocabulary test involving those words than will children from homes where the words are never heard. It is to be expected that small children who have been given Form Board toys as gifts will do better on tests of spatial intelligence involving forms than will children who have never owned such toys. Most intelligence tests are loaded with middle-class content that is bound to be more familiar to white children than to Negro children.

There is a less obvious possibility that may be more important. The variety of experience (perceptual, motoric, and linguistic) enjoyed by a child in the critical period of earliest childhood may permanently affect his learning and problem-solving ability. This possibility was mentioned at the very start of Chapter 1 in connection with an experiment showing that rats reared in an "enriched" environment were at maturity better at learning mazes than were rats reared in an impoverished environment. Now we should like to cite a related experiment that is especially relevant to the interpretation of intelligence test scores.

The experiment (Cooper and Zubek, 1958) was done with two genetically distinct rat strains, strains bred for brightness and dullness over many generations. Representatives of both strains were reared in three kinds of environment, ranging from an extreme of restriction and impoverishment through the normal habitat of a laboratory rat to a highly enriched "playground" equipped with tunnels and slides and swings. The learning abilities of the six groups were assessed at maturity and, while there was a discernible effect of genetic strain, extreme differences of environment overcame it completely. For example, the dull strain, or "race," reared in an enriched environment learned faster than did the bright strain reared in an impoverished environment.

Suppose now that we saw these two groups of rats perform and knew nothing of their actual genetics and were disposed to discount the effects of environment. Imagine that we were bent on assessing innate intellectual potential. One group has earned a better score than the other and so we might uncritically think it the superior race. To be sure, this group probably knows more at maturity and certainly can learn faster. However, if we thought this superior group had been superior from the start and that no effort on behalf of the apparently inferior group could have elevated them, we should be mistaken. We should be mistaken, too, if we thought it necessary to segregate the offspring of the apparently inferior group for fear they would be unable to keep up with the offspring of the apparently superior group.

Given the fact that intelligence test scores can be affected by experience and given the unlike experiences of whites and Negroes, it is possible that the differences in the mean scores of groups are attributable to experience. If they are, they should tend to disappear in circumstances where the experiences of the groups are similar, and that is what happens. It has been repeatedly shown that in the first two years of life, when differences of experience are probably minimal, there are no significant racial differences in intelligence (Gilliland, 1951; Pasamanick, 1946). On an isolated island in the Caribbean, where Negroes are nearer to social equality with whites than they are in the United States, Curti (1960) found no significant racial differences on nine of fourteen intelligence measures. Studies in New York City (Klineberg, 1935) and in Philadelphia (Lee, 1951) have shown that Negro children coming to these cities from the South systematically gain in IQ with each grade completed in the North. In educationally unsegregated communities in Boston and Minneapolis it has been shown that only very minor Negro-white differences in IQ exist.

The evidence on intellectual potential having the greatest practical importance is that provided by the desegregation effort itself. In 1954, Washington, D.C., where Negroes then comprised three-fifths of the students, introduced sweeping well-conceived desegregation. In 1959, the consequences were assessed. Achievement test scores had risen for each grade sampled and each subject tested approached or equalled national norms. Furthermore, both Negro and white students shared in these gains (Pettigrew, 1964). Nor is the Washington experience unique. Louisville also has reported marked improvements in the performance of Negro students and slight improvements in the performance of white students (Pettigrew, 1964).

The evidence we have does not prove that Negro Americans and White Americans have exactly the same intellectual potential; there can be no strict proof so long as opportunities are unequal. The evidence does make it clear that there are no great differences. The evidence does not exclude the possibility, for example, that Negro Americans have an intellectual potential slightly superior to that of white Americans. In these circumstances the stereotype of innate Negro inferiority is objectionable and mischievous in the extreme. There is reason to believe that the accumulated evidence has weakened the stereotype. In 1956 Hyman and Sheatsley found that four out of five white Americans, including a majority of white Southerners, regarded Negroes as their intellectual equals. This is a favorable contrast with the two out of five of 1942. Unhappily the resistance to desegregated education does not seem to have declined in a degree commensurate with the weakening of the stereotype. This is because the stereotype was never the only reason for segregation. It was rather the most discussible reason, the most rational-seeming. It is so no longer.

There has been no persuasion campaign in the United States against stereotypes other than the ethnic. Around every sort of social group a reputation develops; these reputations always overlook individual differences and often may not represent real trends. We have popular conceptions of poets, professors, professional wrestlers, and film stars. Locally there are definite conceptions of Radcliffe girls and Wellesley girls, of Harvard students and M.I.T. students. The M.I.T. student in particular is acquainted with the disagreeable experience of being stereotyped in an unfair way. Introduced into a liberal arts crowd as a man from M.I.T., he feels the stereotype coming down on him like a square steel mold shaving off all his idiosyncratic parts. In fact, he is quite likely to be articulate, seriously interested in philosophy, a good amateur musician, and not an engineer. But it will be presumed that he is a slave of the slide rule.

In spite of the fact that our conceptions of occupations and schools and drivers of automobiles are generalizations about categories, more often based on hearsay than on experience, and frequently inaccurate, there has been no effort to relieve us of them. This is, I think, because they lack the characteristics that make stereotypes truly dangerous. They are not ethnocentric judgments evaluating remote groups by local standards. They do not imply the existence of innate group characteristics, where the evidence is that such characteristics do not exist. The familiar ethnic stereotypes do both of these things and have been used to justify war and discrimination. If our conceptions of ethnic groups ceased to be ethnocentrically evaluative and ceased to imply a nonexistent inborn character, then, even if they were rather inaccurate, there would be little harm in them and we would no longer call them stereotypes.

REFERENCES

Abravanel, E. A psychological analysis of the concept of role. Unpublished master's thesis. Swarthmore College, 1962.

Allport, G. W. *The nature of prejudice*. Cambridge: Addison-Wesley, 1954.

Brigham, C. C. *A study of American intelligence*. Princeton: Princeton Univer. Press, 1923.

Buchanan, W., & Cantril, H. *How nations see each other*. Urbana: Univer. of Ill. Press, 1953.

Clark, E. L. Motivation of Jewish students. *J. soc. Psychol.*, 1949, **29**, 113–117.

Clark, G., & Birch, H. G. Hormonal modification of social behavior. *Psychosom. Med.*, 1945, **7**, 321–329.

Clark, G., & Birch, H. G. Hormonal modification of social behavior. *Psychosom. Med.*, 1946, **8**, 320–331.

Cooper, R. M., & Zubek, J. M. Effects of enriched and constricted early environments on the learning ability of bright and dull rats. *Canad. J. Psychol.*, 1958, **12**, 159–164.

Curti, Margaret W. Intelligence tests of white and colored school children in Grand Cayman. *J. Psychol.*, 1960, **49**, 13–27.

Fortune, W. F. Arapesh warfare. *Amer. Anthropologist*, 1939, **41**, 22–41.

Garrett, H. E. The equalitarian dogma. *Mankind Quart.*, 1961, **1**, 253–257.

Gilbert, G. M. Stereotype persistence and change among college students. *J. abnorm. soc. Psychol.*, 1951, **46**, 245–254.

Gilliland, A. R. Socioeconomic status and race as factors in infant intelligence test scores. *Child Develpm.*, 1951, **22**, 271–273.

Gordon, H. *Mental and scholastic tests among retarded children*. London: Board of Education (Educational Pamphlet No. 44), 1923.

Gross, N., McEachern, A. W., & Mason, W. S. *Explorations in role analysis: Studies of the school superintendency role*. New York: Wiley, 1957.

Havemann, E., & West, P. S. *They went to college.* New York: Harcourt, Brace, 1952.

Hayakawa, S. I. *Language in action.* New York: Harcourt, Brace, 1941.

Herskovits, M. J. On the relation between Negro-white mixture and standing in intelligence tests. *Pediatrics Sem.,* 1926, **33**, 30–42.

Herskovits, M. J. *The anthropometry of the American Negro.* New York: Columbia Univer. Press, 1930.

Hyman, H. H., & Sheatsley, P. B. Attitudes toward desegregation. *Scient. American,* 1956, **195**, 35–39.

James, W. T. Social organization among dogs of different temperaments, terriers and beagles, reared together. *J. comp. physiol. Psychol.,* 1951, **44**, 71–77.

Jenkins, M. D. The upper limit of ability among American Negroes. *Scient. Mon.,* 1948, **66**, 399–401.

Jenkins, M. D. Intellectually superior Negro youth: Their problems and needs. *J. Negro Educ.,* 1950, **19**, 322–332.

Katz, D., & Braly, K. W. Racial stereotypes of one hundred college students. *J. abnorm. soc. Psychol.,* 1933, **28**, 280–290.

Klineberg, O. *Negro intelligence and selective migration.* New York: Columbia Univer. Press, 1935.

Klineberg, O. *Social psychology.* (Rev. ed.) New York: Holt, 1954.

Klineberg, O., Fjeld, H., & Foley, J. P. Unpublished study. Cited by O. Klineberg, *Social psychology.* (Rev. ed.) New York: Holt, 1954.

Komarovsky, Mirra. Cultural contradictions and sex roles. *Amer. J. Sociol.,* 1946, **52**, 184–189.

Kuckenberg, Karolyn G. Effect of early father absence on scholastic aptitude. Unpublished doctoral dissertation. Harvard Univer., 1963.

Lee, E. S. Negro intelligence and selective migration: A Philadelphia test of the Klineberg hypothesis. *Amer. Sociol. Rev.,* 1951, **16**, 227–233.

Maller, J. B. Mental ability and its relation to physical health and social economic status. *Psychol. Clin.,* 1933, **22**, 101–107.

Mead, Margaret. *Sex and temperament.* New York: Morrow, 1935.

Montagu, M. F. Ashley. Intelligence of northern Negroes and southern whites in the First World War. *Amer. J. Psychol.,* 1945, **58**, 161–188.

Nadel, S. F. *The theory of social structure.* New York: Free Press, 1957.

Pasamanick, B. A comparative study of the behavioral development of Negro infants. *J. genet. Psychol.,* 1946, **69**, 3–44.

Pettigrew, T. F. *A profile of the Negro American.* Princeton: Van Nostrand, 1964.

Robinson, Mary L., & Meenes, M. The relationship between test intelligence of third-grade Negro children and the occupations of their parents. *J. Negro Educ.,* 1947, **16**, 136–141.

Seligmann, B. B. The American Jew: Some demographic features. In *American Jewish Yearbook,* 1950, **51**, 3–52. Philadelphia: Jewish Publication Society of America.

Scott, J. P. *Aggression.* Chicago: Univer. of Chicago Press, 1958.

Staats, A. W., & Staats, Carolyn K. Attitudes established by classical conditioning. *J. abnorm. soc. Psychol.,* 1958, **57**, 37–40.

Stern, C. The biology of the Negro. *Scient. American,* 1954, **191**, 81–85.

Terman, L. M., & Oden, M. H. *The gifted child grows up.* Stanford: Stanford Univer. Press, 1947.

Terman, L. M., & Tyler, L. E. Psychological sex differences. In L. Carmichael (Ed.), *Manual of child psychology.* (2nd ed.) New York: Wiley, 1954.

Theman, V., & Witty, P. A. Case studies and genetic records of two gifted Negroes. *J. Psychol.*, 1943, 15, 165–181.

Warner, W. L., & Srole, L. *The social systems of American ethnic groups.* New Haven: Yale Univer. Press, 1945.

Wellman, Beth L., & Pegram, Edna L. Binet I. Q. changes of orphanage preschool children: A re-analysis. *J. genet. Psychol.*, 1944, 65, 239–263.

Wells, W. D., Goi, F. J., & Seader, S. A change in a product image. *J. appl. Psychol.*, 1958, 42, 120–121.

Witty, P., & Jenkins, M. D. Intra-race testing and Negro intelligence. *J. Psychol.*, 1936, 1, 179–192.

Part Three

THE SOCIALIZATION

OF THE CHILD

*T*HE American sociologist, Talcott Parsons, has called the birth of new generations of children a recurrent barbarian invasion. He does not mean barbarian in the sense of Neolithic humans living by hunting and fishing but in the familiar popular sense which holds a barbarian to be an uncultured or unsocialized person. Human infants do not possess culture at birth; they do not have a conception of the world, a language, or a morality. All of these things must be acquired by them, and the process of acquisition is called socialization.

The process of socialization is the meeting ground of social science, of general psychology, and of the psychology of personality. It may reasonably be designated the central topic of social psychology. Waiting for the infant is a society possessing a culture. The infant is set down in the midst of an ordered way of life, and he possesses certain possibilities for processing information and developing desires which make it possible for that way of life to influence him. A major consequence of these influences is the creation of a set of enduring competencies, standards of judgment, attitudes, and motives which together comprise an organized system called a personality. This system has, in its turn, some power to transform the culture that created it.

The selection of topics in the next four chapters is somewhat eccentric for a *Social Psychology* and that is because the conception of socialization they develop departs from traditional conceptions. Socialization is sometimes understood to be simply the control of impulse, sometimes to be the acquisition of values; sometimes as conformity to norms and sometimes as internalization of the parental superego. All of these conceptions take insufficient account of the intellectual side of socialization and of the active, creative role of the child.

For a time in psychology, socialization was more or less equated with weaning, toilet-training, and the curbing of aggression; more generally with the control of impulse. This emphasis was a remote derivative of Freud's writings on psychosexual development. In Chapter 8 a good deal is said about the control of aggression and about Freud's ideas on that subject. However, since weaning and toilet-training have not yet been shown to have any effects on adult personality they will not concern us in the chapters ahead.

The difficulty with the notion that socialization is value acquisition is that values are too often understood to be nothing more than positive and negative valences. In fact, however, they are much more. For one thing values require to be conceptualized. In order to set a positive value on achievement and a negative value on aggression, for instance, one must possess the two conceptions: achievement and aggression. The fact that those of us who write about such conceptions have difficulty defining them should alert us to the intellectual dimension of value acquisition.

Freud, in his fondness for physical metaphors, wrote of socialization as "internalization" or "incorporation"—most directly of the parental superego but, indirectly, of the culture. "Internalization" and "incorporation" can be misleading terms. They are so if they suggest that a child gulps down adult standards in raw form and that these enter into his own superego without undergoing significant transformation. In fact, of course, whatever is taken in by a child is processed by his intelligence and that intelligence changes with age and experience. His understanding of the "same" moral principle is repeatedly transformed as he matures. Adult principle and adult example are only nutriment to the child's mind. The terms "internalization" and "incorporation" need not be misleading if we take them to imply a subsequent digestion and assimilation.

Conformity to the norms is sometimes said to be the end result of a positive or successful socialization. This is much too narrow a conception. The norms of a language are rules of pronunciation, spelling, semantics, and grammar. Some who have learned these rules very well—children, poets, the Beatles—elect on occasion to violate them. Others who know them well undertake to reform them: to make spelling consistent or to strip certain words of ambiguity. Similarly the moral theory an individual forms by working over his moral experience can lead him to reject some part of the conventional morality. He is likely to argue, in support of his position, that the change he favors will make the total morality more consistent or that the substitution he offers will more truly realize the basic values of the culture than does the rejected part. Saints and revolutionaries and reactionaries all take some such position. It does not seem correct to consider such persons to be negative outcomes, failures of socialization. They have successfully internalized the norms but they have made a novel system of them and novel systems sometimes displace established ones.

The conception of socialization developed in the next four chapters may be summarized as follows. The mature persons with whom a child interacts behave in accordance with such systems of norms or rules as are called logic, mathematics, language, morality, aesthetics, political philosophy, physical theory, and so on. For the most part these systems have not been explicitly formulated by the adults whose behavior is governed by them and they will not be explicitly formulated by the child who acquires them. What seems to happen is that the child processes what he perceives of the behavior of mature members of his society in such a way as to extract the rule systems implicit in it. This process is not a simple "passing over" of the systems from one generation to another. What each child extracts at a given age is a function of his idiosyncratic experience and of his present intellectual capabilities. The systems governing the child change as he grows older and they need not, in the end, simply reproduce the rules that prevail in his society. The outcome can be unique and is sometimes revolutionary.

Languages are the cultural systems that have been best described and Chapters 6 and 7 describe English in considerable detail before discussing its digestion and assimilation by the child. The Genevan school of psychology, in which Jean Piaget is the leading figure, has, for more than forty years, studied the child's acquisition of such systems of knowledge as logic, measurement, morality, number, and theory of physical reality. What we do not know about this work is whether the results describe the process of intellectual socialization in European and American society or whether they describe the maturation of intelligence in children everywhere. If the former is correct then Genevan psychology is a major contribution to the study of socialization; if the latter then Genevan psychology is an essential preparation for the study of socialization. Either way it seemed to me a good thing to include Piaget's work in this *Social Psychology*, and Chapter 5 is devoted to it.

The subject of morality and values, with which Chapter 8 is concerned, is one that can be discussed in the round. The dimension of affect or feeling has been treated by Freud and by students of escape and avoidance conditioning; the dimension of moral conduct was studied in the Character Education Inquiry in the late 1920's and has been treated theoretically as a problem of reinforcement learning and learning by imitation; the dimension of moral knowledge and judgment was investigated by Piaget some years ago and is being investigated by Lawrence Kohlberg today. In the domain of morality we are able to have a reasonably adequate conception of what socialization must mean.

The topic of socialization is discussed at length in the next four chapters but it arises also in other chapters, especially the two that follow this section. The Achievement Motive (Chapter 9) and the Authoritarian ideology (Chapter 10) are both aspects of personality that are presumed to be created in childhood by particular kinds of family situation. However in Chapters 9 and 10 our focus is on the adult personality rather than on its creation.

CHAPTER 5

The Development of Intelligence

After Freud, it is Jean Piaget, I think, who has made the greatest contribution to modern psychology. Since 1921 Piaget has been Director of Studies of the *Institut Jean-Jacques Rousseau* in Geneva. The Institute is a research organization affiliated with the University of Geneva. The Institute has arrangements with the schools and preschools of Geneva which make it wonderfully easy to do experimental work with children. Piaget has written approximately 25 books and 160 articles, and these numbers will be out of date by the time you read this chapter. His works concern the development in the child of concepts of causality, chance, quantity, classes, number, measurement; the development, in short, of intelligence.

The entire research program has been governed by a single important goal—to discover the successive stages in the development of intelligence. In his attempts to characterize these stages, Piaget has made sophisticated use of logic and mathematics. The research results from which the stages were inferred have been substantially validated in Great Britain, Scandinavia, Canada, and elsewhere. The work in Geneva over the past forty years is a monumental achievement.

However, American graduate students in psychology in the forties and fifties commonly read only one of Piaget's books and none of his research papers. The book they read was *The Language and Thought of the Child*, which was first published in 1924. It left an impression of unstandardized "clinical" method, highly redundant exposition, and clumsy conceptualization. Furthermore, American investigators were said to have repeated the study and obtained very different results. Few students felt any obligation, let alone temptation, to read further in Piaget.

More important than the unattractive features of *The Language and Thought of the Child* was a difficulty American psychologists had with understanding what Piaget was trying to do. Psychology, we believed, should aim at discovering the variables that control behavior. The central problem was learning—the conditions that facilitate it and slow it down. Piaget seemed to be concerned with description rather than control. The stages he described changed with age, but he had nothing to say about the effect of variables other than age, variables one could manipulate, such as practice and incentive. Even in the fall of 1961 when Piaget's associate, Professor Bärbel Inhelder, lectured in America polite audiences would struggle to think up an appropriate question and hit finally upon: "How could one speed up the child's progress through the stages of intellectual development?" Piaget must have some reason for working out all these stages; surely this was it.

This chapter describes the aims of Genevan research and relates them to the aims of other kinds of psychological research. It also reviews the general conclusions of that research, the description of intelligence in terms of four chronologically successive models: 1) sensory-motor intelligence; 2) preoperational intelligence; 3) concretely operational intelligence; 4) formally operational intelligence. Finally it treats of the relation between Piaget's work and social psychology. Let us begin, however, by becoming acquainted with a representative problem (Piaget, 1941; Piaget and Inhelder, 1941) of the Genevan research.

A Representative Investigation

A five-year-old boy is seated at a table and before him are a pitcher of milk and some glass tumblers. The boy is given two tumblers of identical size; one of the tumblers (T_1) is filled almost to the top with milk. The task is to fill the other tumbler (T_2) to exactly the same height. The experimenter pours milk into the second tumbler (T_2) until there is nearly as much milk in T_2 as in T_1. Now the small boy lines up the tumblers side-by-side and, seeing some discrepancy, asks that a little more be poured into T_2—and a little more—"Wait . . . they are almost even."

The boy is a precisionist and the experimenter must use a medicine dropper to add and subtract tiny quantities of milk until the boy is satisfied and says: "They are just the same."

The experimenter now produces a third glass tumbler (T_3) much taller than T_1 and T_2 but also much narrower. He pours the contents of T_2 into T_3, taking care to empty out every drop. "Now," he asks, "how much milk is there in this glass" (pointing at T_3)? "Is there the same amount as in this glass" (pointing at T_1) "or is there less or is there more?" "There is more," replies the boy. In fact, of course, T_3 contains the same quantity of milk as does T_1 since it has received the full contents of T_2 and T_2 was set exactly equal to T_1.

What makes him think that there is more milk in T_3 than in T_1? "Well," he says, "because the milk is higher in this one," and he points to the top of the column of fluid in T_3 which is indeed higher than the column in T_1. But does he actually think that the higher column means more milk?

Perhaps he simply does not properly understand the words in the experimenter's original question. The experimenter asked about *amounts;* are they the *same*, or is this one *more* or is it *less?* The italicized words are the critical words. A five-year-old might think that they refer to the heights of the columns of fluid without regard to the widths of those columns. His deficiency may be a deficiency in the understanding of certain words rather than a more general confusion about the notion of quantity.

The experimenter could try asking his question in another way. For example: "If I pour the milk in this glass" (T_3) "back into this one" (T_2) "how high up will it come on the glass?" When this is done the boy points to a level above its prior level in T_2 and so above the level of the milk in T_1. It does really seem as if he thinks the quantity of milk has increased in the process of being poured into T_3. He does not seem to realize that quantity is *conserved*, that it remains the same during a process of pouring back and forth provided only that there is no spilling or residue.

How general is the result? Would this boy always say that there is more milk in T_3 and would other five-year-olds say the same? There is one other answer that is common. Another child or even the same boy on another occasion might say that there was *less* milk in T_3. This answer like the other is incorrect. If the experimenter follows it up by asking: "What makes you think that?" the boy will point to the width of the column of fluid and say: "It is not as big here."

For the child with preoperational intelligence, the child younger than six or seven years, the quantity will be judged to be either *more* or *less* but not the *same*. The two incorrect answers resemble one another in that each one follows from attention to a single dimension of the column of fluid. A correct answer must take simultaneous account of the height and width of the column. We can characterize the solutions of the younger children (who are in the period of preoperational intelligence) as treatments of a two-dimensional problem as if it were one-dimensional. Which of the two incorrect answers the child gives may simply depend on the chance *centering* (Piaget's French term is *centration*) of his attention. To respond correctly the child must be able to *decenter* his attention; to shift from one dimension to another.

How general is the one-dimensional solution for other sorts of quantity problem? Using fluids, one can replace the tall, thin T_3 with a collection of very small containers. Pouring milk from T_2 into these, the experimenter might fill three of them to the top. Is there more fluid in the three little jars or in the first glass? If a child notices the height of the column in a single jar he may say there is less. But if he notices that the jars are more numerous he may say there is more.

Quantity can be studied with substances other than fluids, for instance with clay or plasticine, and with transformations other than pouring. The subject judges two round balls of clay to be of identical size. The experimenter then takes one between his palms and rolls it out to make a long, thin sausage. Now how does the quantity of clay in the sausage compare with the quantity in the first round ball? Some children, centering on the length of the sausage, say there is more; some, centering on its width, say there is less.

From quantity we can move to number and discover the preoperational child making errors of the same kind. The experimenter sets before the subject half-a-dozen egg cups arranged in a row with the same small spatial interval separating each adjacent pair. Directly opposite each cup he places an egg and so they stand in one-to-one correspondence, six eggs and six cups. Now the experimenter may take the cups and considerably increase the interval between pairs—stretching out the set into a much longer line. Are there as many cups as eggs? More? Fewer?

Some preoperational children, centering on the length of the line, say that there are more cups. They would be correct if the density of the cups were the same as the density of the eggs, but it is not and they are wrong. Some preoperational children center on the density of the cups and notice that they are less tightly packed than are the eggs. These children say that there are fewer cups. In fact, of course, the number is the same; six in both cases. For the conservation of number, as for the conservation of quantity, it is necessary to take simultaneous account of two dimensions. It sometimes happens that a preoperational child is able to count the cups and eggs and to say that there are six and yet when he looks at the short, tight line of eggs and the long, open line of cups he judges them to be unequal. The ability to apply number-names to numerable things does not guarantee a full understanding of the concept of number.

Now, for contrast, we turn to an older child, say a child of eight years, who is in the period of concretely operational intelligence. He is given the original problem involving milk and tumblers. After pouring, the experimenter asks the familiar question: "Is there the same amount or more or less?" The boy promptly says, "The same," and there is an implicit "naturally" in his intonation. If we continue with other containers of varying size he will become impatient and say, "It's the same, it's always the same."

It is important to watch the older boy's performance carefully. There is a crucial difference between his reaction to each problem and the reaction of the younger boy. The younger boy when he is asked the critical question intently examines the materials before him. The older boy scarcely looks at them. For him it does not seem to be a problem in perceptual judgment. The correct answer appears to have a necessity in it that removes it from the sphere of matters requiring empirical verification.

The necessity in the answer derives from the fact that the subject has witnessed the transformation—the pouring, the molding of the clay, the shifting of eggcups. He knows that such transformations are "reversible." The milk in T_3 could be poured back into T_2 and if this were done the original level would be restored. The clay sausage could be balled up again and the ball would match the original. The eggcups having been moved apart can be moved back together again. For the transformation he has witnessed, the subject knows that there exists a transformation that will exactly restore the original state. Because the original state can be restored, because we can return to our starting point, we believe that something is conserved or preserved through the transformations imposed. Quantity is preserved across pourings and shapings; number across shiftings.

Think what the conservation problems would be like if the subject did not witness the pouring and shaping and shifting. We are shown a round ball of clay and a long sausage of clay and asked whether or not the amounts of clay are the same. We have not seen the sausage in its original form (exactly matching the ball) and we have not seen that it was rolled out without any bits of clay being pinched off. In these circumstances the conservation question would be a hard one. We should want to examine the clay closely and try to judge whether the length of the sausage compensated for its thinness. It would have become a problem in perceptual judgment and we should find ourselves behaving like the preoperational child.

For the adult or the operational child the conservation problems are only problems of perception when the original state and the transformation have not been seen. For the younger preoperational child the conservation problems are perceptual problems even when the transformations have been seen. The very young child centers on a single dimension and answers questions with reference to the way that dimension looks. An older child, who has made some progress toward conservation, will study both dimensions and try to judge whether the loss in one is compensated by the gain in the other. It is still a perceptual problem for him, he still needs to look, but he begins to realize that there are two dimensions involved. When both dimensions change and there is no means of quantitative measurement, perception cannot provide a certain answer to the conservation problems and so the older preoperational child may vacillate in his judgments. The child who has attained operational intelligence *knows* that quantity and number are conserved across the transformations he has seen. It is not a perceptual problem, not something he needs to check by looking. Intelligence corrects and sets aside the judgments that perception alone might dictate.

The conservation of quantity problems manifest the characteristic qualities of Genevan research. These will now be summarized and compared with closely related research approaches.

The Genevan Program

A Genevan research begins with some aspect of common adult knowledge or some sensory-motor performance of which adults are capable. The studies of the 1920's, work reported in such books as *The Child's Conception of the World* (1926), *The Child's Conception of Physical Causality* (1927), and *Judgment and Reasoning in the Child* (1928), begin with such conceptions as nationality, life, dreams, and causality. The method of inquiry is to ask questions; the data are the child's replies.

In the thirties there were studies of infancy, especially the books *The Construction of Reality in the Child* (1937) and *The Origins of Intelligence in Children* (1936). The starting point for these researches is not verbalized knowledge but a set of performances such as grasping an object and looking for an object and recognizing an object. The method of inquiry could not involve asking questions or giving complex directions. It was chiefly naturalistic observation of infant behavior with experimental interventions altering the situation to see what the infant would do. These were often cleverly contrived to settle some question of interpretation. Piaget's chief subjects for these studies were his own three children.

The studies of the forties and fifties (for example: Piaget, 1941; Piaget and Inhelder, 1948; Inhelder and Piaget, 1955) typically begin with systematic adult knowledge, sets of concepts defined in terms of one another and belonging to some branch of formal learning. We have the child's conceptions of number, measurement, geometry, velocity, the law of floating bodies, chance, logical classes, and the like. The method of inquiry is to ask questions and also, usually, to provide materials for manipulation; the data include the child's manipulations as well as his talk.

The research program, in every case, has been to work out the stages by which children commonly attain the adult competence. Ingenuity is required in order to find ways of putting the question to children of various ages. However, because the program is, in general terms, always the same there must be a large amount of positive transfer-of-training from the design of one Genevan research to the design of another Genevan research. This transfer may have helped to make possible the steady, strong flow of results over a period of forty years.

The adult knowledge or performance that is the starting point of Genevan research belongs to cognitive culture in that it is shared among mature members of the society. What we do not know, in many cases, is whether the adult competences are also cultural in that they are socially transmitted and variable from one society to another. It is certain that some Genevan research does include knowledge that is variable from one society to another—conceptions of chance, of physical laws, of morality —and it is likely that social transmission is important for this knowledge. However, as the knowledge becomes more clearly cultural in these respects it is less clearly cultural in the sense of being shared by all mature members of a society. Not every adult in western civilization is as clear about chance and probability and floating bodies as Piaget's Swiss adolescents seem to be. Other aspects of intelligence studied in Geneva—for example, the recognition of objects—are not cultural in any sense. They develop out of the child's commerce with the physical world and do not rely on social transmission; they are the same everywhere. The question is, in what degree Piaget's work is the study of human development and, in what degree it is the study of cognitive enculturation in the civilized world. It is a question to which we will return.

In his youth Piaget worked, for a time, in the laboratory of Binet and Simon in Paris, and Genevan research has a clear relation to the work of the French inventors of the IQ. Intelligence tests take their content from common adult knowledge—the meanings of words, the ability to tell time, and the like. Piaget has, in his own way, studied certain Binet-Simon problems. For example: "I have three brothers—Paul, Ernest, and myself. What is wrong with this statement?" But what Piaget does with such material is quite different from what Binet and Simon did.

In the Paris laboratory Piaget's assignment was to develop age norms for certain reasoning problems, but the norms themselves did not interest him. He was interested in the nature of the incorrect solutions that preceded the correct solutions. For intelligence testers the repertoire of adult knowledge is a vast learning problem set all children in a society. By working out the average age at which items in this repertoire are attained they can determine the comparative speed with which each individual child is getting through the course. A fast mover is presumably more intelligent than a slow mover. Piaget has not been concerned with relative speeds, but rather with the kinds of imperfect understanding that regularly precede mature understanding.

The difference between Genevan research on cognitive development and much American research is of another kind. American psychologists have concentrated on the dynamics of development, the laws of transition from one level to another (Kessen, 1962). In order to discover such laws it is necessary to control the learner's past experience. Consequently, American experimental work with children (as contrasted with intelligence testing which is a practical undertaking) does not take its problems from common adult knowledge. You cannot discover the laws of learning by asking children what they understand dreams to be or what they mean by "telling a lie." This is knowledge they acquire outside of the laboratory and one cannot tell how their individual opportunities to learn may have varied.

In American laboratories the problem presented to the children is usually new to them; they cannot have learned it on the outside. The task may be to form a novel concept or to memorize a list of nonsense syllables or to acquire a conditioned response. The experimenter can manipulate such variables as amount of practice, the spacing of trials, and the interval between response and reinforcement. The differential effects of his manipulations will teach him what variables control performance. This is the way to go about discovering laws of behavior change and the discovery of such laws is certainly a central psychological problem.

There is, however, a danger in the American research strategy. Wanting to use problems new to the child the experimenter is likely to take those that are closest to hand: classical problems of the psychological laboratory such as discrimination learning, serial learning, conditioning, delayed response, and the like. Some of these procedures are adapted from methods used with animals. They are an insufficient set because they are not *representative* of the intellective operations a child can perform. The acquisition of such systematic knowledge as language, number, and physical concepts may involve intellectual learning processes that are not required for the classical laboratory problems; the child's most characteristic processes may be missed.

Beginning with some aspect of adult intelligence Piaget determines its state in children of various ages. Typically the child's intelligence turns out to be quite different from the adult's; he does not understand things as we do. There is often considerable surprise in these discoveries. Consider the conservation of a continuous quantity like milk. This is an aspect of understanding to which we have never really attended. It is so obvious, so "necessary," that pouring a liquid back and forth should leave its quantity unaltered that we had not realized there was any variation among human beings in their grasp of this matter. In ordinary circumstances the child's incomprehension is not exposed. Glass tumblers are often drawn from a same-size set and, in these circumstances, the height of the column of liquid is a sure cue to the quantity of liquid. Once in a while a child is given a choice of quantities of something he likes in containers of various sizes and he may choose the wrong one. We smile and say, "He picked it because it looks like more," but we are not seriously startled because he has not seen the pourings that enable intelligence to correct perception. The Piaget experiment is so devised as to reveal, for the first time, the child's incomprehension. One of the accomplishments of the Genevan work is to instruct adults in the unexpectedly great differences between our intellectual world and that of the child.

The Genevans might have found in their studies that, while all children of a certain age have imperfect understanding of various intellectual matters, the nature of the imperfections is different from one child to another. Or, even if the imperfections were the same, their order might have been different from one child to another. The profoundly important fact is that the imperfections are alike across children and the order in which the stages succeed one another is constant. On many problems there is a standard progression for children in Geneva, at least, very probably for the civilized world, and perhaps beyond.

For each problem a progression is established, a progression described as a sequence of stages. Since each progression is correlated with age, one begins to accumulate facts concerning the character of intelligence at each age level. Children of five years will answer in a certain way questions about quantities of milk and will answer in a certain way questions about quantities of clay and will answer in a certain way questions about numbers of eggs and eggcups.[1] The accumulating facts invite the theorist to

1. Genevan research has been cross-sectional rather than longitudinal and it has not been the Genevan practice to administer a large number of problems to children at a given age level. Consequently the characterization of intelligence at different age levels has not been based on transformations in the performances of the same children over time and the characterization of intelligence at any given age level has not been based on covariation across problems in the performances of the same children. However, more recent longitudinal and correlational studies (Inhelder, 1953) seem to have confirmed the picture that was derived from cross-sectional work.

find their common properties and so to attempt a general abstract characterization of intelligence at each level. Children of five years, on many kinds of problems, seem to be unable to deal simultaneously with two dimensions and to be unaware of the fact that certain kinds of physical operations can be reversed. The lineaments of preoperational intelligence begin to emerge.

Piaget has, from the first, pressed toward a general characterization of the development of intelligence. His books are strewn with concepts he tried out—"egocentric," "animistic," "intuitive," "realistic," etc. These terms provide a description of the development of intelligence which is much more general than the description of progressions with individual problems. He has, however, provided a still more general description.

Intellectual development is now understood in Geneva to be a progression through either three or four major periods (*period* is the more general term and *stage* the less general). The four periods are: Sensory motor intelligence (0–18 months); Preoperational intelligence (18 months–7 years); Concretely operational intelligence (7–11 years); Formally operational intelligence (11 onward). In some treatments the second and third periods are not separated but treated as earlier and later stages of one long period (Inhelder, 1962). For concretely operational intelligence and formally operational intelligence Piaget has provided explicit models. He has in each case set down the logical and mathematical operations to which the child's thought in that period approximates. The two earlier periods are in part characterized by the absence of the later operations and in part by an assortment of positive attributes.

While Piaget sets down usual ages for each period he does not contend that these are absolutely fixed. He simply holds that the periods are ordered, that they will in all cases succeed one another as described. The claim is the same for the stages in each particular progression. Presumably for more intelligent children, the age of attainment of each stage is earlier than for the less intelligent. All children will go through the stages in the same order but the rate of movement will vary from child to child.

The child who has entered the stage of formal operations has not cast off the attainments of earlier periods. He can still do the things that can be done with sensory-motor intelligence; for example, grasping a new object, exploring its possibilities, recognizing it when it reappears. He has, on the other hand, cast off the preoperational ways of thinking about quantity and number, since the displacement of these by the conservations is a part of what it means to attain to operational thinking. In large part, however, the child retains earlier forms of intelligence, integrating them with more advanced forms. The period a child is said to be in is defined by the most advanced performances of which he is capable. The

Genevan position implies really that stages and periods constitute cumulative scales; whoever can perform a more advanced operation ought to be able to perform all less advanced operations.

The underlying Piagetian conception is that there are several qualitatively distinct kinds of mind which are developmentally prior to the mature mind. In terms of a modern metaphor, human intelligence is not one sort of computer but four different models ordered in time. We must next ask what it is that causes one model to be transformed into another?

For some of the Piaget problems it would seem as if the information necessary to a correct solution were very generally available. The conservation of liquid quantity is one such. There would seem to be ample opportunity to pour milk or water from one container to a container of different size and back again to the first and to observe that nothing has been lost or gained in the process. It would seem still more certain that any child who has played with clay has had an opportunity to learn that alterations of shape are reversible. Cups and saucers are in one-to-one correspondence in the ordinary kitchen cupboard and this correspondence can, like the correspondence of eggs and eggcups, be restored after displacements. Why, then, does not a five-year-old child understand all these things? Can it be from insufficient or inadequate experience? Perhaps it is chiefly a matter of biological maturation. Or it may be a readiness that depends upon a very large amount of experience with liquids, with malleable substances, and with discrete objects.

One way to look into the determinants of intellectual change is to attempt, by training, to advance a child from one stage or period into another. This is an undertaking that has never attracted Piaget, but in recent years other investigators have tried. The techniques of training that have been used seem well-conceived for their purpose. Wohlwill and Lowe (1962) made an effort to teach kindergarten children that merely rearranging a set of objects does not alter the numerical value of the set —that number is conserved. They had one group count a set of objects before and after rearrangement and this was done many times. Of course the number was always the same. Smedslund, of the University of Oslo, has tried (1961) to teach children between five and seven years of age that the weight of a lump of plasticine is not altered by changing its shape. This lesson, the conservation of weight, is closely related to the conservation of global quantity. Smedslund gave his subjects thirty-two training trials involving two identical balls of plasticine. The shape of one would be altered and the child would predict whether the two would still have the same weight. He then tested his prediction by weighing the balls on a scale balance and, of course, they were always the same.

There are quite a few studies of this kind, dealing with a variety of Piaget problems and generally employing training procedures that ought to work. The outcomes are not perfectly uniform but the following conclusions are fair (Wallach, 1963). The training has been generally much less effective than we would have expected it to be and in some cases it was totally ineffective. Training has been least effective where the child was much younger than the age at which the knowledge ordinarily develops. With children whose age is near that at which the knowledge normally develops, well-planned training can somewhat hasten the process. However, there are indications that the knowledge acquired by intensive training is not quite the same as knowledge acquired in the normal way whatever that way may be. For example, children given training on the conservation of liquids will sometimes learn to give conservation answers where the several containers are not greatly unlike one another. However, if such a child then sees a glass of water poured into a great tin washtub, such that the bottom of the tub is not even covered, he will often revert to non-conservation and say that there must be less water in the tub.

Smedslund has done a very nice experiment (1961) that uncovered a difference between children who acquired the conservation of quantity by intensive training and children of the same age who gave conservation answers without special training. Both groups were consistently giving correct conservation answers in the problems involving two equal balls of plasticine when the experimenter changed his procedure in a way designed to extinguish the idea of conservation. In the process of altering the shape of one of the balls of plasticine he would surreptitiously pinch off a bit of the substance and so, when the child weighed the two, they were not equal. The experimenter did this a number of times. The children who had acquired the conservation of weight by special training showed no great surprise at the outcomes and reverted to non-conservation answers. The children who had acquired conservation in the usual way refused to relinquish their belief in it. They argued that a piece of the plasticine must be missing—perhaps it had fallen on the floor. In fact they made assumptions which would reconcile the outcomes with the conservation of weight. No mere empirical outcome could upset this necessary relation. And of course their assumptions were, in principle, correct. The reaction of these children to data disconfirming the conservation of weight is like the reaction of psychologists to data confirming extra-sensory perception; most of us say: "There must have been a leak [sensory] somewhere."

Since many of the conceptions studied by Piaget are resistant to change by training there must be a substantial readiness factor involved. Its nature is unknown. For some problems, at least, biological maturation may be involved. Probably readiness is, in part, a matter of massive quantities of experience with a full range of the materials to which the conception applies; for example, liquids in containers of greatly varied shapes and malleable substances transformed into a great variety of shapes.

Now we will examine some of these wonderful problems. Only a sampling can be treated but we may as well organize them in such a way as to convey an idea of the nature of the four great periods of development, the four kinds of intelligence. It will be possible to go beyond the problems to a loose characterization of the general attributes of the four kinds of intelligence.[2] We will not describe Piaget's models from logic and mathematics because these require a very extended exposition which is not justified for our purposes.[3] We will consider the periods in developmental order.

Sensory-Motor Intelligence

Piaget believes that for approximately the first eighteen months of life the child perceives and acts, but does not have internal representations of the world. The sensory-motor period ends with the development of the most primitive form of central representation, which is *imagery*. The infant, being unable to speak, very distractible, deficient in motor skills, and largely unresponsive to directions cannot be set most kinds of experimental task. However, an acute observer, and Piaget is certainly that, can learn a lot about infant intelligence by simply watching infant behavior and can sometimes refine conclusions by altering circumstances and taking note of the consequences. What Piaget has seen of the first two years persuades him that there are important intellectual developments in this period. One of these, the only one we shall discuss, is the conception of a permanent or identical object.

ADULT UNDERSTANDING OF THE IDENTITY OF AN OBJECT

We must first make explicit what it is that adults understand by any single object.[4] Let the object be a particular ashtray—one that usually rests on the coffee table in the living-room, one we could recognize

2. These general characterizations do not stay close to Piaget's own discussions. They are in the first place very incomplete, hardly more than suggestive of the four periods of intelligence. They are in the second place shaped by my own interests and by the limitations of my understanding. They are an assimilation, not a reproduction.

3. Flavell in his book *The Developmental Psychology of Jean Piaget* (1963) offers a good introduction to the models and a comprehensive lucid discussion of all of Piaget's work. Wallach (1963) provides a good review of the empirical work, abstracted from its theoretical context, and Inhelder (1962) has made a brief, recent, and authoritative statement of the Genevan position.

4. This section is particularly remote from Piaget's own discussions.

anywhere. Suppose that we were moving about the room while the ash-tray remained stationary. As you may remember from your study of the perceptual constancies in general psychology,[5] the proximal stimulation delivered to the eye by such an object changes with its distance from the eye, with the angle of orientation to the eye, and with the play of light on the object. One thing we all understand about the ashtray is that it has an identity which is preserved through these transformations of the proximal (or retinal) image.

The Perceptual Constancies. In between paragraphs I am actually peering at a certain bronze ashtray on my coffee table. By setting myself to do it I can notice how the image changes as I move about. The size of the image is, of course, inversely proportional to the distance of the object from the eye. But looking at it in our familiar everyday fashion it does not appear to diminish and enlarge as we move away from it and toward it again. It appears to have a constant size and that is the phenomenon of size constancy which has been intensively studied in experimental psychology.

In a typical sort of size-constancy experiment the subject looks at an unfamiliar white card that stands on a table directly in front of him and perhaps about five feet away. This card, the standard stimulus object, is to be compared with a half-dozen or so other white cards which stand on a table ten feet away. One of the comparison cards is exactly the same size as the standard card; the other comparison cards are either larger or smaller than the standard. The subject is asked to identify the comparison card that objectively matches the standard. The cards have black numerals below them and the subject gives his response by calling out a numeral.

Suppose the standard card is two inches square. A comparison card of the same objective size but at twice the distance creates a retinal image that is only a fraction of the size of the retinal image created by the standard card. The comparison card at ten feet that produces a retinal image of the same size as does the standard card at five feet would be four inches square. If the subject calls out the number of the comparison card that is objectively equal to the standard then he manifests perfect constancy. If he calls out the number of the comparison card that is four inches square, twice the size of the standard, then he manifests zero constancy and appears to be matching retinal images rather than real sizes.

In the usual experiment the standard card is not the same card as any in the comparison series but simply a match in size for one of them. Suppose we change the experiment a little. To begin with, let there be a

5. Gibson's *The Visual World* (1950) gives an excellent treatment and Koffka's profound discussion in *Principles of Gestalt Psychology* (1935) is a classic.

comparison series of cards at the same distance from the subject as is the standard card, five feet, and let the subject select a match for the standard in these circumstances. This he can very easily do since the objectively equal cards will, when they are at the same distance from the subject, create retinal images of the same size. Now, leaving the standard at the five-foot distance let us remove the comparison cards to a ten-foot distance, shuffle their order, and ask the subject to pick out the one he had previously called equal to the standard. In this version of the size-constancy experiment the subject must show that he can tell which of a set of images at a greater distance could belong to the same object as an earlier image at a lesser distance. He must make a judgment of objective identity and not simply a judgment of objective size equivalence. For adults, objective equivalence of size is one of the characteristics of identity and they will respond accordingly. Back now to the ashtray.

Looked at from directly overhead the perimeter of my ashtray is a perfect circle. Lowering my eye somewhat and sighting along the top of the ashtray, the perimeter becomes an ellipse. As the eye continues to move lower the ellipse narrows until its farther edge disappears behind the nearer and the rim is only a straight line. These are transformations of the image accomplished by changes in my angle of view. It does not seem to me, of course, that the ashtray is, like some rubbery amoeba, altering its shape. That would be my impression if the changes in the image were not accompanied by just the right changes of head position. As it is, I think of the shape of the ashtray as constant. This is the perceptual constancy of shape. There is a comparable phenomenon—the constancy of color—which preserves the color of the ashtray through changes in the image produced by altering the quality of light falling on its surface.

The adult conception of an identical object involves, in the first place, the perceptual constancies. Our earlier discussion of the conservations of quantity and number prepares us to appreciate an aspect of the constancies that is not ordinarily brought forward in textbook treatments. For the movement away from the ashtray that reduces its image size there exists a reverse operation—moving toward the object—which will restore all the original sizes in reverse order. For the lowering of the eye that changes a circle into an ellipse there is a reverse operation—raising the eye—which will bring back the circle. Size and shape and color can be thought of as *really* constant through transformations of image because there exist reverse transformations.

If the size-constancy experiment is modified as we modified it above, to require the subject to identify the comparison object that could be the same object as one he has just seen closer up, then the constancy experiment comes to resemble very closely the conservation experiment. In both cases two things (or quantities), A and B, are set equal in equivalent circumstances (either distance or container size). Then one (B) is caused to assume a different appearance (smaller image or taller column of fluid) in new and different circumstances. The subject has in each case the problem of recognizing that the two appearances in different circumstances belong to the same reality, that there is an invariance behind the apparent variation. In both cases the ultimate reason for believing that there is an invariance is the fact that the change of appearance can be reversed. The original apparent match between A and B can be recovered by bringing the comparison card in closer once again or by pouring the milk back into its original container. The difference between the conservation of quantity experiment and the size-constancy experiment, as we have imagined it, is that the child witnesses the pouring of the liquids but we did not let our subject keep track of the movement of the cards. If we were to do so the judgment would be very easy indeed; children of five years certainly would not fail such a problem as they do fail the conservation problems. This may be because the transformations involved in the constancies are learned much earlier than those involved in the conservations.

Until this point the ashtray has held its position on the table. It is of course possible for the viewer to hold his position and ask another person to move the ashtray about. All the transformations of the image that can be produced by moving the viewer can also be produced by moving the object. These operations are also reversible. The transformations of the image so far considered are ordered in a completely general way. They are predictable from the properties of the ashtray as a reflecting surface in conjunction with the laws of optics. There is another sort of transformation that is not predictable in this way—the other side of the ashtray.

Other Aspects of Identity. From the uppermost, the cigarette-receiving, surface, and from optics, one cannot predict the nature of the surface that rests on the table. For the present instance it turns out to be brownish-red in hue and to have the name of the manufacturer scratched in the center. The perceptual constancies, because they follow completely general laws, would not have to be entirely learned; an organism could be "wired" from birth to perceive in accordance with constancy. However the various surfaces of objects are not lawful in the same way; there is nothing in optics or in the ashtray's upper surface that constrains the ashtray to have a certain name scratched on its nether surface. We have long known how large the moon will look when we get there but the surface appearance of the other side of the moon cannot be foretold from this side.

Because the various surfaces of an object are often not related to one another in any regular way our ability to anticipate unexposed surfaces from the surface exposed cannot be innate. We must learn about an object by examining it on all sides. As an adult familiar with a particular ashtray, if I should see it lying bottom side up, I should know that it was not a new thing but the same old ashtray—turned over. This sense of an identity preserved across changes of appearance depends, as do the constancies, on knowledge of certain reversible operations. The turning-over that has exposed the nether surface can be reversed to restore the upper surface.

The invariance we think of as an object is, like the invariance of number or quantity, a set of "permanent possibilities of perception" linked to one another by reversible operations. Think what would have to happen to cause us to judge that the ashtray had changed its state, its nature, rather than its position. If, as we look, it becomes a puddle on the table then it has melted down and is no longer an ashtray since a puddle-appearance is not one of the possibilities of perception that go to make up an ashtray. Suppose that, while we steadily regard it from above, it transforms into an ellipse. Then it cannot be an ordinary inanimate ashtray. The appearance it has assumed is possible for an ashtray but it is not possible given a fixed line of regard from above.

There is still more to our conception of an object. We think of the object as continuing to exist when it is out of sight. If one drops a handkerchief over an object it is not thereby conjured out of existence. Our confidence that it endures is founded, once again, on the existence of a reverse operation. The handkerchief can be lifted and the earlier perception restored. If, when the handkerchief is lifted, the object is not there, which is sometimes the case if the lifter is a magician, we set it down to sleight-of-hand. It has to be an illusion. We are at least as confident of this judgment as were Smedslund's child subjects who knew some plasticine must have been dropped or pinched off since the lump had lost weight.

We think of an object as continuous in time and space. If we know that the ashtray was left in the kitchen sink overnight and that no one has moved it, then we know that it must be in the sink in the morning. While the coffee table is the usual place for the ashtray we would not expect to find the ashtray in that place given the present circumstances. Having been left in the kitchen, the ashtray could only now be on the coffee table if it had in the intervening time occupied spatial positions that lie between the kitchen and the coffee table. Which is to say that it would have to have been carried there during the night.

Suppose a friend arrived carrying an ashtray just like our own but not the same ashtray. If we only saw him and his ashtray, and not our own, we might think he had picked ours up. If, however, we could look one way and see our own and then the other way and see him carrying one of the same kind, we would know there were two. How would we know it? Both visible images—the tray on the table to the left and the tray in a friend's hand on the right—belong to the possible appearances of a single tray. One real tray could produce both images. But not without passing through intervening space and time. There are two trays because the one on my left could not get over to the right in the time allowed and without my detecting its movement. The two appearances now present are linked by an operation—simply sweeping my gaze from left to right— which cannot link appearances that belong to one ashtray.

An object for adults is something that is conserved through changes of position and illumination, something that exists independently of our ex- perience of it, something that has continuity in space-time. What evidence is there that infants do not have this conception?

DEVELOPMENT OF THE OBJECT CONCEPT

The perceptual constancies of size, shape, and color could be innate since the physical conditions for constancy are perfectly lawful. Gestalt psychologists have long taken the stand that the constancies are a feature of the visual world from the very start of life. Helmholtz, before the ad- vent of Gestalt theory, and Piaget, and Brunswik (1956) and others since, have held that the constancies are a result of learning, that the retinal image is "corrected" by experience. The sad fact is that we are not yet sure who is right or in what degree each is right.

On the one hand it has been demonstrated many times that animals, even when they are quite young, have good size constancy (Locke, 1938). In addition, a study by Cruikshank (1941), though not completely con- vincing because of its method, suggests that human infants have consider- able constancy by six months. On the other hand, studies by Lambercier (1946), by Piaget and Lambercier (1951 and 1956), and by Brunswik (1956) find that constancy improves with age though the judgments of even the youngest children in these studies are far from those the retinal images would dictate. In addition there is evidence from persons operated on for visual cataracts which argues that the constancies are not innate but learned.

A blind person usually identifies objects by palpating them with his fingertips. Touch receptors cannot be stimulated from a distance but only by contact and so for a blind person a given object always has the same apparent size. He has no experience of an image that grows smaller with increasing distance. When such a person attains vision in later life how does he judge size? There have been investigations of such cases and Von Senden (1932) has reviewed all the published reports from 1690 until 1931.

Newly sighted persons are at first dazzled by a flood of light and troubled by uncontrolled eye movements. Soon, however, they report awareness of color distinctions and of differences in shape. They are not, however, able to identify familiar objects by vision alone. The subject will know that a cube and sphere held before his eyes are different one from the other but until he touches them he will not know the name of either. Several investigators have carried out reasonably well-controlled studies of size constancy. In one, the patient looked at unfamiliar cards all of the same shape but varying in size and in distance from her. She thought the nearest of the cards the largest. It was in fact the smallest but was so near as to cast a larger retinal image than any of the others. Another patient thought the sun must be about the size of his hat and that a candle flame close up was only a little smaller than his arm. For the most part Von Senden's review suggests that the visual constancies are learned.

Eleanor Gibson reviewing the experimental literature on perceptual development (1963) refers to "the confusion of conflicting evidence for development of perceptual constancy" (p. 156). She attributes the confusion to the fact that constancy judgments are highly sensitive to background conditions, to the nature of the judgment or reaction required, and to the attitude assumed by the subject, and these factors have varied greatly from one experiment to another. For the present, in any case, the importance of learning for the perceptual constancies is not settled. It was worthwhile introducing the constancies, nevertheless, because they are the first of the great invariants that figure in the child's conception of the physical world.

Aspects Other than the Constancies. Conservation of the object involves, in addition to the constancies, knowledge of the several surfaces of the object and these must be learned since they do not follow any general laws. Piaget, observing his own children, saw the knowledge developing (1936, 1937). One of his children would immediately reach for the bottle when it was presented nipple foremost. However, when the butt end of the bottle was toward the child and the nipple out of sight he did not at first recognize it. With more experience he learned to recognize it and to turn it around so that the nipple was presented. From butt to nipple and back again makes two visual impressions linked by a reversible operation.

One day Piaget observed his eleven-month-old daughter Jacqueline suspended in her cloth swing looking down through the open area of the leg hole at her own foot. Jacqueline then looked over the side of the swing and down to get this different view of her foot. Then she looked back and forth between the two views five or six times, very much as if she were practicing the reversible operation and noting the outcomes.

Perhaps the most difficult thing to believe about the infant's conception of the object is that he does not realize that it exists independently of himself. Jacqueline would reach out for something she wanted but when

Piaget concealed it with his hand she immediately ceased to reach. Jacqueline was playing with her celluloid duck one day when it slipped beneath the bedsheet and out of sight. Though she saw it go and had been enjoying her play with it she made no effort to recover it. Did she perhaps not realize that the object out of sight continued to exist?

Some favorite plaything is behind a screen and Piaget brings it forth a little at a time. At first it is not recognized but then when more can be seen the infant's smile of recognition occurs. But, and this is the telling observation, the infant does not attempt to remove the screen or take the object from behind the screen. In Piaget's opinion: "Everything occurs as though the child believed that the object is alternately made and unmade. . . . When the child sees a part of the object emerge from the screen and he assumes the existence of the totality of that object, he does not yet consider this totality as being formed 'behind' the screen; he simply admits that it is in the process of being formed at the moment of leaving the screen" (Piaget, 1954, p. 31).

Almost anything one can say about the infant mind sounds improbably complex; we have only adult language to work with. The safest propositions seem to me to be the negative ones. I cannot feel sure that an infant thinks an object is being created as it emerges into view. I feel a little more confident of the statement that he does not realize that the unseen portion of the object exists now behind the screen.

The continuity of the object in space-time also seems not to be understood. Piaget repeatedly hid a toy at one point (A). The children, a bit older now, learned to look at A and find the object there. Piaget then moved the object, the child watching, to point B and hid it there. The child looked, not at point B, but at A where it had previously been found. It was as though the location A were an attribute of the object rather than one of the infinitely numerous spatial loci it might occupy. In fact it could not be at A in the present case. It had disappeared at B and there was no way for it to move unobserved to A. Adults too sometimes operate in this fashion. Suppose that your car keys are always left on a certain table but on this occasion you believe that you have dropped them in someone else's house. You call that someone else to check. Suppose the reply is negative. Will you not look again on the usual table, the table where the keys ought to be? And again, shaking out a book you have already shaken out and looking under an ashtray too small to conceal the keys. Once more, now, very methodically, one section of the table at a time, each in its order. They must be here somewhere.

On another occasion Piaget held an object in his hand and passed both hand and object behind a screen; the hand emerged empty. Since everything was done under observation the object would have to have been behind the screen. Only that region in the object's trajectory was concealed from view and so that is where it would have to have been if it were anywhere. We know it would have to be somewhere because objects do not pass into the void. The child, however, did not look behind the screen. He seemed not to realize that it must still exist and could only be in the one place.

Our conception of the object requires a certain conception of space and time. Piaget holds that these fundamental categories of experience (which Kant held to be *a priori*) are developed in the period of sensory-motor intelligence. The conception of causality also begins then. And there is the development of prehension (grasping), as well as of the behavior Piaget calls primary, secondary, and tertiary circular reflexes. Behavior begins to manifest the directionality that suggests intention. Finally, the period ends with the first signs of imagery.

In Piaget's view the clearest signs that a child has begun to represent to himself absent objects (to have images) are a particular kind of imitation and a particular kind of play (Piaget, 1945). Deferred imitation is imitation of an absent model. Jacqueline one day saw a child throw a great tantrum in an effort to escape from his crib. The next day she tried it herself, producing an easily recognizable imitation of the tantrum she had seen twelve hours earlier. In such a case Piaget feels it necessary to postulate the existence of a central representation that guides the performance.

Representational play is another kind of behavior suggesting imagery. When a child pretends to be washing his hands without any soap or water or plays at eating when there is no food it seems that he must have images. One afternoon on a preschool playground I watched a small boy who was pretending that a big wooden tub was his horse. The play alone suggested imagery but the suggestion became stronger a moment later. A little girl came over to join him in his play and began to climb into the tub. He yelled: "Not there! That's his head." I could almost see it myself.

It is somewhat arbitrary to settle on representational play and deferred imitation as the definitive signs of imagery. As a student once pointed out to me, some sort of central consequence of experience, some sort of retention must be postulated to exist from the very start of life. Conditioning, the development of habits, the improvement of skills all require retention of some sort. The psychology of the sensory-motor child cannot be exhausted by perception and action alone; there must also be central events. Piaget would agree but he would hold that there are not central *representations*.

Any behavior that shows the effect of prior experience might suggest that there were images of the prior experience. We do not feel any strong necessity to infer the existence of images in the case of a developing motor skill. However, the sensory-motor infant can recognize its bottle. Is it not reasonable to suggest that he does so by comparing the present percept with an image of bottles past? What of the infant who, receiving the bottle wrong-end-to, turns it around? Is it not likely that he had an image of the nipple on the other end? Piaget does not assume imagery in these cases but only with behavior that is more powerfully suggestive of central representation—the imitation and play described. This remains a somewhat arbitrary decision and is perhaps dictated in part by Piaget's belief that imagery makes language possible. And language begins to become important at about eighteen months.

Preoperational and Concretely Operational Intelligence

Piaget's chief contributions to the study of language are: 1) the thesis that the speech of young children is "egocentric" or unsocialized; 2) the provision of data on the development of meaning for such important words as *alive, dream, more, less*, etc.; 3) charting the evolution of the child's understanding of logical classes, which has implications for word meaning. Piaget has not studied the development of the formal linguistic systems (phonology and grammar) but others have done so. Piaget's work and the work of others on the development of language are both considered in the chapters that succeed this one. Here we will be concerned with intellectual developments other than language which take place in the preschool and elementary school years (roughly 2–11).

Preoperational and concretely operational intelligence are here treated together because, in general, the same problems have been used for studying both periods. The two periods are essentially two levels of response to a common array of tasks (Inhelder, 1962); the preoperational being less adequate from an adult standpoint and the concretely operational more adequate. The problems considered are not the same as the problems considered for the sensory-motor child. In order to identify the most advanced performances of which the older child is capable he must be set tasks more complex than grasping and object conservation. It should be understood, however, that intelligence on the sensory-motor level also continues to develop during the operational periods; for example, the exploration of new objects and substances. When we come to the period of formal operations we will again come to a new set of tasks—tasks that will test the limits of adolescent intelligence.

The child after the first two years can move about, recognize objects, handle them, and explore their possibilities. Between two and four he learns to name things, to ask questions, issue commands, and assert propositions and to understand all of these when they come from another. In the long period, from two years until eleven or twelve, he is working out a conception of the world. Once he is in good linguistic contact and reasonably responsive to social pressures he can be interrogated about this conception.

Piaget was always keenly aware of the shortcomings of the method of interrogation. He worried about the possibility of suggesting answers to a child. There is a poignant sentence in *The Moral Judgment of the Child:* "Indeed, it is rather disturbing to find that the children one interviews oneself answer more often in conformity with one's own theory than do the children interviewed by other people" (Piaget, 1948, p. 208). He worried about the child's tendency to "romance," to make up answers for the fun of it or to tease the questioner. He worried about the problems of interpreting the child's words. His way of meeting these problems was to ask questions simply and interestingly and in a great many different forms and to use all his own powers of observation to discover the truth.

The interrogation method produced many interesting discoveries about the preoperational child's conception of the world (Piaget, 1926). He is not, in the first place, clear about fundamental categories; he does not distinguish as we do among mental reality, physical reality, and social reality. Dreams seem to him to be a kind of ethereal image in the room, an image received by the eye. For a time he believes that anything that moves is alive and so clouds are alive and the sun and the moon. A plant, he suspects, can feel the prick of a pin. Like the adult cardplayer or dice-thrower he expects to command the inanimate world and have it obey. Moral law and physical law and psychological law are not clearly distinguished. Clouds move to bring us rain, the rules of marbles have always existed and could not possibly be changed. The names of things belong to them as absolutely as their physical attributes. The moon, he suggests, is called *moon* because it gives light. The child's theory about the origins of reality is "artificialistic." Everything was originally made or created, all things are artifacts. The creators were his parents or early men or Gods. They made the sun, the moon, the stars, the sky, water, stones, and trees. When he gives up the belief that names are natural he decides that they were assigned by the early creators. When the rules of marbles are no longer thought to have existed from all eternity they are explained as a kind of agreement among early men. Everything was created by men and also for men.

The model for artificialism seems to be the way in which the child's parents are, in his experience, the source of everything. Everything seems to work in accordance with their wishes. They are omniscient (all-knowing), omnipotent (all-powerful), and omnipresent (everywhere-existing). They generally work for the child's welfare. They can be moved by entreaty and placated with good behavior. They are, as Freud argued in *The Future of an Illusion* (1927), the model for the child's spontaneous conception of God. When he begins to discover the limitations and faults of his parents he feels the need for a higher being who can be to him what his parents have been.

The preoperational child is "egocentric," that is he is captive within his own point of view, unwittingly captive. He is not aware of other points of view and so cannot assume another's point of view. Being unaware of other points of view he is necessarily unaware of his own—as a point of view. It is simply the way things are.

The egocentrism of the child's language shows in his inability to explain something clearly to another person. He does not take proper account of the informational requirements of his listener but appears to assume that the listener understands in advance everything that is to be explained. Egocentrism of language is discussed in the next chapter.

The egocentrism of the preoperational child appears in a large number of Genevan observations. A child walking away from his home is asked to show where the house is and he points in the direction behind himself. Asked the same question on the return journey, he again points behind himself. The house is conceived to occupy a fixed position relative to ego. Or if he is asked: "When you go out for a walk what does the sun do?" the answer is that the sun follows him around. By night the moon will do the same.

Here is one I have tried with my nephews. "Do you know that your daddy is my brother?" When they were younger than seven years they did not understand this at all. Their daddy was their daddy. *Daddy* seemed to them an absolute designation like a proper name. They did not understand that the term is relative to a point of view. The fact that the same man can be a daddy, a brother, a son, and a husband was beyond their comprehension.

The answers to each kind of question make a developmental sequence, often a sequence of six stages. Very often, however, a major change would occur at about six or seven years suggesting the division into two major periods: four to seven and seven to eleven. Across problems there appeared consistencies which suggested that the thought of the younger children could be characterized as "artificialistic," "animistic," "egocentric," "anthropocentric," "realistic," etc. The thought of the older children was more like adult thought in its separation of the mental from the physical and of social norms from mechanical causation; more adult, too, in its grasp of multiple points of view and of relational concepts. There is much to be learned from this early work. Still the descriptive concepts are a little loose and the data do not always clearly conform to them. In addition, there is always the troubling thought that the child may not have understood Piaget's question or that Piaget may not have understood the child's answer.

The later studies in which verbal interrogation is supported by concrete materials which the child manipulates and judges are more convincing. Furthermore, the results of these studies are more newsworthy. We are not greatly surprised by the child's "childish" answers to questions about the nature of life and dreams and the origin of words because we had not expected him to have adult answers to such questions. The later studies, on the other hand, astonish us with evidence that the child's understanding of the nature of the physical world is quite unlike our own.

THE CONSTRUCTION OF PHYSICAL REALITY

Intellectual development might be said to involve the formation of a theory of reality from the shifting data of perception; a theory that proves to be adaptive. Consider the phenomenon of size constancy. A single object at various distances might be judged to be increasing and decreasing in size since that is what happens to the image. However, the images produced by other objects show proportionate changes of size with similar changes of distance. What is more, if you hang on to the object and move it back and forth you find that images of all sizes can be produced by altering the distance. The best theory to cover data of this kind is that the real size of the object is constant but that the apparent size diminishes with distance.

Size constancy is a superior theory to its major alternative—a theory that the real size of an object is proportionate to the size of its image without regard to distance. If our primitive forbears had subscribed to the latter theory they would have believed that the saber-toothed tiger some yards away, which cast an image no larger than that of a mouse close up, was in fact mouse size and therefore harmless. They would have believed that the antelope a little distance away offered them less food than the rabbit nearby. Primitives with such a theory would not have survived to become anybody's forebears.

The theory of size constancy involves interpreting an immediate partial perception in terms of a more complete set of perceptual data and also in terms of actions that may have been performed and might be performed. The theory that Piaget calls the conservation of the object does the same thing on a grander scale. We see two images one after the other and they are quite unlike. What is the underlying reality? If we do not go beyond immediate and partial perception we will say that there are two different objects. Conservation requires that we consider the angles of view for each object and their distances from the eye and these fuller data must be considered in terms of transformations that have occurred and which may be reversible. If the relations are right we will judge that we have seen one object in different places at different times. Conservation of the objects, which the preoperational child has attained, is a theory about an underlying invariance behind the world of shifting appearance, a *geno-type* behind the *phenotypes*. This again is a theory that works very well.

The preoperational child is less advanced than the concretely operational child in the theory of reality that is normal in the civilized world and in some respects probably normal for adults everywhere. The preoperational child, in many situations, still judges in terms of partial and immediate perceptions. This can be seen most clearly with the problems discussed earlier in this chapter that deal with the conservations of liquid quantity, of substances like clay, and of number for discrete objects. The preoperational child judges by the way things look—usually in terms of just one of the relevant dimensions. He does not shift his attention from one relevant characteristic to another. He does not interpret the present appearance of things in terms of the reversible operation which could be performed. These conservations are like the conservation of the object in that they transcend immediate perception to discover a deeper reality. However, the conservation of the object is achieved in the sensory-motor period; the conservations of quantity and number are not attained until the age of concrete operations. There are other conservations which are attained after seven years. The conservation of weight and volume are attained, in that order, considerably later than the conservation of global quantity. There are conservations basic to the representation of space: the conservations of length, distance, order, and area (Piaget, Inhelder, and Szeminska, 1948).

A Problem of Measurement. The tendency to be governed by immediate and partial perception, which appears in the preoperational child's treatment of quantities, number, and space, appears also in his performance on other problems. One of these concerns the child's ability to measure (Piaget, Inhelder, and Szeminska, 1948). He is shown a tower made of blocks which stands on a table and is asked to build a tower of the same height on another table some distance away. The second tower is to be built of blocks smaller than those used in the first and therefore the problem cannot be solved by piling up blocks in one-to-one correspondence with those of the first tower. In addition the second table is lower than the first and therefore the problem cannot be solved by horizontal alignment of the tops of the two towers. What is required, in essence, is some means of laying off the height of Tower A alongside the height of Tower B.

The youngest children try to do the job by visual inspection, but this cannot be satisfactory as a large screen is erected between the two towers which prevents simultaneous viewing. The youngest child will run over and look at the first and then back to look at his own, trying to hold the image in his eye, as it were, but this does not give good results. Success depends on discovery of a third term (C), a *tertium comparationis*, which can be used to measure tower A and then carried back to measure tower B. If A = C and B = C then we know that A must equal C; the relation symbolized by = is a transitive relation. The younger children do not realize this.

Children in the later stages of preoperational intelligence begin to use a third term, a common measure, but their common measures are more restricted than those of the child with operational intelligence. The preoperational child must have a third term that resembles the towers to be compared. In the extreme case the third term must resemble the towers in every way; it must itself be a tower and the child's method is to match A and B by setting them equal to tower C which he moves from one to the other. If he is a little more advanced, the resemblance need not be so close but the third term must have exactly the same height as the towers. It will often be a part of his body (fingertips to shoulder and the like) which he carries back and forth as a measure. Sometimes he will place his two hands at the base and top of tower A and then try to walk the column of air across the room. As adults we occasionally regress to this level and we know it does not work. When the child is a little older he will utilize a stick or piece of paper for a measuring instrument—provided it is exactly the same height as tower A.

What happens if there is no stick or paper or body part that matches the height of tower A? What happens if the child is given a longer stick or a shorter one and asked if it can help? The preoperational child will dismiss it as useless or else use it and draw incorrect conclusions. The concretely operational child measures off the height of tower A on the longer stick, holds or marks the place, and measures off the same height with tower B. Smaller measuring instruments are more difficult to use but eventually children realize that a shorter length can be measured off repeatedly on A and then the same number of times on B; this is the principle of the yardstick and other standard measuring instruments. For the preoperational child, equality of height is only transitive when the equality is simple: A must equal C exactly and B must equal C exactly if he is to realize that A = B. The child older than about seven years recognizes that if A = $\frac{1}{2}$C and B = $\frac{1}{2}$C then A = B; if A = 3C and B = 3C then A = B and so on. When he understands the transitivity of equality in height in this general way then any object whatsoever can become a measuring instrument. Intelligence has made a consequential advance.

The performance of the preoperational child, even when he uses a third term to measure, is too much governed by perception. His third term must resemble the items to be measured; the resemblance is very close when the third term is itself a tower, less close when it is only a stick matching the towers in height. There is no reason in principle why the measuring instrument need resemble the objects to be measured and it is a limiting requirement. The performance of the preoperational child was also often limited by his failure to shift attention from one aspect to another of the object. A preoperational child often marked only the top of the tower in the air with his hand and then tried to transfer that hand at that height over alongside tower B. Even if his hand had stayed at the same level he would have failed to solve the problem because tower B, resting on a lower table, should not rise to as great an absolute height as A. The correct solution must consider both the bases and the tops of the towers. As in many of the conservation problems the preoperational child centered his attention on only one of the relevant dimensions.

Representation of Perspective. Some of the characteristics of preoperational thought discovered by the earlier question-and-answer method appear again in the child's manipulation of physical materials. There is, for example, a certain "egocentrism" manifest in the child's understanding of perspective (Piaget and Inhelder, 1948). He has before him a three-dimensional pasteboard model of a Swiss scene. In the foreground on his right is a little green mountain with a tiny house at the top. Behind and to the left is a larger brown mountain with a red cross on the summit. In the background stands the largest mountain, a grey pyramid with snow at its peak. A zigzag path runs down the side of the green mountain and a rivulet descends the brown mountain.

The child is always at a certain position (A) facing the scene. A small wooden doll is placed in other positions (B, C, and D) so as to face the model on different sides. The child is to indicate how the scene must look to the doll in each case. There were several tests for this knowledge. One involved laying out ten pictures of the scene taken from different angles; the child was to identify the picture that corresponded to the doll's point of view. One hundred children, between the ages of four and twelve, participated in this research.

Children under seven years responded in an astonishing way. They attributed to the doll, whatever the doll's position, their own point of view. The performance was egocentric in the sense that the representation selected was always the one corresponding to the image available to the child in position A. Children in the period of concrete operations developed the ability to choose correctly according to the perspective available to the doll.

When the younger children walked around the model, the image they saw changed, of course, in accordance with the laws of perspective and this must have been, in some sense, what the children expected since they evinced no surprise. Had the image always been the same, had it always been the view from A, we may be certain that the child would have been surprised. In other words when the child himself occupied the several positions of the doll the views he obtained were not that single view he attributed to the doll and he found this quite natural. On the level of perception the preoperational child is well acquainted with shifts of perspective, but to be perceptually set for shifts in perspective is evidently not the same thing as to *represent* such shifts while holding a fixed position. The former is a process of perception; the latter is an operation of thought. The perceptual achievement occurs in the first two years or so but the related achievement on the level of thought occurs much later.

If the younger child first studies the view from A and then moves to B he is able both to select his own present view and also his immediately previous view from A. What he cannot do is select views for positions he has not occupied; views that are still "virtual." Presumably, immediately previous views can be supplied by imagery which the preoperational child possesses. Virtual views must be constructed by a set of reciprocal mental operations which involve the reversing of left and right and front and back with appropriate changes of position. This is more than the preoperational child can manage. The preoperational child seems to work on the Piaget problems with an intelligence that is of a different order from the intelligence of the concretely operational child. Piaget's most general description of this difference involves the description of a set of logical operations (the *groupements*) which the older child has and the younger does not have. Let us try to summarize the character of both sorts of intelligence without using the logical models, staying at the level of a looser verbal characterization.

GENERAL CHARACTERIZATION

In answering questions the preoperational child shows a greater reliance on present perception than does the operational child. He judges that there is more liquid in the narrow container because it can be seen to rise to a greater height. The perception on which he relies tends to be partial in that it focuses on a single dimension of the problem. He attends to the height of the column of fluid or to its width but does not move back and forth between the two.

Insofar as the preoperational child relies on central representations it is on the kind of representation that is closest to perception—imagery. In the perspectives problem he is able to recognize a view that he has just seen but not able to pick out views he would see from new positions. Presumably this is because the immediately previous view is available as an image and the virtual views are not. The virtual views can only be constructed correctly by one who treats such relations as left and right, before and behind, as relative to a point of view.

What the preoperational child lacks is operations. These are central events whose neurophysiological nature is unknown but which do not imitate perception as does the image. When they become completely general in the stage of formal operations they correspond to such logical and mathematical operations as classification and cross-classification, equivalence and inclusion, addition and subtraction, implication and disjunction, correlations, proportions, combinations, and permutations. In the period of concretely operational intelligence some of these operations are lacking and others are not completely general, but linked with particular content. The concrete child may understand that equivalence of height in building towers is a transitive relation and yet be very far from understanding that the relation symbolized as "=" is always transitive.

Piaget believes that mental operations are somehow derived from overt operations—from actions in the external world. Consider once more the child who must judge whether there are as many eggs as eggcups when the eggs are close together and the cups are far apart. What is required for a correct solution is a mental operation either separating out the cups or gathering together the eggs. This mental operation must be reversible; the child must realize that the one action cancels the other and restores the original state. As a preparation for this mental operation he has often performed a comparable physical operation—the actual rearrangement of objects. Piaget believes this external motor operation somehow becomes internalized as a mental operation.

It sometimes happens with the conservation problems that a child who gives the wrong answer will get the right answer if he is actually allowed to manipulate or to pour back and forth. If he can execute these operations motorically he can give conservation answers, but if he must do the whole thing in his head he cannot. The word *operation* expresses Piaget's conviction that intelligence develops out of motor activity not just out of passive observation. In his phrase: "Penser c'est opérer."

Formally Operational Intelligence

The child who acquires formal operations has the basic intellectual equipment for working as a scientist. The problems the Genevan investigators have used to explore the properties of adolescent intelligence are scientific problems. For instance, a child is given some buckets of water and an odd lot of objects including pebbles, needles, bits of wood, and toys. He is to find out why some things float and others sink; in effect he is set the problem of discovering the Law of Floating Bodies. Or he is given a kind of billiard game with a spring plunger that shoots marbles against a projection wall from which they rebound to the interior of the apparatus. A target is placed in one location and then in another location and the child is to try to hit it. It will help him if he discovers that the angle of incidence equals the angle of reflection. These problems and some of the others involve principles of physics that are taught in school. However the investigators, Inhelder and Piaget, report in their book *The Growth of Logical Thinking* (1958) that their subjects had not yet been given any formal instruction associated with the problems they were set. In effect they were to anticipate some of the achievements of science and yet, the problems were set in such a way that they could be attempted by children whose ages placed them at the preoperational or the concretely operational levels as well as by young adolescents.

OPERATING WITH COMBINATIONS

In understanding the formal operations I find it helpful to begin concretely with a particular problem. As Figure 5-1 illustrates, the child is given four similar flasks containing colorless, odorless liquids which look exactly alike. The bottles are labeled with numbers. The liquids they contain are not named for the child but they are: 1) diluted sulphuric acid; 2) water; 3) oxygenated water; and 4) thiosulphate. There is a fifth bottle, a smaller one, that is labelled g and contains potassium iodide. The experimenter produces two glasses containing perceptually-identical liquids and hands them to his subject. With the child watching, the experimenter pours several drops from bottle g into each glass. The result is that the liquid in one glass turns yellow while the liquid in the other glass does not change its appearance. In fact the liquid that turned yellow when combined with g was a mixture of sulphuric acid (1) and oxygenated water (3) while the liquid that did not turn yellow was water (2). We can summarize these facts by saying that $1 + 3 + g$ will be yellow whereas $2 + g$ will not be yellow. The child has not been told what liquids were in the two glasses and so he knows only that g, added to one liquid, gave yellow while g, added to another liquid, did not give yellow. Now he is given two empty glasses, flasks 1, 2, 3, and 4 and bottle g and simply asked to try to produce yellow.

What is there to be learned? The combination $1 + 3 + g$ yields yellow and will still do so if 2 (water) is added. On the other hand the addition of thiosulphate (4) will bleach the mixture. In sum, $1 + 3 + g$ with or without 2 makes yellow; no other combination does so. How do children in the several periods of intelligence work at this problem?

The child at five and six years with preoperational intelligence chiefly makes a mess. He mixes liquids in an apparently random way. He appears to have no systematic plan for trying the various possibilities and no scheme for keeping track of outcomes. If, by chance, he produces color he can give no adequate explanation for its appearance or its disappearance. The "water" turns yellow, he says, because it was shaken in a certain way

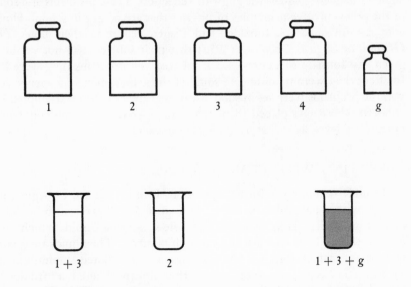

FIGURE 5-1. THE PROBLEM OF COLORED AND COLORLESS CHEMICALS.
Four similar flasks contain colorless, odorless liquids: (1) diluted sulphuric
acid; (2) water; (3) oxygenated water; (4) thiosulphate. The smaller flask,
labeled g, contains potassium iodide. Two glasses are presented to the subject; one contains 1 + 3, the other contains 2. While the subject watches,
the experimenter adds several drops of g to each of these glasses. The liquid
in the glass containing 1 + 3 turns yellow. The subject is then asked to reproduce the color, using all or any of the five flasks as he wishes.

or when the yellow disappears it has melted away or sunk to the bottom.

We know that, in the conservation problems, the child with preoperational intelligence answers in terms of immediate appearances while the
child with concrete operations answers in terms of what has happened
(the previous pouring) and what could happen (the reverse pouring).
The preoperational child's intelligence is limited to the *actual* while the
child with concrete operations can deal with the potential. The immediate
appearance takes its place, for the older child, in a network of possible
transformations. In the present problem in chemistry this characteristic
appears very clearly.

The concretely operational child does not combine liquids at random
but rather begins by combining each one with g: perhaps first 4 with g,
then 2 with g, 3 with g, and 1 with g. He appears to have a systematic
preconception of what might be tried, of the combinations that are possible. He is able to keep track of what he has done. There seems to be a
kind of matrix in his mind, a set of 4 cells defined by g in conjunction with
1, 2, 3, and 4 and he fills these cells systematically.

Still his conception of the possibilities is very limited. In addition to two-at-a-time combinations he is likely to think of combining all at once: 1 and 2 and 3 and 4 and g. But the younger child in the period of concrete operations does not ordinarily think of combining liquids three at a time or four at a time. The older child in this period may try some combinations of this order, perhaps 4 with 2 with g and then 1 with 3 with g. However, he does not make these combinations in any systematic order; he does not for instance first try 1 and g with 2, then 1 and g with 3, then 1 and g with 4. He does not seem to prefigure to himself the full matrix of possibilities but only the simplest entries, the liquids taken two at a time. In other ways, too, the understanding of the child in the period of concrete operations is limited. If he gets the color and is asked what caused it to appear he does not seem to understand that it is the conjunction of liquids that has done the trick. Instead he says that it is some one of the liquids which *really* contains the color. Why, then, are the others necessary? His answers are confused.

Children with formal operations (twelve, thirteen, and fourteen years old) see further into the sphere of the potential than do the concretely operational children. They frequently verbalize the necessity of trying all possible combinations. Some children work them all out on paper, not with the mathematical formulas from probability theory but with listings holding everything constant while the open position is filled by one bottle after another. Even when they do not write down the combinations, the children with formal operations work them out mentally and realize them all: combinations two-at-a-time, three-at-a-time, four-at-a-time, and all five together. This ability to represent in advance a full set of possibilities is a cardinal feature of intelligence on the most advanced level of development.

PROPOSITIONAL LOGIC AND HYPOTHESIS TESTING

In addition, formal intelligence can be characterized as "hypothetico-deductive" and "propositional." To see what these terms imply it will be useful to simplify the chemistry a bit. Suppose we are simply told of the existence of three liquids (A, B, and C) and also told that there are just two outcomes of interest: yellow (y) or not yellow ($\bar{y}$). We are to discover how to make yellow.

As yet we have seen nothing, not even the single liquids A, B, and C and so we do not know whether any of these alone is yellow or not. The possible conditions to be examined are: A; B; C; AB; AC; BC; ABC. We have represented the combinatorial possibilities and would go ahead to realize them. However, formal intelligence can do more.

Suppose we examined each liquid in isolation and found A to be colorless, B to be yellow, and C to be colorless. The child with concrete intelligence might manage to remember these individual empirical correspondences. What he would not do is reason out all the implications of this pattern of evidence. He might very well stop here since he would have discovered a way to get yellow: select B.

However, the obtained data are consistent with many different general principles. Perhaps B is the necessary and sufficient cause of yellow; i.e., B alone or in any combination, whether with A or C or both, may give yellow. On the other hand, it is possible that B is not always sufficient to the production of yellow; perhaps B combined with anything else gives a colorless result. B may not even be necessary to the production of yellow. It might happen that A and C together will look yellow.

These various formulations that are all equally consistent with the data so far examined amount to a set of competing hypotheses. One could go on to test them. We might try A and C in combination. Suppose the outcome is colorless. Does that mean that B is necessary for yellow? Yes, because there remain no unexamined combinations in which B does not participate. Nothing is left to be tried but AB, BC, and ABC. Do our data mean that B is always associated with yellow? No, because any of the remaining combinations may prove to be colorless. Let us then try them.

This process involves more than the prefiguring of a set of possibilities and then their realization. At each stage we have a conception of the general propositions that could be true. These are hypotheses to us; we can deduce their consequences and test their truth. New data react on the hypotheses, disconfirming some, reducing the number still tenable. This is a hypothetico-deductive procedure, a procedure dealing in propositions and logical relations.

The running talk of the children with formal intelligence shows that they are operating in this hypothetico-deductive mode. When they try out 1 with 3 with g and get yellow they do not think of this result as the end of the problem. They know that there may be other ways of getting yellow. They know that 1 and 3 and 4 and g may give yellow and/or that 1 and 3 and 2 and g may give yellow, etc. They are also able to put the immediate successful outcome together with the failure that preceded it. They do not think that the new outcome is consistent with the possibility that 1 and g alone will give yellow or that 3 and g alone will give yellow for the reason that these combinations have been tried and found to be colorless.

In the work of a scientist, a hypothesis or a theory saves labor. Suppose you were experimenting with laboratory animals rather than flasks of liquid and trying to discover the dietary factors conducive to coronary occlusions which cause "heart attacks." The number of conceivable experimental variations in this problem is infinite, one could not try all possible diets as one can try all possible combinations of 5 liquids. Suppose however that the scientist has a hunch that the level of free fatty acids in an animal's blood is related to the probability of coronary occlusions. The hunch or hypothesis establishes priorities among the conceivable experimental variations. It directs him to compare, first, high-fat diets with low-fat diets; it directs him to let those variations wait which he has no reason for trying.

Even in the chemistry problem of Inhelder and Piaget the possible experimental variations are more numerous than the systematic combinations the subjects tried. Suppose the order in which liquids are combined makes a difference; perhaps 1 added to 3 does not give the same effect as 3 added to 1. If we keep track of different orders we deal with permutations rather than combinations and the possible permutations are, of course, more numerous than the possible combinations. An occasional subject did, in fact, try a few permutations but something about the situation or some conception of what is probable in chemistry problems of this kind caused most subjects to restrict themselves to combinations. In addition to order, it would be possible to attend to quantities of liquid and these are endlessly divisible. Are three drops of a liquid equal to two drops? An occasional subject considered this possibility but probably the absence of any apparatus for precise measurement suggested that quantity would not be crucial. The restriction of tests to combinations without regard to quantity is a saving of effort resulting from hypotheses of a very general and unformulated sort. Sometimes, in addition, a subject would seize upon a particular explicit hypothesis and would desert the orderly trial of all possibilities in order to perform at once the crucial experiment.

Sar (twelve years, three months) had made yellow with 1 and 3 and g. It then occurred to him that 2 and 4 might both be water and completely without effect in these chemical combinations. He moved to a direct test: "Give me a glass of water." Sar took the water from the faucet and added it to 1 and 3 and g, the combination that gave yellow. He thereby stepped outside the matrix of combinations and introduced a new element. The water did not change the color of 1 and 3 and g. Now, to determine whether 2 and 4 were water.

The effect of adding water to the yellow mixture is known. If 2 is water then it should act like water, all other things being equal. If 2 and 4 are the same they should have identical effects, all other things being equal. Sar once again made yellow with 1 and 3 and g and then added—not water—but 2. The liquid remained yellow so 2 *could* be water. Yet again Sar made yellow with 1 and 3 and g and this time added—not water or 2—but 4. The liquid turned colorless so 4 could not be the same as 2 and could not be water.

This was a true hypothesis-testing experiment. It involves the notion that one can determine whether factors are the same or different by observing their effects in situations that are otherwise identical. Sar held constant the conditions that made yellow: 1 and 3 and g. He then created comparison cases, changing one variable at a time, and the pattern of evidence taught him that 2 and 4 were different and that 2 and water might be the same. This ability to make observations crucially relevant for a particular hypothesis by following the fundamental experimental logic of the "Rule of One Variable" is another of the characteristics of formally operational intelligence.

FORMAL OPERATIONS AND SOCIAL PROBLEMS

In the final chapter of *The Growth of Logical Thinking* (1958) Inhelder and Piaget suggest that most of the familiar characteristics of adolescent personality are consequences of formally operational intelligence. The formal operations, above all, deal in potentialities or possibilities; what might be done and what would then be likely to follow. Adolescence in European and American culture is the time when one must plan a future life course, when decisions must be made about education, career, residence, and marriage. The social role of the adolescent requires him to deal in possibilities, to entertain alternatives and envision consequences. Formally operational intelligence enables him to do so.

Inhelder and Piaget refer to adolescence as the "metaphysical" age, by which they mean that it is the great age for theorizing. The adolescent theorizes about the nature of man, the nature of good and evil. He thinks about his own society, how he might change it and what would follow therefrom. The adolescent girl often has a theory about raising children and a theory about married love, theories that will enable her to manage these things better than her parents have done. Inhelder and Piaget think that the reformism of the adolescent is marked by a temporary return of egocentrism. The reformer does not accurately estimate the inertia of the social machinery but projects his own readiness for change.

In adolescence one may see clearly that socialism follows inevitably from Christian axioms, that discrimination against minorities cannot possibly coexist with democratic principles, that Cold War tensions would necessarily be eased if we would set an example of trustfulness, that a rational society must exercise economic controls. Or, one sees clearly that a soppy altruistic ethic has destroyed individuality; that collectivism can only be overthrown by a return to personal selfishness, to economic competitiveness, and the insistence on earned privileges. Whatever the conclusions of the adolescent's reasoning on social issues may be the reasoning itself seems to him to be perfectly rigorous, and rigorous thought, he believes, will compel social change. There is a powerful emotional attachment to abstract ideas. As an adolescent one is amazed at adults who do not seem to realize the logical implications of their own ideas and who, still more unaccountably, do not make their actions consistent with their beliefs. The adolescent vows that he will never get to be like that; he will fight off whatever it is that clouds the adult intelligence. And suddenly he is ten years older, uncertain about everything and thoroughly compromised, trying to recall what it was he vowed to preserve.

Inhelder and Piaget acknowledge that adults in civilized societies do not all attain to formally operational intelligence and they assert that there are primitive societies in which no one has attained to this level. While the authors believe that biological maturation establishes a readiness for operational intelligence in early adolescence there is also some kind of necessary social experience. It may be that participation in the complex roles of civilized society somehow produces operational intelligence or it may be that this kind of intelligence is transmitted as a technique of problem-solving from one generation to another.

The ability to think scientifically must function as a momentous change in the evolution of culture. It is prerequisite to the accomplishments of physics, mathematics, biology, and the behavioral and social sciences. The historical order in which these studies have emerged suggests that operational intelligence is not applied to all domains with equal ease; that it is first turned upon realms remote from the self—the non-living world—then upon the living world exclusive of man. Last of all it is turned upon man and his societies. Not everyone in our society who can apply operational intelligence to the stars and to physical mechanics and to white rats can apply it to desegregation and mental health.

Genevan Research and Social Psychology

The central topic of social psychology is probably the socialization or enculturation of the child. To this topic Genevan research must certainly be relevant. However, the nature of the relevance and its extent are still uncertain because we do not know how much of what the Genevans have discovered is cultural.

A culture is a system of rules for the guidance of behavior, a system widely shared within a society. These rules are socially transmitted, the new generation learns them from the old, and they are variable from one society to another. What role does culture play in the development of intelligence as it has been described by Piaget? Let us look at two extreme possibilities: 1) Culture plays no role; 2) culture determines all.

HOW MUCH IS CULTURAL?

If culture plays no role then all of the stages of development should appear in children everywhere and always in the same order. The terminal states of knowledge and operational competence should be the same everywhere. Changes from stage to stage would depend upon maturation and upon learning that is not social, learning from commerce with the physical world. If the Genevan description has this kind of universality it will not perhaps qualify as social psychology in its own right but it will have the greatest possible relevance to social psychology. Anyone who undertakes to study the child's acquisition of a cultural system—a language, a game, an etiquette, a set of values—will want to begin with Piaget's characterization of the development of intelligence. The four kinds of intelligence, described by Piaget, when they are turned upon social norms ought to produce four characteristically different kinds of outcome. If the Genevan progression is a universally valid characterization of age-graded transformations of the human intellectual apparatus it will be the chief foundation of the study of socialization.

What if the progressions are completely determined by culture? In this case the different kinds of answers and performances obtained from children will all have been taught them by other human beings. It will be as if adults, in instructing children about quantity and number and implication and causality and dreams and chance, tell them different kinds of stories according to their ages. Many adults do just this in certain spheres. The child's progression from a belief that Christmas presents come from Santa Claus to a belief that they come from parents is culturally determined and so is his progression from a belief that babies are brought by the stork to a belief that they grow inside mothers. Sequences of this kind are not universal. They extend beyond one nation to the wider sphere of western Europe and North America, as do many of Piaget's progressions, but we should be surprised to find them in Japan, Ghana, and New Guinea.

If the Piaget progressions are standard sequences of belief and competence inculcated by western European cultures then they are themselves important contributions to the enculturation topic within social psychology. The fact that the systems inculcated are intellectual or cognitive rather than affective or evaluative does not prevent them from being cultural. Language is also such a system. The fact that the systems are primarily aimed at guiding the individual in his manipulation of the physical world rather than in his interaction with other humans does not prevent them from being cultural. Instruction manuals for agriculturists or aviators or astronomers constitute such systems. Possibly because there has been so much talk in social psychology about toilet training, weaning, and the control of sex and aggression, the terms "culture" and "socialization" have come to connote affect and value and social relations. But of course there is also an intellectual and impersonal culture that children must acquire.

It is quite clear that the Genevan story of development is neither perfectly culture free nor perfectly culture dependent. It is a mixture but, on the whole, it is nearer the culture-free pole. Some parts of the Genevan characterization of development probably are not socially transmitted and not variable. The developments of the sensory motor period, since this is the time before language becomes important, are likely candidates. The conservation of the object, first conceptions of space and time, the control of grasping and the emergence of primary, secondary, and tertiary reflexes may be universal achievements in the first years of life.

Among the progressions described by Piaget there may be others that are universal; for example the occurrence of non-conservation answers before conservation answers and, among the conservations, a progression from quantity and space to weight and still later to volume. Wallach (1963) summarizing a large number of European and North American replications of the Genevan researches on conservation finds that while there are shifts of a year or two in the age norms ". . . the same general developmental sequences have, on the whole, been obtained by such work" (p. 247). Jacqueline Goodnow (1963) has very recently taken the Piaget problems concerning the conservation of space, weight, and volume to Hong Kong. She administered them to four groups of children, some of them European and some Chinese, some of them having had full schooling for their ages and some almost no schooling. The detailed results are complicated but the author summarizes them by saying that ". . . the most striking result is the very real and close similarity in performance among boys of different nationality and education" (p. 43) and that ". . . replication of Geneva results was fair to good" (p. 48).

Probably because they are older, Piaget's studies of the 1920's have been more often repeated in remote cultures than have the recent studies. Piaget has jokingly referred to the 1920's as his "preoperational period" (Tanner and Inhelder, 1953, p. 93) and the work done then clearly interests him less than what has followed. The earlier investigations were question-and-answer sessions which yielded data less easy to interpret than the data from the later studies, which combined interrogation with manipulation of physical materials. The subject matter of the early studies included the nature of dreams, the origin of names, the concept of life, and the origin of the sun and moon. These seem to me to be matters about which parents are fairly likely to tell stories of the Santa Claus and stork variety, a kind of story that parents do not tell about quantity, area, number, measurement and the like. For these reasons it would not have surprised me if the findings of the 1920's had turned out to be peculiar to Genevan children in the 1920's. They seem to be more general than that but not perfectly general.

Piaget in *The Child's Conception of the World* (1926) attributes to children below the age of five years a "diffuse animism" which is supplanted by a more limited and "systematic animism" that may last until the age of eight or nine. Animism, in general, is a tendency to regard nonliving things as living and is revealed in the child's tendency to say that such things are alive as a bicycle and the sun and fire and the wind and to say that grass can feel, a motor see, and a tree cry. Child animism has been looked for in a good range of cultures, in the United States, England and Sweden and among Chinese children, Hopi children, Zuni children, and the Manus children of New Guinea. Jahoda has reviewed all of this work (1958a) and contributed new data from Ghana in West Africa (1958b). He finds that the results at first look like an inconsistent tangle. However, a critical analysis shows that the minimal prediction that animism will occur in early childhood and decline with age is confirmed by most, though not all, of the studies.

My guess is that the particular progressions discovered in Piaget's later work will have greater generality than the progressions discovered by purely verbal inquiry and that the ordering of the four great periods of intelligence, sensory-motor, preoperational, concretely operational and formally operational, will stand up very well to cross-cultural test. It is interesting to have Margaret Mead's opinion that the ordering of the periods is likely to be "reproducible cross-culturally" (Tanner and Inhelder, 1953, p. 204). In one respect, however, we can be sure that there is cultural variation. Inhelder and Piaget (1958) have themselves predicted it. In some societies no adults have attained to the stage of formal operations. There are societies in which no one seems to use the logic of propositions, correlations, proportions, and experimental method.

With these qualifications I think we can say that the chief importance of Genevan research for social psychology is as a kind of background or preparation for the study of enculturation. We need to know as much as we can about the usual developmental transformations in intelligence before studying the acquisition of language, motives, values, and ideologies. The ways in which knowledge of the development of intelligence can assist social psychology are illustrated in one of Piaget's own books: *The Moral Judgment of the Child* (1932). This work is, by anyone's definition, a contribution to social psychology. It deals with conceptions and rules that are socially transmitted and variable from one society to another and which are used to govern social interaction. It deals with the child's learning of the rules for playing games of marbles and of his understanding of such moral conceptions as lying and justice.

THE RULES OF THE GAME

Children in Geneva and in Neuchâtel, where the work was done, played with marbles according to rules somewhat like those followed by children in America. The rules of a game contrast interestingly with the rules of a language, rules of pronunciation, meaning, and grammar. Both languages and games are truly cultural since both are shared, transmitted, and variable from society to society. However, the rules of a language which enable a child to understand and construct new sentences are not explicitly taught to him and are not a part of his own explicit knowledge until years after he has first learned to use them. The child somehow induces the rules from the speech around him and conforms to these rules long before anyone formulates them verbally for him. In the case of a game like marbles, on the other hand, the child is told the rules, often many times, and he can in turn explain them. Even so it appears that his understanding of the rules at any age is affected by the level of his intelligence.

Piaget watched children between three years and thirteen years play marbles and he talked about the game with some twenty of them. With the marbles before them Piaget would say: "When I was little I used to play a lot but now I've quite forgotten how. I'd like to play again. Let's play together. You'll teach me the rules and I'll play with you" (Piaget, 1948, p. 13). It seems a wonderful idea to make the child the expert and give him the chance to expound. Piaget asked whether the rules had always been the same and where they came from. He asked whether one could make up a new rule, a rule nobody else knew. Would such a rule be real? Would it be fair?

Some of the very youngest children knew nothing of any rules. Watching them play with the marbles by themselves, Piaget found that each child's behavior moved toward a kind of ritualistic regularity, a personal norm not prescribed by any society and not involving others. Children a little older played marbles in an egocentric manner. They sometimes followed rules they had been told to follow or had seen others follow but not in such a way as to play a game against one another. Even when two children played simultaneously the play of one was not integrated with the play of the other. The picture is reminiscent of a group of children with egocentric speech playing in a sandpile; each one talks but not to anyone in particular and no one in particular attends.

Egocentrism, one of the salient features of preoperational language and of thought about the physical world appears also in the preoperational child's understanding of marbles.

The child who plays egocentrically holds the rules to be inviolable and absolute; they cannot be changed by anyone. He imputes to them the force of physical laws. As for their origin? Some children think they have always existed.

There is a transitional stage and then, in the latter part of the period of concrete operations, the boys begin to play an elaborately articulated social game. In fact they become lawyers of the game, arguing the fine points of the rules, imagining difficult cases that the rules might not cover or where the rules might be in conflict. Piaget was amazed at the intricacy of the system and pokes fun at educators who think children of this age are not capable of learning abstract subject matter. Children of this age believe that a rule could be changed if everyone agreed to it. The rules seem to them to derive their validity from the social consensus and so are of a different order from physical laws.

You do not have to learn the rules of marbles unless you want to play the game; you can opt out. There are other rules from which the child cannot exempt himself—rules of cleanliness, courtesy, respect for property, and the like. There are positive sanctions (rewards) for good behavior and negative sanctions (punishments) for bad, so it is important to be able to predict the kind of sanction each act will incur. The level of the child's intelligence influences his conception of the local morality even as it does his conception of the physical world and of the game of marbles.

MORAL CONCEPTIONS

Piaget selected a fundamental problem. What determines the seriousness of a crime? It seemed to him that the relevant variables were of two kinds: the magnitude of the injury or damage and the intention or motive of the criminal. As experimental materials he contrived little stories which systematically vary the magnitude of the crime and the intention of the criminal.

Here are two examples (Piaget, 1948, p. 118):

IA. A little boy who is called John is in his room. He is called to dinner. He goes into the dining room. But behind the door there was a chair, and on the chair there was a tray with fifteen cups on it. John couldn't have known that there was all this behind the door. He goes in, the door knocks against the tray, bang go the fifteen cups and they all get broken!

B. Once there was a little boy whose name was Henry. One day when his mother was out he tried to get some jam out of the cupboard. He climbed up on a chair and stretched out his arm. But the jam was too high up and he couldn't reach it and have any. But while he was trying to get it he knocked over a cup. The cup fell down and broke.

The damage done by John (IA) was greater than the damage done by Henry in a ratio of fifteen to one. John's damage was not intended and it did not occur as a byproduct of any sort of misbehavior. Henry's damage was also not intended but if he had not disobeyed his mother it would not have happened. In other stories the degree of damage and the nature of the motive were given other values. In still other stories the misdeed was theft rather than damage, and magnitude was a matter of the value of the thing stolen.

Piaget's subjects were between six and ten years of age. To make sure that they understood each story, and particularly the motives involved, he asked the children to tell him the story and questioned them about details before going on to the important inquiry. Considering the characters in two stories, for example John and Henry in the stories above: Are they "la même chose vilain?" Or is one naughtier ("plus vilain") than the other? Which one should be punished more?

How would we answer? John's breakage of fifteen cups is an accident, it seems to me. No crime has been committed and no punishment should be administered. Henry is "naughtier" because while he did little damage the story implies that he was being disobedient and the children understood it so. If there were a third story in which a boy broke cups with the intention of doing damage I think we would consider him the "naughtiest" of the three. Piaget did not, in this work, clearly distinguish between willful damage and damage incidental to other misbehavior, and that is certainly an important distinction. His stories usually involve nothing worse than damage that is the byproduct of some other kind of misbehavior, though there is one about a small boy giving a gentleman misleading directions as a joke.

There are other distinctions Piaget did not make in this work which he might have made. An adult reading the two stories about John and Henry will certainly judge Henry to be the "naughtier" and adult judgments of naughtiness or villainy or wickedness seem generally to be based on intentions. Judgments of this sort can be distinguished from something that might be called the seriousness or importance of what happens. Seriousness is most closely related to the magnitude of the damage or theft. Adults can make quite independent judgments of seriousness and wickedness. John's fifteen cups are more *serious* than Henry's single cup but Henry is the greater villain. If a pedestrian is killed by a motorist, that is more serious than if a pedestrian is only knocked down. However, the motorist who has killed a man may be less villainous, less blameworthy, than the motorist who only knocked someone down. It suffices that the motorist who killed someone should have been obeying the law in every respect, so that the death was in no sense his fault, whereas the other motorist was drunk and speeding or, to make it worse, "out to get" the man he hit.

While adults can independently judge seriousness and wickedness, the two dimensions do sometimes interact. The motorist who accidentally kills a man will feel, and is expected to feel, a shock that somehow partakes of remorse. His friends must try to assure him that what happened was in no sense his fault. A parent on the scene when John smashed his fifteen cups would be likely to feel a flash of anger and John, though innocent, might get smacked. Afterwards—recollecting in tranquillity—the parent would realize that he had been unjust and would try to make it up to John. Still the immediate punishment was governed by the magnitude of the objective damage rather than by the wickedness of the intention.

The law, too, often punishes in terms of the objective event rather than the intention. Violations of traffic laws, when they are unintentional, are still punishable. Ignorance of the law is no excuse, perhaps because knowledge and intention are always hard to prove. If the law punishes in terms of the objective event it gives people a reason to acquire knowledge and control their intentions. Still the law does often reckon with intentions; if a man is killed it makes a great difference whether there was "intent to kill."

In the Piaget questions the operative word was "vilain" which may be translated as "naughty." For adults, judgments of naughtiness would be primarily governed by intention rather than by objective consequences. Piaget did not find sharply separated stages in the answers of the children but those in the preoperational period, those under seven years of age, most often judged naughtiness in terms of objective damage. A boy who breaks fifteen cups is worse and should be punished more than a boy who breaks one. A girl who does major damage with a pair of scissors while trying to help her mother is naughtier than the girl who does slight damage while playing with the scissors in mother's absence. A little boy who steals a bread roll to give a hungry friend is worse than a little girl who steals a bit of ribbon for herself. Why? Because "rolls cost more." Older children more often judged naughtiness by intentions; from children over ten years old there were no instances of judgment in terms of objective damage.

In these moral judgments it seems to me that one can see again the perceptual character of preoperational intelligence. Cups and holes cut with scissors and rolls and ribbon are perceptible. Intentions are not; they are psychological states which must usually be inferred from behavior. It would appear that the child's understanding of the contingencies governing blame and punishment begins with perceptually obvious externals. However, if the child understands the contingencies governing reward and punishment in the perceptual way then adult justice will seem to be full of contradictions. Crimes that are objectively small will sometimes be more severely punished than crimes that are objectively large. Such contradictions can only be reconciled by discovery of the psychological variable—motive or intention—to which parental punishments are chiefly attuned. The problem is like one Inhelder and Piaget studied in connection with the period of formal operations—discovery of the Law of Floating Bodies. A child, trying to understand why some things float and others do not, first thinks in terms of such perceptible attributes as size or weight or being made of wood. The contradictions that exist on this level can only be resolved by discovering the concept of specific gravity—the weight of an object compared to the weight of an equal volume of water.

Piaget's investigation of the child's understanding of lies (1948) produced similar results. What is a lie? Children of six years said a lie was "naughty words," words learned in the street like the oath *"charogne"* (carrion). Asked to judge whether certain untrue statements were also lies these children acknowledged that they were. Probably their parents had been made indignant by both naughty words and by untruths and the child had not clearly distinguished the two categories; both are bad things to say.

For children a little older, a lie is simply any statement that does not accord with fact and the reprehensibility of the lie is proportional to the magnitude of the departure from the truth. A boy who tells his mother he saw a dog as big as a cow is more deserving of punishment than a boy who tells his mother he got good grades in school when he did not. Why? Because the dog as big as a cow is the greater improbability. This curious theory is not held by older children, children of ten and eleven. In their view a lie is an untruth with intent to deceive. An obvious improbability such as the report of a dog as big as a cow is not a lie at all because it cannot deceive anyone. It is a *blague*, a joke. The child's conception of a lie, then, like his conception of other misdeeds, begins on an objective perceptual level. It is, first of all, naughty words—a list of proscribed utterances. Then it becomes more abstract and relational but still perceptual—a lack of correspondence between objective facts and assertions. Finally the imperceptible psychological variable of intention becomes critical.

In these developmental sequences the child's morality becomes increasingly inward. This is surely a process of enculturation. It cannot be the case that children's moral judgments follow the same course in all societies. The contrast between the objective morality of the preoperational child and the inward psychological morality of the operational child is, after all, similar to the contrast between the Ten Commandments and the Sermon on the Mount. The Christian ethic is more *psychological* than the Mosaic

Law. It judges by what is in a man's heart, not by what he performs. The Mosaic Law may always have been intended to be understood in an inward sense but it could be understood otherwise and was so understood in Christ's day. In our own day Christianity is understood as a set of external observances at least as often as it is understood in terms of intentions. Indeed the two moralities are in continual contention. The thalidomide tragedy in 1962 caused people to debate whether it was wrong for a woman to have an abortion when her motive was to avoid giving birth to a deformed child.

Piaget's older Swiss children were apparently governed in terms of a largely psychological morality. In the years of preoperational intelligence they did not correctly apprehend this morality but understood it first in perceptual preoperational terms. It cannot be assumed that all children or adults understand morality in a psychological way. It may be the case, however, that the theories of early childhood are bound to be objective whatever the nature of the operative adult system.

Piaget proceeded to an investigation of the child's ideas about "just punishment," asking questions of some one hundred children between six and twelve years. Various kinds of juvenile misdeeds were described and, for each, some alternative punishments. Piaget said that parents often did not know what sort of punishment to use and he thought it would be helpful to have children's opinions on the matter. What seemed to them to be fair in each case?

Two great principles of punishment can be described. Piaget calls one "expiatory punishment"; the idea here is that punishments should be adjusted by intensity to the magnitude of the crime but that they need not, in any other respect, match the crime. The same punishment—a beating or going to bed without any supper—is fair and just for all misdeeds of a certain magnitude, whatever the qualitative nature of the misdeed.

The second principle Piaget calls "reciprocity"; the idea here is to "let the punishment fit the crime"—qualitatively as well as quantitatively. There are numerous subvarieties, many ways to fit a punishment to a crime. One can let the child suffer the natural consequences of his action— if he breaks a window let him sleep in a cold room. One can do to a child what he has done to another—"If you hit your little brother I am going to hit you." One can require him to make good the harm he has accomplished —if he breaks his brother's gun he must make restitution by buying another or giving up his own. And there are other possibilities.

Children younger than seven years generally favored expiatory punishments whereas older children favored reciprocity; by eleven or twelve years 80 per cent of the preferences were for some variety of reciprocity. The several varieties of reciprocity involve relationships which the preoperational child probably could not understand. For example, suppose a child who has pushed his little brother is to be pushed by his father on the principle of doing to him what he has done to another. In order to appreciate the equivalence of the two pushes the child must be able to take another's point of view. To egocentric thought the pushes are entirely different; me pushing someone is not the same as me being pushed. Apprehension of the equivalence depends on the realization that when I push there is someone receiving the push whose experience resembles mine when I am pushed. Unless the child can thus move between points of view and compare them, the two pushes are quite different and there is no apparent justice in the second one.

The same difficulty arises when very young children are expected to "take their turn." Three brothers all want to have a ride on daddy's back and the youngest is to be first but, it is explained to him, he must then stand aside and let the others take their turn. When his time is up he does not cheerfully stand aside but immediately starts crying when he is asked to give up his place. From his egocentric position he cannot see the equivalence of the three rides. To him the rides are either "I ride" or "someone else rides" and so they are different.

The principle of restitution in punishment in which a child makes good the damage he has done involves an appreciation of reversibility which the preoperational child lacks. The principle of punishment by natural consequences, in which the child who breaks a window is left to shiver, will, in some cases, involve causal relationships that are not clear to the preoperational child. In general, then, I think that the child's sense of justice, as well as his notions of naughtiness, reflects the developmental level of his intelligence.

Piaget published *The Moral Judgment of the Child* in 1932 and at that time the four periods in the development of intelligence had not been worked out. Consequently Piaget does not talk about moral development in quite the way that I have. In his view the important factor in the child's moral judgments was the child's slowly developing sense of solidarity and sympathy with others. The younger child is governed by an external authority and his moral judgments are based on the presumed reactions of that authority. Actions are bad in the degree that they are likely to be discovered by authority and are likely to offend that authority. Consequently, objective misdeeds of high magnitude are the worst. When a child develops feelings of solidarity he comes to judge misdeeds in terms of the threat they constitute to the welfare of others. He approves of restitution as a punishment since it makes amends to others. Or he approves of doing to the bad child what he has done to another so that the bad child may learn to feel what others feel. Piaget's argument is very interesting but subsequent research has not supported it (Kohlberg, 1963, p. 320) and so I have not used it here.

The Moral Judgment of the Child makes a small beginning on a great topic: the intellectual side of enculturation. The norms that guide behavior are, after all, an intellectual system of great complexity and it seems likely that the child's understanding of these norms will be a function of the developmental level to which his intelligence has attained. What this book does so magnificently is to expose the intellectual aspect of value acquisition. Under Freud's influence we have long thought of value acquisition as simply a problem of causing children to feel pleasure when they are good and pain when they are bad. Internalization of external sanctions in the form of a rewarding and punishing superego has seemed to be the whole process. But there is also a problem of understanding. When has one sinned and how badly and what is a fair punishment? Values are not simply plus and minus signs; they are plus and minus signs attached to concepts which are organized in systems.

REFERENCES

Brunswik, E. *Perception and the representative design of psychological experiments*. Berkeley: Univer. of California Press, 1956.

Cruikshank, Ruth M. The development of visual size constancy in early infancy. *J. genet. Psychol.*, 1941, **58**, 327–351.

Dennis, W., & Russell, R. W. Piaget's questions applied to Zuni children. *Child Develpm.*, 1940, **11**, 181–187.

Flavell, J. H. *The developmental psychology of Jean Piaget*. Princeton: Van Nostrand, 1963.

Freud, S. The future of an illusion (1st ed., 1927). In *The complete psychological works of Sigmund Freud*, Vol. XXI. London: Hogarth, 1961.

Gibson, Eleanor J. Perceptual development. In National Society for the Study of Education, 62nd Yearbook, *Child psychol.* Chicago: Univer. of Chicago Press, 1963.

Gibson, J. J. *The perception of the visual world*. Cambridge: Riverside, 1950.

Goodnow, Jacqueline J. A test of milieu effects with some of Piaget's tasks. Air Force Contract AF 49 (638)–682, 1963.

Inhelder, Bärbel. Criteria of the stages of mental development. In J. M. Tanner & Bärbel Inhelder (Eds.), *Discussions on child development*, Vol. I. New York: Int. Univers. Press, 1953.

Inhelder, Bärbel. Some aspects of Piaget's genetic approach to cognition. In W. Kessen & Clementina Kuhlman (Eds.), Thought in the young child. *Monogr. Soc. Res. Child Develpm.*, 1962, **27**, No. 2, Serial No. 83.

Inhelder, Bärbel & Piaget, J. *The growth of logical thinking*. New York: Basic Books, 1958.

Jahoda, G. Child animism: I. A critical survey of cross-cultural research. *J. soc. Psychol.*, 1958, **47**, 197–212. (a)

Jahoda, G. Child animism: II. A study in West Africa. *J. soc. Psychol.*, 1958, **47**, 213–222. (b)

Kessen, W. Stage and structure in the study of children. In W. Kessen, & Clemintina Kuhlman (Eds.), Thought in the young child. *Monogr. Soc. Res. Child Develpm.*, 1962, **27**, No. 2, Serial No. 83.

Koffka, K. *Principles of Gestalt psychology*. New York: Harcourt, Brace, 1935.

Kohlberg, L. Moral development and identification. In National Society for the Study of Education, 62nd Yearbook, *Child psychol.* Chicago: Univer. of Chicago Press, 1963.

Lambercier, M. Recherches sur le développement des perceptions. VI. La constance des grandeurs en comparaisons sériales. *Arch. Psychol., Genève*, 1946, **31**, 79–282.

Locke, N. M. Perception and intelligence: Their phylogenetic relation. *Psychol. Rev.*, 1938, **45**, 335–345.

Piaget, J. *Judgement and reasoning in the child.* (1st ed., 1924) New York: Humanities Press, 1952.

Piaget, J. *The language and thought of the child.* (1st ed., 1924) New York: Humanities Press, 1959.

Piaget, J. *The child's conception of the world.* (1st ed., 1926) New York: Humanities Press, 1951.

Piaget, J. *The child's conception of physical causality.* (1st ed., 1927) Patterson: Littlefield, Adams, 1960.

Piaget, J. *The moral judgment of the child.* (1st ed., 1932) New York: Free Press, 1948.

Piaget, J. *The origins of intelligence in children.* (1st ed., 1936) New York: Int. Univer. Press, 1952.

Piaget, J. *The construction of reality in the child.* (1st ed., 1937) New York: Basic Books, 1954.

Piaget, J. *The child's conception of number.* (1st ed., 1941) New York: Humanities Press, 1952.

Piaget, J. *Play, dreams, and imitation in childhood.* (1st ed., 1945) New York: Norton, 1951.

Piaget, J., & Inhelder, Bärbel. *Le développement des quantités chez l'enfant.* Neuchâtel: Delchaux et Niestlé, 1941.

Piaget, J., & Inhelder, Bärbel. *The child's conception of space.* (1st ed., 1948) New York: Humanities Press, 1956.

Piaget, J., Inhelder, Bärbel, & Szeminska, Alina. *The child's conception of geometry.* (1st ed., 1948) New York: Basic Books, 1960.

Piaget, J., & Lambercier, M. Recherches sur le développement des perceptions. XII. La comparaison des grandeurs projectives chez l'enfant et chez adulte. *Arch. Psychol., Genève*, 1950–1952, **33**, 81–130.

Piaget, J., & Lambercier, M. Recherches sur le développement des perceptions. XXIX. Grandeur projectives et grandeurs réeles avec étalon éloigné. *Arch, Psychol., Genève*, 1955–1956, **35**, 257–280.

Smedslund, J. The acquisition of conservation of substance and weight in children. III. Extinction of conservation of weight acquired "normally" and by means of empirical controls on a balance scale. *Scand. J. Psychol., Stockholm*, 1961, **2**, 85–87.

Tanner, J. M., & Inhelder, Bärbel (Eds.), *Discussions on child development.* Vol. I. New York: Int. Univers. Press, 1953.

Von Senden, M. *Space and sight.* (1st ed., 1932) Transl. by P. Heath. New York: Free Press, 1960.

Wallach, M. A. Research on children's thinking. In National Society for the Study of Education, 62nd Yearbook, *Child psychol.* Chicago: Univer. of Chicago Press, 1963.

Wohlwill, J. F., & Lowe, R. C. An experimental analysis of the development of conservation of number. *Child Develpm.*, 1962, **33**, 153–167.

CHAPTER 6

Language: The System and

Its Acquisition

Part I. PHONOLOGY AND GRAMMAR

Every known human society has a language and no animal society has one. This is not to say that animals do not communicate with one another. The male stickleback is able to communicate his claim on a territory and his readiness to defend its boundaries. The worker honeybee can communicate to other workers the location of a nectar source, the distance of the source from the hive and the source's direction. Chimpanzees in the wild employ gestures and calls to summon, threaten and alert one another (Goodall, 1963). Most animal species have some means of communication. What they do not have is the technology of communication called language.

Language is defined by certain design features (Hockett, 1958) which taken together make it possible for a creature with limited powers of discrimination and a limited memory to transmit and understand an infinite variety of messages, and to do this in spite of noise and distraction. If we imagine ourselves to have been assigned the task of designing a communication system that will transmit infinitely many meanings, we will see something of the value of the features that define language.

We might undertake to provide a brief unique sound for each message or meaning. Suppose the message were the one that English encodes as *She is preparing dinner*. It would be easy enough to provide a single distinctive grunt or whistle for this total message. That is the way communication problems are solved among the animals. However, we cannot solve them so in our system. The number of messages to be communicated is very greatly in excess of the number of distinct sounds humans can identify.

We would do better to design on the phonemic principle which is the principle all languages follow. This means beginning with a stock of elementary sounds which are called *phonemes* in descriptive linguistics. Phonemes are, for the most part, vowels and consonants, and they correspond roughly to the letters of an alphabetic writing system. Phonemes are not themselves meaningful; they are semantically empty. No language uses very many. The range in the languages of the world is from about fifteen to about eighty-five, with English using forty-five. Probably the number is small because it is advantageous to use only sounds that can be easily produced and identified. By making sequential arrangements of the phonemes, larger units, very much more numerous than the elementary ones, can be constructed. The larger units are called *morphemes* in descriptive linguistics and are similar to, but not the same as, words. With forty-five phonemes one can build the 100,000 or so morphemes of an ordinary college dictionary of American English without making any sequence very long. Morphemes are not semantically empty; each one has a meaning.

We might build our stock of morphemes by combining the elementary sounds in all possible ways up to some limit of length. If the morphemes used up all possible combinations of phonemes, then a change of a single phoneme, any single vowel or consonant, would always constitute a new morpheme. The transmission and identification of morphemes in such a language would be a precarious business. Any elementary error, such as might easily be caused by noise or distraction, would result in the reception of an unintended morpheme and so of an unintended meaning. Natural languages never do use all possible combinations of phonemes. There are always restraints on combination. English, for example, sometimes uses a cluster of consonants to begin a morpheme, but the language does not permit every conceivable cluster to be used in this way. Of the many thousand possible combinations of one, two, or three consonants, fewer than one hundred are actually employed. As a consequence of such restraints a message may be considerably distorted without being mistakenly identified. If we saw *Shx is pxeparxing dinnxr* we probably would know what was intended. This is, in part, because the combinations with *x* do not constitute English morphemes. They would be morphemes if all possible combinations were used.

From our 45 phonemes, let us imagine that we have created 100,000 morphemes. By some estimates highly educated people learn to recognize and understand as many as this, though it is a rare person who *produces* more than about 10,000 different ones (Miller, 1951). These are large numbers but something short of the infinite set of messages the system is required to be able to convey. The number of distinct signals can be enormously increased, indeed infinitely increased, if we will allow the creation of morpheme sequences, the creation of sentences. In twenty years or so of life, humans do well to learn to produce and understand 100,000 morphemes or words. How do they ever become competent to produce and understand an infinite number of sentences? The relation between a word or morpheme and its meaning is arbitrary and so has to be memorized. Knowledge that *dinner* is the name of a certain meal does not enable anyone to guess the meaning of the word *preparing*. However, the relation between a sentence and its meaning is not arbitrary in this way. Sentences are built by rule. If anyone knows the meaning of the constituent morphemes of *She is preparing dinner* and knows also certain rules concerning subject-object relations and the formation of the present tense and progressive aspect, he can work out the sense of the sentence. The meanings of sentences can in general be derived from the meanings of the morphemes, in conjunction with knowledge of grammatical constructions and the meanings of these constructions. There is not an infinite variety of morphemes or of grammatical constructions but only of the sentences that can be derived from both together.

The design features of our communications system may be summarized and generalized as follows: Fewer than one hundred sounds which are individually meaningless are compounded, not in all possible ways, to produce some hundreds of thousands of meaningful morphemes, which have meanings that are arbitrarily assigned, and these morphemes are combined by rule to yield an infinite set of sentences, having meanings that can be derived. All of the systems of communication called languages have these design features.

Animals other than man do not have languages of their own and, on present evidence, they are all also incapable of learning the language of any human group. Young chimpanzees have been raised by human families as if they were children, but the chimpanzees have not learned to speak the family language, not even when they were given larger amounts of explicit language training than children ever receive (Brown, 1958). Strenuous efforts have also been made to teach language to bottlenose dolphins (Lilly, 1961), but without real success. The dolphin seemed a likely creature because in absolute weight and size his brain is in the human range. What is more, the dolphin brain is in the human range when the measure is a ratio of brain weight to body weight. However, the probability is that it is not chiefly the size of the brain that qualifies a creature for learning language, but rather the organization of that brain (Lenneberg, in preparation).

Not every human brain is adequate for the acquisition of a language. Total mass may play some role. Nowhere in the world does the newborn infant begin at once to imitate the speech it hears. Children everywhere in the world start to babble recognizable vowels and consonants some time in the first year and begin to produce words early in the second year. By about the middle of the second year they start to make two-word sentences. By the end of the third year children use a large part of the basic grammatical apparatus of the local language. Lenneberg (in preparation) believes that this worldwide timetable is governed by biological development.

The neonate's brain is likely to weigh about as much as the brain of a full-grown chimpanzee. It is not until three years that the child's brain approximates adult norms in size, weight, and fissuration. In addition to the growth of the brain there are peripheral biological developments that contribute to a readiness for speech. With the end of the nursing period the suckling pads in the cheeks of the infant are absorbed and his oral cavity takes on a shape more like that of the adult. By the end of the first year he usually acquires some front teeth which provide articulatory surfaces for the tongue in the production of such dental consonants as the initial sound in *thin* (Lenneberg, in preparation).

Biology is critical for language acquisition but learning opportunities also matter. It occasionally happens that a child is discovered living in isolation, hidden away in an attic or cellar, usually an illegitimate child, fed quickly and surreptitiously by its mother. One such child, Isabelle, was found in a house in Ohio, secluded from contact with everyone but a deaf-mute mother (Davis, 1940). Isabelle was six and a half at the time of her rescue and had apparently been isolated since birth. She had no speech and made only a croaking noise. Isabelle was given good care and training, and, in a week's time, began to vocalize. Two years after rescue, at the age of eight and a half, it is reported that Isabelle's speech could not easily be distinguished from the speech of other children of the same age (Davis, 1947). Human children, like Isabelle, who live outside of any speech community, do not invent language, but require a community to provide it.

Learning oportunities may also be responsible for the fact that working-class children lag behind middle-class children on almost any index of speech development (Templin, 1957). Irwin has shown, for instance, that middle-class children talk more and produce a greater variety of vowels and consonants from about eighteen months on. This difference may be partly a matter of innate ability since there are consistent IQ differences favoring children of higher SES. However, Irwin (1960) has shown that learning opportunities are also important. In order to increase the amount of speech exposure in the homes of working-class families he induced the mothers of a group of children from thirteen to thirty months of age to read to them daily for a period of fifteen minutes from illustrated baby books. A second group of children of comparable ages in working-class homes in which no systematic stimulation occurred served as the control. After the age of eighteen months the experimental group was significantly superior in the frequency with which speech sounds were produced.

Beginning at about eighteen to twenty-four months maturation and learning opportunities ordinarily come together in a way that makes it possible to acquire a system for the communication of an infinite variety of messages. What are the uses of such a system? The obvious uses are the social ones. Information that one person possesses can be delivered to others who do not have it but could use it. This kind of transmission is possible between generations as well as among contemporaries, and so, with the emergence of language, life experiences begin to be cumulative. Some animal species are able to transmit a small amount of lore across generations; chiefly knowledge of waterholes, feeding places, and the habits of enemies (Wynne-Edwards, 1962). But most of what the aged anthropoid knows perishes with him. The young chimpanzee starts life, as he did millennia ago, from scratch.

Very much less obvious than the social uses of language are its uses for the mental processes of the individual. This great subject is more easily introduced with reference to writing and reading than to speech. Writing is a secondary linguistic system founded on speech but not usually learned until the early school years. When children are first introduced to writing and reading it might be a good idea to make a classroom demonstration of one of the advantages of literacy.

We would let the children hide, wherever they wished within the classroom, a large number of small desirable objects: coins and tricks and stamps and the like. Then we would ask each child to call out the names of the objects he has hidden and also their hiding places. All the children would be instructed to try to memorize all of the information so that they might recover as many valuables as possible on the following day. The teacher, while all this went on, would stand at the blackboard inscribing certain cryptic signs:

> Dime—In dirt around plant
> Stamp—Page 21 of dictionary
> Metal spider—On top of painting of George Washington.

On the next day one child after another would be given a chance to recover as many treasures as he could directly find while the teacher stayed out of the room. No child would recover more than a fraction of the total. Then everything would be returned to its hiding place and the teacher called into the room. Consulting the blackboard she would triumphantly collect every last object. The preliterate children would gather that there was some powerful "medicine" in those marks on the board, something enabling the teacher to store far more information than they were able to store.

The preliterate has no writing but he is not without technology. There is speech itself. Where the teacher has written herself a message at Time 1 to be decoded at Time 2, the children have spoken themselves such a message. The spoken form does not "keep" as well as the written; but does it perhaps keep better than information not verbalized at all? How would the recovery process have gone for completely prelinguistic creatures? Would they even possess such relational concepts as are named in English with the terms *in* and *around* and *on top of?* Would they know the thing category we call *plant* and the substance we call *dirt?* If they had the conceptions and lacked only the names, would that make a difference in their performance? To these questions about language and thought we will return.

The discussion of language acquisition in this chapter is organized by linguistic systems as these systems are conceived by the science of descriptive linguistics. Descriptive linguistics may be regarded as a branch of cultural anthropology since it is concerned with a cultural system, a set of rules for the guidance of behavior. The late Clyde Kluckhohn used to say that linguistics was the most advanced branch of anthropology. This claim for linguistics rests on the fact that it has found a set of universal categories that can be used for the description of any language. Chief among these are the phoneme, morpheme, morpheme class, and immediate constituent. The use of a common set of categories has rendered the structure of one language comparable with the structure of another. It has also revealed the existence of a large number of "linguistic universals"—ways in which all languages are alike (Greenberg, 1963). From the descriptive studies, generalizations have emerged which are of interest both for the theory of culture and the theory of the human mind.

This chapter, Part I of our discussion of language, concerns two formal systems: the phonological and the grammatical. Any utterance in a language can be represented on these two levels. On the more molecular level it is a phonetic sequence, a sequence of elementary sounds. The description of the phonemes of a language and the rules governing their combination is a description of the phonological system. The rules governing the combination of phonemes only apply to short stretches of speech that fall between the pauses (technically, *open junctures*) which usually separate words. There are no phonological rules across pauses and so no possibility of building up sentences by writing rules for the combination of sounds alone. One must move to a second more molar level of description where the elements are morphemes, the smallest units of meaning. From morphemes, words are composed by "morphological" rules and sentences by "syntactic" rules. Morphology and syntax together comprise what the linguist calls grammar. In discussing phonology and syntax we will describe the nature of the systems as well as what is known of their acquisition.

From the formal systems we will turn, in Chapter 7, to the semantic system and here descriptive linguistics is not able to give us much help. It is just here, of course, that the critical problems of language and thought arise. Chapter 7 concludes with a discussion of the social communicative function of language and the problems that egocentrism makes for this function.

The Phonological System

We will use the term *phone* to designate any particular occurrence of a vowel or consonant. The term *phoneme* will be defined at some length but it refers roughly to a category of phones, a category that is distinctive for native speakers of a language. A *phonemic transcription* of speech is a written record of speech from the point of view of the native speaker; it preserves all, but only, the distinctions that function as such for the native speaker. It is a transcription from "inside" the language. A phonetic transcription is, in linguistic field procedures, a prerequisite to the discovery of phonemes. It is an "external," relatively culture-free, written record. We will follow the established convention of enclosing phonetic symbols in brackets (e.g., [p]) and phonemic signals in slash marks (e.g., /p/).

SPEECH PRODUCTION IN GENERAL

Speech sounds are basically a set of modulations of the stream of air which, when we inhale or exhale, passes through the oral cavity, the nasal cavity, and the pharyngeal cavity. Speakers of English use in-drawn breath for *tsk-tsk!* and occasionally to gasp surprise or even to say a short word like *Yeah*, but our vowels and consonants are all usually created with exhaled air. Other languages make greater use of the in-drawn stream.

Figure 6-1 is a schematic drawing of the principal parts of the human speech apparatus. At the top of the trachea or windpipe, encased in the heavy sheath popularly known as the "Adam's apple," is the larynx or voice box. The larynx contains the vocal cords or bands which are

bundles of muscle and cartilage that can be opened and closed and subjected to various degrees of tension. When these cords are set so that
the stream of air from the lungs causes them to vibrate, the result is
vocal tone. Great variations of pitch and quality are possible for any
speaker and there are also differences between speakers. When vowels or
consonants are produced with vocal tone, they are said to be "voiced."
When the cords are open and air passes freely through, without setting
up vibrations in the larynx, the vowels and consonants produced are
"voiceless."

The speech sounds we call consonants are produced by impeding or
breaking the stream of air with one or another of the mobile articulators
in the mouth. To make the initial sound of the word *big*, for example, the
two lips come together and then release air with a small explosion. The
sounds we call vowels are produced by permitting the air a relatively
free passage but altering the size and shape of the various cavities through
which that air passes. These alterations cause certain frequencies in the
basic complex tone to be damped and set up resonance chambers for
others. The consequence is the kind of variation of vocal quality that
distinguishes *hid* from *had* and both of these from *hide*.

Consonants are most conveniently characterized in terms of a place of
articulation and a mode of articulation. A place is defined by the surfaces
that approach or contact one another. In the examples that follow, of
English consonants produced in various positions, the first member of
each pair is voiced and the second member is voiceless. Bilabial consonants
like [b] and [p] are produced by the two lips. Labiodental consonants,
like [v] and [f] are produced by the lower lip and upper teeth. Apico-
alveolar consonants, like [d] and [t], are produced by bringing the apex
or tip of the tongue to the alveolar ridge which is the hard gum surface
just behind the upper teeth. Dorso-velar consonants, like [g] and [k],
are produced by bringing the back or dorsum of the tongue up to the
soft velum above. These are some of the positions used to make English
consonants; there are also many positions not used in English which
are used in other languages. For example, the apex or tip of the tongue
can easily be brought to the upper lip to produce a sound something like
[b] or something like [d] but different from either of them.

The mode of articulation of a consonant describes the nature of the
interference with the air stream. Consonants like [b], [p], [d], [t],
[g], and [k] are all "stops." The air stream is fully stopped at the position
of articulation and then abruptly released. Consonants like [v] and [f], as
well as the initial sound of *the* (symbolized [ð]) and the initial sound
of *thin* (symbolized [θ]) are "fricatives." There is constriction at the
position of articulation so that the air stream makes a noise in passing
through. Consonants like [z] and [s] are "sibilants" produced by direct-

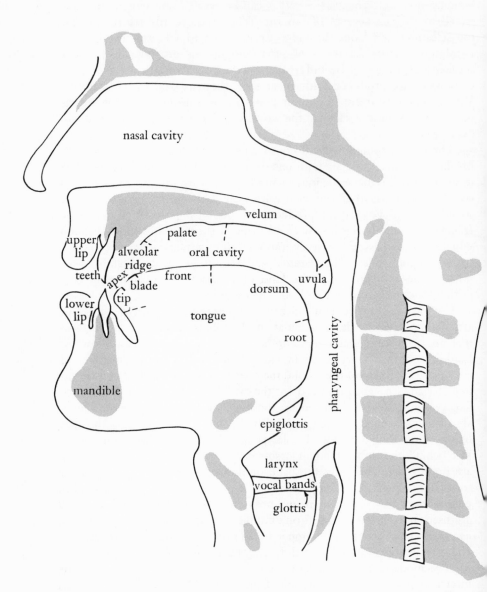

FIGURE 6-1. SCHEMATIC DRAWING OF THE SPEECH APPARATUS
(From W. Nelson Francis, *The Structure of American English*. Copyright
© 1958 The Ronald Press Company)

ing a jet spray of air against a surface. Consonants like [m] and [n] and the final sound of *sing* (symbolized [ŋ]) are "nasals" produced by stopping the oral passage at the position of articulation and so forcing the air stream out through the nose. All of these are modes of production used in English; there are also some that English does not use. A "trill" for example is a very rapid, repeated interruption and release of air. Trills produced by the tip of the tongue are heard initially in such Italian words as *Rigoletto* or *Renata*. Trills produced with the pendulous organ at the back of the throat, which is called the uvula, are heard initially in French *rouge* and German *rot*.

Any number of consonants not heard in English can be created from combinations of articulation mode and articulation place. A fricative mode of production at the place where we form [k] and [g] produces such sounds as are final in Scottish *loch* and German *Buch*. A nasal that one does not hear everyday can be produced by bringing the tip of the tongue to the upper lip and attempting to articulate [n]. Try this exotic nasal (we will symbolize it as [x] in place of [n] on *nose.* Now shift among three versions of *nose:* one with [n]; one with [x]; and one with [m]. You will begin to hear a new nasal, distinct from either [n] or [m].

For the production of vowels the tongue and lips are the most important organs. The tongue can cause numberless variations of size and shape in the cavities through which the air stream passes. Lip rounding as in [o] or [u] produces still other variations. With vowels as with consonants, it is very easy to produce sounds not heard in English. For instance, the front vowel [i] produced with lip-rounding is an un-English umlaut vowel.

The printed letters that stand for vowels and consonants in our writing system appear on the page as discrete entities ordered from left to right. The literate speaker of a language that is written alphabetically quite naturally thinks of the individual phones of speech as a set of discontinuous segments that follow one another in time like a line of marching soldiers. In fact, however, speech is, for the most part, physically continuous. We do not pause after each vowel or consonant, though we do pause between such larger segments as words and sentences. The movement from one phone to another is often as gradual as the transformation from one pattern to another in a continuously rotating kaleidoscope.

The most startling aspect of speech in a completely unfamiliar language is the fact that it does not "segment" to our ears. Segmentation emerges on the perceptual level when we begin to detect recurrences. For someone who had never heard English the word *big* might at first sound like one complex, continually shifting sound. When he had also heard *ban* and *bay* and noticed the difference from *pan* and *pay*, his perception of *big* should change. There would be an initial entity in *big* recognized from its occurrence elsewhere and its distinctiveness from contrasting entities. The transformations of a kaleidoscope would similarly begin to segment when a viewer could say: "Ah yes, there's that murky one again and now comes the pattern that looks like a starry sky."

We can be sure that children have to learn to hear the significant recurrences and contrasts that are the segmental phonemes of the local language. Most of this learning seems to be accomplished in the first two or three years. However, responding to speech as if it were made up of recurrent vowels and consonants is not the same thing as consciously representing speech to oneself as a string of segments. The conscious conception of speech in discrete segmental terms usually does not develop until children learn to read.

The vowels and consonants are called "segmental" phones in descriptive linguistics. Speech always also involves some significant features that cannot be considered segmental for the reason that they do not march with the vowels and consonants but are rather added to or imposed upon the marching line. These "suprasegmental" features are the various stresses and pitches. In English there are four significant (or phonemic) stresses and also four significant pitches. The fact that these are an essential part of English phonology can be demonstrated with an example of a sentence that is uninterpretable in a printed form which omits stress and pitch. "Mary where Jane had had had had had had had had had the teacher's approval." The sense will emerge if we add punctuation and italics to suggest the critical suprasegmentals and pauses. "Mary, where Jane had had *had*, had *had* had; *had* had, had the teacher's approval." Jane, you see, used *had* whereas Mary used *had had* and it was the latter form that the teacher approved.

THE PHONEME

The trained linguist hearing speech in an unwritten language that is completely unfamiliar to him is nevertheless able to hear it as segmented into recurrent patterns. He will have had training in phonetics and this training has equipped him to identify speech sounds that do not occur in his native language or in any of the familiar European languages. Furthermore, he has a set of symbols for writing down what he hears; possibly the International Phonetic Alphabet composed of Roman and Greek and Old English letters and various other forms, plus a set of modifying little marks or "diacritica."

In recent years close acoustic study has shown that the individual phones of anyone's speech are all, in some detail or other, unique. This is true even of those phones that a speaker intends to be the same and thinks of as being the same. No linguist can possibly hear all of the physical differences that exist in the speech he records, but training will have sharpened his perceptual discrimination so that he hears much more phonetic detail than does the untutored ear. It is generally not practical for the phonetician to preserve in his written transcription all of the phonetic detail he can discriminate under optimal conditions. In practice, phonetic records preserve major distinctions in the speech being studied; more distinctions than the native speaker pays any attention to but not so many as the well-trained human ear is capable of hearing and, of course, not the infinite variety physical instruments can register. In a phonetic transcription one aims at a culture-free record that does not prejudge the phonemic structure and at an over-differentiated record that does not miss possibly significant differences.

A phonetic symbol, such as [p'], stands for the class of phones produced by bringing together the two lips and exploding a puff of air without, at the same time activating the vocal cords (i.e., "voicelessly"). The symbol stands for a class of phones and not for a particular unique phone because it does not indicate such additional properties of any particular phone as the general level of intensity and the duration of the sound. The phonetic [p'], also and most importantly, implies nothing about the functional significance of this class of phones for the linguistic community. It does not indicate whether the community thinks of a phone of this type as different from a phone of the type [b], which is like [p'] except that it is "voiced" and not aspirated, nor whether [p'] and [b] are used by the community to distinguish one meaning from another. The phonetic transcription is a rough physical record that is prerequisite to the discovery of phonemic distinctions.

A brief presentation such as the one offered here can give only an approximate understanding of the phoneme. In this paragraph we will have an analogy intended to convey the general lines of the phoneme concept and, in the following paragraphs, we will have the essentials of the definition offered by linguistic science. Imagine, now, that we have undertaken the study of the metal currency of some foreign country. Imagine further that we have a collection of coins belonging to that currency. These will vary from one another in many respects; in color, size, brightness, printing, pictures, milling, smoothness, dirtiness, etc. Examined closely there will be no exact duplicates among the coins even as there are none among phones. In the economic exchanges of the community, however, the various potentially discriminable differences are not of equal importance. Variations of size and color among American coins, for instance, assign a given specimen to one or another functional class; they make of it a penny, nickel, dime, quarter, or half-dollar. Within a class one member is equivalent to another (although potentially discriminable in terms of year, shininess, etc.) and members of different classes are not functionally equivalent. Those of us who habitually operate with American coins think of them as falling into five classes. We regularly attend to size and color because these characteristics determine functional class membership and only under extraordinary circumstances do we notice characteristics of the coins which have no functional importance. Phones like coins are organized into a functional system and the basic classes of this system are the phonemes. The phonemic structure of an unfamiliar language is worked out by the linguist from study of the speech practices of the community. He cannot tell in advance which characteristics of the phones he hears will have functional significance for the community.

In English we have many consonant pairs which are alike except that one is voiced and the other is voiceless. The linguist, whose native language is English, will notice this dimension of variation in any unfamiliar speech to which he is exposed even as the American who studies unfamiliar coins will attend to size and color. However, it is always possible that, in the unfamiliar society, voicing does not distinguish coin types. It is essential that both the linguist and the coin classifier begin their studies with a relatively full description of their materials which does not prejudge the local functional system; for speech this is the phonetic transcription. The functional system must, in both cases, be abstracted from the behavior of community members.

The linguist's phonetic transcription of a collection of utterances will record more phonetic distinctions than are actually functional for native speakers. Some of the phones that have been distinctively recorded by the linguist should be grouped together as one phoneme. Those that belong together will have some articulatory and acoustic similarity and this similarity causes the linguist to consider the possibility that certain phones are one phoneme but similarity alone cannot establish the facts. The final decision depends on the way the phones are distributed among the utterances and on certain judgments obtained from native speakers. There are two kinds of relationship among phones which indicate to the linguist that the phones in question are members of one phoneme. The relationships are called *free variation* and *complementary distribution*.

Phones in free variation are, essentially, phones that are mutually substitutable one for another; the variations among them are unintentional and have no significance for native speakers. Indeed, native speakers are not ordinarily aware of the variations. One can, for example, alter the force and the pitch and the breathiness of the initial [k] sound in *cat* so as to yield a variety of potentially discriminable phones. Native speakers of English, however, will not ordinarily pay any attention to these changes, and, in fact, will think of the pronunciations as all essentially the same. There are several behavioral tests from which the linguist can learn whether phones are free variants in the minds of native speakers. The linguist can tell his informant that he intends to "repeat" a given utterance, e.g., *cat*, and then can deliberately run through the set of phones suspected of being in free variation. If the native speaker accepts these various pronunciations as "repetitions" then the varying phones belong to one phoneme. The linguist can also ask the native speaker to repeat a form and note what variety of pronunciations is offered by the speaker as a set of repetitions. Then there is sometimes the possibility of noting whether phonetically variant forms are used to name the same object. If they are, it is probable that the native speaker thinks of the forms as the same.

Phones in complementary distribution are essentially variant forms of a single phoneme where the variations are predictable from preceding or subsequent phones. In English the initial [k] of *keep* is articulated farther forward on the soft palate than is the initial [k] of *cool*. It is as if the speaker anticipates the placement of the front vowel in making the [k] of *keep* and the back vowel in the [k] of *cool*. And, indeed, the forward [k] in English regularly precedes front vowels and the [k] produced farther back precedes back vowels. These two phones are, for English, in complementary distribution, by which we mean that they occur in mutually exclusive phonetic environments. With a little training a linguist can learn to hear the difference between the two phones but it is not a difference to which the native speaker attaches any significance. Such phones in complementary distribution are called, in descriptive linguistics, "allophones" (or variant forms) of a single phoneme.

Examples of complementary distribution also occur in English printing and these are more familiar than examples from our speech. The upper-case letter, for instance, occurs at the beginning of a sentence and the lower-case letter does not. In this respect, therefore, such letters as *s* and *S* are in complementary distribution; i.e., where the one occurs the other does not. These are printed letters, not spoken forms (pronunciation of *s* and *S* does not vary in any consistent way). The linguist would call *s* and *S allographs* of one *grapheme* in the writing system of English. Allophones, like allographs, are variant forms of a basic type, with the variations being predictable from preceding and following phones—the phonetic environment.

Finally, there is the case of phones that belong in distinct phonemes, the variations in speech that the native speaker does notice and uses to discriminate meanings. Phones that are phonetically distinct are never in complementary distribution. They distribute like free variants, i.e., they occur in some utterances which are otherwise identical. The difference between phonemically distinct phones and free variants lies with the behavior of the native speaker. He will not accept phonemic changes as "repetitions"; he will not offer them as "repetitions"; he will not use utterances that vary in this way for the same referent. In short, using the tests for free variation, a set of results opposite to those described above identifies phonemically distinct phones.

How do the phonemes of one language differ fom those of another? There are two main sorts of difference: a simple phonetic exclusiveness and a difference in the phonemic organization of shared phonetic material. The first difference is the more familiar. We know that speakers of English do not employ the uvular [r] of French *rouge* or the final velar fricative of German *Buch*. This kind of difference on the phonological level has an analogue on the level of the lexicon or vocabulary. The most familiar sort of difference in lexicon is the case where one language has a name for some local custom or site or invention which is simply not represented in the other language. Differences in the cognitive organization of areas of overlap are less familiar and more interesting.

Articulatory and acoustic variations which serve to differentiate phonemes in one language may differentiate allophones or free variants in another language. In English, as we have mentioned, most of our consonants can be paired as voiced and voiceless phonemes. Pittman (1948) reports that in the Oto language (Oklahoma) some of these consonant pairs are in free variation, i.e., one member of the pair is an acceptable substitute for the other, as if *din* and *tin* were the same word. In English we do not distinguish phonemically among the [k] sounds in *ski* and *keep* and *cool*. The first two would belong to different phonemes in Hindi and the second two to different phonemes in Arabic (Gleason, 1961). Speakers of English have an area of phonetic overlap with speakers of Oto and also with speakers of Arabic and of Hindi, but the phonemic organizations are different. There is again an analogy on the level of the lexicon. We shall be much concerned, later on, with the case in which some reference domain, some portion of reality, is named in each of two languages but differently organized in the two.

What are the perceptual consequences of a difference in phonemic structure? Native speakers of English trying to learn Hindi or Arabic will tell you that it is at first difficult to hear any difference between the several [k] sounds. Have we perhaps acquired a special auditory sensitivity to acoustic differences that separate one phoneme from another in our native language and an insensitivity to acoustic differences that fall within the domain of a single phoneme? There is one highly relevant experiment; it was done at the Haskins Laboratory in New York (Liberman, et al., 1957).

DISCRIMINATION BETWEEN PHONEMES

The Haskins Laboratory for many years has been working out the distinctive acoustic features of the various phonemes of English. It utilizes the sound spectrograph, which is a device that transforms speech sound into visible patterns, and the Pattern Playback, which makes the reverse transformation. The pictures produced by the spectrograph are called spectrograms (see Figure 6-2). On a spectrogram, time appears on the horizontal dimension. On the vertical dimension appear acoustic frequencies rising with height on the paper. The relative concentration of acoustic energy at particular frequencies is represented by the darkness of the lines at that level of the spectrogram. In order to compare the acoustic properties of various English vowels a speaker of English might be asked to speak into a microphone the following syllables: *heed, hid, head, had, hod, hawed, who'd,* and *hud.* The spectrograms provide a large amount of acoustic detail for each syllable and suggest the characteristic features of each vowel. In order to find out whether some feature is actually an important one for recognition of a vowel the Haskins people would use the Pattern Playback. The acoustic characteristics can be painted on paper— in an idealized form—and the Playback will transform it into sound. They then see whether the sound is recognizable as one or another English

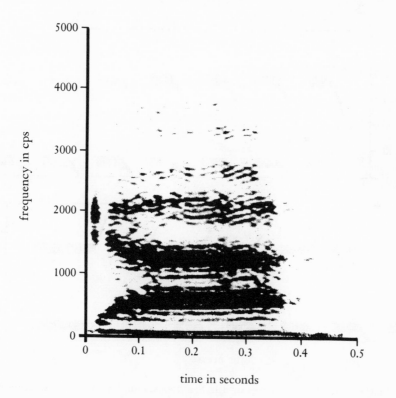

time in seconds

FIGURE 6-2. SPECTROGRAM OF THE SYLLABLE [GA] SHOWING TRANSITIONS AND VOWEL FORMANTS

vowel. The Playback is, in short, a device for synthesizing speech and it figures importantly in the experiment to be described.

If a single speaker produces the various vowels of English it turns out that each vowel can be rather well characterized by the placement in the spectrogram of its first two *formants*. A formant is a frequency band of concentrated energy in the total spectrum; it appears as a dark bar in the spectrogram. The acoustic characteristics of consonants are many and various, but in some cases the cues for several consonants lie along a single physical dimension. This is true of the English consonants [b], [d], and [g]. The dimension involved is the direction and extent of the transition into the second formant of the vowel following the consonant.

Figure 6-3 pictures some idealized painted spectrograms. The placement of the first two formants is the same for all patterns and is such as to produce the central vowel of the word *gate*. The tail on the second formant pictures the transition into that formant and this is the feature that varies in the patterns presented. In the pattern at the extreme left of Figure 6-3

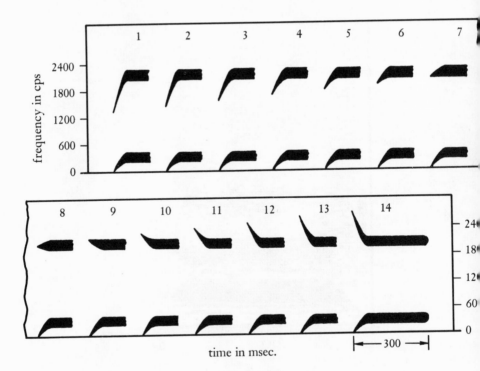

FIGURE 6-3.   ILLUSTRATIONS OF THE SPECTROGRAPHIC PATTERNS FROM WHICH THE STIMULI OF THE HASKINS EXPERIMENT WERE PRODUCED

the transition starts at a point 840 cycles per second below the steady state of the formant. The successive patterns start the transition from ever higher positions until, in the last pattern on the right, it falls to the formant from a point 720 cycles per second above. It is this feature—the direction and extent of the transition—that determines whether the vowel will seem to be preceded by [b], [d], or [g], whether we would hear *bay, day,* or *gay*.

Figure 6-2 is a speech spectrogram picturing the formants and the consonant transition for an actual obtained pronunciation of the syllable [ga]. The formants are the broad horizontal streaks and the transition corresponding to [g] is the tail swinging down into the second formant. The pictures of Figure 6-3 are idealized spectrograms not obtained from actual speech but painted for the Pattern Playback. Patterns 11, 12, 13, and 14 have transitions into the second formant which, if sounded, would produce a [g] sound.

The fourteen patterns of Figure 6-3 were the stimulus materials for the Haskins experiment. The starting points of the transitions rise from one pattern to the next by a constant step—120 cycles per second. In physical terms the differences between all adjacent patterns are identical. English-speaking subjects listened to the patterns, one at a time but in random order, and were asked to say in each case whether the sound was [b], [d], or [g]. When the judgments were plotted against the patterns it became clear that the physical continuum was divided psychologically into three phonemes. The data for one subject appear as Figure 6-4.

A cultural system, a language, breaks an acoustical continuum into phoneme categories. Probably the cutting points are perfectly arbitrary; the language might, equally well, shift the whole set of consonant divisions to the right or to the left. Those of us who have English as our native language have presumably learned to cast the individual sounds into their several phoneme categories; learning to do this would be a part of learning to perceive English speech in the correct way.

The subject who sorts several different sounds into the same phoneme category is not necessarily unable to discriminate among them. He may put them together in the same spirit with which we throw together a large variety of hues and call them, roughly, "red." The question is: Do the cultural categories go deeper than this? Do they affect the ability to discriminate among the sounds?

To learn about powers of discrimination something called an "A-B-X" procedure was used. The sounds were grouped in triads such that there was an A stimulus, a B stimulus, and a third stimulus (X) which was identical either to A or to B. The subjects were instructed to judge whether X was the same as A or the same as B. The measure of discriminability for any two sounds was the percentage of the time that the match

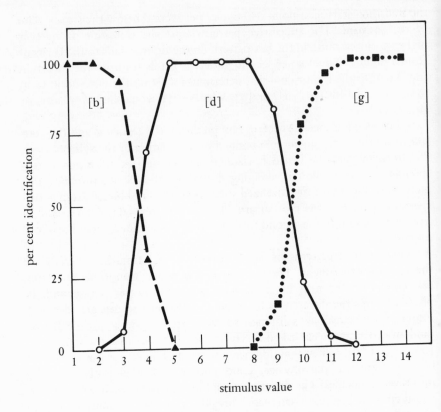

FIGURE 6-4. DATA FROM ONE SUBJECT IN THE HASKINS EXPERIMENT

with X was correct. This is not a procedure that asks for rough categorizations but a procedure that asks the subject to distinguish one stimulus from another if he possibly can do so.

In general, of course, the ability to distinguish sounds improves with the physical distance between them; remote pairs from the set of fourteen were better discriminated than adjacent pairs. The physical difference between all adjacent pairs is a constant 120 cycles per second. Was the discrimination of all such pairs equally acute? More generally, are all pairs having a given physical separation discriminated with the same success? They are not. Stimuli within a phoneme category are less well discriminated than stimuli having the same physical separation that fall on either side of a phoneme boundary. The stimuli numbered 3 and 5 in Figure 6-4 were much more accurately differentiated than were stimuli 1 and 3 or 5 and 7.

Researchers at the Haskins Laboratory have done experiments similar to the one described here with such other English consonant contrasts as

/s/ and /t/, /sl/ and /spl/ (Griffith, 1958; Bastian, Delattre, and Liberman, 1959; Liberman, et al., 1961a, 1961b). The general outcome has been the same in all cases: Discrimination across boundaries is better than discrimination within boundaries.

We are inclined to conclude that learning to speak one's native language causes a sharpening of sensory acuity at boundaries between phonemes relative to the acuity within phonemes. It is important, in an English-speaking land, to be able to distinguish stimulus 3, of Figure 6-4, from stimulus 5; it can be the difference between *buy* and *dye*, *bin* and *din*. Nothing hinges on the distinction between 1 and 3; the word would be *buy* whichever occurred. Apparently differences that are significant come to be detected with greater acuity than differences that are not significant.

The results of the Haskins experiments have another possible explanation. Perhaps English phoneme boundaries are not arbitrarily placed. Perhaps they fall where they do as an adaptation to the natural properties of the human auditory system. If our hearing is innately very acute in certain regions of a continuum then a language might evolve in such a way as to place its phoneme divisions at these points. If this were the case, however, then all languages that employ phonemes like /b/, /d/, /g/, /s/, and /t/ ought to locate them acoustically exactly where English locates them. This is definitely not the case. In addition there is experimental evidence that discrimination of speech sounds can be sharpened by deliberate training (Lane and Moore, 1962). It is fairly certain that the placement of phonemes in a language influences the auditory discrimination of native speakers.

SIMILARITY AMONG PHONEMES

The phonemes of a language will not all be perceptually equidistant from one another. In English the consonants /b/ and /p/ are maximally close together. Both of them are bilabial stops. The difference between them is that /b/ is voiced, whereas /p/ is voiceless. It is the voiced-voiceless feature that is distinctive for this pair. The phoneme /t/ is like /p/ in being voiceless and also in being a stop. The difference between the two is that /p/ is produced by the lips while /t/ is produced by the apex of the tongue. It is the labial-apical feature that is distinctive for this pair. How similar are /t/ and /b/? They differ from one another with respect to both of the distinctive features we have described; /t/ is voiceless and apical whereas /b/ is voiced and labial. In sum, the stops /b/ and /t/ are further apart than either /b/ and /p/ or /p/ and /t/. Two distinctive features separate the first pair whereas only one feature separates the members of each of the other pairs.

A feature of articulation that functions as the only distinction between one pair of phonemes is likely to function, in the same language, as the only distinction between other pairs. In English speech we have many consonant pairs that are perfectly matched, except for the voiced-voiceless distinction. For example, there are: /b/ and /p/; /d/ and /t/; /v/ and /f/; /ð/ of *the* and /θ/ of *thin*. We have also many pairs distinguished by the labial-apical feature alone: /b/ and /d/; /v/ and /ð/; /p/ and /t/; /f/ and /θ/. A feature that is used at all for phonemic distinctions in a language tends to be used for more than one pair. Phonological systems are designed almost as if someone had reasoned that if native speakers are going to have to discriminate a certain feature at all, they may as well discriminate it right along.

If we add a third distinctive feature to the two already mentioned we obtain the three-dimensional plot of Figure 6-5. The third feature is the difference in mode of production between a stop and a fricative. The stop-fricative feature alone distinguishes /b/ from /v/; /d/ from /ð/; /p/ from /f/; and /t/ from /θ/. In Figure 6-5 eight English consonants are

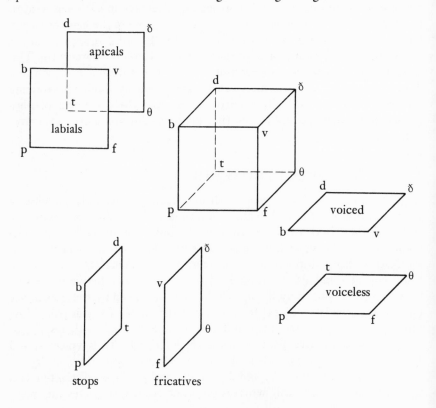

FIGURE 6-5. EIGHT ENGLISH CONSONANTS EMPLOYING THREE DISTINCTIVE FEATURES

classified in terms of three distinctive features. The consonants on the front surface are all labials while those on the back surface are all apicals. The consonants on the top surface are all voiced while those on the bottom surface are all voiceless. The consonants on the left side are all stops while those on the right side are all fricatives. A single straight line segment always represents a difference of one distinctive feature. The number of segments separating any two consonants represents the number of features separating these two consonants.

The theory of distinctive features was first proposed by Jakobson, Fant, and Halle in 1952. These authors argue that a phoneme is a bundle of concurrent distinctive features. They provide a list of such features which is intended to be adequate for the specification of the phonemes of all languages. Each feature is characterized in both articulatory and acoustic terms and, perhaps because the authors were impressed with analogies between the digital computer and the human nervous system, each feature is conceived to operate in a two-alternative or binary fashion.

A distinctive-feature analysis exposes a level of structure even more molecular than the phonemic. It is also a hypothesis concerning the comparative perceptual similarities of the phonemes of a language. In this latter role the distinctive-feature analysis of English has been well supported by research on perception.

When speech is heard in noisy conditions there will be errors of phoneme identification. The prediction made by a distinctive-feature analysis is that phonemes separated by just one feature will be more often confused than phonemes separated by two features and still more often confused than phonemes separated by three features, etc. From Figure 6-5 we can see that if a /b/ is mistakenly identified it should be more easily mistaken for a /p/ or a /d/ or a /v/ than for a /ð/ or a /f/ or a /t/. It should be least often mistaken for a /θ/. Research by Brown and Hildum (1956) and by Miller and Nicely (1955) generally confirms these predictions of a distinctive-feature analysis.

SEQUENCES OF PHONEMES

In order to build meaningful elements, or morphemes, phonemes are strung out in sequences. These sequences have a syntax; that is, there are implicit rules which permit some kinds of sequence and prohibit others. All languages observe such rules but the rules are not the same from one language to another, even when the phonemes are similar.

Figure 6-6 describes the ways in which one can begin an English utterance with one or more consonants. The English language does not use more than three consonants initially. It uses any single consonant except /ŋ/, which is the final nasal sound of *sing*, and /ž/, which occurs in

$$
\text{word} \rightarrow \left\{ \begin{array}{lll}
C_1 & & \\
C_2 & + & r \\
C_3 & + & l \\
C_4 & + & w \\
C_5 & + & y\ w \\
s & + & C_6 \\
\check{s} & + & C_7 \\
sp & + & C_8 \\
sk & + & C_9 \\
str & &
\end{array} \right\} + \text{ vowel } + \ \ldots
$$

yields:	*do, brew, bland, dwarf,*		C_1 all consonants except ŋ and ž
	(pueblo), few, (dupe), skill,		C_2 *b, d, f, g, k, p, š, t, θ*
	(svelte), shmoo, spring, scram,		C_3 *b, f, g, k, p, s*
	string		C_4 d, g, h, k, s, t, (*p, θ, b, š*)
			C_5 *b, f, g, h, k, m, p, v, θ*
also:	*loo, frew, fland, dwill, bule,*		(*d, l, n, r, s, t*)
	smig, shloo, splob, sklit, strab		C_6 *k, m, n, p, t, w, (θ, v)*
			C_7 *l, m, n*
not:	*žay, vrew, tland, fwog, wule,*		C_8 r, l, y
	shap, shpoon, spkay, skbob		C_9 *r, l, w, y*

( ) Indicates possibilities that exist for some speakers of English but not for all.

FIGURE 6-6. PERMISSIBLE CONSONANT ONSETS FOR ENGLISH WORDS (BASED ON WHORF, 1956; HOCKETT, 1958; AND STRANG, 1963)

azure. Speakers of English who attempt to pronounce French words in a French way will use /ž/ initially as in *Jean* of *Chez Jean*, and so have a slightly larger set of onset possibilities. Clusters of two consonants usually involve /r/, /l/, /w/, or /y/ in second position. Clusters of three consonants are very few in number and all utilize /s/ initially.

The formula of Figure 6-6 provides a basis for dividing conceivable phoneme sequences into three classes: those that actually occur in English words; those that do not occur but are possible; those that do not occur and are unlawful. This threefold division is characteristic of linguistic rules on every level and we shall see it again in morphology and syntax. It raises a central question concerning the child's acquisition of language: How does the child in a speech community manage, without explicit instruction, to project the actual occurrences he experiences into the locally accepted population of unrealized but possible occurrences?

The consonant onsets that are actually used in English words constitute the data base from which the formula of Figure 6-6 was derived. Consequently the formula generates all real words; it generates *do, brew, bland, dwarf, few*, and many thousands more. However, the formula generalizes beyond real words. It says in effect that any single consonant or consonant cluster that is used initially at all is available for general use in initial position. The consonant /l/ is now used before certain vowels and vowel-plus-consonant combinations to yield such real words as *loot, law, lie, low, lead, lyre,* etc. The formula says that these uses of /l/ in initial position make it available for new uses before any vowel or vowel-plus-consonant combination. Speakers of English if they need to coin new words to name soaps or detergents or toys are free to invent such forms as *loo, lez, litch, lorbe,* and the like. In short, the formula projects existent combinations into a large population of possibilities. Syntax, even on this simple molecular level, is a *productive* or *open* system.

The formula of Figure 6-6 also proscribes many conceivable combinations; these are the set of unlawful utterances. Any onset that has not yet been used as an initial onset for any real word falls into this last class. Thus speakers of English are not expected to invent such new words as *ngob* or *žay* or *vrew* or *tland.*

It is reasonable to suppose that an unlawful onset, if it were to be produced, would usually be mistakenly identified by speakers of English. Brown and Hildum (1956) have compared the ability of English speakers to identify syllables having unlawful initial clusters with their ability to identify possible combinations that are not actual words. The unlawful syllables included *zdrall, pshoop, fwice, tlib, srate,* and others that cannot be generated by the formula of Figure 6-6. Among their possible syllables that are not actual words were *prall, throop, skice, spib,* and *drate.* All of these can be generated by the formula of Figure 6-6. The possible syllables were identified with much greater accuracy than the unlawful ones.

There must always be some marginal indeterminacy in any formula like that of Figure 6-6, an indeterminacy which is due to individual variations of cultural breadth. The combinations involving consonants in parentheses would be "possible" and pronounceable for some speakers and not for others. Some speakers say *Jean* in the French way and *Schlitz* in the German way but others use the consonant of *judge* for *Jean* and say *Schlitz* as if it were *Slitz.* Some speakers have in their active vocabularies such words as *pueblo, bwana,* and *schwa.* Some say *dupe* and *lure* as if they were *dyupe* and *lyure* and so on. Some use the words *sthenic* and *svelte.* At the present time this formula for English consonant onsets is being radically enlarged by the necessity of speaking such names as *Mboya, Nkrumah, Rwanda, Srinagar,* etc. In Figure 6-6 parentheses have been used to identify combinations that are possible for some speakers of English but not for all.

In any version of the formula for consonant onsets in English the total number of different onsets is well below one hundred. What is the number of conceivable onsets? There are twenty-four consonant phonemes in English. If we accept the, actually arbitrary, upper limit of three consonants to a cluster, then the conceivable combinations of 1, 2, or 3 number 14,424 (Hockett, 1958). In short, the language, in building morphemes, utilizes only a tiny fraction of its combinational possibilities. If it used more of them it could, of course, cut down on long words and morphemes. Why does it not do so?

Are some conceivable combinations simply impossible for the human speech apparatus to produce? Perhaps some are and certainly all of those that the formula proscribes would be judged by native speakers to be very difficult to pronounce. For the most part, however, this difficulty is an acquired one rather than an ineluctable human one. Just about any combination that any language regards as unpronounceable is, somewhere in the world, regularly pronounced—with ease. Serbo-Croatian, for example, which allows for about three times as many onsets as does English, includes among them: /žb/, /žg/, /žd/, and comparable pleasures. Most languages of the Polynesian group, on the other hand, use no consonant clusters at all and we need not wonder what they would think of /skr/, /str/, /spl/, and the like. It is not natural unpronounceability that produces the sequence formula.

It is reasonable to suppose, as we did at the start of this chapter, that one function of the restrictions on phoneme sequencing is to provide redundancy and prevent errors of interpretation (Hockett, 1958). If all vowels were preceded by all consonant onsets, then any error of one vowel or consonant would result in the reception of an unintended morpheme. As it is, many errors of a single segment are simply non-English and so the receiver can check his mistake or guess the nearest real morpheme. Glance again at the real words of Figure 6-6 and see how well they would resist misinterpretation if the more likely errors of perception occurred: *brew* to *braw* or *prew; bland* to *blund* or *pland; dwarf* to *dwirf* or *twarf*. The sequencing formula is not, however, ideally designed for avoiding errors of interpretation and so we can be sure there is more behind it than the provision of redundancy.

Since the rules for consonant onsets are rules governing the combination of formal elements, they are rules of syntax—on a relatively molecular level. They differ from the rules of syntax which govern the combination of morphemes into words and words into sentences in an extremely important respect. Going through the onset formula on one path rather than another changes the word that is generated; for example, from *brand* to *bland* to *swand* to *stand*. Some of the outcomes are words, all are possible words. When the outcomes are words there is a shift in meaning with the rule applied. However, the connection between the new meaning and the new sound sequence is always arbitrary and can be known only by having been memorized. There is no semantic change that is characteristic of the switch from one phonological route to another. Changing from

/r/ to /l/ after /b/ yields *brand* and *bland*. This would not enable anyone to guess the meaning-shift involved in going from /r/ to /l/ after /g/: *grand* to *gland*. However, a shift on the morphological level from, for example, a past tense morpheme to a progressive morpheme produces a consistent and characteristic effect. The change from *brand-ed* to *brand-ing* is just like the change from *sand-ed* to *sand-ing*. A shift on the syntactic level from *Man bites dog* to *Dog bites man* produces the same kind of an effect as the shift from *Cat chases mouse* to *Mouse chases cat*.

In addition to the English formula for consonants preceding the vowel, English has a formula for consonants that follow the vowel. Final clusters are more numerous than initial clusters and there is little overlap of membership between the two sets. Clusters occurring medially in a word can be analyzed into sequences permitted initially or finally or into a combination of such sequences.

With all the rules for the sequencing of phonemes it is natural to wonder whether sentences could not be constructed directly from phonemes. They cannot be, because the phonological restraints do not apply across the kind of short pause that is called, in linguistics, an open juncture (symbolized /+/). The open juncture occurs at the end of most, though not all, words. It functions like a neutral, home position for the articulatory apparatus. The phones produced just prior to the juncture do not constrain those that can occur after it. Here, for example, are some word pairs separated by open juncture, which have consonants on either side of the juncture that could never be directly combined in English: *glimpsed view; banning books; shrimp's range; bird perch*. The syntax of phonemes applies only to the short stretches between pauses. For the longer stretches that are sentences a syntax of morphemes and words is used.

THE DEVELOPMENT OF PHONOLOGY IN CHILDREN

Most of the psychological work that has been done on the development of speech sounds in children has not been concerned with phonemics. Research has concentrated on the frequencies with which the various vowels and consonants occur in the vocalizations of children at different ages (Irwin, 1947a, 1947b, 1947c; Chen and Irwin, 1946). The experimenter has typically taken time samples of the child's babbling or speech, made a rather broad phonetic transcription and then a plot of frequency against phone type. Such plots are useful for answering some questions concerning the development of speech but they are not directly relevant to phonemic questions. The phoneme is a cognitive construct not a motor act. The mere occurrence in child vocalization of certain phone types does not establish these types as members of distinct phonemes for the child. Neither does any particular frequency of occurrence. Adult speakers of both English and Arabic produce, fairly frequently, a relatively forward [k] and also a back [k]. As we know, the two stops belong to distinct phonemes in Arabic but not in English.

There are no studies of the emergence of phonemes in child speech which are fully satisfactory from the point of view of method. There are a few observations of single children made by linguist-parents which point the way. One such was reported in 1943 by Velten.

Using a phonetic transcription, Velten recorded (in order of appearance) all of the meaningful speech forms used by his daughter, Joan, from her eleventh month until her thirty-sixth month. Meaningful forms were defined by Velten as forms used with some consistency of reference. From this linguistic corpus Joan's phonemic system was abstracted according to certain rules. Let us have an illustration. Where two meaningful forms differed with regard to a single phone, e.g., [ba] and [da], Velten thought it possible that the two phones ([b] and [d]) might belong to the same phoneme for the child or that they might belong to distinct phonemes. If [ba] had the same meaning as [da], if the one form were offered as a repetition of the other, then the two consonants were considered to be free variants. If, however, [ba] had a different meaning than [da], then [b] and [d] were thought to belong to distinct phonemes. In Velten's actual materials, as it happened, [ba] seemed to mean *bottle*, whereas [da] seemed to mean *down*. There was also [za] for *that* and Velten concluded that these three consonants were organized by his daughter as distinct phonemes.

Joan's words also made use of the consonants [p], [s], and [t] which are the unvoiced mates of, respectively, [b], [z], and [d]. It was clear from the fact that she had the words [ap], [as], and [at] that the three unvoiced consonants were phonemically distinct from one another, but Velten also asked whether each voiced consonant was distinguished from its unvoiced mate: ([b] from [p], [d] from [t], [z] from [s]). In Joan's vocabulary the voiced consonant was always in initial position and the voiceless consonant in terminal position; i.e., the consonants were in complementary distribution and, therefore, were regarded as allophones (voiced and voiceless versions) of single phonemes. There were, for instance, the words [ba] and [ap] but neither [pa] nor [ab]. Joan did not have two words of different meaning such that the only phonetic distinction marking the difference of meaning was the contrast between voiced and unvoiced. This feature which is "distinctive" for the adult speaker of English was not yet distinctive for Joan.

The psychologist who becomes interested in child phonology will think at once of a number of questions concerning the learning of phonology which cannot be answered by distributional analysis alone but which are open to study by experimentation. Velten might, for instance, have undertaken deliberately to teach Joan to distinguish the voiced-voiceless feature. This could have been done by methods of discrimination-training familiar in both animal and human psychology. Velten might have taken a simple contrasting pair of forms like *bo* and *po* and used them as names for two unlike toys. He could have played a game with Joan in which she was required to bring to him the toy he named. If he then presented *bo* and *po* in random alternation and Joan was able consistently to fetch the indicated toy, there would have been evidence that she had acquired some perceptual control of the voiced-voiceless feature for a particular pair of consonants in a particular pair of words. How widely would this learning have generalized? Would Joan promptly have shown control of the distinction in *go* and *ko*, *do* and *to*, *zo* and *so*? Would she perhaps have distinguished the first two pairs, but not the third for the reason that [g], [k], [d], and [t] are all stop consonants as are [b] and [p] but as [z] and [s] are not?

Another linguist-parent, Ruth Weir (1962), tells us that her son, Anthony, had difficulty with the voiced-voiceless distinction, saying *bik* for *big*, *ret* for *red*, *tiaper* for *diaper*. Anthony also had some difficulty with the distinction between front and back articulation, saying *kray* for *tray* and *waik* for *wait*. Gleason (1961) reports that his daughter learned very early to distinguish labial stops from nonlabial stops and somewhat later voiceless stops from voiced stops. She was much longer learning the distinction between [t] and [k]. The word *cake* would sometimes come out as *cate* or *tate* or *take*. In the girl's speech one could not distinguish such words as *cake*, *Kate*, and *Tate*. In Gleason's opinion the ultimate incentive for distinguishing [k] from [t] was the necessity in English of differentiating the words that contrast in these phonemes alone—such as *cake* and *Kate*.

While we do not have much information about the emergence of phonemes, the distinctive-feature analysis provides us with an interesting hypothesis. Phonemic development may be a process of progressive differentiation resulting from the ability to discriminate more and more distinctive features. The idea may be expressed with reference to the consonant cube of Figure 6-5. A child who only distinguished apicals from labials would have two gross proto-phonemes. The labial one would have, as members, [b], [v], [p], and [f]; the apical would include [d], [ð], [t], and [θ]. If he next added the feature: stop vs. fricative, his proto-phonemes would each divide into two. The result: a labial stop including [b] and [p]; a labial fricative including [v] and [f]; an apical stop including [d] and [t]; and an apical fricative including [ð] and [θ]. Finally the child would add the voiced-voiceless distinction and this would cause each of the four previous phonemes to divide again. The result would be the eight English consonants of Figure 6-5. At this point differentiation should cease. Not because no further differentiation is possible for the auditory system, but because no further differentiation is required by the cultural system. The observations of children that have already been published indicate that phonological development cannot be quite so simple and beautiful a process, but the reports suggest that phoneme emergence is some kind of differentiation process following distinctive-feature lines.

About the child's knowledge of the rules for sequencing phonemes we know almost nothing. To be sure, Ruth Weir's book (1962) about the speech of her two-and-a-half-year-old son, Anthony, reports his use of the majority of the consonant onsets permitted in English. The really interesting question, however, is not which onsets are used. It is whether children have internalized the formula itself. The test of that would be their ability to distinguish possible but unreal words like *fland* and *dwill* and *spib* from unreal and impossible words like *sbap* and *fwog* and *tlib*. Would young children find the latter stranger and less pronounceable than the former? If so, then they would have abstracted the implicit syntax of phonemes and generalized its rules.

The Grammatical System

We are changing levels of analysis. Any linguistic utterance is, we know, a sequence of individually meaningless phonemes but it is also, simultaneously, a sequence of meaningful morphemes. The sentence *The dog chased the cats* is a string of vowels and consonants spoken at different pitches with varying degrees of stress. It is also a string of the following morphemes: {the}, {dog}, {chase}, {–d}, {the}, {cat}, {–s}. In discussing grammatical systems we shall be thinking of utterances in this second way. The morpheme is our element or unit and grammar is the set of rules for combining morphemes to make words and sentences. We shall use braces to enclose symbols that stand for morphemes.

THE MORPHEME

The morpheme cannot be defined as precisely as the phoneme. Morphemes are, roughly, minimal meaningful forms. In the illustrative sentence of the preceding paragraph each of the forms {the}, {dog}, {chase}, and {cat} is a morpheme and also a word. Morphemes such as these, which can stand alone, are called "free morphemes."

The word *chased* is not a single morpheme and neither is the word *cats*, because, while both forms are meaningful, they are not minimal. Each of them can be subdivided into two morphemes. *Chased* is composed of a verb and the ending {–d}. This ending is only used on a verb when the action named occurred in past time, so the ending may be said to mean past time. The word *cats* is composed of a noun and an ending {–s}. This ending means plurality—more than one cat, in the present case. Morphemes that are not words and do not stand alone are called "bound morphemes."

Grammar is conventionally divided into morphology and syntax; the former being rules for building words and the latter rules for building sentences. We will preserve that distinction here.

MORPHOLOGY

Words that are not single morphemes may, in English, be combinations of free morphemes only or of bound morphemes only or of some of each. Words such as *birthday, blackboard,* and *football* are constructed from free morphemes alone. Words such as *circumvent* and *disturb* and *include* and *perceive* contain more than one morpheme but none of the morphemes is free to occur alone. Words such as *cats* and *chases* and *singer* and *simplest* and *disprove* and *uneasy* contain both free and bound morphemes.

Many English bound morphemes are suffixes, and suffixes divide into two categories: "inflections" and "derivational" suffixes. Inflections are suffixes that must be final in a word; nothing can be added after them. The final morphemes of *chased* and *cats* are inflections. Derivational suffixes need not be final. Derivational suffixes serve generally to transform words belonging to one part of speech into semantically related words belonging to another part of speech.

English uses only a few inflections, but these few are used with great frequency. They include the possessive inflection of *John's house;* the plural inflection of *three cats;* the third person present indicative inflection of *he chases;* the simple past of *he chased* and the comparative and superlative forms of the adjective as in *happier* and *happiest.*

Derivational affixes are very much more numerous than inflections but none of them is used as frequently as the inflections. There are some that serve to transform nouns into adjectives: *fault* to *fault-y, fate* to *fat-al, child* to *child-ish,* etc. These are some that do the reverse job: *false* to *fals-ity, stingy* to *stingi-ness, abundant* to *abundan-ce,* etc. There are some that transform nouns to verbs: *beauty* to *beauti-fy; utility* to *utili-ze, saliva* to *saliva-te,* etc. And again some that work in the opposite direction: *arrive* to *arriv-al, sail* to *sail-or, agree* to *agree-ment.*

All of the major parts of speech in English are linked with one another by derivational affixes, though adverbs are peculiar in that, while there are rules for transforming words from something else into an adverb, there are not rules for turning adverbs into anything else. Whenever a word is shifted from one part of speech to another it acquires a new set of possible uses and so the derivational machinery in English is a major source of linguistic productivity.

Inflections for Plurality and Past. Let us look closely at two fragments of English morphology, the inflections for plurality and the simple past tense (appearing on *cats* and *chased* in our sample sentence) to see how morphological rules differ from the rules for sequencing phonemes. Any literate speaker of English who is asked what the rule is for forming the regular plural is likely to say: "You add *s.*" And in writing one does add the letter *s.* Behind that misleading single letter, however, there are in spoken English three phonemically different inflections.

Consider the three plurals: *dogs, cats,* and *horses.* In printed form the letter *s* is the plural element for all three. However, if you attend closely to your pronunciations of the three, you will find that the inflections are distinct. To *dog* one adds the voiced sibilant /z/; to *cat* one adds the voiceless sibilant /s/; to *horse,* which in the singular already has a final sibilant, one adds a midvowel plus the voiced sibilant which yields /ɨz/. There are in short three forms of the regular plural.

The variations in the regular plural are lawful. The voiceless sibilant is used for *cat, duck, map,* etc. What these have in common is a final voiceless consonant on the singular form. The voiced sibilant is used for *dog, bud,* and *lab,* and all other singular forms that terminate in a voiced consonant. The voiced /z/ is also used for singular forms that end with a vowel or semivowel, such as *cow, hoe,* and *tree.* Finally, the /ɨz/ form is used with *horse, maze, niche,* and *judge;* with all singular nouns that end in either a sibilant or a sibilant-like affricate.

The regular past inflection on the verb follows a pattern that is a perfect abstract parallel of the plural pattern. The written form of the inflection seems always to be either *d* or *ed.* Behind these written forms are three phonemically distinct inflections. When the base verb ends with a voiceless consonant, for example, *walk, tip,* or *hiss,* the inflection is the voiceless stop /t/. When the base verb ends with a voiced consonant, for example, *nag, bribe,* or *buzz,* the inflection is the voiced stop /d/. The voiced stop is also used after vowels or semivowels, as in *sigh, toe,* and *pray.* When the base verb itself ends in either /d/ or /t/, one adds the voiced stop plus a neutral vowel, making /ɨd/. Examples are *batted, fitted,* and *padded.*

The rules for both the regular plural and the regular past are covered by the following abstract description. The alternative inflections are voiced and voiceless forms of otherwise identical consonants. The voiceless form is used to follow voiceless consonants, the voiced to follow voiced consonants or vowels. When the base word terminates in a consonant of the same type as the inflections themselves, a neutral vowel is supplied and then the voiced version of the inflection. This abstract description also applies in English to the inflections for possession and for the third-person present indicative form of the verb.

The three forms of the plural and also the three forms of the past, since they are selected by, or conditioned by, immediately preceding sounds, are in complementary distribution. In this respect they are like allophones of a phoneme. However, [s] and [z] cannot be considered allophones nor can [t] and [d] because when they are not functioning as plural or past inflections they are not in complementary distribution. Furthermore, they are used to distinguish one meaning from another as in *seal* and *zeal*, *tin* and *din*. As inflections for plurality /s/ and /z/ and /ɨz/ are called *allomorphs*, or variant forms of one morpheme. And the same is true of /t/ and /d/ and /ɨd/.

The rules of inflection described above belong to a realm transitional between phonology and morphology, which the linguist calls *morphophonemics*. I selected these morphophonemic patterns for detailed description because they are similar to the sequencing rules by which phonemes are combined, but different in a critical way.

Like the formula for possible consonant clusters, the inflection patterns are rules that guide the formation of speech sequences. Both sets of rules divide conceivable utterances into three classes. The first class is that of actual English sequences and, on the morphological level, includes *dog*-/z/ and *cat*-/s/ and *horse*-/ɨz/. The second class is created by generalizing the implicit regularities of the first class and would include, on the morphological level, such acceptable but not actual plurals as *loo*/-z/, *fland*/-z/, *svuff*/-s/, and *litch*/-ɨz/. It is worth noting that when Al Capp invented the word *shmoo* he specified its plural as *shmoon*, but his specification did not prevail. When people talked about the comic strip they referred to *shmoo*/-z/.

The third class of sequences is the set of utterances that are not actual and that violate the regularities defining the second class. These unlawful utterances would include, on the morphological level, *cow*/-s/, *dog*/-s/ and *cat*/-z/, as well as the more exotic forms that might be created by pluralizing prepositions or putting the past inflection on conjunctions. Unlawful utterances on the level of phonology and on the level of grammar violate cultural norms, not natural laws. It is not naturally impossible to form such utterances. But if they are formed in a certain community they will fall outside the linguistic system and either be regarded as incomprehensible or else assimilated to the lawful utterance they most resemble. If someone said *dog*-/s/ and *cat*-/z/, it would probably be assumed that he meant the proper forms but had a vaguely Slavic accent or was drunk or something.

What are the important differences between the inflectional rules and the phoneme-sequencing rules? The chief difference is that the inflections are not just sounds, they are morphemes. A change in an utterance from one phoneme to another will, if it is a permissible change, create a new word and the presumption of a new meaning. If people start to use the word *frew* as a noun it will be assumed that they have in mind some meaning other than *brew* or *crew* or *view*. However, what that meaning may be cannot be derived from the phonemic sequence as such. Meaning is arbitrarily assigned at the level of individual morphemes and so has to be memorized. The case would be quite otherwise if, once the sense of the word *frew* had become established, someone invented *frew-/z/*. The addition is not just a consonant, but is the morpheme for plurality, and so one knows that whatever a *frew* may be, the word *frews* refers to more than one of them.

The change of a morpheme in an utterance, if it is a lawful change, produces a change in the sense of the total utterance that is derivable or predictable because it is *characteristic* of the morpheme in question. The change of a phoneme also produces a change in total meaning but one that is not predictable because phonemes do not produce *characteristic* semantic effects.

The inflection rules are unlike the phoneme sequence rules in a second respect. The inflection rules cannot be stated in terms of phonemes alone. To be sure there is some reference to phonemes; the final consonant or vowel of the base form selects the particular allomorph of plurality or of the past tense. It is because they make such reference that the inflection rules are called *morphophonemic* rather than just morphological. However, it is only the selection among the allomorphs that is phonemically conditioned. The plural morpheme itself, disregarding variations of phonemic shape, is not affixed to particular vowels or consonants. It is affixed to morphemes and these must belong to the class of morphemes called nouns or, more exactly, count nouns. The inflection for the simple past tense cannot be affixed to morphemes of this class but only to morphemes of another class—verbs.

Rules of grammatical sequence are rules for the combination of morphemes. But the morphemes of a language are so numerous that the rules are better stated in terms of classes of morphemes. The familiar parts of speech are examples of very large morpheme classes.

SYNTAX

English is a language having most of its grammar at the level of syntax rather than morphology. It is from syntax that English acquires its greatest productivity. In this section we will illustrate two aspects of English syntax: sequencing rules and hierarchical structure.

Sequencing Rules. Recall our sample sentence: *The dog chased the cats.* We have so far talked about the way in which the two complex words in this sentence are built up by morphophonemic rules. Now we will talk about the words in the sentence which precede the verb. As the sentence stands, there are just two of these: *the* and *dog.* Just for the present discussion of sequential syntax let us add a third word, between these two, the descriptive adjective *old.* There is not much syntax in two words; three will make a better example. These three constitute a noun phrase (NP) in English.

Rules of syntax resemble rules of phonological sequence and also rules of morphology and of morphophonemics in that they divide conceivable utterances into three classes. There is, however, a difference of crucial significance in the definitions of the first and second classes. For the more molecular rules the first class consists of actual English words or morphemes, which one might look up in a dictionary, and the second class of potential words or morphemes, which can be imagined by generalizing the regularities implicit in the actual ones. With syntax we are able to generate phrases and sentences but there is no dictionary or any other kind of book that lists all actual phrases and sentences of English. It is impossible that there should be such a book since the number of grammatical sentences is infinite. When language is considered as a cultural system there is, on the level of syntax, no way of distinguishing between actual and potential utterances. For the individual speaker, however, the distinction between actual and potential utterances does exist. Any one of us, in however long a lifetime, can only have heard some finite set of actual sentences or phrases but from the regularities in these we can think ahead to indefinitely many additional possible sentences which we have not heard. These might, depending on individual experience, include "the old lemur" or "the old lute" or even, for a child, "the old cat."

The third class of conceivable utterance is composed, as it is on more molecular levels, of all the utterances that violate the rules and so fall outside the system. Examples of these are: "the dogs old" and "old the dogs" and "dogs old the." What must the rules be like that will proscribe those immediately above and permit "the old dog" or "the old cat" or "the old lute"?

They are written in terms of morpheme classes. One might begin by assigning each of the morphemes involved in the sample noun phrase to such a class: *the* is an article (Art), *old* is a descriptive adjective (Ad), and *dog* is a count noun (Nc). A morpheme class is a class of morphemes that have similar privileges of occurrence in such larger constructions as words, phrases, and sentences. In the description of a language a morpheme class is defined by its formal privileges without reference to meaning. Count nouns, for instance, are partially defined by the fact that they can take the plural inflection. *Cat* belongs, we know, to the count noun class and so also does *dog*. Count nouns also have the *privilege* of being preceded by articles and by descriptive adjectives. Articles are partially defined by their privilege of preceding either nouns alone or nouns that are preceded by adjectives. Adjectives have the privilege of interpolation between articles and nouns. And so on.

Putting the various class privileges together one can write a simple formula that will generate phrases like: "the old dog" or "an old cat" or "a young man" or "the friendly cat." The formula appears as Figure 6-7. Nouns and adjectives can only be listed illustratively since they are so very numerous. Notice the parallels between this formula and the formula of Figure 6-6 which generates consonant onsets. Both are sequence rules written in terms of classes of linguistic units. The great difference is, of course, that any of the lawful variations produced by the syntactic formula has a meaning derivable from its components, whereas the lawful variations in the consonant onset formula have meanings that are not derivable.

$$NP \rightarrow Art + Ad + Noun$$

$$Art \rightarrow \textit{a, an, the}$$
$$Ad \rightarrow \textit{old, young, friendly, green,} \text{ etc.}$$
$$Nouns \rightarrow \textit{dog, cat, man, house, car, cup, tree,} \text{ etc.}$$

FIGURE 6-7. A FORMULA FOR GENERATING SOME ENGLISH NOUN PHRASES

Parts of speech are very large morpheme classes, but we were not taught in "grammar school" to define them by privileges of occurrence. A noun, they told us, "is the name of a person, place, or thing." At that time, none of us was disposed to point out that, while person and place are clear enough, thing is not. It can only mean all the concepts we nominalize which are neither persons nor places. These include blood, justice, wind, and many others. Morpheme classes do not have enough semantic uniformity to be clearly defined in semantic terms. However, morpheme classes do have semantic tendencies. Most names of persons and places are nouns even if the reverse is not true, and many names of actions are verbs and many names of qualities are adjectives. The tendency that morpheme classes have to be semantically distinct as well as formally distinct is one of the reasons for thinking that a grammar is, in some degree, a theory of reality. The consonant classes of Figure 6-6 do not of course show any semantic consistency.

We cannot go far toward the description of a full English grammar but we cannot let the simple formula of Figure 6-7 stand without suggesting how imperfect and incomplete it is. For example, some of the phrases one could generate with the formula of Figure 6-7 as it stands would not be grammatical. "A old dog" will not do and neither will "an friendly dog." The two indefinite articles are allomorphs governed by the initial phoneme of the word that follows: *an* before vowels and *a* before consonants. There seems to be something wrong also with a sequence such as "a friendly car" or "a young house." It is difficult to decide whether the difficulty is grammatical or only semantic but some grammarians would want to write their rules so as to exclude such sequences.

Suppose we tried to be more ambitious in our grammar. If we became only a little more ambitious and tried to allow for the pluralization of count nouns we should have to subdivide the articles and add a restriction on combination. The definite article *the* can precede count nouns in either the singular or plural but the indefinite articles, *a* and *an*, can only precede count nouns in the singular. The articles of Figure 6-7 do not all have the same privileges when we inflect the noun for number.

Not all English nouns are count nouns. Suppose we wanted to make those alterations in the formula of Figure 6-7 that would make it capable of generating noun phrases utilizing nouns of other kinds. Count nouns name objects that have more or less characteristic sizes and shapes, objects that are discrete and countable, such as *cup, tree, man,* etc. Another class of nouns, mass nouns, consists of names of extended substances such as *sand, air,* and *water.* Mass nouns can be preceded by the definite article (*the sand, the water*) but they cannot be preceded by the indefinite articles *a* and *an* (*a sand? a water?*). Mass nouns also cannot be pluralized. If mass nouns were listed in with the count nouns in the formula of Figure 6-7 that formula would generate such unlawful phrases as *an old sand* or *a green water.* To broaden the range of the formula without producing unacceptable sequences it would be necessary to proliferate morpheme classes and multiply restrictions.

Suppose that we wanted to be really ambitious and describe the proper sequencing of every sort of noun modifier. A loose approximation to the rules appears as Table 6-1. The columns represent morpheme classes designated in a rough semantic way. If members of more than one class are to precede the same noun they must in general appear in the left-to-right order of Table 6-1. One says in English "this train's first four passenger cars" but not "this train's passenger four first cars." One says, "that boy's three unusual young grey Persian cats" but not "that boy's grey three Persian unusual young cats."

HIERARCHICAL STRUCTURE

We have become accustomed to thinking of *The dog chased the cats* as having units of two sizes, phonemes and morphemes. The sentence also breaks up into units larger than either phonemes or morphemes. If one were to show the sentence to an adult speaker of English and ask him to

Table 6-1. Sequential Order of Modifiers in English Noun Phrases

Particles	Possessive	Ordinal number	Cardinal number	Characteristic	Size	Shape	Temperature and humidity	Age	Color	Origin	Noun	Head noun
the							cool		blue	Aegean		sea
a												
this	train's	first	four								passenger	cars
that	boy's		three	unusual				young	grey	Persian		cats
those												
some												
many												
any				remarkably			hot, damp			tropical		climate
your												
his					short	stocky						frame
her												
their												
our												
my	son's			witty			warm		colorful			personality

indicate its chief parts he would probably divide it between *The dog* and *chased the cats*. The first portion he probably would call the subject and the second portion the predicate. The feeling that a sentence somehow "cracks" into such major sub-wholes is a real part of every speaker's feeling for his language.

The largest constituents of any sentence, the ones created by what might be called the first "cut," are called its *"immediate constituents."* The *ultimate constituents* of a sentence, from the point of view of grammar, are its individual morphemes. Between the ultimate constituents and the immediate constituents there can be varying numbers of intermediate structural levels, varying with the complexity of the sentence. Figure 6-8 represents the hierarchy of levels present in our model sentence. The first cut separates subject from predicate; the second separates, within the predicate, the verb from its object. The final cut breaks the sentence into the morphemes that are its ultimate constituents.

For our own language we can identify constituents intuitively and agree with one another fairly well. For other languages the linguist has other techniques. One helpful test for immediate constituents is to substitute single words for various parts of a sentence to see whether the result is a grammatical sentence similar in structure to the original. In place of *The dog* one could use *Rover* or *He*. In place of *chased the cats* one could use *plays* or *howls*. Now try the substitution with a sequence that is not a constituent such as *dog chased*. It is not easy to think of a single word that can replace these two and leave the result a sentence.

The	dog	chase	-d	the	cat	-s.	morphemes
The	dog	chased		the	cats.		words
The	dog	chased		the	cats.		subject-verb-object
The	dog	chased		the	cats.		subject-predicate
The	dog	chased		the	cats.		sentence

FIGURE 6-8.   CONSTITUENT STRUCTURE ANALYSIS OF A SENTENCE

As long as we think of sentences as sequences of morphemes we are likely to think of syntactic rules as rules for selecting morphemes from sets of classes ordered from left to right or, in time, from earlier to later. There are logical arguments which make it seem unlikely that rules of this sort can ever yield a complete grammar of a real language (Chomsky, 1957; Gleason, 1961). The hierarchical analysis of a sentence into constituent structures suggests another sort of syntactic rule. Instead of trying to generate the sentence from left to right we might try to generate it from the top down. Chomsky has devised a system for doing this by starting with the largest constituents and rewriting these into progressively smaller constituents. He calls this kind of grammar a phrase structure grammar.

Figure 6-9 presents in schematic form a phrase structure derivation of our model sentence and in the next few paragraphs we shall be making reference to the figure. On the left-hand side of Figure 6-9 we have the model sentence rewritten in terms that are progressively more specific. On the right-hand side are the grammatical rules governing the process. The rules are all of the same general type; they all rewrite one constituent symbol at a time and always into smaller or more specific constituents. The rule always stands opposite the version of the sentence to which it is applied and the version of the sentence next below on the left is always the representation that results from application of the rule.

Derivation	Rules
Sentence	Sentence → NP + VP
NP + VP	NP → Art + N
Art + N + VP	VP → V + NP
Art + N + V + NP	NP → Art + N
Art + N + V + Art + N	Art → *the*
the + N + V + *the* + N	N → *dogs, cats, man, mouse, lion*, etc.
the + dogs + V + *the* + cats	V → *chased, ate, caught, bit*, etc.
the + dogs + chased + *the* + cats	

FIGURE 6-9.   DERIVATION OF A SENTENCE FROM THE TOP DOWN

We begin with the symbol "Sentence." This is divided into a noun phrase (NP) and a verb phrase (VP). For reasons of economy in the grammar this division is better than the related division into a subject and a predicate. Next the noun phrase (NP) component is rewritten into article (Art) plus noun (N). Then the verb phrase (VP) component is rewritten as verb (V) plus noun phrase (NP). This second noun phrase (NP) is rewritten as article (Art) plus noun (N). At this point we can see the advantage of the initial division into NP and VP rather than subject and predicate. The NP can appear as object of a verb or in a prepositional phrase as well as serving as the subject of a sentence, and one set of rules will serve to expand it in any of these positions.

The sentence now appears as Art + N + V + Art + N. These symbols all represent morpheme classes: articles, nouns, and verbs. The remaining rules are lists of the words that belong to each class; in effect the lexicon listed by syntactic class. The nouns and verbs, being very numerous, are represented by only a few entries. The final steps in the particular derivation of Figure 6-9 involve the selection of specific morphemes from each class and by selecting the right ones we can emerge with our model sentence.

Figure 6-10 is a diagrammatic representation of the hierarchical structure of the model sentence. Any two words that are joined at a node belong to a common constituent at some level of analysis. The words *dog* and *chased* we see do not join and they are not members of any constituent below the level of the sentence itself.

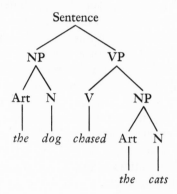

FIGURE 6-10.   DIAGRAM OF THE CONSTITUENT STRUCTURE OF A SENTENCE

A phrase-structure grammar is in several ways superior to a left-to-right grammar. One of its virtues is an ability to represent certain common semantic ambiguities. One can easily generate a string of morphemes which, when considered as a string of morphemes, is ambiguous. Consider the sentence: "They are baking potatoes." Does it mean that certain potatoes are being baked or that certain potatoes are meant for baking? This ambiguous string of morphemes can be generated in two ways by a phrase-structure grammar. One way of doing it is to combine *baking* and *potatoes* into a single predicate nominative construction and this carries the sense of potatoes meant for baking. The other possibility is to make *are* and *baking* into a single present progressive verb and this carries the sense of potatoes being baked. A left-to-right grammar has only one way of representing the sequence and so cannot explain the ambiguity that exists.

For a full discussion of the properties of phrase-structure grammar I must refer you to Chomsky (1957) and to Gleason (1961). In these books, too, you will find treatments of another sort of rule, the grammatical transformation. The phrase-structure grammar, while it is superior to a left-to-right sequencing grammar, has shortcomings of its own. Grammatical transformation rules are designed to remedy these.

The properties of sequential order and of hierarchical structure, which are so evident in language, may characterize every sort of mental and behavioral process. This thesis has been argued in a book called *Plans* by Miller, Galanter, and Pribram (1960). These authors show how sequential order and hierarchical structure can be built into a computer program and how such programs might operate in instinct, learning, and recall.

THE DEVELOPMENT OF GRAMMAR IN CHILDREN

There are several research groups in the United States now studying the development of grammar. The author belongs to one of these[1] and the discussion that follows is, for the most part, based on the work of that group. It is a description of three processes in grammar acquisition.

Some time in the second year of life most children begin to construct two-word utterances; such a one, for instance, as *push car*. A construction such as *push car* is not just two single words spoken in a certain order. As single-word utterances (they are sometimes called holophrases) both *push* and *car* would have equal strong stresses and the falling intonation contours that are terminal in normal English sentences. When *push* and *car* are programed as a single utterance, the primary or strongest stress would fall on *car* and so would the highest level of pitch. *Push* would be subordinated to *car* by a lesser stress and a lower pitch; the unity of the whole would appear in the absence of a terminal contour between the words and the presence of such a contour at the end of the full sequence.

By the age of thirty-six months some children are so advanced in the construction process as to produce all of the major varieties of English simple sentences up to a length of ten or eleven words. Our research group has been chiefly concerned with children who are between eighteen and thirty-six months of age and most recently we have been making a longitudinal study of a boy and girl whom we shall call Adam and Eve. We began work with Adam and Eve in October of 1962 when Adam was twenty-seven months old and Eve eighteen months old. The two children were selected from some thirty whom we considered. They were selected primarily because their speech was exceptionally intelligible and because they talked a lot. We wanted to make it as easy as possible to transcribe accurately large quantities of child speech. Adam and Eve are the children of highly educated parents; the fathers were graduate students at Harvard, and the mothers are both college graduates. Both Adam and Eve were single children when we began the study. These facts must be remembered in generalizing the outcomes of the research.

While Adam is nine months older than Eve, his speech was only a little

1. The group has included Mrs. Ursula Bellugi, Dr. Jean Berko Gleason, Mr. Colin Fraser, Dr. David McNeill, Mr. Samuel Anderson, and Dr. Daniel Slobin. The work was supported in whole by Public Health Service Grant MH-7088 from the National Institute of Mental Health.

more advanced in October of 1962. The best single index of the level of speech development in children is the average length of utterance and in October, 1962, Adam's average was 1.84 morphemes and Eve's was 1.40 morphemes. The two children stayed fairly close together in the year that followed; in the records for the thirty-eighth week Adam's average was 3.55, and Eve's 3.27. The processes to be described appeared in both children.

Every second week we visited each child for at least two hours and made a tape recording of everything said by the child, as well as of everything said to the child. The mother was always present and most of the speech to the child is hers. Both mother and child became very accustomed to our presence and learned to continue their usual routine with us as observers.

One of us always made a written transcription, on the scene, of the speech of mother and child with notes about important actions and objects of attention. From this transcription and the tape a final transcription was made and these transcriptions constitute the primary data of the study. For many purposes we require a "distributional analysis" of the speech of the child. To this end the child's utterances in a given transcription were cross classified and relisted under such headings as: "*A* + noun"; "Noun + verb"; "Verbs in the past"; "Utterances containing the pronoun *it*"; etc. The categorized utterances expose the grammatical regularities of the child's speech.

The dialogue between mother and child does not read like a transcribed dialogue between two adults. Table 6-2 offers a sample section

TABLE 6-2. A SECTION FROM ADAM'S FIRST RECORD

Adam	Mother
See truck, Mommy.	
See truck.	
	Did you see the truck?
No I see truck.	
	No, you didn't see it?
	There goes one.
There go one.	
	Yes, there goes one.
See a truck.	
See truck, Mommy.	
See truck.	
Truck.	
Put truck, Mommy.	
	Put the truck where?
Put truck window.	
	I think that one's too large to go in the window.

from an early transcribed record. It has some interesting properties. The conversation is, in the first place, very much in the here and now. From the child there is no speech of the sort that Bloomfield (1946) called "displaced," no speech about other times and other places. Adam's utterances in the early months were largely a coding of contemporaneous events and impulses. The mother's speech differs from the speech that adults use to one another in many ways. Her sentences are short and simple; for the most part they are the kinds of sentence that Adam will produce a year later.

Perhaps because they are short, the sentences of the mother are perfectly grammatical. The sentences adults use to one another, perhaps because they are longer and more complex, are very often not grammatical, not well formed. Here for instance is a rather representative example produced at a conference of psychologists and linguists: "As far as I know, no one yet has done the in a way obvious now and interesting problem of doing a in a sense a structural frequency study of the alternative syntactical in a given language, say, like English, the alternative possible structures, and how what their hierarchical probability of occurrence structure is" (Maclay and Osgood, 1959, p. 25). It seems unlikely that a child could learn the patterns of English syntax from such speech. His introduction to English ordinarily comes in the form of a simplified, repetitive, and idealized dialect. It may be that such an introduction is necessary for the acquisition of syntax to be possible, but we do not know that.

In the course of the brief interchange of Table 6-3 Adam imitates his mother in saying, "There go one" immediately after she says, "There goes one." The imitation is not perfect: Adam omits the inflection on the verb. His imitation is a reduction in that it omits something from the original. This kind of imitation with reduction is extremely common in the records of Adam and Eve, and it is the first process we shall discuss.

Imitation with Reduction. Table 6-3 presents some model sentences spoken by the mothers and the imitations produced by Adam and Eve. These were selected from hundreds in the records in order to illustrate

TABLE 6-3. SOME IMITATIONS PRODUCED BY ADAM AND EVE

Model utterance	Child's imitation
Tank car.	*Tank car.*
Wait a minute.	*Wait a minute.*
Daddy's brief case.	*Daddy brief case.*
Fraser will be unhappy.	*Fraser unhappy.*
He's going out.	*He go out.*
That's an old-time train.	*Old time train.*
It's not the same dog as Pepper.	*Dog Pepper.*
No, you can't write on Mr. Cromer's shoe.	*Write Cromer shoe.*

some general propositions. The first thing to notice is that the imitations preserve the word order of the model sentences. To be sure, words in the model are often missing from the imitation, but the words preserved are in the order of the original. This is a fact that is so familiar and somehow reasonable that we did not at first recognize it as an empirical outcome rather than as a natural necessity. But of course it is not a necessity, the outcome could have been otherwise. For example, words could have been said back in the reverse of their original order, the most recent first. The preservation of order suggests that the model sentence is processed by the child as a total construction rather than as a list of words.

In English, the order of words in a sentence is an important grammatical signal. Order is used to distinguish among subject, direct object, and indirect object and it is one of the marks of imperative and interrogative constructions. The fact that the child's first sentences preserve the word order of their models partially accounts for the ability of an adult to "understand" these sentences and so to feel that he is in communication with the child. It is conceivable that the child "intends" the meanings coded by his word orders and that, when he preserves the order of an adult sentence, he does so because he wants to say what the order says. It is also possible that he preserves word order just because his brain works that way and that he has no comprehension of the semantic contrasts involved. In some languages word order is not a very important grammatical signal. In Latin, for instance, *Agricola amat puellam* has the same meaning as *Puellam amat agricola* and subject-object relations are signalled by case endings. We would be interested to know whether children who are exposed to languages that do not utilize word order as a major syntactic signal preserve order as reliably as do children exposed to English.

The second thing to notice in Table 6-3 is the fact that when the models increase in length there is not a corresponding increase in the imitation. The imitations stay in the range of two to four morphemes, which was the range characteristic of the children at this time. The children were operating under some constraint on length or span. This is not a limitation of vocabulary; the children knew hundreds of words. Neither is it a constraint of immediate memory. We infer this from the fact that the average length of utterances produced spontaneously, where immediate memory is not involved, is about the same as the average length of utterances produced as immediate imitations. The constraint is a limitation on the length of utterance the children are able to program or plan.[2] This kind of narrow-span limitation in children is characteristic of most or all of their intellectual operations (Brown & Fraser, 1963). The limitation grows less

2. See Brown & Fraser (1963) for additional evidence of the constraint on sentence length.

restrictive with age as a consequence, probably, of both neurological growth and of practice but of course it is never lifted altogether.

A constraint on length compels the imitating child to omit some words or morphemes from the mother's longer sentences. Which forms are retained and which omitted? The selection is not random but highly systematic. Forms retained in the examples of Table 6-3 include: *Daddy*, *Fraser*, *Pepper*, and *Cromer*; *tank car*, *minute*, *brief case*, *train*, *dog*, and *shoe*; *wait*, *go*, and *write*; *unhappy*, and *old time*. For the most part they are nouns, main verbs, and adjectives, though there are exceptions, as witness the initial pronoun *He* and the preposition *out* and the indefinite article *a*. Forms omitted in the samples of Table 6-3 include the possessive inflection -*s*, the modal auxiliary *will*, the contraction of the auxiliary verb *is*, the progressive inflection -*ing*, the preposition *on*, the articles *the* and *an*, and the modal auxiliary *can*. It is possible to make a general characterization of the forms likely to be retained that distinguishes them as a total class from the forms likely to be omitted.

Forms likely to be retained are nouns and verbs and, less often, adjectives, and these are the three large and "open" parts of speech in English. The number of forms in any one of these parts of speech is extremely large and always growing. Words belonging to these classes are sometimes called *contentives* because they have semantic content. Forms likely to be omitted are inflections, auxiliary verbs, articles, prepositions, and conjunctions. These forms belong to morpheme classes that are small and closed. Any one class has few members and new members are not readily added. The omitted forms are the ones that linguists sometimes call *functors*, their grammatical *functions* being more obvious than their semantic content.

Why should young children omit functors and retain contentives? There is more than one plausible answer. Nouns, verbs, and adjectives are words that make reference. One can conceive of teaching the meanings of these words by speaking them, one at a time, and pointing at things or actions or qualities. And of course parents do exactly that. These are the kinds of word that children have been encouraged to practice speaking one at a time. The child arrives at the age of sentence construction with a stock of well-practiced nouns, verbs, and adjectives. Is it not likely then that this prior practice causes him to retain the contentives from model sentences that are too long to be reproduced in full, that the child imitates those forms in the speech he hears which are already well developed in him as individual habits? There is probably some truth in this explanation, but it is not the only determinant since children will often select for retention contentives that are relatively unfamiliar to them.

We adults sometimes operate under a severe constraint on length and the curious fact is that the English we produce in these circumstances bears a formal resemblance to the English produced by two-year-old children. When words cost money, there is a premium on brevity or, to put it otherwise, a constraint on length. The result is "telegraphic" English and telegraphic English is an English of nouns, verbs, and adjectives. One does not send a cable reading: "My car has broken down and I have lost my wallet; send money to me at the American Express in Paris"; but rather, "Car broken down; wallet lost; send money American Express Paris." The telegram omits: *my, has, and, I, have, my, to, me, at, the, in.* All of these are functors. We make the same kind of telegraphic reduction when time or fatigue constrain us to be brief, as witness any set of notes taken at a fast-moving lecture. A telegraphic transformation of English generally communicates very well. It does so because it retains the high-information words and drops the low-information words. We are here using "information" in the sense of the mathematical theory of communication. The information carried by a word is inversely related to the chances of guessing it from context. From a given string of content words, missing functors can often be guessed but the message "my has and I have my to me at the in" will not serve to get money to Paris. Perhaps children are able to make a communication analysis of adult speech and so adapt in an optimal way to their limitation of span. There is, however, another way in which the adaptive outcome might be achieved.

If you say aloud the model sentences of Table 6-3 you will find that you place the heavier stresses, the primary and secondary stresses in the sentences, on contentives rather than on functors. In fact the heavier stresses fall, for the most part, on the words the child retains. We first realized that this was the case when we found that in transcribing tapes, the words of the mother that we could hear most clearly were usually the words that the child reproduced. We had trouble hearing the weakly stressed functors and, of course, the child usually failed to reproduce them. Differential stress may then be the cause of the child's differential retention. The outcome is a maximally informative reduction but the cause of this outcome need not be the making of an information analysis. The outcome may be an incidental consequence of the fact that English is a well-designed language that places its heavier stresses where they are needed, on contentives that cannot easily be guessed from context.

We are fairly sure that differential stress is one of the determinants of the child's telegraphic productions. For one thing, stress will also account for the way in which children reproduce polysyllabic words when the total is too much for them. Adam, for instance, gave us *'raff* for *giraffe;* the more heavily stressed syllables were the ones retained. In addition we have tried the effect of placing heavy stresses on functors which do not ordinarily receive such stresses. To Adam we said: "You say what I say" and then, speaking in a normal way at first: "The doggie will bite." Adam gave back: "Doggie bite." Then we stressed the auxiliary: "The doggie *will* bite" and, after a few trials, Adam made attempts at reproducing that auxiliary. A science fiction experiment comes to mind. If there were parents who stressed functors rather than contentives would they have children whose speech was a kind of "reciprocal telegraphic" made up of articles, prepositions, conjunctions, auxiliaries, and the like? Such children would be out of touch with the community as real children are not.

It may be that all the factors we have mentioned play some part in determining the child's selective imitations; the reference-making function of contentives, the fact that they are practiced as single words, the fact that they cannot be guessed from context, and the heavy stresses they receive. There are also other possible factors—for example, the left-to-right, earlier-to-later position of words in a sentence—but they make too long a story to tell here (Brown & Fraser, 1963). Whatever the causes the first utterances produced as imitations of adult sentences are highly systematic reductions of their models. Furthermore, the telegraphic properties of these imitations appear also in the child's spontaneously produced utterances. When his speech is not modeled on an immediately prior adult sentence, it observes the same limitation on length and the same predilection for contentives as when it is modeled on an immediately prior sentence.

Imitation with Expansion. In the course of the brief conversation set down in Table 6-2, Adam's mother at one point imitates Adam. The boy says: "There go one," and mother responds: "Yes, there goes one." She does not exactly reproduce the model sentence of the child but instead adds something to it or expands it. What she adds is a functor, the inflection for third person on the verb, the very form that Adam had omitted when he imitated his mother.

One of the first things we noticed when we began to study child speech was the frequency with which adults imitated children. Indeed they seemed to imitate more often than did the children themselves. We later came to realize that adult imitations are seldom exact reproductions; they are usually expansions. The mothers of Adam and Eve responded to the speech of their children with expansions about 30 per cent of the time. We did it ourselves when we talked with the children. Indeed we found it very difficult to withhold expansions. A reduced or incomplete English sentence seems to constrain the English-speaking adult to expand it into the nearest properly formed complete sentence. Table 6-4 lists a few sample expansions from the hundreds in the records.

The first thing worthy of attention in the expansions of Table 6-4 is the fact that the words spoken by the mother preserve the order of the words in the child's sentences. To be sure, words and inflections are added but they are fitted in—before, and after, and between the words the child

TABLE 6-4. EXPANSIONS OF CHILD SPEECH PRODUCED BY MOTHERS

Child	Mother
Baby highchair.	*Baby is in the highchair.*
Mommy eggnog.	*Mommy had her eggnog.*
Eve lunch.	*Eve is having lunch.*
Mommy sandwich.	*Mommy'll have a sandwich.*
Sat wall.	*He sat on the wall.*
Throw Daddy.	*Throw it to Daddy.*
Pick glove.	*Pick the glove up.*

used; they are not generally permitted to disturb the order of the child's words. It is as if these latter were taken as constants by the mother, constants to which some sentence had to be fitted. She acts as if she were assuming that the child means everything he says, all the words and also their order, but as if he might also mean more than he says. From the mother's point of view an expansion is a kind of communication check; it says in effect: "Is this what you mean?"

The second thing to notice about Table 6-4 is the character of the forms added to the child's utterances. They include the auxiliaries *is* and *had* and *will;* the prepositions *in, on, to,* and *up;* the progressive inflection *-ing;* the articles *a* and *the;* the pronouns *her, he,* and *it;* and the main verbs *had* and *have.* For the most part the words added are functors and functors are, of course, the words that the child omits in his reductions.

The interaction between mother and child is, much of the time, a cycle of reductions and expansions. There are two transformations involved. The reduction transformation has an almost completely specifiable and so mechanical character. One could program a machine to do it with the following instructions: "Retain contentives (or stressed forms) in the order given up to some limit of length." The expansion accomplished by Adam's mother when she added the third-person inflection to the verb and said "There goes one" is also a completely specifiable transformation. The instructions would read: "Retain the forms given in the order given and supply obligatory grammatical forms." To be sure this mother-machine would have to be supplied with the obligatory rules of English grammar, but that could be done. However, the sentence "There goes one" is atypical in that it adds only a compulsory and redundant inflection. The expansions of Table 6-4 all add forms that are not grammatically compulsory or redundant and these expansions cannot be mechanically generated by grammatical rules alone.

In Table 6-4 the topmost four utterances produced by the child are all of the same grammatical type; all four consist of a proper noun followed by a common noun. However, the four are expanded in quite different ways. In particular the form of the verb changes: It is, in the first case, in the simple present tense; in the second case, the simple past; in the third case, the present progressive; in the last case, the simple future. All of these are perfectly grammatical but they are different. The second set of child utterances is formally uniform in that each one consists of a verb followed by a noun. The expansions are again all grammatical but quite unlike, especially with regard to the preposition supplied. In general, then, there are radical changes in the mother's expansions when there are no changes in the formal character of the utterances expanded. It follows that the expansions cannot be produced simply by making grammatically compulsory additions to the child's utterances.

How does a mother decide on the correct expansion of one of her child's utterances? Consider the utterance "Eve lunch." So far as grammar is concerned this utterance could be appropriately expanded in any number of ways: "Eve is having lunch"; "Eve had lunch"; "Eve will have lunch"; "Eve's lunch"; etc. On the occasion when Eve produced the utterance, however, one expansion seemed more appropriate than any other. It was then the noon hour, Eve was sitting at the table with a plate of food before her and her spoon and fingers were busy. In these circumstances "Eve lunch" had to mean "Eve is having lunch." A little later when the plate had been stacked in the sink and Eve was getting down from her chair the utterance "Eve lunch" would have suggested the expansion "Eve has had her lunch." Most expansions are not only responsive to the child's words but also to the circumstances attending their utterance.

What kind of instructions will generate the mother's expansions? The following are approximately correct: "Retain the words given in the order given and add those functors that will result in a well-formed simple sentence that is appropriate to the circumstances." These are not instructions that any machine could follow. A machine could act on the instructions only if it were provided with detailed specifications for judging appropriateness and no such specifications can, at present, be written. They exist, however, in implicit form in the brains of mothers and in the brains of all English-speaking adults and so judgments of appropriateness can be made by such adults.

The expansion encodes aspects of reality that are not coded by the child's telegraphic utterance. Functors have meaning but it is meaning that accrues to them in context rather than in isolation. The meanings that are added by functors seem to be nothing less than the basic terms in which we construe reality: the time of an action, whether it is ongoing or completed, whether it is presently relevant or not; the concept of possession; and such relational concepts as are coded by *in, on, up, down,* and the like; the difference between a particular instance of a class ("Has anybody seen *the* paper?") and any instance of a class ("Has anybody seen *a* paper?"); the difference between extended substances given shape and size by an "accidental" container (*sand, water, syrup,* etc.) and countable "things" having a characteristic fixed shape and size (*a cup, a man, a tree,* etc.). It seems to us that a mother in expanding speech may be teaching more than grammar; she may be teaching something like a world-view.

Figure 6-11 illustrates some contrasts of meaning that are coded by functors in English. The pictures are from a test of grammatical comprehension that we designed for work with children (Fraser, Bellugi, & Brown, 1963). The two pictures of each pair in Figure 6-11 represent the same objects, actions, and qualities—the aspects of meaning usually coded by contentives. The pictures of a pair differ from one another in the aspect and time of action, in the spatial relations between objects, in the number of creatures performing an action—aspects of meaning that are usually coded by functors.

As yet it has not been demonstrated that expansions are *necessary* for learning either grammar or a construction of reality. It has not even been demonstrated that expansions contribute to such learning. All we know is that some parents do expand and their children do learn. It is perfectly possible, however, that children can and do learn simply from hearing their parents or others make well-formed sentences in connection with various non-linguistic circumstances. It may not be necessary or even helpful for these sentences to be expansions of utterances of the child. Only experiments contrasting expansion training with simple exposure to English will settle the matter. We hope to do such experiments.

There are, of course, reasons for expecting the expansion transformation to be an effective tutorial technique. By adding something to the words the child has just produced one confirms his response insofar as it is appropriate. In addition one takes him somewhat beyond that response but not greatly beyond it. One encodes additional meanings at a moment when he is most likely to be attending to the cues that can teach that meaning.

If expansions do teach the child something we must still wonder how much. An expansion is always an *actual* utterance in the native language —either a morpheme or a word or a sentence. Does a child only learn the particular utterances he is taught? Is language acquisition simply the learning of *actual* utterances on all levels of grammar and phonology, or is it the acquisition of the various productive formulas or rule-systems which generate potential utterances as well as actual utterances? Eventually there must be acquisition of the productive formulas because, for all adults, language is a system that is open on all levels. How soon does the child begin to detect the regularities in actual utterances from which the productive potentialities may be induced? Nothing has been done about studying this question on the level of the phonological sequences that

a. The bird in the cage
b. The birdcage

c. The cup will fall
d. The cup is falling

e. The dog digs
f. The dogs dig

FIGURE 6-11. SOME SEMANTIC CONTRASTS THAT ARE CODED BY FUNCTORS

generate morphemes, so we will take it up on the level of grammar, of morphology and syntax.

Induction of the Latent Structure. The clearest evidence a very young child can give that he is working out the latent structure of language is, paradoxically enough, the production of an unlawful utterance. However, it must be an unlawful utterance of a certain type. Suppose a child comes in from the yard and says, "I digged a hole," or comes back from a drive in the country and says, "We saw some sheeps and oxes." In saying *digged*, *sheeps*, and *oxes* he produces words that are not actual utterances in English. We can be fairly sure, therefore, that he has not heard these from anyone and so is not simply imitating. As long as a child speaks correctly he may only be producing utterances he has heard. We cannot after all, keep track of every morpheme, word, and sentence a child has had a chance to learn to imitate. When he speaks incorrectly or unlawfully he is not likely to be imitating.

In the case of such unlawful utterances as *digged* and *sheeps* we are, in addition, able to guess the source of the creations. They seem to be overgeneralizations of the regular forms of the past and the plural. As it happens English verbs and nouns do not all follow the regular inflectional paradigms. By treating irregulars as if they were regulars the child exposes the inductive operations of his mind and reveals to us his possession of a productive formula.

Jean Berko (now Jean Gleason) invented a way to make a systematic study of children's knowledge of the morphological or word-forming rules of English. A child is shown the small animal of Figure 6-12 and told: "This is a *wug*. Now there are two of them. There are two———." The experimenter holds her voice up to signal the child that he is to complete the sentence; he will usually supply *wug*/-z/. For a different animal

This is a wug.

Now there is another one.
There are two of them.
There are two ——.

FIGURE 6-12. ILLUSTRATION OF JEAN BERKO'S METHOD FOR ELICITING INFLECTIONS

the word is *bik* and the correct plural *bik/*-s/. For a third animal it is *niss* and the plural *niss/*-ɨz/.

Jean Berko (1958) invented a set of materials that provides a complete inventory of the English inflectional system: the plural and possessive endings on nouns; the simple past, the third person present indicative, and the progressive on verbs; the comparative and superlative on adjectives. She presented these materials as a picture-book game to children of preschool, first, second, and third grade levels and worked out the development of the rules with age.

The use of the regular inflections for children seems to be more general than it is for adults. Both kinds of subject were shown a picture of a man swinging something about his head and told: "This is a man who knows how to gling. He glings every day. Today he glings. Yesterday he————." Adults hang suspended among *gling, glang, glung,* and even *glought* but children promptly say *glinged.* Dr. Berko also tested to see whether children who generalize the regular inflection would correctly imitate irregular forms or would assimilate them to the rules. She showed a picture and said, for instance, "Here is a goose and here are two geese. There are two————." Most of her subjects said *gooses* and performed similarly with other irregular forms. These observations suggest that rules of great generality may survive and override a number of counter instances.

Jean Berko's subjects all showed knowledge of the inflectional formulas of English. Her youngest subjects were four years old. This is not the youngest age at which children show knowledge of the productive morphological formulas. Both Adam and Eve began to create overgeneralized plurals and pasts before they were three years old.

Unlawful utterances that result from the overgeneralization of rules are more difficult to identify on the level of syntax than they are on the level of morphology. In Table 6-5 we have listed some utterances produced by Adam or Eve for which it is difficult to imagine any adult model. It is unlikely that any adult said any of these to Adam or Eve since they are very simple utterances and yet definitely ungrammatical. In addition it is difficult, by adding functors alone, to build any of them up to simple grammatical sentences. Consequently it does not seem likely that these utterances are reductions of adult originals. It is more likely that they are

TABLE 6-5. UTTERANCES NOT LIKELY TO BE IMITATIONS

My Cromer suitcase.	*You naughty are.*
Two foot.	*Why it can't turn off?*
A bags.	*Put on it.*
A scissor.	*Cowboy did fighting me.*
A this truck.	*Put a gas in.*

mistakes which externalize the child's search for the regularities of English syntax. We will provide, as an example of this process, the evolution in child speech of the noun phrase.

A noun phrase in adult English includes a noun, but also more than a noun. One variety consists of a noun with assorted modifiers: *The girl; The pretty girl; That pretty girl; My girl*, etc. All of these are constructions which have the same syntactic privileges as do nouns alone. One can use a noun phrase in isolation to name or request something; one can use it, in sentences, in subject position or in object position or in predicate nominative position. All of these are slots that nouns alone can also fill. A larger construction having the same syntactic privileges as its "head" word is called, in linguistics, an "endocentric" construction and noun phrases are endocentric constructions.

For both Adam and Eve, in the early records, noun phrases usually occur as total independent utterances rather than as components of sentences. Figure 6-13 presents an assortment of such utterances. They consist, in each case, of some sort of modifier, just one, preceding a noun. The modifiers, or as they are sometimes called the "pivot" words, are a much smaller morpheme class than the noun class. Three studies of child speech (Braine, 1963; Brown & Fraser, 1963; and Miller & Ervin, 1964) have independently revealed that this kind of construction is extremely common when children first begin to combine words.

a coat	*more coffee*
a celery*	*more nut**
a Becky*	*two sock**
a hands*	*two shoes*
the top	*two tinker toy**
my Mommy	*big boot*
my stool	*poor man*
that Adam	*little top*
that knee	*dirty knee*

NP → M + N
M → *a, big, dirty, little, more, my, poor, that, the, two*
N → *Adam, Becky, boot, coat, coffee, knee, man, Mommy, nut, sock, stool, tinker toy, top,* and very many others

* Ungrammatical for an adult

FIGURE 6-13. NOUN PHRASES IN ISOLATION PRODUCED AT TIME 1

It is possible to generalize the cases of Figure 6-13 into a simple implicit rule. The rule symbolized in Figure 6-13 reads: "In order to form a noun phrase of this type, select first one word from the small class of modifiers and select, second, one word from the large class of nouns."

This is a "generative" rule by which we mean it is a program that would actually serve to build constructions of the type in question. It is offered as a model of the mental mechanism by which Adam and Eve generated such utterances. Furthermore, judging from our work with other children and from the reports of Braine, and of Miller and Ervin, the model describes a mechanism present in many children when their average utterance is approximately two morphemes long.

We have found that even in our earliest records the $M + N$ construction is sometimes used as a component of larger constructions. For instance, Eve said: "Fix a Lassie" and "Turn the page" and "A horsie stuck" and Adam even said: "Adam wear a shirt." There are, at first, only a handful of these larger constructions but there are very many constructions in which single nouns occur in subject or in object position.

Let us look again at the utterances of Figure 6-13 and the rule generalizing them. The class M does not correspond with any morpheme class of adult English. In the class M are articles, a possessive pronoun, a cardinal number, a demonstrative adjective or pronoun, a quantifier, and some descriptive adjectives—a mixed bag indeed. For adult English these words cannot belong to the same morpheme class because they have very different privileges of occurrence in sentences. For the children the words do seem to function as one class having the common privilege of occurrence before nouns. They are an assortment from all the modifier classes of Table 6-1 used in an undifferentiated way.

If the initial words of the utterances in Figure 6-13 are treated as one class M, then many utterances are generated which an adult speaker would judge to be ungrammatical. Consider the indefinite article *a*. Adults use it only to modify common count nouns in the singular such as *coat, dog, cup*, etc. We would not say *a celery; celery* is a mass noun. We would not say *a Becky; Becky* is a proper noun. We would not say *a hands; hands* is a plural noun. Adam and Eve, at first, did form ungrammatical combinations such as these.

The numeral *two* we use only with count nouns in the plural. We would not say *two sock* since *sock* is singular, nor *two tinker toy* since *tinker toy* is singular. The word *more* we use before count nouns in the plural (*more nuts*) or mass nouns in the singular (*more coffee*). Adam and Eve made a number of combinations involving *two* or *more* that we would not make.

Given the initial very undiscriminating use of words in the class M, it follows that one dimension of development must be a progressive differentiation of privileges, which means the division of M into smaller classes. There must also be subdivision of the noun class (N), for the reason that the privileges of occurrence of various kinds of modifiers must be described in terms of such sub-varieties of N as the common noun and proper noun, the count noun and mass noun. There must eventually emerge a distinction between nouns singular and nouns plural since this distinction figures in the privileges of occurrence of the several sorts of modifiers.

Sixteen weeks after our first records from Adam and Eve the differentiation process had begun. By this time there were distributional reasons for separating out articles from demonstrative pronouns and both of these from the residual class of modifiers. By the time of the thirteenth transcription, twenty-six weeks after we began our study, privileges of occurrence were much more finely differentiated and morpheme classes were consequently more numerous. From the distributional evidence we judged that Adam had made five classes of his original class M: articles, descriptive adjectives, possessive pronouns, demonstrative pronouns, and a residual class of modifiers. Eve had the same set except that she used two residual classes of modifiers. In addition, nouns had begun to subdivide for both children. The usage of proper nouns had become clearly distinct from the usage of count nouns. For Eve the evidence justified separating count nouns from mass nouns, but for Adam it still did not. Both children by this time were frequently pluralizing nouns but as yet their syntactic control of the singular-plural distinction was imperfect. The generative rules were very much more complicated than the rule of Figure 6-13.

In summary, one major aspect of the development of syntactic structure in child speech is a progressive differentiation in the usage of morphemes and therefore a progressive differentiation of morpheme classes. At the same time, however, there is an integrative process at work. From the first, an occasional noun phrase occurred as a component of some larger construction. At first these noun phrases were just two words long and the range of positions in which they could occur was small. With time the noun phrases grew longer, were more frequently used and were used in a greater range of positions. The noun phrase structure as a whole, in all the permissible combinations of modifiers and nouns, was assuming the combination privileges enjoyed by nouns in isolation.

In Table 6-6 we have set down some of the sentence positions in which both nouns and noun phrases occurred in the speech of Adam and Eve. It

TABLE 6-6. SOME PRIVILEGES OF THE NOUN PHRASE

Noun positions	Noun phrase positions
That (flower)	*That (a blue flower)*
Where (ball) go?	*Where (the puzzle) go?*
Adam write (penguin)	*Doggie eat (the breakfast)*
(Horsie) stop	*(A horsie) crying*
Put (hat) on	*Put (the red hat) on*

is the close match between the positions of nouns alone and of nouns with modifiers in the speech of Adam and Eve that justifies us in calling the longer constructions noun phrases. These longer constructions are, as they should be, endocentric; the head word alone has the same syntactic privileges as the head word with its modifiers.

For adults the noun phrase is a sub-whole of the sentence, what we have called an "immediate constituent." The noun phrase has a kind of psychological unity. There are signs that the noun phrase was also an immediate constituent for Adam and Eve. Consider the sentences using the separable verb *put on*. The noun phrase, "the red hat" is, as a whole, fitted in between the verb and the particle even as is the noun alone in "Put hat on." What is more, however, the location of pauses in the longer sentence, on several occasions, suggested the psychological organization: "Put . . . the red hat . . . on" rather than "Put the red . . . hat on" or "Put the . . . red hat on."

The unity of noun phrases in adult English is evidenced, in the first place, by the syntactic equivalence between such phrases and nouns alone. It is evidenced, in the second place, by the fact that pronouns are able to substitute for total noun phrases. For example, in the immediately preceding sentence the pronoun "It" stands for a rather involved construction from the first sentence of this paragraph: "The unity of noun phrases in adult English." The words called "pronouns" in English would more aptly be called "pro-noun-phrases" since it is the phrase rather than the noun which they usually replace. One does not replace "unity" with "it" and say, "The *it* of noun phrases in adult English." In the speech of Adam and Eve, too, the pronoun came to function as a replacement for the noun phrase. Some of the clearer cases appear in Table 6-7.

TABLE 6-7. PRONOUNS REPLACING NOUNS OR NOUN PHRASES AND PRONOUNS PRODUCED TOGETHER WITH NOUNS OR NOUN PHRASES

Noun phrases replaced by pronouns	Pronouns and noun phrases in same utterances
Hit ball	*Mommy get it ladder*
Get it	*Mommy get it my ladder*
Ball go?	*Saw it ball*
Go get it	*Miss it garage*
	I miss it cowboy boot
Made it	
Made a ship	*I Adam drive that*
	I Adam drive
Fix a tricycle	*I Adam don't*
Fix it	

Adam characteristically externalizes more of his learning than does Eve and his record is especially instructive in connection with the learning of pronouns. In his first eight records, the first sixteen weeks of the study, Adam quite often produced sentences containing both the pronoun and the noun or noun phrase that the pronoun should have replaced. Perhaps we see here the equivalence in process of establishment. First the substitute is produced and then, as if in explication, the form or forms that will eventually be replaced by the substitute. Adam spoke out his pronoun antecedents as chronological consequents. This is additional evidence of the unity of the noun phrase since the noun phrases *my ladder* and *cowboy boot* are linked with *it* in Adam's speech in just the same way as the nouns *ladder* and *ball*.

The emergence of the noun phrase as a functional unit in child speech motivates us to change the general form of our description of their speech. A certain pattern of combinations of morpheme classes has become recurrent. The pattern appears as the subject of a verb and as the object of a verb; as the object of a preposition; and as a predicate nominative. In writing generative rules for sentences that include a noun phrase it is an economy of description to employ one symbol (NP) for the total pattern, using the symbol wherever the pattern is privileged to appear but expanding the symbol just once for all positions. In short the emergence of the NP gives us a reason to generate the child's speech from the top down rather than as a sequence of selections from ordered morpheme classes.

We have described several processes involved in the child's acquisition of syntax. It is clear that the last of these, the induction of latent structure, is by far the most complex. It looks as if this last process will put a serious strain on any learning theory thus far conceived by psychology. The very intricate simultaneous differentiation and integration that constitute the evolution of the noun phrase is more reminiscent of the biological development of an embryo than it is of the acquisition of a conditioned response.

It seems unlikely that the intellectual apparatus evolved by our species for linguistic operations should be used for those operations alone. In Chapter 3, "Stratification," we drew some parallels between social structure and linguistic structure, in particular between social roles and parts-of-speech or morpheme classes. Social roles, such as male and female, guest and host, doctor and patient, as well as morpheme classes, such as article, noun, and verb, are defined in terms of the privileges and obligations of interaction enjoyed by their members. There are parallels also between the higher levels of linguistic structure and higher levels of social structure. The immediate constituents of a well-formed social event are as psychologically real as the immediate constituents of a well-formed sentence. A marriage ceremony, for instance, has such first level constituents as the procession, the vows, the reception, and the departure of the honeymooners. On a lower level of analysis the ceremony involves such roles as bride, groom, minister, and father-of-the-bride. The ultimate constituents are of course the persons occupying the roles on a given occasion. The parallels between linguistic structure and social structure are not superficial. It seems likely that the two sorts of structure will turn out to be learned in the same way.

REFERENCES

Bastian, J., Delattre, P., & Liberman, A. Silent interval as a cue for the distinction between stops and semivowels in medial position. *J. Acoust. Soc. Amer.*, 1959, **31**, 1568 (Abstract).

Berko, Jean. The child's learning of English morphology. *Word*, 1958, **14**, 150–177.

Bloomfield, L. *Language*. New York: Holt, 1946.

Braine, M. D. S. The ontogeny of English phrase structure: The first phase. *Language*, 1963, **39**, 1–13.

Brown, R. *Words and things*. New York: Free Press, 1958.

Brown, R., & Fraser, C. The acquisition of syntax. In C. N. Cofer & Barbara S. Musgrave (Eds.), *Verbal behavior and learning*. New York: McGraw-Hill, 1963.

Brown, R., & Hildum, D. C. Expectancy and the perception of syllables. *Language*, 1956, **32**, 411–419.

Chen, H. P., & Irwin, O. C. Development of speech during infancy: Curve of differential percentage indices. *J. exp. Psychol.*, 1946, **36**, 522–525.

Chomsky, N. *Syntactic Structures*. The Hague, The Netherlands: Mouton, 1957.

Davis, K. Extreme social isolation of a child. *Amer. J. Sociol.*, 1940, **45**, 554–565.

Davis, K. Final note on a case of extreme social isolation. *Amer. J. Sociol.*, 1947, **52**, 432–437.

Fraser, C., Bellugi, Ursula, & Brown, R. Control of grammar in imitation, comprehension, and production. *J. verbal Learn. verbal Behav.*, 1963, **2**, 121–135.

Gleason, H. A., Jr. *An introduction to descriptive linguistics*. (Rev. ed.) New York: Holt, Rinehart & Winston, 1961.

Goodall, Jane. My life among wild chimpanzees. *National Geographic*, 1963, **124**, No. 2, 272–308.

Greenberg, J. H. (Ed.) *Universals of language*. Cambridge: M.I.T. Press, 1963.

Griffith, B. C. A study of the relation between phoneme labelling and discriminability in the perception of synthetic stop consonants. Unpublished doctoral dissertation, Univer. of Conn., 1958.

Hockett, C. F. *A course in modern linguistics*. New York: Macmillan, 1958.

Irwin, O. C. Development of speech during infancy: Curve of phonemic frequencies. *J. exp. Psychol.*, 1947, **37**, 187–183. (a)

Irwin, O. C. Infant speech: Consonantal sounds according to manner of articulation. *J. Speech Disorders*, 1947, **12**, 402–404. (b)

Irwin, O. C. Infant Speech: Consonantal sounds according to place of articulation. *J. Speech Disorders*, 1947, **12**, 397–401. (c)

Irwin, O. C. Language and communication. In P. H. Mussen (Ed.), *Handbook of research methods in child development*. New York: Wiley, 1960.

Jakobson, R., Fant, G. M., & Halle, M. *Preliminaries to speech analysis*. Cambridge: Acoustics Laboratory, M.I.T., Technical Report No. 13, 1952.

Lane, H. L., & Moore, D. J. Reconditioning a consonant discrimination in an aphasic: An experimental case history. *J. speech hear. Disord.*, 1962, 27, No. 3.

Lenneberg, E. *Biological bases of language*. In preparation.

Liberman, A. M., Harris, Katherine S., Eimas, P., Lisker, L., & Bastian, J. An effect of learning on speech perception: The discrimination of durations of silence with and without phonemic significance. *Lang. Speech*, 1961, 4, Part 4, 175–195 (a).

Liberman, A. M., Harris, Katherine S., Hoffman, H. S., & Griffith, B. C. The discrimination of speech sounds within and across phoneme boundaries. *J. exp. Psychol.*, 1957, 54, 358–368.

Liberman, A., Harris, Katherine S., Kinney, J. S., & Lane, H. The discrimination of relative onset-time of the components of certain speech and non-speech patterns. *J. exp. Psychol.*, 1961, 61, 379 (b).

Lilly, J. C. *Man and dolphin*. Garden City: Doubleday, 1961.

Maclay, H., & Osgood, C. E. Hestitation phenomena in spontaneous English speech. *Word*, 1959, 15, 19–44.

Miller, G. A. *Language and Communication*. New York: McGraw-Hill, 1951.

Miller, G. A., Galanter, E., & Pribram, K. H. *Plans and the structure of behavior*. New York: Holt, 1960.

Miller, G. A., & Nicely, Patricia C. An analysis of perceptual confusions among some English consonants. *J. Acoust. Soc. Amer.*, 1955, 27, 338–352.

Miller, W., & Ervin, Susan. The development of grammar in child language. In Ursula Bellugi & R. Brown (Eds.), The acquisition of language. *Monogr. Soc. Res. Child Develpm.*, 1964, 29, No. 1, Serial No. 92.

Pittman, D. *Practical linguistics*. Cleveland: Mid-Missions (314 Superior Avenue), 1948.

Strang, Barbara H. *Modern English structure*. New York: St. Martin's Press, 1962.

Templin, Mildred C. *Certain language skills in children: Their development and interrelationships*. Minneapolis: Univer. of Minnesota Press, 1957.

Velten, H. V. The growth of phonemic and lexical patterns in infant language. *Language*, 1943, 19, 281–292.

Weir, Ruth H. *Language in the crib*. The Hague: Mouton, 1962.

Wynne-Edwards, V. C. *Animal dispersion in relation to social behaviour*. Edinburgh and London: Oliver & Boyd, 1962.

CHAPTER 7

Language: The System

and its Acquisition

Part II. THE SEMANTIC SYSTEM; LANGUAGE, THOUGHT, AND SOCIETY

The analytic study of phonology and grammar proceeds best in abstraction from problems of meaning. But ultimately of course the formal systems are interesting because they provide a means for communicating an infinite set of meanings. And probably not only a means of communication but also an agency for the creation of meanings. The linguistic systems may even be the vehicle of thought itself.

The Semantic System

There is no description of the total semantic system of any language. Indeed there is no demonstration that the domain of meaning is a single system. There are systematic descriptions of the meanings of small sets of interrelated terms. Consider, for example, the American English terms: *father, mother, son, daughter, uncle, aunt, nephew, niece.* The meanings of these eight terms can be described with three distinctive features or semantic components: sex, generation, and lineality. Each feature has two values. For sex, the values are male and female; for generation, the values

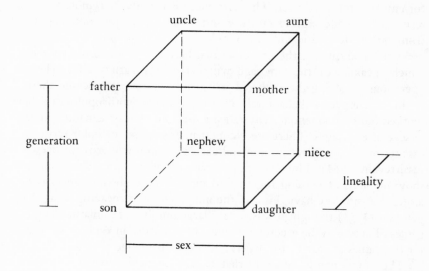

FIGURE 7-1. THE MEANINGS OF EIGHT KIN TERMS

are ascending and descending; for lineality, they are direct and collateral. Since the eight corners of a cube, together, comprise two values on each of three dimensions, it is possible to represent the meanings of the eight kin terms in the manner of Figure 7-1. This representation is like that of Figure 6-5, in which eight English consonants are represented in terms of three binary distinctive features. Figure 6-5 is a representation of some systematic aspects of phonology whereas Figure 7-1 is a representation of some systematic aspects of meaning.

A semantic analysis like that of Figure 7-1 is called a "componential analysis" or, alternatively, an analysis in terms of distinctive features. A componential analysis defines all of some set of words in terms of the same semantic dimensions or components. The meaning of each word in the set appears as a unique bundle of values on the common dimensions. The meaning of *father*, for instance, is: a *male* relative in the *direct* line belonging to the *ascending* (or higher) generation. Or, more briefly, father is: male, direct, ascending. *Niece* has the meaning: female, collateral, descending. And so on.

A componential analysis is economical since it uses fewer semantic components than there are terms to be defined. In our example, eight kin terms are defined by three components having two values each. A componential analysis, furthermore, shows how the meaning of each term in a set is like and unlike the meaning of each other term in the set. A componential analysis also describes the degree of similarity in meaning for any two terms in a set. The term *niece* is maximally remote from the term *father* while *mother* and *son* and *uncle* are all just one step away from *father*. Romney and D'Andrade (1964) have shown that a componential analysis like the one described here is predictive of the way in which speakers of the language will perform a variety of intellectual operations involving the analyzed terms and the concepts behind them.

In recent years behavioral scientists, chiefly anthropologists, have worked out componential analyses for a small number of semantic domains in several languages. There are componential analyses of color terms, disease terms, botanical terms, numeral classifiers, and of words for firewood (Sturtevant, 1964). Thus far, the several particular componential analyses show no signs of coming together to yield a more abstract analysis of a larger domain. We have, instead, the impression that meaning is, as Wittgenstein (1953) thought it was, a very large number of miniature language games. There may be a certain amount of structure in each game, but so far the games appear to be largely independent of one another.

The componential analyses that have been made give us an idea of what a systematic semantics may be like but almost everything in this field remains to be done. We must proceed without a full description of the system itself to ask how linguistic meanings may be learned and what they have to do with thought.

There is one sort of laboratory problem in psychology which, though it has usually been presented to adult subjects, seems to have much in common with the experiences of children learning the meanings of words. It is the concept-formation experiment. Of the several variations on this experiment (Hull, 1920; Heidbreder, 1946; Smoke, 1932; Bruner, Goodnow, and Austin, 1956), I think the one used by Edna Heidbreder in the 1940's is most like the child's experience. Heidbreder's own subjects were adults.

HEIDBREDER'S EXPERIMENT

The pictures in Figure 7-2 comprise five series that were used by Heidbreder. Her subjects did not see the full array of Figure 7-2 but saw the pictures one at a time as each came up on a rotating memory drum. The top picture of the leftmost column appeared first and when it did the experimenter pronounced the word *Ling*. Then came the picture just below and the experimenter called it *Fard* and then the next which was called *Relk* and then *Pran, Leth, Dilt, Stod, Mank,* and *Mulp* in that order.

The subjects in Heidbreder's laboratory were not told to form concepts—and neither are children at home. The experiment was described to the subjects as a study of memorization and their assigned task was to learn the name of each picture. As soon as they could do so, they were to anticipate the experimenter, saying the name before she did. Nothing was said about when the words would begin to repeat and there was no temporal break between the series to mark the cycles of recurrence. However, the first picture of Series II was named *Pran* and the second *Relk* and the third *Dilt* and so on. Somewhere in this second series most subjects must have realized that the names were repeating and the repetition of a name is an invitation to discover the rule governing its occurrence.

Heidbreder's nonsense syllables, *Relk*, *Pran*, *Mulp*, and the others, belong to the class of possible but not actual English words, a class partially described by the formula we have seen in Figure 6-6. The new words are unused but legitimate combinations of English phonemes. Heidbreder's adult English-speaking subjects were prepared by their long training in the local phonological system to accept these sound patterns as possible words. Furthermore they were able to tell that each word was a new word, different by at least one phoneme or one sequential position from every known word. Heidbreder said *Pran* and that would not be the same as *Plan* or *Bran* or *Pram*. Finally, the subjects' long training in the perceptual aspects of phonology had prepared them to recognize the second pronunciation of each word as equivalent to or the same as the first; $Pran_2 = Pran_1$. We know of course that no two pronunciations of the experimenter could have been acoustically identical. But for the enculturated ear pronunciations are "repetitions" so long as the same phonemes are produced in the same sequence.

A new word (or morpheme) is an invitation to find a governing semantic rule, and since meanings are assigned arbitrarily at the morphemic level Heidbreder's subjects would not have expected the sense of *Pran* to be predictable from the senses of *Plan* or *Bran* or *Pram*. Across the series of Figure 7-2 the word *Pran* does not ever name the same picture twice; nor does any other name. The pictures are all different. Which is also the way with things in the real world. In Series I *Pran* names the fourth figure down (one rose lying across two others), in Series II *Pran* names the first figure, in III the last, in IV the second, and in V—? You may have anticipated the answer. It is the second from the last. *Pran* names a category of things, no two of which are identical, but all of which have a common attribute.

How are we able to anticipate new occurrences of *Pran* from experience of old instances? It would seem that we must abstract from the unique detail of the old instances the recurrent attribute, a certain crisscross configuration. Having abstracted the attribute we also generalize to new cases and use the attribute as the cue to say *Pran*. It is this process of abstraction and generalization, inferred from the ability to name new instances correctly, that is called concept formation. The concept is also, of course, a semantic rule, a rule of reference for the use of a new word.

Series I	Series II	Series III	Series IV	Series V

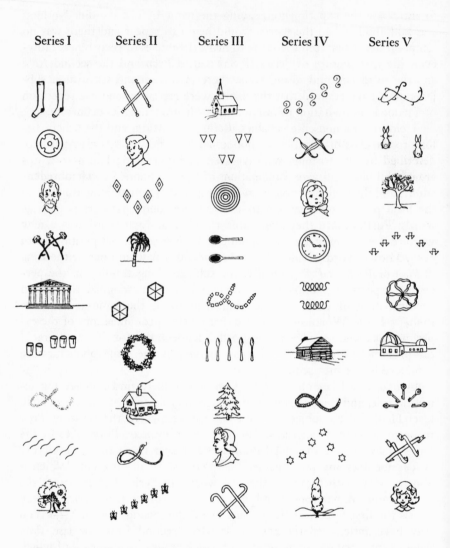

FIGURE 7-2. PICTURES USED IN HEIDBREDER'S STUDY OF CONCEPT FORMATION

THE MEANING OF *FA FA*

Table 7-1 is a chronological record made by Lewis (1957) of his son's growth in knowledge of the concept named in English by the word *flowers*. This record describes an experiment in concept formation having many points of resemblance to Heidbreder's experiment. Mother (M) is in the role of the experimenter who begins by naming instances, none of them identical. The child (C) is in the role of subject who at first listens and observes, then points on request and eventually names new instances. The child's experience of referents is, like the experience of Heidbreder's subjects, distributed and discontinuous in time. Somehow the recurrent word, *flowers* or *Pran*, serves to attract relevant experiences, to sum them over time into a conception governing the use of the word.

One or two incidental aspects of Lewis' record are interesting. The second named instance of flowers, at the age of sixteen months and thirteen days, is the same as the first. Both are yellow jonquils growing in a bowl and so recognition requires only that the child have the conception of an enduring object (see Chapter 5). At this point *flowers* is the name of an "identity category." With the next instance the referent becomes an equivalence category. The flowers are of a new species and a different color but still in a bowl. At age 17:24 an immense abstraction is called for. The flowers are pictures in a book, lacking odor, texture and tri-dimensionality. It is worth noting that the child gives no evidence of understanding ("No response from C") and so it may be that he was not at that time able to take so large a step. At the end of the record, however, he is correctly labeling embroidered flowers and sugar flowers on a biscuit. Throughout the record the child does not use the actual English term in naming but employs his childish equivalent, a reduplicated syllable. His parents accept this equivalent for the time being but later on they probably will start to correct it. Parents sometimes seem to relax their motor performance standards while a concept is growing.

Flowers is a word that names a category of things but of course words do not all name things and grammatical constructions as such never name things. Is it therefore the case that a reference-making, concept-formation procedure cannot be a general model of the acquisition of linguistic meanings, but only a model of the acquisition of thing meanings? What has reference to do with verbs and prepositions and subject-object constructions? Everything, I think.

It is, in the first place, possible to contrive reference-making procedures useful for teaching the meaning of every sort of linguistic form and construction. One can point appropriately and say: "See the boy *walking*," and then point again and say: "See the boy *running*." With a couple of cups and pennies in front of us we might point and say: "See the penny *on*

TABLE 7-1. DEVELOPMENT OF THE MEANING OF FA FA OR FLOWERS
(From M. M. Lewis, *How Children Learn to Speak*, Basic Books, New
York, 1959)

Age	Circumstances	Spoken to child	Child's behavior	Spoken by child
16:12	M brings C near to yellow jonquils growing in a bowl.	*Smell the pretty flowers.*	C bends over them, smells them, and says:	*a . . .* *a . . .* *a . . .*
16:13	C crawling about room.	*Where are the flowers?*	C crawls towards the jonquils and holds out his hand toward them.	
16:16	There are pink tulips in a bowl in another room. M says:	*Baby, where's flowers?*	C points to tulips.	
17:24	Pictures of flowers in a book shown to C. M says:	*Where's flowers?*	No response from C.	
18:14	M holding C at window through which he can see hyacinths in a bowl in the room.		C touches window pane and says:	*fa fa*
18:15	M wheels C's carriage toward bed of tulips and says:	*Where are the flowers?*	C repeats many times:	*fa fa*
18:21	M takes C into a room where there is a bowl of irises and says:	*Where are the flowers?*	C stretches out hand toward flowers and says:	*fa fa*
18:27	C is wheeled beneath branches of a flowering cherry tree.		C looks up toward blossoms and says:	*fa fa*
19:27	C playing in garden. M says:	*Pick a flower and give it to Daddy.*	C picks Virginia stock and brings it to F.	
22:26	C has a biscuit with a tiny sugar flower.		As soon as he gets it C says:	*fa fa*
	C has slippers with embroidered flowers.		C points to flowers with signs of joy and says:	*fa fa*

the cup," and then: "See the penny *in* the cup." Using pictures it is easy to contrast "See the dog chasing the cat" and "See the cat chasing the dog." The pictures of Figure 6-11 are examples of contrasts that could teach the meanings of functors. The principle for devising such reference-making games is always the same. Compose two sentences that are alike in every morpheme or dimension except the morpheme or dimension of which you wish to teach the meaning. Match the utterances, appropriately, with situations that are identical but for some feature relevant to the meaning of the critical linguistic morpheme or dimension. Some meanings (for example, salvation, loyalty, and physical mass) cannot be directly transmitted by making reference. They are built up from propositions but the terms of the propositions will ultimately reduce to reference.

Parents do not often contrive reference-making games like those described above. On the other hand the speech of parents to children or of any adults to children is much more often in the referential mode than is speech between adults. In part this may be because adults believe that children are only able to understand what is here and now. In part, probably, it is because the speech of children is itself largely governed by contemporaneous external stimulation and the speech of adults to children is often an expansion of what the child has said.

The conversation between Adam and his mother, set down in Table 6-2, was mostly about trucks that could be seen in the street below. Adam's mother did not take that opportunity to show her son pictures of every sort of truck, contrasting them with such confusable categories as cars and fire engines and buses. On other occasions, however, she did name other trucks and also cars, fire engines, and buses. I believe that this kind of referential speech is, in effect, a less deliberate and probably less efficient equivalent of the contrived reference-making games we have described.

For some period of time a word like *truck* passes back and forth between a parent and child under the control of vehicles in the street. When it has done so often enough there is created in the child's mind a conception of the vehicles named. The adult can check the outlines of that conception against the one in his own mind by checking the child's usage of the word against his own. Once the child has the conception he can understand and produce "displaced" speech, speech about trucks in the absence of the things themselves. And the community around him, knowing that he has served his apprenticeship on the level of reference, will believe that he understands displaced speech.

DOES LANGUAGE CREATE CONCEPTS?

Some of the problems that Heidbreder set her subjects probably were very different from the problems that new words set for children. Consider the case of the word *Mulp*. This word names some kind of tree in each of the series of Figure 7-2. The concept tree is one that Heidbreder's subjects possessed when they arrived for the experiment; they even had a word for the concept. The problem set by *Mulp* was not therefore a problem of concept *formation* but rather a problem of concept labeling. There was nothing to learn but a new tag for an old concept. In what degree is this also the case for children learning their native language? Do they perhaps have most of the concepts in advance? Have they formed conceptions of trucks and trees and flowers and walking and running and relations of spatial containment before they learn how to express these ideas? We have been assuming that they do not, that the linguistic form sets a problem of concept formation for children and not a problem of naming alone. What reason is there for thinking so?

Let us assume that the conceptual furnishings of an adult mind are not innate but are learned. How might they be learned? There are three major possibilities: 1) Concepts are learned from direct commerce with the physical world without any social mediation; 2) concepts are socially mediated but the mediation is non-linguistic; 3) concepts are socially mediated and the mediation is linguistic. If either of the first two is true then languages are simply codes coordinated to a conception of reality that is formed without their aid. If the last is true then a language is a determinant of the conception of reality, a mold shaping the mind as well as a code connecting minds. It goes without saying that the truth need not vote a straight party ticket. All three kinds of learning probably occur. It will be argued here that the third way is likely to be the most important.

The possibility that concepts are learned without social mediation of any kind is suggested by much of the work of Piaget (see Chapter 5). In the eighteen or so months of infancy, the "speechless" time of life, Piaget reports that children form conceptions of enduring objects located in space and time. This learning seems to be accomplished by manipulating things and observing the effects of manipulation. What is left to be learned about objects after eighteen months? Their linguistic tags, presumably.

In the preoperational and concretely operational years children learn the conservations of quantity, number, area, volume, and so on. These conservations may be regarded as the meanings of certain words and phrases ("same amount"; "more to drink"; "larger"; etc.), since such words and phrases are used to probe for the ideas. Obviously the child must have some opportunity to hear and memorize the words and phrases if he is to answer Genevan interrogations. Again, however, it would appear that the linguistic forms are no more than the tags that make communication possible. The conservations themselves seem to depend upon maturation and experience in operating upon the physical world.

The impression we have from Geneva is that neither language nor any other form of social mediation is important for creating the concept of the enduring object, or for conceptions of space, time, quantity, and area.[1] This is, above all, because such concepts seem to be enforced by the real nature of the physical world and seem certain to be the same for people everywhere. There have been few cross-cultural checks on the Genevan studies of the 1940's and 1950's (see Chapter 5) but we do not expect to find cultures in which quantity is not conserved or in which changes of appearance in an object are confused with changes of state.

For concepts that are universal, social mediation is not likely to be important. However, I think even the Genevans, and certainly the rest of us, would be more inclined to look for social mediation in connection with the concepts that Piaget studied in the 1920's. Conceptions of justice, of lying, guilt, volition, causality, and the nature of life are not likely candidates for cultural universality and so one suspects that such ideas are transmitted by people. If we leave the domains of meaning favored in Geneva and turn to those usually studied in anthropological linguistics we find cultural relativism everywhere.

Differences of Meaning between Languages. In order to make a comparative study of reference-making words it is necessary to have some kind of standard grid or coordinate system that describes the reference domain. One can then compare the mapping of that domain into two or more lexicons. For the domain of colors physics provides a description in terms of the length and magnitude of wave lengths and their mixture; psychophysics offers a description in terms of just-noticeable differences in the three dimensions of hue, brightness, and saturation. Neither of these descriptions is the same as the color lexicon of any ordinary language. The dimension of wave length or hue is represented in the English lexicon by the common terms: *red, orange, yellow, green, blue, violet,* and *purple.* Each term in the lexicon has a certain region of application. Other lexicons map the same domain somewhat differently.

Figure 7-3 roughly represents the lexical mappings (Gleason, 1961) of English, Bassa (a language of Liberia), and Shona (a language of Rhodesia). Bassa makes a single major cut—*hui* is for the blue-green end of the spectrum and *ziza* is for the red-orange end. Shona groups together the reds and purples (the two ends labeled *cips^wuka*) and recognizes two other groups which are approximately the blues and the greens-plus-yellows. Many other segmentations of the spectrum are known. The language of the Zuni Indians groups together the yellows and oranges. Numerous languages have a single word for the entire blue-green range.

Color names are sometimes also the names of objects. Our word *orange* names a fruit which, when it is ripe, exemplifies the hue. The earlier usage is the application to a fruit. The later usage names the range of colors ex-

1. There is recent work which suggests that language may be more critical than the Genevans have thought. See Bruner, 1964.

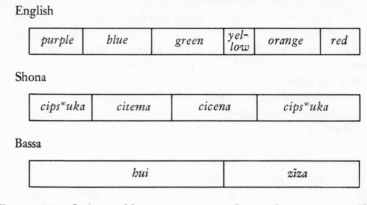

English

purple	blue	green	yel-low	orange	red

Shona

cips"uka	citema	cicena	cips"uka

Bassa

hui	zĩza

FIGURE 7-3. LEXICAL MAPPINGS OF THE COLOR SPECTRUM IN THREE LANGUAGES

emplified by the fruit—wherever those colors appear. In languages that have a single word for blue and green that word is often also the name for the sea. The colors of the sea vary through the full blue-to-green range and that is probably why these hues are named by a common term.

Comparative semantics can also work with reference domains that have no dimensionalized physical description. It is only necessary to have a standard grid that is different from the ordinary lexicon of any of the languages being compared. One can, for example, describe human kinship in terms of biological relationships. When lexicons are laid off on such a grid we find that there are very many different ways of categorizing kinfolk. Our word *aunt* applies to four biologically distinct relationships: father's sister, mother's sister, father's brother's wife, and mother's brother's wife. We do not have single words to name these four varieties and do not usually think of them as distinct categories. Murdock (1949) has reported that in the languages of the world the four genealogically distinct aunts are categorized in almost every conceivable way. One language has a term for each type. Another language has a single term for father's sister and father's brother's wife and a different term for mother's sister and mother's brother's wife. Still another names three kinds of aunt with one term and the fourth kind with a second term.

The branch of anthropology called *ethnoscience* has contributed to our knowledge of what is cultural in cognitive structure. Ethnoscience is a comparative semantics working chiefly with domains for which there are, in western civilizations, scientific taxonomies. The taxonomy is often used as the standard grid. In ethnobotany the Linnean taxonomy is the grid and folk vocabularies for naming plants are laid out on that grid. When this is done unrelated languages prove to have few terms of exactly equivalent range. The Hanunóo of the Philippine Islands have names for ninety-two varieties of rice but all ninety-two varieties are, for the English speaker, simply *rice* (Conklin, 1954). The Hanunóo example serves to illustrate what may be a general principle of comparative semantics. Cognitive domains that are close up are more differentiated than are remote domains. A metaphor from visual perception suggests what I mean. A gravel path stretching away from the perceiver is, at one's feet, composed of individual differentiated stones but in the distance it becomes an unbroken white expanse. For the Hanunóo rice is a staple food and variations in rice are of great importance as they are not for us. I do not mean to say that rice is physically closer to the Hanunóo than to us, though it may be, but that it is closer in a metaphorical sense; closer, that is, to their central concerns. The principle that the world near home has more texture than the world farther away is illustrated by the academic world of Cambridge, Massachusetts. At Harvard, engineering seems a single profession or at most a small number of professions. At the Massachusetts Institute of Technology, on the other hand, they have names for ninety-two varieties of engineering. Psychology, however, is there one of the "humanities"— just barely discriminable from fine arts or history.

The findings of ethnoscience and comparative semantics suggest that it is a rare thing to find a word in one language that is exactly equivalent in reference to a word in an unrelated language. If each lexicon is regarded as a template imposed on a common reality these templates do not match up. On the level of grammar, differences of meaning between languages are more striking and probably of greater significance. Benjamin Whorf (1956) has described some fascinating differences and has argued that they result in unlike modes of thought.

If reality were such as directly to impose itself on the child's mind one would expect it to have imposed itself in that same form on the languages of the world. The ubiquity of linguistic non-equivalence suggests that reality can be variously construed and, therefore, that the child's manipulations and observations are not alone likely to yield the stock of conceptions that prevail in his society. The requirement that a child learn to make correct referential use of a morpheme or a meaningful construction is sufficient to cause the child to form the governing concept if the physical world has not already imposed it upon him. Lewis's son could not make proper use of the word *flowers* (or *fa fa*) without having the concept of flowers. A Hanunóo boy, if he is going to name correctly ninety-two kinds of rice, must be able to conceive of the ninety-two and a Bassa boy, if he is to use *hui* and *zīza* correctly, must think of purple plus blue plus green as similar but distinct from orange plus red. For any concept that is cultural rather than natural the problem set by the need to master its linguistic expression is sufficient to cause the concept to be learned. Sufficient but perhaps not necessary.

NON-LINGUISTIC SIGNS

When Lewis' son first looked upon the yellow jonquils in a bowl and heard them named *flowers* he was also enjoined to smell them and we may guess that his mother leaned over and did just that. When a ball is named *ball* it is also likely to be bounced. When a cat is named *kitty* it is also likely to be petted. Smelling and bouncing and petting are actions distinctively linked to certain categories. We can be sure they are distinctive because they are able to function as symbols of these categories. In a game of charades one might symbolize *cat* by stroking the air at a suitable height in a certain fashion, or symbolize *flower* by inclining forward and sniffing. In Ingmar Bergman's movie *The Silence* a woman in a strange land, knowing no word of the language, asks for food by seeming to transmit something to her mouth and performing munching movements. If there are non-linguistic actions that are distinctively linked with the cognitive categories of a culture why should not the child learn his categories from these actions, rather than from the articulatory actions called speech? And why should he not demonstrate his possession of the concepts with well-timed sniffings, pettings, bouncings, and munchings rather than with well-timed stops, trills, flaps, and fricatives?

How often is it the case that a category which is distinctively named is also treated to a distinctive action? It is often the case but by no means always. Flowers are marked by sniffing actions but there are no actions that distinguish one species of flower from another. The first names given to things seem to fall at the level of distinctive action but names go on to code the world at every level; non-linguistic actions do not.

What determines the name that parents will offer to a child for any thing or person around the house? A first thought is that parents simply give each referent *the* name by which it is called in their language. A dime for instance is called *dime* because that is the English name for that object. But of course it is not the only correct English name for that object. The dime in a parent's hand is a *coin* as truly as it is a *dime*. It is also *money*. It is even an *artifact* or a *thing* and it would be quite correct to call it by any of these terms. More narrowly it may be *a 1952 dime* or even *a 1952 dime that is quite dull and has most of its lettering worn down*. Any particular referent has not one correct name but many correct names.

What determines the name a parent will give a child for a dog brought into the house as a pet? *The* name may be *Prince*. Other correct names are *terrier*, *dog*, and *animal*. Why was Lewis' son taught to call jonquils *flowers*? Why not *jonquils*, which is the name Lewis gave them in his book?

Each name of a referent assigns it to some category. The dime category is larger than the 1952 dime category but smaller than the coin category, the money category, or the thing category. The Prince category is on the level of an identity; it is much narrower than the dog category. The flowers category is larger than the jonquils category but narrower than the plants category. Parents do not consistently assign referents to the narrowest possible category and they do not consistently assign referents to the broadest possible category. What determines the level chosen?

When something is categorized it is regarded as equivalent to certain other things. For what purposes equivalent? How are all dimes equivalent or all flowers or all cats? They are equivalent in the first place in that they can be given certain names, the names *dime, flowers,* and *cat*. But the equivalence goes beyond naming. Dimes are equivalent in that they can be exchanged for certain newspapers or cigars or ice cream cones or for any two nickels. In fact they are equivalent for all purposes of economic exchange. Flowers are equivalent in that they are agreeable to smell and are pickable. Cats are equivalent in that they are to be petted, but gently, so as not to inspire them to claw. The linguistic equivalence is matched in each case by some sort of non-linguistic equivalence. There is an isomorphism between naming behavior and other sorts of culturally patterned behavior. When the sorts of behavior are diverse, as in the case of the dime, it is not easy to make a comprehensible enactive symbol (to use Bruner's term, 1964). When the behavior is very simple, as in the case of flowers, it is easy to make a good enactive symbol.

Why then do parents name each referent as they do for children or, more generally, why do we name each referent as we do for anyone? To answer in one sentence: I think we name each thing so as to categorize it at its level of probable non-linguistic equivalence. For some referents this level will be the same for any auditor. One dime is equivalent to another and different from every nickel or penny for anyone who uses our coinage. An orange is an orange, an apple an apple, for anyone. Since these things function in the same fashion for everyone they are named in the same fashion for everyone. The principle of anticipated non-linguistic equivalence is not proved by such cases. One might feel that these referents are simply given the name that fits what they really are.

But sometimes the same referent is given different names for different auditors. Consider the dog *Prince*. That is not his name always and everywhere. When he roams abroad and is spotted by a child in a strange neighborhood that child is told: "See the doggie." Prince, away from home, assumes generic status. He is a dog equivalent to other dogs; a creature to be called to, conceivably petted, but not fed or bedded down. In the only household that feeds him, Prince is categorized and named uniquely. Or consider a child's father. Abroad he is just a *man* or, if his functions are more particular, a *policeman*. At home he is a one-of-a-kind *Papa*. Notice, incidentally, that we have here further evidence that the world close up is more differentiated than the world at a distance.

Non-linguistic equivalences for children are not always the same as they are for adults. Jonquils are just *flowers* because all the child is expected to do about them is to sniff and not pick. Even a dime need not be called *dime*. Sometimes parents just say *money* for any sort of coin. This seems to be when their children are at the age where the only non-linguistic behavior that matters is "not to put them in the mouth and not to drop them down the register or drain." When a child is old enough to be sent to the store, the name of a dime for him must be *dime*.

While insisting that each referent has many possible correct names it must still be admitted that for many referents there is one name that has a superior status. While a dime *can* be called a *coin* or *money* or *a 1952 dime* we somehow feel that *dime* is its real name. The other categorizations seem like achievements of the imagination. To conceive of the thing as a dime seems to be a passive recognition of its true nature. The word *dime* seems like its true name, the name God gave it. The distinction is like the old philosophical distinction between essence and accident. The essential categorization and the true name are perhaps the ones that reflect its usual and most elaborately developed level of equivalence in our lives. Where there is no one level of equivalence that is either more usual or more elaborate than any of several others there seems to be no feeling of an essential nature and a true name.

Insofar as cultural categories are linked with distinctive non-linguistic actions, as well as with names, the possibility exists that the categories are learned from the actions rather than from the names or from both together. Cognitive development in natural circumstances presents us with a bad experiment with two confounded variables. It is rather as if Edna Heidbreder had, as each picture came up on the memory drum, not only spoken its name but also made some characterizing movement of her hands or head. We should not know which signal had functioned for a subject to mark the equivalence of instances in one category. Probably both would have been used and probably both are used by children.

One of the most consistent differences between the intellectual performances of children and the performances of adults is the tendency children have to define words in terms of actions (Feifel and Lorge, 1950). If a young child is asked what *ball* means he is likely to answer: "You bounce it" or "You throw it." *Cat* means to pet or play with and *flowers* are to smell. It looks very much as if children learn the two kinds of action that may go with a category, the articulatory and the non-articulatory, and offer the latter as a definition of the former. Perhaps the relation is even symmetrical. If an adult were to pretend to bounce something and ask a child: "What does that mean?"—the answer might be "Ball."

Cognitive categories of the first level may be redundantly transmitted by names and by conventional actions. The first level is neither consistently very abstract nor consistently very concrete. It is rather consistently functional. The world is made up of mommy, daddy, flowers, kitty, Prince, and the like. Perhaps a very young child needs the redundancy of signals in two modes. But the first sweep of cognitive enculturation is followed by an endless process of further categorization which moves in both the abstract and the concrete direction. Cats are differentiated into Persians, Siamese, Maltese, and the like; fishes into perch, cod, smelt, and the like. Cats and fishes and many others are summed into animals or vertebrates. For these latter categories there seem to be no characterizing actions. The linguistic system, at first supported by the action system, proceeds on its own. For testing these notions deaf children would be a strategic group. Since they are able to utilize the unspoken but not the spoken signs their enculturation should proceed normally on the first level but not, without special training, on later levels.

Distinctive non-linguistic actions are not arbitrarily associated with categories. Balls are bounced because they can be. Flowers are smelled because it is agreeable to do so. This non-arbitrariness probably helps us to use actions as guides to categories when such actions exist. Linguistic actions (names) *are* arbitrarily linked with categories and may at first need the support of actions that are appropriate and not linguistic. However, arbitrariness is the superior principle in the long run since it can be combined with all the systematic properties of linguistic phonology which lighten the burden on memory and the demands for perceptual vigilance. An arbitrary but systematic and productive signalling system can be used to mark out and stand in place of all the conceptions our minds can fashion.

In the enactive mode we soon run out of appropriate material symbols. There are none for such categories as Persian or smelt or furniture or utility or 1952 dimes. And there are no arbitrary enactive symbols to take over where the appropriate symbols leave off. Our non-linguistic actions do not constitute a productive system of the sort that phonology is. Actions that are not articulatory could of course be made into a system but cultural evolution has not favored this development. The advantages of a movement that leaves the hands free and that can be heard are very great.

Because non-linguistic actions encode only a small part of our shared cognitive inventory it has been possible to invent the *game* of charades in which enactive encoding of concepts like furniture or utility is a trial of skill. There can be no comparable linguistic game because in this mode conventional symbols exist for just about any category we can conceive. No player of charades with even a minimal understanding of the game would, by the way, set his opponent a problem on the first level of cognitive enculturation; such a problem as signalling cat or flowers or dime.

Words or, more broadly, meaningful linguistic constructions surely do help to create conceptions. On the first level of enculturation there are also actions that can create conceptions. The actions probably could do the job alone though, for hearing children, I would expect the words to help. Beyond the first level, insofar as our conceptions are cultural rather than inevitable, it seems as if language must be the determining agent. If we think in terms of meanings that are encoded grammatically rather than lexically I think the role of language is even more evident. Would we conceive of the actions that verbs name in terms of past, present, and future points of reference, in terms of the progressive aspect and the active, passive, and imperative modes, if our grammatical system did not compel us to do so? Think of what is involved in the following sentence: "When he arrived we were having lunch but he had not yet had breakfast."

Child and Adult Understanding of Words. Children even before they are two years old begin applying words to categories of things according to implicit general rules or concepts. From this fact one might suppose that logical classification is a primitive sort of operation which very young children perform as well as do adults. However, there are several studies (Vigotsky, 1934; Piaget and Inhelder, 1959; Bruner and Olver, 1963) showing that when children are set explicit problems of classification they perform very differently from adults and, indeed, that children do not operate in a fully mature way on such problems until early adolescence.

Concept formation in children has been studied in several different ways. Piaget and Inhelder have used a method of "free classification" in which children are given a mixed lot of objects—geometric forms, cutouts of people, animals, plants, and so on—and asked to put together those that are "similar" or which "go together." Adults presented with such a problem are likely to form classes such that all the members or instances of any one class possess the same defining attribute or the same combination of defining attributes. Adults can often formulate the rule governing class membership and this rule will perfectly fit their sorting of the objects. Adults are also often able to arrange classes into hierarchies of subordination and superordination.

If objects presented in a free classification problem were geometrical figures adults might sort into triangles and squares, defining the first as "three-sided closed figures" and the second as "rectangular figures with sides of equal length." Adults would put *all* the figures fitting the one rule together and *all* the figures fitting the other rule together. Adults would know that the class of geometrical figures includes both triangles and squares and that there are fewer triangles (or squares) than geometrical figures.

The performance on problems of free classification of children younger than six years is in many ways unlike that described above. Young children are inclined to sort objects on a part-whole basis rather than on an instance-class basis. For example, a child might put together a toy stove, a sink, a woman, and some food and call the result a kitchen. Each object is, loosely considered, a "part" of a kitchen.

Some children under six years do start out by sorting together similar objects, but when they have put together two or three that have a certain feature they will unaccountably desert that feature and begin adding objects on a new principle. Vigotsky also found this kind of behavior and he called the collections resulting from it "chain complexes."

Piaget and Inhelder found that even children who sort on the basis of consistent similarity are usually unable to supply a rule that will accurately describe their sorting. Sometimes they will give a rule that fits all the objects they have placed together (perhaps squares) but will leave out of their collection some objects that are equally well described by the rule (some squares will be left with the triangles).

Piaget and Inhelder found that the child's understanding of the relations among classes that are organized into a hierarchy is not complete until long after the age of six. One of the difficulties can be illustrated with the category we name *flowers*. The child is shown a collection of pictures of flowers. Most of the flowers pictured are primroses but a few are flowers of other kinds. The materials represent therefore a relation of class inclusion. The superordinate class of flowers (F) includes a large subordinate class of primroses (P) and a small subordinate class of other varieties (O). The child is asked whether a bouquet of all the flowers will include the primroses (P) and also the others (O) and he says that it will and so seems to understand that $F = P + O$. But then the experimenter asks: "Suppose I had a bouquet of the primroses and you had a bouquet of all the flowers; who would have the larger bouquet?" "You would," replies the child. With several variations of procedure the child still insists that the primroses make a larger bouquet than all the flowers. Even though he will also say that all the flowers must include the primroses.

Piaget and Inhelder believe that when the child's attention is centered on a subordinate class (the primroses) he can only compare that class with its complementary (the other flowers) and so find it larger. He has the inclusion relation in mind when he is focusing on the inclusive class, the superordinate, but he loses it when he focuses on one of the subordinates. In effect, though he understands that $F = P + O$ he does not seem to understand that $P = F - O$ and so that $P < F$.

Vigotsky and his associates in most of their work (1934) have not used the method of free classification. Their stimulus materials, a set of twenty-two blocks varying in color, shape, height, and size, are known as the Vigotsky blocks. There are five different colors, six different shapes, two heights (the tall blocks and the flat blocks), and two sizes of the horizontal surface (large and small). On the underside of each figure, which is not seen by the subject, is written one of the four nonsense words: *lag, bik, nur, cev*. Regardless of color or shape, *lag* is written on all tall large figures, *bik* on all flat large figures, *nur* on the tall small ones, and *cev* on the flat small ones. At the beginning of the experiment all blocks, well mixed as to color, size, and shape, are scattered on a table in front of the subject. The examiner turns up one of the blocks (the "sample"), reads its name to the subject and asks him to pick out all the blocks which he thinks might belong to the same kind. After the subject has done so, the examiner turns up one of the "wrongly" selected blocks, shows that this is a block of a different kind, and encourages the subject to continue trying. After each new attempt another of the wrongly placed blocks is turned up. As the number of the turned blocks increases, the subject by degrees obtains a basis for discovering to which characteristics of the blocks the nonsense words refer. A normal adult working on this problem will formulate a hypothesis from the attributes of the first block. If it were a large, flat, yellow triangle labelled *bik*, he might put all the triangles together, regardless of their other attributes, guessing, in effect, that *bik* means triangle. Suppose the experimenter then turned over a triangle that was blue, small, and flat and showed the subject that this triangle was not labelled *bik*. The subject would say something like: "Oh, then it's not the triangles." He would then test another hypothesis—perhaps putting together all the yellow blocks. Eventually he would discover that the *biks* were the tall, large figures and he might be able to verbalize this principle. Throughout he would understand that he must find the attribute or attributes that were invariably associated with *bik* and not with the other syllables.

Young children do not cope with the task in this way. Vigotsky has described a variety of procedures followed by children; one of these was quite common and has also been found by Piaget and Inhelder and by Bruner and Olver. Shown a large, flat, yellow triangle labelled *bik* the child first adds to it another triangle. He may add a third triangle and would seem to be testing a triangle hypothesis. At this point his attention may be taken by the blue color of the most recently added triangle and he next adds a large blue square. He might then choose another large block, one that is neither triangular nor blue. Proceeding in this way the child seems to choose each new block because of some similarity with a block already chosen, but the dimension of similarity is not constant. He deserts attributes without having been given any reason for doing so. In the end he does not have the sort of class in which all instances manifest one or more defining characteristics; he has what Vigotsky calls a "chain complex." A chain complex is like a rope made up of many short fibers, none of them running the length of the rope. In a chain complex there are short-run similarities linking subsets of the total set but there is no similarity linking each with each.

The method of Bruner and Olver (1963) was different again. They offered words two at a time (e.g., *banana* and *peach*) and asked the child to say in what way the two things named were alike (e.g., "both are yellow"). Then additional words were added (e.g., *potato, meat, milk*) and the child was to find a superordinate quality common to all (e.g., "things to eat"). With this procedure, as with the procedures of Vigotsky and of Piaget and Inhelder, children frequently formed chain complexes. "Banana and peach are yellow; peach and potato are round; potato and meat are served together"; etc.

There are, then, some differences between the performances of children and adults on tasks that explicitly call for operations of classification. Children are disposed to sort on a part-whole basis and are disposed to form chain complexes. Children are seldom able to formulate rules that accurately describe the classes they form. Children do not fully understand the relation of class inclusion. Since the use of words to make reference involves classification it is reasonable to suppose that adults and children do not learn or understand words in the same way. For several reasons, however, it is difficult to tell from these studies of concept formation just how much difference of linguistic understanding exists.

The child's tendency to sort together the parts of a whole in Piaget and Inhelder's experiment does not necessarily represent an incapacity to sort together instances of a class. The direction to the children after all was to put together things "that belong together" and the parts of a whole do certainly belong together. Perhaps adults understand this kind of direction to mean that they should put together instances of a class while children understand it to mean that they should put together objects ordinarily contiguous in space.

The adult ability to provide explicit rules which describe sortings of geometrical figures or of the Vigotsky blocks should not be taken to mean that adults are ordinarily able to provide rules describing their use of words. They are seldom able to do so. For a word like *triangle* they can give a definition, but then the definition of triangle is taught in school. Words like *flower* and *dog* and *house* are not easy to define in a descriptive way.

Probably it is the case that adults understand the class inclusion relation and that children do not and in this respect adult and child understanding of some words may differ. However, knowledge of the class-inclusion relation is not required for referential use of a word nor is it required for most propositional uses. One can identify primroses and affirm most of what there is to affirm about primroses without being quite sure how to answer the question: "Are there more primroses or more flowers?"

The intellectual characteristic of children that seems most likely to be a reliable characteristic and to have general implications for their understanding of words is their use of chain complexes. This characteristic has turned up in three investigations using different methods and there is at least anecdotal evidence that it appears also in the child's use of ordinary words. In this latter connection Vigotsky repeats a familiar story. The word *quah* was originally used by a child to name a duck swimming in a pond, the water in a glass, and the milk in his bottle. At this point one would say that he was applying *quah* to liquids. Instead of persevering in this consistent usage he started to apply the word to the picture of an eagle on a coin. Presumably his attention had shifted from liquids to the similarity between ducks and eagles. This practice gave way in turn and the child used *quah* for round coinlike objects. *Quah* seems to have named a chain complex and children's words often seem to do so. There are many examples in Werner's *Comparative Psychology of Mental Development* (1948).

Lewis' account of the development of *fa fa* does not look like the growth of a chain complex. Why is that? Very likely the account is incomplete. It does not, for instance, describe any erroneous identifications and so it leaves us free to suppose that the child was always attending to some such conjunction of attributes as "petalled forms of a color other than green." He may have been doing nothing of the kind. The child first identified jonquils and then tulips. Both of these flowers have cup-shaped corollas on long bare stems and this pattern may have been the attribute governing his behavior. We cannot tell from the account. If the child had been shown another kind of cup-like structure on a stem, perhaps a piece of equipment from the chemistry laboratory, and had labelled it *fa fa* we should have known what attribute he had in mind. When he then proceeded to name hyacinths which do not have cup-shaped corollas we should have looked for a new attribute. The tulips were pink. If the hyacinths were also pink we should have guessed that his attention had shifted to pink and that his word was describing a chain complex.

If the child is disposed to shift attributes and make chain complexes how does he come to use a word like *fa fa* correctly? Would not this word and any word wander out of its proper path? The reason presumably is that adults are there to correct usage. Lewis' child was less free to develop *fa fa* than was the child who developed *quah*. If adults had insisted that *quah* be used properly, perhaps as the name for ducks, the semantic meandering that is a chain complex would not have occurred.

In sum, it is possible that children characteristically attempt to use words as names for chain complexes even though the attempt is not always clearly evident. Adults seldom reveal chain complexes in an explicit study of classification. Do these structures then play no part in adult learning and understanding of words and is this a difference between adults and children?

Vigotsky believes that the chain complex plays a great part in the historical development of language; in particular the process by which a word develops multiple meanings. He cites the semantic evolution of the Russian word *sutki*. Originally it meant a seam, the junction of two pieces of cloth sewn together. Later it was used for any sort of junction such as, for instance, the meeting of two walls to make a corner. Then it was used metaphorically for twilight, which is the junction of day and night, and then for the time from one twilight to another, the 24-hour day. This kind of semantic progression is very much the usual thing in language and if the progression constitutes a chain complex then the complex plays some part in adult thought.

The evolution of *sutki* is in several ways like a chain complex. There is the shift of usage from one attribute to another. Over the total range of usage—seams, corners, twilight, the 24-hour day—there is no single common attribute and also no conjunction of common attributes. However there seems to be a critical difference between the multiple meanings of a word and the chain complexes of a child. Each of the meanings of a word, such as *sutki*, is itself a concept. Seams are a concept, corners another, twilight another, the 24-hour day another. These several concepts have short-range resemblances among themselves. There is no attribute common to all of them but each one resembles some of the others in certain ways. One might perhaps call the meanings of a word a chain of concepts.

The short-range resemblances used by a child are not concepts. *Quah* was not used to name all birds and also all liquids and also all coinlike objects. It was first used to name some liquids and then that usage was given up in favor of some birds and then both of these in favor of some coinlike objects. Vigotsky's child subjects did not use a nonsense syllable to name all triangles and also all blue blocks but rather used it first for some triangles and then for some blue blocks. The component resemblances are not inclusive concepts and do not seem to be added together. There is rather an unaccountable shifting from one attribute to another, none of the attributes being fully exploited. The difference is great between this process and the evolution of a word's meaning.

While historical semantic progressions are not chain complexes it is just possible that the progression in understanding by an adult of any single sense of a word is a chain complex. We do not know very much about how adults learn to understand new reference-making words. It is common to suppose that they work out linguistic meanings as they work out concepts in the laboratory—by formulating hypotheses, testing them against new instances, and revising them in the light of confirming and disconfirming evidence. But this conception of semantic learning may be an idealized one based on discussions in philosophy and in science. The actual process of learning new words may be more like the chain-complex wanderings of the child. The failure of the adult to reveal such complexes in the laboratory may derive from the fact that the laboratory tasks are explicit problems which invite a deliberate technique. The only deliberate technique adults have is their academic idealized technique and that is the one they use in the laboratory, though perhaps not the one they use ordinarily. Children, not having been schooled in scientific taxonomies or in logic have no idealized technique and so, perhaps, perform in the laboratory as they do outside the laboratory. The chain complex may be a model of the classification processes used by children in all circumstances while for adults it may be a model of processes used in casual circumstances but not in explicitly problem-solving circumstances.

UTTERANCES AS EXPRESSIVE SYMPTOMS

Reference is the linguistic function we are most aware of. *Expression*, as it will be understood here, is a function of which we are less aware. Partly on that account, expressive meaning is a rich subject for social-psychological study. So it will be introduced here even though nothing systematic is known about it.

Let us begin with an example. A British physiologist visiting in Boston once identified a student to an American colleague by saying: "He is the nigger in your class." The American was shocked of course; not by the referential meaning of the word *nigger* but by its expressive meaning. In Boston, and almost anywhere in the northern states of this country, the word *nigger* is only used by people who are antagonistic to or look down upon the Negro. *Negro* is an exactly equivalent term of reference used by persons having more favorable attitudes to the group named. *Nigger* functions, then, to tell the listener something about the speaker; it is a symptom of a fairly nasty set of attitudes. However, the British physiologist did not have these attitudes. In Britain, *nigger* is an affectively neutral term used by everyone to designate an ethnic group. The Englishman and his colleague discovered the difference of usage and so removed the misunderstanding. Still the word continued to have differential effects for the two of them. They said it over a number of times, each trying to hear *nigger* as the other heard it but neither quite able to do so.

In the case described the word *nigger* has functioned in two ways: 1) as a name referring to a race; 2) as an expressive symptom of a prejudice against that race. Both functions are founded on a correlation between a word and certain non-linguistic circumstances. Negroes have been referred to as *nigger* and prejudiced persons have done the referring. For the word to fulfill its two functions a listener must have had experience of the two sorts of association. What is the difference between *nigger* functioning as a name and *nigger* functioning as an expressive symptom?

As an expressive symptom an utterance causes an interpreter to infer something about the speaker and this inference will be based on past association between the utterance and some characteristic of speakers. *Nigger* as a name is related to something other than the speaker. This reflexive aspect of the symptom distinguishes the two functions of *nigger* but it will not serve to distinguish names in general from symptoms in general.

Consider a self-referring utterance such as: "I am an American." This sentence would cause an interpreter to infer something about the speaker —that he is a citizen of the United States. It is not, however, an expressive symptom. The critical word *American* names the characteristic that is inferred. But what does that mean? It means, in the first place, that the word is used to make reference in such a construction as "There goes the American." This kind of construction goes with pointing at or denoting a person of a given nationality. In addition the word is used as a surrogate for the referent category in every sort of linguistic construction. "Some Americans live abroad in order to save on income taxes." "The American abroad is less ethnocentric than he used to be." And so forth.

The relation between *nigger* and the class of persons prejudiced against Negroes is quite different. One does not point at a prejudiced man and say: "He is a nigger." One does not use the term as a surrogate for prejudiced people. On the other hand *nigger* is used as a name, as a term of reference and linguistic surrogate, for the racial group. An utterance functions is an expressive symptom when it causes an interpreter to infer something about the speaker but does not name that something.

Meanings which are expressed rather than named have a special social-psychological status. They are not always intended by the speaker. Certainly most of the people who say *nigger* are not deliberately revealing their attitudes. Perhaps because it is not the focus of the speaker's intention an expressed meaning is supposed to be less real, less certainly a social fact, than a named meaning. A Negro could not, I suppose, sue a man for calling him *nigger*. The speaker could always plead that he intended no insult.

Because expressed meanings are often not deliberate but rather un-witting, the interpreter is often especially attentive to them. From this channel he may learn things the speaker would prefer not to disclose. On the other hand, since interpreters are often tuned to expression the speaker or writer will, if there is time and important matters are involved, try to monitor his expressive symptoms. The careful letter-writer spends nearly as much time on the "tone" of his communication as he does on its referential meaning. Tone carries information about the letter-writer, in-formation that is not named.

The several aspects of expressive meaning can best be communicated with a story. The scene was a dinner party; the guests were all political scientists or people in the foreign service and they were all chiefly inter-ested in the problems of newly independent nations. The conversation turned to Nigeria and a young specialist on economic development re-marked: "That's a place I've not been to." A few seconds later a young political scientist said: "I've not been there either and it isn't the only place I haven't been to." The young economist flushed, in his wife's hand the wine glass trembled, the hostess looked embarrassed. There was no explicit acknowledgment of the connection between the two utterances but when, later in the evening, the political scientist tried to make himself agreeable to the economist, everyone knew why. There was a community of understanding through language that extended well below the level of the explicit topic of conversation.

The economist had chosen to express the fact that he had never been to Nigeria by saying: "That's a place I've not been to." This is a self-referring utterance. It serves to place the speaker in the class of persons who have never been to Nigeria. In this role the utterance is not an ex-pressive symptom since it explicitly affirms that the speaker has not visited Nigeria. The economist could have communicated the same information about himself and Nigeria in other ways; for example: "I have never been there." The choice of one form over another, like the choice of *nigger* over *Negro*, serves as an expressive symptom. But the symptom in this case involves a choice among sentence constructions.

Probably the economist was chagrined to be asked about a country he had not visited when there were so many very out-of-the-way places that he had visited. It must have seemed a pity that the group's single sample of his traveling experience should be so very unrepresentative. Would they not, from that unlucky sample, put him down as an un-traveled person? He might have forestalled such an inference by saying: "I have not been to Nigeria but I have been everywhere else." The tone of this is disagreeable; it has the ring of a small boy's braggadocio. The economist might instead have tried: "That is one place I have not been to."

However, this is baldly boastful and the company present might have interpreted the remark as a sign of personal insecurity.

The meaning the economist wanted to convey is a meaning that must be conveyed by an apparently inadvertent expressive symptom. The characteristic of the speaker which is to be inferred by his listeners is a complimentary one. It is bad American manners to affirm good things of oneself. The benefits that may accrue from having the good thing known are likely to be more than canceled by the impression that the speaker is impressed with his own qualities. "I have been everywhere else" sounds like a small boy because small boys often have not learned that virtues must not be trumpeted and they sometimes do trumpet them. "That is one place I have not been to" sounds like an insecure person because such a person may find it necessary to slam across a message of this kind so that even his dullest interpreter will get it. The best style is a symptom subtle enough to risk incomprehension by some.

The sentence used by the economist represents a resolution of three forces: 1) the necessity to confess a particular lack of experience; 2) the wish to make known the general sophistication surrounding the particular inexperience; 3) the tabu on explicit boasting. In a matter of seconds he produced the delicately contrived compromise: "That's a place I've not been to." The ignorance is admitted while the sophistication is disclosed as if inadvertently. However, his rivalrous young colleague, the political scientist, responded as if the disclosure had been a brazen proclamation and so made the company and probably the economist conscious of the calculation behind the tone of the sentence. But it was the political scientist who was the more embarrassed since his unplanned, almost reflexive, response exposed an ugly pugnacity that he would have preferred to conceal.

Expressive symptoms need not be words or sentences. Intonation, tone quality, and pronunciation can all function expressively. When you say "Hello" on the telephone a friend gets, from the characteristic timbre of your voice, an unplanned message exactly equivalent to the assertion: "This is John Doe speaking." Suppose a wife is suspicious of her husband's excuses for arriving home late but she does not want to come out with an accusation. She can give him something to worry about by responding to his telephoned excuse with an ironic intonation on "What a shame." Expressive symptoms need not even be vocal; every sort of behavior, every personal possession, can be expressive.

There is a very good reason for learning to interpret expressive symptoms. They are a safeguard against being deliberately misled. Children learn very early to read expressive symptoms and so "see through" their parents and parents to "see through" their children. A father tells his little daughter that spinach is delicious and eats a gray strand or two with much smacking of the lips but she has noticed that his portion is usually left on his plate and that he never asks for more. A small daughter reports herself too ill to go to school but her mother has, in the past, noticed the rapid recovery that followed upon permission to stay home.

There are so many dimensions to expressive behavior that even advance calculations and rehearsals cannot guarantee that a communication will convey only what one wishes. I have sometimes had a phone call to make where I knew some care must be taken not to reveal a feeling of exasperation. Once or twice the exasperation has been strong enough, and the reason for concealing it compelling enough, to make me work out beforehand the words and tone of voice to be used. Then, still rehearsing subvocally, I would dial the number, get the party, and say a few genial introductory words. His usual response? "What's eating you today?"

Language, Thought, and Society

At the start of Chapter 6 one of the uses of literacy was described. A teacher who could read from the blackboard the names of the places in which various valuable objects were hidden would be able to recover more of these objects at a later date than would pupils who could not read. Both the written and spoken language can transmit information from one person to another and the written language can, in addition, be used by one person to store information for himself from one occasion to another. Has the spoken language also some power to do this? There is a recent experiment on this problem. DeLee Lantz (1963) has shown that the efficiency with which referents can be linguistically coded is related to the efficiency with which they can be stored in memory.

THE CODABILITY OF REFERENTS AND THEIR RECOGNITION

Lantz tells a story that gives a useful overview of her experimental problem. Suppose a housewife wants to buy curtains to match the color of the painted wooden trim in her kitchen and does not want to chip off a bit of the trim to take along to the store. How can she match the two colors, which cannot be viewed side by side? She might look hard at the trim and then take a fast train to the store hoping to remember the color truly. She might alternatively phone the store and describe the color to the woman in the curtain department: "It's a shade of blue but a little on the green side and quite pale." The outcome of Lantz's experiment would suggest that if the one procedure will succeed the other will succeed and if one will not the other will not.

Lantz worked with a set of precision-manufactured color chips from the Farnsworth-Munsell Hue Test. These chips are individually mounted in small plastic caps. They differ from one another in the dimension of hue alone, all being approximately equal in brightness and saturation. The chips run the full circle of the spectrum in small, perceptually equidistant, steps. It is possible to distinguish each chip from each other chip—in a good light and on close examination—but on casual inspection those nearby one another look very much alike.

Lantz's first subjects were given the job of naming (or encoding) each chip in an array of twenty. Before they began naming they were allowed to view the full set of colors mounted on pegs around the circumference of a wheel. After that a subject saw just one chip at a time and was asked to name it in such a way as would enable another person who had not seen the chip to pick it out from the full set on the wheel. Since there were many more colors than there are familiar color terms in the English lexicon subjects could not hope to succeed by using only the single words: *green, blue, purple, red, yellow,* and *orange.* They necessarily had recourse to phrase construction and invented such names as: "dirty gold," "grass after watering," "a light blue sky tinged with pink." Each chip was encoded by twenty people.

The next step was to determine the efficiency of the encodings. New subjects were given the names composed by the first group and asked to identify the colors named. A subject would be given such a name as "dirty gold" and would decide which chip in the full array was most likely to have inspired that name. Each subject decoded a total of eighty messages, four from each of the encoders.

From the decoding data Lantz obtained a score for each color which reflected the average communication efficiency of the names given that color. These scores are called scores of *codability.* A color with a high codability score was one that the first group of subjects generally succeeded in transmitting linguistically to the second group of subjects. The score for a color was calculated across multiple encoders and also across multiple decoders and so it may be considered to be a property of that color in that linguistic community. The only purpose of the experimental procedures until this point was to obtain codability scores for all the colors.

It remained to relate the linguistic variable of codability to a cognitive process; the process was one of perceptual recognition. New subjects were involved and these subjects made no overt use of language. First a subject was allowed to look briefly at the full set of colors. Then, in the simplest experimental condition, he would look at a single chip in a controlled exposure apparatus for just five seconds. The color would be removed and, after an interval of five seconds, he would be asked to try to find, in the full array, the color he had just seen. The array was mounted on a wheel behind an aperture in such a way that the subject could move the colors past his eye one at a time and stop when he thought he recognized the original. Each subject attempted to recognize all of the colors. Some subjects were given a more difficult task of recognition; they saw four chips at once and then had to try to identify all four.

How does one work at this task of delayed recognition? For myself, and for many subjects, it goes like this. When the color initially appears you try to give it a distinctive name, not speaking aloud but verbalizing to yourself. When the color is removed the name can be retained, even rehearsed. Somehow, names are responsive to volition in a way that images are not. Then you search around the perimeter of the wheel of colors, testing each chip against the name to see whether the two belong together. When the chip is found which best deserves the name, that is recognition.

The need to transform the perceived chip into linguistic symbols does not seem to be as great with one color as with four. Some subjects say that the memory image of a single color persists for them long enough to be matched against those in the full array. With four colors to retain, however, most people seem to find it necessary to utilize the linguistic code. In an earlier experiment, closely related to this one, Brown and Lenneberg (1954) found that the importance of linguistic coding also increases with the duration of the interval during which a color must be stored in memory.

The major outcomes of Lantz's experiment are correlations between the codability scores of the individual colors and the recognition scores of the same colors. For the condition in which one color at a time was to be recognized the correlation was .320. For the condition in which four colors at a time were to be recognized the correlation was .711. The success which certain speakers of English enjoyed in transmitting colors by linguistic means was positively correlated with the success enjoyed by other speakers of English in recognizing those same colors. The relationship was much stronger for the difficult recognition problem than for the easier one.

Apparently an entity that can be efficiently transmitted from one member to another of the same linguistic community can be efficiently retained from one occasion to another by a single member of the community. When an effective message can be composed for others an effective message can be composed for oneself. Encoding into the spoken language seems to be useful for information storage and retrieval. It is not as useful in some ways as writing on the blackboard; large amounts of writing will "keep" with less effort than will large amounts of speech. However, what can be stored in an alphabetic writing like ours is ultimately dependent on codability. If the valuable objects hidden in the classroom and also their hiding places were not highly *codable* an alphabetic writing would be incapable of storing the "fact." If the teacher in her classroom had had the problem of retrieving particular Farnsworth-Munsell chips, her performance from the written record would have varied with the basic codability of each chip.

VARIABLES AFFECTING REFERENT CODABILITY

A codability score accrues to a referent in an array of referents for a particular linguistic community. Lantz's experiment holds constant the array of referents (the full set of colors) and also the community (speakers of English) and allows scores to vary with the particular referent. It is easy to see that scores of an individual referent must vary with the array it is in. In the Farnsworth-Munsell series used by Lantz there were a great many off-greens: murky ones, bluish ones, yellowish ones, and so on. Therefore a particular misty gray-green chip had, in that original array, a very low codability. It was difficult to find words that would unequivocally select it out from its mates. Suppose now that this low codability chip were put into a new array made up entirely of brilliant reds and oranges. In the new array the codability score of the green chip would go up. Anyone could easily encode it in such a way as would enable others to identify it. In fact the chip could simply be called *green* since it would be the only green in the new array. The misty gray-green chip, now become simply green, would also be much more recognizable than formerly. With a change of array the codability of the particular referent seems to change and the possibility of recognizing it changes proportionately.

The codability of any referent, not only of colors, will vary with the array of referents from which it is to be distinguished. One zebra in a herd of zebras has low codability. It might be called *the small zebra with one ragged ear* and that encoding still might not serve to distinguish it. The same zebra in a herd of elephants has high codability. The word *zebra* alone would, in these circumstances, transmit its identity to any speaker of English.

The codability of a particular referent in a fixed array of referents will vary with the linguistic community or to put it a little differently, with the resources of the language used. Among the Hanunóo, who have names for ninety-two varieties of rice, any one of those varieties is highly codable in the array of ninety-one other varieties. The Hanunóo have a word for it and so can transmit it efficiently and presumably can recognize it easily. Among speakers of English one kind of rice among ninety-one other kinds would have very low codability and would be difficult to recognize. We may guess that, if the Hanunóo were to visit the annual Automobile Show in New York City, they would find it difficult to encode distinctively any particular automobile in that array. But an American having such lexical resources as *Chevrolet, Ford, Plymouth, Buick, Corvette, hard-top, convertible, four-door, station wagon,* and the like could easily encode ninety-two varieties.

Linguistic communities need not be conceived on so broad a scale as "speakers of English" and "speakers of Hanunóo." These larger communities can be subdivided into smaller ones composed of persons sharing a professional vocabulary or persons sharing terms for local buildings and sites. Somewhere in the United States there must be rice growers and rice graders and rice inspectors for whom ninety-two or so kinds of rice are highly codable and highly recognizable. In the array of buildings that fills the Harvard Yard, Sever Hall and Emerson Hall are more codable for the local linguistic community than for visitors. The principle that the world close up is more differentiated than the world farther off can be restated by saying that the world close up is more finely coded.

CODABILITY OF CATEGORIES

Lantz found that four colors exposed simultaneously were harder to recognize than one color at a time and Brown and Lenneberg found the same. The subject has to invent four distinctive names and remember the lot. Presumably five colors would be harder to recognize than four and six harder still, unless the experimenter hit upon a set of colors which, as a set, had low codability. Suppose our six colors were all greens and were the only greens in the total array. A subject could code the lot as *green* and recognize the lot very easily indeed, more easily than some single chips of low codability. It seems then that there are higher order codabilities above the level of the particular referent. There are in fact codabilities on the categorical level.

Codability scores on the categorical level could be directly determined by procedures of the same general type as those used for codability on the level of the particular referent. Encoders would be shown not one, but a number, of chips in the full array and asked to compose a name that would enable others to distinguish the set from all others in the array. Decoders would be given the names and asked to pick out the named categories from the array. The codability of a category would be the average transmission efficiency of the names given it. Sets having minimum codability would as sets simply be coded as a list of the names given each particular referent in the set. Sets of this kind cannot get very large without exceeding our memory capacity.

Presumably, codability on the level of categories would predict recognition on the same level. A subject would first see the full array of colors on the wheel and would then be shown one collection or set at a time. The set would be removed and he would be asked to try to find them all in the complete array. Sets that can be efficiently transmitted linguistically should be more easily recognized than sets that cannot be efficiently transmitted.

Codability scores on the level of the category, like codability scores on the level of the particular referent, would vary with the contrast array. A set of five girls in an array of girls might be difficult to encode but the same set of girls in an array of men would be easy to encode. Recognition of the set would also be easier in the second case than in the first. Codability scores on the level of the category, again like codability scores on the level of the particular referent, would vary with the linguistic community when the contrast array was held constant. The set of colors that we might call *purple-plus-blue-plus-green* (which is essentially a list of the names of sub-categories) would be more easily encoded among the Bassa (Figure 7-3). They have the word *hui* for the set. On the other hand, the smaller set that we call *blue* would pose more difficulty for speakers of Bassa. They would probably resort to phrase construction, making up something like "the *hui* of the sky."

CODABILITY, LENGTH OF A NAME, AND FREQUENCY

You may have noticed, in passing, that differences of codability, where codability refers to the average transmission efficiency of the names given a referent or category, are often associated with differences in the length of the names. Among other zebras, a certain zebra, if it is to be distinguished, must be called something like *the small zebra with one ragged ear*. The same zebra among elephants is highly codable in the sense that a name preserving its identity can easily be found and the name is a short one— *zebra*. For the Hanunóo one kind of rice out of ninety-two kinds is easily transmitted and a single word will do the job. If we speakers of English tried to encode the same kind of rice we would do it less effectively than the Hanunóo and the name we used would not be a single word but some sort of phrase like *a large-grain, brown-flecked rice*. The association between high transmission efficiency and brevity of the name assigned can be explained.

Zipf (1935) has shown that there exists a tendency in Peiping Chinese, Plautine Latin, and American and British English for the length of a word to be negatively correlated with its frequency of usage. This is true whether word length is measured in phonemes or syllables. The correlation of length and frequency is probably a universal linguistic law and, with this correlation, we are, for once, in a good position to state the direction of cause and effect. In the histories of many particular words increasing frequency has led to abbreviation. New inventions have often been given long names of Greek or Latin derivation and then, as the products became widely known and frequently mentioned, the linguistic community found shorter tags for them. The *automobile* became the *car* and *television* shrank first to *video* and eventually to *TV* in the United States and *tellie* in England. In French, *cinématograph* has dwindled to *cinéma* and, at last, to *ciné*. Within a linguistic subculture, words having a high frequency in local usage may abbreviate, though in the larger community they remain unaltered. At Harvard, *psychology* is *psych.*, *social relations* is *soc. rel.*, and *Humanities 2* is *Hum 2.*

The relation between word length and frequency can safely be generalized into a relation between the length of any sort of name and frequency. Even before television was given the polysyllabic name of *television* it must have had a longer name that was a phrase. Someone, somewhere surely said: "It ought to be possible to invent *a device that would transmit pictures over a distance.*" The lengthy italicized phrase is a name for television but a name of this sort would not long be tolerated once people had frequent occasion to speak of the referent in question. Names that are constructions, names that are created from the combinatorial resources of the language, are surely less often used than names that are words in the conventional lexicon. The implication is that we more often speak of *zebra* than of *the small zebra with one ragged ear*, of *rice* than of *a large-grain, brown-flecked rice*.

Why should a community use one name more frequently than another? The likeliest answer is that the community has more to say about the one referent or category than the other. We do not usually talk just to be naming things. We talk to convey information, to warn of dangers, to transmit values, to guide action. When a community can name a referent or category with a single word, especially a short word, the community probably can formulate a large number of propositions concerning that referent or category. If we asked speakers of Hanunóo to tell us all they know or think they know about Rice No. 92, we probably would get a good flow of talk about its market value, ease of cultivation, and resistance to disease and perhaps some advice to be sure to cook it *al dente*. If we asked speakers of English to tell us all they know or think they know about *a large-grain, brown-flecked rice* they probably would look blank. Speakers of English have ideas about rice generically conceived but not about rices specifically conceived. Speakers of Hanunóo have ideas on the specific level. The world close up is more finely coded than the world farther off because our expectations and superstitions and ideas in general are more differentiated in the regions that concern us.

Why should speakers of one language, for example English, have a short one-word name for the zebra among elephants (or the zebra among any animals other than zebras) and a long name for the zebra among zebras. The answer is the same: We have a certain amount to say about a zebra *as opposed to any other sort of animal* and nothing to say about one zebra as opposed to another. A zebra in contrast to elephants is striped and rather like a horse and not a work animal and so on. *A small zebra with one ragged ear*, as opposed to other zebras, is ————. We have nothing to add. However, if the small zebra were to become the pet of a family two things would happen simultaneously: its name would be shortened to *Stripes* or the like and ideas about Stripes in contrast to all other creatures would accumulate, ideas about his temperament, his intelligence, his likes and dislikes. In effect a linguistic subcommunity is created when the animal is adopted as a pet.

Why should a short name, especially a word as opposed to a construction, be associated with high codability in the sense of efficient transmission? While adults among themselves do not usually talk just to be naming things, adults with children often do talk just to be naming things. Children spend some years learning to match up particular referents and categories with names. Which names? The conventional ones, the ones that are frequently used, words for the most part and, in particular, short words. The adult attempts to transmit to the child the meanings of *rice* and *green* and *Stripes* and *zebra* and he checks the success of his attempts, correcting when necessary. In short we all have had a lot of transmission training on conventional short meaningful forms, training we have not had for phrase names like *a misty gray-green* or *a large-grain, brown-flecked rice*.

It is not only children who are engaged in reference games but any new inductee to a linguistic community. If you go to visit the family that has a pet zebra they will teach you his name. If you go to live with the Hanunóo or among rice growers in this country they will begin by teaching you their ninety-two names. If you undertake to study zoology your teachers will start out by showing you pictures of *protozoa, coelenterates, hydra*, and the like. It is as if every linguistic community, parents at home or nationals of another country or teachers of a science, adopts the same policy toward neophytes: "Let us begin by defining our terms."

The whole point of defining terms is to make it possible to go on and say something useful employing those terms. With children, when we have finished defining, what we go on to say is our total cultural tradition. "*Green* lemons are not ripe and not good to eat." "The *zebra* will kick if approached too closely." "*Rice* is the staple food of the Chinese." Some of these propositions are intended to guide action. They can only do so if the child can "cash" the principal words into referents. He cannot reject green lemons unless he can recognize the color green nor avoid approaching zebras unless he knows what zebras look like. The codability scores of a linguistic community are a reflection of that community's total culture. In acquiring those codability scores the child is acquiring a certain model of the world. When he has it he will be able to receive complex information concerning that model and will be able to act in the light of that information.

Before concluding this section we must drop back to explain an apparent inconsistency. The variations in codability that Lantz worked out for the Farnsworth-Munsell hues were not reflected in variations in the length of the names created. This is because the entire task was at a level of codability below the level of the lexicon. All of the names had to be phrases since the differences among the colors were very slight. Speakers of English in general have nothing to say about any of these colors on the particular level required. However, there were variations in codability in the sense of coding efficiency. These derive from the combinational possibilities latent in our color lexicon, our grammar, and our general vocabulary. We cannot "explain" these codability scores in terms of the larger culture. Even on this level of highly derivative coding, however, the possibility of transmitting to one another was closely related to the possibility of recognizing from time to time.

CODING ABILITY AND EGOCENTRISM

Codability means susceptibility of being precisely coded and is a property of referents. *Coding ability* means comparative personal skill at coding. A coding ability score belongs to a person in comparison with other persons and with regard to some semantic domain. There are both *de*coding and *en*coding abilities (probably closely correlated). Here we will consider only the encoding skill but will refer to it generically as "coding ability."

Coding ability appears in Lantz's data as the differential personal skill at constructing good names. Some subjects were regularly able to create names or descriptions that other speakers of English could accurately decode. Lantz did not actually develop a coding ability score but it is, in a general way, clear how this would be done. A coding ability score would reflect a subject's performance across colors rather than a color's eliciting power across subjects.

What does coding ability require? It is necessary to be able to make an informational analysis of the array of referents so as to identify the distinctive properties of the one to be transmitted. It is necessary to control a lexicon and also the grammar of the language. But something else is needed. The encoder must realistically assess the informational requirements of his decoder. Children are not very good at this last aspect of the game. They have a tendency to project their own information into their auditors, a tendency that Piaget has called "egocentric" (see Chapter 5).

Egocentrism in Child Speech. Some of the experiments that Piaget reports in *The Language and Thought of the Child* (1924) nicely expose the

egocentric element in the child's encoding. In this work he was not concerned with the coding of particular referents or even categories of referents but rather with the coding of processes, actions, and cause-effect
relations.

Piaget's general procedure was to explain something to one child and
then ask that child to explain it to another. In one case, for instance,
the experimenter explained, with the aid of diagrams, the operation of an
ordinary water tap. He pointed out the handle and demonstrated how
to turn it on. Using his diagrams, the experimenter showed that in the
stem of the handle, inside the water pipe, there was a canal or little hole.
When the handle was in "on" position this opening was lined up so as to
permit the flow of water from the pipe above through the opening and
out the spigot. When the handle was in "off" position the opening was
turned the wrong way and so there was no passage for the water and none
came out the spigot. A child who had the benefit of this explanation was
then asked to explain it himself to another child who had been waiting outside. The next paragraph consists of one of these explanations together
with Piaget's parenthetical comments. Both the child who explained and
the one who listened were about seven years old.

"*The water can go through there*" (points to the large pipe in fig. 1,
without designating the exact spot, the opening) "*because the door*"
(which door?) "*is above and below*" (the movable canal *b* which he does
not show) "*and then to turn it*" (turn what?) "*you must do so*" (makes the
movement of turning fingers but without pointing to the handles *a*).
"*There, it*" (What?) "*can't turn round*" (= the water can't get through)
"*because the door is on the right and on the left. There, because the water
stays there, the pipes can't get there*" (the pipe is lying down. Note the inversion of the relation indicated by the word "because." What ought to
have been said was: "The water stays there because the pipes can't . . .
etc.") "*and then the water can't run through*" [Piaget, 1924, 1959, p. 103].

Before looking at the specifically egocentric aspects of the explanation
above we must consider whether its inadequacies result from poor coding
ability or from incomplete understanding, on the part of the encoding
child, of the experimenter's explanation. Fortunately Piaget has effectively
excluded the latter possibility. The child destined to encode was skillfully
questioned first about the operation of the water tap: its parts and processes and the cause and effect relations involved. Piaget was able to correct
for the encoding child's level of understanding in calculating an egocentrism score. The child who composed the explanation quoted above understood the operation of the tap quite perfectly. Nevertheless he and the
others of his age did not effectively transmit what they knew. Their failures were chiefly due to egocentrism.

In the explanation of the water tap that we have quoted there are a
few defects which result from poor control of lexicon and grammar rather

than from egocentrism. The child's use of the word *door*, presumably for the canal or opening that permits passage of water, is eccentric. He also does not control the grammatical expression of cause and effect, which involves linking two propositions with the conjunction *because*, the expression of the effect preceding the conjunction and the expression of the cause following it. He has the order turned around.

In what ways is the explanation egocentric? It is so in the first place by virtue of a failure to appreciate the necessity of starting out by defining terms. The word *door* for instance is not ostensively defined, that is defined by pointing, but it needs to be since it is an eccentric usage. The child operates as if anyone must naturally understand what he, the encoder, means by *door*. He operates as if his usage were perfectly familiar and conventional and so in need of no explanation. Socialized speech always shows some sense of the lexicon of the auditor and defines those terms that are likely to be either totally unfamiliar or unfamiliar in their impending usage.

In the second place the pointing the child does is highly approximate. He says "there" and points in the direction of a large pipe when he has in mind the opening in the pipe. He acts as if his focus of attention were inevitable, as if the aspect of the visual world that an encoder has chiefly in mind must also be the aspect a decoder has chiefly in mind. On this assumption, no very precise pointing would be necessary.

In the third place, the composer of the explanation quoted used pronouns without proper attention to antecedents. He twice speaks of *it* when one cannot tell from the preceding sentences what *it* is. Presumably the encoder knows and, since he knows, his decoder must know. This seems to be the encoding child's assumption, an assumption that the decoding child's performance proved incorrect.

On many problems—story-telling, explaining the operation of a syringe, etc.—Piaget found the coding children below the age of seven or eight to be highly "egocentric." In Piaget's usage, as you can see, "egocentric" does not mean self-referring or self-glorifying. It means self-*centered*, but in a special way. The child is centered in himself in the sense that he does not apprehend the informational requirements of others but tends to attribute to them information they could not possess but which he does possess. Effective coding requires that the point of view of the auditor be realistically imagined.

The work of Piaget on children's coding ability had no interesting follow-up for forty years. At the present time, however, Flavell and his associates (1963) are studying children's coding ability in an imaginative way. They require encoders to transmit the same information to auditors possessing different amounts or kinds of prior information. In one procedure a child was supposed to explain a game, first to a blindfolded adult and then to a seeing adult. Some of the younger children were amazingly inattentive to the peculiar requirements of the blindfolded decoder. Their explanations went: "You must pick up this" (pointing) "and you must put it there" (pointing).

In another experiment Flavell had the encoding child speak simultaneously to three other children; the encoder was the police chief and the decoders were policemen in squad cars. The chief had information units a, b, c, d, and e. One listener (L1) already knew a; another (L2) knew a and b; a third (L3) knew a, b, and c. Some interesting problems were set the chief. For instance, he was asked to send a message that would put all three listeners in possession of the full information and not to send anything unnecessary. Since all knew a, and a was all that L1 knew, the chief had to send b, c, d, and e. This might be called "teaching to the bottom of the class." The problem changes if we suppose that L1, L2, and L3 are free to tell one another what they know. Then the chief need only communicate what none knows. This is "teaching to the top of the class."

Egocentrism in Adult Speech. Adults are not altogether free of egocentrism in their coding. When the driver of an automobile asks a pedestrian or a gas station attendant for directions, what amount of prior information in the driver is likely to be presupposed by the answer? Sometimes an encoder seeks guidance by asking, "Are you from around here?" Sometimes an encoder notices the out-of-state license plate or a foreign accent and gives exceptionally explicit directions that are tuned to the decoder's presumed level of information. However, encoders are sometimes tired or irritable and so just say to a visitor from Ceylon: "Harvard Square? Take the drive to Anderson Bridge, then turn right and keep going until you can see the Yard."

Adults are somewhat rigid too about shifting addressees. Several years ago Shneidman and Farberow (1957) asked some psychologists who study language to analyze a collection of suicide notes and of matched simulated suicide notes. The genuine notes were written by people who had, in fact, killed themselves. The false notes were written, at the investigators' request, by subjects who were asked to imagine themselves on the brink of suicide. They were to write the notes they would leave behind. The students of language were given both sets of notes without distinguishing identification and asked to try to distinguish the genuine cases from the feigning cases.

It was not difficult to tell the one set from the other and one basis for doing so was the occasional inappropriate provision of information in the false notes. The writer who was pretending to be on the verge of suicide did not always write to the point of view of his supposed addressee. A man supposedly writing to his wife would say something like: "I am disappointed in my job with General Motors" or "I hate to leave our son John."

Any wife would know where her husband worked and "my job" would be sufficient specification. She would know that John was her son and the first name alone would identify him for her. However, an outsider could not know where the man worked or who John might be. The writer, pretending to send a message to his wife, had somewhat in mind the psychologists who were actually going to read it and so put in details suited to the informational requirements of the psychologists.

The baseline case in encoding is the case where someone composes a message at Time 1 to be decoded by himself at Time 2. Presumably this is the case in recognition but, in that case, the speech is not vocalized and so cannot be directly studied. Sometimes, however, coding for oneself is explicit and even written down as in lecture notes or lists of things to buy at the store. It is clear that such communications are directed to one's own requirements. When a student is prevailed upon to lend his lecture notes he commonly says: "I don't think you will be able to get anything out of them." There is reason to believe that a message to one's own mind can contain less information than a message for others. Edith Kaplan has done some work (1963) contrasting descriptions (of novel drawings) written for oneself at some future time with descriptions written for others. The former were about half as long as the latter. A message for oneself can make economic reference to idiosyncratic experience: "Looks like the abstraction on my living-room wall."

It might appear that there could be no problem of egocentrism in speech for oneself but actually there can be. One's own mind at Time 1 has not the same information as one's mind at Time 2. The requirements of the latter addressee must be imagined. We know that they can be unrealistically imagined from the fact that lecture notes written to be read just before the exam sometimes fail to communicate.

The speech of preschool children, Piaget found, shows extremities of egocentrism far beyond the failure to define terms and keep track of the antecedents of pronouns. Children will often verbalize aloud in total disregard of the requirements or attention of any auditor. A baby will talk away in its crib as sleep advances upon it though no one is there to hear. Children of three and four years will sit about a sandpile all talking at once with none listening and none concerned to see if he has a listener. Children do more of this than adults but adults do sometimes indulge in such "collective monologues." The verbatim transcription of a conference always shows some simultaneous talk and much discontinuity from one "contribution" to another. It often seems that no speaker had any listeners. The others may have been silent, but they were attending to the inner voices composing contributions to come.

Childhood Egocentrism and Inner Speech. Vigotsky (1934) agrees with Piaget that the speech of preschool children is highly egocentric but he disagrees with Piaget on another matter—the ultimate fate of egocentric speech. Piaget appears to have believed that egocentric speech largely disappears at school age. Vigotsky claims that it has not just withered away but has gone underground to become "inner speech." Inner speech is thought that is verbalized but not vocalized. And since inner speech is verbalization for oneself it requires no auditor and it need not consider the informational requirements of another. It can be low on redundancy, highly abbreviated.

Speech between persons who are very well acquainted can be more abbreviated than speech between strangers. Vigotsky's striking illustration is a passage from *Anna Karenina*. It is the declaration of love between Kitty and Levin by means of initial letters:

> "I have long wished to ask you something."
> "Please do."
> "This," he said, and wrote the initial letters:
> *W y a: i c n b, d y m t o n.* These letters meant: "When you answered: it can not be, did you mean then or never?" It seemed impossible that she would be able to understand the complicated sentence.
> "I understand." she said, blushing.
> "What word is that?" he asked, pointing to the *n* which stood for "never."
> "The word is 'never,' " she said, but that is not true." He quickly erased what he had written, handed her the chalk, and she wrote: *I c n a o t.*
> His face brightened suddenly: he had understood. It meant:
> "I could not answer otherwise then."
> He seized the chalk with tense, trembling fingers, broke it, and wrote the initial letters of the following: "I have nothing to forget and forgive. I never ceased loving you" [*Anna Karenina*, Part IV, Chapter 13].

Since speech can abbreviate in the degree to which two people are of one mind it follows that inner speech can be still more abbreviated since there is but one mind involved. Vigotsky believed that in inner speech, condensation was chiefly accomplished by omitting the subjects of sentences. Inner speech, he held, was a speech of predicates only. He cannot be said to have demonstrated this assertion. Inner speech is not accessible to public inspection and it is not even very easy to study it in oneself.

There are, we have seen, circumstances in which speech for oneself is recorded in an enduring form and can be inspected: the memoranda one writes, lists of engagements and things to be done; notes on lectures and reading. However, lecture notes and memoranda do not achieve compression by omitting subjects and retaining predicates. Most generally they achieve it by omitting functors. Written language for oneself is often telegraphic.

In their telegraphic character, notes to oneself resemble the earliest speech that combines words, the utterances of a child between eighteen months and three years. The earliest speech ought to be the most ego-centric. Perhaps Vigotsky was mistaken in thinking that inner speech suppresses the subject of a sentence but correct in thinking that inner speech is, like externalized speech for oneself, abbreviated. Is inner speech telegraphic?

I can only answer for myself and that with no great confidence. It seems to me that it is not. When it is clear to me that I am *verbalizing* to myself and not thinking without words the sentences seem to be as complete as those I speak aloud. Something that is clearly *inner speech* occurs for me when I am doing some routine thing: shaving or walking for pleasure or having a bath. The sentences are often a recollection of sentences actually spoken or a rehearsal of sentences to be spoken or a wish-fulfilling transformation of sentences spoken into sentences that might better have been spoken. My inner speech can be highly repetitious—the same sentences go round again and again. As a mental operation it is not much like the hard-driven, impatient business of taking notes. When I have inner speech the cerebral engine seems to be idling.

Why should inner speech be telegraphic or predicative or in any way abbreviated? Are we to assume that speech will always be as abbreviated as it can be? If so, it is difficult to see why one should verbalize at all to oneself. Since thought is not all verbal and so need not be verbal, either in Vigotsky's view or Piaget's, why should it *ever* be verbal? One mind unto itself would seem to have no need of words: The thought that lies behind words ought to be enough. In addition, if speech is always as abbreviated as it can be why do not husbands and wives, when they are discussing familiar matters, use telegraphic speech? They would easily understand one another if they used only half as many words as they do use. If speech is always as abbreviated as it can be why did not Kitty and Levin use initial letters for the ordinary business of life as well as for their declaration of love?

Perhaps ordinary speech, whether vocalized or inner, tends to proceed at a stable level of redundancy which represents a comfortable rate of information processing. Writing is a much slower process than speaking. When we write with the full redundancy of speech, when we write every word, we are likely to be processing information much more slowly than if we were speaking. Still, when the addressee is another person, not familiar with our concerns, we must write at full length. The process can be uncomfortably slow but we often fill the time by undertaking to communicate with greater care than in speech; choosing sentences that are apt and have the right expressive tone. When the addressee is oneself as in the case of notes and memoranda it is not necessary to write every word and there is little reason to seek out felicitous phrasing. In these circumstances we settle on a comfortable rate of information processing and, since the motor side of writing is so slow, a very abbreviated, non-redundant English is comfortable. When the notes are being taken at a fast-moving lecture there is an added reason to accelerate and we may have to process information at an uncomfortably rapid rate. We not only omit words, under great time pressure, but omit highly predictable letters and syllables and, taking advantage of the familiarity of our handwriting, leave strokes incomplete, t's uncrossed, and i's undotted. Husband and wife speaking to one another do not abbreviate because they are speaking, not writing, and speaking is the more rapid process.

Levin chose to communicate his message to Kitty in a highly abbreviated way because of the extreme delicacy of that message: "When you answered: it cannot be, did you mean then or never?" She might, after all, have meant "never." If she were not very closely in tune with him, very much of his mind, his inquiry would be embarrassing for them. But if she were not nearly of one mind with him she would not understand his communication by initial letters—or could pretend not to. If she were able to understand it and willing to acknowledge it then she must return his love. It was not simply because of their great mutual understanding that Kitty and Levin communicated by initial letters. They gave up the language of initial letters after this one time. They used it once, not as a simple consequence of their mutual understanding, but as a delicate means of testing the depth of that understanding.

Why we have inner speech or subvocal speech at all remains a mystery to me. Inner speech must stand in relation to thought somewhat as writing does to talking: a slow plodding process. But there are reasons to write. A permanent record can be attained and that record can reach people in other places and times. There does not seem to be any comparable advantage that inner speech has over thought. The speech is not loud enough to be heard by another. If it is for oneself, does one need words to tell oneself what one is thinking?

The difficulty does not lie with understanding why *certain things* that a child might say aloud are not said aloud by adults. As Piaget put it, the child lacks verbal continence, he says everything, and verbal continence is as necessary for social life as are other kinds of continence. A child may express aloud the fact that he hates someone or that he finds someone ugly or that he is badly bored with someone's company. The reaction to talk of this kind teaches us to do an advance content analysis of the sentences we program so that we will not vocalize what is offensive unless we want to. Normal adults in conversation know that there is an inaudible stream of speech in the other which is of greater personal relevance and interest than the one that can be heard. Paranoid adults fancy they can hear it.

It is clear why children learn not to vocalize much that might be vocalized. What is unclear is why some of the sentences that are not vocal-

348 THE SOCIALIZATION OF THE CHILD

ized are subvocalized, are produced as words and sentences but inaudibly. Much that cannot be spoken aloud seems to retreat to the level of pure thought. Why should not everything?

Perhaps Vigotsky did not intend us to understand by "inner speech" a process that is consciously verbal. In what sense, then, would this inner process be speech? Vigotsky makes it clear that inner speech is not intended to include all of thought. Perhaps inner speech is thought that is shaped by language and that follows linguistic rules, especially rules of syntax, but which is not necessarily consciously verbal. If so, then I believe we do have a great deal of inner speech. What I then wonder about is whether we have any thought that is not inner speech.

REFERENCES

Brown, R., & Lenneberg, E. H. A study in language and cognition. *J. abnorm. soc. Psychol.*, 1954, **49**, 454–462.

Bruner, J. S. The course of cognitive growth. *Amer. Psychologist*, 1964, **19**, 1–15.

Bruner, J. S., Goodnow, Jacqueline J., & Austin, G. A. *A study of thinking.* New York: Wiley, 1956.

Bruner, J. S., & Olver, Rose R. The development of equivalence transformations in children. In J. C. Wright & J. Kagan (Eds.), Basic cognitive processes in children. *Monogr. Soc. Res. Child Develpm.*, 1963, **28**, No. 2, Serial No. 86.

Conklin, H. C. The relation of Hanunóo culture to the plant world. Unpublished doctoral dissertation, Yale Univer., 1954.

Feifel, H., & Lorge, I. Qualitative differences in the vocabulary responses of children. *J. educ. Psychol.*, 1950, **41**, 1–18.

Flavell, J. Personal communication. 1963.

Heidbreder, Edna. The attainment of concepts: Terminology and methodology. *J. gen. Psychol.*, 1946, **35**, 173–189.

Hull, C. L. Quantitative aspects of the evolution of concepts. *Psychol. Monogr.* 1920, **28**, No. 1 (Whole No. 123).

Kaplan, Edith. Linguistic characterization of objects in external vs. inner speech. In H. Werner & B. Kaplan, *Symbol formation.* New York: Wiley, 1963.

Lantz, DeLee. Color naming and color recognition: a study in the psychology of language. Unpublished doctoral dissertation, Harvard Univer., 1963.

Lewis, M. M. *How children learn to speak.* New York: Basic Books, 1959.

Murdock, G. P. *Social structure.* New York: Macmillan, 1949.

Piaget, J. *The language and thought of the child.* (1st ed., 1924) New York: Humanities Press, 1959.

Piaget, J., & Inhelder, Bärbel. *La genèse des structures logiques élémentaires: classifications et sériations.* Neuchâtel: Delchaux et Niestlé, 1959.

Romney, A. K., & D'Andrade, R. W. Cognitive aspects of English kin terms. In A. K. Romney & R. W. D'Andrade (Eds.), Transcultural studies in cognition. *Amer. Anthropologist*, 1964, **66**, No. 3, Part 2.

Romney, A. K., & D'Andrade, R. W. Transcultural studies in cognition. *Amer. Anthropologist*, 1964, **66**, No. 3, Part 2.

Shneidman, E. S., & Farberow, N. L. *Clues to suicide.* New York: McGraw-Hill, 1957.

Smoke, K. L. An objective study of concept formation. *Psychol. Monogr.*, 1932, 42, No. 4 (Whole No. 191).

Sturtevant, W. C. Studies in ethnoscience. In A. K. Romney, & R. W. D'Andrade (Eds.), Transcultural studies in cognition. *Amer. Anthropologist*, 1964, 66, No. 3, Part 2.

Vigotsky, L. S. *Thought and Language.* (1st ed., 1934.) Cambridge: M.I.T. Press; and New York: Wiley, 1962.

Werner, H. *Comparative psychology of mental development.* Chicago: Follett, 1948.

Whorf, B. L. *Language, thought, and reality.* (Edited by J. B. Carroll.) Cambridge: M.I.T. Press and New York: Wiley, 1956.

Wittgenstein, L. *Philosophische Untersuchungen.* (Transl. by G. E. M. Anscombe.) Oxford: Blackwell, 1953.

Zipf, G. K. *The psycho-biology of language.* Boston: Houghton Mifflin, 1935.

CHAPTER 8

The Acquisition of Morality

For Sigmund Freud the acquisition of morality meant the installation within the child's personality of an agency—the superego. This agency issues moral imperatives of a "Thou shalt" and "Thou shalt not" variety. It competes for the control of behavior with the id urges of sex and aggression. The superego is able to enforce its edicts by punishing infractions with moral anxiety or guilt and by rewarding idealistic action with a gratifying flow of self-esteem.

It seemed to Freud that the child derives his superego from his parents by a process which Freud called "identification." The content of the superego, the nature of its imperatives, derives, Freud thought, from the content of the culture which the parents represent. Some of this content is found in all cultures, for instance the tabu on incest, and some is specific to particular cultures. In any event the content of the culture is internalized through identification with parents and set up within the child's personality as a socializing and moral agency—the superego.

Freud put the concept of identification to more than one theoretical use. It seemed to him that identification was responsible for the child's unconscious sexual identity as well as for the installation of the superego.

The child has two parents and so has the possibility of making two identifications, one with a parent of the same sex and one with a parent of the other sex. The balance between these two identifications Freud thought must somehow determine sexual identity. The causes of an uncertain identity and of a biologically inverted identity would be found in anomolous patterns of identification.

The abstract conception we have briefly summarized has been enormously influential. It has shaped psychoanalytic theory and therapy and also the empirical study of conscience within academic psychology. It has also influenced the average man's beliefs about himself and his relation to society. The force of the Freudian conception chiefly derives from two propositions: 1) Morality is not instilled by God but is acquired from a society and more directly from two parents; 2) sexual identity is not biologically inevitable but is influenced by family relations.

Most of the ideas about the acquisition of morality which will be presented in this chapter derive from Freud's theoretical writings. The difficulty with those writings is that when one has read them and grasped the intellectual system they set forth one is left with the question: "How much, if any of it, is true?" Consequently we shall not start off with the theories but begin instead with a sample of the evidence from which the theories were derived. The evidence is clinical. For something like forty years Freud spent about ten hours a day, most days of the year, listening to patients talk about themselves in as uninhibited a fashion as they could manage. No one before him had had such an experience; he was the possessor of a body of data unique in history. To evaluate his theories we must have some acquaintance with this kind of data and so we shall begin with a case study, a study that was especially important in shaping the Freudian theory of identification. The study is called *Analysis of a Phobia in a Five-Year-Old Boy* (1909).

This case, the analysis of the boy Hans, recommends itself above all the other case reports Freud wrote because it contains more data, in the form in which they were available to Freud himself, than does any of the other reports. This is because Freud conducted the analysis by mail. Hans's father made the observations, asked the questions, took down the answers, and sent them to Freud in letters. In the case report Freud has quoted at length from these letters and so it is possible for us to examine the data available to him. From the data Freud made certain inferences about Hans, inferences concerning the boy's desires and fears. How clearly do these inferences follow from the data? Would others draw the conclusions Freud drew? You can form an opinion about this for yourself if you will undertake to do the exercise in psychoanalytic interpretation that constitutes the first section of the present chapter.

The second section puts together Freud's theories of identification and of the development of the superego from the many places in his works where he touches on these topics. The third section traces the later history of some of Freud's ideas, particularly those concerning the determinants of superego or conscience strength. There have been a number of non-clinical studies of conscience strength and we shall see how well Freud's ideas have stood the test of these studies.

For Freud the moralization of the child meant little more than the control by guilt of sex and aggression. We cannot be content with so limited a treatment. In the fourth section we will consider the role of imitation in moral behavior, the importance of having a good model to follow. The fifth section focuses on a dimension of morality that Freud scarcely mentions: moral knowledge and moral thought. Not surprisingly it was Piaget who awakened psychology to the intellectual aspect of the problem. Then, having discovered that moralization is a complex process with components of knowledge, feeling, and conduct we will, in the sixth section, consider how well these components hang together. Is morality fragmentary and specific or is it a generalized state of the character? Finally the chapter offers some propositions to guide the future study of moralization and these propositions are far removed from the ideas about the superego with which we now begin.

An Exercise in Psychoanalytic Interpretation

The five-year-old boy, Hans, suffered from a phobia; one of the problems in this exercise is to work out a Freudian interpretation of that phobia. A phobia is an excessive fear, a fear that most people would judge to be not justified by reality. Hans was afraid that a horse would bite him, so afraid that he would not go out of the house. Probably horses do bite—once in a long while—but not often enough to keep most of us at home. The second problem in this exercise is to make an interpretation of a certain phantasy that Hans had. This phantasy may have been a dream or it may have been a waking phantasy. All we know is that he said he thought it and that the events reported, which concerned himself and two giraffes, could not actually have happened.

The phobia and the phantasy are to be given *Freudian* interpretations and so you will need some acquaintance with Freudian theory. Only an acquaintance is necessary not a long familiarity. If you will read (or review) in the *Introductory Lectures on Psychoanalysis* (1915–16)[1] Lectures 1 through 10, they will provide sufficient knowledge of the fund-

1. Also available in paperback under the title *A General Introduction to Psychoanalysis*. New York, Permabooks, 1953. The numbers of the lectures are the same.

amentals of psychoanalytic thought. Many of you will already have such knowledge from other sources.

In addition to psychoanalytic theory you need some data. First we will have short descriptions of the phobia and the phantasy, the problems posed, and then a collection of excerpts from Freud's case history. These latter are descriptions of behavior and reports of conversations sent to Freud by Hans's father. No interpretive statements are included. The excerpts are a small selection from a long history. They appear in chronological order and this is also the order in which Freud received the reports.

To try your hand at clinical inference do the following: Work out an interpretation of both the phobia and the phantasy and muster all the support for your interpretations that you can find in the data from the case report. Be prepared to argue your case. In addition, be critical of what you are doing. How good is the evidence? If most students of the case should hit on the same interpretations would this mean that the inferences were valid? The excerpts published here omit several crucial facts from the original. Try to guess what these are. If you are able to do so, does that validate your interpretation? What might Freud have done, when the case was in process, to test his interpretations? What could be done, more generally, to test psychoanalytic interpretations? Here now is the exercise.

BACKGROUND:

Hans was born in Vienna in 1903. His parents were among Freud's adherents and endeavored to rear Hans with a minimum of coercion. Freud had asked his friends and students to report to him anything they might learn about the development of sexuality in their own children. Hans's father, who was a physician, wrote often to Freud about his son's development. Hans had been born in 1903; in 1906 a second child was born, the girl Hanna. In 1908, when Hans was five years old, he first developed attacks of anxiety and then a phobia. His father wrote in distress to Freud and was advised to attempt to discover the cause of the phobia by talking with Hans and studying the boy's actions. The father took extensive notes and sent them on to Freud. Freud himself had only one interview with Hans.

PROBLEMS FOR ANALYSIS:

1. The phobia. Hans was afraid that a horse would bite him in the street and was unwilling to go out of the house. At one time when he was especially anxious he even said: "The horse'll come into the room." He was particularly afraid of horses pulling heavy loads, drawing carts or buses. At one time or another he said that the horses he feared most were the white ones, especially those that were black about the mouth and had blinders on.

2. *A phantasy*. One morning Hans reported that, in the night, "there was a big giraffe in the room and a crumpled one; and the big one called out because I took the crumpled one away from it. Then it stopped calling out; and then I sat down on the top of the crumpled one" [p. 179].

RELEVANT MATERIALS QUOTED FROM FREUD'S CASE HISTORY APPEARING IN CHRONOLOGICAL ORDER*

a. But the great event of Hans's life was the birth of his little sister Hanna when he was exactly three and a half. His behaviour on that occasion was noted down by his father on the spot: "At five in the morning," he writes, "labour began, and Hans's bed was moved into the next room. He woke up there at seven, and hearing his mother groaning, asked: 'Why's mamma coughing?' Then, after a pause, 'The stork's coming today for certain.'

"Naturally he has often been told during the last few days that the stork is going to bring a little girl or a little boy; and he quite rightly connected the unusual sounds of groaning with the stork's arrival.

"Later on he was taken into the kitchen. He saw the doctor's bag in the front hall and asked: 'What's that?' 'A bag,' was the reply. Upon which he declared with conviction: 'The stork's coming today.' After the delivery of the child the midwife came into the kitchen and Hans heard her ordering some tea to be made. At this he said: 'I know! Mummy's to have some tea because she's coughing.' He was then called into the bedroom. He did not look at his mother, however, but at the basins and other vessels, filled with blood and water, that were still standing about the room. Pointing to the blood-stained bedpan, he observed in a surprised voice: 'But blood doesn't come out of *my* widdler.'

"Everything he says shows that he connects what is strange in the situation with the arrival of the stork. He meets everything he sees with a very suspicious and intent look, and *there can be no doubt that his first suspicions about the stork have made their appearance.*

"Hans is very jealous of the new arrival, and whenever any one praises her, says she is a lovely baby, and so on, he at once declares scornfully: 'But she hasn't got any teeth yet.' And in fact when he saw her for the first time he was very much surprised that she could not speak, and decided that this was because she had no teeth. During the first few days he was naturally put very much in the background. He was suddenly taken ill with a sore throat. In his fever he was heard saying: 'But I don't want a little sister!'

"Some six months later he had got over his jealousy, and his brotherly affection for the baby was only equalled by his sense of his own superiority over her" [pp. 153–155].

b. "At Schönbrunn (a zoological garden) Hans showed signs of fear at animals which on other occasions he had looked at without any alarm. Thus he absolutely refused to go into the house in which the *giraffe* is kept, nor would he visit the elephant, which used formerly to amuse him a great deal. He was afraid of all the large animals, whereas he was very much en-

* From *The Collected Papers of Sigmund Freud*, Volume III, translated by Alix and James Strachey, Basic Books, New York, 1959.

tertained by the small ones. Among the birds, he was also afraid of the pelican this time—which had never happened before—evidently because of its size again" [p. 176].

c. "Hans always comes in to us in the early morning, and my wife cannot resist taking him into bed with her for a few minutes. Thereupon I always begin to warn her not to take him in bed with her, . . . and she answers now and then, rather irritated, no doubt, that it's all nonsense, that one minute is after all of no importance, and so on" [p. 182].

d. ". . . he comes in to me [father] in the morning to see if I have gone away. Unfortunately at the moment I did not understand this, and said to him:
    " 'When you're alone, you're anxious for me and come in to me.'
    "Hans: 'When you're away, I'm afraid you're not coming home.'
    "I: 'And have I ever threatened you that I shan't come home?'
    "Hans: 'Not you, but Mummy, Mummy's told he she won't come back.' (He had probably been naughty, and she had threatened to go away.)
    "I: 'She said that because you were naughty.'
    "Hans: 'Yes.'
    "I: 'So you're afraid I'm going away because you were naughty; that's why you come into me.'
    "When I got up from the table after breakfast Hans said: 'Daddy, don't trot away from me!' " [p. 187].

e. "The position of our street-door is as follows:
Opposite it is the warehouse of the Office for the Taxation of Food-Stuffs, with a loading dock at which carts are driving up all day long to fetch away boxes, packing-cases, etc. This courtyard is cut off from the streets by railings; and the entrance gates to the courtyard are opposite our house. . . . I have noticed for some days that Hans is specially frightened when carts drive into or out of the yard, a process which involves their taking a corner. I asked at the time why he was so much afraid, and he replied: *'I'm afraid the horses will fall down when the cart turns'* " [p. 188–189].

f. Hans has said that he is most afraid of horses with a thing on their mouths.
    "I [father]: 'What is it that they've got on their mouths?'
    "Hans: 'A black thing.' (I think in reality it must be the thick piece of harness that dray-horses wear over their noses.)
    " 'And I'm most afraid of furniture-vans, too.'
    "I: 'Why?'
    "Hans: 'I think when furniture-horses are dragging a heavy van they'll fall down.'
    "I: 'So you're not afraid with a small cart?'
    "Hans: 'No. I'm not afraid with a small cart or with a post-office van. I'm most afraid too when a bus comes along.'
    "I: 'Why? Because it's so big?'
    "Hans: 'No. Because once a horse in a bus fell down.'
    "I: 'When?'
    "Hans: 'Once when I went out with Mummy in spite of my "non-

sense," when I bought the waistcoat.' (This was subsequently confirmed by his mother.)

"I: 'What did you think when the horse fell down?'

"HANS: 'Now it'll always be like this. All horses in buses'll fall down.'

"I: 'In all buses?'

"HANS: 'Yes. And in furniture-vans too. Not often in furniture vans.'

"I: 'You had your nonsense already at that time?'

"HANS: 'No. I only got it then. When the horse in the bus fell down, it gave me such a fright, really! That was when I got the nonsense.'

"I: 'But the nonsense was that you thought a horse would bite you. And now you say you were afraid a horse would fall down.'

"HANS: 'Fall down and bite.'

"I: 'Why did it give you such a fright?'

"HANS: 'Because the horse went like this with its feet.' (He lay down on the ground and showed me how it kicked about.) 'It gave me a fright *because it made a row with its feet*'" [pp. 192–193].

g. "April 9th. This morning Hans came in to me [father] while I was washing and bare to the waist.

"HANS: 'Daddy, you *are* lovely! You're so white!'" [p. 196].

h. "I [father]: 'Are you fond of Hanna?'

"HANS: 'Oh yes, very fond.'

"I: 'Would you rather that Hanna weren't alive or that she were?'

"HANS: 'I'd rather she weren't alive.'

"I: 'Why?'

"HANS: 'At any rate she wouldn't scream so, and I can't bear her screaming.'

"I: 'Why can't you bear it?'

"HANS: 'Because she screams so loud.'

"I: 'Why, she doesn't scream at all.'

"HANS: 'When she's whacked on her bare bottom, then she screams.'

"I: 'Have you ever whacked her?'

"HANS: 'When Mummy whacks her on her bottom, then she screams.'

"I: 'And you don't like that?'

"HANS: 'No. . . . Why? Because she makes such a row with her screaming.'

"I: 'If you'd rather she weren't alive, you can't be fond of her at all.'

"HANS (assenting): 'H'm, well.'

"I: 'That was why you thought when Mummy was giving her her bath, if only she'd let go, Hanna would fall into the water. . . .'

"HANS (taking me up): '. . . and die.'

"I: 'And then you'd be alone with Mummy. A good boy doesn't wish that sort of thing, though.'

"HANS: *'But he may think it'*" [pp. 214–215].

i. "I: 'Where does the stork live?'

"HANS: 'Where? In the box where he keeps the little girls. At Schönbrunn, perhaps.'

"I: 'I've never seen a box at Schönbrunn.'

"HANS: 'It must be farther off, then. Do you know how the stork opens the box? He takes his beak—the box has got a key, too—he takes his beak, lifts up one' (i.e., one-half of the beak) 'and unlocks it like this.' (He demonstrated the process on the lock of the writing table.) 'This is a handle too.'

"I: 'Isn't a little girl like that too heavy for him?'

"Hans: 'Oh no.'

"I: 'I say, doesn't a bus look like a stork-box?'

"Hans: 'Yes.'

"I: 'And a furniture-waggon?'

"Hans: 'And a scallywaggon' ("Scallywag"—a term of abuse for naughty children) 'too' " [pp. 220–221].

j. "Afternoon, in front of the house. Hans suddenly ran indoors as a carriage with two horses came along. I could see nothing unusual about it, and asked him what was wrong. 'The horses are so proud,' he said, 'that I'm afraid they'll fall down.' (The coachman was reining the horses in tight, so that they were trotting with short steps and holding their heads high. In fact their action *was* 'proud.')

"I asked him who it really was that was so proud.

"Hans: 'You are, when I come into bed with Mummy' " [p. 224].

k. "I: 'Then why do you always cry whenever Mummy gives me a kiss? It's because you're jealous.'

"Hans: 'Jealous, yes.'

"I: 'You'd like to be Daddy yourself.'

"Hans: 'Oh yes.'

"I: 'What would you like to do if you were Daddy?'

"Hans: 'And you were Hans? I'd like to take you to Lainz every Sunday—no, every week-day too. If I were Daddy I'd be ever so nice and good.'

"I: 'But what would you like to do with Mummy?'

"Hans: 'Take her to Lainz, too!'

"I: 'And what besides?'

"Hans: 'Nothing.'

"I: 'Then why were you jealous?'

"Hans: 'I don't know' " [p. 231].

l. "Hans: 'I'm not afraid of carriages and pair or cabs with one horse. I'm afraid of buses and luggage-carts, but only when they're loaded up, not when they're empty. When there's one horse and the cart's loaded full up, then I'm afraid; but when there are two horses and it's loaded full up, then I'm not afraid.'

"I: 'Are you afraid of buses because there are so many people inside?'

"Hans: 'Because there's so much luggage on the top.'

"I: 'When Mummy was having Hanna, was she loaded full up too?'

"Hans: 'Mummy'll be loaded full up again when she has another one, when another one begins to grow, when another one's inside her.'

"I: 'And you'd like that?'

"Hans: 'Yes.'

"I: 'You said you didn't want Mummy to have another baby.'

"Hans: 'Well, then she won't be loaded up again. Mummy said if Mummy didn't want one, God didn't want one either. If Mummy doesn't want one she won't have one.' (Hans naturally asked yesterday if there were any more babies inside Mummy. I told him not, and said that if God did not wish it none would grow inside her)" [p. 233].

m. "I: 'You'd like to be Daddy and married to Mummy; you'd like to be big as me and have a moustache; and you'd like Mummy to have a baby.'

"HANS: 'And, Daddy, when I'm married I'll only have one if I want to, when I'm married to Mummy, and if I don't want a baby, God won't want it either, when I'm married.'

"I: 'Would you like to be married to Mummy?'

"HANS: 'Oh yes' " [p. 234].

n. "I: 'You know when the bus-horses fell down? The bus looked like a baby-box, and when the black horse fell down it was just like . . .'

"HANS (taking me up): '. . . like having a baby.'

"I: 'And what did you think when it made a row with its feet?'

"HANS: 'Oh, when I don't want to sit on the chamber and would rather play, then I make a row like this with my feet.' (He stamped his feet)" [p. 237].

o. "On May 2nd Hans came to me in the morning. 'I say,' he said, 'I thought something today.' At first he had forgotten it; but later on he related what follows, though with signs of considerable resistance: *'The plumber came; and first he took away my behind with a pair of pincers, and then gave me another, and then the same with my widdler.'* . . .

"I: 'He gave you a *bigger* widdler and a *bigger* behind.'

"HANS: 'Yes.'

"I: 'Like Daddy's; because you'd like to be Daddy.'

"HANS: 'Yes, and I'd like to have a moustache like yours and hairs like yours' (He pointed to the hairs on my chest)" [p. 240].

INTERPRETATION OF THE PHANTASY

If you have your interpretations of the phobia and the phantasy we can proceed to their discussion though you may want first to have a discussion with other readers. The phantasy is the simpler of the two problems and we will begin with it. From my classes I have always received the following two interpretations and these two have always been more popular than any others.

1. The big giraffe is Hans's father and the crumpled one is his mother. In the dream or phantasy Hans takes his mother away from his father and the father objects, but in vain.

2. The big giraffe is Hans's mother and the crumpled one is Hanna. Hans destroys Hanna or gets rid of her while his mother complains in vain.

TABLE 8-1. Two INTERPRETATIONS OF HANS'S PHANTASY

MANIFEST ELEMENTS	LATENT ELEMENTS	
	Interpretation 1	Interpretation 2
big giraffe	father	mother
crumpled giraffe	mother	Hanna
sitting down on top of crumpled giraffe	possession-"coaxing"-intercourse	destruction

These two interpretations can be schematized by setting the major elements of the phantasy opposite their meanings (Table 8-1). From our review of psychoanalytic theory, and especially of dream interpretation, we know that the elements as they were reported by Hans are called the "manifest content" whereas their parallels in the interpretation are called the "latent content." It is very easy, in both interpretations, to provide depth meanings for the two giraffes but there is difficulty with fixing the depth meaning of "sitting on top of the crumpled giraffe" in the case where the crumpled giraffe is Hans's mother.

The first interpretation is, of course, an interpretation in terms of the Oedipus Complex. Hans is said to love his mother and to be jealous of his father. The phantasy expresses Hans's wish to win his mother away from his father. The scene as a whole has an exact structural equivalence with the scene described in Excerpt *c*. Hans had been accustomed to come, in the morning, to his parents' bed, wishing to crawl in with his mother but meeting objections from his father. In both phantasy and reality there are two large creatures together; Hans approaches them and is welcomed by one but not by the other. In the phantasy Hans's victory is more definitive; he takes the crumpled giraffe away from the large giraffe. This perhaps is the wish-fulfilled that Freud has taught us to look for in every dream.

But now we can see why it is difficult to interpret "sitting on." The fact that the scene is set in mother's bed together with the genital approach implied by "sitting on" in conjunction with the psychoanalytic set we have taken suggest a desire on Hans's part for sexual intercourse with his mother. But the creator of this phantasy is a five-year-old boy and one must consider what a five-year-old boy is likely to desire. Would he even know about the existence of sexual intercourse? Freud asked Hans's father whether, in the earlier years when the boy's bed was in his parents' room, Hans might not have heard or seen what psychoanalysts call the "primal scene." The father assured Freud that this was not the case. Freud, like Hans in Excerpt *h*, seems to have said: "H'm, well."

Even if Hans had been aware of the primal scene he could hardly have formed any accurate understanding of its nature. Children often understand the scene as some sort of violence and are frightened by it. Hans's own word for what he liked to do in bed with his mother was "coaxing with her." This seems to have been a warm, sentimental, secure, and also sensuous experience—erotic in a way, probably including pleasant genital sensations and yet not at all the same as adult sexual intercourse; in fact cuddling or snuggling. Freud, like most of the students who have worked on this case, preferred not to commit his interpretation at this point to any single, sharp adult idea.

The second interpretation of the phantasy invokes the complex of sibling rivalry. Hans is angry at having to share his mother's love with Hanna. "Sitting on" in this interpretation might be taken to mean simply removing Hanna from sight or it might be taken to mean the destruction or murder of the younger sister. The more extreme interpretation here is more acceptable to us than it is in the Oedipal version because, in Excerpts *a* and *b*, Hans himself has said that he wishes he had no little sister. In addition most of us know of cases in which a child has, in supposed play, come near to killing a younger sibling; most of us know that babies need to be given some protection from rambunctious brothers and sisters.

Sibling rivalry is a more obvious theme of the universal family drama than is the Oedipus Complex. Clyde Kluckhohn has written (1954) that from the anthropological evidence it would appear that sibling rivalry is a cultural universal. It is certainly a complex not easily avoided in family life. Modern parents are likely to "prepare" a child for the arrival of a little brother or sister by telling him how much he will love to have a small playmate. When the baby arrives they make great efforts not to lessen their attentions to the older child in order to give him no reason for jealousy. And when the baby comes—it is greeted with mortal hatred. There is some inevitable divergence of attention, some necessity to take the baby's side in conflicts between children, some unavoidable flow of sympathy to the more helpless child. The elder is suddenly the bigger and tougher specimen who will seem selfish and bullying if he is ungenerous to the younger child.

Which of the two interpretations, the one in terms of sibling rivalry and the other in terms of the Oedipus Complex, is correct? We can compare the evidence supporting them. The giraffes figure in both cases as symbols for human beings. A symbol is, in anybody's sense, one thing standing for another: words are sometimes said to symbolize ideas; the American flag may be understood as a symbol of liberty. The Freudian symbol differs from the thing it symbolizes in terms of emotional charge: the branch of a tree is less charged than the phallus, the act of climbing stairs less charged than the act of intercourse. The comparatively innocuous stand-in, the symbol, is linked with its sense by some kind of association, often by some points of similarity. What are the particular points of resemblance that enable us to move from the giraffes to the members of Hans's family?

We are given two animals of a single species (giraffes) and so we may anticipate a pair of latent elements belonging to one class—the two parents in the Oedipal case, the two female relatives in the sibling rivalry case. The two animals are differentiated by one characteristic—"crumpling." Hans's father asked him what he meant by "crumpled" and the boy, in demonstration, took up a piece of paper and crumpled it. What is there about Hanna or about Hans's mother to suggest crumpling?

Hans had seen his little sister soon after her birth. The most striking aspect of her appearance might have been the wrinkled skin of a newborn and so, perhaps, Hans has represented wrinkling as crumpling. This is possible but there is no report of Hans commenting on such a feature as he did on Hanna's lack of teeth. In addition, crumpling would seem to suggest to Hans, in view of his demonstration with the piece of paper, not just a fissured appearance but also a collapsing, a reduction in size. Who, in his experience, has collapsed? His pregnant mother, perhaps. Excerpt *1* suggests that Hans had noticed his mother's increase of size before Hanna's birth and so does much else in the full case history. Perhaps then the crumpled giraffe is his mother—after she has been delivered of Hanna.

Anyone looking for Freudian symbols would find a phallus in the long, stiff neck of the giraffe. If we take a dreambook approach to the interpretation of the phantasy we will surely say that the large giraffe must be Hans's father because of its neck. A dreambook provides a fixed interpretation for any element of dream content, an interpretation to be invoked regardless of the context or the identity of the dreamer. Freud sometimes wrote as if that were his approach to symbolism; see, for instance, the list of symbols and interpretations in Lecture 10 of *A General Introduction to Psychoanalysis*. At other times (1933) he took the position that the meaning of a symbol had always to be discovered in the associations of the particular dreamer. Perhaps there are some symbols that very often have the same interpretation but in the case of a small boy one looks for corroborative evidence before taking a standard interpretation from a dreambook for adults.

From the age of three years at least, Hans had taken a lively interest in "widdlers." He took note of the widdlers on the animals at the zoo and later on when his father drew a Bowdlerized giraffe Hans told him that he had omitted something and the boy added a stroke between the legs. Hans asked his mother one day: "Mama, have you got a widdler too?" and she replied: "Of course" (Freud, 1909, p. 151). It came to be Hans's theory that all the animal creation had widdlers—of a single kind—while inanimate things, tables and chairs and the like, had none. The sight of his little sister in her bath did not disabuse Hans of his theory that females as well as males had widdlers, for he insisted that Hanna's widdler was simply quite small. However, Hans was very curious to see his mother and the maids and other females without their clothing and his father, thinking to make him less curious, finally told him that females do not have widdlers. Hans's phantasy followed his enlightenment on the anatomical difference between the sexes and so it is at least possible that the crumpled giraffe, by contrast with the large giraffe, symbolizes this difference. If so, then the crumpled giraffe is the mother and the Oedipal interpretation is supported.

What connections can we trace between sitting on top of something and the idea of possession or "coaxing"? We have already found some erotic suggestion in the genital approach that occurs in sitting on something. The case for possession is stronger, I think. A small boy who wants to prevent someone from taking away one of his possessions, for instance a toy truck, often sits down upon it. The weight of his body prevents dispossession. It is a kind of "body English" for a primitive conception of private property. When an object that is sat upon is not substantial enough to support a boy's weight, the action of sitting is destructive and so interpreting the phantasied action as a destruction, the sense appropriate to the theme of sibling rivalry, is also quite reasonable.

In the English word *possess* we can still dimly discern the Latin root *sedere* which means "to sit." The German word for *possession*, the word used in the original case report, is *Besitz* and the tie to *sitzen* ("sit") is obvious. The abstract concept of possession has, in the evolution of European culture, grown out of the concrete act of sitting (think, for instance, of "squatter's rights"). Abstract terms in all languages have such concrete ("perceptible") beginnings. The idea of intellectual adherence, for example, in the sense of adherence to a dogma, derives from the sticking together of physical surfaces as in *adhesive* tape. I am not suggesting that Hans had knowledge of linguistic roots and that his dreaming mind drew upon this knowledge in devising symbols. The suggestion is rather that the child mind may arrive at an understanding of abstract concepts by a developmental progression similar to that traceable in the cultural evolution of the same concepts.

There are lines of association to support both interpretations. Perhaps they are somewhat more persuasive for the Oedipal version—the phallic neck, the crumpled *post partum* mother, the crumpled female genital, *Besitz* and *sitzen*. In addition to these element-by-element similarities there is a scene, fitting the Oedipal interpretation, having the same abstract structure as the phantasy as a whole: the scene in the bedroom.

In favor of the sibling rivalry interpretation on the other hand are the many clear expressions of Hans's hatred for Hanna as well as several particular lines of association—a "crumpled" baby, sitting on something fragile as an act of destruction. How can we choose between the interpretations? We might put it up to the patient. But Hans, in conversations with his father that were not included among the excerpts presented here, seemed to accept both interpretations.

Does psychoanalytic theory require that we choose between the two interpretations? It does not. Expository writers who want to be clear try to use each word with a single consistent meaning but the "dream work" is not trying to be clear. It is perfectly acceptable in psychoanalytic theory for more than one interpretation to be correct. In fact the collapsing of two themes into a single representation is an instance of "condensation" which is supposed to be a common aspect of the dream work. The story of the two giraffes can embody both the themes we have considered. Symbols in a phantasy can have more than one meaning but to say this is not the same as to say that they can mean anything whatever. There may be several credible interpretations but there are many others that are not credible. Even though we may not be fully convinced let us proceed.

INTERPRETATION OF THE PHOBIA

Hans's phobia changed in time: He was at first afraid that a horse would bite him but later on he said that when he saw one horse drawing a heavily loaded cart he was afraid the horse would fall down. It will simplify the problem of interpretation to deal with these fears one at a time.

The major elements of the original phobia are just two: a subject and a predicate; the horse and the act of biting. Students of this case are usually agreed that the horse, who is expected to bite, is Hans's father and a strong case can be made for this interpretation. In Excerpt *d* Hans says: "Daddy, don't trot away from me!" It is white horses that Hans especially fears and in Excerpt *g* he says: "Daddy, you *are* lovely! You're so white." In Excerpt *j* Hans was frightened by two horses because they looked so "proud." His father asked him who it really was that was so proud and the boy replied: "You are, when I come into bed with Mummy." Notice, however, that on this occasion Hans feared that the horses would fall down, not that they would bite him. We shall want to return to this fact.

When he was asked to describe the sort of horse that frightened him most, Hans said it was the sort with blinders on and with something black around the mouth. Hans's father had been puzzling over this at about the time he brought his son for a single interview with Freud. Freud took in the black moustache and spectacles on the father and thought he knew whom the horse symbolized. These details of the father's appearance are facts you may possibly have guessed. You may also have guessed on grounds of general probability that Hans and his father would have played "horsie" together. This was the case; the boy's father had been his first horse.

The translation of horse is easy since the evidence in the excerpts is abundant but the translation of biting is more difficult. An occasional student of the case, knowing his Freud, will argue that biting should signify castration, the punishment a boy is supposed to fear will befall him for his love of his mother. This interpretation is not usually put forward with conviction. There is little to suggest it in the excerpted materials and it is surely far-fetched to suppose that a boy would think his father capable of such an act. However two very critical facts have been omitted from the excerpts.

At about three years of age Hans had begun to play with himself, to practice childhood masturbation, especially when he went to bed at night. When he was three-and-a-half his mother tried to break the habit by threatening Hans: "If you do that, I shall send for Dr. A to cut off your widdler" (Freud, 1909, p. 151). More than a year later, after Hans had developed his phobia, his father assured him that horses do not bite, but Hans insisted that "white horses do." One day he had been standing near a white horse with a little girl friend named Lizzi and Lizzi's father had adjured her: "Don't put your finger to the white horse or it'll bite you." A finger is an appendage and biting, like cutting, is an act that severs, and Hans's "white" father had been his horse. Sometimes, very infrequently, a student guesses at events of this kind from certain fragments of evidence in the excerpts.

Recall the very first excerpt, the description of the day Hanna was born. The stork tale told to Hans by his father does not account for the groans the boy heard, for the doctor's bag and the blood in the bedpan. A long time later Hans's father told him that females—his mother and Hanna —do not have widdlers like his own. But is it the case that they never had them? May they not have had them once and lost them? Hans's mother has said that doctors cut off widdlers; he has seen blood in a bedpan and a doctor's bag, his father has told him an absurd story about the stork and later on told him that his mother and Hanna do not have widdlers. And Hans's father was, by profession, a doctor.

If all the ideas described are brought together they are sufficient to have suggested to Hans that he stood in some danger of castration at the hands of his father for his sexual naughtiness in playing with himself and "coaxing" with his mother. In suggesting that Hans may have had such an idea one must add that he almost certainly did not have it in any clear form. Ideas are not all on one level of consciousness. Perhaps you can recall times as a child when you lay awake in the night visited by vague nightmarish thoughts. A large toy animal can seem to have come to life as it stares at you with eyes of fire. For an instant, in which your heart stops, the shadow of the trees on the wall is a hovering menace. Children can follow a regular routine and play happily and yet have a hazy suspicion at times that the father and mother they see are not their real parents; that their smiles and kindness change when his back is turned to malevolent looks and murderous designs. If Hans suspected that his father was a bloody castrator that suspicion only existed in a shadowy half-world where anything can exist.

The phobia changed in time and became a fear that a horse drawing a heavy load would fall down. If the horse is still taken to be Hans's father this phobia may represent a fear that the boy's father will fall down and die. Hans, you remember, was terrified that the horses who were "proud" like his father would fall down. Both Freud and Piaget (1926) have found that children believe in the omnipotence of thought, in the power of an expectation or a wish to bring about an event. We all know from our own experience or from children and adults with whom we are acquainted that it is possible to experience guilt on the death of a parent because one has for a moment thought of the death before it happened and, perhaps, thought that it would be no bad thing. Hans may have wished his father dead and out of his way but if he had such a wish he had a more powerful wish that it should not be so, for Hans loved his father even while he feared and hated him.

During the summer before Hanna's birth Hans and his mother had been alone together a good deal at a summer resort called Gmunden, which is on one of the Austrian lakes. The boy's father had been with them some of the time but he had frequently to leave to attend to his practice in Vienna. In father's absence Hans's loving mother had indulged the little boy's desire to snuggle into bed with her. Hans had had his mother all to himself and he remembered the Gmunden summer as a happy time, almost a honeymoon time. On one of the occasions when his father left for the city Hans, seeing the horse disappear down the road, had wished that his father might never return. But Hans was not of one mind on this subject; the wish was not wholehearted. "When you're away, I'm afraid you're not coming back" (Excerpt *d*). "Daddy, don't trot away from me."

The conflict in Hans was not simply a conflict between love of his mother and fear of his jealous father. There was also the conflict between a desire to be rid of his father and his great love for his father. The hatred he felt for a rival threatened Hans with a fearful physical retaliation but the more shattering threat may have been the danger that he would do away with the rival whom he loved almost as much as he loved his mother.

The Gmunden summer had an unhappy aftermath: not only the return to an interfering father but the arrival of a clamorous new rival (Hanna). This latter occurrence, too, is represented in the phobia of a falling horse. In Excerpt *i* Hans's father asks: "I say, doesn't a bus look like a stork-box?" and Hans answers that it does. Hans assents again in Excerpt *l* when his father suggests: "When Mummy was having Hanna, was she loaded full up too?" In the full case history there is much to suggest that Hans noticed his mother's size in pregnancy and it is possible that the horse with a loaded cart is a pregnant mother. In fearing that such a horse would fall down and spill out the contents of the cart Hans may have symbolized a fear that his mother would give birth again, spilling out another unwelcome sibling. However, the evidence we have cited from the excerpts is not very persuasive for the reason that the suggestions were made by Hans's father and simply assented to by Hans. Psychologists who have worked with children know that a child's assent may have no significance.

However, there is one powerful bit of evidence that argues for the birth interpretation; it is a bit of evidence I find very convincing. In describing the occasion when he actually saw a horse fall down Hans uses an unusual phrase: "It gave me a fright because it made a row with its feet" (Excerpt f). The phrase occurs again at the end of Excerpt n: "Oh, when I don't want to sit on the chamber and would rather play, then I make a row like this with my feet." The occurrence in two contexts of a single odd locution can serve as a psychological tracer, indicating that the two events are somehow associated.

Students of the case often notice the double occurrence of "a row with his feet" but they do not often hit on a good explanation of the occurrence. Because the row that Hans makes with his feet is associated with a wish to be playing one naturally thinks first of the row as expressing impatience but it is not clear what impatience has to do with the fallen horse. It is more profitable to try to think of some connection with birth.

One of the great puzzles that occupies the mind of a child is the nature of birth (Piaget, 1926). How are children born? There is a theory that is very common among small boys. The theory is that childbirth, like defecation, is accomplished anally. There is no other model for birth in a child's experience of his own physical processes. The transfer to the fallen horse of the row with his feet that Hans makes on the chamber surely links the fallen horse and spilled cart with pregnancy and birth. In the full case history there is much additional detail that is corroborative of this interpretation.

As symbolic expressions Hans's phantasy and his phobia have a striking economy and symmetry. The two great latent themes are the Oedipus Complex and the complex of sibling rivalry. These two themes may be regarded as variants of a single, more general theme—resentment of rivals who deflect a mother's attentions. When the rival is a little sister there is not much to be feared by way of direct retaliation and also no great love to conflict with hatred. Therefore the hatred can be rather openly expressed. When the rival is a father there is power to be feared and love to conflict with the wish to eliminate the rival and so the conflict is more severe and the need to disguise fear and hatred more extreme. Both themes are condensed into a single phantasy (or dream) and wish-fulfilling outcomes are provided as Freud argued they always are provided in dreams. Hanna is destroyed and mother is possessed. The phobias express the same two themes but in place of wish-fulfilling outcomes there are fears of dreaded outcomes: castration, the death of Hans's father, the birth of another sibling. Hans's symbolic productions have the symmetry and economy of works of art.

Should we be persuaded by the evidence we have seen? Is it certain that Hans was concerned with sibling rivalry and Oedipal desires and that his phantasy and phobias express the two themes? What we have by way of evidence is a great many bits and pieces that fit the interpretation. Too many to be accidental? We have no way of determining a baseline, no way of knowing how many congruous items it is reasonable to expect by chance. While we cannot set any explicit numerical baseline I think we have a kind of implicit baseline derived from our experience of life. If we are persuaded by the evidence in this case history it is surely because the "fit" between facts and interpretation is, by our experience, too good to be set down as accidental.

But how has this sense of a good fit been produced? The data from Hans were largely obtained by his father who was convinced in advance that Freudian explanations would be found. Again and again the father pressed Hans toward the expression of Oedipal desires and feelings of sibling rivalry. Most of the clearer statements of these themes were made by the father; Hans assented but children will often assent when they do not agree or even understand. As Freud put it: "Hans's father was asking too many questions and was pressing the inquiry along his own lines instead of allowing the little boy to express his thoughts" (Freud, 1909, p. 207).

Not all of the best evidence for the Freudian interpretations was forced out by Hans's father. The white horse with something black about its mouth—the fallen horse making a row with its feet—the possession of the crumpled giraffe by sitting upon it; these fragments and many others were volunteered by Hans to a father who did not foresee them and often did not understand them when they appeared. When we subtract material that was suggested by the interrogator there remains a significant residue of evidence.

The evidence you were given in the excerpts had been sifted three times and all three sifters believed in the Freudian interpretation. From the total stream of behavior in Hans's home over a period of more than two years his father selected certain things to write to Freud—these surely were the things that Hans's father thought Freud would find interesting-significant-interpretable. From all the reports in all the letters Freud selected some sample for quotation in the case history and this sample was surely selected for its consistent interpretability. Finally I have sifted from Freud's case history the most interpretable fragments of all. As one student put it to me, "the result is a jigsaw puzzle that can only be put together in one way, but what relation is there between the cardboard picture that results and the original events in Vienna between 1903 and 1906?" Given a Freudian orientation and a very carefully selected sample of evidence one may obtain a high consensus among interpreters but this fact does not prove that the interpretation is valid for the population of evidence from which the sample was drawn.

AN EXPLANATION IN TERMS OF CONDITIONING

In reading the excerpts you may have been startled when you came upon Hans's statement in Excerpt *f:* "Because once a horse in a bus fell down." The passage is startling because it suggests an alternative to the Freudian explanation of Hans's fear that horses would fall. The alternative is based on principles that are well established in both familiar experience and experimental psychology. Since Hans has actually seen a horse fall and a bus tip over, his fear of similar horses and conveyances could be a simple one-trial conditioned fear response. What need is there to appeal to arcane symbols and dubious theory? The origin of the phobia is as straightforward as the origins of the fears of the child Albert in a famous early demonstration of conditioning carried out by John Watson (Watson and Rayner, 1920).

Watson caused Albert to be afraid of a white rat (which initially delighted the boy) by startling Albert with a sudden loud noise while he was playing with such a rat. A noise of this kind is an unconditioned stimulus to fear and the fear response became attached to the conditioned stimulus of the sight of the rat. The fear generalized to stimuli similar to the conditioned stimulus and so Albert was afraid of rabbits and his mother's coat and a Santa Claus mask as well as the original rat. The falling of a horse and tipping of a bus must surely have created a great clatter; there would have been the noise of neighing and screaming and of wildly striking hooves. Thus noise would have been an adequate unconditioned stimulus for fear in Hans and the sight of horses pulling conveyances a conditioned stimulus. The conditioned fear would serve as a drive, motivating avoidance of situations where such horses and carts might be seen and so Hans stayed indoors.

Using a little more of conditioning theory and making a plausible assumption we can also explain Hans's fear that a horse would bite him. We will assume that at one time or another in the first three years of his life some animal had given Hans a bite and that this bite produced pain and fear. If the event was labeled for him as a "bite" then that word would have become a conditioned stimulus for fear. Later on, we know, Lizzi's father said in Hans's presence: "Don't put your finger to the white horse or it'll bite you" (Freud, 1909, p. 172). The conditioned fear elicited by the word *bite* could have become attached by second-order conditioning to the sight of white horses. The explanation is surely plausible and it assumes only an associationistic psychology. What need is there to invoke the Oedipus Complex?

The Failure to Extinguish. The conditioning explanation dictates a specific therapy—the process called *extinction.* Watson was sure that he could have cured Albert's phobia by presenting the conditioned stimulus without the reinforcement of the unconditioned stimulus. Unluckily (for Albert as well as Watson) there was no opportunity to try the extinction procedure because Albert went home from the hospital before the experiment could begin. However, others have used an extinction therapy for acquired fears and have succeeded in eliminating them (Jones, 1924; Jones, 1930; Wolpe, Salter, & Reyna, 1964). Jones (1930), for instance, subjected several infants to a mildly painful electrical stimulus in conjunction with a tapping noise and the noise came to elicit the emotional response. Jones then presented the noise many times over a period of weeks without the unconditioned stimulus and eventually the noise lost its power to elicit fear. It would seem that this kind of extinction therapy ought also to have cured Hans.

The implication for corrective action of an associationistic psychology was clear to Hans's parents as it would be to any parent: Reassure the boy about horses. And so they told him that horses do not bite and will not fall. They pointed through the window to the horses at the loading platform opposite the house to show Hans that he had nothing to fear. For years the boy saw horses without any further falls or bites or threats of bites but his fears did not extinguish. The fact that they did not extinguish when they should have extinguished, if the conditioning explanation were correct, argues that the explanation is not correct or at any rate not complete. It argues that the fear was fed by some subterranean stream and Freud has told us what stream it may have been.

What are the action implications of the psychoanalytic interpretation? The depth interpretation tells us not to waste time reassuring Hans about horses. This is not the point at which a force can be effectively applied. The symbolic interpretation directs us to apply pressure at a point in the boy's mental processes which is quite remote from the point suggested by the manifest content. He does not require reassurance about horses but rather about his father, about masturbation, and pregnancy.

In his single interview with Hans, Freud told the boy that his father was not angry because Hans so loved his mother but was fond of him in spite of it. Three days after the visit Freud received a letter that began: "The *first real improvement* is to be noted" (Freud, 1909, p. 186). It seems that Hans had found the courage to stand at the street door for an hour watching the horses go by and this was something he had long been too frightened to do. Apparently, then, the depth interpretation suggested a therapy and the therapy was effective. Surely this is clear evidence that the psychoanalytic interpretation was valid.

The story is not so simple. The conditioned fears that Jones managed to extinguish were very mild ones; he notes that his electrical stimulus did not make any child cry. There is reason to believe that some conditioned fears, those of traumatic intensity, are not easily eliminated by the extinction procedure and Hans's fear may have been of traumatic intensity. If we assume that it was of traumatic intensity then the failure to extinguish is consistent with a conditioned response account of the phobia. Furthermore the success of the psychoanalytic account is not perfectly clear because the cure Freud accomplished was not permanent; Hans's phobia returned. We will take the argument a little deeper.

Irreversibility of Traumatic Conditioning. Solomon and Wynne (1953) have produced fear in dogs[2] using the following procedure. The animal stands in one compartment of a two-chambered shuttle box. Suddenly the lights in his compartment go out and a gate is raised so as to convert the wall between the two compartments into a shoulder-high barrier. This complex event is the conditioned stimulus (CS) and, before training, it elicits no marked signs of fear in the dog and, in particular, does not cause the animal to jump the barrier into the second chamber. Ten seconds after the CS the experimenter delivers to the animal a very intense electric shock so intense as to be just subtetanizing. The shock is the unconditioned stimulus (UCS) and like Watson's abrupt noise it produces fear, but there would seem to be a difference in the intensity of the fear. Where Watson's Albert only cried a bit, Solomon's dog screamed, leapt about, defecated, urinated, and before long jumped the barrier to safety. This degree of massive, diffuse reaction of muscles and viscera is called by Solomon and his associates a traumatic (literally "wounding") fear.

The dog's first hurdle jump is an *escape* response; it enables him to get away from the shock. After a few trials, sometimes only three or four, the animal jumps so promptly on delivery of the CS that it is absent from the darkened chamber when the shock is delivered and so altogether *avoids* the UCS. Jumping the barrier within the ten-second interval between CS and UCS is an avoidance response. Watson's Albert also made avoidance responses to the CS: He attempted to get away from the white rat. Hans tried to avoid horses by refusing to go out of doors. The avoidance response, motivated by fear of traumatic intensity, has occupied Solomon and his associates for many years because it has the interesting property of high resistance to extinction. They have had the patience to administer as

2. Lucille Turner and Solomon (1962) have worked on traumatic avoidance conditioning in humans. The problem is complicated in interesting ways by the cognitive processes of the human subject. One man, for instance, did not avoid the shock, though he knew how to do so, because he was afraid it would spoil the experiment.

many as 650 extinction trials distributed over several months and none of their animals showed any signs of extinction. It seemed to the investigators that traumatic avoidance conditioning was inextinguishable by ordinary procedures.

There is more than one reason why traumatic avoidance resists extinction. Once the CS occurred Solomon's dogs generally jumped the barrier in something under two seconds. Since the UCS, the shock, was held off for ten seconds the dogs were long-gone when it was delivered. On extinction trials, of course, it was never delivered. But dogs who promptly jumped when the lights darkened had no opportunity to find out that the shock was missing. In Solomon's phrase they did not "test reality" and so did not learn that their fears were no longer justified. This is certainly one reason why avoidance does not readily extinguish.

Hans, in the degree that he was able to shut out the sight and sound of horses, also removed the possibility of testing reality, of learning that horses did not generally either fall down or bite. It is interesting in this connection to speculate on the role of the verbal reassurances given him by his parents. Their talk about the harmlessness of horses seems to have brought the boy to the point where he could stand at the door or window and expose himself to horses at a distance. Dollard and Miller (1950) have made the persuasive suggestion in connection with psychotherapy that talk about persons and actions which arouse fear reduces the intensity of the fear to the point where a patient can try out new behavior in real life. Something like that seems to have happened with Hans and he did look at horses and they did fail to fall down or to bite. Still his fears did not disappear.

Solomon and his associates, Kamin and Wynne (1953), also induced their dogs to test reality but not by verbal reassurance. When the lights dimmed and the gate was raised a glass barrier fell into place preventing the animal from jumping into the other chamber. The dog stayed in the darkened compartment well beyond ten seconds and so had an opportunity to learn that there was no more shock. After very many trials of this kind a few animals gave up the avoidance response. Others did not, and, in all the dogs, the darkening of the chamber seemed to continue to produce some fear. Solomon and Wynne (1954) concluded that the failure to test reality is not the only reason for the great persistence of the avoidance response. On the basis of their own data and supporting findings of Gantt (1953), Liddell (1944), and others they postulated a partial irreversibility of the conditioned fear itself. It seems to Solomon and his associates that when a fear response is of traumatic intensity then the classical conditioning that attaches it to a new stimulus cannot be completely extinguished.[3] The fear can be much reduced and so the irreversibility is

3. This view has not gone unchallenged. See, for instance, Carlson and Black (1959), Carlson (1960), and Seward and Raskin (1960).

only partial, but the fear survives at some minimal level. The dog will always be afraid when the lights go down in the shuttle box.

If the great clatter of a falling horse gave Hans a fright of traumatic intensity then conditioning theory predicts that his fear of horses ought to have been reduced by extinction procedures but not completely eliminated. So far as one can tell from the case history that is what happened. If the original fright was a mild one then extinction should have been more effective. And now we see that no decision can be made as to the adequacy of a conditioned response account of Hans's phobia. The case history was not written to test such an account and so the report is not sufficiently detailed where we need details. Even with details the decision would be difficult since conditioning theorists have not been able to specify an explicit intensity at which fear becomes traumatic and so irreversible. We can only conclude that a conditioned-response account that includes Solomon's ideas is not ruled out by the facts presented in Hans's history.

Freud's Therapy. A conditioned-response account of Hans's phobia is a possible alternative or supplement to the psychoanalytic account. Conditioning theory does not account, however, for the boy's associations and dreams and phantasies. How does the psychoanalytic account fare in view of the outcome of Freud's attempt at therapy? There was some immediate remission and that is certainly to the credit of the depth interpretation. But what shall we make of the fact that the fears returned? Was Freud mistaken about their source? Perhaps. However, he had very little time with Hans and apparently did not attempt to relieve the boy's mind about masturbation and pregnancy though the depth interpretation makes these concerns central to the phobia. Maybe the difficulty was that Hans's fears had a realistic base that could not be completely eliminated with words. After all, Hans's sensual attraction to his mother had to be curbed; he was expected to give up masturbation and he could not hope to prevent additional pregnancies. Hans's various wishes, all of them centering on the desire to have exclusive and intimate possession of his mother were necessarily opposed by those around him—by his father, his mother, and his little sister. So long as he harbored wishes that others found unacceptable he must fear interference and punishment and the loss of love. Hans's fears had a certain inevitability and were perhaps not resolvable in terms of talk alone. The ultimate inefficacy of Freud's therapy for Hans does not unseat the depth interpretation of the phobia and the temporary efficacy of the therapy does something to establish it. Therapeutic efficacy is easier to evaluate than the congruence of associations and symbols that we found in the case history. Surely it is the success of psychoanalytic therapy rather than the persuasiveness of psychoanalytic interpretations that has caused the world to take Freud's theory so seriously.

PSYCHOANALYTIC THEORY IN RELATION
TO PSYCHOANALYTIC THERAPY

The research literature on treatment of psychopathology shows a curiously persistent tendency to neglect control data. For example, while there are thousands of reports of pharmacological treatment of psychotic states, treatment by tranquillizing drugs, only a handful of the studies reported have controlled for the well-known "placebo" effect. Most papers simply report that some percentage of cases, perhaps some thousands of patients, who were administered chlorpromazine showed definite improvement. Such reports tell us nothing about the effectiveness of chlorpromazine unless they also tell us what percentage of patients show definite improvement when they are given neutral pills that look just like chlorpromazine. It is also necessary that neither patients nor staff should know who has been given the real thing.

One can see why persons in clinical practice so often neglect to collect control data. For the man seeing patients the control case is the patient as he was before the new therapy. With psychotic patients who may have been much the same for months or years a sudden change that follows a new therapy must seem to have been caused by the new therapy. It need not be so. One cannot be sure unless comparable cases, not treated with the the presumed effective agent, fail to show improvement.

Psychoanalytic institutes and mental hospitals and psychiatrists in private practice have often reported on the percentages of cases that improve but they do not report proper control cases. H. J. Eysenck (1961) has measured the effectiveness of psychotherapies, including the psychoanalytic but not exclusively the psychoanalytic, against data on neurotic persons who received no treatment or treatment by general practitioners that included no psychotherapy or custodial care without psychotherapy. About two-thirds of all the cases, whether treated or not, recovered in a few years' time. The comparison may be unfair to psychoanalytic therapy —neurotics who are treated by general practitioners may be less seriously ill than those who undertake psychoanalysis—but in the absence of better data one can only conclude that the value of psychoanalysis has never been proved.

Suppose the value of the therapy were to be proved by adequate group comparisons and statistically significant differences. Would it follow that psychoanalytic theory is valid? I think not. There is, in the first place, great variability in the practices of therapists who call themselves psychoanalysts. Freud himself is said to have performed very strangely as a therapist: he sometimes shouted at his patients and pounded the table. There is not, in the second place, the kind of strictly deductive relation between theory and recommended practice that would make the outcome of practice a test of theory. If the therapy were conspicuously successful it would inevitably reflect some credit on the theory since it was, at any rate, *suggested* by the theory, but conspicuous success would not rigorously establish the theory. And in any case the success of the therapy has not been established.

Why then do we take psychoanalytic theory so seriously? We do so in part because Freud was a powerful writer and a courageous man and because he provided a conception of human nature that can fit into modern thought. But these are considerations apart from truth and falsity; there are also reasons that have something to do with truth. The man who sees patients takes in some early data, interprets them psychoanalytically, and is led to anticipate certain other data. These other data are forthcoming often enough so that the theory seems to work. As in the case of little Hans there are enough "pieces that fit" to generate belief. This is evidence but it is evidence for which we have no exact method of evaluation. The therapist's knowledge also suggests to him little experiments, things to try, interpretations to make. These little experiments, like Freud's reassurances to Hans, often have their anticipated effects and so generate belief. The little experiment, unlike the big experiment on the effect of the total course of therapy across many patients, can be closely related to particular theoretical propositions. However, the proper control case is always lacking in clinical practice and so these little experiments are not really trustworthy. There is a vast amount of empiricism behind psychoanalytic theory and it has produced a band of believers and zealots; but the empiricism is ultimately unsatisfactory.

Freud's Theory of Identification

Hans is not to be regarded as a markedly pathological case. Phobias in children are not at all uncommon and the Oedipus Complex and the complex of sibling rivalry are supposed to be universal human situations, features of normal development. What was perhaps unusual about Hans was the freedom with which he talked about some of his preoccupations and that may have been a consequence of the effort his parents made to be permissive. In any case Hans came back to visit Freud as a young man of nineteen and then was in good health. He had read the case history but could recall nothing of the events described, ". . . the whole of it came to him as something unknown!" (Freud, 1909, p. 288). Hans's problems have a certain inevitability and universality. The normal way out is not through psychotherapy but through a process of identification and repression and postponement.

In Excerpt *o* from the case history Hans describes a thought, or perhaps it was a dream, that he had one morning. "The plumber came, and first he took away my behind with a pair of pincers, and then he gave me another, and then the same with my widdler." Father jumped down his throat with an interpretation: The new behind and the new widdler were bigger models—like daddy's—and this expressed Hans's wish to be like daddy. The boy agreed.

On another occasion, very late in the period covered by the history, something occurred that is better evidence of the development of identification. Hans was playing with imaginary children and his father said: "you know quite well a boy can't have any children." Hans responded: "I know. I was their Mummy before, *now I'm their Daddy*" (Freud, 1909, p. 238). This evidence would be quite at home in contemporary studies where the nature of a child's doll play is often taken to reveal his major identifications.

Identification with his father is the happy ending to Hans's story. It represents what is called the positive (or favorable) resolution of the Oedipus Complex. In identifying with his father Hans adopts his father's morality and so relinquishes his mother as an object of sexual desire. At the same time the boy is confirmed in his masculinity since he takes an adult male for his life's model.

With the concept of identification Freud sought to solve two great problems: 1) the continuity of conscience across generations, the appearance in children of the values of their parents; 2) the institution in children of biologically appropriate sexual identities causing them to have the values, desires, and manners of their own sex. Both problems can hardly be said to have existed until Freud created them. The Victorian mind was not aware that there was anything to be explained about conscience or sexual identity. Conscience had been supposed to be a "still small voice" planted in man by God for the guidance of his conduct. Each person's sexual identity was biologically established and it was biological instinct that caused heterosexual desire to develop in adolescence. The principal challenge to these views was and is the variety of mankind. Instead of the few standard models predicted by the Victorian view, the world is full of a number of things, of criminals, and psychopaths, and martyrs, and persons who perpetually feel guilty. It contains inverts and perverts and occasional homosexuals and persons of confused sexuality. The Victorian mind coped with this diversity by assigning everything but the standard article to the category of things unnatural, degenerate, and inexplicable.

In Freud's view, both conscience and sexual identity were largely learned. "One may reject the suggestion of an original as one might say, natural capacity for discriminating between good and evil" (Freud, 1930, p. 106). "It seems probable that the sexual instinct is in the first instance independent of its object; nor is its origin likely to be due to its object's attractions" (Freud, 1905, p. 148). The varieties of mankind he saw as a set of alternative outcomes to the complicated learning that goes on in childhood, a set of variations of character following lawfully upon variations in family relationships. Where the rest saw natural instincts or the lack of them Freud saw the greatest problems of social learning.

In psychoanalytic theory the agency in the mind that represents morality is called the *superego*. Freud began writing about the moral functions of the mind before 1900, in his letters to his great friend Fliess, but he did not introduce the term superego until 1923. In that year, in a monograph called *The Ego and the Id*, he partitioned the mind into three, now well-known, parts. The *New Introductory Lectures*, which were first published in 1933, described principal aspects of the superego and gave each a name. The observing, judging, punishing aspect, which had been called the censor or censorship in *The Interpretation of Dreams* (1900), was to be called by its familiar name "conscience." The term *ego ideal*, first introduced in the 1914 paper *On Narcissism*, was to be used for the positive standard against which the conscience measures the ego.

How does the superego function? It causes resistance to temptation, guilt for wrongdoing and shame for inadequacy, enhanced self-esteem for either virtue or capability. Freud is chiefly concerned with morality rather than with adequacy or capability. However, in *Group Psychology and the Analysis of the Ego* (1921) he wrote: "And the sense of guilt (as well as the sense of inferiority) can also be understood as an expression of tension between the ego and the ego ideal" (p. 131). It seems to have been his position that the ego ideal represents an ideal of capability and knowledge as well as of morality and that the conscience measured the ego against both kinds of standard. Any failure of the ego to realize ideal standards is cause for disagreeable emotion: guilt if the failure is moral and a sense of inferiority if it is a failing of ability. Feelings of righteousness and capability reward the ego that is close to its ideal.

The functions of the superego—maintenance of proper conduct by contingent rewards and punishment—are the same as the functions of parents and teachers and policemen and others who maintain the norms. Since there are two forces that make for good conduct a man's conduct alone gives no indication of the strength of his superego. Freud recognized (1930) that there are people whose "anxiety relates only to the possibility of detection" (p. 108). The strength of conscience he held can only be assessed from conduct that is not subject to external sanction. How does a man behave when parents, teachers, or police are not about? This essential distinction was taken up years later by Sears, Maccoby, and Levin (1957). When they undertook to assess the strength of conscience in a large number of children they did it by asking the mothers whether their children sometimes confessed misdeeds that had been done behind mother's back.

A society must have some way of controlling conduct when the police are not around because the police cannot always be around. It is possible to get away with very much more wickedness than most of us try to get away with. We could cheat more, seduce more, steal more, and lie more than we do. It is society's internal agent—the superego—that keeps us within bounds and presumably society needs such an agent. However, the agent often goes beyond what is necessary for the maintenance of society. It punishes evil desires even when evil actions are renounced and it punishes sometimes when even the desire is hard to find.

What is the source of the superego? The answer can be given in very general terms with a few brief quotations. In his last work, *An Outline of Psychoanalysis* (1940), Freud wrote: "The long period of childhood, during which the growing human being lives in dependence upon his parents, leaves behind it a precipitate, which forms within his ego a special agency in which this parental influence is prolonged" (p. 16). "The parents' influence actually includes not merely the personalities of the parents themselves but also the racial, national, and family traditions handed on through them as well as the demands of the immediate social *milieu* which they represent. In the same way, an individual's superego in the course of his development takes over contributions from later successors and substitutes of his parents, such as teachers, admired figures in public life, or high social ideals" (p. 17). The immediate sources are parents and parent successors and the remote sources are the cultures and subcultures represented by the parents. What aspects of the parents become the superego? Not primarily their actions, Freud held, but their standards, in fact their superegos. Standards can be preserved from generation to generation without being very adequately realized in anyone's behavior.

What are the determinants of identification and the creation of the superego? The superego is, to quote Freud's almost ritually repeated phrase, "the heir of the Oedipus Complex." So it comes into being as the Complex is resolved and its creation is supposed to accomplish that resolution. Probably Freud's most complete and straightforward account of how this is supposed to go appears in his paper *The Dissolution of the Oedipus Complex* (1924). Here now is a very bald résumé.

Both boys and girls take their mothers as their first sensuous love objects for the reason that love develops out of dependence on a caretaker. A boy's love for his mother becomes increasingly passionate and so his father becomes an increasingly exasperating and threatening rival. At length a threat of castration is made to the boy or imagined to have been made. Chiefly because of this threat but also perhaps because of his anatomical inadequacy, the boy gives up his mother as a love object, represses his desire for her and his hatred of his father, and accepts his father as an ego ideal or model.

What about girls? "At this point our material for some incomprehensible reason becomes far more obscure and full of gaps." Those are Freud's words (1924, p. 177), and it must be admitted that the reason is incomprehensible since so many of his patients were women. It makes one wonder how much of his developmental psychology he got from patients and how much from his self-analysis. How about girls? They also have a complex; in his *Outline of Psychoanalysis* (1940) Freud mentions that it might be called the Electra Complex. Girls are not fearful of castration but rather believe it has already happened to them. They feel themselves incomplete and envy the male his penis. This causes them to turn away from mother who was their first love object and to love the father instead as a means of acquiring a penis or the control of one. In time the desire for a penis from father is supplanted by the desire for a child. The threat of castration is supposed to *end* the Oedipus Complex whereas the supposed fact of castration and an accompanying penis envy are supposed to *initiate* the Electra Complex. What then brings it to an end? Freud really did not know and in *Some Psychical Consequences of the Anatomical Distinction between the Sexes* (1925) he suggested that it must just wear off. And he added a characteristically anti-feminist observation that women seemed to him not to have as exacting and objective a superego as men.

Freud gave some details of the progress of the Oedipus Complex in his 1924 paper and these details are in startlingly close correspondence with the details of Hans's 1909 history. The threat of castration is made in order to curb masturbation. It is usually made by mother though she often says that either father or a doctor will do the deed. The threat is not at first taken seriously (it was not by Hans) and only comes to be taken seriously when the boy discovers that females do not have penises and assumes that they have been castrated. If a boy sees a female at an earlier time he will deny that there is any difference and insist that the female's penis is very small. Hans did just that with Hanna. Can it really have happened that Freud's cases through the years presented him with the same detailed history as did Hans? Or was Hans's case for some reason enormously influential in fixing Freud's conception of the universal Oedipus Complex?

However that may be, the account of the dissolution of the Oedipus and Electra Complexes does not really account for the occurrences of identification. Why does the boy identify with his father? How does his doing so solve the Oedipal problem? When will he not do so? As for the girl it is not even quite clear that she does identify with her mother.

In *Mourning and Melancholia* (1917) and in *The Ego and the Id* (1923) Freud takes up the topic of identification in earnest. When someone beloved dies the ego identifies with or introjects the lost loved one.

The ego seeks to resemble the one who must be relinquished to death. In effect the ego consoles the id: "Look you can love me too I am so like the object." This identification with the lost beloved is "the work of mourning."

It seems now that we have found a determinant of identification. Identification occurs when a love object must be relinquished. Therefore since a boy must give up his mother as an object of sexual love he should identify with his—whoops! It comes out wrong. By this theory the boy should identify with his mother and the girl, since it is her father she must relinquish, should identify with her father. Whenever I read *The Ego and the Id* (1923) and arrive at this point I feel as if Freud himself might have said "whoops!" so patent is his surprise at the conclusion to which his speculation has led him.

Freud tries the theory this way and that way to see if he can make it fit all the data points. In fact, he notes, boys do show some signs of identification with their mothers and girls with their fathers. Identification is not a one-time event; there are numerous identifications and a child can identify in some respects with one parent and in other respects with the other parent. Yes, but if identification confirms the child's sexual identity then the major identification must, in the normal case, be with the parent of the same sex and that is not the way it will work if the parent the child loves sexually and so gives up is to be the major object of identification.

The full Oedipus Complex or Electra Complex, Freud goes on, always involves taking both parents as love objects and also feeling fearful and jealous of both. If so, there should be identification with both lost loves, both parents, for both boys and girls. But then the outcome for the two sexes would be the same. That will not do because Freud wants to use identification to establish sexual identity as well as the superego and so the outcomes must be appropriately differentiated.

Freud begins to swing wildly. The human being's biological nature is always bisexual; there are always both masculine and feminine components. Freud had always held that view. Since both parents have been loved and given up there will be a basis for identifications with both by children of either sex. Which identification is stronger will depend on the relative strength of the masculine and feminine components in the child's nature. Since masculinity will usually be stronger in boys they will usually identify with their fathers and since femininity will be stronger in girls they will identify with their mothers. It works! But it gives the whole problem back to the Victorians. Boys become men because they are biologically male and girls become women because they are biologically female. If that assumption is acceptable to Freud he does not need all the rest of his theoretical apparatus, for the single assumption will establish appropriate sexual identities.

The discussion of identification that appears in *The Ego and the Id* (1923) is probably Freud's most serious discussion of identification and I find the outcome a disappointment. The disappointment is with the over-arching theory, the attempt to unify mourning and conscience and sexual identity, rather than with his insight into each of the three particular phenomena. The attempt to treat all these things, conscience and the work of mourning and sexual identity, as one kind of identification having one kind of source may simply have been foredoomed by the facts. Freud could have extricated himself from his theoretical bind if he had been willing to think of identifications as being of two or more kinds involving two or more sorts of determinant.

Additional determinants of identification were available to Freud from his own writing. In one or another book or paper he suggested all of the following: 1) Identification can occur because the ego sees itself as similar to some other person; 2) identification can occur because the ego envies the success or authority or attributes of another person and wishes to participate in them; 3) identification can occur because another person threatens the ego with aggression and the ego seeks to conquer its fear. The last of these was much elaborated by Freud's daughter Anna (1946). Suppose Freud had been willing to separate out identification$_1$ from identification$_2$: the former to designate the transmission of moral standards having nothing to do with sex role, such as honesty and truth-telling; the latter to designate the transmission of sexual identity including appropriate object choice, appropriate ambitions and tastes, and so forth. Perhaps identification$_1$ is made with the major relinquished love object and so would occur across sex—a boy with his mother and a girl with her father. For identification$_2$ a different determinant could be selected. It might be the recognition of similarities (a boy with his father and a girl with her mother), but this would take us very near the Victorian answer and not allow for the varied outcomes found in nature. Envy of success is more promising, I think, and in one form is very like a contemporary theory that we will discuss a little later, the status-envy theory of John Whiting (1960). Perhaps identification$_2$, the transmission of sex role, is made with that person whom the child sees as most successful in obtaining love from the one the child chiefly loves. This would mean that since boys love their mothers if the mothers love their husbands then boys will identify$_2$ with that man—father. Girls should identify$_2$ with their mothers if the mothers are loved by the fathers whom the girls also chiefly love.

I do not say that any of the above is true. Indeed the virtue of the treatment is that one obtains propositions whose truth is uncertain but conceivably discoverable. Freud's passion to unify and to dogmatize led him to take a different line. It seems to me that most psychoanalysts after Freud have shared his taste for dogma on the subject of identification and the superego. Polemics about the age at which the Oedipus Complex occurs, about the distinctions among guilt, remorse, shame, and fear and when children have these experiences do not advance the great problems Freud exposed. And so we will not turn to the neo-Freudians to find the next step forward, but rather to empirical psychology.

The Strength of Conscience

If everyone had the same sort of conscience, same in content and in severity, then each man should feel guilt proportionate to his wickedness. We know they do not do so. People who are as harmless as anyone can be, may, nevertheless, sink into a guilty depression. On the other hand, psychopaths can murder and torture without suffering guilt. Guilt is not directly proportionate to wickedness and so consciences must vary in content and in severity. Freud has even proposed, in *Civilization and its Discontents* (1930), that guilt is inversely related to wickedness: "The more righteous a man is, the stricter and more suspicious will his conscience be, so that ultimately it is precisely those people who have carried holiness farthest who reproach themselves with the deepest sinfulness" (p. 114). Why should this be so? Reverse the order of Freud's statements and you take away all their surprise—"The stricter and more suspicious a man's conscience is, the more righteous will he be." Of course. Consciences govern conduct and the more severe the conscience the better the conduct. But Freud arranged his remarks differently because he thought the direction of cause and effect was not only from severe conscience to good conduct but also the other way around. Again from *Civilization and its Discontents:* ". . . in the beginning conscience (more correctly, the anxiety which later became conscience) was the cause of instinctual renunciation, but later this relation is reversed. Every renunciation then becomes a dynamic fount of conscience; every fresh abandonment of gratification increases its severity and intolerance . . ." (pp. 113–114).

The superego causes man to renounce some instinctual gratification, in particular to renounce aggression. The energy of the renounced desires becomes available to the superego. The aggression one does not express against others is expressed by the superego against the self. The ferocity of the superego, the intensity of guilt, is proportionate to the fury that goes unexpressed. By extension, then, the child who hates his father mightily but behaves toward him with perfect submission will have the most punishing conscience.

Renounced aggression energizes the superego and so, Freud argues, do externally imposed deprivation and frustration. "As long as things go well with a man, his conscience is lenient and lets the ego do all kinds of things; when some calamity befalls, he holds an inquisition within, discovers his sin, heightens the standards of his conscience, imposes abstinences on himself and punishes himself with penances" (p. 110). Can you testify to the truth of this? Have you suffered a serious illness or injury or the death of someone dearly loved? Is Freud's statement true? It seems to me to be a statement that requires no experimental or psychoanalytic data to validate it; most of us find it validated in our own experience. And yet I cannot recall that anyone formulated the proposition before Freud. Freud formulated many such insightful propositions and I think they justify the honor we pay him.

Severity of conscience then is held to be proportionate to the amount of aggression renounced and to deprivations imposed from without. And there is a third determinant implied by Freud in *Civilization and its Discontents* (1930). He believed that the superego of a boy was derived from his father and so one might anticipate that its severity should be proportionate to the father's. "Experience has shown, however, that the severity which a child's superego develops in no way corresponds to the severity of the treatment it has itself experienced. It seems to be independent of the latter; a child which has been very leniently treated can acquire a very strict conscience" (p. 117). It seems fair to infer that Freud would have predicted that the father who brutally beats his son will not have a son whose conscience is exceptionally strong and in this form the prediction takes us close to some contemporary work. Freud did not clearly formulate the sort of parental discipline that would engender strong conscience in a child but he said again and again that it develops out of "the dread of losing love" (1930, p. 107).

Now we shall see how these several ideas of Freud's have endured the test of non-clinical evidence. Since the strength of a man's conscience is most truly revealed by the way he behaves when no one can know how he behaves, the psychologist who would study conscience has no easy task. What he has often done is to cause the person being studied to believe that behavior is private when it really is not. In an earlier, more innocent age the required conditions could be created with a one-way screen; the observer could go unobserved. Nowadays everyone knows about one-way screens, but in the 1930's, when the workers at the Harvard Psychological Clinic made their famous "explorations" into the personalities of fifty men (Murray, 1938), sophistication was not so general. MacKinnon (1938) was able to give subjects a chance to cheat in circumstances where they did not know that they could be observed.

MACKINNON'S EXPERIMENT

Each subject (there were ninety-three in all) was given twenty problems to solve, working alone in a room that had a rather large mirror on one wall. The experimenter left a couple of booklets with the subject; the booklets contained answers to all the problems and the subject was permitted to look at some of these and prohibited from looking at others. MacKinnon identified forty-three violators of the prohibition and fifty non-violators.

About four weeks later each subject was asked, in private, if he had looked at any of the answers he had been told not to look at. Those who had not, simply said so. Of those who had, about 50 per cent denied it while the other 50 per cent made confessions of varying completeness. To the confessed violators MacKinnon put a question asking whether they had felt at all guilty about what they had done. He could not put this question to the violators who lied or to the non-violators and so he asked them instead whether they thought they would have felt guilty if they had cheated. Of those who had cheated, whether confessedly or not, only 25 per cent reported that they had felt or would have felt any guilt. Of those who had not cheated 84 per cent said that they would have felt guilty if they had cheated. MacKinnon went on to ask: "Do you, in everyday life, often feel guilty about things which you have done or have not done?" Seventy-five per cent of the non-violators, the innocent, said they often felt such guilt and 29 per cent of the violators. What were Freud's words? "The more righteous a man is, the stricter and more suspicious will his conscience be . . ." (1930, p. 114).

The relation MacKinnon found between acquaintance with guilt and comparative righteousness demonstrates, at least, that people do not all have the same conscience. Guilt is not directly proportionate to wrongdoing. In fact, it is, as Freud predicted, inversely proportionate. That may simply mean that people prone to guilt avoid the wrongdoing that will cause them suffering or it may further mean that the wrongdoing that is foregone somehow feeds energy to the conscience. This latter, peculiarly Freudian idea, is not easily proved but MacKinnon found a fragment of evidence in its favor. He recorded the incidental behavior of the subjects when they were working the problems. Nine or so of the violators cussed out the problems while they worked saying such things as: "You bastard" or "These are the God damnedest things I ever saw." None of the non-violators did this. About 31 per cent of the violators indulged in such restless destructiveness as pounding their fists or kicking the legs of the table while only 4 per cent of the non-violators did so. Conceivably the aggressive energy expressed by the wrongdoers was subtracted from the energy available to the conscience while the energy unexpressed by the innocent was made available to the conscience.

Some time after the original experiment MacKinnon undertook to inquire into the childhood experiences of his subjects. He was able to contact twenty-eight of them, all males, thirteen violators and fifteen non-violators. They were asked to check, on a list of common forms of punishment, those most usually employed by each of their parents. MacKinnon divided the punishments into those that were physical—beatings and deprivation of privileges, etc.—and those that were psychological—causing the child to feel that he has fallen short of an ideal, has hurt his parents and lost some of their love. The numbers were very small but it is interesting to find that 78 per cent of the violators checked physical punishments and only 48 per cent of the non-violators. Psychological punishments went the other way, being checked by 52 per cent of the non-violators and only 22 per cent of the violators. What were Freud's words? ". . . A child which has been very leniently treated can acquire a very strict conscience" (1930, p. 117). If psychological punishments are more lenient than physical then the severity of the child's conscience is not proportionate to the severity of the parent's punishment but actually tends to be inversely related.

Probably it is wrong, however, to think of physical and psychological disciplines as two points on a severity scale. There is a sharp difference in the quality of the experience; so MacKinnon's subjects told him and so we all know. A beating arouses fury; one vows to get even. A mother who, with tears in her eyes, tells her son that he has disappointed her may give more pain than the pain of a beating, but it is a different kind of pain; it does not seem to engender anger but shame and the resolve to do better. Freud had observed that gentle parents sometimes produced children with very punishing superegos and so he knew that there was not a direct relation between the intensity of punishment and the intensity of guilt. He was puzzled about the matter, not sure just what sort of relation should exist. The distinction MacKinnon made between punishments different in kind or quality, rather than simply in intensity, points toward the answer.

THE SEARS STUDY

MacKinnon directly studied wrongdoing and guilt but for information about the child-rearing to which his subjects had been exposed he had only their retrospective reports. A study done at the Harvard Laboratory of Human Development in the 1950's (Sears, Maccoby, and Levin, 1957) obtained the mother's own account of her child-rearing practices. The Harvard research team interviewed mothers from two suburbs of Boston; each mother had a child enrolled in a public-school kindergarten. The interviews took about two hours apiece and the questions ranged widely over the behavior of the children and the child-rearing practices of the parents. The transcribed interviews were rated (with high reliability) on 188 different scales. These ratings are the data of the study and it should be remembered that they are all derived from the mother's verbal report.

Sears and his associates at Harvard thought of a clever way to learn something about the strength of the child's conscience. Here now is the question as it was addressed to two mothers (M) by an interviewer (I), and following the question are portions of each mother's answer.

I. We'd like to get some idea of how Sid acts when he's naughty. When he deliberately does something he knows you don't want him to do when your back is turned, how does he act?

M. Very seldom does that. But a few times that he has done something that he shouldn't do, that I don't know anything about, if I'm in the other room, he just can't hold it in very long. And finally he comes in to me and he says, "Mother,"—and I'll say, "What?"—"I did something I shouldn't have done." Instead of leaving it and getting away with it, he usually comes over and tells me what he's done. He usually comes, I mean, and it's not very long after he's done it. He can hardly hold it in to himself, you see.

I. Are there any situations in which he doesn't do this? In other words . . .

M. Never come across one that he didn't. Even when he does something outside that he shouldn't do, and I don't even know about it, he could very easily not say a word to me. Instead he comes in and he says, "You know what I did?" And if something goes wrong in school he'll say, "Something happened today. My teacher had to speak to me." And he doesn't have to tell me, but he does; he comes right over and tells me. I don't know why. I should think if I were a child I'd keep it to myself but he doesn't; he comes and tells me and I would never know about it. I mean it—you know the old saying, "What you don't know won't hurt you." He evidently doesn't know it yet [1957, pp. 377–378].

I. We'd like to get some idea of how Billy acts when he's naughty. When he has deliberately done something he knows you don't want him to do, when your back is turned, how does he act?

M. Well, right now he is lying. If he is caught, he will lie his way out, which is very disturbing to me. If there is anything I can't stand it's lying. I just want him to face the fact he's been naughty, and I will be much kinder with him; but sometimes if he's very bad, I just put him up in his room which has a terrible effect on him. Sometimes I just give him a good scolding, and sometimes I fall back on the old dodge of telling him when his father gets home he will deal with him, which I know is wrong, but I just don't know how to handle him. I'll admit he is a problem [1957, p. 379].

From the mothers' reports the raters credited the first child with a highly developed conscience and the second child with a much less well-developed conscience. In the ratings for development of conscience across all the children there is a finding of some incidental interest. Twenty per cent of the boys were credited with strong consciences and 29 per cent of the girls. This time we remember Freud's words to his discredit. He suggested (1925) that females do not develop such strong superegos as do males.

What is the relation between strength of conscience and parental discipline? The interviews were also rated on the degree to which parents made use of such techniques as: praise, isolation (e.g., sending a child to his room), withdrawal of love, tangible rewards, deprivation of privileges, and physical punishments. The more psychological techniques, the first three above, were positively associated with the development of conscience and the more physical techniques, the last three above, were negatively associated with the development of conscience. The relationships were not large. The largest was that with the technique of physical punishment; of the parents who made much use of this technique 15 per cent had children with strong consciences whereas, of the parents who made little use of physical punishment, 32 per cent had children with strong consciences.

If we take physical discipline to be more severe than psychological the outcome confirms Freud's observation that children of lenient parents sometimes have severe consciences. It goes beyond Freud's observation to confirm MacKinnon's discovery that persons with strong consciences are more likely to have been disciplined in a psychological way than in a physical way. The 379 mothers of the Harvard study were also rated on the general warmth of their behavior toward their children and this variable in conjunction with the use of a particular disciplinary technique served to identify the mothers most likely to have children with strong consciences. It was the generally warm mothers who used withdrawal of love as a major disciplinary technique.

"Withdrawal of love" is a psychologist's phrase. Mothers do not spontaneously report using it and interviewers did not even ask them about it. The ratings had to be made by inference from certain kinds of reported behavior. Do we know what withdrawal of love is like? Mother looks hurt or her voice quavers a little. She has less to say than usual, her movements are brusque, her jawline shows a certain tension. If something slightly disagreeable happens—a cup breaks or the cat gets in her way—she over-reacts, bursting into tears or a temper. Perhaps you recognize it; not only mothers practice it but husbands and wives, sisters and brothers.

Warmth as a rule and withdrawal of love for wrongdoing seem to create conscience. Presumably warmth (or love) is necessary because the threat of withdrawal is proportionate to the value of what has been given. Mothers who were generally cold but who seemed to practice withdrawal of love were not nearly so likely to have children with strong consciences as those who were generally warm.

The question about conscience in the study by Sears and his associates asks how a child behaves when he has done something naughty unbeknownst to his mother; it does not specify any particular kind of naughtiness. One sort of behavior that was naughty in the eyes of almost all of the 379 mothers was aggression against parents. A child ought not to raise his hand against his mother or father, neither should he speak to them in an angry or impertinent way. For a child to be aggressive to his siblings or to children outside the family seemed not nearly so bad to the mothers, though most of them believed this kind of aggression also had to be curbed. The way the mother felt about aggression was related in a very straightforward way to the amount of aggression their children were reported to manifest. Mothers who felt more permissive about aggression got more of it; those who were less permissive got less of it.

Children seem to be punished for aggression more often and more severely than for any other behavior. Yet parents who will not permit aggression do not necessarily stop it with physical punishment. They may simply restrain a child or distract him.

How well does physical punishment work as a check on aggression against parents? Not well. The parents who punished had the more aggressive children. Apparently then punishment fails to produce a generally strong conscience and fails also to check the particular form of wrongdoing against which it is most often directed—aggression against parents.

Very few associations have been reliably established between childrearing practices and child personality. The association between physical punishment and an aggressive child has more evidence behind it than any other. All the vaguely Freudian talk about the importance of weaning and toilet training for the development of personality has come to nothing. To be sure psychologists and pediatricians and government pamphlets have given advice and child care has been revolutionized in a generation (Bronfenbrenner, 1958) but not on the basis of established knowledge about personality development. Reviews of the research literature (e.g. Orlansky, 1949) show that weaning and toilet training are not known to have any consequences for personality. There is considerable support for an association between a parental stress on early independence training and a strong achievement motive in the child (see Chapter 9). However, the evidence relating punishment and aggression is still better.

PHYSICAL PUNISHMENT AND STRENGTH OF CONSCIENCE

It was a shortcoming of the Harvard study that the aggressiveness of the children was not directly determined but had to be rated from what mothers said. However, in another study of which Sears was the senior author (1953) children were observed in nursery school and their observed aggressiveness related to the severity of the punishment their mothers said they suffered for aggression at home. The relationship was the same: Severe punishment went with more aggression. There are many other confirming studies. The Gluecks (1950) found severe physical punishment to be one of the major factors associated with delinquency in young boys. Bandura and Walters (1959) have compared the attitudes of parents of twenty-six hyperaggressive boys with the attitudes of parents of twenty-six normal boys matched with the first in socio-economic status and intelligence. The hyperaggressive boys had all been in trouble with the law and most of them were on probation. The aggressive boys experienced less guilt than the normal boys, their parents used physical punishments while the parents of the normal boys favored psychological sanctions, the fathers of the aggressive boys rejected their sons in greater degree than did the fathers of normal boys.

It has become a stale lesson in psychology that a correlation or association between two variables does not establish the direction of cause and effect. Physical punishment and aggressiveness are correlated variables and our discussion, like the discussions of all the authors cited, has encouraged the reader to think of the parental practice as the cause of the child's characteristic. That may be the correct way to think of it but the correlation in question is susceptible of a very reasonable interpretation which reverses the direction of cause and effect. Perhaps innately aggressive children exasperate their parents into beating them while gentler children do not. The animal evidence of Chapter 4 strongly suggests the existence of innate differences in aggressiveness of temperament. Disciplinary measures used by parents probably constitute a scale of increasing desperation; parents *in extremis* may turn to physical punishment.

The case for thinking of aggression as the cause is reasonable but so is the case for punishment as cause. This form of discipline has a peculiar and interesting property: it is itself an instance of the behavior it is designed to eradicate. Punishment, the response to aggression, is itself aggression. What will the child learn? It is intended that he learn not to be aggressive and if he learns by Thorndikian "stamping out" that is what he should learn. If, on the other hand, he learns by imitating what others do he may learn to be aggressive. He might even learn a subtler lesson that incorporates all the information: Do not be aggressive to parents, since that is punished, but do be aggressive to those smaller or subordinate to yourself as parents successfully do. To learn this subtler lesson he must recognize the non-equivalence of aggression-upward with aggression-downward.

Bandura, Ross, and Ross (1961) have demonstrated that children very readily imitate the aggressive actions of another person so we cannot doubt that punishing parents could create aggressive children. In addition, the Bandura and Walters study of hyperaggressive boys obtained data giving some support to the view that punishment is the cause. These authors interrogated parents about their very earliest attitudes toward their children and the indications are that the fathers had been rejecting long before the boys became exceptionally aggressive. Whichever has priority in the child's history, punishment or aggressiveness, it seems likely that in a short time the two variables must constitute a mutually reinforcing system. Punishment by angering the child and providing him with an aggressive model must increase his own aggression and that increase would stimulate the parents to further violence.

Thinking of punishment as itself a form of aggression has suggested to us that punishment can engender aggression because it constitutes an imitable model of aggression. In a parallel manner the "technique" called "withdrawal of love" can be reconceived as a model of non-aggression under provocation. It may be misleading to call "withdrawal of love" a "technique" or even a "practice" because in many instances love withdrawal does not describe what parents intend to do. Their intention is to not express anger or aggression though strongly tempted to do so. A parent who will not allow himself to hit a child or to scream at a child is nevertheless hurt, frustrated, and angered by the child's misbehavior. Taking care not to "blow up" he arranges his words and his face so as to conceal what he feels, but the deliberateness, the control, are themselves a message. They come through as a certain stiffness, a lack of spontaneity, a chill—the withdrawal of love. If this is true then the withdrawal of love can, alternatively, be described as an imitable model of non-aggression under stress and imitation of the model would produce a non-aggressive child.

MILIEU THERAPY FOR AGGRESSIVE CHILDREN

The contrast between physical and psychological sanctions can be translated from the individual to the institutional level. The Wiltwyck school in New York offers what is called *milieu therapy* for boys who are psychopathic or hyperaggressive or neurotic. It is a precept of Wiltwyck's director Ernst Papanek (1953) that: "Punishing teaches the child only how to punish." The boys at Wiltwyck are allowed to be aggressive within certain limits and the limits are established by means other than counter-aggression. The school offers friendship, permissiveness, and understanding. It is a therapy of the milieu, of the boy's total environment; they live at Wiltwyck. Fritz Redl offered a similar experience for a time at Pioneer House in Detroit (Redl and Wineman, 1954) and Bruno Bettleheim (1950) at the Orthogenic School of the University of Chicago. The idea derives from the experiments in the treatment of delinquency initiated by August Aichhorn (1935) in Austria after the first world war. Milieu therapy is in sharp contrast with the harsh discipline and corporal punishment that keep order in the more usual reformatory. Which is more effective in curbing aggression and strengthening inner controls?

Some of the boys who go to reformatories or schools like Wiltwyck have been diagnosed as "psychopathic children." The word "psychopathy" is sometimes used in a general way to designate any sort of mental pathology or illness, but it has also a narrower sense in which it is the name of a particular psychiatric category. It is a category of the greatest relevance to a discussion of the strength of conscience because psychopathy diagnoses an underdevelopment, specifically, of conscience. It used to be called "moral insanity" and the central feature of the psychopath is supposed to be guiltlessness. "He can commit any act with hardly a twinge of remorse" (McCord and McCord, 1956).

The psychopath commits crimes but he is not the same as other criminals. Most criminals believe in some code and show sympathy and love for some people. The psychopath's capacity for love is blunted and he does not feel the rightness of any code. He seems to be incapable of making a continued effort in the interest of a remote goal; even his crimes are likely to be unplanned and impulsive. Most neurotics are too anxious, inhibited, and guilty to be confused with the psychopath, but acting-out neurotics, and persons with behavior disorders, do resemble the psychopath. The psychopath is not bizarre and disoriented in the way that many psychotics are.

The psychopath is not defective in his *knowledge* of right and wrong. Psychopathic boys at Wiltwyck know the general morality on such matters as stealing, killing, lying, kindness, and generosity; they even endorse the code on a verbal level (McCord and McCord, 1956). Furthermore the behavior of psychopaths, like the behavior of anyone who is not institutionalized, is largely normal. They drive on the right-hand side of the road, brush their teeth, and wear clothing. From time to time they also steal, kill, and rape with complete *sang-froid*. Presumably the psychopath knows what is expected and what is right and is willing to go along as long as he has no strong impulse to do otherwise. He may have impressive social graces, an insouciant charm. But while he knows the moral code he does not feel it and if his impulses conflict with the code he can break it without remorse. Psychiatric theory clearly specifies that the impairment is one of conscience or superego and within the conscience it is feeling that is supposed to be impaired rather than cognition.

What are the causes of psychopathy? There is some possibility that psychopaths are less "conditionable" than normals (Lykken, 1957; Bandura and Walters, 1963). It is probable that brain injury plays some determining role in many cases (McCord and McCord, 1956). However, the most reliable antecedent of adult psychopathy is an experiential one; the psychopath was severely rejected by his parents and in many cases brutally beaten (McCord and McCord, 1956). Cause and effect are uncertain as usual but the association is the one to be expected if psychopathy is the pathological extreme of weak conscience and aggressiveness.

The character of the psychopath may be better communicated by case histories than by definitions. This is a short one from the McCords' book, concerning one of the Wiltwyck boys.

> Paul, a 10-year-old white boy, wore a mask of enmity, creased with scowls and frowns. Extreme aggressiveness and uncontrolled impulsivity, at the age of 3½, had brought Paul to the attention of a psychiatrist.
>
> Since first treatment, Paul's aggression, hyperactivity, and destructiveness had increased. In public school, Paul attacked several children, set fire to the teacher, and ravaged the classroom. After one year, the principal suspended him. Taught at home, Paul drove teacher after teacher from the house. To "have his way," he sometimes resorted to banging his head against the wall. A second psychiatrist concluded: "He has no ability for relating to either adults or children, no comprehension of the consequences of his acts, and no guilt concerning them."
>
> Detailed and frequent neurological examinations have shown no defect or damage in the child's brain.
>
> Paul's family lived in a slum area. His father openly rejected the child and had beaten him severely since infancy. His mother, a weak and ineffectual woman, had no control over the boy.
>
> While stealing from a warehouse, Paul struck a watchman on the head, causing severe concussions. For this offense, the court remanded Paul to a public home in New York City.
>
> At the home, Paul set fire to the furniture and curtains. He horrified the other children by killing goldfish with pins and pulling out their intestines. The children's home moved him to Wiltwyck in July, 1954.
>
> During the research interview (a month after arrival), Paul showed no guilt feelings, a hatred of his parents and other authority figures, and such intense hostility that the interview could not be completed. He left the room saying, "Get me out of this hole!" [pp. 130–131]

Psychopaths, because they are often intelligent and can behave expediently, may stay out of institutions most of the time and play a part in the world's affairs. Leadership in a riot (see Chapter 14) is probably as much prominence as most of them attain but sometimes they seem to go higher.

> G. M. Gilbert, chief psychologist of the Nuremberg trials, described Herman Goering as an "amiable psychopath." Gilbert pointed to Goering's brutal, loveless childhood as typical of the psychopath's background. Goering's father was a stern Prussian official who valued military discipline above all else. Goering's earliest memory was of "bashing his mother in the face with both fists when she came to embrace him after a prolonged absence...."
>
> As a child Goering loved excitement, the glaring splash of military uniforms, and early exhibited his taste for sadistic brutality. Uncontrolled behavior and vicious attacks on his sisters led his parents to shift Goering

from school to school. His mother predicted: "Herman will either be a great man or a great criminal!"

In his youth, Goering's drive for glory, his brutality, his emotional impulsiveness, and his aggressiveness "found its most desirable expression in the military prerogative of his culture." Goering's recklessness earned him the distinction of being one of Germany's top air aces in World War I, but his uncontrolled greed brought him into illegal wartime adventures. He took illicit leaves, accepted bribes, and established a clandestine army supply company.

After the war, he married a rich Swedish countess. Despite his newly found wealth, Goering missed the excitement of war. Attracted by Hitler's militancy, Goering was swept into the Nazi party. He moved from honor to honor as president of the Reichstag, head of Nazi industry, and chief of the Luftwaffe. His objective was expressed in a Reichstag speech: "I am not here to exercise justice, but to wipe out and exterminate!"

Goering's spectacular rise to power provided him with the means of satisfying his craving for pleasure. He turned to drug addiction, mistresses, and "Roman" orgies. As Germany collapsed, Goering pranced through his palace, Karinhall, dressed in a toga, with painted fingernails and lips.

With the fall of Germany, Goering, along with the other Nazi leaders, went on trial for his part in the war crimes. Gilbert, who came to know Goering during the trial, noticed a singular lack of guilt. After seeing a documentary film of mutilated bodies from a concentration camp, for example, Goering commented only: "It was such a good afternoon, too, until they showed that film—they were reading my telephone conversations on the Austrian matter and everybody was laughing with me—and then they showed that awful film, and it just spoiled everything."

Before ending his life with poison, Goering left this message for the West: "You Americans are making a stupid mistake with your talk of democracy and morality. . . . Don't think that Germans have become more Christian and less nationalistic all of a sudden . . . you can take your morality and your repentance and your democracy and stick it up!" [McCord and McCord, 1956, pp. 30–31, based on Gilbert, 1948]

The McCords (1956) have made controlled studies of the effects of the Wiltwyck milieu and these are surely among the best studies we have of the value of any variety of psychological therapy. Since they were chiefly concerned with psychopathic boys and behavior disorders they had to find ways to assess level of aggression and strength of conscience. They used familiar methods such as having the Wiltwyck counselors rate the boys on various characteristics but, in addition, the McCords invented special measures that are well adapted to the Wiltwyck population and to the assessment of the strength of "inner controls." One test was composed of pictures of a dog—Rover—in a variety of situations, all of them frustrating. Rover would see his own ugly reflection in a mirror or would encounter a policeman on his beat or would see his "girl" with another dog, etc. With each picture the boy subject would be asked: "What does Rover want to do?" and three alternatives would be offered. In one of these Rover was pictured as reacting with aggression, in another Rover withdrew from the threat, and in a third he made some neutral, possibly assertive, response. The boy's answers were interpreted as projections of his own inclinations.

In 1953 the McCords administered their battery of tests to thirty-five boys at Wiltwyck and also to thirty-five boys at a "typical public reformatory." They analyzed the results in terms of months of residence at time of testing and obtained evidence that Wiltwyck was having desirable effects on its inmates, whereas the reformatory appeared to be having little effect of any kind. In 1954 the McCords gave the battery to all of the 107 children then at Wiltwyck and again analyzed by term of residence. Boys who had been longer at Wiltwyck appeared to be less aggressive and to have stronger inner controls.

The results suggest the Wiltwyck milieu was the cause of these characterological improvements, the effect being proportional to the time spent in this milieu. This conclusion builds on a hidden assumption which is that the boys who, in 1954, had been at Wiltwyck for varying periods of time had, on their arrival, all shown about the same high level of aggression and low level of inner control. Suppose the assumption were grossly false and that the school had been changing its admissions policy in such a fashion that the boys admitted each consecutive month were more severely aggressive than those admitted the previous month. In these circumstances the boys in 1954 would have had lower aggression scores the longer they had been at Wiltwyck but none need have improved at all in their time there. There is no reason to suppose that the school had changed its admission policy in this way but the logical problem is there and so it is good to be able to report that the McCords also made a longitudinal study. Twenty-five boys who had been recent arrivals at Wiltwyck in 1954 were tested again, eight months later, in 1955. The results of the longitudinal study confirmed those of the cross-sectional study: On numerous measures aggression declined and internalized guilt increased in the psychopathic boys and in the boys with behavior disorders.

The evidence of the longitudinal study is not perfect. There was no control group. Why should one be required? The boys' scores changed significantly in the period of their residence at Wiltwyck and so Wiltwyck must have caused the change. But this conclusion relies on the assumption that the patients would not have changed if nothing had been done for them. Perhaps anyone taking the tests a second time would have changed his answers so as to appear to be less aggressive. Yes, but the changes appeared in more than test scores; they appeared in the ratings of everyday behavior made by Wiltwyck counselors. Well, perhaps it was just age that changed them. Perhaps boys of their age, at Wiltwyck or not, become less aggressive in eight months' time.

Not all of the twenty-five boys studied in 1954 and 1955 were diagnosed either as psychopaths or as behavior disorders. Six boys were diagnosed either as psychotic or neurotic. These boys did not change in the ways that the hyperaggressive boys did; some of the neurotic boys manifested less guilt and more aggression. The neurotic and psychotic boys are a valuable control. Apparently a second administration of the test does not inevitably lower scores and apparently eight months additional age does not do it either. The control is not perfect; it should be psychopathic boys who were not at Wiltwyck. Still I believe I am convinced.

There is no doubt that Freud inspired the research on strength of conscience but it cannot be said that Freudian theory rigorously predicts its outcomes. Freud set the problem; MacKinnon took his experimental hypotheses from Freud; Aichhorn was much influenced by him and Papanek studied with him. Freud said that more severe consciences would be found in more righteous men and that the gratifications foregone by the righteous, especially aggressive ones, fed energy to the superego. MacKinnon found some supporting evidence for these ideas. The best-established proposition, however, is that rejection and physical punishment by parents tend to produce aggressive children with under-developed superegos. The nearest Freud seems to have come to this proposition is his observation that the severity of the conscience is, at any rate, not directly proportional to the severity of parental discipline. It is not clear to me that Freudian theory calls for the kind of milieu therapy created at Wiltwyck. Does it not also suggest that boys could acquire consciences by identifying with an aggressor? Threaten them with castration and they will come 'round. Or perhaps it suggests that the boys should be made to fall in love and then deprived of their love objects. Introduce them to a collection of very attractive Salvation Army girls, then take away the girls and the Salvation Army values will be internalized. In any case I think Freud would have been surprised to find consciences developing at Wiltwyck without the aid of the Oedipus Complex and at an average age of eleven years.

The Role of Imitation (or Learning by Identification) in Moral Conduct

Parents who beat their children for aggression intend to "stamp out" the aggression. The fact that the treatment does not work as intended suggests that the implicit learning theory is wrong. A beating may be regarded as an instance of the behavior it is supposed to stamp out. If children are more disposed to learn by imitation or example than by "stamping out" they ought to learn from a beating to beat. That seems to be roughly what happens. How important in general is imitation for the development of moral conduct?

IMITATION AND LEARNING BY REINFORCEMENT

The analogy between training animals and training children is an obvious one and so the first principle one thinks of using to explain the development of moral conduct is the principle of selective reward and punishment (or positive and negative reinforcement). In one way or another parents often reward good conduct and punish bad conduct and these rewards and punishments should shape the behavior they follow. Parents will react in terms of their own moral values and so these values should eventually be seen as regularities in the behavior of children. Parents are representative of a larger culture and of subcultures and so the behavior of children after the first year or so varies from one society to another and, within a society, from one socio-economic level to another.

How, in terms of reinforcement, should male children learn to be boys and female children to be girls? Parents do not reinforce the same kinds of behavior in the two sexes; the rules of reinforcement are contingent on the sex of the child. Boys are reinforced for being assertive and girls are not; girls are reinforced for learning to cook and sew and boys are not. Boy and girl roles are two distinct reinforcement programs and so are all sex-typed roles such programs. When the boy and girl become adolescent they assume new roles which is to say that the rules of reinforcement change:Lipstick is approved for teenage girls and driving an automobile for teenage boys.

If sex roles are learned by selective reinforcement the child should have no need of a same-sex model. A woman living away from her husband should be perfectly capable of exerting selection pressures that will cause her son to behave in an ideally masculine fashion. She need only have a correct conception of masculinity and the wish to see her son approximate it. If moral conduct is altogether learned by selective reinforcement a child should have no need of a moral examplar. If the parents have a well-developed conception of what moral behavior is and are guided by it in reinforcing the child they themselves should be able to manifest consistent villainy without doing the child's character any harm. A good example should be of no importance if children do not learn by example but only by direct reward and punishment.

Still there is the fact that parents who beat their children for being aggressive nevertheless have aggressive children, in fact children more aggressive than those of parents who administer no beatings. This is not the way things should go if direct reward and punishment were the only determinants of behavior. It is the way things should go if children learn by example. In addition, Brim (1958) has shown that boys who have a sister for their single sibling manifest more feminine traits than do boys whose single sibling is a brother. This looks like learning by example again and this time the learning is of sex-typed behavior.

Freud, we know, thought it important to make his theory of identification work in such a way as to cause a normal child to establish its major identification with the parent of the same sex. Clearly he believed that a model was important for learning sex roles and so he must have believed in learning by example. Perhaps indeed that is what he meant by identification—a kind of imitation except that imitation usually implies some specific action whereas identification is a more general modeling process. This in fact is how some contemporary psychologists (Bronfenbrenner, 1960; Kagan, 1958) use the word *identification*. They write of "learning by identification" and mean imitation of a very general order.

Do children imitate? Of course they do. We even have an experimental demonstration. Bandura and Huston (1961) gave some children, who were busy with a discrimination problem, the opportunity to observe an adult going through various unusual and striking actions unrelated to the child's task. The adult might march about or talk to himself or perhaps knock a small rubber doll off a box. Half of the children saw one set of actions and half saw a different set. Both groups of children later imitated what they had seen and the two groups behaved differently since they had seen different behavior. Bandura, Ross, and Ross (1961) demonstrated that children exposed to aggressive models generalized these aggressive responses to a new setting. In 1963(a) the same authors reported that children who had recently seen aggression in a motion picture reacted aggressively to mild frustration more frequently than did children who had not had the prior exposure to aggressive models. The fact of imitation is established and there is a serious possibility that aggressive children learn by the example of their parents and by the example of aggression shown in the mass media.

Bandura and McDonald (1963) have done an experiment that compares learning by direct reward with learning by imitation and this experiment helps us to understand why a model is important in socialization. There is incidental interest for us in the fact that the experiment made use of pairs of stories like those Piaget used for the study of moral judgment (see Chapter 5). One story of each pair described a well-intentioned act that resulted in considerable material damage and the other story a selfishly or maliciously motivated act that resulted in trivial damage. The child was to say which act was the naughtier. For the children having an "objective conception" of morality, the younger children, the acts with more serious consequences were the "naughtier" ones. For the children having a "subjective conception" of morality, the older ones, the acts that were selfishly or maliciously motivated seemed the "naughtier" ones.

The initial subjective or objective orientation of each child was determined. Thereafter some of the children listened and watched while adults expressed judgments counter to their own orientation. Other children had no exposure to adults but were themselves directly rewarded whenever they expressed judgments counter to their own original orientation. Finally the orientations of the children were once again determined to see what changes had been produced.

Observation of adults produced much more change than did direct reward. One probable reason for the inefficacy of the reward training was the very small number of reinforceable responses emitted by the children. For the most part they continued giving the responses of their initial orientation and so had little experience of reward for giving contrary answers. The desired response had too low a frequency level (too low an operant level) to be selected out by reward.

In the training of animals too one sometimes wants to select out a response that the animal seldom performs. One can often do it by the method of "successive approximations." Perhaps the rat does not initially show any tendency to roll a marble into a cup in the floor of his cage but he can be brought to it. One can begin by giving him a bit of food whenever he moves into the general vicinity of the marble. That will serve to keep him near the marble and will increase the frequency with which he moves the marble. Feed him for that and then for moving in the direction of the cup and at last for dropping the marble into the cup. It is a slow method and it relies on the emission of responses transitional to or in the direction of the response in which we are ultimately interested. Such responses do not always exist. The children chose one story or the other and so long as they were not choosing as the experimenter wished he had no opportunity to reward them.

Apparently once children have attained a certain level of perceptual and motor control they are able to approximate many actions of a model simply from seeing them. A boy can make a good try at "walking like a man" simply from seeing his father do it. If he had only his mother to reward successive approximations, would he ever learn? Perhaps a girl can look demure once she has seen her mother do it, but her father all alone, rewarding expressions that tend to demureness, might never get her there.

DETERMINANTS OF IMITATION

So the presentation of a model as well as the administration of reward and punishment can cause behavior change in children. In life there are always many models and, from one model, many kinds of behavior so we need to know when imitation is likely to occur and when it is likely not to occur; what are its determinants. Some writers, ambitious for reinforcement theory, have argued that we imitate behavior we have seen reinforced in another. Learning by imitation would then figure as "vicarious reinforcement" (Hill, 1960), a new variety of reinforcement to add to "primary" and "secondary." Bandura, Ross, and Ross (1963c) have put the idea to a test.

Children saw films in which someone behaved in a strikingly aggressive way. In one film the very destructive behavior was followed by severe punishment, in another by generous praise and good food, and in a third the behavior had no consequences. In a post-exposure test of imitative behavior the children who had seen the figure in the film punished imitated him the least. The children who had seen him rewarded and the children who had seen him experience no consequences imitated him more, but these two groups of children were not different from one another. The idea of vicarious reinforcement would lead us to expect rewarded behavior to be more imitated than punished behavior but not that behavior having no consequences would be imitated as much as rewarded behavior.

Bandura and his associates did not stop with the single post-exposure test of imitation. All of the children were offered attractive incentives for reproducing the behavior they had seen (Bandura and Walters, 1963, pp. 57–58). These incentives completely wiped out the differences previously observed in the performances of the groups. The results compel us to make a distinction between *learning* the behavior of a model and *performing* it. Apparently all three groups had equally well learned the distinctive behavior of the model but those who had seen the behavior punished were less disposed to perform it overtly. Vicarious reinforcement seems to have some differential effect on performance but none whatever on learning.

The distinction between learning the behavior of a model and performing it has also been made by two other theorists—Eleanor Maccoby (1959) and John Whiting (1960)—though they prefer to speak of role-learning and role-performance. Maccoby has argued that a child must necessarily learn his mother's role since that role is complementary to his own. He stands by his highchair and raises his arms, she lifts him just below the armpits and lowers him toward his chair, he slips his legs in and down and lowers his head as she brings the tray over the top. Here is one habit distributed between two nervous systems. Her behavior is matrix to his patrix and so they must learn one another's ways.

Presumably the child runs through his mother's role in his head since that role guides his own behavior. Mother's role includes her judgments of right and wrong, her praise and censure, and Maccoby's theory, therefore, provides for the literal internalization of a parent. It gets us beyond mere conforming behavior and provides for an agency in the mind something like Freud's superego, a voice standing over against the ego telling it what to do and reacting to what it does.

Maccoby's discussion predicts that one will learn the behavior of another whenever that behavior belongs to a role complementary to our own and that certainly happens. However, we also learn roles that are not complementary to our own. An actor in a play certainly learns all the lines of other actors that cue his own lines and he often does say the other actors' lines to himself. A marching soldier certainly learns all the commands the sergeant barks at him and can bark them out himself if he is asked to drill the squad. However, both the actor and the sergeant learn more than the roles complementary to their own. The actor may learn the entire play including many lines and actions which are not cues to his own performance. The soldier may learn the role of the sergeant *vis-à-vis* the lieutenant though he himself plays no part in this interaction.

We all have learned how to play many roles not our own and not complementary to our own. A young unmarried man, for example, knows the role of expectant father. He must smoke many cigarettes and pace the floor; he had better not go calmly to the movies. That role was learned by observation alone. There was no necessity for vicarious reinforcement and no necessity that the role be complementary to his own.

We learn the behavior of others on some very general principle. I will guess that for short-term learning the behavior need only be novel and attended to. Perhaps any unexpected action that we notice is learned and retained for a short time; novelty is information, and there is an appetite for information in the human species. Most of the behavior that was imitated in Bandura's experiments was highly dramatic behavior. If we internalize fragments of other people on so catholic a principle as novelty then novelty alone will not serve to account for the acquisition of morality or a superego. Our minds are full of other people but they do not all matter in equal degree.

Whiting (1960) has argued that while a child learns or has "cognizance" of many roles he does not have an equal desire to perform them all. Bandura has shown that vicarious punishment and reward have some effect on the performance of immediate imitative responses. Whiting, himself, believes that the primary cause of the wish to perform a role is envy of the status of the person who ordinarily performs it. Whiting's theory is that a child will envy the status of another person when that person has "more efficient control over resources than he has" (Whiting, 1960). Resources are anything the child desires: food, love, cars, dogs, etc.

When a boy sees that his little brother is treated more indulgently than he is himself the elder will envy the status of the younger and will attempt to perform the younger's role. It is commonly observed that elder children displaced by a younger do frequently turn "babyish." Perhaps Hans for a time imitated Hanna; he ought to have done it if this theory is right. Perhaps "status envy" accounts for Brim's (1958) discovery of feminine traits in boys with sisters. Of course many of the roles a child will envy he cannot play. A boy might envy his father's control over the resource of mother's love and wish to play that role and a girl might, for parallel reasons, wish to perform her mother's role. The roles are not appropriate to their age or circumstances and efforts to play them will meet with direct negative reinforcement. In these circumstances, Whiting holds, the child will practice the role covertly, will phantasy himself in the part of the envied parent, will play that part with dolls and soldiers. For many years the child will yearn toward the parental role and as its various aspects become appropriate to him will perform them.

Whiting's theory comes nearer than any other to preserving Freud's explicit ideas about identification and making them into a more sensible package. The boy's identification with his father would, by Whiting's theory, develop out of the boy's love for his mother and envy of his father's success with her. The girl's identification with her mother is also clearly predicted by the theory. If each child chiefly loves its cross-sex parent and if the parents chiefly love one another then "status envy" predicts appropriate sexual identities for both boy and girl.

Bandura has once again done the most valuable experiment, this time again with Ross and Ross (1963b). He has compared the child's tendency to imitate three sorts of model. The essential figures are a child who watches, an adult who controls the use of a collection of magnificent toys, and a second adult. In one condition the second adult was freely given the toys by the adult who controlled them. Both adults later performed striking actions that might invite imitation. The investigators suggest that if the chief determinant of imitation is status envy the child should imitate the adult who was the recipient of the toys since he was the lucky one. If, however, it is *social power* that chiefly attracts imitation, a view put forward by Mussen and Distler (1959) and Parsons (1955), among others, then the child ought to imitate the controller of the toys. The experiment included a third possibility. Some children were themselves the recipients of the toys from the controller; the second adult simply stood by. If children imitated the adult who had shown them preferment that result would have confirmed what is called the nurturance theory of identification. Mowrer (1950, 1958), for one, has argued that a child will wish to act like anyone who is associated with the gratification of his needs.

Children imitated primarily the adult who had social power, the one who controlled the toys. rather than the adult whose status they might have envied. It did not seem to make much difference whether the child or the second adult received the toys; the controller was imitated in about equal degree in the two cases. The result seems to be a defeat for Whiting's status envy theory and a victory for the social power theory. In fact, however, that is not a perfectly clear implication of the results. In most of the examples Whiting gives of a status that is envied the envied person enjoys resources (in the manner of the adult who receives the toys) and also has power over them (in the manner of the adult who controlled the toys). A father may conspicuously bask in the love and affection of a boy's mother and also control that love and affection.

Bandura and his associates have separated two characteristics that might cause a status to be envied: control of resources and consumption of resources. In Whiting's discussion these two things are not distinguished and, indeed, they often go together in life. When they are separated the Bandura experiment shows that it is power that attracts imitation. Perhaps this is because power reliably implies the possibility of enjoying resources while the enjoyment does not so reliably imply control over them.

In general summary, parents can affect the behavior, the conduct, of children in at least two ways: by direct reward or punishment and by providing a model for imitation. It now looks as if power were the prime factor making a model attractive for imitation though such other factors as nurturance and vicarious rewards may also be important. With two parents to manifest power and administer direct reward and punishment there are many possible kinds of family pattern, many kinds of learning problem presented to children. For some kinds of behavior, for example speaking the local language, all forces work in the same direction. Both parents model English and both reward it. For some kinds of behavior the pattern will be complex, for example assertiveness. Perhaps father manifests considerable assertiveness and has more power in the family than his non-assertive wife. Perhaps both parents reward assertiveness in their son and not in their daughter. Both children might be expected to try out being assertive on the model of their impressive father and the son's performance would be confirmed by approval but the daughter's would not be. Does the daughter perhaps retain a desire to behave assertively, a latent identification with her male parent, that leads her to try out assertiveness in new groups where the reinforcement program may be different? Learning by identification is certainly a complex geometry and it is likely that what we now know is not more than the rudiments.

Moral Knowledge and Moral Thought

The investigators who have studied the child's control of aggression generally have had some difficulty defining their critical term. What is aggression? Any injury to another or only a physical injury? Must it be intentional? What if the injury given has been provoked by an injury received? Does it matter whether the provocation comes from someone older, from an age mate, or from someone younger and weaker? The investigators who have struggled to define the category of aggression have seldom asked whether the children they studied had any understanding of the category. And yet understanding of aggression on some level, not necessarily the level of explicit definition, would seem to be prerequisite to the control of aggression. How can one control a class of behavior if the principle of classification is inaccessible?

Morality has an intellectual dimension as well as dimensions of emotion and of conduct. The intellectual dimension is almost completely missing from Freud's treatment and from the work of investigators influenced by Freud. It appears, however, in two non-Freudian researches of the late 1920's and early 1930's, in Piaget's *The Moral Judgment of the Child* (1932), and in the monumental American study called *The Character Education Inquiry* (Hartshorne and May, 1928–30).

There is an interesting contrast in the orientations of the two studies. *The Character Education Inquiry* implicitly conceives of the development of moral knowledge as a gradual piecemeal approach to conventional adult standards, the rate of approach varying from child to child. It is an orientation to moral knowledge comparable to the Binet-Simon IQ orientation to intelligence. Piaget's work on morality contrasts with that of *The Character Education Inquiry* in the same way that his work on intelligence contrasts with the Binet-Simon work on intelligence. Piaget was not interested in the rate of approach to particular adult standards. He was concerned with the forms of understanding that precede mature understanding (see Chapter 5).

THE CHARACTER EDUCATION INQUIRY

The Character Education Inquiry was research on a grand scale. Thousands of children participated and the ground covered included moral conduct as well as moral knowledge. Conduct was studied by giving children opportunities to lie, to cheat, and to steal in circumstances such that they could believe themselves secure against discovery though in fact they were not. We will describe the outcome of this part of the study in the next section. The work on the intellectual aspect of morality employed some twenty paper-and-pencil tests and involved children in the fifth through the eighth grades.

Hartshorne and May (1930) divide their tests into a set involving moral *knowledge* and a set involving moral *opinion*. A knowledge test is made up of items having objectively right answers; for example the following statement is to be marked "true" or "false": "Good marks are chiefly a matter of luck." Items on opinion tests have no objectively right answers.

For example the respondent is to say whether it is or is not his "duty" to do the following: "To report another pupil if you see him cheating." Another item asks whether the following principle is "true" or "false": "To master oneself is a greater thing than to win a battle." Opinion tests were sometimes scored against an adult consensus and sometimes against a kind of ideal code supplied by the investigators. The domain of moral knowledge, precept, and opinion is so vast that there are some questions to which children of any age will give "immature" responses and some to which they will give "mature" responses. Suffice it to say that children in the early grades of school give the answers adults approve to a good many questions. This does not tell us how children understand the questions nor how they reason about moral matters.

PIAGET'S STUDY OF MORAL JUDGMENT

Piaget's methods you may recall from Chapter 5. To learn how children thought about a system of social norms he asked them to explain to him the game of marbles. To investigate their understanding of moral concepts he told them little stories, matched in most ways but unlike in critical ways, and asked the children to say which story described the naughtier action. Here are two such stories:

> There was once a little girl who was called Marie. She wanted to give her mother a nice surprise, and cut out a piece of sewing for her. But she didn't know how to use the scissors properly and cut a big hole in her dress.

> A little girl called Margaret went and took her mother's scissors one day that her mother was out. She played with them for a bit. Then as she didn't know how to use them properly she made a little hole in her dress (Piaget [1932], 1948, p. 118).

Younger children thought Marie the naughtier child for the reason that she had done the greater damage. Older children disagreed because they considered the child's intention to be the crux of the matter.

Piaget summarized his findings in terms of two moralities. The younger child, from four years to about eight years, has a morality that Piaget called *heteronomous*. The term *heteronomous* means "subject to another's law"; the younger child is subject to the law of adult authority. His respect for authority causes him to regard adult rules as sacred, unchangeable things. Moral wrongness is defined in terms of adult sanctions; acts that are wrong are the acts that adults punish. Duty is understood as obedience to authority. The younger child's intellectual limitations in conjunction with his respect for authority cause him to conceive of wrongdoing in highly, literal, objective terms without regard to intentions, to believe that moral values are absolute and universal, and that justice is served by severe arbitrary punishment rather than by restitution to the person wronged.

The second morality, which ordinarily develops after eight years, Piaget called *autonomous*. The word means "subject to one's own law." The autonomous morality is supposed to develop out of the mutual respect that peers feel for one another as well as from advances of a purely intellectual sort. The rules of conduct are regarded as products of group agreement and as instruments of cooperative action. Moral conceptions become psychological rather than objective, relative rather than absolute, and subject to change by group agreement. Justice is a matter of reciprocal rights and obligations and is best served by repairing the harm that may have been done.

The progression from a heteronomous to an autonomous morality did not seem to Piaget to be dependent upon direct adult tuition. He thought the change resulted from the child's continuing spontaneous effort to comprehend within one system his total moral experience. Freud's use, in connection with the acquisition of morality, of such terms as "internalize" and "incorporate" tends to suggest that adult precepts are gulped down in raw form and become superego tissue without undergoing significant transformation. Piaget's conception of moral development would suggest that digesion is a closer analogue of moralization than is ingestion. Moral experience and adult precepts are only nutriment to the organism. In the process of assimilation they are transformed.

Piaget's description of moral development has in some respects been confirmed by later work and in some respects not. Studies by Caruso (1943) in Belgium, and by Lerner (1937) and Macrae (1954) in the United States warrant the conclusion that some of Piaget's dimensions are genuine developmental dimensions for more than one culture. These dimensions include the shift from objectivity to subjectivity and from absolutism to relativism; the clearly developmental dimensions are the more cognitive dimensions. The associations Piaget proposed between heteronomous morality and unilateral aspect for authority and that between autonomous morality and mutual respect between peers have not been consistently validated by later research (Kohlberg, 1963b).

KOHLBERG'S STUDY OF MORAL THOUGHT

In psychology the study of morality is often regarded as equivalent to the study of values. However, philosophy, at least since Kant, has distinguished value theory from ethics or moral philosophy. A sharp distinction between moral values and other values is not easy to make but the central idea is that moral values carry a sense of absolute obligation, of "ought" or "should," whereas other values carry only a sense if desirability, of "I like" or "I want." Aesthetic values, economic values, the values of success and of health generate preferences and yearnings rather than categorical imperatives. Among psychologists who study morality only one, Kohlberg (1958, 1963a, 1963b, 1964), seems to have made a serious effort to separate moral values from other kinds and to invent techniques of investigation aimed at the specifically moral.

Kohlberg is in the Piaget tradition and has asked children to judge the morality of conduct described in stories. Kohlberg's stories are new ones of his own invention and they pose such moral dilemmas as this:

> In Europe, a woman was near death from a special kind of cancer. There was one drug that the doctors thought might save her. It was a form of radium that a druggist in the same town had recently discovered. The drug was expensive to make, but the druggist was charging ten times what the drug cost him to make. He paid $200 for the radium and charged $2,000 for a small dose of the drug. The sick woman's husband, Heinz, went to everyone he knew to borrow the money, but he could only get together about $1,000 which is half of what it cost. He told the druggist that his wife was dying, and asked him to sell it cheaper or let him pay later. But the druggist said, "No, I discovered the drug and I'm going to make money from it." So Heinz got desperate and broke into the man's store to steal the drug for his wife. Should the husband have done that? Why? [Kohlberg, 1963a, pp. 18–19]

The story of the cold-hearted druggist does not inquire about the child's understanding of simple sins and simple virtues in the manner of Piaget's stories. Kohlberg's story opposes a legal-social rule to a human need and asks the child to reason about the morality of the case. Both lines of conduct open to the husband are legitimate, though in different senses. Kohlberg's dilemmas admit of resolutions which subordinate the rule of law or of authority to a higher principle. They admit of a morality by which the conventional morality can itself be judged. Moral judgment does not have to end, as is so often implied, with acceptance or "incorporation" of the local culture. People sometimes change society instead of conforming to it.

Kohlberg's dilemmas are challenging to adults as well as to children. They draw upon more than our understanding of moral conceptions; they stimulate us to reason in terms of a general theory of morality. For instance, one problem asks whether a man in a civilian air-defense post should, after a heavy bombing raid that may have endangered his family, stay at his post and help others or go to his family. Sixteen-year-old Tony (IQ 115) reasoned as follows: "If he leaves, he is putting the safety of the few over the safety of the many. I don't think it matters that it's his loved ones, because people in the burning buildings are someone's loved ones too. Even though maybe he'd be miserable the rest of his life he shouldn't put the few over the many" (Kohlberg, 1963a, p. 28).

Consider what is involved in Tony's answer. He is not working with rules that prescribe concrete conduct but with general moral principles for deciding among legitimate alternatives. His reasoning may be said to start with the principle that one should take the roles of all the people involved—"people in the burning building are someone's loved ones too." He adds the axiom that all persons must be considered to be of equal value—"I don't think it matters that it's his loved ones." And resolves the problem with the utilitarian principle of the greatest good for the greatest number—"he shouldn't put the few over the many."

Kohlberg posed his problems to approximately one hundred boys between the ages of seven and seventeen; some of them were middle class, some lower class, and some officially delinquent. The basic data are extensive interview protocols. Kohlberg (1963a) describes his results in terms of six development stages and some thirty aspects of morality, a total matrix of 180 categories. The first developmental stage is in several respects similar to Piaget's heteronomous morality and the second is similar to Piaget's autonomous morality. Kohlberg does not, however, find evidence that unilateral respect for authority and mutual respect between peers are the causes of these two moralities.

For Freudians who believe that the superego is "the heir of the Oedipus Complex" moral development is considered to be largely complete by the age of five years. For Piaget, whose problems elicited nothing more advanced than autonomous morality, development seemed to be complete by about eight years. It is not surprising, in view of the difficulty of the dilemmas he invented, that Kohlberg finds stages beyond those of Piaget or Freud; development continues through the whole age range Kohlberg studied, from seven to seventeen.

Kohlberg's last developmental stage, stage VI, is particularly interesting. The child in this stage judges conduct in terms of his own internal standards, in comparative independence of his immediate social environment. Furthermore he explains that the chief motive for moral behavior is not social at all. One does what is right to satisfy ones own conscience, to avoid self-condemnation. The child's explanation of his own conduct in terms of a conscience must be distinguished from the simple possession of a conscience. The internal agency may be present from a much earlier age. There is generally a considerable interval in intellectual development between the age at which the child first begins to operate in accordance with a certain intellectual structure and the age at which he can represent that structure to himself. Piaget found that children operate as if space were Euclidean long before they can make Euclidean representations of objects in space. Students of language know that children utilize a grammar long before they have any explicit knowledge of grammar. In the sphere of morality it is reasonable to suppose that we respond to the prompting of an inner voice long before we explain our actions in terms of that inner voice.

Kohlberg agrees with Piaget that the successive moralities of the child are not a set of graded lessons taught by adults but result from the child's spontaneous restructuring of his experience. Kohlberg differs from Piaget chiefly in believing that moral development is long continued and complex rather than being a single step from heteronomous to autonomous morality. It seems to me that Kohlberg approaches morality very much as contemporary students of language acquisition approach the problem of grammar. To speak a language one must have a system of general rules by which infinitely many sentences can be constructed. To distinguish right from wrong, one must have another such system. Parents do not provide lessons in what to do if your wife needs a medicine you cannot afford or in how to resolve the conflicts that may arise in a bombing raid. We have no rote answers to Kohlberg's dilemmas. They can only be resolved by reference to general rules. It is unlikely that moral rule systems are simpler than grammatical rule systems.

Specificity and Generality

The most surprising discovery to come from *The Character Education Inquiry*, more than thirty years ago, was the marked specificity of moral conduct. Some eleven thousand children participated in that study. They were given opportunities to lie, cheat, and steal, in a variety of settings, in classrooms, at home, in athletic contests and in party games. The correlations between bad conduct in one setting and bad conduct in another setting averaged about .34. Even in very closely related circumstances children were likely to be inconsistent; the child who cheated on an arithmetic test as often as not failed to cheat on a spelling test.

Hartshorne and May (1928–30) emphasized the specificity of moral conduct because they were surprised by it. They had expected much more consistency of character. In fact their data also reveal some consistency or generality. Burton, in 1963, showed that the many low positive correlations between one situation and another represent a weak factor of general morality.

The question of specificity or generality can be raised about each of the dimensions of morality. These dimensions include moral knowledge and moral feeling in addition to moral conduct. The acquisition of a moral rule is a process in all three dimensions though individual investigators seem never to study it so. Consider the rule: "One should tell the truth and not lie." Acquisition of this rule entails, in the first place, a kind of knowledge; the terms of the rule, truth-telling and lying, must be correctly conceptualized. Moral knowledge has been the particular concern of Piaget and Kohlberg. The rule is, in addition, a guide to conduct; it prescribes one sort of behavior (truth-telling) and proscribes another sort (lying). Conduct has interested Bandura, Sears, the McCords, and many others. The rule is, finally, a guide to the occasions for moral feeling; one should feel guilty about lying and feel virtuous about telling the truth when there is a temptation to lie. Moral feeling is the dimension of the process that Freud favored.

The question of specificity or generality arises for each of the dimensions of morality and also for the relations among dimensions. Is a person who knows one moral rule likely to know others? Is a person who will feel guilty over lying likely to feel guilty over stealing? Does the knowledge that stealing is bad imply that one will not in fact steal? Is the knowledge that stealing is bad generally associated with the prospect of guilt for whatever stealing one does? The data on these matters, added to what we have already learned, will finish off a certain simplistic view of the acquisition of morality and direct us toward a more reasonable view.

The simplistic view goes like this: 1) A morality is a set of rules shared by all mature members of a society; 2) these rules are organized in the individual personality into the agency called a superego; 3) the superego works in three dimensions: conduct, feeling, and knowledge; 4) the three dimensions are not independent of one another but three faces of the one monolithic moral agency; 5) children do not at first have a superego; they internalize the superego of their parents in its given form in the degree that they identify with the parents; 6) the installation of the superego will be manifest in the simultaneous appearance of conventional moral conduct, feeling, and judgment. If all these propositions were correct we ought to find generality prevailing over specificity. Children should be consistent within the dimensions of conduct, feeling, and judgment and also consistent across dimensions. There should be in each child some level of all-round, evenly developed conventional morality; the level depending on the strength of identification.

Within the dimension of conduct we already know, from *The Character Education Inquiry*, that consistency is slight. More recent work by Weinberger (1959) and by Rau (in press) confirms the earlier finding. The picture is one of positive but small correlations between moral conduct in one situation and moral conduct in another situation. In terms of conventional adult morality the child's development in the dimension of conduct is uneven.

There is some evidence that moral feelings or emotions are also more specific than general. Allinsmith (1960) has attempted to assess the intensity of guilt experienced by 112 teenage boys in connection with different kinds of immorality: theft, disobedience, and wishing someone dead.

He used a projective method; the boys were asked to complete stories describing one or another sort of immoral action. Allinsmith's conclusion, in his own words, is: "Judging from our data, the person with a truly generalized conscience, either 'punitive' or 'psychopathic,' is a statistical rarity. . . . It is necessary to speak of 'guilts' rather than of 'guilt,' and to be sensitive to the complexities of moral learning" (pp. 164, 165).

Moral knowledge and moral thought seem to be more consistent than are conduct or feeling but there is also some inconsistency. The Hartshorne and May paper-and-pencil tests of moral knowledge and opinion scored children's answers against the criterion of an adult consensus. There were alternative forms of the various tests and children's scores on one form generally correlated very highly with scores on another form. Furthermore scores on one test correlated highly with scores on another test. In short, children who gave adult answers to some questions in the moral sphere were likely to give adult answers to other questions in the moral sphere. This was true so long as the tests were all taken in the same social setting—for example a classroom. However, some of the children took equivalent forms of the tests in more than one setting; in the classroom, in Sunday school, at home, at a children's club meeting. The correlations from situation to situation averaged about .40. In the words of the authors: "The wide differences in means of tests taken by the same children in different situations and the relatively low correlations between the scores of the same children indicate quite clearly that a child does not have a uniform generalized code of morals but varies his opinions to suit the situations in which he finds himself" (1930, pp. 107, 108).

Piaget studied moral understanding rather than conventional moral opinion. Consistency or generality on the Piaget problems means giving answers of the same moral type to problems of varying specific content. Piaget reports a developmental progression but it is noteworthy that he chooses not to describe this progression in his usual fashion—as a set of discontinuous stages. Piaget explicitly says that there was too much inconsistency in the moral judgments to justify the presumption of stages in the usual sense. Other investigators (Macrae, 1954; Johnson, 1962) who have worked with the same problems or similar problems have found consistency of response to sets of questions that clearly belong to the same conceptual type but little or no consistency to questions that are conceptually remote, even though these questions are all supposed to draw upon the same morality. Macrae (1954), for instance, found that children who judged the comparative naughtiness of one pair of actions in terms of intentions rather than consequences were likely to do the same with other pairs of actions. However, these "subjective" answers which are supposed to represent a heteronomous morality were not associated with heteronomous notions of a just punishment.

Kohlberg, like Piaget, has studied moral thought but with different and more complex problems. Kohlberg (1963a) reports a developmental progression and some degree of individual consistency. For example, there were fifteen boys whose answers caused them to be characterized as having a predominantly Type I morality (punishment and obedience orientation). On the average 45 per cent of the thinking of these boys satisfied the Type I model. Again we see some consistency but nothing like complete consistency.

In each of three dimensions—knowledge, conduct, and emotion—morality seems to be more specific than general. It remains to ask how one dimension relates to another. Does moral judgment predict moral conduct? Does moral conduct imply moral emotion? The data on these questions are crude; for instance one cannot tell whether a paper-and-pencil questionnaire that asks subjects to rate the intensity of their disapproval of cheating should be regarded as a measure of judgment alone or of judgment-plus-emotion or, most likely of all, as a measure of the respondents' wish for social approval. Hartshorne and May (1930) and Hendry (1960) found no significant correlations between actual resistance to cheating and stated belief in the badness of cheating or in one's unwillingness to cheat. However, Hartshorne and May more generally found low positive correlations between level of moral knowledge and morality of conduct (about .34 on the average). Kohlberg (1964) related moral knowledge, in his sense, to the child's resistance to cheating and to the child's strength of conscience (as rated by teachers) and found correlations at about the same level as were reported by Hartshorne and May. Havighurst and Taba (1949) found small positive correlations (averaging about .24) between their paper-and-pencil measures of a child's strength of belief in certain virtues and the character ratings the child received on these same virtues. Burton (1958) and Rau (in press) have found that the strength of conformity to particular rules is not correlated with indices of the general intensity of guilt or moral anxiety. In general the picture that emerges from studies that relate the three dimensions of morality to one another is like the picture that emerges from studies that relate instances within a single dimension: Low positive correlations are usual, sometimes there is no correlation, high correlations are generally missing.

The evidence for specificity in the moral domain casts general doubt on the simplistic view that adults share a morality which parents introduce to the child which the child incorporates, as given, in all its dimensions. The evidence for specificity causes us to entertain some very different ideas. Perhaps there is no morality shared by all members of a society. Perhaps the morality parents bring is made up of many distinct learning problems. Perhaps the child's progress on these problems is uneven. Perhaps the different dimensions of morality involve different kinds of learning. Perhaps the dimensions of morality are not three faces of a single superego but are systems more complexly related. We cannot prove that these views are correct but the material we have covered in this chapter makes us ready to take a position.

Propositions for the Future

In this last section we will give up our usual practice of presenting the evidence and arguing both sides. There is at once too much evidence and too little that is definitive. But the chapter as a whole, particularly the immediately preceding section, leaves us with some propositions about the moralization of the child which we believe to be more realistic than the propositions that have thus far prevailed. Flatly stated, they read like this.

1. A morality is a system of rules for distinguishing right conduct from wrong conduct very much as a grammar is a system of rules for distinguishing well-formed sentences from badly-formed sentences. Moralities are not static but, like grammars, are always in evolution. Probably moralities change more rapidly than grammars. They change because of internal contradictions, because of the impact of foreign moralities, and because of the creation of new circumstances.

A complex society like the United States does not at any one time have a single morality but rather many moralities distributed among regional and occupational and socio-economic subcultures.[4] The morality of the total culture is not homogeneous but is a patterned diversity. Morality is always in the making, always controversial at some points, as witness the continual evolution of the law through court decisions, the contemporary dispute over the civil rights of Negroes, and the dispute among intellectuals concerning Hannah Arendt's book *Eichmann in Jerusalem* (*Partisan Review*, 1964).

Because moralities are both diverse and dynamic it is not surprising that Hartshorne and May found children inconsistent in their moral opinions. Indeed we should expect, and Hartshorne and May found it to be so, that adults would disagree with one another on many moral judgments.

2. The moralization of the individual proceeds in three dimensions: knowledge, conduct, and feeling. At least four kinds of learning seem to be involved. There is a *cognitive learning* of concepts or rules for which the critical variables include: a) the array of positive and negative instances; b) the number of noisy or distracting attributes; c) the temporal

4. This is a position like that taken by Florence Kluckhohn and Strodtbeck (1961) with reference to value orientations in general. Their view that values are in certain respects universal and that cultural differences represent different patterns of emphasis is persuasive and stimulating.

order of instances; d) the learner's attention to instances; e) the labeling of instances; f) the explicit formulation of the rule or concept; g) the intellectual level of the learner, etc. The second sort of learning is *instrumental learning* or *operant conditioning* in which behavior is shaped by selective reinforcement. Critical variables include the availability of the response, the reinforcement schedule, and the interval between response and reinforcement. The third sort of learning is *imitation* or *learning by identification* in which one person models himself on another. The perceived power of the model seems to be one determinant of imitation and the nurturance of the model may be another. The fourth sort of learning is the *classical* (or *respondent*) *conditioning* of autonomic, especially emotional, responses. Critical variables here include the intensity of the unconditioned stimulus, the frequency with which the conditioned stimulus and unconditioned stimulus are paired, the interval between the two stimuli, and perhaps the innate "conditionability" of the subject (Eysenck, 1960).

The four sorts of learning are not likely to be equally important for the three dimensions of morality. The acquisition of moral knowledge must chiefly involve cognitive learning; conduct seems to depend on both instrumental conditioning and imitation; feeling probably depends on classical conditioning. These coordinations between kinds of learning and dimensions of morality are certainly not perfect. Imitation, for example, has definite cognitive components. The child can imitate a performance only in terms of his understanding of that performance. Watch a small boy drive his father's car and you will see that while he knows the wheel must be twisted and various knobs pulled he is not able to steer, nor is he clear about which knob to pull when. What is more the noises he makes suggest that he is as much motor as driver.

If the several sorts of learning are differentially important for the several dimensions of morality it is not surprising that a child's development in these dimensions should be uneven. The determinants of knowledge are not the same as the determinants of feeling and so one may develop while the other does not. Neither is it surprising that development within a dimension is uneven. Conditions for learning one sort of moral conduct may have been ideal while the conditions for learning another sort of conduct were very poor. If moralization is a matter of many learning problems and several kinds of learning, rather than of the "incorporation" of a parent's superego, uneven development is to be expected.

3. Within the individual, the three dimensions of morality are not all on the same footing. Moral knowledge or theory would seem to be a set of rules for *evaluating* conduct, not a computer program for generating conduct. Conduct which is covered by moral rules, whether it is copying on an exam or attending church on Sunday or playing Eich-

mann's role in the attempted extermination of the Jews, is not simply a resultant of moral judgment. A person can be quite clear that one course of action is immoral and another course moral and yet choose the immoral. This can happen, in the first place, because moral values are not the only values. There are also aesthetic values and economic values and scientific values and the values of health, success, and survival. Any of these may override morality in determining conduct on a specific occasion and morality may also be overriden by fatigue, pain, intoxication, or sexual arousal. It is not to be expected, therefore, that correlations will be very high in children between moral conduct and moral judgment. In the course of a lifetime one works, intermittently, at raising the correlation. To bring conduct under the dominion of morality is a great task; it is the struggle for character.

Moral anxiety, guilt, and shame do not arise always and only where one's moral theory says they should. It is possible to be perfectly clear in your mind about the immorality of stealing a book and yet be able to do it without a twinge. It is possible to be perfectly clear about the indifference to morality of an extended vacation and yet unable to take one without suffering guilt. Knowledge and feeling seem to be largely independent agencies in the mind and that may mean that they are learned in quite different ways. Moral feeling seems to be the true Freudian superego. Guilt is at least partly unconscious and it seems to be possible to defend against guilt by repression and displacement and projection.

Conduct is not an agency in the mind at all but is the battleground on which moral feeling and moral theory meet. They contend for the control of conduct, contend with one another, with other values and with an oscillating physiology. Conduct has also a conflict-free sphere. Routine moral conduct not involving resistance to temptation is probably a set of habits learned instrumentally and by imitation of a model.

4. A child's moral theory is not the unprocessed reflection of an adult morality. The first difficulty with the reflection theory is that there is more than one adult morality and even one will contain inconsistencies. The child's mind is bound to work over what it receives in quest of satisfactory generalizations. The second difficulty with the notion of simple internalization or reflection derives from the child's own intellectual capacities. He can only understand what is offered him according to his present intellectual capabilities. His understanding of the "same" external principle must be repeatedly transformed as his intelligence matures. His effort to organize and reconcile the total data may never be complete. It is expecting a great deal to suppose that all of his views at any point in time will be of a consistent logical type. The irregularities found by Piaget and Kohlberg are probably always present.

5. The end of moralization need not be complete acceptance of the

adult morality. The moral theory an individual forms out of his own idiosyncratic collection of moral data can cause him to reject the larger part of the conventional morality. From a social point of view the ideal outcome of the moralization of the individual is not acceptance of some static set of folkways but participation in the moral argument of his time and civilization. From the individual point of view the ideal outcome is that rare state which has been mistakenly assumed to be usual, some reasonable consistency among judgment, feeling, and action.

REFERENCES

Aichhorn, A. *Wayward youth*. New York: Viking, 1935.

Allinsmith, W. Moral standards: II. The learning of moral standards. In D. R. Miller & G. E. Swanson (Eds.), *Inner conflict and defense*. New York: Holt, 1960.

Bandura, A., & Huston, Aletha C. Identification as a process of incidental learning. *J. abnorm. soc. Psychol.*, 1961, **63**, 311–318.

Bandura, A., & McDonald, F. J. The influence of social reinforcement and the behavior of models in shaping children's moral judgments. *J. abnorm. soc. Psychol.*, 1963, **67**, 274–281.

Bandura, A., Ross, Dorothea, & Ross, Sheila A. Transmission of aggression through imitation of aggressive models. *J. abnorm. soc. Psychol.*, 1961, **63**, 575–582.

Bandura, A., Ross, Dorothea, & Ross, Sheila A. Imitation of film-mediated aggressive models. *J. abnorm. soc. Psychol.*, 1963, **66**, 3–11. (a)

Bandura, A., Ross, Dorothea, & Ross, Sheila A. A comparative test of the status envy, social power, and the secondary reinforcement theories of identificatory learning. *J. abnorm. soc. Psychol.*, 1963, **67**, 527–534. (b)

Bandura, A., Ross, Dorothea, & Ross, Sheila A. "Vicarious" reinforcement and imitative learning. *J. abnorm. soc. Psychol.*, 1963, **67**, 601–607. (c)

Bandura, A., & Walters, R. H. *Adolescent aggression*. New York: Ronald, 1959.

Bandura, A., & Walters, R. H. *Social learning and personality development*. New York: Holt, Rinehart, Winston, 1963.

Bettleheim, B. *Love is not enough*. New York: Free Press, 1950.

Brim, O. G. Family structure and sex role learning by children: A further analysis of Helen Koch's data. *Sociometry*, 1958, **21**, 1–16.

Bronfenbrenner, U. Freudian theories of identification and their derivatives. *Child Develpm.*, 1960, **31**, 15–40.

Bronfenbrenner, U. Socialization and social class through time and space. In Eleanor E. Maccoby, T. M. Newcomb, and E. L. Hartley (Eds.), *Readings in social psychology*. (3rd ed.) New York: Holt, 1958.

Burton, R. V. Temptation influences on fantasy. Unpublished paper, 1958.

Burton, R. V. The generality of honesty reconsidered. *Psychol. Rev.*, 1963, **70**, 481–499.

Carlson, N. J. Primary and secondary reward in traumatic avoidance learning. *J. comp. physiol. Psychol.*, 1960, **53**, 336–340.

Carlson, N. J., & Black, A. H. Traumatic avoidance learning: Note on the effect of response prevention during extinction. *Psychol. Rep.*, 1959, **5**, 409–412.

Caruso, I. H. La notion de responsabilité et du justice immanente chez l'enfant. *Arch. Psychol., Geneva*, 1943, **XXIX**, No. 114.

Dollard, J., & Miller, N. E. *Personality and psychotherapy*. New York: Mc-Graw-Hill, 1950.

Durkin, D. Children's concepts of justice: A comparison with the Piaget data. *Child Develpm.*, 1959, **30**, 59–67.

Eysenck, H. J. The development of moral values in children: The contribution of learning theory. *Brit. J. educ. Psychol.*, 1960, **XXX**, 11–22.

Eysenck, H. J. The effects of psychotherapy. In H. J. Eysenck (Ed.), *Handbook of abnormal psychology*. New York: Basic Books, 1961.

Freud, Anna. *The ego and the mechanisms of defense*. New York: Int. Univers. Press, 1946.

Freud, S. The interpretation of dreams. (1st ed., 1900) In *The complete psychological works of Sigmund Freud*. Vol. IV. London: Hogarth, 1953.

Freud, S. Three essays on the theory of sexuality. (1st ed., 1905) In *The complete psychological works of Sigmund Freud*. Vol. VII. London: Hogarth, 1953.

Freud, S. Analysis of a phobia in a five-year-old boy. (1st ed., 1909) In *The complete psychological works of Sigmund Freud*. Vol. X. London: Hogarth, 1962.

Freud, S. On narcissism. (1st ed., 1914) In *The complete psychological works of Sigmund Freud*. Vol. XIV. London: Hogarth, 1957.

Freud, S. Introductory lectures on psychoanalysis: Parts I and II. (1st ed., 1915–1916) In *The complete psychological works of Sigmund Freud*. Vol. XV. London: Hogarth, 1963.

Freud, S. Mourning and melancholia. (1st ed., 1917) In *The complete psychological works of Sigmund Freud*. Vol. XIV. London: Hogarth, 1957.

Freud, S. Group psychology and the analysis of the ego. (1st ed., 1921) In *The complete psychological works of Sigmund Freud*. Vol. XVIII. London: Hogarth, 1955.

Freud, S. The ego and the id. (1st ed., 1923) In *The complete psychological works of Sigmund Freud*. Vol. XIX. London: Hogarth, 1961.

Freud, S. The dissolution of the Oedipus complex. (1st ed., 1924) In *The complete psychological works of Sigmund Freud*. Vol. XIX. London: Hogarth, 1961.

Freud, S. Some psychical consequences of the anatomical distinction between the sexes. (1st ed., 1925) In *The complete psychological works of Sigmund Freud*. Vol. XIX. London: Hogarth, 1961.

Freud, S. *Civilization and its discontents*. (1st ed., 1930) London: Hogarth, 1949.

Freud, S. *New introductory lectures on psychoanalysis*. New York: Norton, 1933.

Freud, S. *An outline of psychoanalysis*. (1st ed., 1940) New York: Norton, 1949.

Gantt, W. H. Principles of nervous breakdown—schizo-kinesis and auto-kinesis. *Ann. N. Y. Acad. Sci.*, 1953, **56**, 143–163.

Gilbert, G. M. Hermann Goering: Amiable psychopath. *J. abnorm. soc. Psychol.*, 1948, **43**, 211–229.

Glueck, S., & Glueck, Eleanor. *Unraveling juvenile delinquency*. New York: Commonwealth Fund, 1950.

Hartshorne, H., & May, M. A. *Studies in the nature of character:* Vol. I, *Studies in deceit;* Vol. II, *Studies in self-control;* Vol. III, *Studies in the organization of character.* New York: Macmillan, 1928–30.

Havighurst, R., & Taba, H. *Adolescent character and personality.* New York: Wiley, 1949.

Hendry, Louise S. Cognitive processes in a moral conflict situation. Unpublished doctoral dissertation, Yale Univer., 1960.

Hill, W. F. Learning theory and the acquisition of values. *Psychol. Rev.,* 1960, **67**, 317–331.

Johnson, R. A study of children's moral judgments. *Child Develpm.,* 1962, **33**, 327–355.

Jones, H. E. The retention of conditioned emotional reactions in infancy. *J. genet. Psychol.,* 1930, **37**, 485–498.

Jones, Mary C. The elimination of children's fear. *J. exp. Psychol.,* 1924, **7**, 382–390.

Kagan, J. The concept of identification. *Psychol. Rev.,* 1958, **65**, 296–305.

Kluckhohn, C. Culture and behavior. In G. Lindzey (Ed.) *Handbook of social psychology.* Vol. II. Reading: Addison-Wesley, 1954.

Kluckhohn, Florence, & Stodtbeck, F. L. *Variations in value orientations.* Evanston: Row, Peterson, 1961.

Kohlberg, L. The development of modes of moral thinking and choice in the years ten to sixteen. Unpublished doctoral dissertation, Univer. of Chicago, 1958.

Kohlberg, L. The development of children's orientations toward a moral order: I. Sequence in the development of moral thought. *Vita hum., Basel,* 1963. (a)

Kohlberg, L. Moral development and identification. In National Society for the Study of Education, 62nd Yearbook, *Child psychol.* Chicago: Univer. of Chicago Press, 1963. (b)

Kohlberg, L. The development of children's orientations toward a moral order: II. Social experience, social conduct, and the development of moral thought. *Vita hum., Basel,* 1964.

Lerner, E. *Constraint areas and the moral judgment of children.* Menasha: Banta, 1937.

Liddell, H. S. Conditioned reflex method and experimental neurosis. In J. McV. Hunt (Ed.), *Personality and the behavior disorders.* Vol. I. New York: Ronald, 1944.

Lykken, D. R. A study of anxiety in the sociopathic personality. *J. abnorm, soc. Psychol.,* 1957, **55**, 6–10.

Maccoby, Eleanor E. Role-taking in childhood and its consequences for social learning. *Child Develpm.,* 1959, **30**, 239–252.

MacKinnon, D. W. Violation and prohibitions. In H. A. Murray, *Explorations in personality.* New York: Oxford Univer. Press, 1938.

MacRae, E. A test of Piaget's theories of moral development. *J. abnorm. soc. Psychol.,* 1954, **49**, 14–18.

McCord, W., & McCord, Joan. *Psychopathy and delinquency.* New York: Grune and Stratton, 1956.

Mowrer, O. H. Identification: A link between learning theory and psychotherapy. In O. H. Mowrer, *Learning theory and personality dynamics.* New York: Ronald, 1950.

Mowrer, O. H. Hearing and speaking. An analysis of language learning. *J. speech hear. Disord.,* 1958, **23**, 143–152.

Murray, H. A. *Explorations in personality.* New York: Oxford Univer. Press, 1938.

Mussen, P., & Distler, L. Masculinity, identification, and father-son relationship. *J. abnorm. soc. Psychol.,* 1959, **59**, 350–356.

Orlansky, H. Infant care and personality. *Psychol. Bull.,* 1949, **46**, 1–48.

Parsons, T. Family structure and the socialization of the child. In T. Parsons and R. F. Bales, *Family, socialization, and interaction process.* New York: Free Press, 1955.

Papanek, E. Training school-program and leadership. *Fed. Probation,* June, 1953.

Piaget, J. *The child's conception of the world.* (1st ed., 1926) New York: Humanities Press, 1951.

Piaget, J. *The moral judgment of the child.* (1st ed., 1932) New York: Free Press, 1948.

Rau, L. Conscience and identification. In R. R. Sears, R. Alpert, and L. Rau (Eds.), *Identification in children.* In press.

Redl, F., & Wineman, D. *Controls from within: Techniques for the treatment of the aggressive child.* New York: Free Press, 1954.

Sears, R. R. The growth of conscience. In I. Iscoe, and H. Stevenson (Eds.), *Personality development in children.* Austin: Univer. of Texas Press, 1960.

Sears, R. R., Maccoby, Eleanor E., & Levin, H. *Patterns of child rearing.* Evanston: Row, Peterson, 1957.

Sears, R. R., Whiting, J. W. M., Nowlis, V., & Sears, Pauline S. Some child-rearing antecedents of aggression and dependency in young children. *Genet. Psychol. Monogr.,* 1953, **47**, 135–234.

Seward, J. P., & Raskin, D. C. The role of fear in aversive behavior. *J. comp. physiol. Psychol.,* 1960, **53**, 328–335.

Solomon, R. L., Kamin, L. J., & Wynne, L. C. Traumatic avoidance learning: The outcomes of several extinction procedures with dogs. *J. abnorm. soc. Psychol.,* 1953, **48**, 291–302.

Solomon, R. L., & Wynne, L. C. Traumatic avoidance learning: Acquisition in normal dogs. *Psychol. Monogr.,* 1953, **67**, No. 4 (Whole No. 354).

Solomon, R. L., & Wynne, L. C. Traumatic avoidance learning: The principles of anxiety conservation and partial irreversibility. *Psychol. Rev.,* 1954, **61**, 353–385.

Turner, Lucille H., & Solomon, R. L. Human traumatic avoidance learning. *Psychol. Monogr.,* 1962, **76**, (Whole No. 40).

Watson, J. B., & Rayner, Rosalie. Conditioned emotional reactions. *J. exp. Psychol.,* 1920, **3**, 1–14.

Weinberger, G. The measurement of resistance to temptation. Unpublished master's thesis, Stanford Univer., 1959. Cited by R. R. Sears, The growth of conscience. In I. Iscoe & H. Stevenson (Eds.), *Personality development in children.* Austin: Univer. of Texas Press, 1960.

Whiting, J. W. M. Resource mediation and learning by identification. In I. Iscoe & H. Stevenson (Eds.), *Personality development in children.* Austin: Univer. of Texas Press, 1960.

Wolpe, J., Salter, A., & Reyna, L. J. *The conditioning therapies; the challenge in psychotherapy.* New York: Holt, Rinehart, Winston, 1964.

Part Four

PERSONALITY

AND SOCIETY

*E*ACH of the two chapters ahead is devoted to a single
dimension of personality: Chapter 9 to the Achievement Motive and
Chapter 10 to the Authoritarian ideology. For each of these dimensions
there is a specific technique of assessment. The development of the techniques, their known properties, and the major criticisms of them are all
described. Since each of the techniques has been used in hundreds of researches there are substantial traditions to discuss. These traditions and
the theories associated with them have a scope that is still extraordinary in
social psychology. From the childhood origins of the motive and the
ideology in specified kinds of families created by specified kinds of social
conditions we move to the effects of the two variables in many areas of
adult life and then, full circle, to the effects on society of adult personalities manifesting extremes of authoritarianism and achievement motivation.

Neither the concept of attitude (an ideology like authoritarianism is
an organization of attitudes) nor the concept of motive was invented by

psychologists. Like the concepts of ability and trait and value, attitude and motive belong to the set of categories which laymen use in construing personality. The informal assessment of persons (see Chapter 12) is now and has always been everyone's concern. Psychology has begun, as newly formalized studies always do begin, with what folk-science has to say about its subject matter.

What are the everyday senses of attitude and of motive which have started psychology on its own work? An attitude has always a focus; it may be a person, a group, a nation, a product, anything whatever really. When the focus is known to many, as in the case of statesmen, ethnic groups, and nations, the corresponding attitude can be used for the comparative characterization of many persons. The dimension of characterization extends from positive (or favorable) through neutrality to negative (or unfavorable). Persons are thought of as occupying positions on this dimension corresponding to their disposition to behave favorably or unfavorably toward the focus.

A motive has not a focus but a goal object or goal condition, some class of goods or persons or circumstances. When the goal is one that many know, as in the cases of food, sex, knowledge, and achievement, the motive can be used for the comparative characterization of many persons. The dimension of characterization extends from a low intensity of motivation to a high intensity of motivation. Persons are thought of as possessing motivation of a given strength either for the moment (as in the case of hunger) or typically (as in the case of the Achievement Motive).

Neither motives nor attitudes are directly available to the senses; if they are not to be regarded as primitive intuitions they must be regarded as constructions founded on sense data. Their discovery in others must in the latter case be an inference from behavior. And one can see what the aspects of behavior are that give rise to the two kinds of inference.

Imagine the existence of a minority ethnic group called Wallonians. In what circumstances would an observer infer the existence in a population of attitudes favorable and unfavorable to Wallonians? We shall imagine that the observer is able to keep track of behavior focused on Wallonians: talk about them, things said to them, actions taken in connection with them. We shall also imagine him to be capable of identifying the favorable or unfavorable tendency of behavior with reference to its focus. The inference that there is, in the population he observes, an attitude toward Wallonians and that the members of this population may be thought of as ranged along the favorable to unfavorable dimension will depend, then, on two patterned aspects of the Wallonian-relevant behavior of the population.

The total collection of acts and sayings focussing on Wallonians will be non-random in two important respects. In the first place the acts and sayings will covary across persons. A man who makes a certain antagonistic remark about Wallonians will, eventually, make certain other antagonistic remarks and also take antagonistic actions. This cluster of sayings and actions will, not invariably but with detectable consistency, appear also in other persons. Favorable actions and sayings will form their own clusters. The observer should form the idea after a time that the man who has made antagonistic remark A_1 and taken antagonistic action A_2 is likely in time to produce the usual correlates of A_1 and A_2, to wit antagonistic behaviors A_3, A_4, A_5, etc. One way of thinking about these patterned data is to attribute to the man who has emitted A_1 and A_2 a disposition or readiness to emit A_3, A_4, A_5, etc. And it is just such a disposition that psychology would call an anti-Wallonian attitude. The index of the attitude in this everyday case is the behavior already produced, A_1 and A_2. The behavior predicted but not yet produced is expected to appear when relevant circumstances arise. In the meantime, there is assumed to exist in the person, a disposition to it or readiness for it. The disposition is the attitude.

The notion that an attitude constitutes a dimension on which persons can be compared could arise from the following patterned aspect of Wallonian-relevant behavior. Imagine that the observer has identified clusters B (made up of B_1, B_2, B_3, etc.) and C (made up of C_1, C_2, C_3, etc.). He finds that it sometimes happens that one person will emit a mixture of A and B behavior (e.g., A_1, A_2, B_2, B_3, etc.); there is overlapping in persons of A and B. He further finds that it sometimes happens that one person will emit a mixture of B and C behavior (e.g., B_1, B_3, C_2, C_3, etc.); there is overlapping in persons of the B and C clusters. Finally he notes that no one ever combines elements from A with elements from C; these clusters do not overlap. The observer should form the idea that cluster B lies between clusters A and C, that persons manifesting pure-B behavior must be intermediate in attitude between persons manifesting the extremes of pure-A and pure-C.

The inference of a dimension would be supported in various ways. For instance, members of the population would occasionally cease to produce one cluster and begin to produce another cluster. This sort of change would be more likely to occur from A to B or B to C than from A to C. The pattern of attitude change, in short, would reinforce the prior conception of the attitude scale itself. The argument made here for three points on a dimension, A, B, C, can be extended to any number of points. The theory of attitude scaling in social psychology is a continuation and refinement of these ideas.

The patterns in human behavior that suggest the notion of motive will be sketched more briefly. Imagine again a population and an observer. We must, in addition, posit some object or circumstance that is to be identified as the goal of motivated behavior. Let us be contemporary and make the circumstance attendance at a performance by the Beatles. How can an observer tell whether a young girl is motivated to hear the Beatles? The basic pattern in behavior is one we might call "directionality". More is involved in directionality than getting there. The simple observation that the girl is in attendance at a performance of the Beatles does not establish directionality for the reason that she might have gone along to keep her sister company or just to fill an empty evening. Our example is a little unfortunate, at this point, because the competition for tickets to the Beatles is so intense in 1964 that it can be fairly safely inferred that anyone found at such a performance was motivated to be there. However, if the entertainment were a less widely popular one, a routine political appearance or a road-company performance of Gounod's *Faust*, attendance would not strongly imply motivation. Of course if the event were even less popular attendance would again imply motivation.

A person manifests directionality when he behaves like a guided missile. He not only arrives at a certain point, he manifests perseverance and adaptability in getting there. As circumstances change and impediments are thrown up he shifts course in such a way as to stay on target. The young girl who "seeks" the Beatles will try to buy a ticket and, failing, try to get a job as an usher and, failing, climb the fence or crawl through the ventilating system or disguise herself as Ringo's mother. She may be credited with directionality. The notion that the same motive exists in a number of persons with varying intensity would seem to depend primarily on the observation that one person will maintain direction in circumstances that deter another. Not every girl who will buy a ticket to the Beatles will, when she fails, climb the fence.

A clinical psychologist trying to work out the motives and attitudes of a patient might actually work over quantities of naturally-occurring behavior or at any rate reports of quantities. The right answers are sometimes hard to find, especially when the patient's reports of his own attitudes and motives are misleading. A man's real goals in his work and real attitudes toward members of his family are not necessarily known to him. The research psychologist cannot work in the time-consuming clinical way. His first need is for a measure that takes little time but which reveals more than a person can report of himself.

CHAPTER 9

The Achievement Motive

You are about to take a test of your creative imagination. If the test were to be administered in the usual way you would be shown a picture for about twenty seconds and then given about five minutes in which to write a story about the picture. Instead, however, you will simply be asked to imagine a certain kind of picture and write a story about that imagined picture.

There are four questions which should be answered in your story: 1) What is happening? Who are the persons? 2) What has led up to this situation? That is, what has happened in the past? 3) What is being thought? What is wanted? By whom? 4) What will happen? What will be done? Plan to spend about a minute on each question. If you do so, you will cover all the elements of a plot in the time allotted. Obviously there are no right or wrong answers; you should feel free to make up any kind of story you like about the imagined picture. Try to make the story vivid and dramatic since this is a test of your creative imagination. Do not simply describe the picture that comes to mind. Tell a story about it. Make it interesting. Now comes the description. Read it, and take 5 minutes to write a story.

Description of the picture: A boy about eighteen years old is sitting at his desk in an occupied classroom. A book lies open before him but he is not looking at it. The boy rests his forehead on one hand as he gazes pensively out toward the viewer.

*   *   *

The task you have just performed is a variation on one part of a procedure for measuring the strength of the Achievement Motive, a procedure devised by David McClelland and his co-workers, (major sources are: McClelland, et al., 1953; McClelland, 1955; Atkinson, 1958; McClelland, 1961). In the full procedure you would see the picture we have described and also three others and would be asked to write stories for all four pictures. The test is truly concerned with creative imagination but the products of the testee's imagination are analyzed for a certain kind of content, content indicative of achievement motivation. You will shortly know enough about the scoring to be able to tell whether your own story contains any of the content that is scored as achievement motivation.

Here now are two stories written by students for the picture described. The first contains a great deal of achievement imagery and the second none at all.

HIGH STORY

1. This chap is doing some heavy meditating. He is a sophomore and has reached an intellectual crisis. He cannot make up his mind. He is troubled, worried.

2. He is trying to reconcile the philosophies of Descartes and Thomas Aquinas—and at his tender age of eighteen. He has read several books on philosophy and feels the weight of the world on his shoulders.

3. He wants to present a clear-cut synthesis of these two conflicting philosophies, to satisfy his ego and to gain academic recognition from his professor.

4. He will screw himself up royally. Too inexperienced and uninformed, he has tackled too great a problem. He will give up in despair, go down to the G—— and drown his sorrows in a bucket of beer (Atkinson, 1958, p. 697).

LOW STORY

1. The boy in the checkered shirt whose name is Ed is in a classroom. He is supposed to be listening to the teacher.

2. Ed has been troubled by his father's drunkenness and his maltreatment of Ed's mother. He thinks of this often and worries about it.

3. Ed is thinking of leaving home for a while in the hope that this might shock his parents into getting along.

4. He will leave home but will only meet further disillusionment away from home (Atkinson, 1958, p. 697).

McClelland has used his method of analyzing linguistic content on folk tales and on stories in children's readers as well as on stories made up by individuals in a testing situation. There is good reason to believe that such an analysis of popular tales provides an index of the strength of achievement motivation in the culture from which the tales are drawn. Here now are very literal translations of two stories containing different degrees of achievement emphasis. The high-achievement story is Turkish.

A STRANGE SALARY

One day a young man came to the director of a large commercial firm and asked for a job. The director liked the young man's manners and speech. Around those days they needed a person in bookkeeping. Perhaps he could be useful in something. But one had to test him and to observe his knowledge and work closely.

The director said to the young man, "All right, I want to give you a job, but first I must put you on a training program. Work with us for a month. If we are satisfied, we shall take you with a regular salary. Of course, you will receive a certain sum for this experimental period. Go and see the bursar, please."

The young man left the room.

A little later the bursar came to the director. He said, "I've spoken with the young man you sent me."

"How did you find him?"

"He seems like a nice person, but the salary he asked for is very strange."

"How?"

"I offered him a hundred dollars for the experimental month. He did not accept. He said, 'I do not want a flat salary. I must earn my daily pay.' Look at the salary he demands, one cent for the first day."

"What, one cent?"

"Yes, one cent. If we are satisfied, two cents for the second day, four for the third, eight for the fourth. In short, for every day he works well, he wants to be paid twice the amount that he received for the previous day."

The director looked at the bursar in amazement. "How strange! What can he get at the end of the month with this one, two, four cents?"

The bursar shrugged and answered, "Why should we care? As long as he wants it this way."

"All right. If he desires so, let it be so. Let him start tomorrow."

The young man was really worthy and conscientious. He worked like a clock, did all his work with immaculate neatness, and finished everything quickly. He pleased everybody in the bureau by his every act.

The month came to an end.

The young man went to the bursar and asked for his salary. The bursar raised his head unworriedly. "I have not calculated it yet. Would you please figure it out and bring it to me?"

The young man had already figured it out. He pulled a piece of paper out of his pocket and handed it to the bursar.

The bursar started to read. "According to the conditions agreed upon; namely, one cent for the first day, after that the daily wage being obtained by doubling the amount for the previous day, the sum for the 30-day experimental period is $10,737,418.23."

The bursar's eyes nearly jumped out of their sockets, he looked at the figures carefully again, he paused for a while; then collecting himself, he fixed his gaze on the young man and said loudly, "You seem to have lost your mind!"

"Why? The calculation is obvious. If you want to, please check it over."

There wasn't the slightest mistake in the calculations. This was the exact amount the young man had to be paid. The bursar was dumbfounded.

When they went to see the director, the bursar was in no condition to speak. His mouth was dry and his tongue was twisted. He uttered a few incomprehensible words and handed the piece of paper to the director. He too was utterly dumbfounded when he read the paper. He gulped a few times, looked at the bursar with knotted eyebrows; but he could not say a word. Even all the capital of the company was not enough to pay this debt.

There was deep silence in the room.

When the young man, who until then had been calmly watching the pitiful condition of the two men, saw that they were unable to speak, he said with a sweet smile on his lips, "When I asked for this salary, I knew perfectly well what it would amount to at the end of the month. I also knew that there wasn't the slightest chance of your being able to pay all this money. My purpose was to show you how attentive I am in financial matters, especially in those that involve long calculations."

The contract was signed that day. The young man joined the company with a fat salary (McClelland, 1961, pp. 459–60).

The story that is not written on an achievement theme is from India.

DON'T EVER OWE A MAN

The world is an illusion. Wife, children, horses and cows are all just ties of fate. They are ephemeral. Each after fulfilling his part in life disappears. So we should not clamour after riches which are not permanent. As long as we live it is wise not to have any attachments and just think of God. We have to spend our lives without trouble, for is it not true that there is no end to grievances? So it is better to live knowing the real state of affairs. Don't get entangled in the meshes of family life.

Just learn that a wife and children are ties of fate, listen to this story:

There was once a certain man in a village. As soon as his wife gave birth to a child he took it to the graveyard and placed him in a hole there. After sprinkling some water on the child he asked the child, "Who are you? Why are you born to me?"

The child replied, "Sir, in my last life I used to live selling firewood. One day you purchased a load of it and did not pay me its worth in money. I am born to you so that I can get it." The man asked him, "How much do I owe you?" The child replied, "Two dollars." The man then asked, "Will you go away if I give you two dollars?" The child said, "Yes." As soon as he placed two dollars on the child it died.

Afterwards the man buried him and went home. He did the same for the next three or four children. His wife began to suspect that her husband was burying live children.

One day she asked her husband whether it was fair on his part to do so. Then the man said, "You give me the child this time. I will get it back to you." This time the man did the same thing to the child, as he did to the first one. It told him, "I was an oil monger in my previous life. You owe me money for one pint of castor oil."

The man asked "Will you go away if I give you a pint of castor oil?" The child said, "Yes." Promising the child that he would give him the castor oil he carried him back to his wife. He gave his wife a pint of castor oil and told her that the child will live while the castor oil lasts. The wife started anointing the child with castor oil. When a small amount of oil was left the child became ill. The illness became worse and the mother, after losing hope that the child would live, took him to the verandah and started crying. The child was fighting for its life. Then the woman went to her husband and said to him, "I can't see him suffering so much. It looks as though it is better if he dies. The pint of oil is gone. Why is he still suffering?"

The man told her, "See whether something is still left in the pot. Clean it well with your hand and rub it on the child." After she did it the child died. From that day she did not oppose whatever her husband did. Again she gave birth to a child. When the man questioned the child, it replied, "Sir, in my last life I deceived you of a couple of thousand dollars. I have come to repay that amount." Then he carried the child back to his wife and said, "This is your son. Look after him carefully. Don't take anything, not even a betel leaf from him. As long as you do that he is your child. If you take anything you won't get him back." So she carried out his orders.

The child grew up and after learning all the arts began earning money. Still his parents never used to take a penny from him. One day after deciding to go to another town on some work, he dressed himself up and took a small bag in his hand and went to the front of his house to get on his horse.

The horse would not allow him to get up. Seeing his mother nearby he asked her, "Mother, hold this bag. After I get on the horse I will take it back." So saying, he gave his mother the bag. Before he could get on the horse, the horse kicked him with its hind legs. Immediately he died. The mother started crying. The father who had gone out returned and after hearing the story, asked his wife to open the bag and see what it contained.

There was exactly two thousand dollars in his bag. He consoled his wife, saying, "You killed your own son by not heeding my words. Why do you cry?" (McClelland, 1961, pp. 454–56)

The contrasting stories will have given you some idea of what it is one looks for in scoring for the Achievement Motive. The development of this method and its use in research during the past ten years is a major accomplishment of social psychology.

Development of the Scoring System

This account begins in an improbable way; it begins with a study of the hunger drive (Atkinson and McClelland, 1948). In the animal laboratory when a psychologist wants to use intensity of motivation as an independent variable it is usually hunger that he undertakes to manipulate.

It can be done so easily. The rats can be deprived of their bran mash for varying periods of time and the presumption is that the intensity of the drive will be proportional to the period of deprivation. Suppose one were to deprive humans of their bran mash and ask them to make up stories. Could we pick up the various intensities of the hunger drive from the content of their stories? The human animal can do what rats cannot, it can verbalize. Can one detect variations of drive in this peculiarly human behavior?

In *The Interpretation of Dreams* (1900) Freud argued that dreams invariably expressed the fulfillment of a wish. In the daydreams of adults and in the nocturnal dreams of small children the wishes are often very clear— to win first prize on a quiz show; to be given a pony or to go hunting in Africa. In the nocturnal dreams of adults it is often difficult to discern the fulfillment of a wish but Freud held it was always there and could be identified if we learned to penetrate certain disguises and symbolisms. The wishes were such as the adult would not like to acknowledge and the disguises were there to disarm the objections of a censorious conscience. A dream, Freud argued, is essentially a response to the stimulus of an insistent wish; fulfillment in fantasy leaves the sleeper undisturbed. Suppose we are not interested in accounting for the occurrence of dreams but rather in discovering the desires of individual human beings; something a psychotherapist must try to do. Freud's theory now directs us to study the individual's dreams because these fantasies are responsive to desire and potentially expressive of desire.

Dreams are a kind of imaginative story produced on an unpredictable schedule and as reactions to unknown stimuli. Why not ask patients to dream to order? Why not provide controlled stimuli so that we may compare the production of one patient with that of another? A line of thought resembling this one led Henry Murray and his associates (1938) to invent the Thematic Apperception Test (commonly called the TAT). The TAT is a set of twenty pictures, each of which is used by a subject as the starting point of a story. The stories are to be analyzed like dreams.

A picture like the one we have described above does not provide objective answers to such questions as: "What is being thought?" "What is wanted?" The talespinner must fill out the pictures from his own motivational substance. The process of apperception means going beyond perception, beyond the recognition of objects and events, to a full interpretation based on one's life experience.

HUNGER AND PHANTASY

It was the TAT that suggested to Atkinson and McClelland that they look for traces of hunger in stories. Their study was different in one critical respect from what others had done with the TAT. In clinical practice the TAT was and is a very popular instrument. There are several scoring methods and interpretative schemes, some of them objective and some not. Atkinson and McClelland started with an established independent measure of a motive—deprivation of food—and checked TAT stories against this measure to see whether the stories were truly responsive to motivation. They began, knowing the answer to their subjects' motivation, and checked to see whether the content of phantasy could have told them the same answer.

The subjects were men at the U.S. Naval Submarine Base in New London, Connecticut. At the time of testing, one group of men had been without food for just one hour; a second group had been without for four hours and so they were due for a meal; a third group had gone overnight, missed breakfast, and they were due for lunch, adding up to sixteen hours of deprivation. The mixup on meals was managed cleverly so that it did not seem to have any connection with the test of creative imagination. The men wrote stories for eight pictures, some of them from the TAT and others designed for the experiment, some of them unrelated to food and some explicitly involving food.

The stories were scored in terms of a variety of categories. One was called "Food-related imagery" and included any reference that had to do with food or eating. Another was called "Food deprivation thema" and was scored whenever deprivation of food was the central plot of the story. Another was called "Need food" and was scored when there was an actual statement that someone in the story wanted food. There were more than a dozen such categories and a scorer simply made a tally for a category whenever a story contained the designated content.

As hunger increased, from the one-hour group to the four-hour group to the sixteen-hour group, there was no increase of "Food-related imagery." The straightforward expectation that food or eating would be more often mentioned as hunger increased was not confirmed. However, some other categories did show an increase: in particular the percentage of "Food deprivation themas," of characters expressing a need for food, and of activities successful in overcoming deprivation. In some dimensions then the content of the stories seemed to be responsive to the strength of a motive. By assigning values of $+1$ or $+2$ to these responsive categories it was possible to assign a composite "need for food" score to each story, across stories to subjects, and across subjects to three deprivation groups. The mean scores for groups significantly increased as the period of deprivation increased. Furthermore one could, from an individual subject's score, make a usually correct guess of the deprivation group to which he belonged. The important demonstration is that when degrees of hunger were known from an antecedent manipulation this information could be recovered from the content of phantasy. Hunger is detectable in the stream of imagination as well as in the blood stream.

We are not concerned with hunger as such and this first experiment serves only to give us a position from which to jump. We want to study the achievement motive but we cannot even be sure that it exists. For hunger, or the several hungers, one can specify the nutrients that are goal objects, the physiological states created by deprivation and the consummatory responses that are set off by attainment of the goal objects. For the achievement motive none of these things can be specified. As evidence for its existence we have nothing but intuition and common report. People talk about one man having more "drive" than another, being more concerned to do a thing well, to succeed. But not even common report is clear about the existence of the Achievement Motive as we shall conceive it. We posit the existence of a generalized concern with meeting standards of excellence, such that one person is comparable with another in terms of the degree to which each has this concern even though, for one, the concern may be directed to scientific effort, for another, to artistic effort, for another, to business.

MANIPULATING ANTECEDENT CONDITIONS

We are going to take our first steps in finding a measure by close and deliberate analogy with the hunger experiment. What we need is a range of antecedent conditions that create varying degrees of achievement motivation even as the varying periods of food deprivation created degrees of hunger. Subjects whose internal states may be presumed to vary will be asked to write stories and we will look, in these stories, for the kinds of content that increase with increasing achievement motivation. The difficulty with this program is that there is not, for achievement motivation, an established technique of manipulation, equivalent to the deprivation approach to hunger. What to do? Plunge in—as best one can.

McClelland and Atkinson and their co-workers were at Wesleyan University and their subjects were male students at that university. The essence of the experimental design was the creation of contrasting social situations such that one extreme situation should be evocative of high motivation to achieve and the other extreme not at all evocative of such motivation. I will call the former situation the Aroused condition and the latter the Relaxed condition. McClelland actually created four conditions in an effort to produce as many degrees of arousal; in reducing my description to two extremes I am not violating the logic of the work.

For both conditions the experimental materials were a set of simple paper-and-pencil tasks and four pictures to be used as stimuli for the creative imagination. For the Relaxed orientation the test administrator was introduced to a college class as a graduate student who wanted "to try out some tests on them." The graduate student, affecting a conspicuously easygoing manner, said that the tests were in a developmental stage and needed to be tried out so they could be improved. He was clearly more interested in testing the tests than in testing the students. With this orientation the subjects seemed to enjoy the paper-and-pencil tasks as they would a series of trifling parlor games. The story telling task came last and was introduced with the familiar spiel about "creative imagination."

For the Aroused condition the test booklets were passed out without explanation and the first task administered with the admonitions to pay close attention and work rapidly. Subjects were then told how to correct the test and calculate their own scores. They were directed to put their names on the booklet, the names of high schools and colleges they had attended with estimated class standing in each; IQ if known; and an estimate of their general intelligence as "above average, average, or below average." The administrator then very gravely made remarks along the following lines:

> The tests which you are taking directly indicate a person's general level of intelligence. These tests have been taken from a group of tests which were used to select people of high administrative capacity for positions in Washington during the past war. Thus in addition to general intelligence, they bring out an individual's capacity to organize material, his ability to evaluate crucial situations quickly and accurately; in short, these tests demonstrate whether or not a person is suited to be a leader.
>
> The present research is being conducted for the Navy to determine which educational institutions turn out the highest percentage of students with the administrative qualifications shown by superior scores on these tests. For example, it has been found that Wesleyan University excels in this respect. You are being allowed to calculate your own scores, so that you may determine how well you do in comparison with Wesleyan students [Atkinson, 1958, p. 66].

At this point the administrator quoted norms for Test 1 that were so high that practically everyone in the class failed badly. The remaining tests were given and then, for the total scores, false norms were again reported which were so high as to make almost everyone feel he had failed. There were numerous signs that students were taking the task seriously and were dismayed by their own performances. At this critical moment they wrote four stories having been given creative imagination directions identical with those used for the Relaxed group.

We all have intuitive notions about the kinds of situations that mobilize achievement motivation and probably we can agree that the Aroused orientation would do so while the Relaxed would not. The Aroused subjects are given to believe that their performances are diagnostic of critically important personal abilities; they are induced to evaluate their performances in terms of definite standards of excellence. Finally they are given an experience of failure which if we think of it as deprivation of success seems likely to create achievement drive even as deprivation of food creates hunger. The Relaxed subjects are not led to think of the tests as diagnostic of ability; are not encouraged to evaluate them in terms of any standard, and are not deprived of success.

The next step was to score the two sets of stories for various kinds of content in order to discover which categories were responsive to motivation. The categories were numerous. For example, "General achievement imagery" was scored if a story dealt with some long-term problem of getting ahead in connection with career, schooling or the like; "Instrumental activity" was scored if the person in the story did something about achieving his goal; "Outcomes" were scored as happy $(O+)$ or unhappy $(O-)$ or doubtful (O_0). The authors then looked to see which of the content categories showed a significant increase from the Relaxed to the Aroused condition. All of those that showed such an increase were to become part of a composite score for assessing the level of motivation in individuals. Those that did not increase, and the Outcome categories were among these, were dropped from further consideration. This experiment was essentially a search for content that responded to contrasting social situations as one would expect the Achievement Motive to respond to these situations.

A PERSONALITY MEASURE

At this point McClelland's thinking took a crucial turn. He had a set of categories that responded to situational manipulations of the general level of achievement motivation in groups. By assigning each instance of content that fell in one of the responsive categories a value of $+1$ he obtained composite scores for each story and across stories for each subject. The average score in the Aroused condition was necessarily very much higher than in the Relaxed condition. Suppose now that one were to administer the creative imagination test to a group of subjects with an orientation intermediate between the Relaxed and Aroused, a Neutral orientation. In these circumstances there will still be a wide variation among subjects in composite achievement content scores. What interpretation shall we give to this variation? It is not a response to situational variation; insofar as the situation can be controlled it is the same for all subjects. It must then be variation that comes from within the individuals. Perhaps it can be taken as diagnostic of a personally characteristic strength of the Achievement Motive. In the same situation some persons seem to be highly motivated to achieve and some are not so motivated at all. The difference is a difference in the individual's readiness or inclination to be concerned with achievement.

The level of achievement motivation in a particular person at a particular time is conceived to be a function of two major factors: 1) the situation; 2) the enduring strength of the motive in the individual personality. With the situation roughly constant for a set of subjects the variation in scores should be chiefly diagnostic of the second factor. If this conception is correct what ought to happen if the same subjects are tested (with comparable sets of pictures) on three occasions with three different atmospheres: Relaxed, Neutral, and Aroused? Since scores are responsive to orientations there should be a general rise from the Relaxed to the Neutral to the Aroused condition. However, insofar as scores are diagnostic of stable personality characteristics the rank order of the persons tested should tend to be invariant. Table 9-1 presents an invented set of scores displaying this effect in ideal form. Unfortunately actual data of this kind have not been collected but there are data for repeated assessments in a single kind of situation.

If testing situations are kept the same, perhaps just neutral, then absolute scores as well as relative order ought to remain the same if it is true that scores are chiefly determined by the controlled orientation and by a stable personality characteristic. There are, however, other possible determinants. Individual scores might be chiefly determined by recent random events. Plays seen on television the night before, a novel just put down, a conversation before class could all affect the stories people tell on a given occasion. Insofar as these events are the effective determinants, scores would not remain constant or preserve their order.

TABLE 9-1. INVENTED SCORES SHOWING IDEAL EFFECTS OF SITUATION AND PERSONALITY

		ORIENTATIONS		
		Relaxed	Neutral	Aroused
	15			
	14			
	13			A
	12			B
	11			C
	10			D
	9		A	E
ABSOLUTE	8		B	F
SCORES ON THE	7		C	G
ACHIEVEMENT	6		D	
MOTIVE	5	A	E	
	4	B	F	
	3	C	G	
	2	D		
	1	E		
	0	F		
	−1	G		
	−2			

If the same four pictures were to be presented on two occasions with only a short interval between them the stories told first would almost certainly affect those told later. For this reason when Lowell (1950) did a test and retest study with a week between he used different sets of pictures which were known to be roughly equivalent (Atkinson, 1950). It is disappointing to find that the product-moment correlation between the two sets of scores was only .22, a value that was not significantly different from zero. This result does not encourage us to believe that the test is measuring a stable personality characteristic. However, the two sets of scores agreed to the extent of 72.5 per cent in placing subjects above or below the median. In short, neither absolute scores nor relative rankings were preserved in any significant degree over an interval of just one week. However, individuals did tend to preserve crude positions defined simply as above or below the median. On the basis of Lowell's early study the authors concluded that they could justifiably compare groups of high and low scorers and assume some stability of individual placement.

Birney (1959) has reported results for a single set of subjects tested in August 1955, October 1956, February 1957, and April 1957. The intercorrelations vary from +.03 to +.56; all are positive but only two of the six are significant. The Fels Research Institute in Yellow Springs, Ohio, has data on certain individuals from early childhood until adult life. At the time the first longitudinal data were collected at Fels, McClelland's measure did not exist. However, TAT stories were taken at various ages and these stories can now be scored in the McClelland manner. Kagan and Moss (1959) have studied the stability of Achievement Motive scores on three such testings taken over a period of six years. All of the three correlations are positive and two of them are significant.

Scores on McClelland's measure are far from having the perfect stability one would like in an index of a presumably enduring personality characteristic. However, the weight of the evidence is in favor of a small positive relationship over periods as long as six years. This is a rather remarkable outcome. The measure is a twenty-minute sample of the contents of consciousness, a tiny spinal tap from the lifetime stream. It is remarkable that an assay of so small a quantity of material should yield results having any stability at all.

Reliability in Scoring

The content categories have been discovered and Figure 9-2, in conjunction with the present paragraph, summarizes them in a systematic way. Each symbol represents a category of content that is scored. Motivation starts with the individual's experience of a state of need (N). He may also be anticipating successful attainment of his goal (Ga+) or, perhaps, anticipating failure (Ga−). He may engage in activity that is instrumental to the attainment of his goal and this instrumental activity may be either successful (I+) or unsuccessful (I−). Sometimes his progress to the goal will be blocked and the obstacle or block might be located in the external world (Bw) or it might be a deficiency of the person himself (Bp). He may experience strong positive and negative affective states while attempting to reach his goal; positive states are likely to be associated with progress toward the goal (G+) and negative states with the thwarting of his efforts (G−). Someone may help him toward his goal or sympathize with his goal-directed behavior and this kind of helpful push is called a Nurturant Press (Nup).

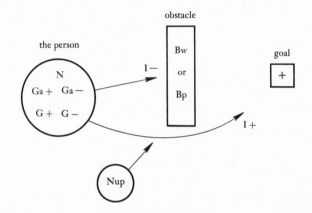

FIGURE 9-1. POSITION OF THE SCORING CATEGORIES IN A MOTIVATED BEHAVIORAL SEQUENCE (FIGURE 4.1 from *The Achievement Motive* by David C. McClelland, John W. Atkinson, Russell A. Clark, and Edgar Lowell. Copyright 1953, Appleton-Century-Crofts, Inc. Reproduced by permission of Appleton-Century-Crofts.)

Now let us have a brief overview of the scoring itself. The basic decision a scorer must make is whether or not the story contains any reference whatever to an achievement goal. The categories summarized above and in Figure 9-1 are all subcategories of achievement imagery and are not scored unless the story as a whole is judged to show some concern with achievement. The basic scoring of AI (Achievement Imagery) is made when some character in the story shows *concern with competing successfully with some standard of excellence.* The standard can be of any kind, the scoring is responsive to every sort of goal. If the story meets the requirements for AI it receives one point and the scorer goes on to look at the subcategories, adding +1 for each one that can be scored. Stories that involve a task, but where the task is approached as a matter of commonplace routine, are scored TI (Task Imagery) and receive no points (a score of 0). Where a story contains no suggestion whatever of an achievement goal and does not even involve a routine task, it is scored UI (Unrelated Imagery) and given the value −1. These three basic categories, UI, TI, and AI are points on a dimension of increasing certainty that a story is concerned with achievement. If and only if AI is scored does one go on to the subcategories.

Need for Achievement (N) is scored if there is a statement in the story that someone wants to reach an achievement goal (e.g., "He wants to become a doctor" or "He hopes to succeed"). Overt or mental activity by one or more characters that is instrumental to goal attainment is the occasion for scoring Instrumental Activity (I). One scores I+, I−, or I? according as the outcome is successful, unsuccessful or in doubt. Instrumental activity is only scored once per story. If someone in the story anticipates goal attainment or anticipates failure to reach the goal then Ga+ or Ga− will be scored. Both of these may be scored but only once each per story. Blocks or obstacles located within the person are scored Bp and blocks in the world outside are scored Bw. If there are personal forces in the story which aid the character who is striving to achieve then Nup is scored. Evidence of positive affective states connected with goal attainment are the occasion for scoring G+ and evidence of negative states for scoring G−. Both kinds of affective content may be scored once each, in the same story. Finally there is a possible extra point for Achievement Thema (Ach Th) which is scored when the achievement imagery is elaborated into the central plot, or theme, of the story. The highest possible score for a story is 11 points, which would require all of the following: AI, N, I (+, −, or ?), Ga+, Ga−, Bp, Bw, Nup, G+, G−, Ach Th.

Try now to score your own story with these brief definitions to guide you and try also scoring the High Story that appears on page 424. I cannot, of course, give you the correct scoring for your own story, but for the High Story it is: AI, N, I−, Ga−, Bw, G−, Ach Th, which makes a total of 7 points. It is almost certain that your scoring of this story will not exactly correspond with the correct scoring. Evidently the definitions of the content categories do not perfectly communicate the author's understanding of these categories. Can such scores ever provide objective data?

Data are objective when various investigators can agree on what the data are. For some topics in psychology, measurement is actually physicalistic and there is no problem of objectivity. Reaction times are read from a chronometer and psychogalvanic reflexes from a galvanometer. The basic "reading" is a judgment of the coincidence of two lines—the pointer and a position on a scale. This is a judgment that can be made with very high agreement without the necessity for any special training of the judges. Interpretation of the data does of course require considerable training but the determination of what the data are, does not. There is no necessity to assess the reliability with which various judges make the readings. It suffices to have a single meter-reader since a consensus among conceivable readers may be taken for granted.

There is another sort of psychological measure which, while it does not involve physical instruments, is, nevertheless, perfectly objective. This is the "objective" paper and pencil questionnaire, inventory, or examination. The basic judgment is one of determining which of several alternatives has been checked. No special training is needed to get a consensus among judges though there can be errors from oversight. In fact the process can be mechanized, which is a sufficient demonstration of its objectivity.

With content analysis, the method used to measure the Achievement Motive, we cannot say that judges are immediately able to agree on the data. Does the High Story on page 424 contain an instance of N, an instance of Ga+, an instance of G−? Are these things there or are they not there? Even with some special training—the abbreviated definitions you have been given for the content categories—a consensus is not obtained. However, a high consensus can be obtained if the training is more extensive.

For the Achievement Motive there is a scoring manual (Atkinson, 1958). An investigator who wants to use McClelland's measure must study the manual until he can score stories as McClelland and his associates score them. He will begin by reading carefully the full definitions of the content categories; there is much more in these than the brief definitions I have supplied. Then he will try his hand at scoring some actual stories in the manual without knowing, of course, what the correct scores are. When he checks his own scores against the "answers"—and the answers are the scores given by the authors of the measure—he will find a very imperfect agreement. He must then reexamine each story and read the author's justification for each category scored. The novice will try again with new stories and check again. When he is beginning to do quite well he will calculate a coefficient of reliability between a set of his own scores and the correct answers. This coefficient is simply a correlation indicating the degree of agreement between a new scorer and an established scorer. When the coefficient is high, above .90 for instance, the investigator is ready to measure the Achievement Motive in new subjects.

This is a rather curious process. In a real sense McClelland's measure does not exist in the external world. It must be built inside the investigator's head from McClelland's blueprints. The aim is to construct a set of mental bins into which story contents can be sorted. This can be done and there are by now hundreds or, perhaps, thousands of investigators who are able to score for the Achievement Motive.

Not every psychologist is willing to accept content analysis as an objective technique and yet I cannot see what is lacking. Objectivity is only social consensus and a consensus on content can be achieved. It is, to be sure, a consensus that must be created by training. The necessity for scorer reliability is absolute. Unless such reliability is demonstrated one cannot tell whether or not investigator A who reports certain findings concerning achievement motivation is talking about the same thing as are McClelland, Atkinson, and their associates. The necessity is only a subvariety of the general requirement in science that terms make unequivocal reference.

But you may wonder why investigators all over the United States and in many other nations should trouble to learn McClelland's scoring. The answer to that is, essentially, that McClelland's scores have proved to be very fruitful in the study of behavior—they are related in important and consistent ways to other aspects of behavior. If they had not proved to be fruitful in this way the measure would have died with McClelland's first publications as many other schemes of content analysis have died for this reason.

There is a difficulty about the accumulation of a large research tradition that involves a particular scoring method. It tends to freeze the method. It may be that by now McClelland suspects that the scoring ought to be changed in certain ways, that a different way of doing it would result in a more valid index of achievement motivation. But if one were to change it, then new results obtained by the new method would become incomparable with all prior results. To make a change is to introduce a sharp discontinuity and one naturally hesitates to do it.

Validity of the Measure

The problem of scoring reliability is the problem of agreement on what the data *are*. The problem of validity is the problem of what the data *indicate*. Have we measured what we have undertaken to measure? In one very limited sphere the notion of test validity has a precise meaning. If a psychologist has devised a test for the purpose of selecting men who will be able to do well on some job or task then the validity of the test is the correlation between test scores and quality of job performance. The job is the *criterion* for the test and the test's validity is measured against its criterion.

In the nature of the case there is no single clear criterion for a measure of the Achievement Motive. However, we have certain ideas about how achievement motivation ought to operate. The most fundamental of these is the notion that persons who have a strong Achievement Motive ought to do better work than persons of comparable ability who have a weak Motive. One can, in a loose sense, validate a measure of the Achievement Motive by determining whether or not scores on the measure relate to other scores as our conception of the Motive suggests they should. This kind of inquiry is called "construct validation."

The method used for the discovery of scoring categories is itself a kind of validation. One of the expectations we would have of achievement motivation is that it would increase in situations which stress successful competition and would decrease in situations where quality of performance and competition do not signify. The content categories were selected for precisely this kind of responsiveness and so we know that for Wesleyan students, at least, the measure is affected by situations as the motive ought to be. In fact we know this for populations other than Wesleyan college students. Several investigators have obtained similar results for other collections of American college students. Angelini (1955) has repeated the basic Arousal techniques in Brazil with Portuguese-speaking subjects and obtained effects on phantasy very similar to those obtained at Wesleyan. Lowell (1950) created contrasting Relaxed and Aroused situations for twenty-one ninth-grade Navaho Indian boys in New Mexico. He somewhat modified the procedure to suit the setting but found that telling these boys that they were taking tests which would show how "smart" they were served to increase the amount of achievement phantasy. The detailed content changed was unlike that produced by Wesleyan students but the scoring categories are independent of particular content and AI is scored just as surely when a boy wants to be a "good sheepherder" (Navaho) as when he wants to be a "good doctor" (Wesleyan).

The findings so far reported have all been for male subjects. However, Veroff (1950), Wilcox (1951), and Field (1951) have all experimented with female subjects. The scores of girls do not increase significantly from the Relaxed to the Arousal conditions. It seems likely that this is because girls are not so stimulated as are men by talk about "intelligence" and "leadership." In Field's study the female scores did go up when the Arousal conditions stressed "popularity" and "social acceptance." Status ranks for girls and women in the United States, which are assigned to them personally and not derived from their husbands or fathers, have more to do with social grace and popularity than with leadership and it seems that their achievement motivation is geared to their status system. Because the scores for female subjects did not respond to this first validating procedure as did scores for male subjects, the research with McClelland's measure has focused on males. What we shall hereafter say about achievement motivation must be taken to have reference to males only.

A minimal sort of construct validity for McClelland's measure was guaranteed by the very procedure for obtaining a scoring system. Further validation is provided by relationships between scores on the measure and other kinds of data. Strodtbeck (1958) has reported a result that quite perfectly satisfies our expectation that the strength of the motive should be related to quality of performance when ability is constant. For a sample of New Haven high-school boys Strodtbeck had intelligence and achievement test scores as well as school grades. Each boy's performance on the tests was inspected and his "expected" school grades were calculated as the grades that were earned, on the average, by boys at his level of intelligence. When the individual boy's grades exceeded the expected performance he was classified as an "over-achiever" and when his grades fell short of the expected performance as an "under-achiever," McClelland's measure was administered to all the boys and over-achievers had significantly higher scores.

A study was done at M.I.T. by Everett (1959) that demonstrates a relation between scores on the measure and another sort of under- and over-achievement. Everett was a Sloan Fellow at M.I.T.; Sloan Fellows are men in management positions who spend a year at the Institute to study economics, psychology, industrial relations, and other subjects useful in management. In Everett's firm there was one department in which there were one hundred men who had been hired with quite similar academic attainments and then given comparable opportunities to advance by taking night-school courses, Everett worked out an index of occupational achievement for these men which was complex in detail but amounted to an indication of how far each man had advanced and how fast. Everett administered to them McClelland's measure and also a number of other paper-and-pencil measures which he had invented and thought might very well serve as indices of achievement motivation. Everett had an idea, I think, that it would not be very difficult for a smart businessman to think up a measure as good as McClelland's. It was instructive to him that none of his own measures was related to the index of occupational achievement, whereas scores on McClelland's measure were slightly, but significantly, related.

Numerous researchers have studied the relations between actual task performance and Achievement Motive scores. Lowell (1950) found that when subjects were asked to do anagrams (i.e., to unscramble scrambled words) high and low scorers started at about the same level but high scorers showed marked improvement with time whereas low scorers did not. He took this to mean that high scorers were sufficiently interested in doing the task well to learn how to do it better as they went along. Wendt

(1955) assigned high and low subjects a set of arithmetic problems which required simple addition and subtraction. He found that the higher the motivation the better were the performances, in terms both of the number of problems done and the number correct. In addition, Wendt asked subjects to report on how bored they were by the task and the subjects with low achievement motivation were more bored.

French (1955) assigned subjects a decoding task that involved substituting numbers for letters. She had assessed achievement motivation some months earlier, not with McClelland's measure but with one related to it. Subjects did the task with three different kinds of orientation and the relation between performance and assessed motivation shifted with these orientations. One group of subjects was asked to cooperate with the investigator but given a relaxed approach to the rather routine task. Achievement motivation was not significantly related to performance. Other subjects were given to believe that the task measured an important ability that would be related to their future careers. For these subjects, motivation was strongly related to performance. A final group of subjects was told that the five men who had made the best scores would have an hour's free time whereas the others would have to go on working. With this incentive, which is extrinsic to achievement, there was again no significant relation between performance and motivation.

These various results generally conform to our prior conception of an achievement motive. People who have high scores perform better in terms of long-term occupational and academic goals, and also do better on brief immediate tasks when the reason for doing so is to satisfy some standard of excellence and not just to accomplish a dull routine or to obtain some extrinsic gratification. There are dozens of other studies that are roughly validating. High scorers have better memory for tasks they have left uncompleted, and so presumably are more motivated to finish something once begun (Atkinson, 1955); they are more active in college and in their communities (McClelland, 1961); when asked to choose working partners they prefer successful strangers to unsuccessful friends (French, 1956); they are more prone to volunteer as subjects for psychological experiments (Burdick, 1955). The measure appears to be drawing upon something that corresponds with our intuitive understanding of achievement motivation.

The Expressive Style of the High Scorer

One summer I went to the Edinburgh Festival in Scotland. Edinburgh is a wonderful-looking city with a great castle on the heights and curious churches of black stone in a spiny, thistle-like, Scottish Gothic style. In the stores, certain articles—for example women's gloves and men's scarves —appear in all the different Scottish clan tartans. If you buy gifts in Scotland you become interested in learning to distinguish the various tartans and also to name them—the Royal Stewart, the MacDonell of Glengarry, the Hunting Macpherson, and so on. You also find that you have definite preferences among the tartans. Because of this little bit of background I was interested when I learned that Knapp (1958) had developed a Tartan Test and had demonstrated that the preferences of high Achievement Motive people are quite different from those of low Achievement Motive people.

Subjects examine a standard set of thirty tartans placed in a random order at eye height on a long bulletin board. Preferences are indicated by grouping the tartans along an eight-point scale. The relations between rankings of individual tartans and motive scores were small. However, the ten tartans that had the strongest tendency to be liked by high scorers were, in certain ways, consistently different from the ten that tended to be liked by low scorers. First, and most obviously, the tartans liked by high scorers were somber and those liked by low scorers were all very bright. The single aspect of these complex patterns that most clearly distinguished the two sets of tartans was the dominant color. High scorers liked tartans with a good deal of blue in them and low scorers liked red.

This single difference in color preference does not greatly advance our understanding of the motive. It might simply stem from a socio-economic difference; conservative tastes go with higher status. Perhaps it means more than this. I remember hearing DeWitt Parker, a famous professor of aesthetics, remark many years ago: "People who particularly like blue are trying to cool their fires." It is an interesting notion that hard-driving people, who "burn" to succeed, like the cool colors whereas more phlegmatic types prefer warm colors.

Knapp (1958) prefers to build his speculations on the fact that blue is regarded as a "soft" and a background color while red is a "hard" and imposing, figural color. A high-motive person, he suggests, is intent on playing an active role, on imposing his will on the environment. Such a person likes a soft, unobtrusive, passive background. The low-motive person is himself the softer, more passive element and he favors a hard, imposing color. Knapp points out that subdued and conservative dress characterizes North European Protestant cultures where, as we shall see, the Achievement Motive seems to be stronger than it is in Catholic Mediterranean cultures, where dress is more colorful. He notes also the sobriety of taste that was characteristic of the Puritans whose achievement motivation seems to have been very high. In the contemporary United States, middle-class dress favors the dull grey look whereas working-class dress is brighter and more colorful. And there are data showing that a higher level of achievement motivation obtains in the middle class than in the working class. Even so I suspect that all of these are accidental historical coincidences.

Knapp's conception of the high-motive person as one who is concentrated on active manipulation of the environment led him to guess that to such a person time might be exceptionally precious and would be conceived as moving rapidly. Certainly the busy achiever does seem always to be counting time, trying to "save" it because he is chronically "short" of it. Knapp devised an ingenious way of discovering how high scorers conceived of time.

Conceptions like time, birth, love, and death have many aspects and so provide the ground for many metaphors. A metaphor will bring forward certain characteristics of the original concept and suppress others. Death can be conceived as "a trumpet," as a "chilling frost," as a "grinning butcher," as "the end of a song," or a "compassionate mother." It is potentially all of these, but you may find some of the metaphors more apt than others and in this preference reveal something of your personal view of death. Knapp decided to provide subjects, whose Achievement Motive scores were known, with a collection of twenty-five metaphors for time and ask them to judge the appropriateness of each one (Knapp and Garbutt, 1958).

There was a very striking difference between the metaphors preferred by high scorers and those preferred by low scorers. High scorers liked: "a dashing waterfall," "a galloping horseman," "a bird in flight," "a winding spool," "a speeding train." Low scorers liked: "a quiet motionless ocean," "a stairway leading upward," "a string of beads," "a vast expanse of sky." The former set involves speed, even haste; the latter set is relatively quiescent. For the most part, the metaphors liked by high-motive people suggest directionality or purposiveness as well as speed. It does seem reasonable to suppose that the high-motive person measures his achievements against time as well as against a standard of quality. You remember that the index of occupational achievement used by Everett (1959) was essentially a matter of how far, how fast. For a man working "against time" time may very well appear to be rushing past at a great rate.

Have you ever looked at a collection of your own doodles? They can usually be found in the margins of lecture notes. Over a year and across the years there are stylistic consistencies which distinguish the doodles of one person from those of another. The patterns on paper are a record of free expressive movement and may be expected to have correlates in personality. Aronson (1958) has shown that in certain dimensions the scribbles of high-motive people are different from those of low-motive people. Before reading what these dimensions are, you may wish to go through a rough version of the Aronson procedure so as to have data of your own to examine.

Do not look yet at the next page. When you do you will see a complex design which is to be glanced at for only a fraction of a second. It is intended that the time be too short for you to get a detailed impression of the design. Having glanced at it you are to reproduce it to the best of your ability, to draw what you think was there. Go ahead.

*   *   *

The drawing you have made is not of course a spontaneous doodle and it may be less characteristic than such a doodle. The difficulty with spontaneous doodles as data is the requirement that they be spontaneous. How does one go about obtaining such productions from a number of people in a relatively short time and in relatively comparable form? Aronson's solution is to present a model design, which contains many of the different kinds of scribbles people make and to make the exposure brief enough to exclude the possibility of an exact copy. The presumption is that one will select from the many possibilities in the vaguely apprehended original those that are congenial personal expressions.

In Aronson's experimental procedure the design was projected on a screen for less than a second. Subjects had previously taken the standard four-story Achievement Motive test and Aronson examined the drawings of high scorers and low scorers in search of consistent contrasts. He found five kinds of them:

1. Discreteness vs. Fuzziness. High scorers made a preponderance of single, unattached, discrete lines while low scorers produced mostly fuzzy, overlaid lines.

2. Unused Space. High scorers left a smaller margin at the bottom of the page than did low scorers.

3. Diagonal Configurations. High scorers produced more diagonals than did low scorers.

4. S-shaped Lines. High scorers produced more S-shaped (two-directional, non-repetitive) lines than did low scorers.

5. Multiwave Lines. High scorers made fewer multiwave lines (lines consisting of two or more crests in the same direction) than did low scorers.

The contrasts were discovered from the drawings of one group of subjects. From these contrasts, Aronson worked out a way of assigning Achievement Motive scores to the drawings of a subject in the hope that such scores would, for new subjects, be correlated with McClelland's scores from verbal material and so might be considered an alternative index of the same motive, a non-verbal index.

With such complex multi-dimensional data it was perhaps inevitable that some contrasts should be found that were related to achievement motivation. In order to determine whether the contrasts were specific to the drawings examined or were, perhaps, general enough to serve as an alternative measure Aronson collected drawings and stories from new groups of subjects. His scores for graphic expression showed low but generally significant correlations with the scores from stories, correlations as high as those that have been obtained for different sets of stories. Therefore the graphic measure may reasonably be regarded as an alternative form of McClelland's measure, as good as an alternative set of pictures.

A non-verbal measure gives access to subjects who could not otherwise be reached. The TAT measure does not work well with children younger than about eight years. Children need not write stories, of course; they can simply tell them while the investigator writes. Under eight years, however, it is difficult to get children to tell connected stories but relatively easy to get them to scribble. It is also difficult for an English-speaking investigator to use the verbal measure with subjects who speak a language other than English and especially a language that is not Indo-European. Words in one language often do not have exact semantic equivalents in another language and scores on this measure may hinge on very delicate semantic connotations. Scores on the graphic measure may be more nearly free of cultural bias. Finally the graphic measure has made possible some fascinating studies of ancient civilizations. By scoring designs on pottery estimates have been made of the level of achievement motivation in Periclean Athens, in Ancient Egypt, and in Pre-Incan Peru.

Childhood Origins of Achievement Motivation

The introduction into American psychology of a new measuring instrument—suggestive and not too difficult to use—has something of the effect of the introduction of the hula hoop or yo-yo into the larger American society. Everyone takes it up—for a time. Soon after the Achievement Motive measure was invented, the journals were full of reports of one-shot studies correlating the new kind of score with all the old kinds of score or, when there was more inventiveness, with other new kinds of score. Each research report dutifully drew a set of conclusions; conclusions that invariably required "further study" to establish them. They seldom got any further study. Innovation exploded everywhere but consolidation lagged. The total picture became difficult to integrate, then impossibly blurred. The profession began to feel a little queasy at the mention of the Achievement Motive even as it had been made downright ill, several years earlier, by undigested F-Scale studies (see Chapter 10). In

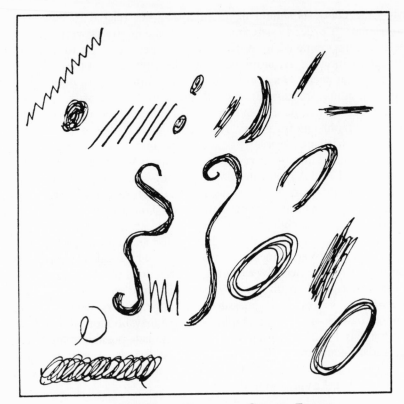

FIGURE 9-2.   THE MODEL DESIGN FOR GRAPHIC EXPRESSIONS
(Courtesy of D. Van Nostrand Company, Inc.)

the late 1950's, I think, the Achievement Motive tradition was about to die.

It was revitalized by a powerful new idea which McClelland supplied. He had continued to think about the total collection of findings, trying to make them fit together, to find their meaning. At length a number of them fell into a really compelling pattern, a pattern relating the motive to world history and to contemporary problems of economic development. Probably the single research result that was most crucial in effecting this expansion of scope was Marian Winterbottom's study of the childhood origins of achievement motivation (1953).

Winterbottom obtained Achievement Motive scores from twenty-nine boys aged eight to ten years. They told their stories instead of writing them and they responded to verbal cues rather than to pictures. One such verbal cue was: "Brothers and sisters playing. One is a little ahead." Each boy told a story about that situation. In addition, Winterbottom interviewed the boys' mothers, asking questions about how children ought to be raised.

The most significant part of the interview was a questionnaire concerning demands for independent action. Each mother was asked to tell by what age she expected her child to: 1) know his way around the city; 2) try new things for himself; 3) do well in competition; 4) make his own friends; and attain other such goals.

On the four items listed above mothers of high-scoring sons expected the accomplishment at a markedly earlier age than did mothers of low-scoring sons. However, there were not differences of this kind on all of the demands about which Winterbottom inquired. The demands yielding such differences all seem to be concerned with doing *new* things independently. Demands that a child take over certain necessary caretaking tasks from the parents were not made at an earlier age by mothers of high-scoring sons. Such tasks as getting dressed and getting ready for bed are duties a parent must perform if a child does not. Mothers of high-scoring sons are not concerned with unloading these duties at an early age. Their concern is rather that a boy should begin early to move out on his own, to acquire skills and explore possibilities. Winterbottom conceptualizes their attitude as a concern with early independence training.

There were some further differences between the two sets of mothers. Those with low-scoring sons believed in more restrictions on behavior; for example, "Not to fight with children to get his own way." These mothers also kept the restrictions on until a later age. When the two sorts of mothers were asked how they rewarded their sons for doing what was expected of them it turned out that mothers of sons with a strong Achievement Motive were more likely to use primary physical manifestations of affection like hugging or kissing.

In Chapter 4 it was suggested that personalities are formed by early roles and, once formed, affect the selection of, and performance in, later roles. Winterbottom's questions of mothers, asking what they thought their sons should do and when, constitute an inquiry into role definition. She was, after all, obtaining maternal prescriptions or guides for the behavior of sons; the contingencies governing administration of rewards and punishments.

In many ways the role definition was the same for all mothers. They all expected their sons eventually to feed themselves, make their own friends, do well in school, have their own interests and hobbies, etc. These are probably the lineaments of the general average American definition of a son's role. There was some variation, however, in the role definitions; specifically in the ages at which independent skills were supposed to be mastered and in the number of restrictions on behavior and the length of the period in which such restrictions were thought to be necessary. All mothers employed sanctions—rewards for good role performance and punishments for bad—but there was variation in the tendency to use the particular sanction of physical affection. The important fact is that the differences of role definition were related to differences of personality in role occupants. Mothers who wanted early independence and little restriction and who rewarded a good performance with hugs and kisses had sons whose achievement motivation was high. Such sons we will find make characteristic choices of occupational role and play their roles for achievement kicks. It is as if the boy as a son internalizes his mother's stress on early independent achievement and generalizes it into a feeling that achievement in this world earns hugs and kisses.

We had better enter some qualifications. The evidence for a connection between stress on independence in child training and high achievement motivation is, we shall see, quite strong. But the evidence is all correlational. Correlational evidence, evidence that two things go together or co-vary, cannot establish relations of cause and effect. We are disposed to see independence training as the cause of high achievement motivation but there is an alternative possibility to be kept in mind: perhaps high achievement motivation in the son and expectations of early accomplishment in the mother are both produced by the son's innately determined level of competence.

Even if it is the mother's expectations, her role definition, that cause the son's high motivation we cannot be sure that setting an early age for independence is the effective cause. It may be that most of the significant differences between mothers of high-scoring sons and mothers of low-scoring sons are of no consequence for the sons' motivation. Everything may stem from a single item; for instance expecting a son "to do well in competition." It may not be independence in general that matters but competitiveness.

On the other hand the truly effective difference between the mothers may not even have been represented in Winterbottom's interview. Perhaps what counts is that the mother admires her husband and wants her son to grow up to be like his father. If that difference happened to be correlated with expectations of independence we could get the Winterbottom results but these results would not reveal the effective variable. It is likely that the questionnaire differences are a small indication of rather general differences of role definition in the sphere of achievement. The total role, the total home atmosphere, may be the effective agent. It is unlikely that any particular expectation or set of expectations can create high achievement motivation. A mother who read Winterbottom's results and decided to produce a highly motivated son by expecting her son to "know his way around the city," "do well in competition," and "make his own friends" before he was eight years old might be disappointed by the results. Motive creation cannot be that simple.

From Winterbottom's study we know what mothers report about their long-term expectations of a son. Such expectations or role definitions are only a blueprint for behavior—they leave us curious to know what parents do, in direct interaction with their children, that is relevant to the

Achievement Motive. Rosen and D'Andrade (1959) went to private homes to observe how parents reacted to their sons when the sons were trying to achieve something.

The investigators visited forty families of which twenty included a son with a high Motive score and twenty a son with a low Motive score. Each son was asked to build a tower out of some very irregularly shaped blocks; the task was made difficult by blindfolding him and restricting him to the use of one hand. Father and mother were allowed to look on and to say anything they liked but forbidden to touch the blocks. The parents were told that the "average" boy could, in these circumstances, build a tower of eight blocks. The parents were asked to estimate in advance, and confidentially, how high they thought their son could build the tower. This kind of advance estimate is called a "level of aspiration." Both the mothers and fathers of high Motive sons set higher levels than did the parents of low Motive sons. With other kinds of tasks it continued to be the case that more was expected of boys with high achievement motivation.

While the blindfolded boy worked at the precarious business of piling blocks, parents urged him on, gave him directions, exploded in happy laughter when he succeeded. But there were differences in the character of this behavior for the parents of the two kinds of sons. Parents of high scorers, especially the mothers, worked up a lot of hopeful encouraging tension over the performance and when it went well poured out happiness and warmth. This is a result consistent with Winterbottom's finding that mothers of high scorers reward accomplishment with hugs and kisses. For low-scoring sons there was something distinctive in the father's behavior. He tended to give them specific directions, and to make decisions for them, to urge them on and react with irritation when things did not go well. It appears that a father who is domineering and authoritarian in behavior is not likely to have a son with high achievement motivation.

There are several other studies of the childhood origins of achievement motivation but I will only describe one of them. This is an early modest study, important to recall because it introduced into this literature the study of a unit larger than the personality; it initiated the use of Achievement Motive scoring to characterize differences between total cultures. The investigators' general plan was to assess the two variables of Winterbottom's study, training for independence and achievement motivation, on the cultural level.

What kind of data would enable one to assign characteristic motivation levels to a culture. It might be done with great effort and expense, by administering the standard measure to a representative sample of persons belonging to a culture. The average of the individual scores could be taken as the cultural score. Instead of trying this, McClelland and Friedman (1952) argued that for simple non-literate cultures one might reasonably score popular folktales and take that average score as characteristic of the culture. In a non-literate culture a folktale cannot be written down by the natives and so if it survives it must be through frequent repetition. It is reasonable to suppose that people will only repeat a tale that is somehow satisfying to themselves and their auditors. If some parts of a tale were not agreeable those parts would probably be dropped or changed. In its standard form a tale should deal in a satisfying way with matters that concern the society that has produced it.

The investigators collected a dozen tales for each of eight American Indian societies. In order to reduce extraneous sources of variation, stories were selected which had the same central character—Coyote, a trickster hero who appears in the tales of many Indian tribes. It proved to be possible to score folktales for the Achievement Motive without making any changes in the standard categories and the total scores across the dozen stories of a group was taken as the score for that culture.

To determine the amount of concern with early independence training in each of the eight Indian cultures, all of the ethnographic materials, all of the descriptive information on each culture, were read and used as the basis of a rating. The ratings of independence training had actually been done by other investigators for an earlier study and those investigators had no knowledge of McClelland's measure. The ethnographic materials included interviews with parents concerning the rearing of children as well as reports of direct observation of parents and children.

McClelland and Friedman found that there was a significant positive relation between the amount of stress on early independence training and the level of achievement motivation in folktales. However, they worked with only eight cultures and the research procedures used had several defects. In a more recent study, Child, Storm, and Veroff (1958) used thirty-three primitive societies and improved on the procedures of the earlier study. They found that it was direct training for achievement rather than a stress on independence or self-reliance that was related to the motivation levels revealed in the folktales of the cultures. If we look at all of the data that have now been collected on child rearing and achievement motivation we cannot be sure of the exact dimension of parental behavior that is effective. It is somewhere in a cluster having to do with independence, achievement, aspiration, and self-reliance. Furthermore, it has not been proved that the childhood correlates of achievement motivation are actually childhood *sources* since there are no data adequate to establish a cause and effect relationship. Still, McClelland seemed to be convinced that it was just that and this conviction together with the realization that there was an empirical method for determining the level of the Motive in whole societies prepared him to make one of the more audacious investigations in the history of social science.

Weber's Thesis

In *The Protestant Ethic and the Spirit of Capitalism* (1904) Max Weber put forward the thesis that the Reformation had produced a characterological revolution, infusing a more vigorous spirit into both workers and entrepreneurs and ultimately bringing about the development of modern industrial capitalism. Weber had noticed that the rise of Protestantism in Germany, Switzerland, England, and the Netherlands coincided historically with the rise of capitalistic enterprise and rapid economic growth. It was his impression that Protestant working girls worked harder and longer than Catholic girls; that they saved their money for long-range goals. Protestant entrepreneurs, he noticed, more often rose to the top of the business world than did Catholic entrepreneurs even though the initial advantage of wealth was often with the Catholic families. An entrepreneur, incidentally, may be defined as someone who exercises some control over the means of production and produces more than he can consume in order to sell it for individual or household income. In the tenets of the various Protestant sects Weber discovered certain ideas that might conduce to entrepreneurial enterprise and so he argued that the religious movement was the cause of the economic development.

Protestantism in general preached that salvation was not to be earned by monastic withdrawal from the world or by the scrupulous observance of the church's rites or even by the accumulation of good works. A man's whole life constituted his claim on eternity. Each man had a "calling" and performance of the duties of that calling was the highest command. For entrepreneurs and workers alike, devotion to one's calling was likely to result in the accumulation of wealth. Protestantism sharply limited the uses that could be made of this wealth. In reaction against the softness and luxury of Rome, Protestantism was ascetic and forbade expenditures on pleasures of the flesh. One of the few things one could in good conscience do with savings was to "plow them back into the firm" or, more modestly, open a shop of one's own.

In Calvinism there was a doctrine that one might have thought would discourage economic enterprise or any other kind of effort. Predestination, a corollary of God's omnipotence, is the belief that the "Elect," those who will be saved, are saved from the beginning of time and nothing one can do will achieve salvation if one is not chosen by God. This is a doctrine whose implicit imperative seems to be: "Take it easy and wait and see." Calvin was aware that such a vulgar interpretation might be made and he did not advise a great emphasis on predestination in preaching for the common folk. Correctly viewed, however, predestination does not invite lassitude.

While one cannot achieve salvation if it is not ordained that he shall be saved, one can create the *conviction* of salvation. No man knows God's decisions; no man knows if he belongs to the Elect. But the Elect can be recognized by others and by themselves from certain outward signs. These outward signs might, of course, have been simplicity and piety. But in fact they included self-denial and a devotion to duty. There was also a belief that God caused His Elect to prosper. In Cromwell's England there was an understanding that business success was a mark of election. While the tenets of Protestantism are not an explicit imperative to economic enterprise there is a way of interpreting those tenets which makes self-denying economic activity advisable.

The Key Hypothesis

Weber's famous thesis makes a link between two large-scale social movements. What McClelland has done is to suggest a mediating social-psychological mechanism. A Protestant ideology should cause parents to stress achievement, self-reliance, and self-denial, in order that the role of the child will properly prepare for the role of an adult belonging to the Elect. The Protestant values in child rearing seem to be that very cluster which Winterbottom and others have found to be associated with high achievement motivation—in the United States today. If child rearing worked in the past, as it seems to work in the present, the Protestant family should have produced sons with high achievement motivation. And this motivation may have found its expression in entrepreneurial enterprise and led to the rapid economic growth of England, Germany, Switzerland, and the Netherlands. This growth greatly exceeded that of Catholic countries like Spain, France, and Italy in the same period. Figure 9-3 diagrams the hypothesis.

Perhaps the law that worked once in the sixteenth and seventeenth

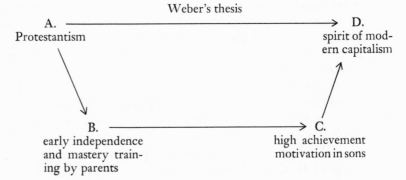

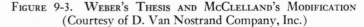

FIGURE 9-3. WEBER'S THESIS AND McCLELLAND'S MODIFICATION
(Courtesy of D. Van Nostrand Company, Inc.)

centuries is working still and achievement motivation is, in the modern world, a prime determinant of the national rate of economic growth. Here is a thesis with the scope and relevance we would wish to see in social psychology. Social movements that matter are linked by a social psychological mechanism. But it is a thesis difficult to test. It seems to call for science-fiction research, that is, research too complex ever to be performed.

PROTESTANTISM AND LEVEL OF ECONOMIC DEVELOPMENT

Is there, first of all, a link between Protestantism and economic development in the modern world? The argument over Weber's thesis by historians and sociologists has featured the selective citation of confirming or disconfirming instances: on the one side the impressive economic development of Protestant England, Germany, and Scandinavia and, on the other side, the accomplishments of Catholic Belgium, the rapid advances today in Catholic Italy, and the past ascendance in commerce of Catholic Venice. McClelland's approach is more systematic. He compared the levels of development in 1950 of all countries in the temperate zones. It was not easy to find a sound index of development; McClelland settled on kilowatt-hours of electricity consumed per capita. There was a striking difference favoring Protestant countries. The difference is not easy to interpret. For one thing there are great differences of natural resources, especially water power, which favor the Protestant countries. Making sensible corrections

TABLE 9-2. AVERAGE PER CAPITA CONSUMPTION OF ELECTRIC POWER, FOR PROTESTANT AND CATHOLIC COUNTRIES OUTSIDE THE TROPICS OF CANCER AND CAPRICORN (Courtesy of D. Van Nostrand Company, Inc.)

Countries	Consumption of electricity kwh/cap 1950	Countries	Consumption of electricity kwh/cap 1950
Protestant		*Catholic*	
Norway	5,310	Belgium	986
Canada	4,120	Austria	900
Sweden	2,580	France	790
United States of America	2,560	Czechoslovakia	730
Switzerland	2,230	Italy	535
New Zealand	1,600	Chile	484
Australia	1,160	Poland	375
United Kingdom	1,115	Hungary	304
Finland	1,000	Ireland	300
Union of South Africa	890	Argentina	255
Holland	725	Spain	225
Denmark	500	Uruguay	165
		Portugal	110
Average	1,983	*Average*	474

where this could be done, McClelland was left with a reduced but still significant difference between Protestant and Catholic nations.

MOTIVATION AND ECONOMIC GROWTH IN THE MODERN WORLD

The novel part of McClelland's thesis is the part that is difficult to test: the Achievement Motive should be correlated with the national rate of economic growth. With preliterate societies, folktales could be scored to get an estimate of the general level of motivation in the total cultures, but in the modern world the oral tradition has died and there are no genuine folktales. The highly imaginative solution was to score the stories in standardized children's readers. Margaret Mead has suggested that these stories are primary means by which a culture gets across its values to new members. When the Japanese conquered the Philippines they saw fit to delete from the local readers references to friendship with the United States on the probably sound presumption that such readers shape children's minds. Stories for children are usually short and simple and since they are fictional they are a form of phantasy. Indeed, many of them are ultimately derived from folktales. McClelland set out to get two stories from each nation in his sample, stories from readers for the second to fourth grades, which means stories intended for children in the age range from eight to ten years.

Because the thesis was adventurous it would take strong and unimpeachable evidence to win serious consideration. A "slight" study, using a small and convenient sample of nations, would have been ineffective. So McClelland started out by trying to include all the nations in the world outside of the Tropics. Those in the Tropics were excluded from the start because their development is low and the necessary data almost certainly could not have been obtained. Inevitably some of the remaining countries dropped from the sample because the necessary storybooks either do not exist or could not be obtained. There remained twenty-three countries in the sample for the years 1920–29 and forty countries for the years from 1946 into the 1950's.

Stories were picked so as to fall in length between the limits of fifty and eight hundred words. Literal translations were made and typed in a standard form. So that the country of origin could not be guessed by the person scoring for Achievement Motive girl's names were replaced by Mary, Jane, Judy, and the like; boy's names by Peter, Bob, and the like; towns were referred to as Big Town or Little Town. All the stories were assigned code numbers and shuffled so that those of one nation did not appear together and they were scored by two judges who had established high scoring reliability.

The scores on the stories manifested one extremely important property. Since there were twenty-one for each nation it was possible to divide them into sets of ten and eleven and correlate across nations the Achievement Motive score on one set with the score on the other set. If the amount of achievement imagery in a story were purely a function of the personality of its author, and in no sense a reflection of the national atmosphere, one would expect the two sets of scores for a single nation to be unrelated. In fact these correlations were impressively large; for the stories collected in the 1920's the correlation was .671 and for the later set it was .594. This fact argues strongly that the amount of achievement content in these stories at a given time is a national characteristic.

The basic research plan was to compare national levels of achievement motivation with national rates of economic growth. The earliest period from which stories were collected was the decade 1920–29 and these will be referred to as the 1925 sample. The second sample centered on 1950 and will be referred to as the 1950 sample. There were twenty-three countries that appeared in both samples and for these twenty-three it was possible to obtain two estimates of the level of achievement motivation with an interval of twenty-five years between the estimates. If a high level of achievement motivation is an important determinant of economic growth then the national level in 1925 ought to be related to the amount of economic growth between 1925 and 1950. The stories scored were written for children eight to ten years old and so the boys who read them in the 1920's would have had a chance to become enterprising entrepreneurs in the 1930's and 1940's and by 1950 their countries should have been showing the effects of their enterprise. Levels of motivation for 1950 ought not be related to economic development between 1925 and 1950 since motivation that succeeds development cannot be the cause of the development.

The measurement of economic growth across countries with different currencies is a difficult problem. McClelland did a lot of reading in economics and listened to a lot of advice before settling on the two indices which seemed to him to be the best. One of these indices makes use of an "international unit" (IU) defined by Colin Clark (1957) in such a way as to have the same meaning in various countries. "One IU of real income was taken as the quantity of goods exchangeable in the U.S.A. for one dollar over the average of the decade 1925–1934" (Clark, 1957, p. 18). Clark then determined how much it would cost in terms of local currency in other countries to purchase the same goods and services as one dollar would have purchased in the United States during the reference years and he expressed the income per capita in the country in terms of the resulting standard international unit.

Some serious criticisms of Clark's procedure have been made. It assumes, for instance, that people in different countries want more or less the same things in the same degree and this is not a fully warranted assumption. In addition, the estimates Clark has had to make of the value of certain items in particular countries at particular times have often seemed to be based on insufficient information. However, no economist has provided any better national income data which are anywhere near as complete in their coverage of countries and time periods. One independent method of estimating incomes for some of the countries involved (Watkins and Hagen, 1956) yields figures that correlate .93 with those arrived at by Clark. For these reasons one of the estimates of national income in 1925 and 1950 used by McClelland was that provided by Clark's international units.

Economic development in the modern world is chiefly a matter of the production, service, and use of modern machinery. Electricity is the form into which most of the energy that runs our machinery is converted. Consequently it seems reasonable to take the amount of electricity produced in a country as a kind of sample, a representative index, of the level of total economic activity. Electrical output has the practical advantage of being measured in the same unit everywhere—the kilowatt-hour. Consequently production in various countries is directly comparable without any complex transformations of the data. Since the figures on electrical output were available for the countries and periods with which he was concerned McClelland settled on this as his second index of economic development.

We now have estimates of economic development for two different dates and we want to know how fast each country has been growing between the earlier date and the later date. It would seem as though their absolute increases from 1925 to 1950 would provide the answer, but in fact they do not. The problem is that economic development regularly accelerates once a country reaches a certain absolute level. If the earlier level is fairly high then it is always to be expected that the absolute increase will be larger than if the earlier level is low. In order to estimate how well each country has been doing we need to find a way of describing its growth relative to the growth that is to be expected given its starting point. Has a country developed more or less rapidly than countries ordinarily do when they start from its particular baseline?

The problem is analogous to that of the psychologist who wants to know whether a student is doing better or less well than he should in his schoolwork given his particular level of intelligence. If the student has a very high intelligence and is doing average work he is "under-achieving" but the same level of schoolwork from a student of low intelligence would be "over-achievement." With the economic data McClelland decided to evaluate increases or gains in terms of the regression line that best fit the over-all relationship between initial level and gain. The regression equation predicts how much a country starting from a particular initial level could be expected to gain on the average. If it gains more than is to be expected for one of its initial level it is an "over-achiever" and if it gains less an

TABLE 9-3. ESTIMATES OF NATIONAL ECONOMIC DEVELOPMENT BETWEEN 1925 AND 1950 COMPARED WITH ACHIEVEMENT MOTIVE LEVEL IN CHILDREN'S READERS IN 1925 AND 1950 (Courtesy of D. Van Nostrand Company, Inc.)

Country	Achievement Motive Level 1925	1950	National income in International Units per capita; gain or loss over expected values in SD units	Electricity produced in kilowatt-hours per capita; gain or loss over expected values in SD units	Average gain or loss in SD units
Sweden	2.19	1.62	+2.35	+3.17	+2.76
U.S.A.	1.90	2.24	+1.28	+1.86	+1.57
New Zealand	1.48	2.05	+.63	+1.86	+1.25
Canada	2.67	2.29	−.04	+1.73	+.85
Great Britain	2.10	1.67	−1.71	+1.65	−.02
Australia	2.81	2.38	+.61	+1.13	+.87
Finland	1.24	1.52	+1.10	+.74	+.92
Union of S. Africa	1.05	2.33	+.70	+.69	+.70
Ireland	3.19	2.29	+.14	+.33	+.24
Denmark	2.00	1.05	−1.23	+.14	−.55
Poland		.86	−.44	+.03	−.21
Norway	1.33	1.71	+.44	−.03	+.21
Netherlands	.29	1.48	−.78	−.10	−.44
Austria	1.57	1.86	−1.02	−.12	−.57
Hungary	1.29	1.81	−.47	−.26	−.37
Chile	1.29	1.19	+.27	−.43	−.08
Japan		1.29	−.52	−.44	−.48
Portugal		2.10	−.19	−.52	−.36
Greece	.38	2.29	−1.28	−.52	−.90
Bulgaria		2.24	−.47	−.52	−.04
France	.81	2.38	−.92	−.55	−.74
Argentina	1.86	3.38	−.50	−.61	−.16
Italy		1.33	−.45	−.62	−.54
Uruguay	1.48	1.86		−.62	
Spain	.81	2.33	−1.93	−.63	−1.28
Belgium	1.00	.43	+1.57	−.75	+.41
Germany	1.38	2.14	−.51	−.79	−.65
Mexico		1.57		−.82	
Switzerland		1.20	+1.29	−1.26	+.02
Russia	.95	2.10	+.39		

"under-achiever." Both indices of development, Clark's international units per capita and the kilowatt-hours per capita, were treated as gains or losses over expected values. They appear in this form in Table 9-3.

At last McClelland had the complete data: Achievement Motive Scores for 1925 and 1950 and economic gains expressed in international units and in *kwh* per capita. He also estimated economic growth by combining the two indices, simply averaging them together since there seemed to be no reason to weight one more than the other. The correlations between national motivational level in 1925 and each of the three indices of economic performance are positive as predicted. They appear in Table 9-4. In the cases of the *kwh* per capita index and the combined index the correlations are statistically significant. The proposition that achievement motivation is a determinant of economic advancement is supported by these positive relationships. It is further strengthened by the absence of any significant relationship between economic gains and the level of motivation in 1950— a date subsequent to the gains. The 1950 levels did prove to be positively and significantly related to rates of economic gain in the period 1952–58. The generation reading the stories in 1950 could scarcely have become entrepreneurs by 1952–58 but of course the 1950 stories or stories comparably loaded with achievement imagery may have been used for some years prior to 1950.

TABLE 9-4. CORRELATIONS OF READER ACHIEVEMENT MOTIVE SCORES WITH DEVIATIONS FROM EXPECTED ECONOMIC GAINS (Courtesy of D. Van Nostrand Company, Inc.)

Achievement Motive level by year	IU/cap 1925–1950 $N = 22$	Kwh/cap 1929–1950 $N = 22$	Both combined $N = 21$
1925	.25	.53, p < .01 pd	.46, p < .02 pd
1950	−.10	.03	−.08

pd = predicted direction.

The measurement problems in this research were truly formidable. Some of them we have not even discussed; for example, the need to take some account of the amount of war damage suffered by various countries. McClelland has done what could be done to meet every objection, has analyzed his data in every reasonable way. The striking fact is that through all the corrections and re-analyses the thread of significant relationship remains: the level of achievement motivation is predictive of a subsequent increase in the rate of economic growth.

MOTIVATION AND ECONOMIC GROWTH IN EARLIER TIMES

With great ingenuity the thesis has been tested for other times and various places. Spain reached a peak of economic development in the sixteenth century and the literature of Spain (not children's readers but the great works like *Don Quixote*) shows a greater concentration of achievement imagery in the two centuries preceding this peak than it does afterwards. Samples of English literature were scored in half-century periods from 1400 through the beginning of the Industrial Revolution around

1830. The level of achievement motivation describes a curve that is strikingly similar to the curve described by economic development except that the motivation is generally thirty to fifty years ahead. A similar relationship was found for the United States from 1800 to 1950 with textbooks scored for the Motive and as an economic index the number of patents granted per one million population. In these data for the United States the motivation is not so consistently in advance of economic development.

Two of McClelland's tests are so ingenious that I want to give you a few details. For Ancient Greece from B.C. 900 to 100, levels of achievement motivation could be estimated from literature, but the assessment of economic development for a society that did not leave us any statistics is a difficult matter. Greece in that period traded chiefly wine and olive oil and both of these were transported in large earthenware jars. Heichelheim (1938), a student of Ancient Greece, has listed all the places in the Mediterranean world where these jars have been found. The jars have also been dated by the centuries in which they were produced. From the locations of Grecian jars for a given period it was possible to make a very crude estimate of the total area with which the Greeks were then trading. The extent of the trading area may reasonably be interpreted as an indication of the level of economic development. It turns out that a rise of motivation preceded the period of maximum trade.

Ancient Greece is sufficiently difficult for a psychologist to study but Pre-Incan Peru from about B.C. 800 to A.D. 700 is still more so. The problem in both cases is to project a modern measure backward in time. If the measure requires the collection of extraordinary data, for example, tachistoscopic recognitions or psychogalvanic reflexes, prior ages are inaccessible to it. With the Achievement Motive, however, the essential measure is a system for scoring verbal materials. It is not necessary that the materials be collected in the standard way; the scoring can be applied to any literary fragments. For Ancient Greece there are such fragments but for Pre-Incan Peru, though the dates are not more remote, there are no such fragments. Can anything psychological be learned from the material remains of a civilization?

There is a basis for making a quantitative estimate of cultural growth in Willey's (1953) work describing the amount of public building done at various periods in Peru. Since there are no written records from this civilization the system of verbal content analysis cannot be used. However, Aronson's method (1958) of scoring graphic patterns or doodles can, with some assumptions and qualifications, be applied to decorative ceramic designs. And such designs appear on Peruvian pottery. In particular there is a sequence of funerary urns, dated by carbon-14 determinations; these were scored for diagonals, S-shapes, and multiple waves. Over the total historical span there appear to have been two periods of high achievement motivation and two periods of low motivation. The high periods were followed by marked cultural growth as indexed by the volume of public buildings and the low periods by the conquest of Peru by outside civilizations. Believe it or not.

Complication of the Key Hypothesis

The diagram of McClelland's key hypothesis presented as Figure 9-3 is too simple for the data we have already described and much too simple to encompass all of the researches described in his book *The Achieving Society* (1961). There are several kinds of revision necessary. In making them we shall deprive the hypothesis of its former pleasant simplicity.

ALTERNATIVE INDICES OF THE VARIABLES

The major variables of the hypothesis are concepts, not measures or indices. For each variable, numerous indices are possible. Achievement motivation can be assessed by scoring the content of verbal materials or by Aronson's scoring of graphic patterns. Since the letter C is the general designation in the hypothesis for the motivation variable, we ought really to represent this variable as C_1 (for the verbal index) and also as C_2 (for Aronson's graphic index). If C_1 and C_2 are both appropriately labelled C; that is to say if they are indeed two indices of a single variable, then scores on the two ought to be correlated. In Aronson's study deriving the graphic measure such a correlation was obtained. It was the correlation, in fact, that justified Aronson in thinking of the new method as an alternative measure of McClelland's Achievement Motive. The list of indices is not closed. Elizabeth French (1958) has created another and still others may be created.

The variable labeled D, which is roughly economic development or capitalistic enterprise has, in various studies, been operationalized as national income, output of electricity, area of trade, volume of coal imports, shipping tonnage, amount of public building done, and number of patents issued per one million population. These are presumably so many D's with subscripts and again the list is not closed. If they are all truly indices of the same variable they should be correlated. Very few correlations have been calculated for the reason that in many studies not more than one index could be obtained. In the major investigation that concerned achievement motivation in children's readers several indices of economic growth were taken and did prove to be correlated.

The two remaining variables, A and B, are like C and D in having multiple indices. In Figure 9-4, as in Figure 9-3, each variable in McClelland's hypothesis is represented by a letter; but Figure 9-4 also lists, as Figure 9-3 did not, several indices of each variable, the indices being designated by letters with subscripts. The two-headed arrows of Figure 9-4 represent the intercorrelations that should exist among the indices of a variable. If the work on McClelland's hypothesis had proceeded according to an orderly ideal the first studies would have firmly established the relations among all these indices. However, the work has been distributed across many independent investigators and across many years and its progress has not been very orderly. Some of the correlations implied by Figure 9-4 have never been taken but the indices have nevertheless been interpreted as equivalent measures of the variable. Other correlations have been taken once and then, because the correlation was significantly greater than zero that once, the indices have thereafter been considered essentially equivalent. As a result it has become difficult to keep track of the evidence on some points.

When Aronson (1958) first used the graphic measure of the Achievement Motive with American college students it proved to be correlated with the verbal measure of the motive. However, when McClelland (1961) obtained both verbal and graphic scores for boys from Brazil, Germany, Japan, and India none of the correlations was significantly different from zero. In the meantime, however, the graphic scores had been taken as an index of the Achievement Motive in studies relating motivation to other variables in McClelland's hypothesis. How now shall we evaluate these latter studies? What, for instance, shall we make of the findings for Pre-Incan Peru where designs on funerary urns were scored for achievement motivation?

POSSIBLE RELATIONS AMONG THE VARIABLES IN THE KEY HYPOTHESIS

The studies suggested by the two-headed arrows of Figure 9-4, studies correlating indices, are incidental to the key hypothesis, they do not test the hypothesis. The key hypothesis is that a rise in A causes a rise in B which causes a rise in C which causes a rise in D. The evidence that most strongly substantiates these claims is evidence showing a relation between two contiguous variables as well as the correct time order; such evidence as the finding that a high level of achievement motivation in 1925 was *followed by* a rapid rate of economic growth between 1925 and 1950. It is often not possible to get data in which time order is preserved. In America today Protestantism and independence training and achievement motivation all exist contemporaneously. One cannot easily separate these out in time so as to see if the rise of Protestantism is followed by changes of child training and these changes by new levels of achievement motiva-

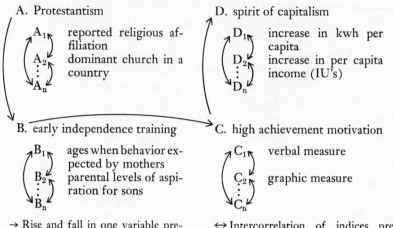

FIGURE 9-4.   MCCLELLAND'S HYPOTHESIS WITH THE VARIABLES FRACTIONATED
INTO INDICES

tion. Where the order in time cannot be known a weaker sort of confirmation can be sought by correlating contemporaneous values of the variables. If it turned out that Protestants in America expected earlier independence from their children than did Catholics, this would support the thesis. The notion that Protestantism causes a certain type of child training requires that a correlation exist and so is supported by such a correlation even though the notion of causality involves more than correlation.

The principal kind of study suggested by the key hypothesis is then a study of the correlation between pairs of contiguous variables: A with B, B with C, etc. However, now that we have multiple indices of each variable (not just A but A_1, A_2 ... A_n) the possible studies relating contiguous variables are very numerous. It is no longer simply a matter of correlating C_1 with D_1. One could correlate C_1 with D_1, C_1 with D_2, C_2 with D_2, and so on to realize all possible pairs of indices across the two variables. This means in the present instance that one might correlate verbal Achievement Motive scores with *kwh*'s per capita and also correlate graphic Achievement Motive scores with *kwh*'s per capita and also verbal scores with national incomes in IU's, etc. The resultant possible studies are suggested by Figure 9-5. Some of them have been done and some not.

The possibilities are still more numerous than Figure 9-5 suggests. Not only each pair of contiguous variables should be correlated, but also any pair whether contiguous or not. The hypothesis implies that Protestants (A) would have higher achievement motivation (C) than Catholics as well

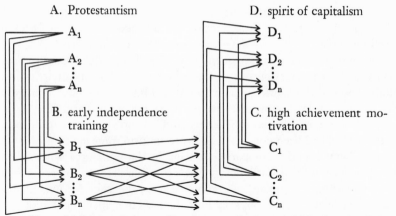

A. Protestantism
D. spirit of capitalism

B. early independence training
C. high achievement motivation

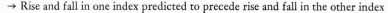

→ Rise and fall in one index predicted to precede rise and fall in the other index

FIGURE 9-5. McCLELLAND'S HYPOTHESIS VIEWED AS A SET OF PREDICTED RELATIONS BETWEEN INDICES OF THE MAJOR VARIABLES

as earlier independence training (B). Countries showing rapid rates of economic growth (D) ought to practice earlier independence training (B) than countries showing slower rates as well as higher achievement motivation (C). In short, each major variable might be correlated with each other major variable. Since in practice the variables must become indices, it is really each index of one variable with each index of another variable. The possibilities are numerous indeed and we have not added to Figure 9-5 the lines that would be required to represent them because the result would be a tartan too tangled for any taste. Most of the implied studies have not been done. McClelland's measure has been used in very many studies but because the studies have accumulated unsystematically the matrix of possibilities they suggest is far from filled.

REFORMULATION OF A VARIABLE IN THE KEY HYPOTHESIS

The studies that have been done linking the major variables are not uniformly confirmatory. Disconfirming results in a science do not always lead to a rejection of a hypothesis; they can motivate a reformulation. Consider a set of results involving the A variable—Protestantism. Protestantism is a movement in the history of Christianity and so plays no part in Pre-Incan Peru or Ancient Greece. But there were rises of achievement motivation followed by economic growth in both of these civilizations. Protestantism also was not the cause of the great age of Spanish conquest. These studies might be said to relate the absence of Protestantism (A) to levels of achievement motivation (C) and economic development (D). They clearly show that Protestantism is not necessary for the latter two developments. Perhaps, however, Protestantism is a sufficient cause of the various effects linked with it in the key hypothesis. McClelland's contrast between the electrical output of Catholic and Protestant countries in the modern world did work out as predicted. This was a study linking variables A and D; let us now see how A works out with B and C.

In the state of Chiapas in Mexico, McClelland's research team located a village that had been converted to Protestantism some eight or nine years earlier. They found a comparison village in the same area where the religion was a modified Catholicism. Such possible determinants of achievement motivation as climate and ethnicity were the same for inhabitants of the two villages. Schoolboys in both had their achievement motivation assessed by the graphic method and the boys in the Protestant villages made higher scores (McClelland, 1961). However, there were numerous difficulties about comparing the data in addition to the doubt we must have about the validity of the graphic measure.

Levels of achievement motivation were obtained, you remember, from children's readers in 1925 and in the 1950's for a large number of modern nations. The Motive was related to the rate of economic growth but we did not report whether the Motive scores were higher for Protestant than for Catholic countries. They were very slightly, but not significantly, so (McClelland, 1961). We have reason, then, to doubt the link between A and C of the key hypothesis.

Veroff, et al. (1960) have done a valuable study with a representative sample of the population of the United States. They asked the questions about age of independence training that were used by Winterbottom and they also obtained Achievement Motive scores using the verbal measure. The outcome is very damaging for the simple notion that Protestantism leads to early independence training and high motivation. Protestants set very slightly earlier ages for independence but the difference is not significant. The two groups did not differ significantly on Motive scores and, furthermore, the slight difference obtained favored the Catholics. Jews, on the other hand, had significantly higher scores than either Catholics or Protestants.

It is clear from the data cited and much besides that Protestantism in the simple sense of nominal affiliation with a Protestant church is neither a necessary nor a sufficient cause of the factors that follow it in the key hypothesis. It may have been such a cause when it was still a movement of social protest and that is the period Weber had in mind. But in the modern world no simple relations exist between church affiliation and child rearing or achievement motivation. It is undoubtedly necessary to make finer distinctions among communicants in terms of their socio-economic level, their ethnicity (Italian Catholics and Irish Catholics are not the same), and the intensity of their religious fervor.

Surveying all of his material relating religions to achievement motivation, McClelland finds that such broad religious categories as Protestant, Catholic, Jew, Buddhist, and Hindu will not serve to order the data. He suggests that we look for values that may be represented in one or another sect of almost any religion. It seems to him that a religious outlook which might be called "individualistic mysticism" is the critical element. Religions that make compliance with formal rituals the essence of a good life, religions that make the priest a necessary intermediary between man and God, are not likely to produce high achievement motivation. More likely to do so are religions that stress the importance of direct mystic communion between each individual and God, religions that make all man's deeds relevant to salvation and not certain ritual acts alone. What this means in terms of the schematic diagrams of Figures 9-3, 9-4, and 9-5 is that the A variable must be reformulated, under the impact of negative results, into a more psychological term. It is a value rather than a simple church affiliation.

FRACTIONATION OF A VARIABLE IN THE KEY HYPOTHESIS

There are other changes which need to be made in the conceptualization of the major variables. The final variable in the sequence, variable D, which is labelled as the "spirit of capitalism" needs to be subdivided into some three variables: D, E, and F. Some fractionation of D has actually been necessary from the start—even for Weber's thesis.

Protestantism was supposed to produce most directly the spirit of modern capitalism which is presumably manifest in a certain kind of human character and this kind of character, in time, was supposed to produce economic growth. To be sure one could simply think of the various indices of growth—rise of national income, electrical output, coal imports, etc.—as evidence that the capitalist spirit exists. But even Weber went beyond such economic statistics to write of the tendency of the Protestants to work harder and for longer hours, to save for remote goals, to invest their savings, and the like. These observations are a crude sort of evidence for the development of a character type which was understood to intervene between Protestantism and economic growth.

McClelland seems to me to have further differentiated variable D; for him there really are three variables at the end of the sequence. McClelland arrives at these variables because he makes an essential distinction that economists have missed—it is a distinction we have stressed in Chapter 4—the distinction between role and personality. The term *entrepreneur* is used in economics to designate a kind of character or personality and also to designate a kind of occupational role. The entrepreneurial role is roughly that of the business manager, one who makes decisions and bears both responsibility and risk. The entrepreneurial character is, roughly, a person who likes to be responsible for his own work, who likes work with tangible outcomes that clearly define success and failure, who likes to plan ahead and to take moderate calculated risks such that good judgment can pay off. In McClelland's theory high achievement motivation will belong to this cluster of entrepreneurial character traits. Such characters will be produced by training for independence and accomplishment. They will be drawn to entrepreneurial occupations which are the roles that provide the best fit for their personalities. When entrepreneurial roles are filled by people of this type a society will have a rapid rate of economic growth.

How shall we diagram this view? We have a D which is the entrepreneurial character and an E which is the entrepreneurial role and an F which is an increase in the rate of economic growth. If we thoughtlessly assume that the relations among these new variables are the same as the familiar cause-effect relations of the major hypothesis we will produce Figure 9-6a. That figure suggests that child training produces high achievement motivation which produces the entrepreneurial character which produces the entrepreneurial occupation which produces economic growth. This is absurd.

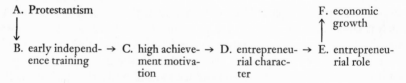

a. All variables in a simple cause and effect chain

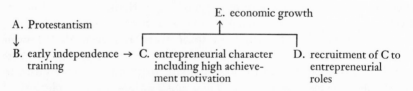

b. One variable a contingency outside the chain of cause and effect

FIGURE 9-6.   McCLELLAND'S HYPOTHESIS WITH THE FINAL VARIABLE
DIFFERENTIATED

High achievement motivation does not produce the entrepreneurial character; it is a part of it. Variable C then ought to be the entrepreneurial character which includes such traits, in addition to achievement motivation, as a tendency to plan ahead, a preference for moderate risks and a liking for personal responsibility. I take it to be McClelland's view that certain child-training practices tend to create this character type. Therefore we do not need a C to go with D but rather a redefinition of C from high achievement motivation to the entrepreneurial character.

The entrepreneurial role seems to me to require a change of quite a different type. It is not actually an independent link in a causal chain. It works like this: if the entrepreneurial characters produced by child training are recruited to entrepreneurial roles then the result will be economic growth. Variable B produces variable C and if C is accompanied by D, which may be defined as recruitment of the right character-type to managerial occupations, then the result will be E. In other words there are two conditions which are immediate prerequisites of E and these two conditions are not themselves causally related. In fact, one of these conditions, variable D, is outside the causal chain of McClelland's hypothesis. The hypothesis does not say what it is that causes entrepreneurial characters to be recruited to entrepreneurial roles. The result is the diagram of Figure 9-6b.

These new modifications in the theory suggest new kinds of study; some of them have been done and the results are interesting. One sort of study relates achievement motivation to other entrepreneurial characteristics. For example, McClelland (1958) engaged five- and six-year-old children in a game of ring toss leaving each child free to set his own distance from the peg. Standing very close gives a very high probability of success, but one could suppose that success under these circumstances would not produce a very strong feeling of accomplishment. If one were to stand very far away then a success would be very improbable and if it occurred would seem more like "luck" than skill. Children with high achievement motivation mostly chose to stand at a moderate distance where success was reasonably probable and chiefly dependent on skill. They behaved, if you will, like an enterprising business man, not like a reckless gambler and not like a Timid Soul.

Another study that I particularly like was done by Mischel (1961) in Trinidad with lower-class Negro children. The experimenter was introduced as an American from a college in the United States who was gathering information on the children in the various schools of the island. After a short session with a questionnaire the experimenter expressed his wish to thank them. He said he would like to give each of them a candy bar of a type he showed them but that he did not have enough of these with him. He gave each of them the choice of receiving immediately a smaller candy bar or waiting a week for him to return with one of the larger bars. In the abstract it was a choice between having a small reward at once or a larger reward after a time. Choices of this kind test a person's will power or ego strength. A young man confronts such a test when he must decide whether to go to work at once for a fairly good salary or to do without the salary and get more education to the end of ultimately earning a larger income. A test of this kind confronts the moderately successful businessman who must decide whether to settle back and enjoy the profits he is currently earning or to reinvest the profits and drive hard to expand his business. In Trinidad it was the children with higher achievement motivation who elected to wait for the bigger candy bar.

There is another kind of study suggested by the new formulation. In a country that has enjoyed rapid economic growth, such as the United States, do we find that men in entrepreneurial occupations have higher Achievement Motive scores than do men in other kinds of occupation? The business schools at both Harvard and M.I.T. have educational programs for men in middle management positions. The men in these programs are sent by their companies because they are good candidates for advancement. McClelland (1961) did obtain significantly higher scores from such men than from a comparison group of male college graduates. Another study (McClelland, 1961) compared the Achievement Motive scores of managers in four countries (the United States, Italy, Turkey, and Poland) with comparison groups of professional men. The scores of the managers were higher in all countries except Turkey.

STATE OF THE EVIDENCE ON THE KEY HYPOTHESIS

Not all of the evidence on these last links in the chain is as good as the results I have cited. The thesis as a whole is vastly more complex than it was back in Figure 9-3 when we had four simple variables, and the data as a whole now leave many things doubtful. Protestantism *per se* does not appear to be consistently related to either achievement motivation or independence training. It is not certain just what dimensions of child rearing are related to achievement motivation; early independence training has not been related in all studies. Perhaps the strongest link, on present evidence, is the link between high motivation and economic growth. Happily this is also the most original aspect of the thesis and it opens an important frontier in relating psychology to economics.

The complication of the original thesis is, in part, a sign of its increasing adequacy. The shift from Protestantism to certain individualistic religious values is bound to be a nearer approach to truth. The addition of variable D, not itself a part of the causal chain but an essential contingency for the step from C to E probably needs to be matched by contingencies at other points. It may be, for example, that the sequence as a whole will not lead to economic growth unless the country in question has a moderate climate and minimal natural resources. Simple cause and effect chains are not likely to be adequate to problems of this scope.

In the work relating the Achievement Motive to economic growth it seems to me that empiricism and research inventiveness have been too exuberant; empirical consolidation and theoretical integration have lagged. There are too many indices of uncertain quality for most of the variables. The major measure, the verbal measure of the motive, does not alone seem to have sufficient validity to carry the load it is carrying. Nevertheless, this work has shown that a motivational variable plays a role in economic history. If everyone has always known that this must be true, we have not always known that the variable could be measured and its role demonstrated.

Achievement Motivation and Job Performance

Work done with something as practically important as achievement motivation ought to have practical consequences but the work has not yet had such consequences. Since a measure has been created for something that is relevant to job performance anyone's first thought would be to use it as a selection device. In filling a job, almost any job, an employer hopes to find someone with "drive." Why not screen applicants with McClelland's measure? Economic programs designed to aid underdeveloped countries often seem to fail because the men in charge of local operations do not have the motivation to make them succeed. There appears to be a scarcity in some lands of characterological resources. Again, why not use the measure to guarantee that the few men who are right for the critical jobs are in those jobs? McClelland seems never to have suggested that his measure be used for this purpose, nor has he implied that it could ultimately be used in this way, though most of us would feel tempted to do so because of the wish to establish the practical relevance of psychology.

A principal impediment to use of the measure as a selection device is the strong probability that applicants would be able to obtain high scores at will. In one study (McClelland, et al., 1953), subjects were told that the test concerned achievement motivation, understood in the popular sense, and were instructed to try to fake high scores. The results indicate that they were able to obtain moderately high but not extremely high scores; the general definition of achievement imagery is close to common sense but the detailed scoring system can hardly be anticipated by a naïve subject. However, if the measure were seriously used in selecting for desirable positions the detailed system would quickly be learned. Beyond the fact that the scoring could not be kept "secure" the measure is simply not a powerful enough predictor of performance to justify its use in selection. As we have seen there are some statistically significant relations with job performance but these are not large enough to have practical significance.

The work with achievement motivation has discovered some possible antecedents of high motivation: individualistic religious values and child training that stresses independence and accomplishment. Since antecedents are known why do we not turn social engineer and create more persons with high motivation? But how? Religious values and child training practices are not easily changed. Even if parents were induced to alter deliberately certain specific expectations for their children we can guess that the expectations altered would turn out not to be the essence of the matter and something more fundamental in the home atmosphere would probably have been preserved and would continue to turn out boys with low motivation. In addition, of course, the antecedents identified are not certainly and generally related to the Motive; the evidence is simply not strong enough to induce anyone to attempt drastic social action.

McClelland has, quite recently, been trying to increase achievement motivation in individual subjects by a method that, at first, sounds terribly wrong-headed but, on reflection, seems more promising. He has been teaching subjects the scoring system and training them to write stories that would earn high scores in the expectation that such training would increase the strength of the motive. Surely this will not work. Subjects would easily learn to write such stories but it is difficult to believe that motives are so easily changed. The imagery in the stories when it is obtained in the usual way reflects the motive but to expect to increase the motive by training someone deliberately to put such imagery in his stories seems rather like trying to give someone a fever by teaching him to put the thermometer in hot water.

Of course the thing that could be most easily taught would be the writing of a single high motive story on some particular theme. It would take more time and be more difficult to learn how to write an indefinite number of such stories on a variety of themes. If a subject learns to attend to the achievement dimension in many kinds of situations for the purpose of writing stories will he perhaps begin to do this when he is not writing stories? Will he perhaps begin to see his daily life in achievement terms and to trace his own history in achievement terms? One might be training someone to write stories ultimately train a habit of thought and it is not absurd to suggest that such a habit of thought may be what the achievement motive is. In any case I feel some suspense about the outcome of this new work.

The work with the achievement motive done to date does not enable us either to create the motive or to select for it. Everything that might be done practically is in the realm of more effective utilization in a given situation of the motivation found there. The point of maximal leverage at present is social structure rather than psychology. In American industrial settings there are often circumstances which prevent the achievement motivation of workmen from being directed upon their work. There may be norms in the workgroup requiring a restriction of output so that the expectations of management do not become onerous for anyone. Violations of such norms can mean ostracism. Most men in the group probably detach work from motivation and do their achieving at home in the garden or in their basement workshop. Occasionally someone will buck the restriction norms. It is interesting to find, in reading interviews with such people, that their talk is often loaded with achievement imagery. Witness the following excerpt:

> I want to work with people who take pride in their work. . . . I believe in taking an interest in the job and getting it done right.
>
> I sound like a company man, but I believe people should do the job right and make the best of it. . . . That's the way my mother brought me up.
>
> The one thing I won't do is work slow. I just plain get tired working slow. I don't know what it is, but when I'm working fast, the day just goes by. I think I get more tired when I try to slow down.
>
> I try to build a good [product]. I always do the job the best way I know how. When I first went on the bench, they used to [do a particular operation] by hand. I straightened that out. I got an electric screw driver and fixture. Now they produce 200 more [products] a week. I arranged to build 100 [products] at a time instead of 25, the way they used to do it around here. Before I came there were three more men on the bench than now, and they never produced as much as I do [Zaleznik, Christensen, and Roethlisberger, 1958].

The direction of achievement motivation toward work objectives can sometimes be accomplished by radical changes in the work situation. Several years ago, men in M.I.T.'s Industrial Relations Section devised a plan for accomplishing such changes. Their plan, the Scanlon Plan, has been successful in some fifty companies. The Scanlon Plan is not a scheme of piecework payment and not a profit-sharing plan in the ordinary sense. Neither is it aimed at weakening the union but, on the contrary, the Scanlon Plan works best with a strong union that has intelligent leadership.

The general idea is to provide a formula whereby the work force shares in any savings that are produced by reducing the cost of labor. The work force does not share in profits unrelated to its own efforts; for example, the company gets the profits from an improved use of its assets. The first task in instituting the Scanlon Plan is to find a "normal" labor cost for the company involved; this will be a ratio for some standard period between total payroll and the sales value of the goods produced by that payroll. Once this ratio has been established then the workforce profits from any reduction in normal labor costs. The bonus is paid in the month it is earned so that a direct relation may be experienced between effort and reward. No matter where the saving was accomplished everyone in the force benefits from it and so a man who tries to achieve an improvement helps the entire group rather than himself at the expense of the group. The bonus is not a substitute for wage increases. These are negotiated quite independently of the bonus.

There is a great deal of psychological wisdom in the Scanlon Plan: 1) the direct link between achievement and reward; 2) the immediate payment of rewards; 3) the sharing of rewards by the entire group. Restriction-of-output norms tend to be given up under the plan. People may work harder and certainly work more steadily but the major increases in productivity are not brought about by a speed-up of the ordinary kind. The plan has a remarkable ability to release the knowledge and imagination of the work force. Suggestions for improving methods of production are invited and evaluated by production committees. At one company, the Lapointe Machine Tool Company, 513 suggestions were received in a 24-month period and 380 of these were accepted. The man who makes a useful suggestion is not a "company man" but a benefactor of his fellow workers since they all profit from his accomplishment.

There is more to the Scanlon Plan than I have indicated and it is not equally successful in every company, but in very many cases it has produced a remarkable psychological reorientation. The plan identifies the worker's private interest with the interests of the other workers and of the company as a whole. Workers at Lapointe, in the days before the plan, used to be rather glad to hear that the company was using red ink in its books. Since the plan was instituted they take the lead in figuring out ways to meet external competition. Formerly, a man who expressed his achievement motivation by working harder endangered his bonds of solidarity with his coworkers. Usually he would not do it, he would be unresponsive to various management incentives for the very sensible reason that the quite limited rewards management could offer were not very important compared with the friendship of his workmates. For the man in a managerial position the company can offer rewards of status and income that are great enough to compete successfully with the solidarity he can have with his peers if he does not outstrip them. But it has nothing comparable to offer the workingman. When occupational achievement is no longer antagonistic to solidarity but even becomes contributory to it the level of achievement goes up. There seems to be plenty of motivation in most Americans; the problem is to provide social arrangements which permit such motivation to be focused on occupational objectives.

For the economic development of countries McClelland has made some suggestions that again amount to social engineering rather than psychological engineering. The critical need as he saw it, in his book *The Achieving Society* (1961), was some scheme for guaranteeing that motivated men would be placed in the entrepreneurial roles. He did not suggest psychological selection but rather that the forces of social selection which ordinarily operate in a competitive American industry be also permitted to operate in overseas efforts at national development. It seemed to him that direct efforts of the United States Government and efforts of foreign governments stimulated by financial aid from the United States Government often did not insist on a continuing high-level performance. He believed that American businessmen, or businessmen in other economically advanced countries, were the ones most certain to insist on such standards. The free-enterprise system had, he thought, a built-in crude mechanism for eliminating inefficient producers. This led him to argue that the best way for a more developed country to help a less developed country would be for business firms in the more developed country to aid similar firms abroad. The U.S. Government could facilitate the process by subcontracting more of its aid plans to U.S. private business. The American private business firm could probably send better men abroad than could the U.S. Government directly and, in addition, the American company would be in a position to set manpower standards in the foreign company. Such a program would have to involve aid from American business, not ownership, since foreign ownership would have serious drawbacks for the foreign country.

As this chapter draws to an end, think back to the ideas that McClelland and his associates had when they invented their measure. It was to be a measure of generalized motivation for achievement. The scoring categories specified a concern with excellence but this excellence could be in any field—poetry, wrestling, inventing, or in dentistry. It is surprising, therefore, to find that the measure has turned out to be chiefly a measure of motivation for business or economic achievement. This gradual shift in emphasis has been an unanticipated outcome of the efforts made at validating the original measure.

Since there is no single clear criterion against which to validate a measure of achievement motivation we found that the validation process amounted to a demonstration that scores on the measure related to other kinds of behavior in such a way as to satisfy our intuitive notions of achievement motivation. In the end, however, something more than this has come of the very numerous studies relating Achievement Motive scores to other data. The scores are higher for managers than for other sorts of professional men; they are related to economic growth; they go with a taste for moderate risks, long range planning, and tasks that involve clear criteria of success and failure. The process of validation has turned into a process of reconceptualization. The measure now seems to be primarily concerned with motivation for economic achievement rather than with achievement motivation in general. It may have worked out this way because one of the original four TAT pictures shows two men standing over a machine. This is a picture that frequently elicits stories about inventors—Henry Ford, Thomas Edison. It may be that the picture has more stimulus value for men with economic or business goals than for men with other kinds of achievement goals. The standard pictures may be a little more effective for eliciting achievement imagery in the economic sphere than they are for eliciting such imagery in other spheres.

The technique of measurement developed for the Achievement Motive has now also been utilized for the Affiliation Motive and the Power Motive. The essential procedure has been the same in all three cases. Scores are obtained from a standardized reliable content analysis of TAT stories. Scoring categories were selected because they shifted in frequency from a situation in which one would judge the motive to be but little aroused to a situation in which one would judge the motive to be strongly aroused. The studies of the Affiliation Motive and of the Power Motive are not nearly so numerous as are those of the Achievement Motive but they are accumulating. At Wesleyan University, ten years ago, McClelland and his students noted that the most neglected topic in experimental psychology was the study of human motivation. They judged this neglect to be a consequence of the dearth of appropriate measures and to be reparable by the invention of such measures. They were right.

REFERENCES

Angelini, A. L. Un novo método para avaliar a motivação humana. Unpublished doctoral dissertation. Brazil: Universidade de São Paulo, 1955.

Aronson, E. The need for achievement as measured by graphic expression. In J. W. Atkinson (Ed.), *Motives in fantasy, action, and society*. Princeton: Van Nostrand, 1958.

Atkinson, J. W. Studies in projective measurement of achievement motivation. Univer. of Michigan. Abstract in Univer. Microfilms, Vol. X, No. 4; Publication No. 1945, 1950. Cited by D. C. McClelland, et al., *The achievement motive*. New York: Appleton-Century, 1953.

Atkinson, J. W. The achievement motive and recall of interrupted and completed tasks. In D. C. McClelland (Ed.), *Studies in motivation*. New York: Appleton-Century-Crofts, 1955.

Atkinson, J. W. (Ed.) *Motives in fantasy, action, and society*. Princeton: Van Nostrand, 1958.

Atkinson, J. W., & McClelland, D. C. The projective expression of needs. II. The effect of different intensities of the hunger drive on thematic apperception. *J. exp. Psychol.*, 1948, **38**, 405–410.

Birney, R. C. The reliability of the achievement motive. *J. abnorm. soc. Psychol.*, 1959, **58**, 266–267.

Burdick, H. A. The relationship of attraction, need achievement, and certainty to conformity under conditions of a simulated group atmosphere. Unpublished doctoral dissertation. Univer. of Michigan, 1955.

Child, I. L., Storm, T., & Veroff, J. Achievement themes in folk tales related to socialization practice. In J. W. Atkinson (Ed.), *Motives in fantasy, action, and society*. Princeton: Van Nostrand, 1958.

Clark, C. *The conditions of economic progress*. (3rd ed.) London: Macmillan, 1957.

Everett, J. L. (III). Motivation and job success. Unpublished master's thesis. Cambridge: School of Industrial Management, Mass. Inst. Technol., 1959.

Field, W. F. The effects of thematic apperception upon certain experimentally aroused needs. Unpublished doctoral dissertation. Univer. of Maryland, 1951.

French, Elizabeth G. Some characteristics of achievement motivation. *J. exp. Psychol.*, 1955, **50**, 232–236.

French, Elizabeth G. Motivation as a variable in work-partner selection. *J. abnorm. soc. Psychol.*, 1956, **53**, 96–99.

French, Elizabeth G. Development of a measure of complex motivation. In J. W. Atkinson (Ed.), *Motives in fantasy, action, and society*. Princeton: Van Nostrand, 1958.

Freud, S. The interpretation of dreams. (1900). In A. A. Brill (Ed. and transl.), *The basic writings of Sigmund Freud*. New York: Modern Library, 1938.

Friedman, G. A. A cross-cultural study of the relationship between independence training and *n* achievement as revealed by mythology. Unpublished honor's thesis, Harvard Univer., 1950.

Heichelheim, F. *Wirtschaftsgeschichte des altertums*. Leiden: A. W. Sijthoff, 1938.

Kagan, J., & Moss, H. A. Stability and validity of achievement fantasy. *J. abnorm. soc. Psychol.*, 1959, **58**, 357–364.

Knapp, R. H. *n* Achievement and aesthetic preference. In J. W. Atkinson, Ed., *Motives in fantasy, action, and society*. Princeton: Van Nostrand, 1958.

Knapp, R. H., & Garbutt, J. T. Time imagery and the achievement motive. *J. Pers.*, 1958, **26**, 426–434.

Lowell, E. L. The effect of need for achievement on learning and speed of performance. *J. Psychol.*, 1952, **33**, 31–40.

Lowell, E. L. A methodological study of projectively measured achievement motivation. Unpublished master's thesis Wesleyan Univer., 1950. Cited by D. C. McClelland, et al., *The achievement motive*. New York: Appleton-Century, 1953.

McClelland, D. C. (Ed.), *Studies in motivation*. New York: Appleton-Century-Crofts, 1955.

McClelland, D. C. Risk-taking in children with high and low need for achievement. In J. W. Atkinson (Ed.), *Motives in fantasy, action, and society*. Princeton: Van Nostrand, 1958.

McClelland, D. C. *The achieving society*. Princeton: Van Nostrand, 1961.

McClelland, D. C., Atkinson, J. W., Clark, R. A., & Lowell, E. L. *The achievement motive*. New York: Appleton-Century, 1953.

McClelland, D. C., & Friedman, G. A. A cross-cultural study of the relationship between child-training practices and achievement motivation appearing in folk tales. In G. E. Swanson, T. M. Newcomb, & E. L. Hartley (Eds.), *Readings in social psychology*. New York: Holt, 1952.

Mischel, W. Delay of gratification, need for achievement, and acquiescence in another culture. *J. abnorm. soc. Psychol.*, 1961, **62**, 543–552.

Murray, H. A. *Explorations in personality*. New York: Oxford Univer. Press, 1938.

Rosen, B. C. Race, ethnicity, and the achievement syndrome. *Amer. sociol. Rev.*, 1959, **24**, 47–60.

Rosen, B. C., & D'Andrade, R. G. The psychosocial origin of achievement motivation. *Sociometry*, 1959, **22**, 185–218.

Strodtbeck, F. L. Family interaction, values, and achievement. In D. C. McClelland, A. L. Baldwin, U. Bronfenbrenner, & F. L. Strodtbeck, *Talent and society*. Princeton: Van Nostrand, 1958.

Veroff, J. A projective measure of achievement motivation in adolescent males and females. Unpublished honors thesis. Wesleyan Univer., 1950.

Watkins, M. H., & Hagen, E. E. *Estimate of world income, 1953*. Cambridge: Center for International Studies, Mass. Inst. Technol., 1956.

Weber, M. *The Protestant ethic and the spirit of capitalism*. (1st ed., 1904) Transl. by T. Parsons. New York: Scribner, 1930.

Wendt, H. W. Motivation, effort, and performance. In D. C. McClelland (Ed.), *Studies in motivation*. New York: Appleton-Century, 1955.

Wilcox, Sue. A projective measure of the achievement motivation of college women. Unpublished honors thesis. Univer. of Michigan, 1951.

Willey, G. R. Prehistoric settlement patterns in the Viru valley, Peru. *Bureau of Amer. Ethnology Bulletin*, 155, Washington, D.C., 1953.

Winterbottom, Marian R. The relation of childhood training in independence to achievement motivation. Univer. of Michigan. Abstract on Univer. Microfilms, publication No. 5113. Cited by D. C. McClelland et al., *The achievement motive*. New York: Appleton-Century, 1953.

Zaleznik, A., Christensen, C. R., & Roethlisberger, F. J. *The motivation, productivity, and satisfaction of workers*. Boston: Harvard Univer., Division of Research, Graduate School of Business Administration, 1958.

CHAPTER 10

The Authoritarian Personality

and the Organization of Attitudes

In 1934 Hitler became chancellor of Germany. In 1938 E. R. Jaensch, a psychologist and also a Nazi, published the book *Der Gegentypus*. This book reported the discovery of a consistent human type—the *Gegentypus* or Anti-Type. The Anti-Type was also called the S-Type because Jaensch found that he was synaesthetic: one who enjoys concomitant sensation, a subjective experience from another sense than the one being stimulated, as in color hearing. Synaesthesia, which we are likely to regard as a poet's gift, seemed to Jaensch to be a kind of perceptual slovenliness, the qualities of one sense carelessly mixed with those of another. In other perceptual tasks Jaensch found the Anti-Type to be characterized by ambiguous and indefinite judgments and to be lacking in perseverance.

On the assumption that personalities manifest a *Stileinheit*, or "unity of style," Jaensch filled out his characterization of the S-Type more from imagination than evidence. The S would be a man with so-called "liberal" views; one who would think of environment and education as the determinants of behavior; one who would take a childish wanton pleasure in being eccentric, S would say "individualistic." S would be flaccid, weak, and effeminate. His general instability would be likely to stem from a racially mixed heredity. Jews are Anti-Types and "Parisians" and Orientals and communists.

The contrasting personality, an ideal for Jaensch, was the J-Type. J made definite, unambiguous perceptual judgments and persisted in them. He would recognize that human behavior is fixed by blood, soil, and national tradition. He would be tough, masculine, firm; a man you could rely on. His ancestors would have lived from time immemorial in the North German space and within the North German population; it would be these ancestors who had bequeathed him his admirable qualities. J made a good Nazi Party member.

In 1950, in the United States, *The Authoritarian Personality* was published. The research reported in this book undertook to discover the psychological roots of anti-Semitism. The anti-Semite in America turned out to be generally ethnocentric, generally antagonistic to groups other than his own because he thought of these groups as having various disagreeable innate qualities. Politically the anti-Semite tended to be conservative, a firm believer in "free enterprise," nationalistic, a friend of business and an enemy of labor unions. A person with this combination of opinions sounded like a potential Fascist. The authoritarian type in his perception and thought appeared to be rigid and intolerant of ambiguity. He was, more or less, Jaensch's J-Type, but J, who was a hero to Nazi social science, was a villain to American social science. What Jaensch called "stability" we called "rigidity" and the flaccidity and eccentricity of Jaensch's despised Anti-Type were for us the flexibility and individualism of the democratic equalitarian. The typologies of Jaensch and of the authors of *The Authoritarian Personality* were much the same but the evaluations were different.

The Authoritarian Personality had the greatest possible relevance to the social issues of its day. The Soviet Union had been our ally in the war against fascism. American intellectuals generally accepted the Marxist interpretation of fascism as a movement of the extreme political right, as a conservatism driven to desperation by the economic problems of capitalism. The Equalitarian opposite to the Authoritarian held the leftish liberal views of a New Dealer in the 1930's. They were views common to humane liberals, to Henry Wallace's Progressive Party, to non-Stalinist communists, the authors of *The Authoritarian Personality*, and most American social psychologists. The Equalitarian was ourselves and the Authoritarian the man in our society whom we feared and disliked.

The research reported in *The Authoritarian Personality* was done at the University of California at Berkeley. The work was subsidized by the Department of Scientific Research of the American Jewish Committee. One of the authors of the book, a social psychologist with very great talent, was Else Frenkel-Brunswik. Mrs. Brunswik and her husband, the eminent psychologist Egon Brunswik, had been students and teachers at the University of Vienna during the period in which Hitler rose to power. They were Jews and well acquainted with anti-Semitism.

After the War, came the realignment of world powers into communist and democratic blocs. In this country the wartime solidarity with Russia was forgotten and Soviet Communism replaced German fascism as the principal villain in world affairs. American intellectuals were not as ready as the national majority to anathematize communists; the two fascist themes of prejudice and political reaction seemed worse evils to us. One of the first indications of general American anxiety about internal communism was the decision of the Regents of the University of California to require a loyalty oath of all its faculty members. This seemed to most of us an egregious infringement of academic freedom and we sympathized with those who refused to sign. We were generally alarmed by the communism phobia which at length led to McCarthyism and to the stigmatization of liberal intellectuals as "eggheads."

Unquestionably there was some gratification for American social psychology during this period in the theory of the authoritarian personality which exposed the fear, the stupidity, and the sadism in nationalistic and reactionary politics. Was there perhaps also some distortion of truth in the service of values? If so, it was not so blatant as Jaensch's, not so obviously unsupported by evidence, not in the service of the state, perhaps not there at all. Still the authors of the 1950 study were not much interested in what has come to be called authoritarianism of the left. Interest in authoritarianism of the left apparently had to wait upon a change of the political climate, a time when disillusionment with communism was general among American intellectuals. It is not easy to do sound social psychological research on contemporary issues because any finding is, in these circumstances, a social force. The study called *The Authoritarian Personality* has affected American life: the theory of prejudice it propounded has become a part of popular culture and a force against racial discrimination. Is it also true? You must judge.

The Widening Circle of Covariation

In 1946 Jean-Paul Sartre published his *Réflexions sur la Question Juive* which appeared in English in 1948 under the title *Anti-Semite and Jew*. The null hypothesis, which is disproved by *The Authoritarian Personality* is, by coincidence, also Sartre's null hypothesis. He puts it this way:

"At the same time, accustomed as we have been since the Revolution to look at every object in an analytic spirit, that is to say, as a composite whose elements can be separated, we look upon persons or characters as mosaics in which each stone coexists with the others without that co-existence affecting the nature of the whole. Thus anti-Semitic opinion appears to us to be a molecule that can enter into combination with other molecules of any origin whatsoever without undergoing any alteration. A man may be a good father and a good husband, a conscientious citizen, highly cultivated, philantropic, *and* in addition an anti-Semite. He may like fishing and the pleasures of love, may be tolerant in matters of religion, full of generous notions on the condition of the natives in Central Africa, *and* in addition detest the Jews" (p.8).

Both Sartre and the California researchers conclude that the above statements are not true: a man who holds anti-Semitic opinions will reliably hold certain other opinions quite different from the opinions of a man who is not anti-Semitic. This is the discovery of the first part of the book. The later parts tell us what kind of a husband, father, and citizen the anti-Semite is.

Two kinds of behavior are said to covary when a change in one is associated in some regular way with a change in the other. The thousand pages of *The Authoritarian Personality* tell the story of behavior that co-varies with attitudes toward Jews. The account moves from anti-Semitic attitudes to ethnocentric ideology to political and economic conservatism to implicit antidemocratic trends to needs and traits revealed in interviews, TAT stories, and answers to projective questions. It is all an account of covariation, of how one kind of behavior is associated with another.

In following the ever widening circle that centers on anti-Semitism we well cross one major methodological boundary. Anti-Semitism, ethno-centrism, political and economic conservatism, and implicit antidemocratic trends are all assessed with fixed-alternative questionnaires. In the re-mainder of the work, research methods are used which do not provide al-ternative responses but leave the subject free to construct his own answer; these include interviews, requests to tell stories about pictures, and requests to respond to projective questions. The fixed-alternative questionnaire item is like the multiple-choice examination question and the open-ended inquiry is like an essay question. Scoring the former is a mechanical process but the latter requires trained judgment and is handled by a method called content analysis.

The fixed-alternative questionnaire is primarily a method of survey research and the first part of the study is essentially an opinion survey. Interviews, TAT's, and projective questions are primarily methods of clinical psychology and the second part of the study is essentially a clinical investigation of a small number of persons. The subjects for the clinical inquiry were selected on the basis of their scores on the Ethnocentrism (E) Scale; they were high scorers and low scorers, ideological extremes.

One of the innovations of *The Authoritarian Personality* was the combination in one study of the two kinds of method.

In addition to crossing a methodological boundary we will in this study cross a conceptual boundary; the two boundaries are related but not exactly coincident. The data are all verbal behavior, answers to questions of one kind or another. However, the authors of the Berkeley research conceptualized the data in two ways. They were, in the first place, concerned with ideology which they thought of as an organization of opinions, attitudes, and values, in political, economic, and religious spheres. They were in the second place concerned with personality which they thought of in the Freudian tradition, as an organization of needs varying in quality, intensity, and object; needs sometimes in harmony and sometimes in conflict. It was the effort to relate ideology to personality that made the California study strikingly original.

It is natural to anticipate that the survey part of the study which used questionnaire items would yield the data on ideology and that the clinical part of the study would yield the data on personality. In fact the coincidence is not quite that sharp. The Anti-Semitism (A-S) Scale, the Ethnocentrism (E) Scale, and the Political and Economic Conservatism (PEC) Scale are all concerned with explicit ideology. However, the F Scale is concerned with personality. It represents an attempt to assess by questionnaire the personality trends that are also assessed by interview and by projective methods. The methodological-conceptual coincidence is further blurred by the fact that the interview protocols and the TAT stories contain some material that is relevant to attitudes and ideologies. Apart from the present study, fixed-alternative questionnaires have very often been used to elicit personality data and open-ended questions have come to be widely used in opinion surveys.

COVARIATION OF QUESTIONNAIRE DATA

The investigators obtained most of their subjects by approaching organizations and asking to survey opinions in the entire membership. Among the subjects of these surveys were students from the University of California, from the University of Oregon, and from George Washington University. There were public school teachers, public health nurses, San Quentin Prison inmates, patients at the Langley Porter Psychiatric Clinic, veterans' groups, labor union groups, and Kiwanis clubs. More than two thousand persons took one or another of the attitude scales. Data from members of important minority groups were deliberately excluded. The majority of the subjects could be characterized as white, non-Jewish, native-born, middle-class Americans and the authors guessed that their findings would hold for this population.

All of the questionnaire items written for the survey portion of the research assumed the same form; they are called, in the terminology of attitude scaling, Likert-type items. Subjects were asked to mark each statement according to the degree of their agreement or disagreement with it by using the following scale:

+1: slight support, agreement   −1: slight opposition, disagreement
+2: moderate support, agreement −2: moderate opposition, disagreement
+3: strong support, agreement   −3: strong opposition, disagreement

Notice that no zero position of neutrality was provided.

In what follows we will be describing the development by the Berkeley research group of four paper and pencil scales: the Anti-Semitism (A-S) Scale, the Ethnocentrism (E) Scale, the Political and Economic Conservatism (PEC) Scale, and the Implicit Antidemocratic Trends (F) Scale. In this work we will be chiefly interested in the way in which one sort of opinion is found to be associated with another, in the widening circle of correlation that suggests the existence of a general ideology of authoritarianism.

For each scale we shall be reporting four critical things: first, the authors' general definition of the attitudes being measured; second, some illustrative questionnaire items; third, a mean correlation between one-half of the items and the other half of the items (usually called a split-half reliability correlation). The split-half reliability correlation provides a rough indication of the degree to which the specific opinions within a scale tend to be associated one with another. It tells us, for instance, whether people who agree with one set of statements that express hostility to Jews also agree with another set of such statements. In the fourth place we will report the mean correlation between total scores on the new scale and total scores on all the scales previously developed. This value is a rough indication of the degree to which attitudes assessed by one scale tend to be associated with attitudes assessed by the other scales. This is the essential framework in what follows, though there are also incidental remarks to be made about each scale.

The Anti-Semitism (A-S) Scale. The investigators' general conception of anti-Semitism was that it consists in "stereotyped negative opinions describing the Jews as threatening, immoral, and categorically different from non-Jews, and of hostile attitudes urging various forms of restriction, exclusion, and suppression as a means of solving the "Jewish problem" (Adorno, et al., 1950, p. 71). They wrote fifty-two questionnaire items to tap this attitude. The authors classified their fifty-two items under five subheadings: 1) offensive items described Jews as conceited, sensual, dirty, and the like; 2) threatening items described them as ruthless, competitive, radical, and the like; 3) attitudes items recommended various discriminative actions to be taken against the Jews; 4) *seclusive* items credited the "clannish" Jews with a desire to keep apart from gentiles; 5) *intrusive* items, on the other hand, attributed to Jews a desire to move in where they are not wanted.

All of the items were written so as to affirm an anti-Semitic opinion and so consistent agreement with items would produce a high A-S score. The authors discussed the possible objection to their procedure that a subject who was somehow "set" so as to agree with statements might mechanically produce a high score without in fact being intensely anti-Semitic. For various reasons they considered this unlikely but as we shall see, when we make a critique of the study, their decision was unwise. The items of all the subsequent scales, with the exception of the Political and Economic Conservatism (PEC) Scale, were also written so as to affirm the attitude in question.

The A-S Scale items were phrased so as to express a subtle hostility without seeming to offend the democratic values that most subjects would feel bound to support. Each item has a kind of fair-minded and reasonable veneer. It is sometimes rather difficult to find the sting. The following item is a good example: "The trouble with letting Jews into a nice neighborhood is that they gradually give it a typical Jewish atmosphere." How could it be otherwise? Surely Jews will produce a Jewish atmosphere. They will at any rate do so if one thinks of Jews as "categorically different from non-Jews." However it is just this saliency of "Jewishness" which the authors consider the beginning of anti-Semitism.

In the second place, if one thinks of "Jewishness" as a set of acquired traits which are subject to change then it is not inevitable that Jews should produce a characteristic neighborhood atmosphere. The atmosphere might chiefly depend on the occupation and education of the residents—Jewish or no. If however the ethnic category has innate ineluctable qualities then the "typical" atmosphere must always be there.

Notice next the use of the expression "letting into." One can only "let in" someone motivated to enter. If the outsider did not wish to come in he would have to be invited or urged or dragged in. How easily we assume that "letting into" is the only possible expression and yet by doing so we attribute to the ethnic category an "intrusive" impulse and that is part of the investigators' definition of an anti-Semitic frame of mind.

Finally there is hostility to this intrusive group in the clever use of the words "trouble" and "nice." Clearly the neighborhood is expected to be less "nice" if it acquires a typical Jewish atmosphere. The item, then, contains all the essentials of anti-Semitism, but they are so artfully expressed that the statement at first appears innocuous.

Here are some other items from the A-S Scale:

1. "One trouble with Jewish businessmen is that they stick together

and connive, so that a Gentile doesn't have a fair chance in competition."

2. "I can hardly imagine myself marrying a Jew."

3. "No matter how Americanized a Jew may seem to be, there is always something different and strange, something basically Jewish underneath."

The original fifty-two items of the A-S Scale were divided into two sets of twenty-six items each and the two sets were administered to the same subjects a week apart. The correlation between the scores was .92. Correlations among the subscales ranged from .74 to .94. There was ample evidence that these opinion items clustered together; a person agreeing with one of them was likely to agree with others.

The Ethnocentrism (E) Scale. We come now upon a very important fact: People who are antagonistic to Jews are likely also to be antagonistic to Negroes and to "Japs," "Okies," foreigners in general. "Of course," one says at first, but there is no logical necessity in the fact. If the reputation of an ethnic group with a particular man were dependent on that man's personal experience with members of the group it is not clear why a man who thinks ill of one minority would think ill of the others nor why a man who thinks well of one should think well of all. Because this is the case it seems likely that neither the behavior of minorities nor our acquaintance with a sample of that behavior is the critical determinant of our attitudes toward them.

Anti-Semitism most commonly appears as a single manifestation of ethnocentrism. The latter term was introduced by William Graham Sumner in his book *Folkways* (1906). Sumner defined ethnocentrism as a tendency to be rigid in the acceptance of the culturally alike and in the rejection of the culturally unlike. The emphasis in this definition is a little different from that in our own definition offered in Chapter 4 but Sumner's emphasis is the more appropriate one for the present case.

The Berkeley investigators wrote thirty-four Likert-type items for the diagnosis of ethnocentrism. Some of these were concerned with Negroes, some with such other minorities as "Japs," "Okies," Filipinos, zootsuiters, foreigners, members of small political parties, criminals, and subnormals. In some items the emphasis was not so much on the odious qualities of minorities and outsiders as on the superior qualities of one's own family and the American Way.

Here are some sample items:

1. "Negroes have their rights, but it is best to keep them in their own districts and schools and to prevent too much contact with whites."

2. "Zootsuiters prove that when people of their type have too much money and freedom, they just take advantage and cause trouble."

3. "Certain religious sects who refuse to salute the flag should be forced to conform to such a patriotic action, or else be abolished."

4. "America may not be perfect, but the American Way has brought us about as close as human beings can get to a perfect society."

The correlation of one half of the items in the Ethnocentrism Scale with the other half of the items, was .91. The correlation between Ethnocentrism and the original 52-item A-S Scale was .80. These results are evidence that antagonism to the culturally unlike is a generalized sentiment.

The Political and Economic Conservatism (PEC) Scale. By the end of the nineteenth century it was widely believed in both Europe and the United States that political views and political institutions could be ranged on a continuum from the radical left to the conservative right. The conservative right has believed in self-enrichment by personal exertion and in the rightness of the social and economic inequalities that follow from such individual competition; it has been opposed to such interferences with rugged individualism as social welfare legislation, state regulation of economic activity, and to the association of working men into labor unions. More generally conservatism has championed the *status quo*, religion and tradition over science and humanitarianism. The radical left has chiefly stood for economic and social equality, for full suffrage, civil liberties, labor unions, welfare legislation, change and science. Fascism, which emerged in the 1930's in Germany and Italy, was interpreted by Marxists and most intellectuals as a movement of extreme right conservatism and the Berkeley researchers made this same interpretation. German fascism was notably ethnocentric and anti-Semitic. The Berkeley group expected to find that its anti-Semitic and ethnocentric subjects would have the political and economic values of the American conservative right wing.

The Berkeley group took the definitive component of conservatism to be an attachment to "things as they are," a resistance to social change. Primary values for the American conservative seemed to include practicality, ambition, and financial success. "Most people get pretty much what they deserve," the conservative holds. The rich have earned their wealth and the poor their poverty. The radical or liberal sees poverty as a symptom of disorder in the political and economic system. He favors economic planning, strong labor unions, welfare legislation.

Here are some items written for the Political and Economic Conservatism (PEC) Scale:

1. "A child should learn early in life the value of a dollar and the importance of ambition, efficiency, and determination."

2. "The best way to solve social problems is to stick close to the middle of the road, to move slowly, and to avoid extremes."

3. "The only way to provide adequate medical care for the entire population is through some program of socialized medicine."

4. "In general, full economic security is harmful; most men wouldn't work if they didn't need the money for eating and living."

Item three asserts a liberal opinion and reactions of *disagreement* with this item increase the PEC score. This scale, unlike the A-S and E scales includes items affirming both sides of the issues with which it is concerned.

The split-half reliabilities of the PEC scales are lower than the reliabilities of the A-S and the E scales; for PEC the average r = .73 while for A-S and E the correlations are between .8 and .9. This shows that the components of conservatism identified in this research cluster with some consistency but the consistency is less than in the case of the components of anti-Semitism or ethnocentrism.

Finally the scores of the PEC Scale did not correlate as highly with scores on the A-S Scale and the E Scale as did the scores on the latter two scales with one another. The mean correlation for PEC with E is .57 and for PEC with A-S only .43. The range of correlations is very great, from .14 to .86. It is noteworthy that, of the thirty or so correlations calculated for different groups, none was negative. In short, neither ethnocentrism nor anti-Semitism ever showed a tendency to go with leftist liberal views; the conservative was always more ethnocentric and anti-Semitic but the association was not strong.

Conservatism and radicalism or liberalism do not, in these data, appear to be perfectly consistent ideologies. As an ideological continuum the conservative-liberal dimension is not closely aligned with either ethnocentrism or anti-Semitism but is in some degree aligned with them. Antagonism to minorities is more likely to be combined with conservative political views than with liberal views but the latter combination is also common and so, too, is a combination of conservatism with little antagonism to minorities.

The Implicit Antidemocratic Trends or Potentiality for Fascism (F) Scale. The authors of the F Scale call it by both of the titles listed above. So far as one can determine they never refer to the F Scale as the Authoritarianism Scale in their book *The Authoritarian Personality*. However, since the F Scale is supposed to identify the kind of personality the book is talking about, it is reasonable to suppose that the scale could also be correctly called the Authoritarianism Scale. At any rate it has been so called in many subsequent research reports (Christie, 1954).

The Berkeley researchers do not explain the variation in their names for the scale and the personality type. It is likely that the preference for one name over the others on any given occasion was dictated by the appropriateness of the connotations of each term to the authors' thinking as of that date. In the book as a whole the authors probably intend the several terms to be understood as equivalents. In one important respect, however, they are not equivalent. Fascism implies conservative right-wing views while "antidemocratic" and "authoritarian" do not. Eventually, as we shall see, it became a matter of serious dispute whether the F Scale assesses only fascism (authoritarian of the right) or assesses authoritarianism in general (right or left).

With the F Scale the Berkeley researchers believed that they were moving to the level of personality. While the scale items are statements of opinion and have the same form as items on the A-S, E, and PEC scales they do not make assertions about minority groups or about political and economic issues. The scale is intended to measure implicit authoritarian or antidemocratic trends in a personality, trends rendering the personality susceptible to explicit Fascist propaganda.

The thirty-eight items of the initial form of the F Scale are a greatly varied lot. In part they were suggested by fascist writings and by the speeches of anti-Semitic agitators. In part they were suggested by persistent themes in the interview protocols of ethnocentric subjects and in their TAT stories. For these data, which we have not yet described, had been collected and studied before the F Scale was written. Indeed the F Scale represents an effort to capture in a questionnaire the insights of the clinical studies.

The items are subclassified under nine general terms. These terms are supposed to constitute the antidemocratic or potentially fascistic syndrome. *Syndrome* is a word used in medicine for a collection of concurrent symptoms of a disease. The nine antidemocratic symptoms are not bound together by logic. If it turns out that they hang together empirically, that persons who have one tend to have all, then the explanation of this fact must be found in the disease process. In the present case that process is conceived as a system of personality dynamics.

Here now are the nine characteristics briefly defined and with two items to illustrate each one.

a. *Conventionalism.* A rigid adherence to conventional, middle-class values.
1. "Obedience and respect for authority are the most important virtues children should learn."
2. "The businessman and the manufacturer are much more important to society than the artist and the professor."
b. *Authoritarian Submission.* A submissive, uncritical attitude toward idealized moral authorities of the ingroup.
1. "Young people sometimes get rebellious ideas, but as they grow up they ought to get over them and settle down."
2. "Science has its place, but there are many important things that can never possibly be understood by the human mind."

c. *Authoritarian Aggression.* A tendency to be on the lookout for, and to condemn, reject, and punish people who violate conventional values.

1. "Sex crimes, such as rape and attacks on children, deserve more than mere imprisonment; such criminals ought to be publicly whipped, or worse."
2. "If people would talk less and work more, everybody would be better off."

d. *Anti-Intraception.* An opposition to the subjective, the imaginative, the tender-minded.

1. "When a person has a problem or worry, it is best for him not to think about it, but to keep busy with more cheerful things."
2. "Nowadays more and more people are prying into matters that should remain personal and private."

e. *Superstition and Stereotypy.* The belief in mystical determinants of the individual's fate, the disposition to think in rigid categories.

1. "Some day it will probably be shown that astrology can explain a lot of things."
2. "Some people are born with an urge to jump from high places."

f. *Power and "Toughness."* A preoccupation with the dominance-submission, strong-weak, leader-follower dimension; identification with power figures; overemphasis upon the conventionalized attributes of the ego; exaggerated assertion of strength and toughness.

1. "People can be divided into two distinct classes: the weak and the strong."
2. "Most people don't realize how much our lives are controlled by plots hatched in secret places."

g. *Destructiveness and Cynicism.* A generalized hostility, vilification of the human.

1. "Human nature being what it is, there will always be war and conflict."
2. "Familiarity breeds contempt."

h. *Projectivity.* The disposition to believe that wild and dangerous things go on in the world; the projection outwards of unconscious emotional impulses.

1. "Wars and social troubles may someday be ended by an earthquake or flood that will destroy the whole world."
2. "Nowadays when so many different kinds of people move around and mix together so much, a person has to protect himself especially carefully against catching an infection or disease from them."

i. *Sex.* Exaggerated concern with sexual "goings-on."

1. "The wild sex life of the old Greeks and Romans was tame compared to some of the goings-on in this country, even in places where people might least expect it."

2. "Homosexuals are hardly better than criminals and ought to be severely punished."

Do you know him—the Authoritarian, the Antidemocrat, the Pre-Fascist? It seems to me that I do. Item after item in the F Scale is something I have heard or very like something I have heard. Furthermore the people I know who have made one of these statements have usually gone on to make others of them. I am less confident of the reality of the nine subscales. The characteristics naming them are not clearly defined and it is not obvious to me that items within a scale cluster together more tightly than do items across subscales. What did the authors find?

The items as a whole had something in common. There was for the first version of the scale a split-half reliability of .74 and, for the final version, that reliability averaged .90. For the F Scale we have more information about internal consistency than for the A-S, E, and PEC scales. For the final version, responses to each item were correlated with responses to each other item. The average of these correlations was .13 and the range was from −.05 to .44. In addition, scores on each single item were correlated with total scores for the remaining items and the mean of these correlations was .33. At a later date the authors of the F Scale made their original data available to Melvin (1955) who did a factor analysis of it and found a very strong general factor running through all items (cited by Eysenck, 1954, p. 152). The Berkeley authors had found a superficially heterogeneous set of opinions that had, as a total set, some kind of psychological unity. However the items within a subscale were not more closely correlated with one another than they were with numerous items outside the subscale. The nine symptoms or characteristics (e.g., "conventionalism," "projectivity,") were not, in short, shown to be psychologically real.

With the F Scale the Berkeley group hoped to identify a personality system that was potentially fascistic and so they expected F Scale scores to correlate with the explicit tenets of fascism expressed in the A-S, E, and PEC scales. This proved to be the case. For the first form of the scale the mean correlation with A-S was .53, with E it was .65, and with PEC, .54. The F Scale was revised several times by dropping items that did not correlate with total scores or that were not predictive of A-S and E scores. For the final version of the scale the mean correlation with an E Scale that included anti-Semitic items was .75; the correlation with PEC was only .57.

It was ethnocentrism, anti-Semitism, and potentiality for fascism that were most strongly interrelated. These attitudes and personality characteristics tended to be associated with conservatism in political and economic matters but not so strongly as they were associated with one another. This pattern suggests that there may have been quite a few ethno-centric and antidemocratic subjects who were leftish liberal in the politi-cal and economic sphere. That is a fact to remember because it is related to later developments.

COVARIATION OF INTERVIEW AND PROJECTIVE DATA

We are crossing the methodological line from fixed-alternative ques-tionnaires to free-response interviews and projectives. It has been said that this is a line similar to that between multiple-choice examinations and essay examinations. Many teachers believe that the best way to sample a student's knowledge is to combine the two kinds of examination. Multiple-choice tests, and also questionnaire items, present a certain problem of communication: the student or subject must try to make out what the teacher or researcher means by the item. The greater burden of decoding is on the one who answers. Essay examinations, and also interview proto-cols and projective data, present the complementary problem of communi-cation. The respondent is free to formulate his own answers, but the in-quirer must try to figure out what he means by them. The greater burden of decoding is on the one who asks. The Berkeley investigators, like some teachers, seem to have believed that the best hope of discovering the truth lay in a combination of the two methods.

Teachers do not ordinarily make a reliability check on their evaluations of essays. When this has been done the results have sometimes revealed a discreditable degree of unreliability. The interpreter of interview and projective protocols usually has a more delicate job to do than the grader of essays and so it behooves him to be more concerned about reliability. In the present research we do not have the simple problem of sorting total productions into categories comparable to the letter-grade categories. Rather we have the problem of searching total productions for various kinds of content, the problem of coding content so as to make it quanti-fiable. Consequently, reliability of scoring is an important consideration.

Interview Collection and Coding. The interview study dealt only with persons whose questionnaire responses identified them as ideologically extreme. There were eighty interviewees, of whom about half had placed in the highest quartile (25%) of the E Scale distribution and about half in the lowest quartile. Forty subjects were men and forty were women. You may remember that most subjects in the survey studies were recruited through some formal group. The researchers now wanted to select out particular interviewees but did not want to alarm them by saying that they had been picked because of the extremity of their attitudes. Conse-quently interviewees were told that they had been selected on the basis of age and regional origin. They were identified by birthdate only, in order to preserve anonymity.

High scorers are supposed to be anti-intraceptive and one item they are likely to have endorsed is: "Nowadays more and more people are prying into matters that should remain personal and private." Such subjects might, therefore, have been reluctant to submit to an intensive interview lasting one-and-a-half to three hours. Largely as an inducement to such interviewees the researchers offered a three-dollar fee; they report that this fee was helpful in obtaining their subjects.

The nature of the interview schedule used in this research must be appreciated if we are to make a sound evaluation of the results. There were six general areas to be covered: 1) Vocation; 2) Income; 3) Religion; 4) Clinical Data; 5) Politics; 6) Minorities and Race. There were subtopics in each area. Clinical data, for example, included: 4a) Family Background: Sociological Aspects; 4b) Family Figures: Personal Aspects; 4c) Childhood; 4d) Sex; 4e) Social Relationships; and 4f) School.

Within each subtopic the interviewer was to have in mind a set of critical underlying questions which were to be answerable from the talk of the interviewee. In the case of subtopic 4b (Family Figures: Personal Aspects) the underlying questions concerned the "Subject's Conception of Parent Figures" and the "Pattern of Power Relations between Father and Mother." These underlying questions were not to be asked in any direct form. One does not ask: "What was the power relation between your father and mother?" The interviewer's task was, instead, to ask more specific questions couched in familiar language and to continue asking such questions until he judged that material had been obtained which would enable a coder of the protocol to answer the underlying question. It was not for the interviewer himself to answer the underlying question. His job was simply to have those questions in mind and to keep asking about particulars until it seemed to him that there was material which would make it possible to answer the underlying questions.

For the particular direct questions to be used in probing for relevant material there was no required set and no required sequence but only a list of suggestions. For example, the interview schedule recommends the following inquiries as means of learning about the "Pattern of Power Relations between Father and Mother:"

How did your parents get along together?
In what ways were your parents most alike?
In what ways were they different from each other?
Who made the decisions usually? (Get specific information e.g., re finances, recreation, discipline of children, residence, etc.)
Disagreements arise in every family from time to time; what bones of contention did your parents sometimes have? [Adorno, et al., 1950, p. 314]

Finally, interviewers were instructed to make a close study, in advance of the interview, of all the questionnaire responses of the interviewee. The Berkeley investigators believed that such advance knowledge would help the interviewer to focus on critical topics. They believed that there was no danger that the results would be biased by the interviewer's knowledge of his subject since the interviewers were not scheduled to code the data but only to collect it. The coders, of course, would not know anything about the questionnaire scores of the subjects since such knowledge could affect what they would "see" in a protocol. The priming of interviewers with knowledge of the questionnaire results is an aspect of the research procedure that was to be severely criticized.

Since the interviewers were oriented to a set of underlying questions it would be reasonable to anticipate that the coding of the data would simply have been a matter of sorting the answers to each underlying question into a set of mutually exclusive categories. Such is not the case. Consider, for example, the underlying question: "Pattern of Power Relations between Father and Mother." One might have guessed that there would be three response categories such as Father Dominant, Mother Dominant, and Parental Equality. Each subject would then be counted as having produced one of these three alternatives. This is not the way the investigators conceived of their questions and not the way they handled their data. The so-called "questions" are actually very general areas of inquiry and the inquiries produced complex multi-dimensional data which the authors coded in any way that promised to distinguish prejudiced subjects from unprejudiced subjects.

There were about ninety coding categories and the categories were somewhat different for men than for women. Before they made up the scoring manual the investigators read through most of the interviews. From this preliminary examination they formed impressions as to the differences between the high-prejudice subjects and the low-prejudice subjects. These impressions, together with a developing theory of the causes of prejudice, guided the formulation of coding categories and the writing of the Scoring Manual. The categories were conceived as pairs and the manual identified one member of each pair as a presumedly High category and the other as presumedly Low. A High category was one that was expected to be scored for high-prejudice subjects and a Low category for low-prejudice subjects. The third alternative in each case was a Neutral category and it was to be scored whenever there was not enough relevant material to justify either the High or the Low or where the material was too conflicting for either High or Low to be scored. Each pair of categories was supposed to be rated independently of all the others but subsequent to a study of the complete interview protocol.

Some of the pairs of categories are clearly related to particular underlying questions. In connection with "Power Relations between Father and Mother" there is the pair: "Denial of parental conflict" vs. "Open and objective verbalization of such conflict." The first member is the High category, the category expected to be associated with high prejudice, and the second member is the Low category. Also relevant to the same underlying question would be the pair of categories: "Father domination" (High) vs. "Mother orientation" (Low). These two pairs of categories are responsive to the same single underlying question but they do not function as four mutually exclusive alternative answers. They are rather two dichotomized dimensions laid across interview material relevant to parental power. Each protocol is scored for both dimensions. For some of the underlying questions (e.g., "Subject's Conception of Parent Figures") the coded dimensions of response are more numerous.

Some coding categories are not responsive to any particular underlying question. For example, subjects were given scores on various aspects of character structure. Did a subject manifest "counter-cathectic rejection of 'erotic' orality" or "positive expressions of 'erotic' orality?" (The terminology is psychoanalytic.) Did he have an "externalized superego" or an "internalized superego," a "weak ego" or a "strong or moderately strong ego?" These categories would have had to be coded as impressions from the total protocol. They illustrate the fact that many categories were not responsive to any particular underlying question and also will serve, I think, to show that some categories were both subtle and elaborately interpretive. Reliability in coding such categories would be difficult to achieve. All references to minority groups were deleted from the interviews and the raters did not see the questionnaires of the subjects. This means they did "blind" coding, coding without knowledge of a subject's position on the prejudice dimension. There were two coders, one male and one female. Both had training in psychology and both had participated in discussions devoted to the development of the coding scheme.

The information given on rating reliability is very sketchy. The two raters coded different interviews, each did approximately equal numbers of male and female subjects and of high and low prejudice subjects. The interview results for any given subject are, therefore, based on a single coding. Had the two coders both done all the interviews would they have produced closely similar results? To find this out the authors picked nine interviews to be coded by both raters. There was reason to believe that two of these interviews were exceptionally difficult to code. Unfortunately we are not told how well the raters agreed on each particular pair of categories in each interview. Instead the authors give, for both raters, the percentage of High categories scored in each total interview. For the most part these are closely similar.

Projective Collection and Coding. The work done with two other clinical instruments is very much like the interview study. The instruments were Murray's Thematic Apperception Test (TAT) and a set of projective questions. For the TAT, subjects are asked to tell a story about each of a standard set of pictures. In the present instance each subject saw ten pictures, some of them from Murray's standard set and some of them photographs selected for the study because they showed members of various minority groups. There were eight projective questions. Here are two of them:

1. "We all have times when we feel below par. What moods or feelings are the most unpleasant or disturbing to you?"

2. "We all have impulses and desires which are at times hard to control but which we try to keep in check. What desires do you often have difficulty in controlling?"

With both the TAT and the Projective Questions a comparison was made between subjects from the highest quartile of the E Scale results and subjects from the lowest quartile. Both sets of data were examined in search of High-Low contrasts before the Scoring Manuals were written. The scoring categories were defined so as to capture quantitatively the differences suspected to exist. In these respects the procedures were the same as in the case of the interview study.

Both TAT stories and answers to projective questions are data that must be coded. The TAT stories were all analyzed "blind" (i.e., in ignorance of the storyteller's E score) by two coders: one a research staff member and one a graduate student with no previous experience on the study. Each story was separated from other stories told by the same subject and randomly placed among the total collection of stories. For the projective questions each individual answer was keyed, separated from the other answers of a subject, and randomly placed in the total set. There were two independent codings of all data. In both of these studies the coding was done under more demanding and more satisfactory circumstances than in the interview study. The reported precentages of agreement in coding answers to a question as High, Low, or Neutral are satisfactorily high. However, as in the case of the interview study, the authors do not tell us how well coders agreed on the particular content categories considered to be High, Low, or Neutral.

Two Special Groups of Subjects. Among the many groups of subjects who participated in the Berkeley study there were two of particular interest: 110 inmates of San Quentin Prison and 121 patients at the Langley-Porter Psychiatric Clinic. Both groups of subjects filled out the E, PEC, and F scales. The psychiatric patients were slightly but not significantly lower than the mean of all other groups tested on the E Scale. There was a tendency for neurosis to go with low scores and psychosis with moderately high scores.

The prisoners produced the highest mean scores of all groups tested on the E, PEC, and F scales. The criminal types represented in the San Quentin population were not, it seems, rebels against established authority. On the contrary, they were politically and economically conservative types, highly patriotic, and filled with hatred for submerged ethnic groups.

Twelve of the prisoners were interviewed; of these, eight scored high on the E Scale and four scored relatively low. Among the high scorers there were three subjects whom the researchers characterize as "overt fascists." These three were not actually members of any self-styled fascist party and so their high scores on all scales cannot be taken as a validation of the characterization of these scales as measures of political fascism. The three subjects were labelled fascist by the authors because they explicitly endorsed the use of force to suppress minorities and to protect business againt labor unions. They dispensed with the pseudo-democratic façade that was important to most prejudiced subjects.

The criminal interviews were not coded or treated quantitatively but they are quoted at length in *The Authoritarian Personality* to establish the authors' position that criminal authoritarianism had the same fundamental personality dynamics as did the authoritarianism that was within the law. Some of the quotations, especially those from the three prisoners who were labelled fascistic, are hair-raising. They suggest that we could find, in this country, willing recruits for a Gestapo.

Concerning Negroes: "They're very closely linked with the jungle. They're built for it." Concerning Jews: "Most all of them Jews talk about sex mostly, or beatin' a guy out of his money." (This latter is from a man who had been arrested for sexually molesting his own children.) Concerning labor unions: "Take away their charters. . . . Abolish them." Concerning parents: ". . . always tried to teach me the right thing; being in prison is not my folks' fault." Concerning the determinants of human behavior. "If I ever did anything wrong, it was the Latin in me." And so on.

For the patients at the Langley-Porter Clinic the study centered on their first psychiatric interview—an interview concerned chiefly with the patient's description of his problems. These interviews were held by members of the regular clinic staff who had no knowledge of the research project and no expectation that the interviews would be studied by outsiders. This is an important fact because, as we shall later see, it exempts the present interview study from a very serious criticism that must be made of the major interview study.

The initial interviews for twenty-eight subjects who scored high on the E Scale and thirty-one who scored low were coded for seven characteristics. Before the coding categories were defined all of the interviews were examined for content that seemed to distinguish prejudiced subjects from unprejudiced subjects. This again is an important fact because, as we shall see, it means that the study of the patient interviews was subject to one serious criticism that must also be made of all the other studies involving content analysis.

Most of the coding categories were similar to categories used in other parts of the study. For example, prejudiced subjects were expected to be anti-intraceptive and extrapunitive. Several categories adapt traits of ordinary authoritarians to the special case of psychiatric patients. Prejudiced subjects were expected chiefly to complain of somatic or physical ailments such as dizziness, tremor, fast heartbeat, and the like, while unprejudiced subjects were expected to complain of such psychological ailments as anxiety, conflict, and depression. In addition, prejudiced subjects were expected to blame their troubles on particular unlucky external events —an illness, a divorce, a death. Unprejudiced subjects would be more likely to see their symptoms as having been present in milder form for years, possibly since childhood.

All of the interviews were coded by two judges who were thoroughly familiar with the hypotheses and findings of the total research. In addition, however, there were seven control raters who were completely unacquainted with the research as a whole. Each control rater coded all interviews for *just one variable*. In the content analyses of the major interview study each rater coded all variables and that means that knowledge of one could easily have biased the coding of another. The study of psychiatric interviews was free of this flaw.

Coding reliabilities were calculated for the two coders who did all the interviews and also for one of these coders and all the control coders. We are given the percentages of coding agreement on *each coding category*, which is the proper report to make on reliability for data of this sort, a report that was not made for the other content analyses. The average percentage agreement between the main rater and the seven control raters was 77 per cent.

Results. In all three sets of clinical data, in the interview protocols, the TAT stories, and the answers to the projective questions, the investigators found numerous statistically significant differences between prejudiced subjects and unprejudiced subjects. Some of the differences occur in content categories that are already familiar to us from the F Scale. "Anti-Intraceptive" is a content category for the analysis of interview protocols as well as a rubric under which certain F Scale items were classified. In both sets of data it is the prejudiced subjects who are anti-intraceptive. Some of the distinctive content categories are very closely related to F Scale rubrics; the Pseudo- or Anti-Scientific category for interview analysis is very like the Superstition and Stereotypy of the F Scale. Again and again quotations from the subjects' freely composed responses echo the items of the F Scale. In considerable degree, then, the projective data confirm the covariation of implicit antidemocratic trends with prejudice which was demonstrated by the questionnaire data.

Analysis of the projective data also added many new items of behavior to the circle of covariation. Prejudiced subjects in interviews showed a tendency to separate sex and affection while unprejudiced subjects were likely to fuse the two. In the TAT stories of prejudiced subjects there was more primitive, impulsive aggression; the heroes of their stories were more often dependent on the demands and regulations of authority. In response to a projective question about the "worst crimes a person could commit" prejudiced subjects were likely to list crimes against the physical person while unprejudiced subjects were likely to list crimes against the personality—psychological cruelties and violations of trust.

All of these data are verbal, all of them roughly contemporaneous. They add up to a list, a very long one, of correlated differences. I have not the patience to write them all down and you would not find it interesting to read or possible to remember. But when the authors interpret the list it becomes a pattern, in more than one dimension, and the pattern is somewhat lifelike.

The transformation from list to personality is accomplished in the following way. Some of the things subjects said are assumed to have historical truth, to be realistic accounts of past events and so a genetic dimension is added. Some of the things subjects said are understood literally, others are interpreted as revelations of unconscious wishes and so a dimension of psychological "depth" is added. Some of the things subjects said are set alongside other things with which they are in conflict and so dynamic forces are added. The construction as a whole is guided by a general blueprint of human personality, the blueprint is psychoanalytic theory.

The widening circle of covariation has become too wide to keep in view and so we will stop describing uninterpreted data. The results of the studies of projective material are more interesting and memorable as parts of the intellectual construction called the authoritarian personality than as unpatterned fragments. The citation of data will be highly selective, chiefly from the interviews, but copious enough, I hope, so that you can judge the adequacy of the evidence.

Construction of the Personality

We can begin with findings which suggest that the prejudiced person has a more consistently favorable impression of himself than does the unprejudiced person. The most directly relevant contrast in the coding categories is: "Self-glorification" as opposed to "Objective self-appraisal."

Prejudiced persons say such things as: "I have always tried to live accord-ing to His Ten Commandments" or "Think one of my best assets is my poise" or "I've always had a happy disposition, and I've always been honest with my family." From unprejudiced subjects come such appraisals as: "I'm rather shy, don't like competition" or "I don't mean I am in love with my mother, but I have a dependency complex . . . married a woman older than myself."

There are other interview categories which contribute to our im-pression that the prejudiced person has an exceptionally good opinion of himself. In describing their sexual experiences, for example, prejudiced men boast of their conquests and represent themselves as ideals of mascu-linity while women speak of having "scads of boys friends." By contrast, an unprejudiced woman says: "I am avoided by the male sex perhaps be-cause I am heavy" and a man reports that he has "alway been rather inhibited about sex."

In addition to having a good opinion of themselves prejudiced persons have a good opinion of their parents. The most directly relevant interview categories are: "Conventional idealization of parents" vs. "Objective ap-praisal." Prejudiced subjects say of their fathers: "He is very sincere and very well liked by his friends and employees" and "He is exceptionally good looking, dresses well, has gray hair" and "I've always been very proud to be his son." Of their mothers they say: "Most terrific person in the world to me" and "She's friendly with everybody." The prejudiced person does not have a father and a mother for parents; he has "Father's Day" and "Mother's Day."

Unprejudiced subjects said of their fathers: "Father tries to be ra-tional but is not always so" and "I think he wanted a boy, so he paid little attention to me." Of their mothers they say: "She is practical and sensible, but she gets too much interested in fads" and "She gives me too much advice."

Very generally, prejudiced subjects do not describe themselves or their parents as fearful or dependent or slothful or aggressive against properly constituted authority or as having any of the traits of the other sex. Un-prejudiced subjects are more likely to ascribe such faults and shortcomings to themselves and their parents. Here then are some new correlates of prejudice. We could stop here, with the simple listing, but instead we will attempt to figure out what the difference means, how it comes about.

One ought, in the first place, to consider the possibility that the two kinds of self and of parental appraisal are the simple truth. Prejudiced people and their parents may, in fact, be superior to the unprejudiced. As you might guess this was not the view of the Berkeley researchers. Their interpretation is actually revealed in the labelling of the categories: "Self-glorification" vs. "Objective appraisal" and "Conventional idealization of parents" against "Objective appraisal." These titles make it clear that the reports of unprejudiced subjects are presumed to be accurate or truthful ("objective") whereas the reports of prejudiced subjects are presumed to be inaccurate ("idealized" or "glorified"). What ground have they for treating the prejudiced as liars and the unprejudiced as truthtellers? Is this a prejudice of their own, a device to evade the unpalatable conclusion that prejudiced people are generally pleasanter people than the unprejudiced?

One might doubt the accuracy of the prejudiced subjects' glowing appraisal of himself and his parents on the ground of manifest improbability. People are simply not that good. Characters are always flawed by fearfulness or dependency or antagonism. People do not greatly differ in the degree to which they possess faults and shortcomings but only in their awareness of such unwelcome traits. Where character flaws are not explicitly confessed it must be because the subject does not want to be aware of them.

Ambivalent feelings are mixed feelings, positive and negative sentiments concentrated on the same object. As Chapter 11 argues and as Freud always assumed, it is human nature to abhor ambivalence. Behind this abhorrence, I suspect, is the fact that ambivalence must tend to paralyze action. If one likes an object or person the thing to do is to approach and if one dislikes to retreat. Ambivalence must activate both tendencies but it is impossible to act on both.

While human beings do not welcome ambivalence there are ways of coping with it. One can differentiate the object for example, oneself or one's parents—into parts, some of them good and some bad. A mother can be practical and sensible but inclined to give too much advice; a father can be affectionate but not handsome or not practical. Ambivalence is resolved by cognitive complication, by making distinctions among the manifestations of an object, the traits of a person, or the members of a minority. The unprejudiced subject seems to cope with inevitable ambivalence by consciously recognizing both the good and bad parts.

On the presumption that some ambivalence of feeling for oneself and one's parents is inevitable it would seem that the prejudiced person is unable to cope with it by complicating his conceptions. He maintains the unity of the object of feeling and handles ambivalence by denying (perhaps repressing) one part of his feelings. Since it is important to think well of oneself and one's parents it is the negative feelings, the unfavorable judgments, that are denied. This argument holds that the person who reports only favorable judgments of himself and his parents is motivated to deny contrary judgments and the basis for that interpretation is the assumption that in any human life there must be grounds for such judgments. The prejudiced person keeps his consciousness clear and unambivalent by denying or repressing what is unwelcome.

This is not the whole story. Prejudiced subjects do not always give perfectly ideal portraits. There are in the interviews with prejudiced subjects some negative self-appraisals. "I have let myself slip, let my carnal self get away from me. . . ." "Except for my industriousness. That just doesn't exist." "I guess I just got that from the other side of the family." Concerning parents, too, there were some unfavorable remarks. "She [mother] was very nervous. Irritable only when overdoing." "He [father] has a hot temper." In the TAT stories and in the answers to projective questions there was additional evidence that many prejudiced subjects were somewhat ambivalent about themselves and their parents.

So then we have direct evidence that prejudiced subjects hold some unfavorable feelings and we are not, after all, forced to posit the existence of such feelings on the grounds of simple probability. This is fine, but the drawback is that we appear to have lost the distinction we started with since both kinds of subjects are manifestly ambivalent. This is not the view of the California researchers. They and their coders judged that the negative feelings expressed by prejudiced subjects could be seen to have a quite different psychological status from the negative feelings of unprejudiced subjects. The criticisms of self and parents voiced by the prejudiced were, to use a psychoanalytic term, "ego-alien." The criticisms were not being consciously faced as such. They were foreign particles, excrescences, impositions from without.

How on earth could one tell whether a criticism is ego-alien? By any of several signs. The prejudiced subject said: "I have let my carnal self get away from me." The carnality is distinguishable from himself, it is not really he. Another subject said that his lack of industriousness was inherited from one side of his family. It was imposed on him, not something for which he himself could be held to account. In speaking of their parents prejudiced subjects frequently began with generalized glowing praise and then seemed to let slip some specific criticism. Such criticisms were often promptly retracted: "He forced some decisions on me" but "He allowed me to do as I pleased; arguments were about things he didn't want me to have" but "He never denied me anything I needed." There is an impression that the criticism pops out against the subject's intention and is then denied or blamed on an external cause or isolated from the essential self or parent.

In the TAT stories as well as the interview protocols it is said to be possible to recognize ego-alien negative feelings. What are the signs? One prejudiced subject told no stories in which the hero was aggressive against either a father or any sort of "father-figure." Since the storyteller is presumed to identify himself with the hero we might say that there was no consciously accepted aggression of this kind. However, aggression of this kind was exhibited by characters in the story whom the storyteller took pains to reject. The heroes identified themselves with authority but figures from whom the subjects dissociated themselves attacked authority. It is this kind of pattern that is taken to be evidence of ego-alien aggression.

Both prejudiced and unprejudiced subjects seem to have aggressive feelings about themselves and their parents but in the former subjects these feelings are ego-alien which means that they are repressed, denied, or isolated while in the latter subjects these feelings are integrated into objective conceptions. What difference does it make whether a feeling is ego-alien or integrated? Are there differential consequences? The first thing to note is that the subjects for whom negative feelings are ego-alien are the prejudiced subjects, the subjects who attribute undesirable characteristics to outgroups. The sins and weaknesses we miss in their self-descriptions and in their descriptions of their parents turn up in what they say about minority groups.

From the minorities section of the interviews come these assertions. "Jewish people are more *obsequious*." "Since the Negro has that feeling that he isn't up to par, he's always trying to show off. . . . Even though he can't afford it, he will buy an expensive car just to make a show." "The Jew is always crying." "They [Jews] suffer from every lust." "They [Negroes] all carry knives; if you do something they don't like, they will get even with you, they will slice you up." "But they [Jews] are so clannish and aggressive and loud that sometimes I can't stand them."

Let me summarize the case for the prosecution of authoritarians: Certain characteristics that are undesirable are not accepted as characteristic of the subject and his parents. However, there is reason to believe that these characteristics exist in the subject and his parents, leading a kind of covert, submerged life. Finally, these characteristics are confidently attributed to others, in this case to minority groups. This is exactly the pattern of evidence that Freud called projection. Something present in oneself but unwelcome, is projected outward. When we add that the unwelcome "somethings" are chiefly sex and aggression, the important drives in Freudian theory, then projection does indeed seem to be the word for it.

If you are a psychological functionalist it is not enough to label prejudice as projection. One must ask what is projection for? What is its utility for the prejudiced person? One answer is suggested by certain quotations from the interviews. A man who bought a fur coat for his mother from a Jewish salesman took advantage of the fact that the salesman misread the price tag and so quoted a price one hundred dollars below that on the tag. "That was a case where I out-Jewed a Jew." "I am not particularly sorry because of what the Germans did to the Jews. I feel the Jews would do the same type of thing to me." Finally, "I think the time will come when we will have to kill the bastards." The prejudiced person has aggressive impulses but he dare not direct them at members of the in-group. He can direct aggression against minorities if he believes the minorities are themselves aggressive and so deserve to be attacked.

Projection seems also to have a functional role in the southern white man's sexual use of Negro women. If one can believe that Negro women are inherently sensual and promiscuous, then one can believe that they seduce a man against his better impulses. On the other hand, if anything happens between a white woman and a Negro it must be rape since the woman could not desire the Negro while he is certain to desire her. As Chapter 14 shows, Negro men have often been lynched for rape when there was strong reason to believe that a white woman had acted provocatively.

By projecting his own unacceptable impulses to sex and aggression the prejudiced man is able to enjoy some direct expression of these impulses. The direct expression is justified by the supposed sexual and aggressive nature of his out-group targets. Since the beliefs which support the prejudiced man's actions are not the true causes of his actions they may be considered "rationalizations" as well as projections. From a set of static correlates the authors have inferred a dynamic sequence which is put in psychoanalytic terms. Repression of impulses leads to projection which functions as rationalization for an expression.

Why is it that some people are particularly bent on maintaining an idealized image of themselves and of those close to themselves? The evidence suggesting an answer is distributed across many categories coded from the interviews. It goes like this.

The prejudiced subject is exceptionally concerned with status and success and rather little concerned with solidarity and intimacy. He puts friendship, love, and marriage in the service of status-seeking. Anyone with whom he might become intimate or even acquainted is evaluated in terms of status points. The prejudiced man always asks: "What can he do for me?" Prejudiced men sometimes expressed a wish to marry a wealthy woman and usually said they wanted a wife who could help a man advance himself; a woman who would do a man credit. Since a woman's socio-economic status is largely derived from her husband, prejudiced women are more intent than are men on assessing the status potential of a possible spouse. "I'd like to marry someone, for instance, who is going into a profession—maybe a doctor." Speaking of a former boyfriend, a prejudiced woman said: "very wealthy family but he didn't have the drive and ambition that I want."

In speaking of the qualities they would hope to find in a spouse, unprejudiced subjects often mentioned beauty, sensuality, shared aspirations. They used the language of romantic love rather than the language of status calculation. Friends were not chosen because of their positions but because of their personal qualities. Desires for solidarity, intimacy, and love were strong in the unprejudiced.

The status and success that so much concern the prejudiced subject are conceived in a very external way. He speaks of money and material acquisitions and social esteem and power. "Every man has a certain ego that he has to satisfy. You like to be on top. If you're anybody at all, you don't like to be on the bottom." Another man said. "I never had any relations with anyone that didn't have money connected with it." Contrast the unprejudiced subjects: "Money has never meant much to me. . . . Maybe it is stupid and unrealistic. But it is the work itself that gives me satisfaction." And from another unprejudiced subject: "I like to work with young people . . . satisfaction of helping someone. . . . It doesn't pay financially, but . . . you are happier . . . makes good friends. . . ."

What is it that causes the prejudiced person to be so much concerned with status and success? The answer seems to be in the interview categories: "Family status-concerned" vs. "Family status-relaxed." Prejudiced subjects made the following observations "Well, they [parents] didn't want me to run with some kind of people—slummy women—always wanted me to associate with the higher class of people." "We lived in a nice house but really couldn't afford it. It was quite an effort to get into social circles." One man's father did not want him to work as a boy because he thought "it was beneath me." An unprejudiced subject made the following remark: "My mother had and accepted a very simple way of life." Another said: "We had a sort of scorn for people who wanted too much."

It is easy to see that parents who are insecure about their own status may produce children who are bent on success. This is little more than a simple transmission of values. But what is the connection between status anxiety and prejudice? Parents who are anxious about their own status should be very concerned to see that their children are properly brought up; that they are children no one could confuse with the offspring of the lower classes. They will want little ladies and gentlemen, not dirty, brawling brats.

How does one create little ladies and gentlemen out of tiny primates? It is clearly a job for an animal trainer, someone who can "lay down the law in no uncertain terms." Status anxiety might cause parents to interpret the roles of parent and child in terms of authority and submission. Here are some things prejudiced subjects said about their parents as disciplinarians. "Well, my father was a very strict man. He wasn't religious, but strict in raising the youngsters. His word was law, and whenever he was disobeyed, there was punishment." Another man remarked: "Father had to give us one look and we knew what he meant."

The parents who were anxious about status probably set their authority firmly against weakness and passivity and unresponsibility. Probably too they firmly sex-typed behavior, requiring a stereotypical unmixed masculinity from their sons and femininity from their daughters (see Chapter 4). The exercise of so much authority would be bound to engender aggression but this seems to have been put down with a firm hand. A prejudiced woman says of her father: "You always did what he said, but it was right; there was no question about it." A man said: "We did what the elders told us to." (Ever question it?) "Well, I never questioned." A man speaks of overhearing, on the street, a child "sass" his mother and adds: "If I'd have said that to my mother, I wouldn't be able to sit down."

With the psychoanalytic concept of displacement we can make the connection to prejudice. Parental discipline frustrates the child and the frustration creates aggression. This aggression cannot be directed against its legitimate target, that would be insurrection against parental authority, and so the aggression is displaced to a less dangerous target—minority groups. Jews and Negroes and "Okies" and foreigners are inviting targets for displaced aggression because of historical circumstances that have caused them to be underprivileged and to have well-established bad reputations.

We see at last why the authors of *The Authoritarian Personality* have argued that the empirical clustering of beliefs that are not logically related argues for the existence of a dynamic psychological relationship. Why should people whose parents were anxious about status have an idealized image of themselves and of their parents and a very bad opinion of minorities and foreigners? It is because status anxiety produces authoritarian discipline which produces repression of faults and shortcomings and of aggression against authority. It is the fate of repressed faults and shortcomings to be projected to minorities and outsiders. It is the fate of the repressed aggression to be displaced from authority and directed against minorities and outsiders. Finally the projected faults and shortcomings rationalize the aggression. Prejudice plays an integral role in the total ideology but the role is psychological rather than logical.

Not all of the characteristics attributed to the authoritarian personality can be neatly fitted into the above construction but many can be; for example, the fact that the prejudiced person is anti-intraceptive. On the F Scale he agrees that there is too much prying into matters that ought to remain personal and private, that when one has a problem the best thing to do is not think about it and just keep busy. From the interviews it appears that he is not given to reflection or introspection. He does not strive for insight into his own psychological operations, he does not see their role in what happens to him. When things go wrong for the prejudiced person it is because of external forces. He is disposed to be "extrapunitive"—to blame others rather than himself. "She's mean and inconsiderate and doesn't give a darn about anyone else but herself."

Among the prejudiced subjects, even those who were patients at the Langley-Porter Psychiatric Clinic resisted psychological interpretations. In their initial interviews they stressed their somatic or physical symptoms —dizziness, tremor, fainting, breathlessness. As causes they favored particular external events—a death, an illness, a shock. They sometimes spoke of psychological illness as if it were a breakdown of a machine; as if some "part"—the nerves or the mind—had given way under external stress. Because the prejudiced man's psychic equilibrium is founded heavily on repression one would expect him to avoid introspection and psychological inquiries. And so anti-intraceptiveness fits in with the total construction. The unprejudiced subjects tended to construe human life much in the manner of modern psychology. A man is his own fate. Very much of what happens to him is a consequence of his character. For those of us who have become addicted to psychological inquiry there seems to be a dimension missing from the prejudiced person; he lives his life but does not examine it.

The Cognitive Style of the Authoritarian

We come now to the California researchers' independent discovery of Jaensch's typology. Among the coding categories applied to the interviews were two that are concerned with general cognitive style: Rigidity vs. Flexibility, and Intolerance of Ambiguity vs. Tolerance of Ambiguity. Prejudiced subjects were judged to be more rigid and also more intolerant of ambiguity than the unprejudiced.

By what reasoning did the authors arrive at their predictions in the sphere of cognitive style? Intolerance of ambiguity is a generalization of the prejudiced subject's intolerance of emotional ambivalence. Ambivalence exists when both love and hate are felt for the same person. The prejudiced man wants his loves and hates to be wholehearted; he idealizes himself and his parents and anathematizes out-groups. The unprejudiced person objectively appraises both, which means that he lives with a mixture of love and hate and so with uncertainties and conflicts that are not in the consciousness of the prejudiced.

Ambivalence is uncertainty of value and ambiguity is uncertainty of meaning. An ambiguous picture is one that might be either this or that; an ambiguous word is one that might signify either this or that. The prediction that prejudiced subjects will be generally intolerant of ambiguity derives from the assumption that personality manifests a unity of style. The intolerance of ambivalence which is motivated by status anxiety and the ban on aggression against authority is expected to spread into areas where it is not specifically motivated, to become a general style, the prejudiced person is expected to manifest intolerance of ambiguity in all perception and thought.

For the interview protocols it was suggested that the subject who is tolerant of ambiguity will make much use of limiting and qualifying language forms. The subject intolerant of ambiguity would take a more absolute tone. Of course the coders were free to consult the total protocol and so may simply have coded intolerance of ambiguity where there seemed to be intolerance of ambivalence or any of the other stigmata of authoritarianism. Consequently the interview results are not good evidence that prejudiced subjects were intolerant of ambiguity.

Rigidity is a term from common parlance with a root meaning that makes reference to the physical world. To produce changes of form in a substance a degree of resistance must be overcome. When this resistance exceeds our expectations—when a joint moves stiffly or a lump of clay is not malleable—we are likely to call the substance "rigid." Abstracting from the physical case we attribute rigidity to thought and behavior when they are exceptionally resistant to applied forces. An elderly person who cannot change his ideas with the changing times manifests rigidity; a patient in psychotherapy who does not relinquish his defenses, in spite of the therapist's insightful interpretations of them, manifests rigidity. The prejudiced person is supposed to show rigidity in his refusal to give up ethnic stereotypes which are presumably contradicted by common experience (see Chapter 4).

The prejudiced person is also supposed to be rigid in a somewhat different but related sense. His ideas are thickly walled off, one from another. He can, for instance, believe that Jews are both clannish and intrusive, and this espousal of propositions that are particularly contradictory suggests that beliefs are rigidly partitioned from one another. It is postulated that rigidity like intolerance of ambiguity would pervade all of the cognitive processes of the prejudiced.

We are not told in *The Authoritarian Personality* what cues coders were instructed to use in rating for rigidity. It is instructive to learn that rigidity was coded whenever intolerance of ambiguity was coded and where one was not coded the other was not coded. In short, the two formal attributes were treated as equivalent. The probability is strong that both were coded whenever a protocol revealed the more obvious signs of authoritarianism. The interview results are not good evidence that prejudiced subjects showed a pervasive cognitive rigidity.

It is never made clear whether the two formal attributes, rigidity and intolerance of ambiguity, are intended to be conceptually distinct. Usually they are treated as equivalent to one another and to such other attributes as "concreteness" and "stimulus-boundness." In the experimental problems devised to test the idea that prejudiced subjects have a distinctive cognitive style the two concepts usually predict the same kind of style.

Else Frenkel-Brunswik (1949) tested for intolerance of ambiguity with a perceptual problem remote from the sphere of ethnic attitudes. Her subjects were prejudiced and unprejudiced children. A picture of a dog was shown and then followed by a number of pictures representing a gradual transformation of the dog into a cat. At every stage the children were asked to identify the object pictured. The prejudiced children tended to hold on for a longer time to the original interpretation about which they had been certain. They were slow to respond to changes in the picture, reluctant to see things that could not be reconciled with the original interpretation, and inclined to shy away from transitional interpretations.

One could say that the prejudiced children manifested rigidity insofar as they resisted perceptual change by adhering, in the face of contrary evidence, to a first interpretation. They may be said to have shown intolerance of ambiguity insofar as they failed to report that transitional pictures were not clearly dog or clearly cat or anything else, but rather interpretable in a number of ways. The aspects of the performance could be separated but in the report of results they are not.

Rokeach (1948) utilized for the assessment of rigidity in problem-solving a task employed by Luchins (1942) to show the powerful effects on thought of *Einstellung* or "set." Subjects are supposed to determine how they could measure out various quantities of water using bottles of specified sizes. Each bottle can exactly measure only its full volume as no gradations are marked. The best solution is the shortest possible method. The experimenter demonstrates the solution of some such problem as this:

> *Given:* Containers of capacities: 31, 61, and 4 quarts.
> *Obtain:* 22 quarts.
> *Solution:* Fill the bottle that holds 61 quarts; from it fill the 31 quart bottle; from the remainder withdraw 4 quarts twice. In short $61 - 31 - 4 - 4 = 22$.

The first six problems or so can all be solved by the same method which may be abstractly characterized as: Largest—Second Largest—Smallest, two times. These are the "set" problems. Subjects ordinarily see that there is a formula which handles all problems and are pleased to have found it. Beginning with the seventh problem, while the previously used formula continues to apply, a shorter solution also becomes available. For example:

> *Given:* 49, 23, 3
> *Obtain:* 20
> *Solution:* $49 - 23 - 3 - 3 = 20$ or $23 - 3 = 20$.

The effect of the set is very strong and most subjects will continue to use their formula solution. With each additional problem the probability of finding the new shorter possibility increases. The formula answer is so quick and easy that subjects naturally ask themselves what the point can be in going on unless there is more to the problems than they have discovered. Wertheimer and Luchins in their use of this task were not primarily interested in individual differences of performance. For Rokeach the test became an index of generalized mental rigidity with the score being the number of problems presented before the subject found the short answer. Rokeach found that children scoring extremely high on ethnic prejudice were significantly more rigid on these problems than were children scoring low on prejudice. He also found that college students above the median on ethnocentrism were more rigid than students below the median.

Rigidity on this task means perseveration on a mode of thought in the face of information that clearly calls for a new mode. It is a little difficult to see how intolerance of ambiguity would be involved in the present case. One might contend that in order to discover improved solutions a subject must think of the problems as susceptible of a variety of solutions and this may be a kind of ambiguity.

Perhaps the clearest experimental rendering of intolerance of ambiguity is that provided by an experiment of Block and Block (1951). A subject sees a point source of light in a totally dark room that is unfamiliar to him. Although the light is actually stationary it will appear, to almost everyone, to move. This is the autokinetic phenomenon and its exact explanation is not known. If the subject is asked to estimate at intervals the amount of movement in the light he will at first give quite varied estimates. Sooner or later he will settle on a rather limited range which has been called his individual norm (see Chapter 13).

It is the "sooner or later" aspect that interested Block and Block. To vary one's estimates is to tolerate ambiguity as to the amount of movement occurring; to stabilize one's judgments is to eliminate ambiguity. Highly ethnocentric subjects stabilized their judgments on fewer trials than did subjects who were less ethnocentric. Presumably the ethnocentric finds the perceptual uncertainty disagreeable and so resolves it rapidly.

To establish the existence of distinct cognitive styles in the prejudiced and unprejudiced it would be necessary to do the following: 1) conceptualize the two styles with a clarity that would make it possible to invent multiple measures of the two; 2) demonstrate that the styles are enduring general characteristics by showing that the various measures are intercorrelated and reliable; 3) demonstrate that the styles are significantly associated with prejudice and the absence of prejudice. This program has not been accomplished for the styles called "rigid" and "intolerant of ambiguity." What we have are a few studies showing that one or another cognitive performance has in a particular case shown a statistical relationship with prejudice. It is not clear that the various performances operationalize the same concept and it is not known that subjects who are rigid on one would be consistently rigid on all.

We can illustrate the deficiencies in the evidence with the later history of Rokeach's discovery of a relation between prejudice and waterbottle rigidity. Dee Applezweig (1954) repeated the study and did not get the same result; Coulter (1953) repeated it in England and did not get the same result. Brown (1953) made repeated unsuccessful attempts to replicate the result with hundreds of students at the University of Michigan. Brown did find that the relationship appeared when the testing atmosphere was made very competitive and that suggests that it is not rigidity in general but rigidity under stress that correlates with prejudice. The general conclusion of these studies must be, however, that it is problematical whether prejudiced people manifest waterbottle rigidity.

Critique of The Authoritarian Personality

It is probable that no work in social psychology has been given a more meticulous methodological and conceptual examination than has *The Authoritarian Personality*. There is even a follow-up volume of evaluative papers called *Studies in the Scope and Method of "The Authoritarian Personality"* (Christie & Jahoda, 1954). The definitive critique of method is the paper in that volume by Hyman and Sheatsley. We cannot review all of the criticisms that have been made but will cover vital ones.

SAMPLING AND THE ORGANIZATION OF ATTITUDES

While the authors of the Berkeley study guessed that their findings could be generalized to the population of white, non-Jewish, native-born, middle-class Americans they recognized that the sample of persons actually studied was not a representative or random sample of this population or of any other specifiable population. To mention only one restriction, the subjects were almost all members of at least one formal organization since the major method of recruiting subjects was through such organizations. It is known that people who belong to at least one formal organization are in very many respects different from people who belong to no organizations (Christie, 1954). The authors of the Berkeley study took the position that sampling considerations were not vital to their work because they were not interested in estimating the incidence of certain attitudes but rather in establishing relationships among attitudes.

Hyman and Sheatsley take issue with the notion that sampling does not matter in a study of relationships among variables: "Correlation coefficients, just like means or percentages, fluctuate from sample to sample and may well vary in different populations." It is conceivable that persons belonging to formal organizations, and this was the kind of person studied, are more concerned with the social issues that form the content of the A-S, E, and F scales than are persons who belong to no organizations. Concern with issues may create a high degree of organization (intercorrelation) among attitudes. Perhaps the conclusion that certain attitudes cohere into what may be called an antidemocratic ideology is only true of Americans who belong to organizations.

The record of related and subsequent researches on the intercorrelation of attitudes is instructive. These intercorrelations do indeed fluctuate from one sample to another and some of the fluctuations are interesting. E. L. Horowitz (1947), for instance, has shown that the intercorrelations among different kinds of prejudice in children, increase with age and grade in school. Prothro (1952) found that the correlation between anti-Semitic and anti-Negro attitudes for a sample of 383 middle-class adults in Louisiana was only .49, which is well below usual values obtained from adults in the North. Almost all of Prothro's subjects were anti-Negro; that was the subculture norm. Not everyone who was anti-Negro was anti-Semitic; though practically everyone who was favorable to the Negroes was also favorable to the Jews. This result shows that where a prejudice is a definite norm the people subscribing to that prejudice may not be the same kinds of people as those who subscribe to it where the prejudice is not a clear norm. Many Southerners go along with the norm concerning Negroes though they are not otherwise ethnocentric. At the same time anyone strong enough to oppose the norm about Negroes seems to have an equalitarian ideology which is also manifest in his favorable attitude toward Jews.

Whereas the magnitude of the correlations among A-S, E, and F fluctuates from sample to sample there is one impressive invariance— no negative correlations seem ever to have been reported (Christie, 1954). It does seem fairly safe therefore to conclude that A-S, E, and F were organized together for middle-class Americans in the 1940's and 1950's. The Berkeley researchers certainly were not justified in generalizing their conclusions as widely as they did, but they seem to have been lucky. They hit on a finding that is as highly reliable and highly general as they, on insufficient evidence, thought it was.

ACQUIESCENCE RESPONSE SET

The questionnaire items of the A-S, E, and F scales are all worded in such a way that agreement with the items represents, respectively, anti-Semitism, ethnocentrism, or potential fascism. The authors were aware that it is generally better practice in opinion-attitude scales to include both positive and negative items. In connection with the construction of the A-S Scale the authors set forth the considerations that persuaded them to write all the items of each scale as authoritarian assertions (Adorno, et al., 1950, p. 59). It is now clear that they made a mistake.

In a 1946 publication Cronbach discussed the problem of response sets in paper and pencil tests; for example, a subject might consistently tend to agree with assertions—regardless of their content. If all the items in a scale assert in the same direction a high score might be as much a manifestation of this sort of acquiescence response set as of agreement with the particular content of the assertions. Cohn (1953) was one of the first to propose that the F Scale was in part a measure of such acquiescent tendencies. He found a correlation of $+.41$ between agreement with a mixed lot of questions from a personality inventory (the MMPI) and a version of the F Scale. The storm really broke in 1955 when Bass composed reversed versions of the F Scale items and administered both the original scale and the reversed scale to the same subjects. If authoritarian content were the only determinant of responses then agreement with an F Scale item ought always to be associated with disagreement with that item's reversal. The resulting correlation between scores on the F Scale and the reverse scale should approximate -1.00. The obtained correlation was only $-.20$ and so it was evident that the degree of authoritarianism manifested on the F Scale was not usually matched by the degree of authoritarianism manifested on the reversed scale. Further analyses showed that some subjects consistently acquiesced with both authoritarian assertions and their reversals whereas some subjects consistently disagreed with both kinds of assertions. The acquiescent subject, had he been given the F Scale alone, would have appeared to be authoritarian and the disagreeing subject would have appeared to be equalitarian. Indeed one treatment of his data (shown by Messick and Jackson in 1957 to be unwarranted) suggested to Bass that acquiescence was more important than authoritarianism as a determinant of F Scale scores.

The discovery of the role of acquiescence in the F Scale made uncertain the interpretation of many studies showing consistent correlations between F scores and scores on other paper and pencil tests. Many of these other tests were also written so that most items asserted in a single direction and so these tests like the F Scale were measures of acquiescence. Consequently many results that had been interpretated as manifestations of the generality of authoritarianism now appeared to be interpretable as manifestations of the generality of acquiescence. This unsettling possibility applied to the original correlations among A-S, E, and F scores since all of these scales were unbalanced. An assortment of researches confirmed the importance of acquiescence as a determinant of

F scores though, in general, it did not appear to be more important than authoritarianism as Bass had thought. In 1958 Christie and his associates added some depth to the discussion and also some superior data.

What does it mean to "reverse" an F Scale item? Consider the item: "Some people are born with an urge to jump from high places." One investigator constructed as its reverse: "No people are born with an urge to jump from high places." This latter is the logical contrary of the former and so agreement with both would suggest either a lapse of memory or extreme illogicality. However, disagreement with both would not be illogical. For while the two are contraries they do not between them exhaust the realm of possible opinions. One might hold that, in the absence of definite knowledge, the best view is that there may or may not be people who are born with an urge to jump from high places. An equalitarian who held this view would disagree with both the original F Scale item and its reversal.

Here is another reversal: "Science has its place, but there are many important things that can never possibly be understood by the human mind" becomes "All the mysteries surrounding our lives will sooner or later be cleared up through the progress of science." While the latter is intended to be an equalitarian assertion reversing the former, it impresses me as somewhat more authoritarian than the original. The use of the quite unjustified, dogmatic *all* should recommend it to authoritarians, even those who have agreed with the original version providing only that they do not recollect the detailed content of the original.

It is fun to consider various reversals of F Scale items because in the process you discover some subtleties of linguistic meaning. Think back to our discussion of the A-S Scale and the item: "The trouble with letting Jews into a nice neighborhood is that they gradually give it a typical Jewish atmosphere." Suppose we try a psychological rather than a strictly logical reversal, substituting favorable terms for the unfavorable. "One delightful consequence of having Jews in a neighborhood is that they contribute a charming Jewish quality to the neighborhood atmosphere." It sounds like a gushy clubwoman overcompensating for a covert but especially vicious anti-Semitism. If she were speaking the sentence we would see her mouth give a wry twist and her voice break on "Jewish" in "charming Jewish quality." It is not an item that appeals to the equalitarian in spite of the intended reversal of sentiment.

It is probably not possible to write items that are perfect psychological contraries to the assertions of the F Scale. Each of these latter conveys a very complex pattern of connotations. To reverse that full pattern is not an easy trick. However, as Christie and his associates have shown (1958) the reversals can be better than those we have cited. Witness their: "An urge to jump from high places is probably the result of unhappy personal experiences rather than something inborn" and their "The findings of science may some day show that many of our most cherished beliefs are wrong." Even Christie's items are not invariably rejected when their reversals have been accepted, but the tendency across numerous subject samples has been in that direction. With these items it is possible to compose F Scales with equal numbers of authoritarian and equalitarian assertions.

Behavior that is consistent for one person over a range of situations and also different from one person to another is a personality characteristic. Response sets to agree or disagree first appeared as sources of error in personality inventories but we have come to realize that they are also personality characteristics in their own right; they may be characteristics of greater interest than most of those that the inventories were designed to measure. In 1960, Couch and Keniston gave names to the two personality types involved—"Yeasayers" and "Naysayers."

Couch and Keniston made a powerful demonstration of the existence of the two kinds of response set. They administered hundreds of items from a large and diversified collection of inventories and assigned each subject an "Over-all Agreement Score" (OAS). Subjects with a high OAS are the Yeasayers and subjects with a low OAS are the Naysayers. Yeasaying and Naysaying were demonstrated to be relatively stable and generalized traits by showing that subjects with a high OAS continued to agree with items from new tests of various kinds and subjects with low OAS continued to disagree. Clinical studies of extreme scorers on the OAS suggested that Yeasayers are individuals with weak ego controls who accept impulses without reservation whereas Naysayers are individuals who control and suppress impulses.

For present purposes the important point is the connection between OAS scores and F Scale scores. Using a short form of the F Scale in which the items are all worded in the same direction (as authoritarian assertions) the correlation with OAS was $+.37$. Apparently, then, yeasaying is a factor in F Scale scores but it only accounts for about 14 per cent of the variance which means that the content of the items is still the major determinant of scores.[1]

It had occurred to several investigators that Yeasaying, since it seems to be a matter of accepting authoritative statements, might itself be a manifestation of authoritarianism. However, Couch and Keniston demonstrated with pure measures of Yeasaying and of authoritarianism

1. Peabody (1961) has reported evidence that it is chiefly negative or anti-content responses that are valid. One can feel more confident that low scorers are opposed to authoritarianism than one can that high scorers are authoritarian. High scores in Peabody's data were largely attributable to acquiescence and seem to represent an absence of definite attitudes.

(using a balanced scale) that the two personality characteristics are completely independent.

In general summary, then, it seems to be certain that a tendency to acquiescence has been a factor in standard F Scale scores but not the major factor. Since acquiescence or Yeasaying is also a factor in many other personality inventories correlations between F Scale scores and other inventory scores may have been generated by acquiescence rather than authoritarianism. In the original Berkeley research the correlations demonstrating the generality of authoritarianism, the correlations among A-S, E, and F scores were probably somewhat elevated by the acquiescence set that was free to operate in all of them. It may be significant that the correlations of A-S, E, and F are somewhat lower with PEC (about .55) than with one another since the PEC scale was balanced with some items asserting conservative attitudes and some asserting liberal attitudes. It is equally certain that acquiescence is not a strong enough factor to have produced all of the correlation among A-S, E, and F and that significant evidence for the generality of authoritarianism remains intact. The results with interviews, TAT stories, and projective questions are exempt from the effects of response set, since with these methods one does not suggest an answer. The fact that the relations demonstrated in this work generally confirm the findings with questionnaires increases our confidence that the questionnaire findings were not entirely generated by response set. Future studies of authoritarianism should employ balanced F Scales, such as have been developed by Christie, and by Couch and Keniston, in order to eliminate the effects of response set.

CRITICISMS OF CONTENT ANALYSES

Content analyses were made of the interviews of both normal subjects and psychiatric patients, as well as of projective sentence completions, and the TAT stories; in short for all data except the questionnaire responses. The methodological criticisms that must be made of these analyses are numerous and serious. The criticisms do not all apply to any one analysis but there was no analysis exempt from all criticism.

Interviewer Knowledge of Questionnaire Responses. In the main interview study forty highly prejudiced persons and forty unprejudiced persons served as subjects. "In each case the interview was preceded by the study, on the part of the interviewer, of the information gathered previously, especially a detailed study of the questionnaire responses" (Adorno, et al., 1950 p. 302). The investigators adopted this practice because the questionnaire responses could help to guide the interviewer in his probing for answers to the underlying questions of the interview schedule.

The coding of the interview protocols was to be done by persons not acquainted with a subject's questionnaire responses. It was perfectly clear to the investigators that if a coder knew he was dealing with the protocols of a prejudiced subject he might be more disposed to find "Rigidity" and "Intolerance of Ambiguity" and "Idealization of Parents" than if he knew he was dealing with the protocols of an unprejudiced subject. Blind coding was employed to obviate the possibility of inducing unreal associations between scale scores and the content of interview protocols. However, the danger warded off in the coding stage had already been welcomed aboard in the interviewing stage.

You may remember that the interview schedule left the interviewer free to determine the particular questions he would ask and the order of their asking. Is it not probable that when an interviewer knew he was dealing with a highly prejudiced subject he tried a little harder to obtain evidence of "Rigidity," "Idealization of Parents," and the like, than when he knew that he was dealing with an unprejudiced subject? Indeed there is fragmentary evidence in the interview quotations of the use of leading questions. Thus, when a respondent spoke of premarital sex relations, the interviewer asked, "All momentary relationships?" (Adorno, et al., 1950, p. 393) If bias did not enter into the questioning itself it may have done so in the interviewer's subsequent effort to make a verbatim record from his own shorthand notes. Expectations we know can have a selective effect on recall.

The "too knowledgeable" interviewer is a defect that occurred only in the major interview study. The interviews with psychiatric patients were taken by social workers and physicians who knew nothing about the authoritarian personality research. Interviews were not involved in the TAT study and the sentence completion study.

Examination of Data in Advance of Coding. This is one criticism that applies to all four content analyses; the investigators invariably examined their data in search of contrasts between prejudiced and unprejudiced subjects before they made up a scoring manual. The coding categories were defined so as to capture the contrasts that seemed to be in the data. The blind coding from the manual is simply an effort to show that differences which appear to exist when one knows whether or not a subject is prejudiced can also be found when one does not know. And also, of course, to show that the content categories can be communicated from one person to another.

If one closely examines two sets of complex multi-dimensional data it will usually be possible to find some differences between the two that are consistent enough to be statistically significant. Suppose all of the conceivable dimensions of contrast were, in the full population of subjects, unrelated to the dimension that governs the division of our data into two sets. Suppose that across the whole population of middle class Americans none of the coding categories that might be used in an analysis is significantly related to being prejudiced or unprejudiced. It could nevertheless happen that in any small sample from this population some categories would be related to prejudice at such levels of significance as a p of .05 or .01. Consider what the .05 level of significance means: differences as great or greater than the one obtained would not occur more than five times out of a hundred in samples of this size if there were no difference in the population in question. If we had predicted our differences in advance and they were significant at this level we could be reasonably confident that these were not chance outcomes. However, if we permit ourselves to pick over the data until we find something significant then we may simply be seizing upon those few of the hundreds of conceivable contrasts which will in any particular sample fall by chance into a five-times-in-a-hundred pattern of contrast.

What ought to have been done? Probably the investigators needed to search at least one collection of data for contrasts between the prejudiced and unprejudiced. One would have thought, however, that one such free search would have sufficed to establish the personality dynamics we have described: Represssion to Projection and Displacement and Anti-intraception to Aggression against Minorities. In subsequent studies the contrasts of content should have been predictable from this theory and these subsequent studies would then have tested the theory. Or, in any particular study, they might have examined only one-half of the data in advance and used the remaining half as a test of expectations generated in the first half. These things were not done in any study but, instead, the full collection of data was always examined in advance.

The Coding of Multiple Variables from the Same Content. In the main interview study something like ninety variables were coded from each total protocol. Remember that the coders in this case were members of the research staff who were thoroughly familiar with the research hypotheses. These hypotheses suggest that one entire set of coded categories will hang together in the protocols of prejudiced subjects and another set in the protocols of unprejudiced subjects. Suppose now that in a given protocol a coder has found some quite unmistakable expressions of Anti-intraception and some clear indications of Extra-punitiveness and so has begun to think of the protocol as the production of a prejudiced person. Suppose it is now time to code for "Conventional Idealization of Parents" vs. "Objective Appraisal." What will he do with the following statement: "Mother was, of course, a very wonderful person. She was very nervous. Irritable only when overdoing" (Adorno, et al., 1950 p. 342). It would seem as though the statement might be interpreted either as "Idealization" or as "Objective Appraisal." If the coder has already decided that he is working on the protocol of a prejudiced subject will he not be more likely to decide on "Idealization" which is a prejudiced category than if he has decided that he is working on the protocol of an unprejudiced subject? The statement in question was in fact coded as "Idealization."

It is to be expected in these circumstances that two coders, both acquainted with the research hypotheses, will make similar decisions and so show high scoring reliability. However, we cannot tell which of the ninety content categories are truly associated with prejudice and which only seem to be so associated because their scoring has been influenced by the scoring of other categories. The Berkeley investigators undertook to prevent this scoring bias (which they call a "halo effect") by instructing coders to adopt an analytic attitude—dealing with one category at a time in isolation from all others. Probably the coders tried very hard to do this. The difficulty is that we cannot be sure that they succeeded.

It was only the protocols from the main interview study that were coded for multiple variables by the same rater. The interviews with psychiatric patients were coded by seven control raters with each rater scoring *just one variable*. Consequently this smaller interview study is exempt from the present criticism. The TAT stories and responses to projective questions were shuffled so that the several productions of a subject could not be linked together. However, it was possible to score a single response—a story or an answer to a projective question—for more than one category and so there was the possibility of some halo effect. The scoring of one category on a story could influence the decision about another category. The analysis of these data was then somewhat less subject to the present criticism than was the analysis of the main interview protocols but it was not completely exempt.

The Reporting of Reliabilities in Terms of Coding Categories that are too General. For the main interview study nine protocols were coded by two raters. There were some ninety categories to be coded and these were put together as pairs such that one member was identified as a High Prejudice category and the other as a Low Prejudice category. We should like to know how well the authors agreed in their decisions for each pair even though there could only be nine items per pair. We are not given this information but instead *The Authoritarian Personality* reports for both raters the percentage of High categories scored in each total interview. For the most part these are closely similar but closely similar overall percentages do not guarantee closely similar decision patterns on particular categories. Both raters, for example, could have scored half of the pairs as High and half as Low but they might have exactly reversed one another in terms of the particular categories scored each way.

The reliability data reported suggest that coders can agree as to whether a total protocol is more likely to be the product of a prejudiced or an unprejudiced subject. But that reliability is not to the point since the discussion of the interviews chiefly concerns the particular content categories characteristic of the two kinds of subject. The study does not report the data that would tell us whether the individual categorical judgments can be made in a reliable fashion.

For the TAT and projective question studies, the judgments for which reliability coefficients are reported are not so crude as in the interview study but they are also not at the level of particular content categories which is the level of the discussion of results. For example, the first item among the projective questions asks subjects to say what moods they find particularly unpleasant or disturbing. The Low categories are: "Conscious conflict and guilt; Focal dependency and love-seeking; Open hostility, by self or others, toward love objects." The High categories are: "Violations of conventional values; Threatening or nonsupporting environment; Rumblings from below; and Omissions." The authors tell us that for answers to this question there was a mean agreement of 93 per cent as to whether an answer was High, Neutral, or Low. But two coders could agree that an answer was High and for one this might be because the response seemed to fall into the category "Violations of conventional values" while for the other it might seem to go in the category "Threatening or nonsupporting environment." We are not told how well coders agreed on particular content categories but conclusions are drawn in terms of these content categories.

It is only in the case of the psychiatric interviews that reliabilities are reported for coding judgments at the level of specificity appropriate to the treatment of results and to the theoretical discussion. Each variable was separately coded and the percentage agreements between a control rater and a principal rater are reported.

AUTHORITARIANISM AND EDUCATION—IQ—SES

In *The Authoritarian Personality* there is a chapter that reports on the relations of ethnocentrism with IQ and with education. Table 10-1

TABLE 10-1. MEAN WECHSLER-BELLEVUE IQ SCORE FOR EACH QUARTILE OF THE ETHNOCENTRISM SCALE (PSYCHIATRIC CLINIC, MEN AND WOMEN)

(From *The Authoritarian Personality* by T. W. Adorno, et al. Copyright 1950 by The American Jewish Committee. Reprinted with the permission of Harper & Row, Publishers, Incorporated.)

Form 45 E Scale quartiles	Range on E	N	Mean IQ
Low quartile	10–24	8	125.3
Low middle quartile	25–36	5	117.8
High middle quartile	37–50	13	113.9
High quartile	51–70	11	107.3
		37	114.9

TABLE 10-2. MEAN NUMBER OF YEARS OF EDUCATION FOR EACH QUARTILE
OF THE ETHNOCENTRISM SCALE (PSYCHIATRIC CLINIC, MEN AND WOMEN)

(From *The Authoritarian Personality* by T. W. Adorno, et al. Copyright 1950 by
The American Jewish Committee. Reprinted with the permission of Harper & Row,
Publishers, Incorporated.)

Form 45 E Scale quartiles	Range on E	N	Mean yrs. education
Low quartile	10–24	29	13.8
Low middle quartile	25–36	28	12.7
High middle quartile	37–50	27	11.8
High quartile	51–70	28	11.2
		112	12.4

presents one set of findings for IQ and Table 10-2 a set of findings for
education. From one subject sample to another the correlations vary in
size but they are invariably negative (E scores rise as IQ or years of education fall), generally significantly greater than zero but generally below
.5. The authors conclude that there is a significant but not very large
relation between ethnocentrism and the other two variables.

Hyman and Sheatsley (1954) in their critique of the Berkeley Study
report data from a National Opinion Research Council survey showing
the associations between five particular F Scale items and years of education. These are reproduced as Table 10-3 and they show a perfectly
consistent decline of authoritarianism with increasing education. Hyman
and Sheatsley also point to a number of differences between the prejudiced and unprejudiced, attributed to personality dynamics in the original
study, that have a more obvious and plausible explanation in terms of
education. For example, one of the projective questions asked: "What
great people do you admire most?" Unprejudiced subjects named Whit-
man, Pushkin, Beethoven, Voltaire, Comte, Freud, and Pestalozzi among
others. Prejudiced subjects named General Marshall, General MacArthur,
Lindbergh, the Pope, Henry Ford, and Bing Crosby among others. The
researchers conceptualize the difference by saying that the unprejudiced
value intellectual, scientific, aesthetic, and social achievements while the
prejudiced value power, control, and conservative Americana. There is
a simpler rubric: the names listed by the prejudiced are known to everybody in the United States while those listed by the unprejudiced are only
known to the better educated.

IQ and years of education are, of course, positively correlated. In
addition, years of education is one index of socio-economic status (SES)
and is somewhat correlated with such others as income and possessions.
In addition there are certain less obvious correlates of the individual
variables: probably more schooling goes with being moderately young

TABLE 10-3. AGREEMENT WITH F SCALE ITEMS AND EDUCATION

	College N = 217	High school N = 545	Grammar school N = 504
Agree that:			
The most important thing to teach children is absolute obedience to their parents	35%	60%	80%
Any good leader should be strict with people under him in order to gain their respect	36	51	66
Prison is too good for sex criminals. They should be publicly whipped or worse	18	31	45
There are two kinds of people in the world: the weak and the strong	30	53	71
No decent man can respect a woman who has had sex relations before marriage	14	26	39

rather than elderly since the availability of education has increased in our lifetimes. Consequently we must suppose that ethnocentrism and authoritarianism are somewhat related to a great bundle of variables having something to do with socio-economic status; the relationship seems to be negative.

How strong are the correlations between ethnocentrism and IQ, education, or other related variables? There have been a number of studies on this point, and Christie (1954), after reviewing them, estimates that the correlation between either IQ and F scores or years of education and F scores would, for a representative cross-sectional sample, range between −.50 and −.60. In the Berkeley studies the range of intelligence and education was, for the most part, quite restricted and restriction of range would operate to keep down the value of correlation coefficients. Christie found that in the various studies that have been reported the size of the correlation increased as the range increased. For this reason he argues that −.50 to −.60 is a reasonable estimate for correlations based on a full range on both IQ and F scores. IQ, and years of education are themselves positively correlated. Christie estimates that with education partialed out the correlation between intelligence and F scores is only about −.20. It seems to be chiefly education or cultural sophistication, rather than intelligence *per se* that reduces authoritarianism.

What is the implication of the fact that the components of the authoritarian syndrome are correlated with education and SES? You remember that the Berkeley researchers held that the covariation of a mixed lot of attitudes and traits having no clear logical relationship argues for the existence of a unifying personality dynamic. Critics have contended that this position is destroyed by the demonstration of a correlation with education and SES. The numerous components of authoritarianism are found together in a person simply because they are the norms of his subculture—the little-educated, less bright, low SES subculture. To this we must respond by asking: Why does this subculture put its norms together as it does? Why should self-glorification, parent idealization, impunitiveness, anti-intraception, and prejudice cohere as a set of norms? The question is there whether you ask it for the individual or for the group.

It is possible, however, that low IQ, education, and SES can account for the syndrome without recourse to personality dynamics. Perhaps parents with low SES stamp out all aggression against authority in their children because it is likely to lead to delinquency and trouble with the police. Perhaps people with low SES are prejudiced against Negroes because it takes severe discrimination to keep the Negro beneath them in status. They may be prejudiced against Jews because the stereotype of the ruthless, clannish Jew accounts in an agreeable way for his occasional economic ascendance. Perhaps the person of low SES is not reflective or introspective because he is too busy hustling to earn a living. We can easily imagine plausible reasons for the association of each authoritarian trait with the cluster that includes low IQ, little education and low SES and so the explanation of the covariation among the traits is simply their several particular ties to the same underlying factors.

In what way does the above account differ from the one offered by the Berkeley group? Both explain the covariation of traits but the question is whether those traits are a bundle or a system. If we account for their coherence entirely in terms of particular ties with income and education and the like then the coherence is simply incidental to their common dependence on the same factors. The components hang together but are not interdependent. The Berkeley group contends, however, that the proscription of any aggression against authority requires ethnic prejudice because aggression must somehow be released. Proscription of aggression against authority in combination with ethnic prejudice requires that there be little introspection or reflection because self-examination would disturb the system of repression, displacement, and rationalization. It is the view of the Berkeley group that the components of the authoritarian syndrome hang together because they are a working system. If it is true that these components are the norms of an underprivileged subculture then I think the contribution of the Berkeley research is to show that this combination of norms makes a viable pattern for human personalities. Norms are not put together at random or incidentally.

When they stabilize into a particular combination it must be because that is a combination that works for human personalities.

In *The Authoritarian Personality* some importance is assigned to SES. It is status concern or anxiety that is presumed to cause certain parents to interpret their parental role in an authoritarian way and from this role-interpretation all the rest is supposed to follow. In 1954 Else Frenkel-Brunswik wrote a paper called *Further Explorations by a Contributor to "The Authoritarian Personality"* (Christie & Jahoda, 1954) in which she described an extensive study of prejudice in children and adolescents. In this work there were interviews with parents of children who were extremely high in prejudice and also with parents of children low in prejudice. Frenkel-Brunswik reports that the subjective feeling of socio-economic "marginality" on the part of the parents rather than their objective SES was the crucial factor in ethnocentrism. A feeling of marginality is said to exist when there is a discrepancy between actual status and the status one aspires to. "Marginality" seems to be much the same as the status concern of the original study.

However, while marginality may be the crucial factor it is evident that Frenkel-Brunswik also found the familiar negative correlation between F scores and SES. She reports a "relatively high percentage of ethnocentric families among the workers . . ." (p. 233). It is easy to imagine a reconciliation of the two aspects of SES that seem to engender authoritarianism. Perhaps the feeling of marginality is the critical factor but feelings of marginality may be especially likely to arise at the lower end of the SES scale, among the working class. The latter part of this reconciliation does not sit well with the liberal intellectual since fascism is supposed to be a movement of the lower middle class rather than of the proletariat.

Nevertheless the evidence is strong that the lower the SES the higher the F score. The idea that marginality creates ethnocentrism, on the other hand, is highly dubitable. MacKinnon and Centers (1956) used a brief F Scale in a public opinion survey of Los Angeles County. With regard to objective SES they found the usual thing: working-class, lower-education groups were exceptionally authoritarian. In addition, these investigators asked each informant to say in what class he placed himself and to rate the strength of his sense of membership in that class. For those who identified themselves as middle class and also for those who identified themselves as working class, those who also identified themselves as "borderline," the "peripheral" members of the classes were *least* authoritarian. If the "borderline" of MacKinnon and Centers is the same as the "margin" of Frenkel-Brunswik then somebody is wrong. Actually the two studies may not be contradictory; it is possible that the so-called "borderline" cases of MacKinnon and Centers were simply unconcerned about social classes rather than insecure about their own positions.

In summary, SES, intelligence, and education are all negatively related to F scores and the relationships are stronger than the Berkeley authors had realized. Of the various negative correlates it seems to be education that is strongest. Kornhauser, Sheppard and Mayer (1956) found that among men who were all auto workers, those with an eighth grade education or less were more authoritarian than those with a greater amount of education. Cohn and Carsch (1954) showed that among workers in a German cosmetics factory, those who had attended *Hochschule* had lower F scores than those with less education. Authoritarianism may be the world-view of the uneducated in western industrial societies. It may be that this world-view hangs together because of the dynamic inter-relations among the parts posited by the Berkeley research.

After the Critique

What of *The Authoritarian Personality* survives the many devastating criticisms of its methods? Hyman and Sheatsley (1954) summarize their masterful methodological critique by saying: "Our major criticisms lead us inevitably to conclude that the authors' theory has not been proved by the data they cite . . ." (p. 119). Notice the care with which this conclusion is formulated: the theory has not been proved by a particular set of data. A methodological critique cannot conclude that a theory is mistaken. Ultimately of course it is the correctness of the theory that we care about. What would be the best opinion on this important matter? By this time you have probably formed an opinion and so have I. How well do we agree?

There are really two sets of methodological criticisms dividing neatly into those that apply to the work with questionnaires and those that apply to the work with projective methods. The most serious defects in the questionnaire work are the inadequate sampling and the operation of response sets. Both criticisms are sound. In spite of their cogency it seems to me that there is a substantial residual probability that the chief conclusion of the questionnaire work is correct: attitudes of anti-Semitism, ethnocentrism, and authoritarianism do generally go together.

You remember that studies done since the original book, though never based on fully adequate samples, do very consistently find significant relations among these attitudes. There seems never to have been a report of a negative relationship. Response set has certainly magnified the size of these relations but, from the evidence, the effects of response set are not great enough completely to wash out the relations. Finally, some of the findings of the questionnaire study were replicated in the projectives study and, while this latter work has its own deficiencies, some account must be taken of the convergence in the two sets of data.

Christie and Cook (1958) have published a bibliography of research relating to the authoritarian personality through 1956. They list 230 titles. In their summary of the work they write: "Although there are serious problems in evaluating research, the over-all picture shows consistency of findings in many of the most intensively studied areas. The E and F Scales are found to be significantly correlated in a wide array of samples and predictions of relationships with attitudinal measures are almost invariably confirmed" (p. 189). I take this conclusion to be about the same as mine.

The flaws in the study of projectives are more serious: interviewer knowledge of the interviewees' questionnaire responses; derivation of scoring categories from prior examination of data; coding of multiple variables from the same data; inadequate reports of coding reliability. Each study of projective materials was flawed by at least one of these and so there are grounds for dismissing the evidence of each study. My own evaluation differs from that of Hyman and Sheatsley in that I should like to give some weight to the congruence of evidence across the main interviews, TAT's, projective questions, and psychiatric interviews.

There is only one criticism that applies to all four studies: the derivation of scoring categories from prior examination of data. What the authors ought to have done in their first study is to examine a part of their data in search of discriminating categories and use the remainder to test. The four studies taken together suggest that the categories would have survived such a test. Suppose we consider one of the studies, for example the main interview study, as the preliminary examination of data in search of categories. Since the other studies employ some categories that are the same as or closely similar to those used with the main interviews it would seem that the authors could have used these studies as tests and need not have made preliminary examinations of data. The fact that they did make such examinations does not completely vitiate the force of the convergence in the findings.

Finally we can be more affirmative than Hyman and Sheatsley because we are not doing a critique of the Berkeley study but are trying to decide on the tenability of its conclusions in view of all the studies that have been done. Perhaps the least well-supported of all the findings in the Berkeley study are those concerning the genesis of authoritarianism in childhood. To begin with, the data were all obtained from adult recollections and such recollections can be grossly inaccurate. Secondly, the data were nearly all obtained in the main interview study and not directly checked in the projective materials; the main interview study had many methodological defects. However, Frenkel-Brunswik has directly studied prejudice in childhood and adolescence. She reports confirmation of most of the original findings.

"It was found that, at least after the age of ten, children's personalities tend to fall into patterns similar to those observed in the adults described in *The Authoritarian Personality*. Thus ethnocentric young-sters tend to display authoritarian aggression, rigidity, cruelty, supersti-tion, externalization, and projectivity, denial of weakness, power orienta-tion, and tend toward dichotomous conceptions of sex roles, of kinds of people, and of values" (Frenkel-Brunswik, 1954). In the homes of the ethnocentric children discipline was strict, rigid, and punitive. Unpreju-diced children were more apt to see both positive and negative features in their parents; they were more able to accept feelings of love and hate for the same persons. Prejudiced children seemed compelled to see their parents as wholly good though there were indications that they also saw them, covertly, as wholly bad. Prejudiced children conceived it to be the chief business of both parents and teachers to discipline their charges and keep them in line. While Frenkel-Brunswik published several partial reports of this work (1949, 1953, 1954), she never made a complete re-port and that is unfortunate in view of its considerable importance.

On the level of covariation, of one variable correlated with another, the findings of *The Authoritarian Personality* seem to me to be quite well established. Anti-Semitism goes with ethnocentrism goes with anti-intraception goes with idealization of parents and self goes with authori-tarian discipline in childhood goes with a rigid conception of sex roles, etc. Two of the presumptive correlates are not well established: status-concern or marginality and the cognitive style characterized by rigidity and intolerance of ambiguity.

On the level of interpretation, the level on which repression is sup-posed to lead to displacement, rationalization, and anti-intraception, things are less certain. These ideas about personality dynamics cannot be proved by correlation. Studies of an entirely different kind are needed. Is it the case, for example, that if an authoritarian somehow became able to tolerate ambivalence, to see faults in himself and his parents, that he would thereupon lose his prejudices or at any rate become able to adjust them to fact? One would have to find a way of bringing ambivalence into consciousness (psychotherapy? hypnosis?) without in any way directly attacking the prejudice. It would not be an easy kind of research to do and it has not been done.

The major alternative to the personality dynamic explanation of the covariation is the suggestion that the traits of the authoritarian cohere simply because they are the norms of people with little education and low SES. For each particular trait one could work out some plausible derivation from one or another aspect of SES. The dynamic explanation would make the coherence tighter by showing how one trait supports another, not logically but in terms of the needs and defenses postulated by psychoanalytic theory. It is likely that both sets of forces—the dynamic interrelations as well as the ties with status and education—cooperate to hold this mosaic together.

Is There an Authoritarian of the Left?

The best measure of authoritarianism is the F Scale. It is objective and quantitative and much easier to use than interview protocols or projective data. However, the F Scale was characterized by the authors in two ways: 1) As a means of identifying fascistic proclivities or an authoritarianism of the right; 2) as a means of identifying authoritarianism in general and this presumably could be of the left as well as of the right. The authors do not actually demonstrate a connection between F Scale scores and affiliation with fascistic political parties. The three inmates of San Quentin who were called fascists were so labelled by the researchers because of their violently antidemocratic views rather than because they were members of a fascist party. We shall first inquire whether the F Scale can identify genuine political fascists to see if it is a measure of authoritarianism of the right. If it is we shall then want to know whether it is only a measure of authoritarianism of the right or whether it can also identify authoritarians of the left—if such there be.

THE F SCALE SCORES OF FASCISTS AND COMMUNISTS

In the 1930's, more than a decade before the publication of *The Authoritarian Personality*, Stagner developed a scale for the assessment of fascistic attitudes. In German and Italian fascistic writings he identified seven characteristic content areas: 1) nationalism, 2) imperialism, 3) militarism, 4) racial antagonism, 5) anti-radicalism, 6) middle-class consciousness, and 7) a benevolent despot or strong-man philosophy of government. The first five of these areas suggest the content of the A-S and E scales and scores on these scales are highly correlated with F Scale scores. The last two seem to have been directly covered in the F Scale. Some of Stagner's items have near-matches in the F Scale; for example, from Stagner's scale we have: "America has plenty of plans—what it needs is strong men who are willing to work for recovery"; the F Scale includes: "What this country needs most, more than laws and political programs, is a few courageous, tireless devoted leaders in whom the people can put their faith." In sum, the ideological content found to be characteristic of fascism in Stagner's independent study (1936) is very similar to the content of the scales used to assess authoritarianism.

During World War II there were opportunities to investigate the personality characteristics of captured Nazis. Dicks (1950) conducted psychiatric interviews with 138 German POW's, some of whom were fanatical Nazis and some of whom were either politically uninvolved or else active anti-Nazis. At several points Dicks' description of the traits characteristic of the fanatical Nazis resembles the Berkeley characterization of the authoritarian. The fanatical Nazi was lacking in rebellion against his father; he showed sadism, projectivity, and a tabu on tenderness.

These fragments of indirect evidence are helpful but one waits for the decisive demonstration. What are the F Scale scores of members of fascist parties? Cohn and Carsch (1954) had the scale translated into German and they administered it in 1952 to 140 workers in a German cosmetics factory. The mean F score was 5.26 and the standard deviation was .86. This mean score was, at the time, the highest that had ever been reported; The San Quentin prisoners had the highest mean of the groups studied in the Berkeley research but that mean was only 4.73. If one makes the assumption that these German workers were former Nazis then the data support the validity of the claim that the F Scale measures fascistic tendencies. However, we do not know that the workers had all been Nazis. In addition, the sample was working class, and low SES groups everywhere have had high F scores. Further, some students of the F Scale (e.g., Peabody) doubt that it is possible strictly to "translate" the complex and subtle assertions of the scale from English into another language.

Can the scale be validated with English-speaking political fascists? The problem is to find them. In the immediate postwar period they could not be found in the United States. Today there are the George Lincoln Rockwell Nazis but they have not been studied. Luckily (from the research point of view) England has had an avowedly fascist group—the followers of Sir Oswald Mosely.

Coulter (1953) administered the F Scale to forty-three English Fascists, also to forty-three English Communists, and also to eighty-three English soldiers who did not belong to either political extreme. All subjects are said to have been of the working class. Coulter's research was done under the direction of H. J. Eysenck of London's Maudsley Hospital and we will, a little further on, discuss the several results of this study in connection with Eysenck's theory of the organization of attitudes.

The mean score of the Fascist men (Christie, 1956a, has calculated the means from Eysenck's report in *The Psychology of Politics*, 1954) was 5.30. The range of possible scores on the F Scale is from 1.0 to 7.0 with 4.0 the theoretical neutral point. American college students usually score in the range from 3.0 to 4.0. The highest group mean published before Coulter's study was the 5.26 reported by Cohn and Carsch (1954) for German workers. The Coulter result is therefore a strong confirmation of the claim that the F Scale measures fascistic trends.

The mean score of the forty-three working-class Communists (according to Christie, 1956a,) studied by Coulter was 3.13 and the score of the "politically neutral" soldiers was 2.50; the Communists were slightly above the soldiers but far below the Fascists. Eysenck draws from Coulter's data the truly extraordinary conclusion: ". . . we have found Communists to make almost as high scores on this scale as Fascists" (Eysenck, 1954, p. 149) and argues that the F Scale is not just a measure of fascistic tendencies but of authoritarianism in general. It would seem to be a more reasonable summary of the data to say that Communists scored slightly above neutrals but much below Fascists and so the F Scale is primarily a measure of authoritarianism of the right though slightly sensitive to the authoritarianism of the left. However, even this version must be questioned.

As Christie (1956a) has pointed out, Coulter's "neutral" soldiers were an extraordinarily equalitarian group. Their mean F Scale score is the lowest-but-one of the fifty or so group means known to Christie. It is well below the usual level of American college students and also well below some means obtained by Rokeach (1960) for samples of English college students. It looks as if Coulter's Communists are more authoritarian than the "neutrals" only because the neutrals are very exceptionally non-authoritarian.

The Communists' score of 3.13 falls in the lower part of the range of data available on American groups and on English college students. In absolute terms the mean is on the equalitarian side of the theoretical neutral point on the scale which falls at 4.0. Neither relatively nor absolutely is it clear that Coulter's Communists are authoritarian.

Among the subjects tested in the original Berkeley study there were nine who identified themselves as Communists and fifty-four who were attending the California Labor School, an organization designated by the Attorney General as under the domination of the Communist Party. The F Scale scores of these subjects unfortunately are not separated out in *The Authoritarian Personality*. However, Christie (1956a) has shown by some ingenious reasoning and comparing of tables of data that these scores must have been relatively low.

Finally, Rokeach (1960), visiting in Great Britain, obtained F Scale scores from thirteen Communist college students. Their mean was the lowest of five political groups studied and it was significantly lower than the means of Liberal Party students and Labor Party students of the Atlee-ite persuasion.

All of these Communist samples have been absurdly small and probably unrepresentative of total membership. Still the consistently low scores, always on the equalitarian side of neutrality and apparently near the bottom of the range for all groups tested, strongly indicate that Communists *in democratic countries* do not produce high scores on the authoritarianism scale. This can mean either of two things: 1) The F Scale only measures authoritarianism of the right or fascism; 2) the F Scale measures general authoritarianism, in some sense, but communists in democratic countries are not authoritarian. In any event the Berkeley researchers seem to have been correct in their belief that the F Scale is a measure of fascism.

In 1944 Edwards, in an article on fascism in America, quoted a Washington newspaper as follows: "Anyone whose opinion differs from our own is now known as fascist" (p. 301). For more recent times that statement could stand but with *communist* substituted for fascist. A great many of us have lived through both periods and have been "worked up" against both enemies. The F Scale and the research on the authoritarian personality provides a single dimension for the description of political ideologies and on this dimension our two ideological antagonists are opposite extremes. That is not a cognitively satisfying state of affairs. It makes it difficult, for instance, to find an attractive ideological stance for the United States; a rather empty moderation or neutrality is the only consistent position that will justify our antagonism to two extremes. Beyond that it is not satisfying, somehow, to feel that two villains are totally unlike. As we shall see in Chapter 11 the human mind prefers to think of the evil things in this world as clustered together in opposition to the good things. There is an agreeable cognitive simplicity in dichotomous evaluation. It would be most satisfying to find that communism and fascism are somehow alike and that we have, all along, been consistently opposed to this quality they have in common. Perhaps it is this strain toward cognitive simplicity that caused Eysenck to see in Coulter's data the greater authoritarianism of both Fascists and Communists rather than the closeness of Communists to neutrals.

Of course there are some real similarities between the fascist and communist movements of our time. Shils (1954) has pointed out that Italian and German fascism were conservative or right wing in their concern with national traditions and the value they set on private property, but they were leftist (in nineteenth-century terms) in their governmental regulation of industry and in this respect similar to Soviet Communism. The latter movement has been leftist in its humanitarian social welfare plans and in its attitude to private property but it has resembled fascism in its suppression of civil liberties.

Throughout *The Authoritarian Personality* there are intimations that one dimension may not be adequate to the description of modern ideologies. The authors toy with a distinction between active, militant liberals and passive, inhibited liberals and with a distinction between "genuine conservatives" and "pseudoconservatives." Shils has taken them to task for not making more of these distinctions; he believes that the Berkeley group was oversold on a liberal-fascist dichotomy. There have been recent attempts to find more dimensions in the structure of attitudes and, in particular, a dimension that will put communism somewhere close to fascism.

THE R AND T FACTORS

Eysenck has proposed (1954) that two independent (orthogonal) dimensions will do the job. His dimensions were not political deductions but inductions from data on the intercorrelation among attitudes. He began by examining some five hundred opinion items drawn from a great variety of published attitude scales. From this set he selected every item that had proved to be "of importance or relevance in any previous research." Eysenck wanted a total of forty items and since he did not find that many that were of established importance he filled up the quota by random selection from the original five hundred. For each item a subject could respond on a 5-point Agree-Disagree scale. Eysenck's analysis of the data is based on 750 middle-class subjects; 250 each from the Conservative, Liberal, and Socialist parties.

Factor Analysis. The two orthogonal dimensions were discovered by the method called *factor analysis.* In this method one begins by correlating the scores on each item with each other item. From the resultant correlation matrix the analyst works out a set of reference dimensions (his factors) which will provide an economical description of the total pattern of relations. He can then select items that are good measures of these dimensions and throw away those that are not.

The mathematical techniques of factor analysis are complicated (see Guilford, 1954), but the basic idea is as simple as correlation itself. A correlation indicates whether two tests possess some common element. Binet applied this reasoning when he decided that, since his intellectual tests were all substantially intercorrelated they must all be influenced by a single general factor of intelligence. Spearman (1904) developed the basic theory of factor analysis in connection with the study of mental ability. Since almost all ability tests are intercorrelated Spearman held that there is evidence of a very general intellectual ability (Spearman's "G") but since the correlations are not perfect there is also evidence of many particular abilities, specific to the individual tests. Spearman and his students found that many correlation matrices included tests having something in common among themselves that was not shared with all tests. They, at first, spoke of "overlapping specific factors" but nowadays we speak of group factors. From a factor analysis of fifty-six cognitive tests Thurstone (1938) discovered six predominant group factors which he called the primary mental abilities. In factor analyzing scores on forty attitude items Eysenck was looking for the group factors that constitute the primary dimensions of ideology.

Thurstone's analysis has not proved to be an ultimate statement about the way human abilities are organized. Three of the primary mental abilities were suggested by the content of tests that clustered together: Verbal (V), Number (N), and Spatial (S). The other three were named in terms of cognitive processes that seemed to be involved in the tests: Word fluency (W), Memory (M), and Reasoning (R). Guilford (1957), as an outcome of a long series of studies of intellectual perform-ance, distinguishes four kinds of content, five cognitive processes, and, in addition, six kinds of cognitive product. Guilford's types of content and types of process are not identical with Thurstone's. Guilford's processes, for instance, are: Memory, Cognition, Convergent Thinking, Divergent Thinking, and Evaluation. Since there are, in Guilford's system five processes, four content categories and six products there are 120 different combinations and 120 different conceivable mental abilities.

Guilford's is only one of a number of factor-analytic descriptions of mental abilities (Cronbach, 1960) offered as alternatives to the Thurstone description. This outcome of the application of factor analysis to the study of mental abilities warns us that any one factor analysis of the attitudinal domain, such as the one made by Eysenck, is unlikely to be the last word. In the analysis of any particular matrix of correlations there are several matters which are resolved by the in-vestigator's judgment rather than by completely determinate mathe-matical procedures. In addition the factors found in one set of items for one sample of subjects may not be found with different items or different subjects.

A correlation table describes similarities between one attitude item and each other attitude item. The factor analyst suggests reference axes for describing all such similarities. Cronbach (1960) puts it this way: "The process is like that of describing the location of a home. Jones lives next to Smith and Adams, and half a block from Brown and White, three blocks from James, Thomas, and Schultz. This description (which resembles a row in the correlation table) is useless if the person seeking Jones does not know where those others live and inconvenient when he does know. So we introduce a reference system. We locate Jones as north of Main Street and west of State. Or we say he lives on this side of the highway, across the railroad tracks and beyond the ice plant. We can place any home in relation to these reference lines"

(p. 255). As you know, if you think of the various ways of describing the location of any particular building, there are always many alternative descriptions—all equally correct but employing different reference lines. In quite similar fashion there are always numerous alternative descriptions of the similarities among attitude items, descriptions that employ different reference axes.

Rotation is a process by which the analyst of a correlation matrix seeks to find the best location for his axes. Thurstone (1947) favored rotation to what is called "simple structure." One of the things one does in rotating to simple structure is to place the axes so that as many tests as possible are nearly perfect measures of just one factor. The factor loading of a test is the correlation between the test and a factor, and simple structure exists when many tests have high loadings on single factors and near-zero loadings on all other factors.

In practice, unfortunately, correlation matrices occur for which there are several solutions all equally near to simple structure and so no unique solution can be said to exist. In such cases the analyst turns to other criteria which are in general less compelling. One such is to locate the axes where they make the best psychological sense but this involves the tricky business of naming and conceptualizing the axes or factors.

Interpretation of a group factor is essentially an effort to induce a concept from a number of particulars. One takes note of the tests that have substantial loadings on the same group factor (are highly inter-correlated) and contrasts them with tests having low or zero loadings on this factor. If it were a matrix of ability tests we might find that tests loaded on one factor all involved verbal understanding while tests not loaded on the factor, but substantially loaded on a second factor, might all involve numerical operations. A pattern of this kind would suggest a verbal factor and a numerical factor. The interpretation of a factor is, properly considered, only a hypothesis. The so-called verbal factor might, with more tests, prove to be word fluency or vocabulary comprehension or verbal reasoning or something else. What the factor analyst should do, but very often does not do, is to test this conceptualization by writing new tests or items which, according to his understanding of the factor, ought to show a high loading. If these new materials are included in a new administration and are intercorrelated as his concept has predicted then he can feel more confident that the concept is correct. In rotating axes so as to give them psychological meaning one seeks to find locations that can be given an interpretation in psychological theory. This was an important consideration in Eysenck's solution of the matrix obtained from attitude items.

It is fairly obvious that the factors obtained in any given analysis are a function of the tests or attitude items employed. With a small number of rather homogeneous verbal tests and a small number of homogeneous arithmetical tests we might get factors that would suggest the terms Verbal and Numerical. If, to the original tests, we added a diverse collection of new tests the original factors might differentiate into several varieties of verbal ability and the Number factor into Arithmetical Operations, Mathematical Reasoning, Spatial Visualization, Mathematical Background, etc. Thurstone's Primary Mental Abilities identified the common elements in the tests he used and these were the common tests of the day. Thurstone could not find ability factors for which no tests had been devised and one reason for the contemporary proliferation of mental abilities is simply the contemporary proliferation of tests. Similarly any description of the structure or organization of social attitudes that is based on factor analysis is relative to the attitude items analyzed.

While it may be obvious that an analysis depends on the items used it seems to be less obvious that a given set of items need not always have the same factor structure. For the analysis also depends on the subjects involved. The structure of abilities is probably more stable across subject samples than is the structure of attitudes. We shall want to consider seriously the possibility that, for people of moderate political views, people who belong to the major institutionalized political parties, all kinds of *extremist* attitudes may be equally unacceptable and so cluster together. However, for a sample that includes various kinds of political extremists these views may separate out into two or more dimensions; the views acceptable to one extreme group being unacceptable to another and vice versa.

Conceptualizing R and T. From the intercorrelations of 40 items across 750 subjects Eysenck extracted two factors. The items defining the first factor were grouped into two opposing sets. On the one hand we find a belief that private property should be abolished, that the death penalty should go, that Sunday observance is old-fashioned, that patriotism is a force that works against peace, and the like. On the other hand, we find a belief that nationalization of industries is inefficient, that we should go back to religion, that Jews are too powerful and colored peoples are inferior, that conscientious objectors are traitors, and the like. Eysenck called this factor *radicalism-conservatism* (the R Factor) and this conceptualization is supported by the differential item responses of the members of the three British political parties. For the most part, items having a high positive saturation with the factor (conservative items) were more acceptable to Conservative Party members than to Socialists. For items having a high negative saturation the pattern of acceptance was reversed. The mean factor scores of three parties, that is scores on the items defining the radicalism-conservatism dimension, distributed the parties from left to right in the order: Conservative-Liberal-Socialist.

The second factor is more problematical. At one extreme the beliefs that: Our troubles have moral causes; birth control should be illegal; we should abolish the death penalty and aim at curing criminals rather than punishing them; and the like. The contrasting set includes the beliefs that: war is inherent in human nature; compulsory sterilization of persons with serious hereditary defects is desirable; the Japanese are cruel by nature; and the like. It is not very meaningful to wind up these two lists with the phrase "and the like" because the like of those listed is not obvious. They are a rather heterogeneous collection. So also are the items in the radical and conservative cluster; the only "concept" one can discover in conservative beliefs is a preference for things as they are or used to be as opposed to the radical's taste for change. However, the radical-conservative dimension is a familiar political reality and the characterization of the factor is validated by the performance of political groups having well-known positions. There are no terms in familiar political parlance that fit the second factor.

Eysenck found his terms in a book by William James (1907) where they refer to two supposed poles of human temperament: the *tender-minded* and the *tough-minded* (T Factor). James lists the presumed characteristics of each.

The tender-minded	The tough-minded
Rationalistic (going by "principles")	Empiricist (going by "facts")
Intellectualistic	Sensationalistic
Idealistic	Materialistic
Optimistic	Pessimistic
Religious	Irreligious
Free-willist	Fatalistic
Monistic	Pluralistic
Dogmatical	Skeptical

It is as impossible to find a conceptual contrast in James's two lists as it was to find them in Eysenck's original items. The lists may nevertheless have a psychological coherence but one suspects that they were a better description of the opposed poles of late 19th and early 20th century philosophy (see especially Ralph Waldo Emerson) than they are of the ordinary man's ideology. Beyond this the "fit" between James's lists and Eysenck's items is not very good. There seem to be no items relevant to such pairs as "Monistic-Pluralistic" and "Intellectualistic-Sensationalistic."

James's list does not include a contrast "Humane" and "Inhumane" but that is a contrast that seems appropriate to very many items; e.g., the tough-minded favor the death penalty, harsh punishment of criminals, even flogging while the tender-minded favor re-education of criminals, are pacifistic, and do not regard conscientious objectors as traitors. The humane-inhumane opposition is, of course, suggested by the terms "tender" and "tough." In the end it may be this connotation plus the linking in James's scheme of religious and tender against irreligious and tough that constituted its appeal for Eysenck.

In support of his two-dimensional theory of attitude organization Eysenck has reanalyzed results reported by other investigators, all of them American, and found that the data could reasonably be represented with the radicalism-conservativism, tender-minded and tough-minded axes (1944). He also reports (1954) that the forty items of his inventory have been administered to American, German, and Swedish groups and that the results obtained were similar. However, these empirical studies of intercorrelations can never finally establish a particular dimensional analysis. Ferguson (1939), for instance, made a careful factor analytic study of attitudes that overlap those studied by Eysenck and came out with a different solution. Ferguson also found two main independent factors but he located them differently and identified them as *religionism* and *humanitarianism*. There is greater intellectual appeal in Eysenck's description chiefly because of the way he proposes to handle communism and fascism.

Our problem, you remember, is that communism and fascism are opposite extremes on a left to right or radicalism-conservatism dimension. But we think we see similarities between the two and we are sure that we would like to see them since our antagonism to both would then have a simple explanation. The solution Eysenck has proposed is elegant. We must conceive of modern politics as a two-dimensional rather than a one-dimensional arena. Opposites on one dimension can be near neighbors on the second dimension. And so communism and fascism though respectively the extreme left and right are both tough-minded. The solution appears in Figure 10-1 as a schematic diagram.

R and T in Relation to Learning. In addition to proposing an elegant resolution of our political quandaries Eysenck has developed his two-dimensional theory in such a way as to relate political attitudes to general psychological theory. His fundamental proposal is that we conceive of attitudes as habits which are learned, a proposal that Doob (1947) and others have also made. Eysenck then declares himself in agreement with the many psychologists who have recognized two fundamental kinds of learning: instrumental learning in accordance with the reinforcement principle, and classical conditioning in accordance

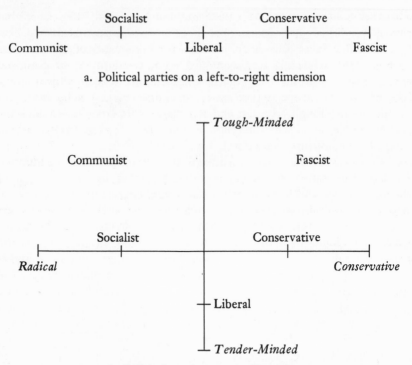

a. Political parties on a left-to-right dimension

b. Political parties on two dimensions

FIGURE 10-1. SCHEMATIC DIAGRAMS ILLUSTRATING TWO HYPOTHESES
REGARDING THE POSITIONS OF POLITICAL PARTIES

with the contiguity principle. Finally, it is Eysenck's position that the attitudes called radical and conservative are instrumental habits acquired because they bring rewards whereas the attitudes called tender-minded and tough-minded reflect different degrees of classically conditioned inhibition.

In reviewing the two kinds of learning it will help to have two model experiments in mind. For instrumental learning we can think of the rat in a Skinner box learning to press a lever because that action is instrumental to the production of food pellets. For classical conditioning the case that is most closely related to Eysenck's argument is the conditioned fear experiment in which an animal hears a buzzer shortly before it is given an electric shock. After a number of trials the fear originally aroused by the shock, but not by the buzzer, will be aroused by the buzzer before any shock is delivered.

Among learning theorists there is not perfect agreement on the exact nature of the distinction between these two kinds of learning nor on what they are to be called. What Hilgard and Marquis (1940) call instrumental conditioning, Skinner (1938) calls operant conditioning. The Law of Effect that Thorndike discerned in this kind of instrumental learning (1911) is more commonly called the reinforcement principle today. The second sort of learning is called classical conditioning by Hilgard and Marquis and respondent conditioning by Skinner.

Among theorists who have accepted the idea that there are two kinds of learning of the kind described, it is O. H. Mowrer (1950) whom Eysenck most closely follows. Mowrer held that instrumental learning involves the skeletal muscles and the central nervous system, that it corresponds roughly to what is popularly called voluntary action. Classical conditioning, in Mowrer's (1950) view, involved the glands and smooth muscles and the autonomic nervous system and the responses conditioned are those that are popularly called involuntary. The actual parallels are not quite so neat (Kimble, 1961) but this is the position Eysenck (1954) assumes.

There is very substantial evidence to show that, in Great Britain, the United States, and elsewhere, political attitudes, party affiliations, and voting are all closely related to socio-economic status. The nature of the relationship is, of course, that people of higher status are more likely to be conservative while persons of lower status are more likely to be radical. This, declares Eysenck, is simply the operation of the Law of Effect in social life. Each social class has learned to adopt the attitudes and take the political actions that bring reinforcement. The upper classes have been rewarded by conservatism and vote accordingly; for the lower classes it is radicalism that pays. Converse (1958) has shown that the strength of the relationship between politics and socio-economic status has not been constant from one American presidential election to another. In the United States it has been greater in times of economic need than in times of affluence and it is probably when economic goods are scarce that class interests are most sharply divided.

The argument connecting tender-minded and tough-minded attitudes with classical conditioning is a little bit complex. The visceral response experienced as fear which might be conditioned to a buzzer is not directly useful or agreeable. It can, however, have great survival value for the organism since it can serve as a signal of danger. The buzzer that forewarns of shock may motivate the rat to take some action that will enable it to avoid the shock. Mowrer (1950) has very effectively argued that this kind of conditioned fear is for human beings a major part of the socialization process. It may be that parental punishments condition us to feel fear when we depart from community standards. It may be classically conditioned fear that restrains us from brute aggression and unlawful sexuality. Perhaps conformity to every sort of norm is maintained by the conditioned fear that follows upon deviance.

Some of the attitudes that Eysenck calls "tough-minded" are concerned with violent aggression (e.g., war is inevitable, criminals should be flogged, etc.) and some would seem to provide for rather free sexual experience (birth control, easy divorce, and legal acceptance of abortion are all desirable). In order to hold such attitudes a person would have to be comparatively free of socialized fear. Could we not argue that the tough-minded are undersocialized, relatively free of conditioned fears, while the tender-minded are oversocialized, heavily inhibited by fears. Remember now that communists and fascists are supposed to be tough-minded. Nazism is renowned for brutality, libertinism, and sexual perversion; Stalinist communism was known for brutality.

What could cause individual variations in the degree of socialized inhibition? Eysenck suggests two possibilities. The variations may result from differences in individual conditionability. Pavlov (1941) noticed marked differences in the ease with which his experimental animals acquired conditioned reflexes and he suggested that such differences in humans might be a basis of important personality differences. There is much evidence of individual differences in conditionality for human subjects in particular experimental situations (Eysenck, 1957; Franks, 1961). In part, then, individuals may be predisposed to tender-mindedness and tough-mindedness by innate conditionability.

In the second place, undersocialization could result from a life history in which there has been little training in socialization. If parents do not punish them children will not learn inhibiting fears. In some of Eysenck's data members of the working class are more tough-minded and members of the middle classes more tender-minded. The first Kinsey report seemed to Eysenck to reveal that the working classes were less inhibited sexually than the middle classes. The work of Allison Davis (1947) in America suggested that the working classes were also less inhibited about physical aggression than were the middle classes. Eysenck concludes that class differences in the amount of socializing pressure account for class differences on the T dimension with conditioned fear the mediating variable.

There is even more than this to Eysenck's grand integration. High conditionability and tender-mindedness are linked to the personality variable called "introversion" and to the pathological condition called "anxiety neurosis." The contrasting state of low conditionability and tough-mindedness are linked to extraversion and to the neurotic state called "hysteria." For this total integration he supplies some new evidence of his own and shows how a large amount of evidence collected by others can be interpreted as supportive (Eysenck, 1957; 1961).

R and T in Actual Relation to Fascism and Communism. It is Eysenck's resolution of our quandary concerning fascism and communism that constitutes the strongest appeal of his two dimensional theory of political attitudes. The resolution pictured as Figure 10-1b is a schematic diagram not a drawing from data. Is it, in fact, the case that communists and fascists resemble one another by virtue of their tough-mindedness? There are two major research findings in support of the claim but both have been seriously questioned.

There is in the first place, Coulter's (1953) study which was mentioned above. The subjects were 43 Communists, 43 Fascists and 83 "neutral" working men. On the F Scale, you recall, the neutrals were extraordinarily equalitarian in comparison with the many other American and British groups who have filled out that scale. The Communists had slightly higher F scores than the neutrals but were still on the equalitarian side of neutrality. The Fascists had much higher scores than the other two groups and in fact scored higher in authoritarianism than any other groups that have been tested. These same subjects were given scales that measure the R and T factors. The crucial data for Eysenck's two-factor analysis of political parties are the T scores; Communists and Fascists ought to have similar scores and both should be more tough-minded than neutrals.

Curiously enough Eysenck does not report the mean scores of the three groups but Christie (1956a) has been able to estimate them from the data that are reported. The higher the score on this scale the greater the tender-mindedness. For neutrals the mean is 14.2; for Communists 11.05; for Fascists 7.85. Does this pattern constitute confirmation or disconfirmation? Eysenck construes it as confirmatory; he notes that both Fascists and Communists are more tough-minded than neutrals. Christie, in a critique (1956a), sees it differently. After all the Communists are almost exactly midway between neutrals and Fascists and so best described as intermediate in tough-mindedness rather than as similar to Fascists. Beyond that, remember that this neutral group produced very exceptionally low F Scale scores and F Scale scores are correlated with T Scale scores. The probability is that the neutrals were extraordinarily tender-minded and the Communists only about average in tough-mindedness for British working-class males.

There is one other major study cited by Eysenck in support of his thesis that Communists and Fascists are similar to one another in that both groups are very tough-minded. This was a study done by Eysenck himself (1954), utilizing groups of middle- and working-class members of the Liberal, Socialist, and Communist parties. In accordance with prediction the Communist mean T Scale score is the lowest of the three. However, Rokeach and Hanley (1956) have looked at the item-by-item

TABLE 10–4. FREQUENCY OF RESPONSES BY CONSERVATIVES, LIBERALS, SOCIALISTS, AND COMMUNISTS TO THE ITEMS ON THE TENDER-MINDEDNESS SCALE

		PROPORTION OF "YES" ANSWERS			
Item and direction of scoring	Class	Conservative	Liberal	Socialist	Communist

Items on which Communists are most tender-minded:

Item and direction of scoring	Class	Conservative	Liberal	Socialist	Communist
1. Coloured people are innately inferior to white people. (T −)	Middle	.42	.27	.19	.00
	Working	.30	.33	.16	.06
3. War is inherent in human nature. (T −)	Middle	.67	.57	.34	.02
	Working	.70	.67	.60	.02
5. Persons with serious hereditary defects and diseases should be compulsorily sterilized. (T −)	Middle	.69	.59	.63	.46
	Working	.96	.83	.89	.71
8. In the interests of peace, we should give up part of our national sovereignty. (T +)	Middle	.32	.60	.76	.74
	Working	.37	.38	.50	.65
10. It is wrong that men should be permitted greater sexual freedom than women by society. (T +)	Middle	.66	.71	.80	.93
	Working	.74	.78	.76	.91
13. Conscientious objectors are traitors to their country and should be treated accordingly. (T −)	Middle	.28	.16	.09	.02
	Working	.67	.22	.27	.06
36. The death penalty is barbaric, and should be abolished. (T +)	Middle	.30	.42	.64	.96
	Working	.19	.11	.20	.83
39. The Japanese are by nature a cruel people (T −)	Middle	.58	.37	.19	.00
	Working	.74	.44	.27	.06

Items on which Communists are most tough-minded:

Item and direction of scoring	Class	Conservative	Liberal	Socialist	Communist
9. Sunday-observance is old-fashioned, and should cease to govern our behaviour. (T −)	Middle	.36	.44	.68	.92
	Working	.59	.33	.69	.95
15. The laws against abortion should be abolished. (T −)	Middle	.28	.40	.53	.90
	Working	.33	.11	.51	.65
16. Only by going back to religion can civilization hope to survive. (T +)	Middle	.65	.56	.36	.00
	Working	.74	.61	.27	.05
23. Divorce laws should be altered to make divorce easier. (T −)	Middle	.33	.42	.61	.96
	Working	.37	.22	.53	.91
28. It is right and proper that religious education in schools should be compulsory. (T +)	Middle	.66	.55	.32	.00
	Working	.70	.78	.13	.05
29. Men and women have the right to find out whether they are sexually suited before marriage (e.g., by companionate marriage). (T −)	Middle	.35	.40	.62	.98
	Working	.37	.22	.36	.77

data and uncovered a startling fact: Of fourteen T Scale items the Communists were the most tough-minded on six items but they were the most tender-minded on the remaining eight items. What is more there is a consistent difference of content between the set of six and the set of eight which suggests that it is highly misleading to call the Communists tough-minded.

Table 10-4 shows the patterns of response for the total set of fourteen items. Rokeach and Hanley suggest that the eight tender-minded responses of Communists might best be conceptualized as "humanitarian" while the six tough-minded responses might best be conceptualized as "anti-religious." The data have not been reported which would show how the tough-mindedness of Fascists breaks down item by item. It is possible, however, that they would tend to be tough where the Communists were tender and tender where the Communists were tough. Communists would then be humanitarian and anti-religious while Fascists would be religious and inhumane. The two might not be similar at all.

The factor analysis from which the unitary T factor emerged was done on data from Conservatives, Liberals and Socialists; no Fascists or Communists were included. A factor structure found in one set of scores cannot be taken as the invariable structure of scores on the tests in question. Members of moderate political parties might tend to reject or accept the views of extremist parties as a unitary set. But the members of the extremist parties, Fascists and Communists, might accept one sort of extremist view and reject the other, destroying the unity of the factor. For a sample that includes both Fascists and Communists there might be no T factor.

The rancorous debate between Eysenck (1956a and 1956b) on the one side and Christie (1956a and 1956b), Rokeach and Hanley (1956) on the other as to whether communists are tough-minded is a very complicated one. I have only reported what I consider to be the more deadly criticisms of Eysenck's position—and I do think they are deadly. The conclusion that has the best chance of being correct is, I think, that fascists and communists in democratic countries are not equally tough-minded in the same sense of the term. If there is indeed a similarity between the two ideologies it seems to lie elsewhere.

ROKEACH'S DOGMATISM

Rokeach (1960) has a suggestion of his own as to what is wrong with communists that is also wrong with fascists. He is convinced that the F Scale is a measure of right-authoritarianism rather than authoritarianism in general. A measure of general authoritarianism, he suggests, must be free of ideological content since it is to be found in people of every political persuasion as well as in Freudians, Unitarians, and art critics. In short, general authoritarianism is best conceived as a mode of thought rather than as a set of beliefs. In identifying intolerance of ambiguity and rigidity as characteristics of authoritarian thought the Berkeley investigators came nearer the identification of general authoritarianism than they did with the F Scale. Rokeach has chosen to call the cognitive style that is general authoritarianism by the name *dogmatism*. He provides an elaborate conceptualization of dogmatism, which is far from identical with popular understanding of that term, and then goes on to construct a questionnaire measure of the concept.

Rokeach does not report data on Fascists but he did manage to find some Communists in England, all students and only thirteen of them. Both the F Scale and the Dogmatism Scale were given to five English groups. As we have seen the Communists obtained the most equalitarian mean score of all five groups and this mean was significantly lower than the means of Conservatives, Liberals, and Atlee-ite Labor Party members. Only the Bevanite left wing of the Labor Party was not significantly higher than the Communists. These results indicate that the F Scale is indeed a measure of authoritarianism of the right and Communists are not high on that measure. Are they high on Dogmatism, which is put forward as a measure of general authoritarianism?

On the Dogmatism Scale the Communists have the highest mean score of all five groups. However, none of the differences between the means attains a conventional level of statistical significance; the difference between Liberals and Communists comes close. No data are presented on the Dogmatism of explicit Fascists.

CONCLUSION

My conclusion, then, is that it has not been demonstrated that fascists and communists resemble one another in authoritarianism or in any other dimension of ideology. No one thus far has shown that there is an authoritarian of the left. Still the impression persists that such a type exists and that some communists belong to it. I believe that both Rokeach and the Berkeley authors have, at several points in their writings, hit upon a promising characterization of general authoritarianism but it is not the characterization they develop or use as the basis of their scales. Perhaps the authoritarian is a person who is best characterized by the kind of information that will induce him to change his attitudes (see Chapter 11). The authoritarian will reverse his evaluations on the simple say-so of an authority figure. If Stalin signs a pact with Berlin then Nazism becomes acceptable for the authoritarian Communist; if Khrushchev devaluates Stalin the Communist authoritarian does the same. The authoritarian liberal would change his views on Communism if Franklin Roosevelt had told him to do so. I would characterize the authoritarian in terms of the kind of information that is sufficient to induce a change of his attitudes.

The non-authoritarian will also change his attitudes but the requisite information is different. The endorsement of an authority will not be sufficient. Most generally he will need to see that the objects of his attitude are related to his more basic values in ways that he had not formerly realized. This is by no means a completely "logical" business and it is not clear that the contrast of authoritarian and non-authoritarian is on a dimension of rationality. I am simply proposing that it is a difference in the weight given to the unsupported opinions of an authority.

The proposed definition is dynamic rather than static. One could not diagnose authoritarianism from an inventory of beliefs but only from knowledge of the circumstances that will change belief. This means that the measurement problem is certain to be more difficult than when authoritarianism is defined in static terms and so one can understand a reluctance to accept such a definition.

By the proposed definitions not all communists will be authoritarian, not all fascists, and not all liberals. It is, however, possible that dynamic authoritarianism would be more often found in conjunction with some ideologies than with others. The focus on single, enduring, and very powerful authorities in fascist and communist states suggests that dynamic authoritarianism may be more common there than in democratic states. The apparent popular acceptance of radical transformations of attitude on little more than the say-so of dictators suggests that this is the case. When Russia invaded Hungary there were wholesale defections from European Communist parties which argues that many members were not dynamic authoritarians. On the other hand there were many who swallowed the Hungary treatment and also de-Stalinization and also the Soviet-German pact before the war.

The idea that all persons affiliated with an extremist political party should have the same personality characteristics is much too simple-minded. It is some improvement to recognize the kinds of personality differences among people adhering to a common ideology that are suggested by a dynamic conception of authoritarianism. But there are other differences that must exist. As Lasswell (1954) has argued an organization as complex as a political party must have a great variety of differentiated roles. The Nazi Party had use for a great many rigid, sado-masochistic, anti-intraceptive, anti-Semites of the kind described in the Berkeley study. But it also had need of clever propagandists, clear-thinking ministers, sensitive diplomats, and courageous military men. There may be some essential quality that occupants of all of these roles had to have in order to be Nazis but, in addition, they had to have distinctive characteristics. An institutionalized political movement could not have operated with personalities of a completely uniform type.

The Berkeley study of the authoritarian personality does not leave many people indifferent. Cool objectivity has not been the hallmark of this tradition. Most of those who have participated have cared deeply about the social issues involved. If it has been difficult for any one investigator to avoid ideological bias there have always been others of contrary bias to keep the argument moving in the direction of truth.

REFERENCES

Adorno, T. W., Frenkel-Brunswik, Else, Levinson, D. J., & Sanford, R. N. *The authoritarian personality*. New York: Harper, 1950.

Applezweig, Dee G. Some determinants of behavioral rigidity. *J. abnorm. soc. Psychol.*, 1954, **49**, 224–228.

Bass, B. M. Authoritarianism or acquiescence? *J. abnorm. soc. Psychol.*, 1955, **51**, 616–623.

Block, J., & Block, Jeanne. An investigation of the relationship between intolerance of ambiguity and ethnocentrism. *J. Pers.*, 1951, **19**, 303–311.

Brown, R. W. A determinant of the relationship between rigidity and authoritarianism. *J. abnorm. soc. Psychol.*, 1953, **48**, 469–476.

Christie, R. Authoritarianism re-examined. In R. Christie, & Marie Jahoda (Eds.), *Studies in the scope and method of "The authoritarian personality."* New York: Free Press, 1954.

Christie, R. Eysenck's treatment of the personality of Communists. *Psychol. Bull.*, 1956, **53**, 411–430. (a)

Christie, R. Some abuses of psychology. *Psychol. Bull.*, 1956, **53**, 439–451. (b)

Christie, R., & Cook, Peggy. A guide to published literature relating to the authoritarian personality through 1956. *J. Psychol.*, 1958, **45**, 171–199.

Christie, R., Havel, Joan, & Seidenberg, B. Is the F Scale irreversible? *J. abnorm. soc. Psychol.*, 1958, **56**, 143–159.

Christie, R., & Jahoda, Marie (Eds.), *Studies in the scope and method of "The authoritarian personality."* New York: Free Press, 1954.

Cohn, T. S. The relation of the F Scale to a response to answer positively. *Amer. Psychol.*, 1953, **8**, 335. (Abstract)

Cohn, T. S., & Carsch, H. Administration of the F Scale to a sample of Germans. *J. abnorm. soc. Psychol.*, 1954, **49**, 471.

Converse, P. E. The shifting role of class in political attitudes and behavior. In Eleanor E. Maccoby, T. M. Newcomb, & E. L. Hartley (Eds.), *Readings in social psychology.* (3rd ed.) New York: Holt, 1958.

Couch, A., & Keniston, K. Yeasayers and naysayers: Agreeing response set as a personality variable. *J. abnorm. soc. Psychol.*, 1960, **60**, 151–174.

Coulter, Thelma. An experimental and statistical study of the relationship of prejudice and certain personality variables. Unpublished doctoral dissertation. Univer. of London, 1953.

Cronbach, L. J. Response sets and test validity. *Educ. psychol. Measmt.*, 1946, **6**, 475–494.

Cronbach, L. J. Essentials of psychological testing. (2nd ed.) New York: Harper, 1960.

Davis, A. Socialization and adolescent personality. In T. M. Newcomb, & E. L. Hartley (Eds.), *Readings in social psychology*. New York: Holt, 1947.

Dicks, H. V. Personality traits and national socialist ideology. *Hum. Relat.*, 1950, **3**, 111–154.

Doob, L. W. The behavior of attitudes. *Psychol. Rev.*, 1947, **54**, 135–156.

Edwards, A. L. The signs of incipient fascism. *J. abnorm. soc. Psychol.*, 1944, **39**, 301–316.

Eysenck, H. J. General social attitudes. *J. soc. Psychol.*, 1944, **19**, 207–227.

Eysenck, H. J. Primary social attitudes as related to social class and political party. *Brit. J. Sociol.*, 1951, **2**, 198–209.

Eysenck, H. J. *The psychology of politics*. London: Routledge & Kegan Paul, 1954.

Eysenck, H. J. The psychology of politics: A reply. *Psychol. Bull.*, 1956, **53**, 177–182. (a)

Eysenck, H. J. The psychology of politics and the personality similarities between fascists and communists. *Psychol. Bull.* 1956, **53**, 431–438. (b)

Eysenck, H. J. *The dynamics of anxiety and hysteria*. New York: Praeger, 1957.

Eysenck, H. J. Classification and the problem of diagnosis. In H. J. Eysenck (Ed.), *Handbook of abnormal psychology: An experimental approach*. New York: Basic Books, 1961.

Ferguson, L. W. Primary social attitudes. *J. Psychol.*, 1939, **8**, 217–223.

Ferguson, L. W. The stability of the primary social attitudes: I. Religionism and humanitarianism. *J. Psychol.*, 1941, **12**, 283–288.

Fisher, S. Patterns of personality rigidity and some of their determinants. *Psychol. Monogr.*, 1950, **64**, No. 1 (Whole No. 307).

Franks, C. M. Conditioning and abnormal behaviour. In H. J. Eysenck (Ed.), *Handbook of abnormal psychology; An experimental approach*. New York: Basic Books, 1961.

Frenkel-Brunswik, Else. Intolerance of ambiguity as an emotional and perceptual personality variable. *J. Pers.*, 1949, **18**, 108–143.

Frenkel-Brunswik, Else. Further explorations by a contributor to "The authoritarian personality." In R. Christie, & Marie Jahoda (Eds.), *Studies in the scope and method of "The authoritarian personality."* New York: Free Press, 1954.

Frenkel-Brunswik, Else, & Havel, Joan. Prejudice in the interviews of children: I. Attitudes toward minority group. *J. genet. Psychol.*, 1953, **82**, 91–136.

Guildford, J. P. Psychometric methods. (2nd ed.) New York: McGraw-Hill, 1954.

Guildford, J. P. A revised structure of intellect. *Reports from the Psychological Laboratory of the University of Southern California*, 1957, No. 19.

Hilgard, E. R., & Marquis, D. G. *Conditioning and learning*. New York: Appleton-Century-Crofts, 1940.

Horowitz, E. L. Development of attitude toward Negroes. In T. M. Newcomb, & E. L. Hartley (Eds.), *Readings in social psychology* (1st ed.) New York: Holt, 1947.

Hyman, H. H., & Sheatsley, P. B. "The authoritarian personality"—A methodological critique. In R. Christie, & Marie Jahoda (Eds.), *Studies in the scope and method of "The authoritarian personality."* New York: Free Press, 1954. Pp. 50–122.

Jaensch, E. R. *Der Gegentypus.* Leipzig: Barth, 1938.

James, W. *Pragmatism.* New York: Longmans, Green, 1907.

Kimble, G. A. *Hilgard & Marquis' conditioning and learning.* (2nd ed.) New York: Appleton-Century-Crofts, 1961.

Kornhauser, A., Sheppard, H. L., & Mayer, A. J. *When labor votes.* New York: University Books, 1956.

Lasswell, H. D. The selective effect of personality on political participation. In R. Christie & Marie Jahoda (Eds.), *Studies in the scope and method of "The authoritarian personality."* New York: Free Press, 1954.

Luchins, A. R. Mechanization in problem-solving. *Psychol. Monogr.*, 1942, **54**, No. 6 (Whole No. 248).

MacKinnon, W. J., & Centers, R. Authoritarianism and urban stratification. *Amer. J. Sociol.*, 1956, **61**, 610–620.

Melvin, D. An experimental and statistical study of two primary social attitudes. Unpublished doctoral dissertation. Univer. of London, 1955.

Messick, S. J., & Jackson, D. N. Authoritarianism or acquiescence in Bass's data. *J. abnorm. soc. Psychol.*, 1957, **54**, 424–425.

Mowrer, O. H. *Learning theory and personality dynamics.* New York: Ronald, 1950.

Pavlov, I. P. *Conditioned reflexes and psychiatry.* Transl. and ed. by W. H. Gantt. New York: Int. Publishers, 1941.

Peabody, D. Attitude content and agreement set in scales of authoritarianism, dogmatism, anti-Semitism, and economic conservatism. *J. abnorm. soc. Psychol.*, 1961, **63**, 1–11.

Prothro, E. T. Ethnocentrism and anti-Negro attitudes in the deep south. *J. abnorm. soc. Psychol.*, 1952, **47**, 105–108.

Rokeach, M. Generalized mental rigidity as a factor in ethnocentrism. *J. abnorm. soc. Psychol.*, 1948, **43**, 259–278.

Rokeach, M. *The open and closed mind.* New York: Basic Books, 1960.

Rokeach, M., & Hanley, C. Eysenck's tender-mindedness dimension: A critique. *Psychol. Bull.*, 1956, **53**, 169–176.

Sartre, J. P. *Anti-Semite and Jew. (Réflexions sur la question Juive,* 1st ed., 1946.) Transl. by G. J. Becker. New York: Schocken, 1948.

Shils, E. A. Authoritarianism: "Right" and "left." In R. Christie, & Marie Jahoda (Eds.), *Studies in the scope and method of "The authoritarian personality."* New York: Free Press, 1954.

Skinner. B. F. *The behavior of organisms: An experimental analysis.* New York: Appleton-Century-Crofts, 1938.

Spearman, C. "General intelligence" objectively determined and measured. *Amer. J. Psychol.*, 1904, **15**, 201–293.

Stagner, R. Fascist attitudes: An exploratory study. *J. soc. Psychol.*, 1936, **7**, 309–319.

Sumner, W. G. *Folkways.* Boston: Ginn, 1906.

Thorndike, E. L. *Animal intelligence.* New York: Macmillan, 1911.

Thurstone, L. L. *Multiple factor analysis.* Chicago: Univer. of Chicago Press, 1947.

Thurstone, L. L. Primary mental abilities. *Psychometric Monogr.*, No. 1, 1938.

Part Five

SOCIAL PSYCHOLOGICAL

PROCESSES

PROCESS is change and in the next four chapters we go in quest of laws of change for attitudes, impressions of persons, groups, and large collectivities. The abstract problem is this. A certain structured state at time$_1$ (T_1) is transformed into another structured state at time$_2$ (T_2) and various events have intervened. In what ways are such transformations lawful?

The following are some T_1 states of attitude, impression, small group, and large assemblage. A collector of Korean pottery has purchased, very cheaply, a celadon bowl that he considers superb and now excitedly shows it to an esteemed friend who is curator of a famous museum's collection of Oriental art. A psychologist from the Soviet Union is met at the airport by several American colleagues and impresses them as a cold, taciturn, but brilliant man. Six unacquainted graduate students assembled for the first meeting of a seminar sit apart from one another and leave the talking to the instructor. Ten thousand opera-lovers assembled in the great arena at Verona achieve a perfect hush on which the soprano floats her top "C."

The T_2 states are like this. The collector of pottery has lost all respect for the judgment of the curator of Oriental art. The American psychologists agree that they had been mistaken about their Soviet colleague, that he is really a warm and humorous person whose ideas about psychology are a little old-fashioned. The graduate students at their eleventh meeting sit in twos and threes; one man talks a lot and one not at all; the group prevails on the talker to agree to get some beer for their final session. The ten thousand at Verona are piled up at the exits shouting and shoving one another.

What events have intervened? The curator pronounced the celadon bowl a fake. The Soviet psychologist had a good night's sleep and the following day lectured on his own research. The graduate students have worked together on a number of problems and some have had good ideas, some not; some have been considerate of others, some not. And at Verona there was a sudden deluge of rain on the open arena.

In order to find lawfulness in events such as these it is necessary to render some episodes identical and others minimally different. The only way to do that since each interaction is, in detail, unique is by abstraction. In the process of abstraction we would lose the celadon bowl, the Soviet psychologist, the academic seminar, and the Verona arena and would be left with persons (p) and objects (o) and attitudes (+ or −), with trait lists, sociometric rankings and a ratio between audience size and exit capacity.

Most of the abstract theories to be described stay within a given topic: attitude change or impression formation or group dynamics or crowd psychology. However there is one, the theory of consistency or balance, which can be applied more broadly. The theory of consistency is utilized in three chapters, in 11, 12, and 13. The most detailed presentation is made in the chapter that immediately follows, Chapter 11 on attitude change.

CHAPTER 11

The Principle of Consistency

in Attitude Change

The general experimental design for discovering determinants of attitude change is a simple one. Some sort of an attitude must be measured before and after the interpolation of persuasive communications which differ from one another in some known respect. The design has been often actualized and the effects tested of varying the emotionality of a communication, the credibility of the communications source, the order of the arguments presented, and so on. The work has been well done, especially the studies constituting the Yale series (Hovland, Janis, and Kelley, 1953; Hovland, et al., 1957; Janis, et al., 1959; Rosenberg, et al., 1960) but it lacks something of intellectual interest because the results do not fall into any general compelling pattern. They summarize as a set of elaborately contingent, and not very general, generalizations.

In recent years the topic of attitude change has picked up in interest because of a series of audacious attempts at systematic theory, all of them utilizing the same principle, the principle of cognitive consistency. The human mind, it seems, has a strong need for consistency and attitudes are generally changed in order to eliminate some inconsistency. This principle derives in part from the many experimental studies that antedate its systematic formulation.

We will study three systematic uses of the consistency principle. The first of these is the most detailed and explicit. It is a kind of model or abstract simulation of attitude change. Its operations are a program that a machine could follow. This model says in effect that when certain kinds of information are fed into the human psychological apparatus, certain perfectly determinate changes of attitude will result. We will call this one the *congruity model*.

The second model is less determinate in its predictions. It does not undertake to specify the particular effect of new information but only a set of effects from which the particular one will be drawn. The *balance model*, as we shall call it, predicts the occurrence of one from a small number of possible changes—all of them working in the direction of increased consistency.

The third formulation is too loose to be considered a model or simulation of attitude change. We will call it a theory, the *dissonance theory*, even though the principles involved do not stand in the kind of deductive relation that the word *theory* implies. Dissonance theory is actually a collection of loosely related ideas.

Clarity and determinancy decline as we move from congruity through balance to dissonance, but quantity of experimentation and also the imaginative quality of the experimentation increase. Consequently we will give more space to research results in the section on dissonance theory than in the sections on the congruity model and the balance model. Before describing the three systematic formulations of the consistency principle we will warm up to the subject with a fairly rich example of the kind of behavior involved.

The Norton-Silvers Problem

The distinguished drama critic of the *Boston Record*, Mr. Elliott Norton, conducts a weekly television program during the theater season on which he interviews stars of shows appearing in Boston. A large number of new productions have their pre-Broadway tryouts in Boston and one of these, in the winter of 1960, was the musical *Do Re Mi*, which starred Phil Silvers. Mr. Norton interviewed Mr. Silvers on one of his programs and the interview generated a quality of personal tension that is very seldom encountered on television.

Elliott Norton is a forthright critic. He had written a very unenthusiastic notice of *Do Re Mi* in advance of the television interview and, at the start of the interview, he said quite unmistakably that he did not think much of the show. Mr. Silvers, on the other hand, thought very highly of the show and, in any case, was bound to it by contract. A simple disagreement between two persons is not uncommon on television; there are numerous Sunday afternoon discussions that confront one party-line Democrat with one party-line Republican over one partisan issue. The result is a conflict between persons but not a conflict within persons. And somehow we know that in this situation neither participant will change his opinion nor even feel any strong pressure in the direction of change. The special discomfort produced by the Norton-Silvers conversation is in part derived from the fact that there was internal or intrapersonal conflict for each participant and this sort of conflict creates a force toward attitude change. In addition, however, the participants were prevented from discharging this tension by making the usual kinds of attitude adjustment because they were operating within a set of social constraints that proscribed such adjustments. The result was fifteen minutes of very hard psychological work for the main figures and also for the sympathetic viewer.

The protagonists of the drama began by expressing great admiration for one another: Phil Silvers was in Elliott Norton's opinion one of our great comedians; Elliott Norton was in Phil Silvers' opinion a dean of the American theater. In these circumstances it was very disagreeable for Mr. Silvers to know that Mr. Norton disliked the show, and it was very disagreeable for Mr. Norton to find Mr. Silvers appearing in such a show. In the more usual Republican vs. Democrat set-to, each participant has an advance low opinion of the political position of his opponent and expects to find that opponent espousing views he himself rejects. There is a battle between the two on familiar lines but no serious division of mind within either man.

It seems to be a general law of human thought that we expect people we like and respect to associate themselves with ideas we like and respect and to dissociate themselves or disagree with ideas from which we dissociate ourselves. These latter disapproved ideas we expect to find espoused by the wicked and the stupid—those we do not like or respect. The "goods" in the world in the way of persons, things, and ideas are supposed to clump together and oppose the "bads," who are expected to form their own clump. This is a consistency principle. It describes the way the world ought to go, and as long as things work this way nothing much happens to our attitudes. But when a new girl friend dislikes our favorite music or an admired professor ridicules our religious beliefs or an esteemed critic attacks a play in which we are appearing, the mind starts working.

It is time to make a first try at modeling the Norton-Silvers problem. This first try will not be identical with any of the three detailed models which are later to be described, though it will be similar to all of them. The idea is to give ourselves some experience in the game of abstracting from a complicated social interaction what we hope are the essentials.

The first abstraction is an enormous simplification which throws away all sorts of detail from the original; it is like deciding to use a blob of blue ink to represent Lake Superior on a map of the United States. We shall represent the situation in each of the two minds by a simple drawing (Figure 11-1) in which the names of persons and things appear on vertical lines from + through 0 to −. The idea is that to have an attitude is to be either for or against something; that the essence of attitude is a value scale on which persons, objects, ideas—the contents of a mind—can be placed. For things that can be evaluated we shall use the term *cognitive objects*. We assume that the important objects in Mr. Norton's mind are Phil Silvers and *Do Re Mi*; the former is good (hence at a + position) and the latter bad (hence at a − position). For Mr. Silvers the important cognitive objects are Mr. Norton and *Do Re Mi*, and both are good.

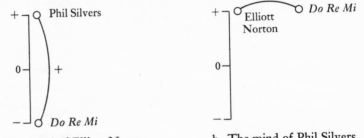

a. The mind of Elliott Norton   b. The mind of Phil Silvers

FIGURE 11-1. THE NORTON-SILVERS PROBLEM

So far our model comprises a generalized attitude scale and cognitive objects placed on such a scale. There is one remaining class of formal element—the bond or link between valued cognitive objects. Bonds are represented in Figure 11-1 as curved lines linking objects, and labelled either + or −. The + bond in Mr. Norton's mind is intended to represent the fact that Mr. Silvers and *Do Re Mi* are known to be associated; in a way Phil Silvers is contained in *Do Re Mi*. The − bond in Mr. Silvers' mind is intended to represent the fact that Mr. Norton has criticized *Do Re Mi*, has withheld his approval from the show; these two are dissociated. In general, associative or + bonds between objects exist in a mind when the two objects are known to like one another or to be bound together, and dissociative or − bonds exist when there is dislike or withdrawal. At this point the model is a static picture of a situation. It remains to set the parts in motion.

The parts will not move so long as the picture satisfies the consistency principle which we shall regard as a kind of equilibrium, but they will move when this principle is not satisfied. This conception of a psychological equilibrium of consistency is the great common property of this first trial model and of the three more serious versions that will later be described. We have already suggested its nature. The human mind expects good things to cluster together and to be opposed to the cluster of bad things. In terms of the model this means that positively valued objects should be linked by associative bonds and, similarly, negatively valued objects should be linked by associative bonds. Between positively valued objects and negatively valued objects there should be only dissociative bonds. If these conditions are satisfied, all is well with the world and there is no need to change one's mind about anything.

If you look now at the Norton-Silvers problem of Figure 11-1, you will see that it does not represent a state of equilibrium. For Elliott Norton there is an associative bond between something good (Phil Silvers) and something bad (*Do Re Mi*). For Phil Silvers there is a dissociative bond between two things that are good (Elliott Norton and *Do Re Mi*). Disequilibrium, we shall assume, sets up a tension or force toward the restoration of equilibrium, and so there must be such a force in both of the minds with which we are concerned. By what means can equilibrium be restored? Primarily by changing the scale positions of objects or the signs of the bonds linking them, and that means—to return from the model to life —changing attitudes between the persons or toward the show.

There are three simple resolutions possible for the Norton-Silvers problem. If Norton would change his mind and like the show, that alone would eliminate the tension; or, alternatively, if Silvers would agree that the show is no good, that would do it; or, finally, the men might give up thinking well of one another and then their disagreement on the show would not represent a disequilibrium. Each of these conceivable changes would alter just one element in each mind: the position of an object or the sign of a bond. Such an alteration of a single element is what we mean by a *simple* resolution. More complicated resolutions, which we shall not describe (though you may find it interesting to work them out), can be attained by shifting more than one element at a time.

Let us look more closely at the simple resolutions to see just how each would serve to restore equilibrium. Figures 11-2a and 11-2a′ represent the actual disequilibrium conditions that constitute the problem. Notice that the one figure requires the other. If there is a + bond between Silvers and *Do Re Mi* in Norton's mind, then it follows that *Do Re Mi* must be positively valued in Silvers' mind. Similarly, the dissociative bond in Silvers' mind between Norton and *Do Re Mi* requires that *Do Re Mi* have a negative position in Norton's mind. The three modes of resolution that follow in Figure 11-2 are likewise to be read as pairs in which the change in one mind requires a certain change in the other mind.

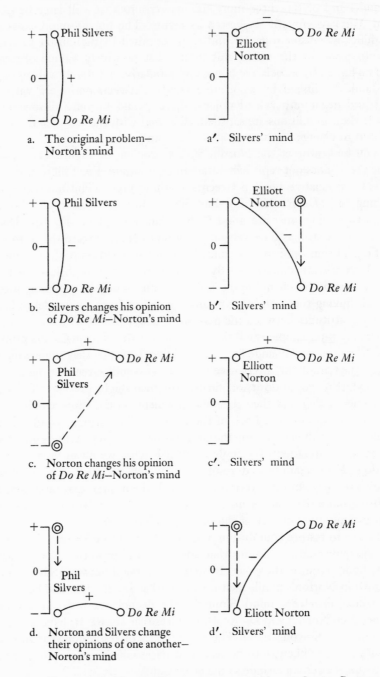

a. The original problem—
   Norton's mind

a′. Silvers' mind

b. Silvers changes his opinion
   of *Do Re Mi*—Norton's mind

b′. Silvers' mind

c. Norton changes his opinion
   of *Do Re Mi*—Norton's mind

c′. Silvers' mind

d. Norton and Silvers change
   their opinions of one another—
   Norton's mind

d′. Silvers' mind

FIGURE 11-2. SIMPLE RESOLUTIONS OF THE NORTON-SILVERS PROBLEM

In Figure 11-2b we see that if Silvers would change his mind about *Do Re Mi* that would change the associative bond in Norton's mind to a dissociative bond and so restore equilibrium. That change would be represented in Silvers' mind (Figure 11-2b′) by a shift of *Do Re Mi* to a negative position. Notice that the broken arrows show the paths of change for valued objects and double circles their former positions. A second possibility is for Norton to change his opinion of *Do Re Mi* to one of approval, which would produce a + bond in Silvers' mind (Figure 11-2c′) and would move *Do Re Mi* to a consonant positive value in Norton's mind (Figure 11-2c). Thus far we have equilibrium restored by one of the two participants changing his opinion of the show. A third possibility is for the two gentlemen to change their opinions of one another. Elliott Norton could decide that Phil Silvers is not much of a comedian, after all, and drop him to a negative value (Figure 11-2d) and, at the same time, Phil Silvers could decide that he does not think much of Elliott Norton as a critic and, without changing the bonds to *Do Re Mi*, both minds would be in equilibrium.

Attitude change of one sort or another is the usual consequence of the kind of disequilibrium we have described, but in the present instance a peculiarly restrictive set of conditions forced the participants to find their way to another solution. Neither man was free publicly to change his judgment of the play. Norton's opinion was in print, and Silvers could hardly speak against the show in which he was starred. They could, of course, change their opinions of one another and, several times, when a voice sounded testy, I thought this would be the outcome. But the two were face-to-face, and so if one turned antagonistic he could expect the other to do the same. Each time this resolution seemed imminent they turned away from it and renewed their vows of mutual esteem. There was a kind of social contract not to use mutual denigration. The constraints all derive from the fact that this was a public encounter. The various attitude changes that could not be revealed on television may have occurred in their secret thoughts. Perhaps one or the other began to think less highly of the other. On the covert level there may well have been a resolution different from the one the viewer saw.

It was Phil Silvers who hit on an acceptable public solution. He recollected that conditions backstage had been hectic during the opening-night performance. During an important scene a sandbag overhead had begun to leak down on him, and he had feared it would fall. This kind of thing had seriously thrown off his own performance, and, in addition, the show had been in fairly rough shape. Numerous scenes and songs had been shuffled or rewritten since opening night. In fact, Phil Silvers found that he had to agree with Elliott Norton that the show Norton had seen on opening night was not very good. It deserved to be panned. But the show which Silvers must necessarily praise was *Do Re Mi* as it was now constituted and as it would be on Broadway. Norton could not very well have a poor opinion of that *Do Re Mi* because he had not seen it. There was no disequilibrium in the fact that a great comedian liked one show and a great critic disliked another show.

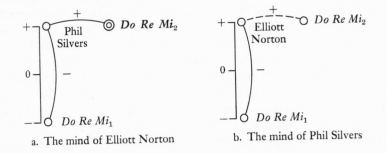

a. The mind of Elliott Norton   b. The mind of Phil Silvers

FIGURE 11-3. RESOLUTION OF THE NORTON-SILVERS PROBLEM BY DIFFEREN-
TIATION OF *Do Re Mi*

This very satisfactory solution can be abstractly described as an agreement to differentiate the original global *Do Re Mi* into *Do Re Mi*$_1$ (opening-night performance) and *Do Re Mi*$_2$ (the show at present). Figure 11-3 shows one of several ways in which the differentiation answer can be pictured. Elliott Norton sees the admired Phil Silvers as dissociated from the not-admired *Do Re Mi*$_1$. This much is certain: that Silvers is associatively linked with *Do Re Mi*$_2$, which Norton has not seen but might conceivably admire. Norton's opinion of *Do Re Mi*$_2$ is not known, but if equilibrium prevails it will be positive. The fact that *Do Re Mi*$_2$'s placement in Norton's mind is inferential is indicated in Figure 11-3a by using a double circle and bold letters for the position of *Do Re Mi*$_2$ in Norton's mind, and a broken line for the inferential positive bond between Norton and *Do Re Mi*$_2$ in Silvers' mind.

The program ended amicably, though with a slight underlying anxiety about the inferential status of *Do Re Mi*$_2$ for Elliott Norton. Before Silvers left he urged Norton to come back and see the show (*Do Re Mi*$_2$) again. Norton assured him that he would like nothing better. In its later history *Do Re Mi*$_2$ was praised by the majority of the New York critics, and this fact may have bolstered Phil Silvers' confidence in the show to the point where he decided that even opening night had been good. Elliott Norton, he may have concluded, was not much of a critic; or he may have been more generous and differentiated Mr. Norton into an astute critic of the drama and a bad judge of musicals. The New York reviews probably caused Mr. Norton to differentiate among New York reviewers; it was not the discerning critics who liked the show.

It has happened more than once that Elliott Norton has disliked the vehicle of an admired star, and I have several times seen the participants find their way to the differentiation answer. Once, however, it failed. Miriam Hopkins, trying hard to understand how a critic of Elliott Norton's stature could dislike her show, introduced the fact that another admired Boston critic had seen and liked the same opening-night performance. Thereby she made things difficult. In order to differentiate, a generic object must be divided into subvarieties along a line that accounts for the inconsistencies of evaluation. The chronological line separating the past performance seen by the critic from the future performances in which the star must appear obviously recommends itself. But by bringing into the problem two admired critics, both present on opening night, Miss Hopkins excluded the usual solution.

However, before the fifteen-minute program finished, Miss Hopkins hit upon another basis for differentiation. With sudden inspiration she asked, "Which side of the house were you sitting on?" "The right side," answered Mr. Norton. "I thought so. This whole show is played to the left. You were getting my back the whole evening and the other critic, my face." Unluckily, Miss Hopkins had neglected to allow for the fact that what is called the "right" side of the house from in front is the "left" from the stage and, too late, it dawned on the participants that it was Mr. Norton who had been getting the expressive half of Miss Hopkins. As the program ended, two white, strained faces showed what disequilibrium feels like.

The three treatments of attitude change to be described in the remainder of this chapter differ among themselves on numerous points, but are agreed that it is disequilibrium of inconsistency that initiates change and that the change generally operates in the direction of equilibrium restoration or consistency. The treatments have different names for their conditions of equilibrium and disequilibrium. In the first case we have congruity-incongruity (Osgood and Tannenbaum, 1955); in the second case balance-imbalance (Abelson and Rosenberg, 1958, 1960); in the third case consonance-dissonance[1] (Festinger, 1957). We shall identify the three treatments by the respective titles: congruity, balance, and dissonance, and this is also the order of description.

1. The credit for originating the line of thought developed in all three treatments unequivocally belongs to Fritz Heider (1944, 1946, 1958). Cartwright and Harary (1956) and Harary (1959) generalized Heider's balance theory to a greater range of empirical cases and also resolved several ambiguities in the theory by utilizing as their formal model the mathematical theory of linear graphs. Newcomb (1953) has made very fruitful use of Heider's notions of balance in an analysis of communicative acts. The three treatments described in the present chapter were selected because of the interesting empirical work they have inspired and because they include all the major variations on the consistency principle.

The Congruity Model[2]

We begin with a now-familiar assumption: that attitudes in a particular mind can be represented by a vertical line from + to − with the names of the objects of attitudes ranged along this line. The drawing of Figure 11-4 is simpler than previous drawings because we are dealing with just one mind at a time. The scale of Figure 11-4 has, however, quantitative aspirations, and so there are numbers along the line. I have placed the names of some attitude objects on this line so that we may operate with concrete examples. The objects and their placement do not belong to the model; its operations are the same whatever the objects may be and however they are placed. Some such lineup as the one in Figure 11-4 existed in many American minds in January of 1964. We thought often of the tragic assassination of John Kennedy. The new President had just delivered his State of the Union Message. There was a little talk about likely Democratic nominees for the Vice-Presidency and quite a lot of talk about likely Republican nominees for the Presidency.

In social psychology the theory of attitude scaling is a relatively sophisticated development. The standard methods for developing scales—the methods of Thurstone, Guttman, Likert, and Coombs—all begin with concrete statements concerning an attitude object (the Negro, the church, communism, and so on) and elaborate techniques for ordering such statements. The congruity model bypasses all this sophistication of measurement and offers a generalized attitude scale that is content-free, a line from −3 to +3, on which any object whatsoever can be placed. In support of their use of a general evaluation scale the authors of the congruity model (Osgood and Tannenbaum, 1955) report that scores on such a scale correlate with scores on Thurstone attitude scales toward the church, the Negro, and capital punishment with the values .74, .82, and .81.

The illustrative objects of Figure 11-4 are a mixed lot, including persons, publications, and legislative proposals. Anything that can be named and valued can go on such a scale, and that includes almost everything. In order to find an entry for the neutral point it is necessary to pick the conspicuously arbitrary and empty proper name—John Doe.

In addition to objects of attitudes there is, in the model, a class of elements called bonds or linkages; these are, as in our preliminary model, of

2. The congruity model was developed in connection with the work of Charles Osgood, George Suci, and Percy Tannenbaum on a measure of connotative meaning (1957). Using factor analytic methods, these authors have found that the three major dimensions of such meaning are evaluation, potency, and activity. The first dimension—evaluation—they have equated with the concept of attitude. The congruity model is thought to have very general application to problems of cognitive interaction as well as particular application to attitude change. The full theoretical and empirical context of this model is of great interest, but it need not be described here since we are focusing on attitude change.

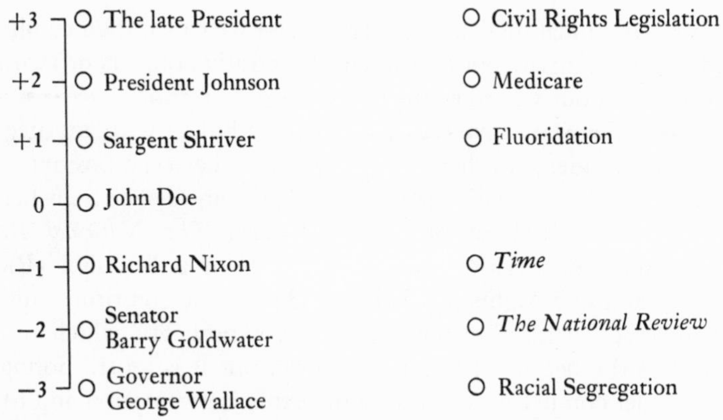

+3 — ○ The late President	○ Civil Rights Legislation
+2 — ○ President Johnson	○ Medicare
+1 — ○ Sargent Shriver	○ Fluoridation
0 — ○ John Doe	
−1 — ○ Richard Nixon	○ *Time*
−2 — ○ Senator Barry Goldwater	○ *The National Review*
−3 — ○ Governor George Wallace	○ Racial Segregation

FIGURE 11-4. A CONGRUITY SCALE WITH ILLUSTRATIVE COGNITIVE OBJECTS

two kinds: associative and dissociative. Associative bonds can be verbal expressions of approval or solidarity and they can be actions. When Khrushchev locked Fidel Castro in an amiable bear hug, the whole world recognized the creation of an associative bond and felt a new pressure on its attitudes.

THE EQUILIBRIUM CONDITION

In the present model there is supposed to be no change of attitude when associative bonds are created between objects at the same scale position. When President Kennedy (+3) in 1963 championed civil rights legislation (+3), the congruity model holds that there should have been no change of attitudes in the mind represented by Figure 11-4. There ought also to have been no change when Governor Wallace (−3) defended the practice of segregation (−3). This is not to say that nothing at all should have happened to the person whose mind we are considering. There may have been great emotional engagement but the model holds that there should have been none of the tension from incongruity that is thought to produce attitude change. The congruity model also holds that no changes of attitude will result from the creation of dissociative bonds linking objects that occupy mirror image positions, i.e., positions tagged with the same number but opposite signs. If Governor Wallace (−3) were to attack civil rights legislation (+3), or if Senator Goldwater (−2) were to attack Medicare (+2), no attitudes should change in the mind we are describing. In general, then, equilibrium in the congruity model encompasses all associative bonds between equally polarized objects (same numerical value) of like sign and all dissociative bonds between equally polarized objects of unlike sign.

The equilibrium conditions for this model are more narrowly defined than in our provisional model. In the latter case we called it an equilibrium if there were associative bonds between two positive objects or two negative objects—without regard to the degree of polarization—and it was also an equilibrium if any positive was dissociatively linked with any negative. The congruity model says that some associations between positives (such as Sargent Shriver [+1] with Medicare [+2]), some associations between negatives (such as Richard Nixon [−1] with *The National Review* [−2]), and some dissociations between objects of unlike sign (Richard Nixon [−1] and civil rights legislation [+3] do not constitute equilibria and will produce attitude change. We cannot now say which of these assumptions is the better reflection of reality, but it is worth noting that making a model compels us to make some explicit assumption and to raise an empirical question of general significance.

CHANGE FROM ASSOCIATIVE BONDS

The occurrence of any associative and dissociative bonds other than those defining equilibria creates forces toward attitude change. Let us consider first an associative bond between Mr. Shriver and President Johnson. Suppose the two gentlemen were to have a friendly private talk about the Vice-Presidency. This is not an equilibrium bond since the objects have different values. It would be an equilibrium bond under either of two hypothetical conditions: If Mr. Shriver were to stay where he is and President Johnson were to be moved to that same +1 position, or if President Johnson were to stay where he is and Mr. Shriver were to be moved to that same +2 position. These hypothetical positions of equilibrium are indicated on Figure 11-5 by double circles and boldface italicized letters. In the present model the forces of attitude change are always toward reestablishment of equilibrium. This would seem to mean movement toward the hypothetical positions. But how much and by which object?

In this model we assume that the total force toward change, the total scale distance to be traveled, is equal to the difference between the actual scale position of either object and its hypothetical position of equilibrium.

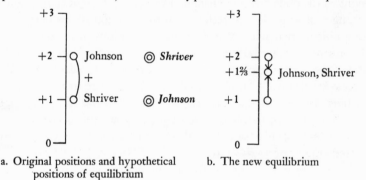

a. Original positions and hypothetical   b. The new equilibrium
   positions of equilibrium

FIGURE 11-5. THE EFFECT OF A SLIGHTLY INCONGRUOUS ASSOCIATION BOND

This value is necessarily always the same for the two objects and, in the present case, is one unit. Which object will travel the distance? At this point the congruity model makes some assumptions which intuition says are sound and yet, we think, are not obvious. The assumption is that both objects associated will be subjected to forces of change, but the more extremely polarized object (the one having the higher number and so farther from zero) will feel the lesser force. In general, it is assumed that the total scale distance to be traveled (one unit in our example) will be divided between the objects in inverse proportion to their respective polarizations.

Think of the one unit to be traveled in our example as divided into thirds. President Johnson is more polarized than Mr. Shriver; they are at the positions of +2 and +1 respectively. Mr. Shriver, who will absorb the greater force, must move two of the three thirds of a unit to be covered and President Johnson just one of the three thirds. This brings the two men to the same position, +1⅔, where the associative bond that links them is congruous and so equilibrium is restored and the mind comes to rest.

It seems to us that in everyday "folk psychology" we think of the effect of an associative verbal bond (for example, one man speaks well of another) as the setting up of a single force—a force on the person spoken about. The object of the assertion is usually assumed to absorb the full force of the change. However, in extreme cases, we recognize that a verbal bond can also affect the speaker. If, for instance, any American presidential candidate were to speak favorably of Fidel Castro, the recoil force of the bond would be very great. Castro might improve his standing somewhat in some American minds, but the candidate would have damaged his own standing greatly. In calculating the persuasive effects of various assertions we make, most of us reckon with a single force: the one we intend to create, the one that acts on the object spoken about. The congruity model makes a different assumption, a less obvious but probably superior assumption that bonds affect both participants in the bond.

In assuming that the amount of change in the value of an object is inversely proportional to the extremity of its initial value, the model incorporates a principle that is backed by some research (Birch, 1945; Klapper, 1949) as well as intuition. Extreme attitudes are less easily changed than moderate attitudes. There is in this simple mechanical model an inertia factor which increases as you move out on the scale. In the special case where one object is at the neutral point (John Doe in Figure 11-4), the model assumes that this least polarized object will absorb the full force of the pressures to change, and so if Senator Goldwater were to praise John Doe, the latter would move all the way down to −2. This may seem to predict a stronger effect than one would find in fact, but that is a question of the adequacy with which the model represents reality, and we had best suspend this kind of question until we are more thoroughly familiar with the formal machinery itself.

In order to acquire some facility in handling the model, here are a few additional examples of change. If Senator Goldwater came out in favor of fluoridation then the two would move towards one another across the three scale units that separate them. Fluoridation, being less polarized, would move two of those units (2 being the value of Senator Goldwater), and Senator Goldwater would move one unit (1 being the position of fluoridation), and the two would reach equilibrium at −1. If Richard Nixon were to praise Governor Wallace, then Nixon would move three parts of the distance (3 being Wallace's scale position), and Wallace would move one part of the distance (1 being Nixon's scale position). Since there are two scale units separating the objects, it is handy to think of these units as four halves, and then Nixon would fall three halves to −2½ and Wallace would rise one half to the same position, thus restoring equilibrium.

CHANGE FROM DISSOCIATIVE BONDS

The general principles governing change from dissociation are the same as those governing change from association, but it takes some practice to see how they are applied. As a working example let us suppose that Senator Goldwater has criticized (−) Sargent Shriver. It is easiest to begin by locating hypothetical positions of congruity. Since dissociative bonds are in equilibrium when they link objects of equal polarization and opposite sign, it follows that there would be an equilibrium if Shriver were at +2 with Goldwater steady at −2, or if Goldwater were at −1 with Shriver steady at +1. Movement will be towards equilibrium, which means the dissociation will elevate Goldwater (for this mind) and also elevate Shriver. There is considerable surprise in this prediction, but let us hold off considering whether the prediction is sensible until the mechanics are clear.

With dissociation as with association both objects will be subjected to forces of change, and the strength of the force will be inversely proportional to the polarization. In the present case, then, Shriver should move more than Goldwater. The scale distance to be traversed is, as with an associative bond, the difference between either object's actual position and its hypothetical equilibrium position—in this example one unit. That unit will be divided in the ratio of two parts to Shriver (Goldwater's position is 2) and one part to Goldwater (Shriver's position is 1). This brings Shriver to +1⅔ and Goldwater to −1⅔; in which positions the dissociative bond is congruous.

Again let us acquire facility. When one object in a bond is at the neutral position (John Doe) and the other is polarized (for example, President Johnson), the neutral object absorbs the full force of the incongruity and moves to the mirror image position of the polarized object (in this

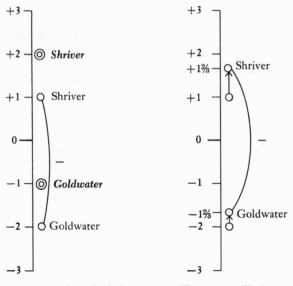

a. Original positions and hypothetical   b. The new equilibrium
   positions of equilibrium

FIGURE 11-6.   THE EFFECT OF A SLIGHTLY INCONGRUOUS DISSOCIATIVE BOND

case −2). In late 1963 an initially neutral object, Lee Harvey Oswald, allegedly dissociated himself in an extreme way from a national hero, President Kennedy, and the neutral object did indeed plummet to −3 or beyond. For some hours after the assassination nothing was known of Oswald except the fact that he was supposed to have killed the president. All over the world, human minds fleshed out the presumed assassin with characteristics that would make his act congruous; each mind assumed that Oswald must have the characteristics of that mind's darkest villains, the characteristics of its −3 objects. In the Soviet Union it was assumed that Oswald was a member of the extreme right wing, probably a John Bircher. The mind of Figure 11-4 probably assumed that Oswald was, like Governor Wallace, a Southern racist. To millions of other American minds it seemed obvious that Oswald must be a communist. The facts were congruous for this latter group and they simply accepted them. The Soviet Union did not change its attitude toward communism but practiced instead the mechanism of denial: "ruling circles" were using the communist story as a cover-up. The mind of Figure 11-4 reconstituted Oswald as an "insane extremist" (−3).

A greatly simplified version of Senator Joseph McCarthy's career might hold that he entered the public consciousness near the neutral position, and by persistently and fiercely dissociating himself from the −3 of communists-in-Government, boosted himself to a positively valued mirror-image position. Once there, his dissociative bonds were greatly feared by figures not so popular as he, since they would tend to reflect these men into negative positions—until, of course, Senator McCarthy attacked persons and institutions more positively valued than himself—General George Marshall and the U.S. Army. These dissociations started him on a descending course, and as he passed others it became expedient for them to join the attack.

We have now reviewed the basic operations of the model. The parts begin to move when there is an associative bond between objects not identically valued or a dissociative bond between objects not in mirror-image positions. Both members of the bond experience forces toward change, but the size of the individual force is inversely proportional to the extremity of the object's polarization. The parts stop moving when the objects arrive at new positions of equilibrium. To these basic assumptions the authors add a pair of special corrections, and these are next to be described.

THE CORRECTION FOR INCREDULITY

Probably the most widely known technique of persuasion (or of propaganda) is prestige suggestion. The idea is that someone's attitude toward an object can be made more favorable by telling him that a person or institution of high prestige thinks favorably of the critical object. Prestige suggestion appears in the congruity model as the case in which an object of lesser value is positively linked with an object of greater value. There have been many experimental demonstrations of prestige suggestion and one of these (Lewis, 1941) turned up a result that illustrates the need for an incredulity correction in the congruity model.

Lewis worked with a set of ten political slogans ("America First," "Balance the Budget," "Share the Wealth," and so on) and with the names of three politically prominent men: Franklin D. Roosevelt, Herbert Hoover, and the then General Secretary of the Communist Party of the U.S.A., Earl Browder. Some of the subjects in the experiments were Republicans, some Democrats, and some Communists. One set of subjects evaluated the slogans themselves in terms of such variables as "social significance," "approval," "author's intelligence," and the like. Another set of subjects (matched with the first in terms of political affiliations) evaluated the slogans after having been told how the same slogans had been evaluated by Roosevelt, Hoover, or Browder. The latter evaluations were made up on various patterns of probability and improbability. A Communist reading that Earl Browder had a high opinion of the slogan "Workers of the World, Unite" would not be disturbed in his views, but a Communist (or a Republican for that matter) who was told that Herbert Hoover had approved the same slogan might experience some surprise. For our present purpose the important point about the results of the experiment is that some subjects—not a great many—refused to believe that such unlikely endorsements were genuine. Presented with a very improbable picture of Earl Browder's judgments, one girl said indignantly, "Do you really expect me to believe that these are Browder's rankings?"

This reaction of incredulity supports our general assumption that people expect associative bonds (such as endorsement) between objects of like value. When such bonds link objects of unlike value the congruity model predicts attitude change. Where the discrepancy is very great (Earl Browder at -3 and "America First" at $+3$), an associative bond should bring both objects to the neutral point. In fact, however, the model as described blows a fuse. The subject refuses to believe in the associative bond and there is no attitude change. In terms of our illustrative array of valued objects in Figure 11-4 it is as if we were told that Governor Wallace had come out in favor of advanced civil rights legislation. Our reaction might very well be, "Who are you trying to kid?"

Osgood and Tannenbaum incorporate in their model a correction for incredulity that serves to "damp" or reduce the change that would be predicted by the unmodified basic rules. As the authors have arranged things, this damping effect reaches its maximum when the departure from equilibrium is at a maximum, in other words, an associative bond between a $+3$ and a -3 or a dissociative bond between either two $+3$'s or two -3's. The corrected model says in fact that people will not shift their attitudes if you tell them that Eisenhower favors Communism, or that Hoover applauds the sentiment, "Workers of the World, Unite," or that Eisenhower disapproves of democracy. They will not change because they will not believe you. At maximal incongruity, then, disbelief is supposed to wash out attitude change. What will it do when incongruity is less extreme?

Since incongruity represents the expected way of the world, it seems reasonable to suppose that disbelief or incredulity will increase as incongruity increases, but Osgood and Tannenbaum confess that their notion of the exact form of this function is a pure hunch. They propose that there will be no incredulity so long as both objects in an associative bond are of the same sign; no incredulity for Johnson favoring Shriver or for Shriver favoring Johnson, even though these various positives have different scale values. For dissociative bonds there will be no incredulity if the two objects are of unlike sign; any $+$ can attack any $-$ without raising suspicions. There will also be no incredulity if either object in a bond is a neutral one. In all the remaining cases—associations between objects of unlike sign, dissociations between objects of like sign—there will be some incredulity. The incredulity correction is always subtracted from the change that would otherwise be predicted. It is a positively accelerated function, that is to say it grows larger at an increasing rate as the incongruity rises, and ultimately, as we have seen, equals and so cancels out the force toward change.

THE ASSERTION CONSTANT

In describing the basic rules of operation, we counted it a special virtue that the model represents associative and dissociative bonds as forces changing attitudes toward both members of the bond, and not simply as a force on the object talked about. It seemed to us that this representation was superior to the everyday assumption that only the thing talked about, the thing approved or condemned, is affected. But perhaps we were too quick to reject everyday opinion.

Suppose that Johnson praises Shriver or that Shriver praises Johnson. What would really happen here? The model, as far as we have described it, says that these events are the same and that the changes would be identical. But would they be? Does it make no difference whether an object is the source of the praise or the object of the praise? Common sense says that it does make a difference. The everyday view is right, we think, in suggesting that the object of the bond will be *more* affected than the source of the bond. However, the model as we have described it seems to us to be right in suggesting that both will be somewhat affected. Probably the best position to take is a compromise one: there will be forces on both participants in the bond, but there will be, other things equal, a somewhat greater force on the object. If Shriver is praised by Johnson, Shriver should experience more change of value than if he (Shriver) praises Johnson.

Once again Osgood and Tannenbaum are ahead of us. The full model incorporates a correction along the lines suggested above. The assertion constant is a value added to the change that would otherwise be predicted for the object of praise or blame. The constant is of the same sign as the predicted change and the authors set it at $\pm.17$ of a scale unit on the seven-point value scale. This figure was suggested by some results obtained in the authors' major empirical test of their model (Tannenbaum, 1953).

The congruity model is a magnetic intellectual construction. It retrieves from memory phenomena that fit the model and phenomena that do not fit. We shall come to some that do not fit but let us first recall a few that do. They are not evidence; they are just an indulgence we are entitled to after having been systematic for so long.

CONGRUITY IN ADVERTISING AND SALESMANSHIP

Efforts to sell a product are sometimes messages in the mass media and sometimes messages in face-to-face conversation. The fact that a potential buyer can send messages to his would-be persuader in the second case but cannot in the first case makes a difference to the strategy of persuasion. Both strategies, however, fall within the domain of congruity theory.

In advertising—a sales message delivered by a mass medium—the most general principle is to link the product with some person or thing highly valued by the consumer and by this means to cause the consumer to think highly enough of the product to buy it. Prestige suggestion is simply a subvariety of the more general technique of value association. In an earlier, more innocent era advertisers paid ballplayers to endorse Wheaties, or aristocratic beauties to credit their complexions to Ponds' face cream. The associative bond, in terms of the model, had to be paid for. After a time the word got round among consumers that money was changing hands and a certain amount of incredulity set in. This is an incredulity which the model does not predict since it does not arise from extreme incongruity.

Nowadays advertisers do not often trouble to suborn real nobility or real athletes since their goal can be more effectively accomplished by using anonymous models—who are incidentally not very expensive—and bonds of physical association rather than verbal endorsement. These are models who look more like English lords and ladies than do real lords and ladies, and if the advertiser poses them with his product in rich surroundings, some positive value will accrue to the product. Since the advertisement uses no real names and makes no explicit assertions, it disarms our incredulity and accomplishes its effect.

When people are living well above the subsistence level—when food, drink, transportation, and shelter are all adequate—they begin to be interested in buying expressive symbols. A desirable symbol is any product that will suggest that its owner is the kind of person he wants to be—rich, virile, devil-may-care, thoughtful, youthful, cultivated, or what-you-will. One can make a product into a desirable symbol by placing the product in an appropriately suggestive setting and spending a lot of money to expose the result to a lot of people.

Consider the famous series of *New Yorker* ads for Hathaway shirts. The medium guarantees a sizeable readership with a taste for elegance and sophistication. Each advertisement pictures the same very distinguished-looking chap wearing a distinctive black eye patch and occupied with spending conspicuous leisure—yachting, playing polo, sipping sherry in the library. And wearing a Hathaway shirt. The implicit proposition may be teased out as *any man who wears a Hathaway shirt is rich, glamorous, cultivated, and distinguished*. Presumably it can be taken for granted that the reader would like to feel that these adjectives apply to himself, and they will apply if he will buy. There is a small difficulty in that Hathaway shirts are not readily recognizable if you cannot read the label. It is for this reason, perhaps, that Countess Mara puts her name on the front of her expensive neckties. Probably, however, a man can enjoy sending himself a symbolic message and feeling enhanced in value as he puts on his Hathaway. Of course, a really smart consumer would leave the expensive Hathaways in the store and buy a black eye patch.

We have never been convinced that there is anything immoral about this kind of selling. Outraged parties sometimes point out that the greater part of the cost of producing such products as perfumes and face creams —and maybe Hathaways—is the advertising cost. But then it is the advertising that creates the symbol, and it is the symbol, not the chemicals or cotton, that the consumer is buying. It seems to us that he gets what he pays for, and we should not expect a symbol-using animal to be interested in nothing but food and drink. A few years ago the Viceroy cigarette campaign called *The Man Who Thinks for Himself* provided a *reductio ad absurdum* of the value-association technique. The many ads trying to get people to buy a product in order "to project an attractive image" had generated a certain revulsion against this sort of external orientation. This fact, in conjunction with a lively contemporary literature attacking conformism and "other-direction" had combined to make independence of mind once again a positive value for Americans. Even among businessmen it was common to hear, "X is a little offbeat, but that's all in his favor." And so an advertiser undertook to persuade people that his product would enable them to project the value which had become important as a reaction against the appeals of advertising.

A characteristic ad pictured a man with firm jaw and steady gaze smoking a Viceroy. This was coupled with a text that read in part, "This man thinks for himself. Knows the difference between fact and fancy. Trusts judgment, not opinion." The implicit logic is: *If the reader doesn't want to appear to be the sort of weak-minded dupe who is taken in by "other-directed" advertising, let him smoke the cigarette smoked by people who are not susceptible to such advertising (according to such an advertisement).* I have heard that this was not a very successful advertising campaign, and I like to believe that it is so.

The whole path from simple endorsement to buying what others buy in order to feel independent stays within the range of the congruity model. There have been changes in what people value and changes in the credibility of different sorts of bond which the model does not predict and was not designed to predict. Behind the changes is the enduring law that associative bonds which are believed, linking object A to an object of higher value, will enhance the value of A.

In face-to-face salesmanship there is two-way communication, and this makes possible a persuasion technique that is not possible in the mass media. Suppose that a young woman comes into a furniture store intending to buy a sofa and is captured by salesman John Doe who appears on her evaluative scale at zero. An inept salesman might immediately express strongly favorable judgments of various high-priced sofas. These sofas, by virtue of their prices and perhaps also their appearances, are likely to have negative values for the customer, and weightless John Doe (since the zero position has no inertia) would by his associative bonds move himself down to join the sofas on the negative side.

A more skillful salesman will not at once reveal his own preferences but will allow his customer to look over the possibilities and to express her taste. When she likes something, he will hasten to agree, and the positive bond will draw him toward the valued sofa; when she criticizes, he will hasten to agree, and the dissociation from the ugly sofa will boost him to a mirror-image position. When he has established himself as a man of good taste (when he is safely perched high on the positive side), he can venture some esteem capital by speaking out for a sofa whose costliness renders it mildly negative for the customer and hope to draw that sofa sufficiently high on the value scale to bring it across the purchase threshold.

Of course, there is more to the salesman's technique than the model indicates. Probably his expressions of agreement with a customer's taste, after that taste has been expressed, are somewhat suspect because of their obvious instrumentality. If he has an alert mind and if his customer's enthusiasms follow some rule, he will abstract the dimensions governing her approval-reaction and project ahead to a sofa just around the corner. A woman who favors warm primary colors, lavish ornament, and rich materials is sure to admire "a beautiful red velvet love seat I'd like you to see." Such advance associative bonds probably should be credited with more power than after-the-fact bonds if a model were to be designed for this particular problem.

The salesmanship technique described above can be generalized as a technique of persuasion by reaction. One person (the persuader) expresses an attitude toward some object, and that object is therefore placed on the familiar vertical scale. The persuader is himself an evaluated object in the mind of the one to be persuaded. Bonds of association, then, are reactions of agreement or approval from the persuader that follow the other person's expressions of attitude, and bonds of dissociation are reactions of disagreement. With these rules of correspondence we see that a neutral persuader (John Doe) can, indeed, enhance his own value by agreeing with the judgments of the other person, but this is only one of many possible effects. If the persuader occupies a positive position, he may be able to raise the other person's evaluation of something by selective reaction to evaluative assertions. If the persuader occupies a more negative position than the attitude object, his endorsement of favorable statements will only further depress the object.

The congruity model, in a loose sort of way, "fits" many familiar phenomena in the sphere of persuasion and attitude change. But what is it that fits? Chiefly the principle that incongruity is a force for change, and this principle appears also in balance theory and in dissonance theory. We do not easily think of familiar phenomena that confirm the numerical aspects of the congruity model and it is the numbers that make the model unique.

EVALUATION OF THE CONGRUITY MODEL

There are three dimensions to the quality of a model. The first of these is the clarity and economy of the formal structure in itself and without reference to the world outside the model. Is it clear what causes the parts of the model to move, how much, and in what direction they move, and when they stop moving? The strength of the congruity model is its formal structure. It handles both associative and dissociative events with the same concepts of incongruity and relative polarization and the operations are unambiguous.

Rules of Correspondence. Since a model is intended to represent something outside itself, it must tell us how its parts and operations correspond to parts and operations in the real world. The rules for moving back and forth between a model and reality are called rules of correspondence. The rules of correspondence for the congruity model are inadequate. The formal elements for the congruity model are objects that can be evaluated and bonds (of two sorts) between objects. Objects, we are told, correspond to persons, groups, offices, countries, ideologies or concepts—any nameable mental content. Associative bonds are statements or actions which suggest that one object approves of another or is associated with another. These rules are suggestive but imprecise and the result is that one can "map" almost any real situation into congruity terms but one can almost always conceive of several alternative and equally persuasive mappings.

Suppose that Senator Goldwater, at a press conference, is asked what he thinks of Sargent Shriver and that the Senator responds: "No comment." Is the response a dissociative bond, as our knowledge of politics and the press conference idiom might suggest, or is it no bond at all as the words taken literally might suggest?

If the bond is dissociative, who and how many are the parties to it? Are they only the Senator and Sargent Shriver, or do we consider that the Republican and Democratic parties are also involved? Has the Senator perhaps dissociated himself from the Peace Corps and from the Roman Catholic Church as well as from Mr. Shriver? The model does not tell us how to deal simultaneously with multiple bonds in a total conceptual arena. The rules of correspondence can be made clearer by limiting the application of the model to paper-and-pencil problems in which the names of objects and also the bonds are supplied by the experimenter. However, the model loses much of its interest if it is restricted to so artificial a domain.

There is a third dimension to the quality of a model. Once the formal elements and operations are coordinated with "real" counterparts, one can use the formal rules to generate predictions about "real" events. These predictions can be checked against empirical outcomes and if they are confirmed our respect for the model will increase. We may come to believe that the congruity apparatus can be used as a paper-and-pencil simulation of complex processes of influence and persuasion.

Accuracy of Prediction. For his doctoral dissertation Tannenbaum (1953) carried out a test of the congruity model. He used the before-after design that is usual in attitude-change experiments and he, as experimenter, supplied both the objects to be evaluated and the bonds linking them. There were six objects: Labor Leaders, *Chicago Tribune*, Senator Robert Taft, Legalized Gambling, Abstract Art, and Accelerated College Programs. The first three functioned as sources of opinions and the last three as objects of opinions. Subjects first evaluated all six objects on seven-point scales,[3] then were exposed to communications linking some of the sources and concepts, and finally evaluated the six objects once again.

Five weeks after the initial assessment of attitudes toward unbonded sources and concepts, subjects were exposed to "highly realistic newspaper stories" which included assertions linking the members of the three pairs. There were 405 subjects, students of elementary psychology participating in small classroom groups. Each group read a favorable newspaper story for one of the three pairs, an unfavorable story for a second pair; and, for the final pair, had no story at all. Immediately after reading the stories, subjects were asked to rate, for a second time, the six individual sources and concepts.

The baseline condition is that in which no news stories were presented—the neutral or control cases. In these cases there was a period of five weeks between the first and second assessments with no interpolated relevant communication. Whatever the subjects' initial attitudes to sources and concepts, there was, under these conditions, no significant change.

The congruity model predicts, in a general way, that evaluation of concepts will rise when associative bonds are created with highly valued

3. There is a complication about the method by which Tannenbaum measured evaluation. The objects were not simply placed on a single seven-point Good-Bad scale, but rather the evaluation procedure required the subject to scale an object on each of six scales labeled with such evaluative terms (in addition to Good-Bad) as: Fair-Unfair, Worthless-Valuable, Pleasant-Unpleasant. The evaluation score for an object was actually the sum of a subject's six ratings. The use of six scales to represent the evaluative dimension is founded in the work of Osgood, Suci, and Tannenbaum (1957) with the Semantic Differential.

sources, whereas the evaluation should fall when associative bonds are created with disliked sources. Dissociative bonds, on the other hand, should result in a rise for the concept when the source is disliked and a fall when the source is admired. The general directions of change were in accordance with these predictions.

Since both source and concept are objects of evaluation in the congruity model, the predictions for change of attitude toward sources with favorable and unfavorable assertions are the same as the predictions for concepts. In this case, too, the prevailing directions of change agreed with the model. The distinction between source and concept has only one consequence in the model: other things equal, the concept is expected to undergo more change. In Tannenbaum's results this was almost invariably the case, and the size of the Assertion Constant was actually fixed on the basis of these results.

The congruity model also holds that susceptibility to attitude change should be inversely proportional to the polarization or extremity of the attitude. With a few minor exceptions it is true of Tannenbaum's results that the amount of attitude change falls off with the degree of polarization in the original attitude.

Tannenbaum does not analyze his data in such a way as to check the model's quantiative prediction for each subject and attitude. His analysis is in terms of large groups of subjects and it permits only a general test of the major assumptions of the model. I think we do not need any data to convince us that the individual quantitative predictions of the model would often go far wrong. You may have noticed some that would be wrong when the model was being described and may have been impatient with the formal details of a scheme that obviously does not work. Let us briefly list a few of the predictions the model makes for the mind of Figure 11-4 which one would be surprised to see confirmed.

If John Doe were to speak critically of Governor Wallace, Doe's value should go up to $+3$ and that would make him almost as great a hero as the late President. High esteem is not so easily won. The same bond between the same persons would come nearer to having this large effect if Wallace were the source and Doe the object. In life there is a great difference between the case in which a relatively neutral person talks about a famous and highly polarized person and the case in which a highly polarized person talks about a neutral person; this difference does not appear in the model.

If President Johnson should say something favorable about either Sargent Shriver or fluoridation, then the President ought to fall in value. But would he? Might it not be the case that Shriver and fluoridation are regarded with unequivocal favor by the mind of Figure 11-4 but not highly polarized because they are not highly salient or prominent? The model does not distinguish salience from approval and disapproval.

If *The National Review* should speak approvingly of Shriver then Shriver ought to lose value in the mind of Figure 11-4. If the same magazine should speak disparagingly of Shriver's administrative abilities he ought to rise in value. But would these things happen? Is there not some advantage in being the object of praise and some disadvantage in being the object of criticism, that is independent of the source?[4] The model does not say so.

Each particular prediction that is improbable suggests some general addition to or correction of the model and these in turn suggest empirical tests. That is why a very explicit model can be useful even when it is inadequate. The congruity model has been useful in this way (Abelson, 1962) and probably will continue to be.

The aspects of the model that are intuitively sound and which are also supported by Tannenbaum's experiment are: the idea that incongruity is a force for change, a force that is exerted on both objects, a force having a greater effect on the less polarized object. Much of the quantitative detail in the model is intuitively dubious and unsupported by published data. These facts suggest that we need a model that is like the congruity model in its general working, but which eliminates the numbers. Actually we used such a model on the Norton-Silvers problem. Its more formal statement is the balance model which we consider next. In eliminating numbers the balance treatment certainly eliminates some very unlikely individual predictions. However, it also eliminates the differences in polarization which predict with some success the relative amounts of change that will occur in two objects that are unequally polarized and incongruously bonded.

The Balance Model

There are a number of very similar balance models;[5] we will use the version set forth in 1960 by Abelson and Rosenberg.[6] In some respects,

---

4. Rosenberg (1962) has reported data indicating that it is indeed agreeable to be the object of a positive bond and disagreeable to be the object of a negative bond whatever the source.

5. Some of the other balance models are those of Heider, 1944, 1946, 1958; of Cartwright and Harary, 1956; and of Newcomb, 1953.

6. In their first published presentation of the balance model, Abelson and Rosenberg (1958) do not provide their cognitive elements with the +, 0, and − signs and do not define the condition of balance in terms of such signs. A later presentation (Rosenberg, Hovland, McGuire, Abelson, and Brehm, 1960) describes the model as it is described here. The change in the model is not, however, so great as it might appear; for many problems the analyses provided by the two models are essentially the same. This is true because, in the first version but not in the second, the list of cognitive elements ordinarily includes the ego and ego's relations (+, 0, or −) with all other relevant elements taken into account. If ego as an element has a + relation with

this balance model is identical with the congruity model and we will begin with the common ground.

ELEMENTS AND RELATIONS

Where the congruity model speaks of objects the balance model speaks of "cognitive elements." These are said to be "things," either concrete or abstract. Cognitive elements include persons, institutions, practices, traits, groups, etc. In English, elements are usually named with nouns or noun phrases which the authors call "substantives." Cognitive elements listed by Abelson and Rosenberg include: "President Nasser"; "Yale students"; "The State Department ban on reporters going to Red China"; "Getting good grades"; "All Suez tolls belonging to Egypt."

Where the congruity model speaks of "bonds" which can link "objects" the balance model speaks of "relations" that can link "elements." Relations are of three kinds. Positive relations (symbolized "p") are equivalent to associative bonds and so include positive affect (liking) and any sort of similarity or connection. Some examples cited by the authors are: "Likes"; "Promotes"; "Is consistent with"; "Is equivalent to." Negative relations (symbolized "n") are equivalent to dissociative bonds and so include negative affect (dislike) and any sort of detachment or estrangement. Some examples cited by the authors are: "Dislikes"; "Opposes"; "Is incompatible with"; "Is alternative to." Null relations (symbolized "o") are equivalent to the absence of any bond at all in the congruity model. Examples of null relations include: "Is indifferent to"; "Does not affect"; "Is unconnected with." In English, relations are named by verbs or verb phrases—as the examples above indicate. Not all English predicates qualify as relations, however. The authors specifically exclude such affect-free predicates as: "Is next in line to" and "Is north of." These would also not be counted as bonds in the congruity model. Until this point the congruity and balance conceptions are identical.

A DIGRESSION

Abelson and Rosenberg acknowledge the close kinship between their model and earlier models created by Heider (1944, 1946, 1958) and by Cartwright and Harary (1956). There are, however, some differences in the several treatments of cognitive relations and these are worth a short

---

another element, e.g., "getting good grades at Yale," this is the same thing, really, as assigning a + value to that element. So long as ego is an element in the analysis of a problem in terms of the first model, it turns out that elements are being assigned +, 0, and − values, though this is accomplished in terms of a relation between ego and something else rather than simply in terms of single valued elements—which is the method of the second version.

digression because they bring to light a major continuity in social psychology.

In Chapter 2 of this book we discussed the basic dimensions of interpersonal relationship. One of these dimensions turned out to be solidarity and in the course of our discussion of solidarity we stressed the fact that similarity and proximity and association seemed to go with affective liking. The English language makes the connection obvious since one can say that: "Likeness goes with liking." Heider is one of the theorists we cited in support of this assertion. Our discussion of solidarity also stressed the fact that similarity or likeness is a symmetrical or reciprocal relation, if A is like B, then B is like A. Affective liking we found tends also to be, in fact, symmetrical (Tagiuri, 1958) and tends, very strongly, to be thought of, or perceived, as symmetrical (Tagiuri, 1958; De Soto, 1960; De Soto and Kuethe, 1959). If A likes B, we expect B to like A. All of this is confirmed in an interesting way by the several models of cognitive balance.

Heider in his formulation of the principle of balance (1958) makes a distinction that Abelson and Rosenberg do not make. Heider separates out affective liking and disliking (symbolized "L" and "DL") from unit-forming and unit-segregating relations (symbolized "U" and "not U") which include similarity, proximity, interaction, causality, and ownership. Abelson and Rosenberg collapse Heider's relations of sentiment and unit formation into the single pair of relations: positive (p) and negative (n). Osgood and Tannenbaum do the same thing but use the terms association and dissociation. What is it that justifies the merging of sentiment relations and unit relations?

In Heider's formulation of balance the first principle is that a positive unit relation calls for a positive sentiment relation (L implies U) and that a negative sentiment relation calls for a negative unit relation (DL implies not U). This principle is exactly equivalent to our assertion in Chapter 2 that similarity and proximity and interaction are associated with positive sentiments or liking. The model-builders who have eliminated the distinction between sentiment relations and unit relations, collapsing them into positive relations and negative relations, are very strikingly acknowledging the force of Heider's first principle and of our assertion. Their models say, in effect, that the tendency to balance liking and unity is so strong that a model can assume it to have been always perfectly accomplished and proceed as if the two analytically distinguishable relations were identical. In effect the treatment of relations in the congruity model and in Abelson and Rosenberg's balance model is a kind of first derivative of the treatment in Heider's model. This is the first continuity.

Cartwright and Harary also make a distinction among relations which is omitted by Abelson and Rosenberg and largely by the congruity model.

Each relation is given a direction. Instead of simply saying that there is a positive relation (e.g., "likes") between two persons, A and B, Cartwright and Harary distinguish "A likes B" from "B likes A." They also distinguish "A dislikes B" from "B dislikes A." Abelson and Rosenberg ignore the direction of relations and simply distinguish positives from negatives. What is it that justifies the merging of the two directions?

In Cartwright and Harary's formulation of balance one of the principles is that a positive relation from A to B calls for a positive relation from B to A and a negative relation for a negative relation. By their formulation no cognitive structure can be balanced in which there is an asymmetry between the two directions. Their principle is equivalent to our assertion in Chapter 2 that liking tends very strongly to be thought symmetrical; if A likes B then B should like A. The model builders who have dropped the distinction of direction in relations are acknowledging the force of Cartwright and Harary's principle and of our assertion. Their models say, in effect, that the tendency in balance theory which makes for symmetry is so powerful that a model can assume that symmetry always exists and so ignore the analytically possible distinction of direction. In effect, then, the absence of any distinction of direction in the balance model we are now considering can be derived from Cartwright and Harary's more refined model. In general, the Abelson and Rosenberg model achieves simplicity by assuming that two kinds of forces toward balance will always have perfectly accomplished their effects. These are the continuities we mentioned and this is the end of the digression.

BALANCE, IMBALANCE, AND CHANGE

Elements, in the balance model, are the objects of attitudes; they assume values in someone's mind. The objects of the congruity model range in value from -3 through zero to $+3$. The elements of balance are only given signs; they are either negative $(-)$, zero (0), or positive $(+)$. The equilibrium condition, for balance as for congruity, is defined in terms of the values assigned to elements and the relations between elements. There is equilibrium so long as elements of identical sign are linked by positive relations or by null relations $(+p+, -p-, +0+, -0-)$, and so long as elements of opposite sign are linked by negative relations or by null relations $(+n-, +0-)$. This is the definition of equilibrium that we used for our analysis of the Norton-Silvers problem and it is the same definition as is used in the congruity model except that numerical values are not involved.

Abelson and Rosenberg take as an example the issue of whether Yale should admit coeds or not. For some Yale students the principal elements in this attitudinal arena are Having Coeds at Yale (C) and Getting Good Grades (G). Suppose a student was for Getting Good Grades (G+) and also for Having Coeds at Yale (C+). If he believed that the presence of coeds would make it easier for him to get good grades, then he would be in a state of mental equilibrium on this issue, since he believes that G is positively related to C or that there is a +p+ link. If, however, he believed that the presence of coeds would interfere with his getting good grades, then he has a +n+ bond and is not in equilibrium. Figure 11-7 shows how one might diagram a bond that is balanced because the objects linked positively are both positively valued. Note that for balance theory, relative standing within the positive region means nothing. If now we imagine the congruity scale from −3 to +3 and suppose that Having Coeds at Yale has the lower value of the two positive elements, it is clear that what is an equilibrium in the balance model need not be but may be an equilibrium in congruity. In general terms it may be said that the conditions of congruity are more exacting than the conditions of balance—congruity requires matched values as well as matched signs. It follows that there will be more balanced situations than congruous situations, that balanced conditions include and extend beyond congruous conditions. Since congruity is more narrowly defined, there will be a larger residual class of incongruous situations than of unbalanced situations, and, in fact, cases of incongruity will include and extend beyond cases of imbalance.

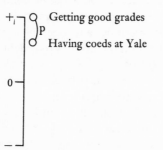

FIGURE 11-7.   A Bond that Is Balanced but not Necessarily Congruous

At this point congruity and balance theories differ only in that one aspires to the power that numbers can give and the other does not aspire so high. We come now to a more fundamental difference between the two. A condition of imbalance is not alone sufficient to generate change in the present case. Putting it another way, we may say that while incongruity is identical with disequilibrium, imbalance is not. In the balance model a person must think about the elements and relations in question before he will be motivated to change. Undiscovered unbalanced bonds are not sufficient to produce change. In effect, one must notice his unbalanced relations before he will become concerned about changing them. The congruity model makes no such stipulation.

If we turn from these models to experimental efforts made to test them, we shall find that the formal difference in conditions prerequisite to change has not so far made any difference. All of the experiments that have been done require subjects to report on their cognitive elements and the relations between them, and so presumably subjects are forced to think about the attitudes in question. In order to give real substance to its novel assumption, the balance model should tell us how to obtain evaluated elements and relations in two ways: 1) so that the subjects will not think about them and 2) so that the subject will think about them. Until operations corresponding to the formal distinction are specified, the formal distinction, in spite of its great plausibility, cannot be tested.

The present model allows for three general outcomes of thought about such unbalanced bonds as Coeds at Yale $(C+)$ would interfere with (n) Getting Good Grades $(G+)$. The first sort of outcome is to change the signs of one or more elements or to change the sign of the relation between them. If one can believe that coeds will not interfere with or will even facilitate getting good grades, then there is the balanced bond $C+$ p $G+$. If one can decide that one does not want Coeds at Yale under any circumstances, then there is a balanced $C-$ n $G+$. Finally, for these minimal balancing changes, there is the possibility of preferring not to get good grades $(C+$ n $G-)$. In addition to these adjustments, which change only one thing at a time, balance can be brought about by a variety of more complex changes in the signs of elements and the relations between them.

The second general outcome, and one for which the initial Norton-Silvers problem demonstrated the need, is to redefine or "differentiate" one of the elements. It would be possible, for example, for the "unbalanced" Yale student to make a distinction between good grades in the sense of a satisfactory passing C and good grades in the sense of all A's. He could go on to realize that coeds probably would make it difficult for him to get A's, but would not interfere at all with getting C's. And, luckily, C's are all he really wants; he has never cared about getting A's. The result is a happy, though possibly precarious, balance.

Differentiation is an important alternative to attitude change. For certain recurrent attitudinal dilemmas there are differentiations that belong to our culture. The religious student whose scientific education pushes him toward a negative evaluation of the Bible is offered a differentiation between the "literal" or "historical" Bible which he can discount and the "figurative" or "spiritual" Bible which he can continue to revere (Abelson, 1959). There is another recurrent dilemma in the fact that almost everyone finds it necessary to tell some lies and yet to disapprove of lying. Consequently, almost everyone can make use of a differentiation between "fibbing" or "telling white lies," which is what we *do* and the other sort of lie which is what we disapprove of.

The final sort of outcome, recognized by the balance model, is made possible by the provision that thinking is necessary to make imbalance into disequilibrium. One can, therefore, restore equilibrium by ceasing to think about the matter in question. There may even develop some clever strategies for keeping away from areas of potential internal contradiction.

I count it an advantage of the balance model that it allows for more kinds of outcome—particularly such very plausible outcomes as differentiation and stopping thinking—than does the congruity model. However, the gain in flexibility is at the cost of a loss in precision or power. The balance model, as far as it has been specified, does not predict which of the three major outcomes will occur in a given case of disequilibrium, nor does it choose among the various changes of sign that could produce balance. The congruity model predicts a completely determinate quantitative change from its assumptions about congruity, inertia due to polarization, incredulity, and the assertion constant. The balance model says that any one of a number of rather general things may happen as a consequence of disequilibrium. The congruity model says that one very particular thing will result from any given disequilibrium, though, it must be added, there is not yet any experimental work that tests the individual quantitative predictions of congruity.

The congruity model is designed to deal with one pair of bonded objects at a time and as presently specified it can only deal with more than one pair of bonded objects by taking them up in succession. The congruity model does not tell us how to calculate the total amount of incongruity, the total pressure for change, in a complex ideational sphere involving many objects and many bonds. Abelson and Rosenberg (1958) do provide formulas for working out the total amount of imbalance in a set of related ideas (and so, incidentally, do Cartwright and Harary, 1956). In order to obtain the total set of elements involved in a complex topic such as "Having an honor system at Yale," Abelson and Rosenberg recommend asking the subject to list all the words or short phrases that come to mind as he mulls the topic over. From one student they obtained six elements in connection with the honor system problem. To complete the matrix the authors recommend asking the subject to relate each element to each other element. The complexity of imbalance in such a matrix can be calculated and the simplest ways of redressing the imbalance discovered. The fact that the balance model can cope with multiple elements is clearly in its favor. There have not, however, been many empirical studies of balance in complicated structures. I think this is because the research techniques for determining the number of elements in a conceptual arena are not very good.

For the basic assumptions of the balance model there is some research support (Jordan, 1953; Burdick and Burnes, 1958; Kogan and Tagiuri,

1958). We will describe just one study. It was done by Abelson and Rosenberg (Rosenberg et al., 1960), and it makes use of the technique of role-playing. The exasperating difficulty with testing a theory of attitude change is the necessity of collecting attitudinal data before and after the introduction of some change factor without exposing your purpose to your subjects. It is commonly supposed that if subjects discover the experimenter's purpose they will give "artificial" responses that are not representative of life outside the laboratory. If this is true, deception may be necessary. Tannenbaum used deception in his test of congruity theory since he pretended that his contrived news stories were the real thing. The trouble with deception, morality aside, which it usually is, is that one cannot be sure who is being deceived. Did Tannenbaum's subjects believe him? Does any of our subjects ever believe us? Role-playing offers an alternative to deception. Instead of concealing experimental manipulations one can reveal them and ask subjects to help.

FENWICK'S ART DISPLAY

Most people can do a satisfactory job of playing the part (or role) of someone else if that part is well described and not completely outside their experience. In the present experiment, subjects were to play a role defined in terms of certain feelings and beliefs which taken together constituted a cognitive structure with a built-in dilemma. Would role-playing subjects resolve their dilemmas in accordance with the predictions of balance theory?

All subjects were Yale undergraduates. Each man was given a pamphlet which on its first page told him that he was to try to put himself into another person's position and exhorted him to "try to *be* this man." The assigned role was that of "the owner of a large department store in a middle-sized, Midwestern city." As part of the content of the role each subject was told to adopt a specific attitude on each of three matters. In the first place all subjects were to set high positive value on "keeping sales at the highest possible volume in all departments of your store." This is the unchanging aspect of the role—a store manager could not credibly set low value on sales—but the other two attitudes were varied among subjects so as to create three different versions of the role.

One group of subjects was also instructed to feel positively toward Modern Art and toward Fenwick, the manager of the rug department. In a second group the assigned role required that the subject feel negatively toward Modern Art and positively toward Fenwick. For a third group both Modern Art and Fenwick were to be negatively valued. In summary, one attitude—setting positive value on sales—was an invariant part of the manager role but favorable and unfavorable attitudes toward two other objects (Modern Art and Fenwick) were varied to yield the three roles diagrammed in Figure 11-8.

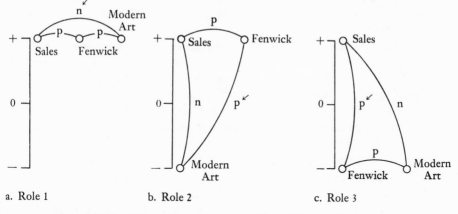

a. Role 1   b. Role 2   c. Role 3

FIGURE 11-8.   THREE VERSIONS OF THE STORE MANAGER'S ROLE
INDICATES LOCUS OF IMBALANCE

The assigned role also involved beliefs about the relations among the three concepts, and the beliefs were identical for the three roles. They were: 1) Displays of modern art in department stores *reduce* (n) sales volume; 2) Fenwick *plans to mount* (p) such a display in the rug department; 3) Fenwick in his tenure as rug department manager has *increased* (p) the volume of sales. These three beliefs were persuasively backed with paragraphs of alleged facts. Belief 1 above, for intance, was supported by the following:

> One year ago a report by the Merchandising Institute appeared in a leading market research journal. It warned against modern art exhibits in stores merchandising popular household products to lower- and middle-class customers. The conclusions were based on a thorough and well-conducted research study which found that 55% of a representative sample of American consumers did not like modern art. Probably it was this basic attitude which underlay the further finding that 46% were offended or distracted by modern art displays and thus tended to spend less time and money in stores featuring such displays [Rosenberg, et al., 1960, p. 126].

Each subject then has a role defined by a set of three elements bound in pairs by three relations. The three relations are identical for all subjects, but the attitudes toward Fenwick and toward Modern Art are varied. The result is that each of the three roles of Figure 11-8 involves an imbalance, but the locus of the imbalance shifts as indicated in the Figure by small arrows. For Role 1, with all elements positively valued, a state of balance requires that all relations be positive, and it is the single negative bond between Sales and Modern Art that is the locus of imbalance. For Role 2 the negatively valued Modern Art ought to be negatively related to both positive elements, and the fact that Modern Art is positively related to Fenwick is inconsistent. For Role 3 the single positively valued element—Sales—ought to be negatively related to both negatively valued items, and so the positive bond with Fenwick is inconsistent.

A subject in any one of the three roles can achieve peace of mind, can balance his cognitive structure, in a number of different ways. However, the simplest solution is, in each case, to change the sign of the single unbalanced relation. Consider Role 1, where a change of sign for the negative relations between Sales and Modern Art (i.e., believing that a display of Modern Art is likely to increase Sales rather than to decrease them) would resolve the dilemma. The problem could also be solved by leaving the negative relation intact, setting a negative value on Modern Art, and changing the relation between Fenwick and Modern Art to a negative one. In other words, if the store manager can decide that he actually dislikes Modern Art and can believe that Fenwick really has no intention of mounting a Modern Art display, he can comfortably continue to think well of Fenwick, to want high sales, and to believe that a Modern Art display would lower sales volume. This is a more complicated resolution because it entails changing two aspects of the original structure. For each role there are numerous possible resolutions that require changes in two or more aspects of the structure. The specific hypothesis of the experiment is: *The order of preference for paths toward restoring an unbalanced structure to balance will correspond to an ordering of the paths according to the number of sign changes required, from the least to the most.*

The first phase of the experiment involved training some ninety-nine subjects (distributed about evenly among the three roles) in the attitudes and beliefs constituting a particular initial cognitive structure. In order to see whether subjects had fully grasped the structure, had successfully internalized it, the experimenters required them, after training, to rate the elements and state the relations between them. It is an interesting incidental fact that for each role a small number of subjects brought about premature balancing, i.e., they did not grasp the role correctly and in fact distorted it so as to eliminate the imbalance. For Role 1 a total of twelve subjects somehow understood that displays of Modern Art would *promote* Sales in spite of the perfectly clear paragraph saying that such displays *lower* Sales. The otherwise balanced set of elements and relations seems to have implied a favorable relation so strongly that some subjects thought that relation actually existed.

For the remainder of the experiment only those subjects who had correctly learned their roles were used. These subjects went on to read three communications that were represented as issuing from three different store officers; each communication had something to say that was relevant to the general dilemma involving Fenwick and the rug department. One communication (hereafter called the Art-Sales communication) contended that displays of Modern Art actually *increase* Sales volume; i.e., it reversed the unbalanced bond of Role 1. A second communication (hereafter called the Fenwick-Art communication) argued that Fenwick really *does not plan* to put up a display of Modern Art in his department; i.e., it reversed the unbalanced bond of Role 2. A third communication (hereafter called the Fenwick-Sales communication) argued that Fenwick has actually *failed* to maintain Sales volume in his department; i.e., it reversed the unbalanced bond of Role 3. In effect, then, there was for each role a communication designed to balance the role structure in the simplest possible way.

All subjects in each role read all three communications and then rated each communication in terms of how much it pleased him, how much it persuaded him, and how accurate it appeared to him to be. The general prediction was that subjects in each role would find most acceptable the communication tailored to the imbalance in that role. In addition, however, it is possible to work out the implications for each role of accepting the other two communications; if a communication were to be accepted, how complicated would be the changes necessary in order to achieve balance? In the case of Role 1 the Art-Sales communication would directly correct the inconsistent bond, and so should be most acceptable to subjects in this role. The Fenwick-Art communication establishes a negative bond (Fenwick will not set up a Modern Art display) which requires one additional change: Modern Art must assume a negative value if balance is to be attained. The Fenwick-Sales communication (which holds that Fenwick has *failed* [n] to maintain sales volume) requires two additional changes for balance: Fenwick and Modern Art would both have to assume negative values. The order of acceptability for the messages to persons in Role 1 ought then to be Art-Sales (1 change), Fenwick-Art (2 changes), Fenwick-Sales (3 changes). In similar fashion detailed predictions can be worked out for Role 2 and Role 3.

The data provide very strong confirmation of the hypothesis. The simplest resolution is indeed the preferred one, and the less simple resolutions are preferred in the order of their simplicity. Imbalance reduction within a structure of attitudinal cognitions will tend to follow a least effortful path. In a second experiment, which reproduced the essential features of the first, this result was replicated. The role-playing design does seem to permit the testing of detailed implications in a model of attitude change without relying on elaborate techniques of deception.

Dissonance Theory

The theory of cognitive dissonance was propounded by Festinger in 1957. It has inspired a large number of empirical studies and the evidence from nearly forty of these was reviewed in 1962 by Brehm and Cohen in a book called *Explorations in Cognitive Dissonance*. At this writing, early 1964, the principles of cognitive dissonance are probably the most influential ideas in social psychology.

THE THEORY IN ROUGH OUTLINE

The concept of dissonance is similar to the concepts of incongruity and imbalance. However, these last two are more like one another than either is like dissonance. In comparing dissonance with the other two conceptions of inconsistency, I will use the terms *balance* and *imbalance* as generic forms, inclusive also of congruity and incongruity.

A state of cognitive dissonance is said to be a state of psychological discomfort or tension which motivates efforts to achieve consonance. *Dissonance* is the name for a disequilibrium and *consonance* the name for an equilibrium. Two *cognitive elements*, A and B, are dissonant if one *implies* the negation of the other; i.e., if A implies not-B. Two cognitive elements are consonant when one implies not the negation of the other element but the other element itself; i.e., A implies B. Finally, two elements, A and B, are *irrelevant* when neither implies anything about the other. Dissonance is comparable to imbalance; consonance to balance; and irrelevance to null relations.

The Norton-Silvers problem can be analyzed in the terms of cognitive dissonance. One cognitive element (A) would be the proposition: Elliott Norton does not like *Do Re Mi*. The other element (B) would be the proposition: Phil Silvers likes *Do Re Mi*. The same two propositions are in the minds of both men and the combination is dissonant for both because, in their minds, A implies not-B and B implies not-A. The two elements do not "fit together"; they are somehow "inconsistent." If either man would change his evaluation of the show the combination of elements would become consonant.

The notable influence of the theory of cognitive dissonance cannot be explained by the fact that it is a formulation of the inconsistency principle; imbalance and incongruity, we will see, are more precise formulations. Dissonance theory is influential because it has emphasized a very interesting kind of inconsistency, some interesting aspects of the magnitude of inconsistency and some interesting ways of reducing inconsistency.

If a dissonance theorist were to analyze the Norton-Silvers problem he would highlight the fact that Phil Silvers had a contractual commitment to appear in *Do Re Mi* and was, in fact, appearing in it nightly. A commitment to action is commonly thought of as the result of a prior attitude favoring the action. But perhaps Phil Silvers did not himself much like *Do Re Mi* when first he read the book and heard a playthrough of the score. Perhaps he only signed for it because he respected the director or liked the prospect of a regular paycheck. If we imagine these circumstances to be true we have an instance of the sort of inconsistency that especially interests dissonance theorists. Someone has taken an action that is inconsistent with his attitudes. The dissonance lies in the combination of these two propositions: I chose to be in *Do Re Mi*; *Do Re Mi* is no good. The mind does not rest easy. The contractual commitment is relatively inflexible and so it may be necessary to change the attitude to fit the deed. Some of the spell cast by dissonance theory may derive from the fact that it is a variation on the existentialist theme that man is motivated to choose his fate.

The magnitude of the dissonance generated by inconsistent action or commitment to action is thought to be greater as the original inducement to action is slighter. If an action cannot be adequately accounted for by factors other than a favorable judgment, then there is a very great need to make the judgment favorable in order to motivate what has been done. If Phil Silvers went into *Do Re Mi* knowing the salary was a little low and the supporting cast only so-so, then any suggestion that the show was no good would be more intolerable than if the pay and supporting cast were extraordinary. These ideas are provocative. The basic idea that inconsistent action is a force for attitude change suggests, for instance, that if we want to reduce discrimination against Negroes in this country we ought not to assume that attitudes must first be made favorable. If the prejudiced person can be induced by extraneous means to take a favorable action toward Negroes he may then change his attitude to account for his action. The magnitude of dissonance principle suggests, in addition, that the way to maximize the pressure on his attitudes is to minimize the extraneous inducement to favorable action. The poorer the excuse for this action the greater the need to make it rational by means of attitude change.

The adequacy of the inducement to take inconsistent action is only one of the presumed determinants of the strength of cognitive dissonance. Another is the degree of hardship or unpleasantness associated with that action. Suppose that Phil Silvers had had a particularly difficult time learning his role in *Do Re Mi*. His dissonance would be greater than if he had had an easy time. The problem can be summed up in the inconsistent propositions: I chose to be in this show and worked especially hard preparing for it; the show is no good. The position of dissonance theory is that the pressure to change the second element, to think well of the show, is greater in these circumstances than if the action itself had been easy. The idea is that the harder one works at something or the greater the hardships endured, the greater the dissonance generated by any suspicion that the goal has not been worth it; the greater the necessity of believing that it has all been worthwhile.

Dissonance theorists have also been imaginative in thinking up ways that one might reduce inconsistency. Consider the man who believes both of these positions: Smoking cigarettes is dangerous to life; I smoke cigarettes. He might reduce dissonance by giving up smoking and so relinquishing belief in the second of the two propositions, or he might somehow believe that smoking is not truly dangerous. In addition, however, Festinger (1957) suggests that he might control his flow of information, seeking out reports of reassuring research (financed usually by tobacco companies) and avoiding the lung cancer statistics. He might also seek out other smokers who would give him social support. Perhaps Phil Silvers read again and again the good reviews that *Do Re Mi* received and sought out the company of those who liked the show.

Now we will see how these various aspects of dissonance theory have been realized in experimental work. Afterwards we will return to the basic concepts of the theory in a more critical spirit.

COGNITIVE CONSEQUENCES OF COMPLIANCE

This experiment was done by Festinger and Carlsmith (1959). All subjects spent an hour at some very tedious tasks; one of which was to put twelve spools into a tray, empty the tray, refill it, and so on. When the experimental task had been completed, all subjects were told a cover story purporting to explain the purpose of the experiment. The story was largely untrue; much condensed and in my own words it goes like this: "You have participated in an experiment on the effects of expectation or 'set.' Some subjects, like yourselves, are doing the experimental tasks without being given any particular expectation concerning the tasks. Other subjects, before they start the tasks, encounter someone who has supposedly just finished with the tasks and they are told that the procedure is 'intriguing,' 'very enjoyable,' 'a lot of fun.' The person who tells them this is a paid confederate of ours. We are concerned in this experiment with the effect on performance of the anticipation that the tasks will be enjoyable." All subjects heard this cover story, all subjects had worked at the dull tasks and, *in fact*, all subjects had worked without having been given an expectation that the tasks would be fun. From this point on the treatment of subjects is differentiated on three lines.

Control subjects were given to believe that the Psychology Department was checking up on the value of the experiments done under its aegis. A departmental representative asked them to rate the procedure they had just gone through for "interest" and "scientific importance" and the like, on scales from -5 to $+5$. This rating of the tasks was also done by subjects not allotted to the *control condition* but only after the interpolation of one or another of two experimental treatments.

One experimental treatment is called the *one-dollar condition* and the other the *twenty-dollar condition*. These conditions were alike in that subjects were told, following the cover story about "set," that the confederate who ordinarily played the part of the person who had just completed the tasks was absent. "I'll tell you what we had in mind: the thing is if you could do it for us now, then of course you would know how to do it, and if something like this should ever come up again, that is, the regular fellow couldn't make it, and we had a subject scheduled, it would be very reassuring to us to know that we had somebody else we could call on who knew how to do it. So, if you would be willing to do this for us, we'd like to hire you to do it now and then be on call in the future, if something like this should ever happen again" (Festinger and Carlsmith, 1959, p. 205). In effect the subject was asked to serve as the experimenter's confederate and such service, of course, required him to lie about the experimental tasks; to say that the dull chores had been "a lot of fun." For the favor of perjury some subjects were offered one dollar (one-dollar condition) and some were offered twenty (twenty-dollar condition). Following their service as confederates, the subjects in both experimental conditions, like the subjects in the control condition, were interviewed by a supposed representative of the Psychology Department and asked to rate the experimental tasks for interest and value.

From the nest of plots and subplots that constitute the procedure of this experiment we must extract the essentials. Three groups of subjects rated a set of tasks for interest and value. The mean rating given the tasks by control subjects was $-.45$ (on a scale from -5 to $+5$) and that indicates that the tasks, as they were intended to be, rather dull. When the experimental subjects, serving as confederates, called the tasks a "lot of fun," we may presume, judging by the control rating, that they felt themselves to be lying. The prediction made by the authors of the study was that the experimental subjects, those who had reported falsely and so taken an action dissonant with their beliefs, would rate the tasks as more interesting than would control subjects.

Some experimental subjects had been paid little for lying (one-dollar condition) and some had been paid a lot (twenty-dollar condition). The authors predicted that those who had been paid little would give the tasks the highest rating on interest for the reason that the sum received was inadequate fully to account for the lie. Not having been paid well enough to excuse perjury, it was cognitively necessary to eliminate the lie by changing the attitude to fit the statement. The more adequately compensated subjects in the twenty-dollar condition could better afford to continue to think the tasks dull for the reason that they had been paid well enough to justify a lie.

The mean ratings of the tasks were: $-.45$ for the control condition; $+1.33$ for the one-dollar condition; $-.05$ for the twenty-dollar condition. This is the predicted order of outcomes. Not the least interesting aspect of the results is the fact that they contradict a reward or reinforcement principle. To rate tasks as enjoyable is linguistic behavior similar to the spoken declaration that these tasks have been a "lot of fun." One might have expected that the subjects who were most strongly rewarded for the declaration would pick up a linguistic habit and so be most inclined to the favorable rating. It turned out otherwise, however. The outcome of the Festinger and Carlsmith experiment is not an obvious one, in terms either of psychological theory or of common sense. The non-obviousness of their predictions is a characteristic in which dissonance theorists take pride.

SEVERITY OF INITIATION AND LIKING FOR A GROUP

Anyone who has, more or less voluntarily, done time in the armed services is likely to have a problem in cognitive dissonance when he is mustered out. The dissonance may be expressed in the following two propositions: I chose to do a three-year hitch in the services; that hitch was totally valueless. It is not pleasant to believe at one and the same time in these two propositions. Most of us cannot bear to write off large chunks of a past we have chosen. We usually handle the problem by discovering that the past has after all conferred some benefits; they may be vague ones. "It was good experience" or "it helped me to decide what I really wanted out of life."

We seem to try to transform any bad experience we have chosen into a good one. Suppose someone works for several years educating himself toward a particular profession and then finds that he cannot qualify, the work has been in vain, and he must choose a new path. Not many people are able to snap their fingers and say: "Well, that's that, the best years of my life down the drain!" We say rather: "It has been good preparation which I do not in the least regret." And what of personal relationships that people choose and for which they suffer, but which end badly; what of broken friendships and divorces? "I figure that I needed my marriage to Zeena to give me maturity and teach me what marriage should be." Maturity—always the last resort—that at least increases as life goes on.

It seems as if the greater the sacrifices voluntarily made, the more arduous the preparation for an experience, the greater the need to retrieve what actually happens. It is probably the man who selects the Marine Corps, knowing how tough Marine boot camp is and how dangerous Marine assignments often are, who has the greatest need to believe that his years in the service were valuable. It is certainly the person who has had to sacrifice in order to make a trip to Europe who has the greatest need to believe that the trip was wonderful. We notice that from among our own group memberships—clubs, fraternities, fields of concentration, professions—we value most the ones that have imposed on us the most severe initiations. Dissonance theorists argue that when a voluntarily chosen group or experience turns out badly, the fact of the choice motivates us to try to think that it has turned out well. Furthermore, they argue, the greater the sacrifice or hardship associated with the choice, the greater the dissonance generated by an unhappy outcome and the greater the need to think of the outcome as happy.

Do we need dissonance theory to account for the fact that people who suffer to attain a goal will value it highly? There must be a self-selection factor such that those who are willing to endure privation or hard work or painful initiations on the way to a goal value the goal very highly. Common sense says that the value causes the willingness to suffer rather than the other way around. In order to determine whether the dissonance effect, the "other way around" effect, also operates, one would have to assign people at random to endure more or less severe initiations. Then with the variations of strength in their antecedent motivation randomized, one could see whether those who suffered more set a greater value on what they attained. This is what Aronson and Mills (1959) have done in an experiment.

The subjects were college women who volunteered to participate in discussions of the psychology of sex with the understanding that the research was concerned with the dynamics of group discussion. Each woman was interviewed privately and told that the researchers felt it was important not to include anyone who would be severely inhibited in a discussion of sex. Did she feel that she could participate without embarrassment? All but one did and if the subject had been assigned (at random) to the *control condition* she was thereupon accepted.

Experimental subjects underwent one of two initiations. All of them were told that the subject's assurance that she would be able to talk freely was not quite enough. It would be necessary to take an "Embarrassment Test." For those who had been assigned to the *severe condition* the test involved reading aloud to the male experimenter a list of obscene words and also some very highly colored passages from contemporary novels. The experimenter was supposed to be forming a clinical judgment of the subject's degree of embarrassment. Those in the *mild condition* were asked to read aloud such sex-related but not very startling words as: *prostitute, virgin,* and *petting.* All subjects were told that they had passed the test.

Experimental subjects after their initiations and control subjects without initiation next listened to a recording of an actual discussion of the psychology of sex. Each subject was given to believe that this was a discussion held by the group she would join. The discussion itself, the same for all subjects, was dull and banal in the extreme. It was an inconclusive, halting discussion of the secondary sexual behavior of lower animals. After it was over the subject was asked to rate both the discussion and the group members on such evaluative scales as "dull-interesting" and "intelligent-unintelligent."

In essence, the experiment was designed to provide all subjects with the following pair of dissonant beliefs: I chose to participate in certain group discussions; these group discussions are dull. The experimenters intended to make the dissonance stronger for experimental subjects by modifying the first proposition so that it assumed the form: I underwent a disagreeable initiation in order to join certain group discussions. In all cases the dissonance could be relieved by transforming the second proposition into the form: These group discussions are interesting. The authors predicted that subjects in the severe condition, since they would experience the greatest dissonance, should have the greatest tendency to give positive ratings to the discussion and the group members. That is the way it came out.

COGNITIVE DISSONANCE AND SOCIAL SUPPORT

This research takes us out of the laboratory and into the midst of a group waiting for the end of the world. The full report appears in *When Prophecy Fails* (1956) by Festinger, Riecken, and Schachter. Some years ago in Lake City (to use the name given in the research report) a Mrs. Marian Keech was receiving messages from outer space which she recorded in automatic writing. Late in September there came to her from the planet Clarion a prediction that, on December 21, Lake City would be destroyed by a great flood. The newspaper report of this prophecy was read by Festinger and his collaborators, the three of them then at the University of Minnesota. They made an interesting prediction from dissonance theory about what ought to happen when a clear prophecy of this kind was clearly disconfirmed by events (as they felt sure it would be). The investigators flew to Lake City and infiltrated the group of followers collected about Mrs. Keech so as to be present on December 21. It would be fun to report that they were drowned while taking notes on that date, but in fact Lake City was not flooded on that December 21.

Judicious prophets do not make predictions that are subject to unequivocal disconfirmation, but a very sincere novice like Mrs. Keech may do so. For Mrs. Keech and for some members of the circle of believers that she acquired, there was a deep commitment to the prophecy. Some of her followers even quit their jobs and freely spent their money, so firm was their expectation of the end. What happens when Lake City is still there on December 22? The obvious thing to do to resolve the dissonance is to lose faith in the prophet. However, where the commitment to the belief is so great that reversal would involve severe hardship and embarrassment, and where there are others with you who are in the same position, dissonance theory predicts a different outcome. The followers will become very active proselytizers, trying to win others to their cause—to bolster the endangered belief by additional social support. This demonstrates the same principle as does the smoker who seeks out elements consonant with his obstinate habit, except that in the case of the apocalyptic social movement the members seek to create consonant elements in the form of new believers.

There have been several historical instances of the disconfirmation of a prophecy followed by a heightened proselytizing, and one can even argue that primitive Christianity is such a case. Some of the disciples of Jesus seem to have believed that He was destined to become King of the Jews in His lifetime and on earth, though Jesus Himself seems not to have said anything of the kind. For the disciples with this secular view the ignominious fate of crucifixion must have constituted a clear disconfirmation. The subsequent apostolic zeal was of course one of the great forces of history.

Mrs. Keech's movement was divided between the Lake City group that met at her home and a group at the nearby town, Collegeville, centering around one Dr. Armstrong who worked in the university health center. The date of the prophecy, December 21, fell during the Christmas vacation, and so the Collegeville followers, mostly students, were dispersed to their homes and had to meet disconfirmation without social support. The Lake City group met the disconfirmation all gathered together at Mrs. Keech's home, and so could supply one another with support. The prediction was that those without support would relinquish their faith, and those with support would increase their proselytizing.

The collection of ideas that emerged from Mrs. Keech's many automatic writing sessions was a wonderful mélange of mysticism, science fiction, and Christianity. The Guardians who spoke to her from outer space told the group that they, the Seekers, would be spared in the great flood. They were to stand by on the twenty-first, prepared to be picked up by flying saucers. If one reads Mrs. Keech's teachings with a skeptical eye, one suspects that she was having delusions of grandeur.

Not the least interesting aspect of this study is the example it provides of a deluded person playing an influential role that might have become of historic importance. Mrs. Keech was fortunate in having a well-protected social position. She did not hold a job, and so her delusions did not get her into trouble with employers and fellow workers. Furthermore, she had an extraordinarily indulgent husband who did not believe in her Voices and yet let her have her meetings while he went about his business. He slept soundly through the night of December 21.

Attempting an experimental study in this setting created some very special methodological problems. In order to keep full records, the false members frequently had to hide in the bathroom or on the porch, where they frenziedly scribbled notes. It is always a problem in psychological work for the experimenter to avoid influencing the process he studies, but in the present instance this problem was exceptionally difficult. If the false members were too enthusiastic in their role as followers, they might intensify the convictions of others; if they were too cool, they might dampen enthusiasm. The effort to avoid a too-direct participation reached a droll climax when one of the false members was asked to act as medium and receive messages from the Guardians. He kept a long silence and finally Mrs. Keech said with some irritation, "What do you see?" "Nothing," he replied. "That's not nothing," he was told, "that's the Void."

Late in the morning of December 20 Mrs. Keech received a message instructing her group to be prepared to be picked up at midnight. They would be escorted to a parked flying saucer and whisked away to safety in outer space. The day and early evening were spent in preparation—rehearsing passwords, removing metal from their clothing (because they had been told that metallic objects would be dangerous on the saucer). As the clock hand approached midnight the group of ten believers sat in strained expectation of an other-worldly knock at the door. The clock ticked past the hour and for a few minutes there was discussion of who had the right time and whose watch was fast. But it became clear that —by anyone's timepiece—the hour had passed without the prophesied delivery. At first there was no visible reaction—just frozen, expressionless faces. Gradually and painfully, feelings of despair engulfed them. They re-examined the prophetic messages in search of some explanation. Near 4:00 A.M. Mrs. Keech began to cry and to say bitterly that she knew some in the group were beginning to doubt her. At 4:45 Mrs. Keech summoned the group together to hear a message; with radiant face she announced: "For this day it is established that there is but one God of Earth, and He is in thy midst, and from His hand thou hast written these words. And mighty is the word of God—and by His word have ye been saved—for from the mouth of death have ye been delivered and at no time has there been such a force loosed upon the earth" (Festinger, Riecken, and Schachter, 1956, p. 169). More followed in this same high solemn style, which apes the King James version even to the archaic pronouns *thou* and *ye*. The gist of the message was that the world had been spared a cataclysm because of the impressive faith of the small group of believers. This elegant explanation was received with high enthusiasm.

In the aftermath of the disconfirmation the members of the Lake City group took turns telephoning newspapers and wire services to publicize their explanation of the failure of the prophecy. Before the disconfirmation, the group had avoided publicity but afterwards they were very active proselytizers. The Collegeville members, on the other hand, who passed the prophetic midnight waiting for their individual rescue saucers in isolation from the group, responded to disconfirmation by relinquishing their faith or by having greatly diminished confidence in the prophet. The prediction of the social psychologist prophets (Festinger, Riecken, and Schachter) was confirmed, and the importance of social support was rather well demonstrated. Even so, these prophets wrote a book to proselytize for dissonance theory.

The empirical studies of dissonance theory that we have sampled are very unlike the studies we know of congruity and balance. Can the principle of consistency that is involved in dissonance theory be the principle we know from the balance and congruity models? Two cognitive elements, A and B, are said to be dissonant if one implies the negation of the other. The terms that require explication in this definition are *cognitive elements* and *implies*. We turn now to the task of explicating these and other basic concepts of dissonance theory.

COGNITIVE ELEMENTS

By "cognitive elements" Festinger says that he means: ". . . any knowledge, opinion, or belief about the environment, about oneself, or about one's behavior" (1957, p. 3). Brehm and Cohen say: "Knowledge of one's feelings, behavior, and opinions as well as knowledge about the location of goal objects, how to get to them, what other people believe, and so forth, are examples of cognitive elements" (1962, p. 3). The defining terms used in these statements, "knowledge," "opinion," "belief," are at least as obscure as the terms to be defined, but one does notice a difference from the definitions of cognitive elements in the balance models. There is no mention of persons, or objects, or things.

Table 11-1 presents an assortment of cognitive elements drawn from discussions of dissonance theory and from experiments inspired by the theory. The elements are arranged in dissonant pairs such that each A implies the negation of a corresponding B. These elements are different from those that balance theorists cite. Here we have no President Johnson or Civil Rights Legislation or Fenwick or Modern Art; no persons or things which can be named, as Abelson and Rosenberg put it, with nouns or "substantives." Elements in dissonance theory appear to be propositions which are most easily expressed as sentences.

TABLE 11-1.   SOME COGNITIVE ELEMENTS ARRANGED IN DISSONANT PAIRS

A_1 Phil Silvers likes *Do Re Mi*	B_1 Elliott Norton dislikes *Do Re Mi*
A_2 I chose to be in *Do Re Mi*	B_2 *Do Re Mi* is no good
A_3 I smoke cigarettes	B_3 Smoking cigarettes is dangerous to life
A_4 The experimental tasks were dull	B_4 I said the tasks were interesting
A_5 I underwent a disagreeable initiation in order to join certain group discussions	B_5 The group discussions are dull
A_6 On December 21 the world will end	B_6 On December 21 the world did not end
A_7 I am a registered Democrat	B_7 I intend to vote Republican

The difference in the way that elements are defined in dissonance theory and the way they are defined in balance models does not represent a disagreement about the kinds of cognitive combinations that are inconsistent and motivating. It is only a difference in the level at which elements are conceived. For dissonance theory a set of elements with nothing else added can be dissonant or consonant or irrelevant. For the other theories, elements alone, however numerous, can be neither balanced nor imbalanced because these two states are defined in terms of values and relations as well as in terms of elements. Values and relations do not explicitly appear in dissonance theory but they are hidden within the propositions which are the very molar "elements" of that theory. We can see how this works with the Norton-Silvers problem.

The most natural way of representing that problem in the terms of dissonance theory is as an inconsistency between two elements, which are in this case propositions: Elliott Norton dislikes *Do Re Mi;* Phil Silvers likes *Do Re Mi.* Mapping the problem into a balance model would yield three elements which are persons or things: Elliott Norton; Phil Silvers; *Do Re Mi.* These three elements by themselves are neither balanced nor imbalanced. The imbalance in the situation only appears when we add values and relations. Notice that to set a positive value (+) on *Do Re Mi,* for the mind of Phil Silvers, is exactly equivalent to the proposition: "Phil Silvers likes *Do Re Mi.*" To create a negative relation or predicate (n) between Elliott Norton and *Do Re Mi* is exactly equivalent to the other proposition: Elliott Norton dislikes *Do Re Mi.* In short, the dissonance analysis in terms of propositions can be broken down into a balance analysis in terms of elements, values, and relations, or the dissonance analysis can be built up from the balance analysis. I have found that the combinations of ideas that would be considered inconsistent by the one analysis would usually also be considered inconsistent by the other analysis. The exception, shortly to be discussed, is the case in which the dissonant propositions do not express evaluations. For the most part balance models and dissonance theory are operating in the same domain.

The more molecular element is characteristic of balance representations and the more molar element characteristic of dissonance representations. Unfortunately, we cannot use this difference to show the exact logical relationship between the theories and we cannot use it to work out exact rules for translating from one sort of representation to another. This is because the definitions of elements in both kinds of theory are imprecise hodgepodges of logic, grammar, and common sense cognitive psychology. In addition, the actual practice of investigators working with the models is not sufficiently consistent to enable us to find clear definitions of our own.

IMPLICATION

What does it mean to say that one element (A) implies the negation of another element (B)? The fact that the elements are usually propositions, together with the use of the term *imply*, suggests that the relation is logical. Festinger holds that while the implication is not always logical, it is so in some cases. In illustration he cites the two beliefs: Man will in the near future reach the moon (A); Man will not be able to leave the earth's atmosphere (B). The first of these is said logically to imply the negation of the second. This is incorrect, however. There is no *necessary* contradiction between A and B. After all, someone might figure out a way of moving the earth close to the moon so that we could step across without leaving our familiar atmosphere.

There appears to be a logical contradiction between A and B above because each of us supplies such very plausible additional premises as: Only if man builds a device that can leave the earth's atmosphere will he reach the moon. The only way in which there can be a logical contradiction between just two propositions is for one to negate the other. It is logically contradictory to believe at one and the same time that man will reach the moon and that man will not reach the moon. However, no study of cognitive dissonance has been concerned with cases in which people believed both A and not-A. I do not see how people ever could believe both A and not-A, though of course they can be undecided between A and not-A. The implication that figures in the definition of dissonance is never logical implication.

What sort of implication is it that links A with not-B in cases of dissonance? I think Brehm and Cohen (1962) have it right when they say it is a question of "what else a person expects when he holds a given cognition" (p. 3). A belief (A) is dissonant with a belief (B) when (A) alone causes the person to judge that not-B is more likely than B. Given that someone is a registered Democrat (A) it is more likely that he will not vote Republican (not-B) than it is that he will vote Republican (B). Given that someone thought an experiment dull it is more likely that he will not say it was interesting (not-B) than it is that he will say it was interesting (B). So the relation between propositions that generates dissonance is not a matter of logical implication but of psychological expectation.

Psychological expectation is a broader concept than imbalance. Imbalance only applies to valued elements, whereas expectation need not involve values or attitudes. Abelson and Rosenberg (1960) specifically excluded from the domain of the balance model such relations as "is north of" and "is next in line to." With such relations one can, however, generate combinations of ideas that are dissonant. For example, the propositions: Canada is north of the United States; Windsor is south of Detroit. (It really is, by the way, because of a twist in the international boundary.) This combination is dissonant but not imbalanced. Imbalance is one variety of dissonance, the variety concerned with values or attitudes.

Some psychological expectations or implications are founded on frequent sequences of events. The sentence: "There was a lot of thunder and lightning but no rain" may be dissonant because we have noticed that when there is a lot of thunder and lightning there usually is rain. However, the sentence: "Canada is north of the United States but Windsor is south of Detroit" is not dissonant because it violates an observed sequence. Nor is observation the basis of the dissonance in the sentence: "Man will soon reach the moon but he will not be able to leave the earth's atmosphere." The dissonance in these and many other cases seems ultimately to depend on logic rather than on experience.

Suppressed Premises. Two cognitive elements, A and B, are supposed to be sufficient to generate dissonance and two elements of the kind listed in Table 11-1 cannot alone generate a logical contradiction. It is correct, therefore, to say that dissonance, as defined, is never a matter of logical contradiction but always of psychological expectation. However, if we seek out the sources of these various expectations we will find that some of them are ultimately logical. The two elements the theory recognizes are not the only ones involved. There are also often some unexpressed premises which, in combination with the elements that are made explicit, can generate logical contradictions.

Why is it that we are disturbed by the propositions, Canada is north of the United States; Windsor is south of Detroit? We are disturbed, I think, because we hold such additional unexpressed beliefs as: Windsor is a part of Canada; Detroit is a part of the United States. If we did not have these additional beliefs, if we thought Windsor was in the United States and Detroit in Canada, there would be no dissonance. A combination of ideas that is dissonant for one person, then, need not be dissonant for another. It depends on what else each person believes.

It follows that an investigator who wishes to determine the effects of some dissonant combination of ideas (A and B) on a set of subjects should begin by showing that the combination is in fact dissonant for those subjects. The most obvious way of doing so would be to ask them, or subjects like them: "Given A, would you say that B or not-B is the more probable?" So far as I can discover this is never done; there is never an independent behavioral specification of dissonance. The combination of ideas is assumed to be dissonant by the investigator because he somehow knows it has to be. In this respect dissonance studies are radically different from studies of imbalance, since these latter always begin by determining or creating the values and relations that will produce imbalance. Could one assume that subjects will think well of Elliott Norton and ill of *Do Re Mi* and so find a positive bond between the two incongruous? Clearly not. Neither could one know, without inquiry, what combinations of Robert Taft and Legalized Gambling or Fenwick and Modern Art would be incongruous or imbalanced.

How has it been possible for students of dissonance to do without independent behavioral evidence? The answer is, I think, that they have worked with situations that are likely to be dissonant for almost everyone. In the Festinger and Carlsmith (1959) experiment, for instance, the propositions involved are: I found the experiment dull; I said the experiment was interesting. This combination is dissonant because of an unexpressed premise: I say what I believe. Probably this premise is one that almost everyone holds and so the Festinger and Carlsmith manipulations can safely be assumed to be a cause of dissonance. However, to eliminate the dissonance it is only necessary to hold the premise: I am a liar and habitually say what I do not believe. Ergo, I have said that the dull experiment was interesting. For very many experiments on dissonance the underlying premise is one complimentary to the self. A thoroughly negative self-conception would eliminate the dissonance from most of the experimental manipulations.

As one reads dissonance studies, it is interesting to try to identify the unexpressed premises upon which the dissonance depends. These turn out to be a curious set of ideas. Here are some of them: 1) I say what I believe; 2) I do what I want to do; 3) If I willingly endure something unpleasant it always turns out to have been worth it; 4) What I choose is better than anything I reject. Very many of the experimental manipulations that have been used would fail to generate dissonance in one who believed: I am a liar with bad luck, poor judgment, and no will power. Perhaps not many take this view of themselves. Still, since dissonance derives from premises about oneself and the world, it must vary with self-concept and world view. It ought to be possible, for example, to contrive situations that would be dissonant for authoritarians, but consonant for equalitarians (see Chapter 10). The dissonance would build on such implicit premises as: I and my family are generous and wholesome; Jews are grasping; Negroes are unclean.

The Linguistic Expression of Dissonance. In English, there is a class of words that we regularly use to code a relation of non-implication or cognitive dissonance between two propositions. This is the class of contrastive conjunctions of which *but* is the most frequently used member. The class includes *nevertheless, although, even so,* etc. If you look at the pairs of propositions in Table 11-1 and try the effect of linking them with conjunctions, I think you will agree that *but* is more appropriate in each case than the non-contrastive *and.*

The contrastive conjunction is also used to mark inconsistency in combinations of three ideas, including those with which we are already familiar from discussions of balance. For example: I detest modern art and Fenwick is crazy about modern art *but* I like Fenwick *anyway.* The word *anyway* stresses the unexpectedness of the final proposition. The contrastive conjunction is again appropriate for those elementary imbalances that figure in the formulations of Heider and of Cartwright and Harary but which are assumed to be resolved by the Abelson and Rosenberg model. For example: He is just like me *but* I dislike him; He likes me *but* I don't like him. In all of these cases the non-contrastive *and* seems less appropriate.

The general function of contrastive conjunctions is, I think, to signal the reader or listener that what is coming next is not what he might expect. It warns him that his normal expectations, streaming out ahead as they always do, will not be a reliable guide to what now impends. He needs to pay attention; information is in the offing. If cognitive dissonance is simply the relation coded by the word *but,* it is not surprising that most people quickly pick up the sense of the concept.

MAGNITUDE OF DISSONANCE

Not all dissonant relations are of the same magnitude. One determinant of magnitude is supposed to be the relative importance of the ideas involved. Suppose that someone does not like children's piano recitals but has, nevertheless, decided to attend one. This combination is dissonant but the magnitude of dissonance is presumably lower than in the case of someone who has made a decision to undergo surgery though he hates and fears surgery. The greater importance of the two elements in the second case is supposed to produce a greater dissonance.

While a relation of dissonance or of consonance is defined in terms of just two elements, there would usually be additional elements in a person's mind which are relevant to these two. Each of these additional elements might be either consonant or dissonant with either of the original two. In the case of the man who elects to attend a child's piano recital, we may suppose that there is an additional element consonant with that decision, the recitalist may be his daughter. The man who is going to submit to surgery probably also has in mind another consonant element; surgery alone can save his life. Festinger suggests that if we think of the magnitude of the various cognitive elements as constant, then the total dissonance between one element and all the rest of a person's thinking should depend upon the proportion of relevant elements that are dissonant with the one in question. Of all the ideas that have something to do with attending a child's piano recital, what proportion consists of dissonant ideas?

A student of social psychology at Harvard, Mrs. Victoria Steinitz, has pointed out to me that there are numerous superficially dissonant or imbalanced ideas that people hold to very stubbornly. To understand these we must look at the total set of relevant ideas. Many patriotic Americans who regard nuclear testing as a severe health hazard are, nevertheless, firmly convinced that the United States should resume nuclear testing. The only way to understand this conviction in terms of the consistency principle is to suppose that nuclear testing is thought to be consonant with the deterrence of enemies and the preservation of peace.

In order actually to determine the total magnitude of dissonance in a person's thinking about any single element, one would need to have a means of eliciting and counting the total population of relevant elements and also a means of assessing their relative importance. There is no adequate procedure for eliciting and counting elements and cannot be so long as the element is not clearly defined. In connection with undergoing surgery one might think of such dissonant matters as blood, pain, bedpans, the sight of suffering, bossy nurses, etc. Is each of these an element or is each experience of any one of these an element? We have no idea how much cognition makes an element and no possibility of computing total dissonance. It is sometimes possible, however, to say whether a new element would have the effect of reducing the total dissonance or adding to it and so of checking the major principle that dissonance engenders efforts at reduction.

THE CASE OF COMMITMENT

As it is defined cognitive dissonance applies to any pair of inconsistent beliefs. However, experimental studies of dissonance have been largely restricted to one kind of inconsistent pair: a belief or attitude and knowledge of action or commitment to action that does not follow from the belief or attitude. Examples of this kind of pair are: I believe that cigarette smoking is dangerous but I smoke cigarettes; I thought the group discussion dull but I rated it as rather interesting. Why should research have concentrated on this sort of dissonance?

Brehm and Cohen (1962) pointed out the direction that dissonance research had taken and offered two plausible explanations. In the first place the relation of implication between a belief and a corresponding action is perhaps obvious enough to require no independent behavioral specification. This I would suggest is because the underlying premise is one that is very widely shared and very firm: I act in accordance with my beliefs. The second reason suggested by Brehm and Cohen for the concentration on commitment to action is that in this case the probable direction of dissonance-reducing effects can be predicted. Cognition about action (such as, I said the experiment was interesting; or, I sold my worldly goods and committed myself to the Seekers) may be assumed to be more resistant to change than the opposing attitudes or beliefs. Efforts at reducing dissonance will probably be directed at supporting the stronger element and modifying the weaker. This brings us back to the three empirical studies with which we began. How does the theory we have studied derive the outcomes of these experiments?

The Festinger and Carlsmith (1959) experiment created dissonance by inducing subjects to bear false witness concerning the interest of a set of tasks. The knowledge that one has lied is presumably a stronger element more resistant to change than the evaluation of the tasks. Total dissonance can be reduced by cognitive elements that are consonant with this stronger element. Knowledge that one has been paid twenty dollars seems a more powerful element than knowledge that one has been paid one dollar and so dissonance is more drastically reduced for subjects with the former knowledge than for subjects with the latter knowledge. Since the twenty-dollar subjects suffer less dissonance, they have less need to modify the weaker element which is the evaluation of the tasks.

The Aronson and Mills (1959) experiment created dissonance by inducing subjects to volunteer for discussions and then giving them to believe that the discussions would be dull. The commitment to participate is presumably the stronger element. Total dissonance can be reduced by cognitive elements consonant with the commitment. Knowledge that one has voluntarily undergone a severe initiation in order to join the group seems a more powerful element than knowledge that one has undergone a mild initiation. Consequently subjects with the former knowledge experience more dissonance than subjects with the latter knowledge and have more need to alter the weaker element, which is the negative evaluation of the discussion heard.

In *When Prophecy Fails* dissonance is attributed to persons who have committed themselves to the Seekers when an event expected by the Seekers fails to materialize. The social support provided by the company of other Seekers is consonant with the commitment and so makes the commitment a stronger element than the fact that the world has not ended. Persons with social support consequently attempt to add further elements consonant with the commitment and so proselytize for their beliefs. For persons lacking social support the continued existence of the world is the stronger element and it overthrows the commitment.

This presentation of dissonance theory has been a sympathetic one. It has, I hope, included enough that is interesting to account for the contemporary influence of the theory. However, there are very serious criticisms to be made. They cannot be exhaustively listed (for that, see Jordan, 1963, or Chapanis and Chapanis, 1964), but we can provide samples with reference to the three experiments with which we are now familiar.

THE LOGICAL STRUCTURE OF THE THEORY

The basic concepts of the theory are: cognitive element, implication, magnitude of dissonance, and commitment. We have tried to understand each of these in turn. This has been a search for solid footing in a quagmire. Each time we tried to rest some weight, the ground most dismayingly has given way. Trying to be a good guide I have repeatedly jumped back before we went under and tried to take us round by another route.

With its basic concepts unclear, it is not possible that dissonance theory should have a rigorous logical structure. The derivations of the outcomes of the many experiments are not true deductions but only an arbitrary selection from the many possible ways of thinking about these experiments. Consider, for example, the logical structure of the research reported in *When Prophecy Fails*.

Dissonance was created in the minds of the Seekers by the disconfirmation of a specific belief. The disconfirmed belief may be expressed in these words: "There will be a great flood on December 21 and the believers will be picked up by flying saucers." For those Seekers who enjoyed social support at the time of the disconfirmation the commitment to the belief was expected to hold firm. Furthermore, the supported Seekers were expected to proselytize for the belief in an effort to bolster it with new consonant cognitive elements. The authors write as if that is what, for the most part, happened. But that is not what happened.

If the Seekers had retained their commitment to the belief which was specifically disconfirmed, they would have had to believe that the flood and the delivery therefrom had occurred on schedule. Proselytizing for this belief would have meant asserting that the world had been destroyed and the Seekers whisked away in saucers. Nobody did anything of the kind. To have done so would have been to deny the clear evidence of everyone's senses.

What did the Seekers continue to believe? The disconfirmation of Mrs. Keech's prophecy was not denied. However, the logical matrix of that prophecy was adjusted so as to blunt the impact of the disconfirmation. The happy discovery made in the hours after midnight was that the cruel facts could be disarmed by adopting certain after-the-fact assumptions. The essentials of the argument go like this. Mrs. Keech is a good prophet who receives messages that are true as far as they go. The Guardians had intended to destroy the world. Unless—and this they did not convey to Mrs. Keech since it would have spoiled their test— unless the Seekers should show great faith by believing in the prophecy. Such faith was shown and the Guardians were moved to compassion. The logic is very like that involved in the Old Testament story of God's command to Abraham that he sacrifice his son, Isaac, and then, at the last minute, God's revocation of the command.

Is all of this or any of this predicted by dissonance theory? Certainly not in any explicit deductive way. Is the outcome then a disconfirmation of the theory? The authors of the study do not say so, they conclude that the theory has been confirmed. They must be privy to some assumptions and understandings which the theory does not make clear.

The muddled state of the theoretical derivations in *When Prophecy Fails* is not unique in the dissonance literature. The muddle is less evident in most of the other studies but ultimately it is usually there. If these are the circumstances what is it that is confirmed by the many confirming experiments on the subject of dissonance? It is not a set of general propositions that might be called a theory of cognitive dissonance. It may, in part, be the general importance of an inconsistency principle for understanding attitude change. Beyond that the experiments only confirm the imaginative powers of a group of investigators. However they do it, the dissonance theorists are repeatedly able to think up interesting manipulations that have the effects they are expected to have. Which is clever of them, but not the same thing as a theory.

ALTERNATIVE INTERPRETATIONS OF RESULTS

The outcome of almost any dissonance experiment (Jordan, 1963) can be explained without recourse to the principle of dissonance. And usually there are several ways of doing it. Consider the Aronson and

Mills (1959) finding that persons who went through a very embarrassing initiation gave higher ratings to a discussion held by a group they expected to join than did persons who went through a mild initiation. What other than cognitive dissonance could be involved?

Perhaps the reading of obscene words and of racy passages from novels was taken as a sign that the discussions on the psychology of sex would be pretty lively. Possibly the recorded discussion then seemed fairly lively because the subject could see where it was leading and what these discussants really had in mind. On the other hand, the initiation may have seemed to forecast some rather vulgar and tasteless discussions. The subject may have been greatly relieved by the politely intellectual tone of the recorded discussion and registered her approval with high ratings. Perhaps, finally, the girls quite enjoyed the supposedly severe initiation and expressed their approval of the total proceedings in the only way available to them, by rating the discussion high. One could understand it if the girls, whose "Embarrassment Test" consisted of reading aloud such words as "virgin" and "petting," were somewhat disenchanted by the total proceedings.

Brehm and Cohen (1962), whose book strongly supports dissonance theory, nevertheless admit that many of the experimental outcomes can be explained by concepts other than dissonance. They point out, however, that these other concepts are not a unified theory but just an odd lot of ideas invoked to suit the occasion. Only dissonance theory they hold can explain the lot. But dissonance theory itself is a mixed bag of ad hoc ideas. There is nothing common to all the derivations but a notion of inconsistency and a certain vocabulary.

SUBJECT LOSS

There are also methodological problems with the dissonance experiments. The most general and serious of these was formulated by Brehm and Cohen (1962). In most of the dissonance experiments at least a few subjects are likely to refuse to complete the experiment and so their data are lost. The disturbing thing about this subject dropout is that there is usually good reason to expect it to vary by experimental conditions in such a way as to favor the dissonance prediction. The Festinger and Carlsmith (1959) experiment can be used as an example.

There is no reason why subjects in the control condition should have dropped out, but when the subjects in the experimental conditions were asked to lie, we would expect some to have refused. Which ones? Probably those offered only one dollar in payment would be more likely to refuse than those offered twenty dollars. Probably, too, those who had found the tasks extremely dull would be more likely to refuse than those who had found them only moderately dull since, for the former subjects, the report that the tasks were interesting would obviously be a falsehood. What would it do to the results if there was a loss from the one-dollar condition of just those subjects who thought the tasks most dull; subjects with a comparable opinion of the tasks being retained in the other conditions? The dependent variable was the rating of the tasks and the main prediction was that the tasks would be rated most interesting or least dull by subjects in the one-dollar condition. If the subjects who would have given the lowest (most dull) ratings dropped out from this condition and not from the other conditions, that fact alone would favor the outcome.

It is very generally the case in studies of dissonance that the most plausible pattern of differential subject dropout by experimental conditions is one that favors the dissonance prediction. Has the dropout actually occurred and has it produced the results? A full answer would require the detailed study of all the original data and no such study has been made. The possibility alone is extremely disquieting. In addition, some of the research reports describe some dropout that fits the pattern. In the Festinger and Carlsmith experiment (1959), for example, eleven subjects out of seventy-one dropped out. Of these eleven, there were seven from the one-dollar condition, four from the twenty-dollar condition, and none from the control condition. There are various reasons for thinking that this dropout pattern did not in the present case produce the confirming pattern of results. However, it does not inspire confidence in this literature as a whole to find that the dropouts were, as we feared they would be, most frequent in the condition offering weaker inducement.

Inconsistency and General Psychological Theory

The strongest feature of the three treatments of attitude change is the one they have in common, the principle that human nature abhors incongruity-dissonance-imbalance (Zajonc, 1960), or, as we shall loosely say in this last section, inconsistency. So good an idea is never invented. The antecedents of the authors we have discussed have also their antecedents, and in the end, we find, the idea seems always to have existed. What has changed is the precision of its statement and the implications which are developed.

Fritz Heider's papers in the 1940's directly inspired the current formulations of attitude change. In the 1930's, however, we have extremely cogent analyses of psychological conflict developed by Kurt Lewin

(1935) for human behavior and by Neal Miller (1944) for the laboratory animal, which, though they do not mention attitude, remind us of the recent work. Lewin first and Neal Miller after him distinguished three major varieties of conflict: The Approach-Avoidance Conflict; the Approach-Approach Conflict, and the Avoidance-Avoidance Conflict. We will map one of these into the balance model just to show the similarities that exist; they exist also for the other treatments of inconsistency.

An Approach-Avoidance Conflict for the laboratory rat can be created by feeding him at a certain point in a maze and also subjecting him to electric shock at a point just before he reaches the food. If the hungry animal is then placed some distance away from the food, he may be said to be in an Approach-Avoidance Conflict, since he will wish to approach the food but cannot do so without moving toward the shock which he would prefer to avoid. If we describe the rat's state of mind in terms of the balance model, it is clear that the food is positively valued and the shock negatively valued. In addition, there is a positive bond between the two cognitive objects, since an approach to one is also an approach to the other—they go together. A positive bond between objects of unlike sign is a condition of imbalance.

The three basic kinds of behavioral conflict can all be translated into the terms of imbalance or incongruity or dissonance. It appears, then, that the new formulations are very similar indeed to the old. Is this, then, another one of those embarrassing cases in which psychology has freshened up some familiar truisms with a new vocabulary and mistaken them for scientific advances?

The inconsistency theories are not just conflict theory in a new guise. Lewin and Miller were mainly concerned with predicting the gross actions of moving toward or away from objects. They worked out the way in which forces to approach or avoid would fall off with distance from the object. From this analysis it followed that in the case of an Approach-Avoidance Conflict there would be a point short of the object where the two sets of forces would exactly balance one another and the organism in conflict would stop there. Approach-Approach Conflicts, it developed, should be easily resolved, since locomotion towards one goal would cause the forces in that direction to increase and opposing forces to decrease. The Avoidance-Avoidance Conflict should set up a field of forces such as to make the most attractive action moving out of the field away from both objects; thus the rat between two points where shock threatens will make frantic efforts to claw his way out of the box. Conflict theory, in short, is focused on the direction of gross actions of approach and avoidance, whereas balance theory is concerned with cognitive adjustments.

Starting with an identical set of disequilibrium conditions the two theories have explored completely different sets of implications. The one theory has not made the other superfluous. Rather, there is here a rich opportunity for theoretical integration. One immediate gain for inconsistency theory from the identification with conflict theory is that we are enabled to understand why human nature abhors inconsistency. A situation of inconsistency is one that calls for mutually incompatible actions —to smoke and not to smoke, to criticize Fenwick and not to criticize Fenwick, to approach food and not to approach it. Inconsistency in the mind threatens to paralyze action.

The conflict theory of Lewin and Miller owes something to the more general notion of conflict of impulse developed by Sigmund Freud. Classical psychoanalytic theory is an intricate structure which was often changed and is full of ambiguities, but the general line on which Freud thought is very clear. The early writings on neurosis, on dreams, and on slips of the tongue all argue in the same way. Freud begins with some item of behavior that appears to be unmotivated—a paralysis of the hand that has no organic cause, a dream of murder, a slip of the tongue in which a man announces that a meeting is adjourned when it was supposed to have been opened. In each case the behaving person insists that he has not wished to act as he has acted and indeed has wished to act in just the contrary way. The insistence is vehement. Freud then proceeds to adduce evidence that while the person is right in reporting that he wished to act in one way, it is also the case that he has wished to act in a directly contrary way. In fact, there is a necessity to divide the psyche into contending forces such as to allow for simultaneous directly opposed wishes. However, the executive agency in the mind abhors this untidy conflict of impulse and commonly admits into consciousness only one impulse at a time. The other impulse is suppressed or repressed or denied, but finds expression in one or another disguised form. In psychoanalytic theory there is a central assumption of the existence of inconsistency and also of a drive to consistency.

Consider Freud's beautiful case study called *Analysis of a Phobia in a Five-Year-Old Boy* (1909), which we have discussed in Chapter 8. Little Hans, the five-year-old, in classical Oedipal fashion hated his father and wished to be rid of him but also loved him and wished him to be close by. Most of the time only the loving impulse was in consciousness and the hatred and fear were "displaced" to horses. It was the boy's exaggerated fear (or phobia) that a horse would bite him that caused Hans's father to ask Freud's advice.

Hans's mother had been accustomed to take the little boy into bed with her when they awakened in the morning. She had done this particularly often during a summer in the country when father was away most of the time. Later on, however, father had interfered with this cozy practice and ordered Hans out of bed. Hans's father was a physician and through an unlucky chain of associations it had been suggested to Hans that physicians sometimes punished sexual naughtiness in small boys with castration. There was a link in Hans's mind between his beloved father and the feared and hated castrator who was his rival in love.

The conflict in Hans's mind could be diagrammed as an unbalanced positive bond linking a beloved father and a hated castrator. It is also, of course, a situation of Approach-Avoidance Conflict, since Hans cannot move toward his beloved father without moving toward the feared and hated castrator. There is a third way of describing such a situation, the description that Freud favored. Hans might be said to have ambivalent feelings, feelings of love and hate toward the same person—his father.

It is very generally true that cognitive inconsistency amounts to ambivalence. The man who enjoys smoking but believes that it may cause cancer is surely ambivalent about smoking. The department store manager who likes Fenwick and detests modern art but believes that Fenwick will mount an exhibit of modern art is ambivalent toward both Fenwick and modern art (Rosenberg et al., 1960). If objects of unlike sign are bound together positively, one may think of the charge on either object as flowing toward the other and creating ambivalence. If objects of like sign are bound together negatively, one may think of a contrary charge flowing toward each object and generating ambivalence.

In the case of young Hans the ambivalence of inconsistency would be extreme and the abhorrence of the ambivalence extraordinarily intense. In such cases the human being may resort to modes of resolution that are more exotic than attitude change or differentiation or stopping thinking.

Freud said that the fear and hate inspired by the father were "displaced" to the horse so as to leave in consciousness unalloyed affection for a parent. At the same time the boy's phobia worried his father and interfered with his father's routine, and provided a reason for Hans to stay close to home and mother; in short, the phobia served some of the purposes of the repressed hatred and yet kept the conscious mind free of imbalance. This is a resolution reminiscent of differentiation: in its elaborate effort to deny any tie between the good and bad. The bad father becomes something quite different—a biting horse—which can only be traced back to the parent by way of a set of trivial and easily overlooked lines of association.

In Freudian theory, as in Lewin's and in Miller's conflict theories, we have a clear antecedent of the present concern with inconsistency, but again the antecedent does not make the contemporary development superfluous. Inconsistency theory explores cognitive adjustments and especially attitude change; conflict theory explores actions of approach and avoidance in both animals and man; Freudian theory explores a range of extreme and sometimes pathological adjustments in both mind and body which occur as reactions to intense ambivalence. There is encouragement in this overlap of ideas. There is the promise that psychology will produce something more satisfying than a collection of models for particular problems, that it will find a truly general theory.

REFERENCES

Abelson, R. P. Modes of resolution of belief dilemmas. *J. conflict Resolut.*, 1959, **3**, 343–352.

Abelson, R. P. Computer simulation of "hot" cognition. In S. Tompkins & S. Messick, *Computer simulations of personality.* New York: Wiley, 1963.

Abelson, R. P., & Rosenberg, M. J. Symbolic psychologic: A model of attitudinal cognition. *Behav. Sci.*, 1958, **3**, 1–13.

Aronson, E., & Mills, J. The effects of severity of initiation on liking for a group. *J. abnorm. soc. Psychol.*, 1959, **59**, 177–181.

Birch, H. G. The effect of socially disapproved labeling upon well-structured attitudes. *J. abnorm. soc. Psychol.*, 1945, **40**, 301–310.

Brehm, J. W., & Cohen, A. R. *Explorations in cognitive dissonance.* New York: Wiley, 1962.

Burdick, H. A., & Burnes, A. J. A test of "strain toward symmetry" theories. *J. abnorm. soc. Psychol.*, 1958, **57**, 367–370.

Cartwright, D., & Harary, F. Structural balance: A generalization of Heider's theory. *Psychol. Rev.*, 1956, **63**, 277–293.

Chapanis, Natalia P., & Chapanis, A. Cognitive dissonance: Five years later. *Psychol. Bull.*, 1964, **61**, 1–22.

De Soto, C. B. Learning a social structure. *J. abnorm. soc. Psychol.*, 1960, **60**, 417–421.

De Soto, C. B., & Kuethe, J. L. Subjective probabilities of interpersonal relationships. *J. abnorm. soc. Psychol.*, 1959, **59**, 290–294.

Festinger, L. *A theory of cognitive dissonance.* New York: Row, Peterson, 1957.

Festinger, L., & Carlsmith, J. M. Cognitive consequences of forced compliance. *J. abnorm. soc. Psychol.*, 1959, **58**, 203–210.

Festinger, L., Riecken, H. W., Jr., & Schachter, S. *When prophecy fails.* Minneapolis: Univer. of Minn. Press, 1956.

Freud, S. *The complete psychological works of Sigmund Freud.* Vol. X (1st ed., 1909) London: Hogarth, 1955.

Harary, F. On the measurement of structural balance. *Behav. Sci.*, 1959, **4**, 316–323.

Heider, F. Social perception and phenomenal causality. *Psychol. Rev.*, 1944, **51**, 358–374.

Heider, F. Attitudes and cognitive organization. *J. Psychol.*, 1946, **21**, 107–112.

Heider, F. *The psychology of interpersonal relations.* New York: Wiley, 1958.

Hovland, C. I., Janis, I. L., & Kelley, H. H. *Communication and persuasion.* New Haven: Yale Univer. Press, 1953.

Hovland, C. I., Mandell, W., Campbell, Enid H., Brock, T., Luchins, A. S., Cohen, A. R., McGuire, W. J., Janis, I. L., Feierabend, Rosalind L., & Anderson, N. H. *The order of presentation in persuasion.* New Haven: Yale Univer. Press, 1957.

Janis, I. L., Hovland, C. I., Field, P. B., Linton, Harriet, Graham, Elaine, Cohen, A. R., Rife, D., Abelson, R. P., Lesser, G. S., & King, B. T. *Personality and persuasibility.* New Haven: Yale Univer. Press, 1959.

Jordan, N. Behavioral forces that are a function of attitudes and of cognitive organization. *Hum. Relat.,* 1953, **6**, 273–287.

Jordan, N. Fallout shelters and social psychology—The "theory" of cognitive dissonance. HI–244–D, June 11, 1963. Croton-on-Hudson: The Hudson Institute.

Klapper, J. T. The effects of mass media. Mimeographed manuscript. Bureau of Applied Social Research, Columbia Univer., 1949.

Kogan, N., & Tagiuri, R. Interpersonal preference and cognitive organization. *J. abnorm. soc. Psychol.,* 1958, **56**, 113–116.

Lewin, K. *Dynamic theory of personality.* New York: McGraw-Hill, 1935.

Lewis, Helen B. Studies in the principles of judgments and attitudes: IV. The operation of prestige suggestion. *J. abnorm. soc. Psychol..* 1941, **45**, 229–256.

Miller, N. E. Experimental studies of conflict. In J. McV. Hunt (Ed.), *Personality and the behavior disorders.* Vol. I. New York: Ronald, 1944.

Newcomb, T. M. An approach to the study of communicative acts. *Psychol. Rev.,* 1953, **60**, 393–404.

Osgood, C. E., Suci, G. J., & Tannenbaum, P. H. *The measurement of meaning.* Urbana: Univer. of Illinois Press, 1957.

Osgood, C. E., & Tannenbaum, P. H. The principle of congruity in the prediction of attitude change. *Psychol. Rev.* 1955, **62**, 42–55.

Rosenberg, M. J. Some content determinants of intolerance for attitudinal inconsistency. Office of Naval Research Technical Report. Ohio State University, 1962.

Rosenberg, M. J., Hovland, C. I., McGuire, W. J., Abelson, R. P., & Brehm, J. W. *Attitude organization and change.* New Haven: Yale Univer. Press, 1960.

Tagiuri, R. Social preference and its perception. In R. Tagiuri & L. Petrullo (Eds.), *Person perception and interpersonal behavior.* Stanford: Stanford Univer. Press, 1958.

Tannenbaum, P. H. Attitudes toward source and concept as factors in attitude change through communications. Unpublished doctoral dissertation. Univer. of Illinois, 1953.

Zajonc, R. B. The concepts of balance, congruity, and dissonance. *Pub. Opin. Quart.,* 1960, **24**, 280–296.

CHAPTER 12

Impressions of Personality,

Including One's Own

The subject of this chapter ought really to be introduced with a motion picture of persons unfamiliar to us so that we might first form impressions of them and then analyze the process of impression formation. A motion picture is impossible to provide and so here instead is an introduction in words to a person we none of us know.

> Jim left the house to get some stationery. He walked out into the sun-filled street with two of his friends, basking in the sun as he walked. Jim entered the stationery store which was full of people. Jim talked with an acquaintance while he waited for the clerk to catch his eye. On his way out, he stopped to chat with a school friend who was just com- ing into the store. Leaving the store, he walked toward school. On his way out he met the girl to whom he had been introduced the night before. They talked for a short while, and then Jim left for school [Luchins, 1957b, p. 34].

The paragraph about Jim is very flat prose, not just because nothing dramatic happens but also because the terms are so purely behavioral. There is nothing interpretive or internal in the paragraph. What do we know for sure about Jim? That he has gone to school, has "basked" in the sun on the way, has seen at least four friends or acquaintances and has stopped to talk with a girl. The motion picture camera could not make so dead a record.

The human mind is not disposed to stop with the facts it is given; it tranforms the facts and it streams ahead of the facts. From the above report of actions performed by Jim most people form an impression that Jim is a "friendly" person. The step from certain data—basking in the sun, stopping to talk with friends, etc.—to the personality trait "friendly" is the essence of impression formation. We will look closely at what is involved.

Data and Constructs

The process we call *forming impressions of personality* is sometimes called *person perception*. Bruner (1958) has argued that the process of perception tends, in general, to accomplish two things: 1) a recoding of the diversity of data we encounter into a simpler form that brings it within the scope of our limited memory; 2) a going beyond the information given to predict future events and thereby minimize surprise. For example, suppose you make a rapid canvass of stations on the car radio, actually hearing a few measures of music, a speaking voice, and a singing voice. These might be perceived as the *Eroica*, a news broadcast, and a commercial jingle. It is easier to remember the above list than it is to remember the particular sequence of notes from the symphony, the sentences of the newscaster, and the drivel of the jingle. The list is an economical recoding. The recoding is an elaborate prediction as well as an economy. The *Eroica* goes on in such and such a foreordained fashion. The news broadcast cannot be predicted in such detail but it will consist of a selection from a rather stable repertoire of disasters, Republicans and Democrats, disarmament talks, and weathers. The jingle is completely determined but brief and there will be new information at that position of the dial within a few seconds. The two accomplishments of perception specified by Bruner, economical recoding and prediction, are also the accomplishments of the process of impression formation.

The term *friendly* is easier to remember than the list of data: 1. Walked with two friends; 2. Basked in the sun; 3. Talked with acquaintance; 4. Chatted with school friend; 5. Stopped to talk with girl. From "friendly" we can roughly, but not perfectly, recover the particular data. People who are friendly are likely to walk to school with friends rather than alone, likely to be willing to stop and chat with acquaintances and new girl friends, perhaps likely to enjoy the sun's warmth though this seems less sure. The word "friendly" is a summary formula for the disposition to do all these things. It is not a scientific formula (Bruner, 1958). It does not permit perfect reconstitution of particular data in the way that $s = gt^2/2$ does for falling bodies. However, "friendly" is a fairly good summary of what we know about Jim.

"Friendly" says a great deal about Jim that the paragraph has not specified; it projects a trait of personality from a few data points. We expect Jim to have a smiling face and a warm manner, not always but more often than most people. We expect him to enjoy parties and to be the sort of person who introduces himself to strangers. We expect to find him likeable and we expect most people to find him likeable. The impression is very elaborately predictive. The predictions cannot all be made with high confidence and they are not all made with equal confidence but we are "set" in a very complicated way for future contacts with Jim.

Our impression or *perception* of Jim relies upon a considerable amount of past experience, upon what psychologists sometimes call an *apperceptive mass*. From hearsay and from direct observation we have learned that certain kinds of behavior hang together, not invariably but probabilistically. People who like parties also introduce themselves to strangers and stop to chat with friends and smile easily and so on. In English this cluster of behavior is called "friendliness." When we learn that Jim has performed a few actions from the total set we give him the name of the set ("friendly") which is easier to remember than the list of particular actions performed and is, at the same time, predictive of all the actions not yet performed but ordinarily entailed. Friendliness is what philosophers call a dispositional construct, it summarizes a great many actions a person is disposed to take.

All impression formation moves from data of some kind to personality constructs of some kind. However there are many kinds of data and many kinds of dispositional construct. Before considering particular research problems in the formation of impressions we need to make a brief survey of the variety of data and constructs.

PERSONALITY CONSTRUCTS

These will be the terms used for the everyday characterization of personality; the categories of what might be called the naïve or lay theory of personality. There is considerable overlap between the naïve theory and the scientific, or at any rate academic and medical, theory of personality. The overlap exists, in part, because academic theory starts from naïve theory and takes motives, attitudes, abilities, traits, emotions, and moods for its initial constructs. In part, the overlap is there because naïve theory borrows novel constructs from professional theory; sophisticated laymen conceive of themselves and their friends in terms of unconscious motives, mother complexes, and oral traits. Everyone wants to construe personalities in as powerfully predictive a way as possible and good terms for doing so, even terms that are only promising, spread rapidly.

We can illustrate a good variety of constructs with the paragraph about Jim. One might infer from the paragraph in question that he was "feeling happy," that he was in a "happy mood" on the day in question. This characterization in terms of mood or feelings summarizes the same set of data as does the characterization in terms of the trait of friendliness. Mood and feeling are also dispositional or predictive but the disposition in question is not thought to be as enduring as is the trait of friendliness and so predictions from mood do not reach as far into the future. If Jim was in a good mood we should expect a smile on his face and no furrow on his brow and easy, relaxed behavior in school and at home. But Jim's good mood today does not predict anything about tomorrow or a month from now whereas the trait of friendliness does. Of course a mood can be characteristic of a person over time, and friendliness can be a temporary disposition instead of an enduring trait. In English we easily convert terms between mood and trait characterizations. Compare "Jim is in a happy mood" with "Jim is a happy person" and "Jim is a friendly person" with "Jim is in a friendly mood."

The construct of emotion is close to the construct of mood and to the construct of trait; in English there are overlapping vocabularies. Emotions are not so enduring as traits; they are more intense than moods and likely to have some assignable cause whereas moods are often conceived as cyclical, unmotivated "ups and downs." Emotions, like all the other personality constructs, are predictive. From the fact of a red tense face and clenched fists we infer a roiling of the viscera and a disposition to take aggressive action. The paragraph about Jim does not provide good data for inferring an emotion; there is not enough intensity in his behavior.

From the fact that Jim of the paragraph stops and speaks to the girl he met the night before one might form the impression that he "likes" that girl. To do so is to credit him with a disposition to wish to be with the girl, to enjoy her company, to try to please her. The term *like* and its opposite *dislike* contrast with trait names like *friendly* or mood terms like *happy* or ability terms like *intelligent* in that they require the specification of an object. We do not say that someone is a "liking person" or that someone is in a "liking mood." You like someone or something. It is a disposition, either enduring or transitory, that has an object. Likes and dislikes between persons have been much studied in social psychology (see, for example, Tagiuri, Bruner, and Blake, 1958).

There are other kinds of constructs that the paragraph about Jim does not suggest; for example, abilities, motives, and ideologies. If it had been reported that Jim got the best score in his class on the day's mathematics assignment we might have credited him with a high level of mathematical ability and so predicted future success with problems involving numbers. If Jim had brushed off his friends in order to get a few extra minutes for study we might have credited him with a high level of achievement motivation (see Chapter 9) which predicts the continuing pursuit of excellence. If he had met a picketing worker outside the stationery store and, on that account, refused to go in the store we might have called Jim a "liberal" and figured we could anticipate his position on desegregation, loyalty oaths, a fluorinated water supply, and Barry Goldwater. In every case a fact or two is projected into a more general disposition.

In studies of impression formation the data collected are almost always verbal; subjects write down the words they are prepared to apply to the personality in question and these are such words as "friendly," "cheerful," "angry," "intelligent," and "reactionary." One of the deeper and more difficult problems in impression formation is to work out the relation between such labelling and what people do in ordinary circumstances. Suppose we were introduced to someone at a party and that we have a conversation that day with our new acquaintance and another conversation some days later. Would we, in our mind, be trying out various verbal formulas for this person, attempting to decide whether he should be called "friendly" or perhaps only "temporarily good-humored"? I do not think that we do that. Do we perhaps try to fit the person to the categories the words name even if we do not say names to ourselves? That is harder to answer from introspection. What I feel surest of is that we are always forming probabilistic expectancies about new people. We seldom formulate these explicitly but we can tell that they are in our mind in some form because of the surprise we feel when they are disconfirmed. If we had thought someone generally friendly and it turns out that he was only having a rare good day we know what we had thought chiefly from the fact that his subsequent coolness startles us. Words for traits seem to come to mind only when there is some reason to communicate an impression to another, to put another person in possession of our expectancies. The words seem to chop up our continuous and shifting expectancies into crude categorical blocks called "friendly," "ignorant," "humorous," and the like.

PERSONALITY DATA

The word *data* is from the Latin *datus* meaning "that which is given" and in experiments on impression formation the data are literally the "givens." In the paragraph about Jim the data are the paragraph which is a report of behavior. From this report, from something known, additional things are inferred by the subject. These additional things are the projections or constructions, the subject's impression. In general, impression formation is the study of relationships between "givens" and guesses in the realm of personality.

In life outside the laboratory we also make a distinction between data and construct, a distinction that is epistemological. Data are thought to be nearer to uninterpreted reality; nearer to being nature's "given," nearer to being stimuli. Data are less dependent on interpretation, they draw less from the apperceptive mass than do constructs. This distinction is a relative one. Movement, color, and contour seem to us to be data relative to the impression of a face and the face to be data relative to the impression of the person's character. In impression formation and in perception generally we never do seem to reach the level of absolute data. There is always some admixture of interpretation. The epistemological sense of "data" is a dubious one to my mind, but it is very widely shared and making it explicit helps to keep things straight.

In most studies of impression formation the experimenter's "given" is nearer nature's "given" than is the subject's inference. The paragraph describing Jim's actions seems to involve less interpretation, to be more inevitable, more nearly imposed by reality than does the inference that Jim is friendly. In studies of expressive behavior experimenters have often provided photographs of emotional faces, recordings of voices or samples of handwriting and asked for inferences about emotion or character. In such studies the experimenter's "given," his stimulus materials, seem to involve less interpretation than do the judgments of feeling and character.

In some studies the inferences have been very remote from the data. Michotte's (1954) investigations of the perception of causality, for example, employ inanimate physical objects but subjects often perceive human interaction. For example, a square black object (A) moves along a straight path until it reaches a square gray object (B); A then stops and B begins to move, away from A and on the same straight line. These are the data. If A's rate of approach is faster than B's subsequent movement, the moving away of B is usually interpreted as caused by A and sometimes as motivated by anger at A. If A's rate of approach is slower than B's subsequent movement then B's movement is often seen as flight motivated by fear of A. Here are human emotions or motives inferred from certain movements of abstract inanimate objects. Heider and Simmel (1944) have shown subjects animated cartoons of three geometric figures —a large triangle, a smaller triangle, and a disc moving around in and out of a large rectangle. These very simple data were often interpreted as human beings in interpersonal conflict; sometimes as two men in rivalry for a girl. The large triangle seemed aggressive and bullying; the small triangle defiant and heroic; the disc timid and female. In this case traits of human character were read from patterns of movement in abstract figures.

The experimenter's data have not invariably been less "interpreted" than the subject's impressions. Asch, in his 1946 studies which did a great deal to stimulate the contemporary interest in person perception, used lists of traits as data. For example, he told his subjects that the following characteristics belonged to a particular person: "energetic-assured-talkative-cold-ironical-inquisitive-persuasive." The subjects were to form an impression of this person and in considerable part their filled-out impressions consisted of additional traits, such as: "popular, opportunistic, skeptical, arrogant, selfish." Bruner, Shapiro, and Tagiuri in their 1958 study also used trait names as "givens" and then required subjects to estimate the probability that certain other traits would be associated with the one given. Given, for example, that someone is "intelligent," how likely is it that he will also be "boastful"? In studies such as these the two senses of "data" diverge. Within the frame of reference of the experiment, one set of traits is given or "known" and another set is "unknown" and must be inferred. In everyday impression formation, however, the experimenter's knowns (e.g., energetic, intelligent) and his unknowns (e.g., popular, boastful) would be on the same epistemological level; they would involve equal amounts of inference or interpretation. Since both data and inference in studies of this kind are personality constructs, some authors have said that these studies are concerned with the naïve, or lay, *theory* of personality rather than with impression formation or person perception. These latter designations seem more appropriate to studies in which the data are faces or behavior or movement and the inferences are constructs.

There are even studies in which the experimenter's data are more like constructs and the inferences more like stimuli. The existence of such studies shows the logical independence of the experimental and epistemological senses of "data." Linda Johnson, for example, in an unpublished study (1955) described by Secord (1958), read to subjects the following two descriptions of persons:

A. "This man is warmhearted and honest. He has a good sense of humor and is intelligent and unbiased in his opinion. He is responsible and self-confident with an air of refinement."

B. "This man is ruthless and brutal. He is extremely hostile, quick tempered, and overbearing. He is well known for his boorish and vulgar manner and is a very domineering and unsympathetic person" (Secord, 1958, pp. 305–306).

Subjects were then asked to consider a long list of *facial* characteristics and decide which ones would probably be found in A and which in B. Two very unlike physiognomies emerged: A would have neat hair, a direct gaze, wide and bright eyes, a smooth brow and a smiling mouth; *B* would have slicked-down or disheveled hair, an averted gaze, narrow eyes, a knitted brow, and a turned-down mouth. See almost any comic strip or adventure movie to find these stereotypes made flesh. Linda Johnson's study reverses a much more common research design in which traits are guessed from faces. The data she gave to her subjects were traits and the inferences they drew were faces but faces are more nearly data, in the epistemological sense, than a.e traits.

We have surveyed the varieties of data and construct employed in studies of impression formation and made some guiding distinctions. It remains to map out what is ahead. We will begin by telling the rest of the story about Jim. The paragraph you have read functioned as data in studies by Luchins (1957) which were chiefly concerned with the role of order in the reception of data on a personality. This section is called "First Impressions." It is followed by an account of the oldest research problem in the field of person perception—the identification of emotions. This is a problem that involves moving from stimuli (faces and voices and gestures, which are epistemological data) to something unobservable— emotions. Then we will take up one of the problems that Asch introduced in his work (1946) with trait lists, the problem of the central trait. This is followed by a consideration of accuracy in impression formation and finally by an argument that the Self also must be perceived or conceived and that Self Perception is tightly interlocked with Person Perception. These are not all the problems that have been studied in impression formation; they are a selection of lively ones.

First Impressions

The paragraph we have seen about Jim was written by a psychologist named Luchins, and Luchins also composed a second paragraph.

> After school Jim left the classroom alone. Leaving the school, he started on his long walk home. The street was brilliantly filled with sunshine. Jim walked down the street on the shady side. Coming down the street toward him, he saw the pretty girl whom he had met on the previous evening. Jim crossed the street and entered a candy store. The store was crowded with students, and he noticed a few familiar faces. Jim waited quietly until the counterman caught his eye and then gave his order. Taking his drink, he sat down at a side table. When he had finished his drink he went home [Luchins, 1957b, p. 35].

The Jim of the second paragraph is presented with some options very closely matched with options presented to the Jim of the first paragraph. The two Jims make unlike choices. The second Jim elects the shady side of the street, avoids the girl he recently met and chooses to sit alone rather than with friends. Luchins calls the first paragraph the "E" or "extravertive" description and the second the "I" or "introvertive" description. Hundreds of subjects have read the E paragraph and, on the basis of the information it contains, gone on to write personality profiles of Jim and to answer very specific questions about Jim's character, appearance, and likely behavior. Hundreds of other subjects have filled out impressions of Jim from the I paragraph alone.

In some versions of his experiment Luchins asked subjects to infer characteristics that are extremely remote from the contents of the paragraph. Here are a few of the questions (Luchins, 1957b, pp. 187–189) about Jim:

1. "Do you like him?"
2. "How does he look?"
3. "How does he talk?"
4. "Jim was waiting for his turn in the barber shop. The barber overlooked him to call on another customer who had just come in. What did Jim do?"
5. "Is he: (a) shy; (b) more shy than forward; (c) more forward than shy; (d) forward; (e) none of these?"

It is remarkable that only a very few subjects said: "How am I supposed to know these things?"

The impressions generated by the I and E paragraphs differed significantly in many respects. The character that was drawn from the E paragraph approximated to the stereotype of an extravert. He was sociable, friendly, popular, likeable, and happy. He was muscular or athletic, had an average rate of speech, walked with a good posture, and would protest if the barber did not call him in his turn. The character from the I paragraph approximated to the stereotype of an introvert. He was shy, reserved, quiet, lonely, unfriendly, and unpopular. He was thin, weak, slight, or spindly, had a slow rate of speech, walked with a poor posture and made no protest to the barber.

The E and the I paragraphs are written so that they can be run together as a single paragraph in the order EI or in the order IE. The EI account tells us that Jim goes to the stationery store, then to school, after school to a candy store, and then home. The IE account tells us that after school Jim goes to a candy store, then home, then to the stationery store, then to school. There are no space-time discontinuities either way but what of the characterological discontinuities? For, of course, in the EI and IE accounts the two blocks of information accrue to the same character and these blocks in isolation are known to generate sharply opposed impressions.

Luchins wanted to determine whether the order of presentation of information about a personality influences the impression formed and his experiment is nicely devised to do that. The full design calls for four groups of subjects, each group reading one of the following accounts: E or I or EI or IE. How would one test to see whether the information presented first is more influential in forming the impression or whether the information presented last is more influential or whether the order has no effect? If the first information is given the greater weight, then the impressions formed from reading IE ought to resemble the impressions from I more closely than would the impressions formed from reading EI and the impressions from EI ought to resemble those from E more closely than would the impressions formed from reading IE. These are the predictions made by a "primacy" effect. A "recency" effect, i.e., a greater weight given the last or more recent information, predicts the opposite pattern: the impression from IE should be more like the impression from E than should the impression from EI and the impression from EI should be more like I than should the impression from IE. If the order of presentation makes no difference, then IE and EI should not differ in any consistent way.

A very large primacy effect appeared for both E and I in three different experiments. Consider, for example, the trait of friendliness. In one experiment 90 per cent of the subjects who read account E said that Jim would be friendly, 71 per cent of those who read EI said the same; only 54 per cent of those who read IE and 25 per cent of those who read I thought he would be friendly. Some subjects were not willing to call Jim either friendly or unfriendly but 55 per cent of those who read I thought him unfriendly, 31 per cent of those who read IE thought the same; only 19 per cent of EI thought him unfriendly and 0 per cent of those who read E. And that is the way the data very consistently went: the impression generated by either compound paragraph more closely resembled the impression generated by its first half alone than it did the impression generated by its second half alone. Other investigators using other methods (e.g., Asch, 1946) having also found a primacy effect in the utilization of information about personalities. "First impressions" appear to be as critical as secretarial schools have always said they were.

How do subjects reconcile the rather sharply conflicting information combined in the IE and EI paragraphs? Consider the EI account in which Jim first acts in a sociable way, then goes to school, and afterwards acts in a rather unsociable way. The first information is likely to be considered more characteristic, nearer Jim's essential nature, than is the later information. The later information can be explained by assuming special contingencies. Something disagreeable may have happened in school or Jim may simply have been tired after school or the people he saw after school may not have been people he liked or the girl he talked to before school could have turned out to be boring or disagreeable. These integrated impressions show the effect of primacy. The first information suggests a kind of baseline disposition for Jim; he has a friendly outgoing nature. This theory is not relinquished when conflicting information appears but is preserved by assuming special circumstances.

There are ways of integrating the information which do not show the primacy effect. One can give equal weight to both the sociable and unsociable behavior and decide that instability is characteristic of Jim. He is a moody person or a nervous person or he is an adolescent. There are also integrations that show a Recency effect. A good breakfast and a bright day made Jim fleetingly cheerful and sociable but he soon reverted to a more characteristic withdrawn manner.

Most subjects reported no great difficulty integrating the information in the compound account and many had not even noticed any conflict. We may guess that the case would have been otherwise if, initially, they had been told that the two paragraphs described two persons and then had been told that both paragraphs were really about the same person. Asch (1946) did this kind of experiment with the trait descriptions: A. intelligent-industrious-impulsive; B. critical-stubborn-envious. His subjects who had thought of A and B as two persons found it very difficult to reconceive them as a single person. When the traits were attributed to one person from the start, integration was not difficult; the interpretation of each trait and the inferences from it were influenced by the others in the combination. When the combinational problem is not set from the start, the interpretations and inferences from the parts are free to go off in contradictory directions.

Although the effect of primacy is large and consistent, Luchins (1957a) has shown that it is easily overcome. The effect was almost completely cancelled, for instance, by warning subjects before they read the paragraphs about the dangers of first impressions and advising them to suspend judgment until they should have finished reading. Luchins tried another variation and produced a major recency effect; he warned, as before, about the danger of being misled by first impressions and then gave subjects a first block of information to read. After reading the first block they did not go on at once to read the second block. Luchins gave them an unrelated task to perform (five minutes of elementary arithmetic problems) before giving them the second block of information. In these circumstances the impression formed of Jim was dominated by the more recent block of information. Since life is filled with unrelated interpolated tasks, recency may actually be thè more usual effect.

The original Luchins experiment, with the IE and EI stories, presented all there was to know about Jim in a short continuous narrative. In life outside the laboratory we do not ordinarily receive information about others in this fashion. There is usually more information to come and its reception is ordinarily interrupted by unrelated matters. Suppose you move into a new community and are introduced to twenty-five people or so in the first week. The running dossiers you keep on these people can grow for many years but for each one there will be intervals, of varying length, in which no new entries are made. In these circumstances retention of information becomes difficult and so the more recent material is probably disproportionately influential. We have an adage for recency that is as well known as the one about first impressions. "In the opinion of others a man is only as good as his latest show—novel—examination—or whatever."

The Identification of Emotions

Charles Darwin introduced the typical experiment. He put together a collection of photographs intended to represent various emotions and showed them to twenty people, asking them to judge the emotion from the expression. Among his judges there was much agreement on some pictures and little agreement on others. Darwin was surprised because when he had first seen the pictures and been told what emotion each one represented he had found the representations perfectly satisfactory. He concluded that some of the pictures were not truly expressive.

The surest principle in psychology is that whenever man first undertakes to conceive of his mental processes, to represent them to himself, he grotesquely distorts them. We stand in relation to the mental world as the five-year-old child does to the perceptible world. The child of that age operates in the perceptible world with considerable precision: he finds his way about a large geographical area; he recognizes thousands of things and faces; he detects at once even very small changes in his milieu. But when he sits down with paper and crayon to represent that world his father emerges as a blob with buttons down the front; walls are transparent and streets rise straight up in the air; birds are about half the size of people. When we adults advance from simply manifesting mentality to representing it we produce our own blobs with buttons.

Psychology's first notion about the identification of emotions was that they appear in the face, a different expression for each named emotion, and are read off like so many signs along the highway. When you point out to a five-year-old that one cannot really see through the wall of a house to the furniture within, as his picture suggests, he will agree with you. The history of experimental work on the recognition of emotions is largely a history of such obvious discoveries, obvious once they were made. We are still trying, in this field, to bring our representation of the process into reasonable correspondence with what we are able to perform.

There are scholarly reviews of this literature by Woodworth and Schlosberg (1954) and by Bruner and Tagiuri (1954) which may be consulted for full bibliographies. Here we will review a few critical "discoveries" and the view to which they lead.

The stimulus material for studies of the perception of emotion has usually been the expressing face and psychologists have been very ingenious in what they have provided. Hulin and Katz (1935) used photographs of the actor Frois-Wittmann registering seventy-two different emotions. Piderit (1859) made line drawings to illustrate a theory of emotional expression and Boring and Titchener (1923) made a collection of interchangeable facial parts from these drawings. From an assortment of brows, eyes, noses, and mouths (the "Piderit features") they built up 360 compounds to be judged. Landis (1924) tried to get real emotions in the laboratory and this led him into such extremities as cutting off the head of a rat while the subject looked on. However, his subjects' expressions did not change greatly across a three-hour session; most of them produced a continuing forced smile suggestive of a determination to endure the ordeal. Munn (1940) used candid photographs from *Life* and *Look* to represent real emotions.

The results are highly contradictory. Some investigators have reported that subjects labelled emotional expressions with considerable accuracy (e.g., Feleky, 1914; Ruckmick, 1921; Woodworth, 1938; Munn, 1940). Other investigators have reported only "chance success" in recognizing emotions (Sherman, 1927; Guilford, 1929; Landis, 1924). The explanation of the disagreement is one of the "discoveries" of this research tradition.

DIMENSIONS OF EXPRESSION

Recognition problems vary in difficulty and errors of recognition vary in size. One investigator might ask his subjects to distinguish love from hate and astonishment from boredom; another might ask his subjects to distinguish among anger, annoyance, chagrin, irritation, tension, and pique. It is not to be expected that the two investigators would find the same level of success. One subject, in a given experiment, might mislabel contempt as disdain and another in the same experiment might mislabel contempt as astonishment. If the first error were counted as one unit from the correct answer should the second error also be counted as one unit from the correct answer? Our intuition tells us that the two errors are not the same size, that the second is larger than the first. In general we have some sense of a space in which emotions are located, a space in which emotions can be closer together or farther apart. Many experimental studies have disregarded this space and treated emotions as equidistant entities and that has made one study incommensurable with another.

Woodworth (1938) found a way to describe the distance between emotional expressions. He discovered that a linear scale was implicit in the recognition errors made by subjects in the various experiments. Suppose we were dealing with colors instead of with emotional expressions and did not know that hue could be scaled from red through orange and yellow, to green, blue, and violet. Suppose we had some one hundred chips of color, all different, and subjects saw them one at a time and afterwards tried to recognize each one in the full set of five hundred. We should find that any one chip would be often confused with a few other ones, occasionally confused with still others, and never confused with still others. If we arranged the chips in a long line such that chips often confused with one another were close together and chips never confused were far apart we should discover the order of the spectrum, from long wave lengths to short: red, orange, yellow, green, blue, violet. Woodworth did just this with emotional expressions; he ordered them in an array such that one found maximum confusion between neighboring pairs, with the confusion diminishing as members of a pair moved farther apart. The result was a six-step scale: 1) love, happiness, and mirth; 2) surprise; 3) fear and suffering; 4) anger and determination; 5) disgust; 6) contempt. Woodworth re-analyzed the data from several studies (Ruckmick, 1921; Gates, 1923; Feleky, 1924; Kanner, 1931) and showed that the results were more consistent than had been thought; subjects seldom missed by more than one step on the scale.

The hue dimension is a circular rather than a linear scale since the violets resemble the reds as much as the blues. Schlosberg showed (1941) that the scale of emotional expressions is also circular; faces usually judged to be expressive of mirth are likely to be sometimes judged expressive of contempt. In 1952, Schlosberg obtained evidence that the scaling of emotional expressions could be improved by the use of two dimensions rather than one. One dimension he labelled Pleasant-Unpleasant; it has love and mirth at one extreme, anger at the other. The second dimension he labelled Attention-Rejection since the expressions at one extreme show the eyes, nostrils, and sometimes the mouth wide open as if to receive stimulation, while the faces at the other extreme show eyes, lips, and nostrils forcibly closed. Surprise is an emotion at the open end and disgust an emotion at the closed end.

The neglect of the dimensionality of emotional expression can account for much of the disagreement among studies of the accuracy with which emotions are recognized. Large errors in the scaled space are uncommon but errors of one scale step are very common. How can one reconcile the error scores with the facts of ordinary human interaction? Could human interaction go as smoothly as it does if people often confused contempt with mirth, suffering with surprise, anger with determination? Mistakes of this kind are common in the laboratory and they seem to suggest that the perception of emotions is not accurate enough to support ordinary interaction. The answer to this difficulty is found in a second "discovery."

THE CUES TO EMOTION

The still photo of a face alone is a radically reduced situation; in life there are more cues and so more accuracy. Reading an emotion from a still photograph of a face is rather like trying to identify animals from the tracks they leave in the snow; the level of accuracy is below that which can be attained when the whole animal is present. The still photo cannot provide all the cues of living faces for the reason that it is still and emotional faces move. In addition, the faces from which we read emotions in life are ordinarily familiar to us while those in the laboratory are not. It is probable that some knowledge of the range of expression a person uses is an important aid in the interpretation of any particular expression. Emotions in the natural case are, in addition, expressed by muscles other than those of the face. The voice is especially expressive. Dusenberry and Knowrer (1939) had someone speak the letters A to X as though he were in various states of emotion. The speakers were recorded and subjects attempted to recognize the intended emotions. They did about as well as judges ordinarily do with facial expression alone. Body tension, posture, and gesture can also be expressive of emotion. Carmichael, Roberts, and Wessel (1937) took both still and motion pictures of the hands of a skilled actor as they protruded through a screen. Judges were able to recognize emotions from the movements of hands alone about as well as emotions can be identified from faces. Hands and voice and face all work together in life and so the reading of emotion should be more exact than it is when the several cues are isolated.

So far we have only considered the cue value of *expressive behavior*, behavior that has no effect on the world beyond communicating the state of mind of the actor. But a person in a state of emotion also produces what Allport (1961) calls *coping behavior*. The emotional person seeks to accomplish effects beyond pure expression and, in doing so, is expressive in still another way. Smashing someone in the face with your fist may be a means of coping with reality but it is also a notably clear expression of some feeling other than affection. Running in fear, asking forgiveness, making an abusive speech are good symptoms of emotion.

Finally there is a kind of cue that seems to be different from the others, there is the situation in which the emotion occurs. Munn (1940) showed the faces he clipped from *Life* and *Look* both with and without the surrounding picture. The surrounding pictures gave only a partial knowledge of the situation but this partial knowledge often produced a marked improvement in the precision of the judgments. One picture of a man's face elicited judgments ranging from surprise to disgust with only a very slight build-up on anger. However, when subjects were allowed to see that the face belonged to a man who was clutching a strikebreaker by the collar the judgments concentrated heavily on anger and hate. Knowledge of the situation then can greatly increase the social consensus and also presumably make that consensus accurate (see also Hunt, Cole, and Reis, 1958).

Situations provide cues for the identification of emotions but we do not accord these cues the same status as the cues in the face, voice, and musculature of the emotional person. We think of the latter as "expressions" or *manifestations* of the emotion and the former as *determinants* of the emotion, as circumstances in which various emotions are more or less probable. As an analogy think of the perceptual problem involved in identifying the printed English word *cold*. The several letters of this word are like the several expressive signs of an emotion. If the perceiver saw only —*ld* he might guess *bald* or *bold* as easily as *cold;* if he saw -*old*, *bald* would be excluded as an interpretation while *bold* would continue to be possible. We could provide quite another sort of cue, an environmental or situational cue, by printing: *hot*- —*ld*. The situation would select *cold* almost as effectively as would the provision of the missing letters but no one would say that *hot* was a part of the word *cold*. *Hot* is like the situation of the man expressing an emotion; both are environments in which some events are probable and others are less so.

IDENTIFICATION OF ONE'S OWN EMOTIONS

We identify and name emotions belonging to ourselves as well as to others. Is the identification process different in the two cases? Emotions in others are recognized from three kinds of cues: context or situation, expressions, and coping behavior. All three kinds of cue are apprehended by exteroceptors, by sense organs like the eye and ear that receive stimulation from outside the body. Emotions of oneself present a fourth kind of cue: sensory feedback from relaxation and tension in the muscles and viscera, feedback which can be experienced as effortfulness in a smile, a hollow feeling in the stomach, a thump of the heart. Cues from the viscera are apprehended by interoceptors and cues from the muscles by the proprioceptors. These data come only to the person having the emotion. How importantly do they figure in its identification?

In the everyday psychology with which we all operate the data from the interoceptors and the proprioceptors are accorded a kind of ultimate status. They *are* the emotion itself whereas the data available to everyone's exteroceptors are occasions for an emotion or symptoms of an emotion but not the thing itself. Clenched teeth and a red face are not anger; they are symptoms of anger. The fact that someone has rudely shoved the person with clenched teeth is also not anger; it is only an occasion for anger. Anger itself is a private feeling.

Emotions unlike physical objects present two views, an insider's view and an outsider's view, and we think of the insider's view as the real thing. We conceive of the private feelings as a kind of criterion and the overt manifestations as so many predictors. Since the criterion is accessible to us in the case of our own emotions it seems unlikely that we would pay any attention to mere predictors. Surely we need not study our face in a mirror, scrutinize our objective circumstances and watch to see whether we hit anybody in order to find out what emotion we are having. We experience it directly. Identification of emotions in oneself appears to rely on different cues than those used for identification of emotion in others.

Internal Cues. If words like *happy* and *angry* and *excited* are said of oneself on the basis of private internal cues, how do children ever learn to use such words appropriately? B. F. Skinner (1945) has given a very sensible answer. Adults, parents especially, are able to see that the child's eyes are shining and that his face is smiling and they know that the occasion is Christmas Eve. In these circumstances they would experience the feelings that in English are called *happiness* and so they tell the child: "You're happy, aren't you?" And he noting his present state of mind learns to call that state *happiness*. If he had said: "I feel anxious" or "I feel bemused" they could have corrected him on the ground that it is extremely improbable that a four-year-old with shining eyes is feeling bemused on Christmas Eve. There is a correlation between the manifestations available to an outsider and the feelings available to an insider. Therefore the adult can correct the child's usage on the basis of external manifestations and thereby cause the child to learn to name his private feelings in the way that other people name theirs.

If we identify emotions in ourselves exclusively on the basis of cues from the proprioceptors and the interoceptors then it must be the case that there are distinctive combinations of such cues for each of the emotions we can name. Such combinations have not as yet been discovered by physiologists. William James proposed in 1884 that an emotion is essentially a pattern of sensation from the muscles and viscera, that palpitations and constricted breathing and a dry mouth are the essence of emotion. However, Cannon pointed out in 1929 that visceral feedback at any rate, is diffuse and non-distinctive and does not seem to change from one emotion to another. Furthermore, visceral changes occur in circumstances where the person does not attribute any particular emotion to himself. Recent studies of the physiology of emotion (Wolf and Wolff, 1943; Ax, 1953; Lindsley, 1951; Schachter, 1957) have sometimes found differences between emotions that we think of as unlike, but often differences have not been found. Certainly physiologists have not found a variety of patterns of visceral activity sufficient to match the variety of terms for naming emotions. It is very doubtful therefore that there are internal cues, especially visceral cues, which could, by themselves, govern our identification of emotions in ourselves.

If we read our own emotions from internal cues alone then it should follow that, if appropriate cues were created by an extraordinary means, such as administration of a drug, we would report an emotion. The sympathetic division of the autonomic nervous system functions at a high level in such emotions as anger and fear. It speeds breathing and heart rate and decreases cutaneous blood flow while increasing muscle and cerebral blood flow. The drug adrenalin is said to be *sympathomimetic* because it produces effects almost exactly duplicating these and so an injection of adrenalin may be said to produce the visceral aspects of certain emotions. Marañon (1924) asked subjects who had been injected with adrenalin to report their experiences. The majority of them simply reported their physical symptoms and said nothing of any emotion. It seems then that the internal cues from the viscera are not alone enough to cause most subjects to attribute emotions to themselves.

The physiological evidence is imperfect but at present it does not suggest that we do or could identify emotions in ourselves from internal cues alone. Not enough distinctive physiological patterns have been discovered to serve as the semantic bases for the words we use. Marañon's study, and the replications by Cantril and Hunt (1932) and by Landis and Hunt (1932) show that a visceral pattern associated with emotion is not enough alone to cause most people to describe themselves as in a state of emotion. Of course the studies that have failed to find distinctive physiological patterns may not have measured finely enough or extensively enough; most of them have concerned visceral feedback alone and not included proprioception. Nevertheless it seems probable that in identification of emotions in ourselves we build on more than internal physiological cues.

A minority of Marañon's subjects did report emotions but they spoke of these emotions in a peculiar way. One said he felt *as if* he were afraid; another *as if* he were awaiting a great happiness. The naming of fear and happiness suggests that visceral arousal plays some role in the identification of emotions in oneself but the use of "as if" suggests that internal cues are not the only ones, that other cues (usually present) are missing. The fact that one subject speaks of happiness and another of fear suggests that the missing cues may be necessary to determine the quality of the emotion. Perhaps the missing cues are the ones we use in identifying emotions in others: situation, expression, and coping behavior.

Knowledge of the Situation as a Cue. It occurred to Schachter and Singer (1962) that the subjects in Marañon's experiment knew they had been given an injection of adrenalin and that they probably had some idea of the effects to be expected from this drug. When the tremor and palpitations and the like came along they knew the cause of these symptoms and, on that account, perhaps, were not disposed to treat them as cues of emotion. Those subjects who did report emotional feelings may have expressed their knowledge of the fact that the drug had caused these feelings by use of the qualifying "as if." What would happen if you could introduce adrenalin without the knowledge of the subject by causing him to breathe it in or to drink it with his coffee? When his symptoms developed would he not look for some cause in the situation and perhaps label his mental state in accordance with what he found? If there were something that could produce mirth the subject might conclude that he was mirthful. This is the experiment Schachter and Singer dreamed of; the one they were able to perform (1962) required some compromises. They did not try to conceal from their subjects the fact that they were being given a drug and in fact subjects were free to refuse, but Schachter and Singer did misinform them as to the name of the drug and greatly misinformed some of them about the effects to be expected from the drug.

Subjects were recruited for a study of the effects of vitamin supplements on vision. They were told that the name of the supplement to be given them was Suproxin. The subject was given a small injection which was in fact adrenalin. Some subjects were told that the compound Suproxin has side effects. They were to expect palpitations, hand tremor, and a warm and flushed face. These are the major consequences of adrenalin and so these subjects, in the *informed* condition, knew what to expect and how to account for it. They were in the position of Marañon's subjects and should have had little reason to interpret their symptoms as an emotion.

What should subjects be told so that they would not attribute their symptoms to the drug but would be prepared to mistake the symptoms for an emotion? One might tell them that Suproxin is a mild drug having no side effects, and this was said to some subjects. However, it could be argued that subjects who anticipated "side effects" from a drug would be emotionally tense or apprehensive as a consequence while subjects expecting no side effects would be less apprehensive and that difference of real emotion could complicate the experimental induction of emotion. And so, although Schachter and Singer used this procedure with one group of subjects, another of their groups seems to provide a better comparison and we will discuss that group only.

Subjects in the *misinformed group* were told to expect side effects (and so had some occasion to feel apprehensive) but were told that the side effects would be a feeling of numbness in the feet, itching sensations over parts of the body and a slight headache. They were not led to expect palpitations and tremor and so were presumed not to be prepared with an explanation for these effects which might then be taken as signs of emotion.

The essential plan was to produce in all subjects visceral arousal that could be emotional but to let some subjects know that the arousal was drug-induced and to conceal this fact from other subjects. The experimenters thought that when the visceral arousal could not be accounted for by the drug it would be interpretable as an emotion of some kind. The particular interpretation should depend on the social situation in which the subject found himself; for different situations there should be different interpretations. A subject set down in the midst of a gay party might think himself high spirited. A subject confronted with a beautiful woman might think himself smitten with love. This again is the dream experiment rather than what was done.

After his injection the subject was told that it would be necessary to wait twenty minutes before taking the vision test so that Suproxin might have time to take effect. For these twenty minutes the subject was joined by another person, supposedly also a subject, also waiting for Suproxin to take effect. The two were left alone by the experimenter. The second subject was a stooge prepared, in one experimental condition, to put on a show of extreme high spirits. He went through a routine involving "shooting baskets" with crumpled paper balls, flying improvised airplanes, and comparable shenanigans. The question was whether the real subject would be caught up in the "fun" and whether he would later describe himself as having felt really high spirited. The subject's actual behavior was observed through a one-way window; his description of his mood was obtained by questionnaires.

For subjects in a contrasting experimental condition the stooge put on a show of anger and behaved in a disagreeable, aggressive way. Everything else was as before except that subjects who were not given a correct explanation of their symptoms were simply told that Suproxin was a mild drug with no side effects. The question was whether such *uninformed* subjects would interpret their palpitations, tremor, and flushing as the emotion of anger.

The experimental outcomes were very much as Schachter and Singer had predicted. When the subject did not anticipate his symptoms and was not led to believe that the drug could cause such symptoms, he behaved like the stooge and reported for himself a mood such as the stooge manifested. More exactly, the *misinformed* subjects were nearer the stooges in action and mood than were the correctly informed subjects. These results seem to mean that when an individual is in a state of physiological arousal for which he has no explanation he will label this state in terms of the situation in which he finds himself. By manipulating this situation it is possible to change the labelling of the emotion without necessarily having changed the physiological state. It looks as if the identification of emotions in oneself as in others is somewhat dependent on external cues.

Is the perception of emotion in oneself *at all* dependent on internal visceral cues? Subjects who were *uninformed* or *misinformed* about the effects of Suproxin and who were given adrenalin tended to pick up the emotion of the stooge. Would this effect have been any weaker if the subjects had not taken adrenalin? Was it really important for them to have visceral cues? To answer this question Schachter and Singer included control subjects who were given injections of a saline solution which produces no visceral sensations whatever. The results from these "placebo" subjects were not completely consistent. By making internal analyses of their data, Schachter and Singer (1962) were able to find evidence that visceral cues do play a part in the perception of emotion in oneself. Several other experiments by Schachter and his associates (Schachter and Wheeler, 1962; Singer, 1961; Latané and Schachter, 1962) reinforce this proposition.

Writing about these experiments of Schachter's and the theory of emotion they suggest Mandler (1962) has proposed a memorable analogy. He calls it the juke-box theory of emotion but is careful to point out the limitations of the mechanical analogy. There are two major actions involved in the operation of a juke box: insertion of a coin and selection of a musical number. Both are necessary, neither alone is sufficient, for the production of music. The coin is a kind of energizer that makes it possible to play any record in the machine but the coin is not partial to any one tune. Perhaps visceral arousal or sympathetic activation is analogous to the insertion of the dime, a condition necessary for the production of many emotions but not distinctively patterned in the several emotions. Selecting the tune may then be analogous to apprehension of the situation. If others are laughing the tune will be *happiness*, if others are aggressive the tune will be *anger*.

The Central Trait

An impression can start from trait names rather than from appearance or behavior. That is what happens with a letter of recommendation: "Mr. Jones is an exceptionally *intelligent* and *skillful* experimentalist. In all his course work he has been unusually *industrious*. He has a *warm* manner that makes him popular with his peers. He is *determined* to become a research chemist and I believe he will be a good one. He is able to see the *practical* implications of chemical research and yet is *cautious* in his interpretation of data."

One sweep of abstraction leaves us with a trait list: *intelligent-skillful-industrious-warm-determined-practical-cautious;* this is the list that Asch used in a pioneering study (1946) of the integration of traits into an impression. Asch read the list to subjects, pretending that the traits applied to some real person, and he asked them to give a brief description of the person the traits brought to mind. One of these descriptions, written from the traits alone, describes someone very like the Mr. Jones that we have imagined. "A scientist performing experiments and persevering after many setbacks. He is driven by the desire to accomplish something that would be of benefit" (Asch, 1946, p. 263).

The independent variable in Asch's study was the fourth trait in the list. For subjects in groups designated "Warm" the trait was *warm* (as above), but for subjects in groups designated "Cold" it was *cold;* the lists were otherwise identical. The change from *warm* to *cold* made a profound difference in the personalities imagined. Here is an impression generated by the list with *cold* in it. "A rather snobbish person who feels that his success and intelligence set him apart from the run-of-the-mill individual. Calculating and unsympathetic" (Asch, 1946, p. 263).

Qualitative differences were clear in the paragraphs subjects wrote; in order to obtain quantitative differences, data of another sort were collected. Subjects were given a check list of eighteen pairs of traits, mostly opposites, and were asked to indicate for each pair the term that best fitted the impression they had formed. The positive terms of each pair appear in Table 12-1, which also contains the frequency with which each was selected by groups "Warm" and "Cold."

It is worthwhile looking closely at the checklist. When the original set of traits (the stimulus list) included *warm*, most subjects thought the person involved would also be *generous, humorous, sociable,* and *popular.* When the stimulus list included *cold*, most subjects thought the person would not have these agreeable traits. Some other traits on the list seemed about equally likely to be checked whether the person was *warm* or *cold*. In either case, subjects thought he would be *persistent, serious,* and *restrained.*

The full portrait projected from a list of seven traits is markedly changed by the substitution of *cold* for *warm* and so *warm* and *cold* are highly "central" terms. They are central to their list, not because they occupied a middle position but because they proved strongly determinative of the impressions derived from the list. Asch, in another study (1946), replaced *warm* and *cold* in the preceding series with *polite* and

TABLE 12-1. PERCENTAGES OF SUBJECTS INFERRING VARIOUS QUALITIES
FROM TRAIT LISTS

| | EXPERI-MENT I | | | EXPERI-MENT II | | EXPERI-MENT III | |
	"Warm" N=90	"Cold" N=76	Total N=56	"Warm" N=23	"Cold" N=33	"Polite" N=20	"Blunt" N=26
1. generous	91	8	55	87	33	56	58
2. wise	65	25	49	73	33	30	50
3. happy	90	34	71	91	58	75	65
4. good-natured	94	17	69	91	55	87	56
5. humorous	77	13	36	76	12	71	48
6. sociable	91	38	71	91	55	83	68
7. popular	84	28	57	83	39	94	56
8. reliable	94	99	96	96	97	95	100
9. important	88	99	88	87	88	94	96
10. humane	86	31	64	91	45	59	77
11. good-looking	77	69	58	71	53	93	79
12. persistent	100	97	98	96	100	100	100
13. serious	100	99	96	91	100	100	100
14. restrained	77	89	82	67	94	82	77
15. altruistic	69	18	44	68	27	29	46
16. imaginative	51	19	24	45	9	33	31
17. strong	98	95	95	94	96	100	100
18. honest	98	94	95	100	92	87	100

blunt. The differences then obtained in the projected list (Table 12-1) were markedly weaker. Within this stimulus list the traits *polite* and *blunt* are a less central pair than *warm* and *cold*. The centrality of the terms *warm* and *cold* does not seem to be absolute, however, for Asch obtained evidence that in other lists this pair had less power.

What causes a trait to be central or critically determinative for a given combination? The work mentioned early in this chapter by Bruner, Shapiro, and Tagiuri (1958) on the trait-to-trait inference network gives us a clue. These investigators were interested in predicting the inferences made from trait combinations on the basis of the inferences made from the individual traits in isolation. For example, can one predict the inferences that will be made from *intelligent* and *inconsiderate* and *independent* when one knows the inferences that are made from *intelligent* alone, from *inconsiderate* alone, and from *independent* alone? Suppose that it seems to most people that a man who is *intelligent* will be *reliable*, that a man who is *inconsiderate* will be *unreliable*, and that a man who is *independent* may or may not be *reliable*. What will happen when all three predictors are combined? If it seems to most people that a man who is *intelligent*, *inconsiderate*, and *independent* will be *unreliable* then the inference from *inconsiderate* has prevailed and one might say that it shows greater centrality (or determinative power or weight) than the other traits in the combination.

Bruner and his associates found that inferences from combinations were indeed predictable from inferences based on the single components. In the first place, when each of the traits in a combination pointed, on its own, to the same inferences, or when two traits out of three pointed to the same inference, then the total combination pointed to that inference. For example, most subjects judged that an *intelligent* person would be *aggressive* and most subjects judged that an *inconsiderate* person would be *aggressive* and so they judged that a person both *intelligent* and *inconsiderate* would be *aggressive*. In the second place, when the individual traits, in a combination of two, led to opposed inferences then the inference from the combination conformed to the single inference that was the stronger of the two. For example, *intelligent* alone suggested *honest;* *inconsiderate* alone suggested *dishonest*. However the inference from *intelligent* alone was weaker than the inference from *inconsiderate* alone; fewer subjects were definite about it. And so the combination *intelligent* and *inconsiderate* was dominated by *inconsiderate* and led usually to the inference *dishonest*.

There is more to the results of Bruner and his associates than we have described. However, the main point is that the inferences made from a combination of traits and the relative weights of each trait in the combination proved to be predictable from knowledge of the inferences made to each trait singly. Wishner (1960) has shown that Asch's result and "centrality" in general can be predicted from data of this sort.

Asch's materials consisted of a fixed stimulus list of six trait names (*intelligent, skillful, industrious, determined, practical, cautious*), two pairs of critical traits (*warm-cold; polite-blunt*), and a check list of eighteen opposites (*generous-ungenerous, happy-unhappy, etc.*). When the word *warm* was used in the open slot on the stimulus list 90 per cent of Asch's subjects in one experiment thought the person described would also be *happy;* when *cold* was used only 34 per cent thought he would be *happy*. When the word *polite* was used 75 per cent thought the person would be *happy* and when *blunt* was used 65 per cent thought he would be *happy*. In short the pair *cold-warm* was more central (or more heavily weighted) than the pair *blunt-polite* in making the inference to *happy* from the given list of traits. Across the checklist as a whole the *cold-warm* pair tended to be more heavily weighted. This is the difference that Wishner set out to explain and he did it, essentially, from the inferences linking each single trait to each other single trait.

Asch had told his subjects that the traits on the stimulus list were descriptive of some real person but a person not known to the subjects.

Bruner and his associates had not pretended that they were talking about any specific individuals but had simply asked subjects to infer one trait from another on the basis of their ideas about what people in general are like. The inferential net linking one trait to another has been called "lay personality theory" (Bruner, Shapiro, and Tagiuri, 1958) and "implicit personality theory" (Cronbach, 1955). Cronbach has suggested that the network could be determined from judgments of real people as well as from pure inference and Wishner did obtain his network in this way. He used all of the traits Asch used: those on the stimulus list, the critical pair, and all those on the checklist. The 214 students in ten laboratory sections of a course in introductory psychology rated their instructors on the whole set. Wishner then estimated the correlations of each single trait with each other trait across all subjects. The correlation between any two traits, A and B, represents the degree to which subjects who attributed A to an instructor also attributed B to that instructor. The correlation between *warm* and *sociable*, for instance, was +.70 whereas the correlation between *warm* and serious was +.02. This means that when an instructor was called *warm* he was also usually called *sociable* but he was about as likely to be called *frivolous* as *serious*. These correlations are not pure measures of inference, of course. They would also be responsive to *real* covariation of traits in the instructors who were rated.

From his elaborate matrix of trait-with-trait correlations Wishner was able, in some degree, to predict, and explain, Asch's results. There were three characteristics of the correlation matrix that made it possible for *warm-cold* to be a powerfully determinative or central trait in Asch's list.

The correlations between *warm-cold* and the six traits of the fixed stimulus list were all small. This means that such stimulus traits as *intelligent* or *cautious* were about as likely to go with *warm* as with *cold*. The pair *warm-cold* did not strongly covary with any trait on the fixed stimulus list and so the appearance of *warm* or *cold* on the list represented new information. What *warm* or *cold* may have had to say about the total personality had not already been said by the other traits on the stimulus list. This was a necessary condition if *warm-cold* was to be a powerfully determinative trait.

The six traits on Asch's fixed stimulus list were also not strongly correlated with the traits on the checklist. For example, the checklist trait *happy* did not correlate above .36 with any of the fixed traits on the stimulus list. Consequently *happy* was not strongly anchored in the impression by any trait in the standard stimulus list and was free to come or go according as the trait in the open position was *warm* or *cold*.

Finally, the traits on the checklist were highly correlated with the critical pair *warm-cold*. The correlation between *sociable* and *warm*, for example, was .70 and Asch had found that when *warm* was in the stimulus list 91 per cent of the subjects thought the person would be *sociable* whereas with *cold* in the list only 38 per cent thought so. *Warm-cold* was central to the impression because it was correlated with the inferred traits and because it was not correlated with the other traits in the stimulus list and these other stimulus traits were not correlated with those on the checklist.

The weight or centrality of *warm-cold* did not hold for all the traits of the checklist. In Table 12-1 you will see that *strong, honest, persistent, serious,* and some others were little affected by the shift from *warm* to *cold.* The power of Wishner's analysis is especially clear in its ability to explain these cases. One or more of the three necessary conditions was lacking in each instance. Consider the trait *persistent;* Asch found, in his Experiment I, that with *warm* in the stimulus list, 100 per cent of the subjects checked *persistent* but with *cold* in the stimulus list *persistent* was still inferred by 97 per cent of the subjects. In short, *cold-warm* carried little weight in this case. Why so? Wishner found the correlation between *cold-warm* and *persistent* to be only .18. In addition, the correlation between *persistent* and *determined* was +.60 and *determined* was always in the stimulus list. *Persistent* had little tendency to covary with *warm* and *cold* and a large tendency to covary with *determined* and this latter tendency anchored it in the impression. Wishner's data very nicely predict the traits for which *warm-cold* carried weight and those for which it did not.

Wishner's analysis demands that the difference in over-all centrality between *warm-cold* and *blunt-polite* be accompanied by a difference favoring the former pair in the correlations that made for centrality. At some points this seems to have worked out as it should. For instance, the checklist trait *happy* which was so much influenced in Asch's experiment by the shift from *warm* to *cold* was less influenced by the shift from *polite* to *blunt.* When *polite* was provided, in Asch's Experiment III, 75 per cent of the subjects inferred *happy* but 65 per cent still did so when *blunt* was substituted. The probable explanation appears in Wishner's correlations; that between *happy* and *warm-cold* was +.54 while that between *happy* and *polite-blunt* was only +.20. While Wishner's data were, at such points as this, confirmatory of his analysis, the total data for *polite-blunt* were not what they should be if Wishner's analysis were a complete explanation of the peripherality of *polite-blunt.* It looks rather as if there were some factor operating in addition to those Wishner identified.

There is no doubt, however, that the three aspects of the correlation matrix isolated by Wishner are important determinants of the weight given a trait in forming an impression. The best possible evidence is that Wishner was able to use his principles to synthesize a personality impression which had exactly the properties he predicted. He worked from a correlation maxtrix to produce a new stimulus list and a new checklist such that the traits on the two lists were uncorrelated. Then he selected, as traits to vary, *humane* and *ruthless* which were uncorrelated with the traits on the stimulus list, highly correlated with half of the traits on the checklist and uncorrelated with the other half of the traits on the checklist. He predicted that in an impression-formation experiment the varied trait would carry great weight for the traits on the checklist with which it was correlated and little weight with the others. That is exactly how it worked out.

Wishner's re-analysis of Asch's work on trait centrality has considerable power, but I should not like to leave the impression that it accounts for everything Asch observed in this study. When combinations of stimulus traits are changed it is not only the inferences to other trait names that are changed, but also the meanings of the stimulus traits themselves. Asch studied, for instance, the semantic transformation of *warm* occasioned by moving the word into the list: obedient-weak-shallow-*warm*-unambitious-vain. This was no longer the warmth of the dedicated, humanitarian scientist suggested by the earlier list. It had become a "passive" warmth, a "doglike affection." A more radical transformation occurred when *warm* was embedded in another list: vain-shrewd-unscrupulous-*warm*-shallow-envious. The beauty of this case is that the words on the list other than *warm* point to the inference *cold*. Consequently the list simultaneously communicates a trait and its negation; the trait is stated and the negative is an irresistible inference. What can the human mind make of such a message? It can distinguish two levels of reality: "I assume the person to appear warm rather than really to be warm" (Asch, 1946, p. 267).

Accuracy in Impression Formation

Investigations of the *process* of impression formation are concerned with inferences from data; investigations of *accuracy* are concerned, in addition, with the validity of the inferences. A process investigation might determine that one man was judged to be more intelligent than another when judges knew nothing of the two except the sounds of their voices reciting the alphabet. An accuracy investigation would in addition determine whether the one man was, in fact, more intelligent than the other. If he was, then the judge who said so was accurate and might be said to have demonstrated some skill in person perception. He could claim to be what Freud called a good *menschenkenner*. Freud confessed, by the way, that he himself did not qualify for the title.

It is often said that accuracy of person perception in everyday life must be high since social interaction ordinarily works smoothly. Certainly we need to have and do have great accuracy in foreseeing what people will do when we interact with them, but much of this foresight is at the level of roles rather than of personalities. A knowledge of social structure alone will take one smoothly through a large part of the day's routine. If a man takes his breakfast in a restaurant he needs to know what to expect of countermen or waitresses but it is not necessary to know anything of the persons in the roles. If he stops at the bank he needs to know the functions of tellers but not their individual characters.

Suppose, however, that a man wants to ask a "favor" of a teller, he would like the teller to "phone in" the deposit he will make and thereby save him an overdrawn charge. A "favor" is a thing that can be done by occupants of a role but which is not an obligation of the role. In deciding whether to ask a favor one would like to know more than the role of teller, one would like to know something of how each person plays the role. At this point accuracy in the perception of personality becomes important to smooth interaction. Two of the three tellers in my bank do not do "favors," and one could guess that from the way they snap rubber bands on packs of bills.

A study of accuracy presupposes a criterion against which judgments may be validated. If the judgments were of intelligence then scores on a good test of intelligence might serve as criterion. If age, sex, or profession were to be inferred from voice or handwriting or the like, then there would be objective facts to serve as criteria. If the problem were to identify the emotions expressed in various faces then the intention of an actor or the self report of a layman might be criteria. If the problem were to make ratings on extraversion-introversion or some other personality trait one might use scores on a paper-and-pencil test that purports to measure the trait. Alternatively the judge's rating might be validated against some better-informed rating such as one that was the consensus of close friends.

These criteria are not very satisfying. Those that are obviously valid (age, sex, profession, intelligence) are not very interesting to judge. Those that are more interesting are of doubtful validity. What does the judge understand "extraversion" to mean and what does the extraversion the questionnaire measures have to do with non-verbal behavior? When an actor "registers" an emotion for judges to identify, how do we know that the actor's pose is not a stage convention remote from the expression of genuine emotion. Even the layman who is genuinely experiencing some emotion is not, we have seen, an unimpeachable authority on the best name for that emotion.

Accurate perception of persons is supposed to be important because it permits prediction of behavior which is essential for smooth interaction. Why not then ask "perceivers" or judges to predict particular actions and use as criteria the way in which the actions are performed. Let the judge guess whom X will marry; what name he will give his first male child, what movies he will see in a month, the meal he will select from a menu. Unfortunately, such actions make poor experimental data. Some are too infrequent, the timing of some is likely to be inopportune, some are so much influenced by adventitious circumstances as to be of necessity unpredictable from person perception. The easiest behavior to collect in quantity and to record is verbal behavior and the verbal behavior that is easiest to process is a choice among fixed alternatives. Let the person to be judged go ahead and answer the extraversion-introversion questionnaire responding to such items as: "Do you like to be alone a considerable part of each day? ☐ Yes ☐ No." However, instead of summing the answers to yield a score, treat each item-response as an action to be predicted. The judge then, is to attempt to fill out the questionnaire as the person has done. Or—ask each of the six members of a group privately to write down the name of the member he likes best. Then let each member guess the choices of all the other members. Or—let the person give himself numerical ratings and set the judge the problem of guessing those self-ratings. In all of these variations, the discrepancy between predicted and actual responses becomes the basis for computing an accuracy score.

DETERMINANTS OF ACCURACY IN RESPONSE-PREDICTING

The response-predicting technique has been very popular in social psychology. It has the three qualities that make for a vogue in our science. As a procedure it is simple and objective. As a procedure it is susceptible of infinite variations which are rather easily thought up. Finally, the procedure is one that seems to go to the heart of subtle and important mental processes. Response-predicting is obviously a way of measuring accuracy of person perception, but it can equally well be considered a measure of more interesting processes; for example, empathy or the ability to "feel what another feels" (Cottrell and Dymond, 1949). The technique can reasonably be considered a measure of social understanding or social insight, a measure of the ability to take the role of another. It is not surprising that the technique has been popular.

Response-predicting has lost its simplicity and some of its popularity in recent years thanks to the cogent analyses of Cronbach (1955, 1958); Gage and Cronbach (1955); Bender and Hastorf (1953); Bronfenbrenner, Harding and Gallwey (1958); and others. We will imagine a typical sort

of response-prediction study in order to illustrate the problems of interpretation that arise.

Six college men, strangers to one another, are convened for two hours
to discuss some campus issue. This is the period of mutual exposure in
which person perception has a chance to occur. All participants start from
the same baseline of zero acquaintance with one another. Following their
two-hour talk each subject is asked privately to rate himself on a set of
bipolar traits appearing as the extremes of seven-point scales; e.g., "Interesting (1) to Dull (7)." Having rated himself, each subject is asked
to guess the self-ratings of each other subject, in short, each man makes
the full set of ratings, six times, once for himself and once for each of
the others. A subject's accuracy score is the average discrepancy between
his ratings of the others and their self-ratings. It turns out that the judges
vary greatly in accuracy scores and these differences might be interpreted
as variation in the ability to perceive and interpret the expressive cues that
individuals produce. The trouble is that there are many ways in which
one judge can come to have a higher accuracy score than another and
yet not have greater skill at person perception.

Projection. Suppose that both the more accurate judge (A) and the
less accurate judge (B) were inclined to assume that the other students
in the group were much like themselves and so used their own ratings as
a basis for guessing the ratings of others. There is evidence that many
judges do rate others in this projective fashion. If both A and B have
rated projectively then the higher "accuracy" score would be attained by
the judge who happened to be more similar to, more typical of, the persons being judged.

A judge would not often project the full detail of his own rating
profile onto another person and still less often would he project that
profile onto all the persons in a set. However, there are subtler forms
of projection that a judge can practice without awareness of what he is
doing. A judge might, for instance, attribute scores to others in such a
fashion as to cause the average of these scores to coincide with his own
self-rating. Suppose that such a judge rated himself at the value 2 on a
bipolar scale labelled "Interesting-Dull" and ranging from the value 1 to
the value 7. This judge, in rating five others, might give them the values
1, 2, 2 , 2, and 3 and thereby cause the ratings of the five others to average out to the value of his own self-rating. There are other non-obvious
forms of projection. A judge might simply confine his ratings of others
to the range within which all of his self-ratings fall. Suppose he always
rated himself at 2, 3, or 4. He could do the same for everyone else and
yet never duplicate in detail his own rating profile. For judges A and B
who practiced one of these subtle forms of projection, as for judges A

and B who practiced the extreme and obvious form of projection, "accuracy" would be a function of typicality.

If Judge A has been more accurate than judge B what difference does it make whether or not A came to be so by projection? It makes a difference when we try to think about accuracy in relation to other concepts. Here is an example. Several investigators have found that leadership in a group, especially sociometric popularity, which means being listed as one "liked" by many others, is correlated with the ability to predict accurately the group opinion on issues relevant to the group life (Chowdhry and Newcomb, 1952; Gage, 1952). Our interpretation of this correlation will depend on our interpretation of the "accuracy" scores. If we take them to be an index of comparative skill at person perception then we will probably guess that the correlation between accurate perception of the group and popularity in the group indicates that the person perception skill is a qualification for leadership. And go on to guess that the person who can form accurate impressions of the views of others is, on that account, well equipped to influence them. How greatly our interpretation changes if we think of the accuracy as a consequence of projection. The leader or popular person knows the group's views because they are his own; he is the modal person in the group. Then we may remember the proposition about popular leadership set forth by Riecken and Homans (1954) to the effect that a member of a group will be popular in the degree that he realizes the norms and values of the group. Or we may think of the closely related idea in balance theory (e.g., Heider, 1958) that people are attracted to those who are similar to themselves. The person having the greatest aggregate similarity to others will have the greatest aggregate popularity and will be the best (projective) judge in this group. The difference to our theory of leadership is profound (see Chapter 13). Leadership appears to be a consequence of typicality in a group and therefore specific to the group.

Knowledge of a Group. Judge A might be more accurate than judge B not because of typicality and projection but also not because he is able to perceive and interpret the expressive cues that individuals produce; judge A might simply have a better grasp of the average position of the group being assessed. The six subjects in the hypothetical experiment we have described were all male college students. Male college students constitute a subculture with a great many views in common. If judge A had an accurate conception of this subculture and judge B a very inaccurate conception, then A might do better at predicting the responses of six particular male students without relying on perception of their individual expressive behavior. The possibility will be more evident if we imagine that A is himself a present-day college student and that B is an elderly, very rich man who graduated from Princeton in the twenties and has an

F. Scott Fitzgerald image of college life. Probably A could do a better job than B of predicting the political and social views and the personal aspirations of six contemporary college men. But A could do this better job if he and B never "perceived" the six men at all because A has a more accurate notion of the subculture to which the men belong.

Knowledge of a group need not extend to detailed information about the group's distribution of responses on every particular item in order to produce a superior accuracy score. Simply knowing the general range of response or having some idea of the mean response would be of enormous help. Suppose A and B were guessing the IQ's of six college men and A thought the mean IQ for such men would be 115 and that most scores would fall between 105 and 140, whereas B thought the mean would be about 100 and that most scores would fall between 80 and 140. Judge A would be likely to make the more accurate guesses about any particular six college men.

In the degree that A's accuracy derives from knowledge of the subculture to which the persons being judged belong, A has no real need of direct contact with these persons. Gage (1952) has shown, in a very dramatic way, that this is true. He first asked judges to predict the questionnaire responses of subjects, whom they had never seen but who were identified as college students, and subsequently gave the judges a period of direct exposure to the students in question. The judges then made a new set of predictions. They were somewhat less accurate after exposure than before. Apparently the new information provided by expressive behavior was misleading. The judges' stereotype of college students provided a better approximation to particular students' behavior than did impressions founded on direct experience. A judge with good knowledge of a subculture might do well to close his eyes when invited to observe the behavior of individuals from that subculture. Effects of this kind have been obtained more than once (Kelly and Fiske, 1951) and a probable explanation is that judges, after experience, strain for sensitivity and therefore widely differentiate individuals who are really close to the mean of their group.

Impressions of a subgroup may, of course, be founded on person perception but it is a kind of person perception that is distinguishable from the perception of differences among individuals in a subgroup. Knowledge of a subgroup does not necessarily imply contact with any persons; opinion polls and novels are two alternative sources of knowledge. Whether it is founded on perception or not, the ability to predict the typical responses of a group seems to be empirically independent of the ability to differentiate among individuals in the same group. Bronfenbrenner, Harding, and Gallwey (1958) have reported evidence to this effect, and so have Cline and Richards (1960). The former authors point out that both kinds of knowledge, knowledge of groups and knowledge of individuals, are important in practical life. A buyer for a department store needs to know what the public, in general, will buy. The salesmen on the floor would like to know what the particular customer will buy. A teacher may have a good idea of the kind of thing that third-graders are able to learn but no very clear idea of the differences among members of her third-grade class. The two kinds of knowledge are analytically distinguishable and, on present evidence, are empirically independent.

Response Sets. There is a third factor, other than skill in perceiving individuals, that can cause one judge to be more accurate than another; he can have a certain set or approach to rating people that happens, incidentally, to promote accuracy. Suppose a judge is disposed to think well of everyone and tends to rate everyone at the more favorable or socially desirable end of such scales as: "Interesting (1)—Dull (7)." He is likely to appear to be a rather accurate judge because, as the extensive work of Allen Edwards has shown, subjects generally attribute socially desirable characteristics to themselves. In one study (Edwards, 1953) a large number of people rated the social desirability of each of 140 personality-trait items. Another large number answered the items as a personality inventory, responding "Yes" to those that characterized themselves and "No" to those that did not. The correlation between the ratings on social desirability and the proportion of respondents who answered "Yes" was .87. There is evidence from Gage and Cronbach (1955) and from Dubin, et al. (1954) that judges in perception studies do differ in their over-all tendencies to respond favorably or unfavorably to others. Those who incline to be favorable should, for that reason alone, tend to be "accurate."

Again we must ask whether it makes any difference how a judge comes to be accurate and again the answer is that it makes a difference to our interpretation of the demonstrated accuracy. A judge who owes his accuracy to a benign outlook and the self-esteem of others may not be skilled at reading expressive behavior. If he has to judge subjects who think ill of themselves or who are perhaps only objective about themselves, he will do poorly. If he is asked to make ratings or to answer questions where the options do not differ in social desirability he will be helpless. Indeed, questionnaires and scales are now often balanced for social desirability in order to eliminate the effects of this powerful response set (see Chapter 10 for a discussion of response sets).

There are other kinds of sets that can make for accuracy or inaccuracy. Judges will often give a characteristic "spread" to their ratings, one judge showing a large amount of variation in his ratings and another judge keeping all his ratings close together. If a judge is extremely good, has very accurate knowledge of the criterion, then he will do well to let the variation in his judgments approach that of the actual criterion values, though his variation should never be greater than that of the criterion. If the judge is in the more usual position of making inferences from inadequate cues, he will do well to restrict the variability of his ratings, giving people closely similar values. Indeed, if two judges have the same not very high correlational validity, the judge who differentiates less will obtain the better absolute accuracy score. In fact there is a rule for determining the optimum amount of variation in a set of estimates, a rule that invokes the statistical concepts of correlation and standard deviation. The optimum standard deviation for a set of predictions in terms of the accuracy score is not the standard deviation of the criterion ratings, but this standard deviation times the correlation between estimates and criteria. This will be a smaller figure than the standard deviation of the criterion ratings except in the case of a perfect correlation between estimates and criteria. In general then, if two judges are equally skilled at person perception but distribute their ratings with unequal variability, the one who varies them less is likely to earn the higher accuracy score (Cronbach, 1955).

This is not the end of the artifacts and complications that have been found in the "simple" response prediction technique but it is enough. Experimental studies using this technique over the years have varied greatly in the adequacy with which they have treated these complications and that makes it difficult, we shall see, to determine what the findings of these studies come to. The two great questions about accuracy in impression formation have been the same from the start. They are: 1) Is accuracy a general trait; are there judges who are consistently good and judges who are consistently poor? 2) What are the qualities of a good judge and what are the qualities of a poor judge?

ACCURACY AS A GENERAL SKILL

The first question is badly put. It should rather be: In what dimensions is accuracy general and in what dimensions not general? It might, for instance, be general across persons judged with the trait held constant but not across traits with persons held constant. Perhaps a good judge of extraversion-introversion is a good judge of that dimension for whomever but not a very good judge of intelligent-unintelligent. Alternatively the person who is a good judge of college students may be good whatever the traits and yet be poor at judging other groups.

The dimensions in which generality is likely to appear are affected by the processes underlying crude accuracy. A "projecting" judge will be accurate for people resembling himself but not otherwise. A judge who credits everyone with socially desirable characteristics will be accurate for people who think well of themselves providing the traits involved are unequally desirable. Generalities of this kind are not what investigators are looking for, they are trying to find a general skill at perception rather than an unwitting practice that causes judges to be right in certain restricted circumstances. However, the only studies than can give clear evidence on the generality of the skill are those that have eliminated the effects of the habits.

Some of the well-designed recent studies find in favor of the conclusion that the skill is not general (for example, Crow and Hammond, 1957), but there is one that finds in favor of generality (Cline and Richards, 1960) and we will say a little about this one. As stimulus material from which to form impressions Cline and Richards used ten color and sound films of interviews. There was some variety among the interviewees; they included a nineteen-year-old engaged male geology major at the University of Utah, a sixty-five-year-old widow with two married children working as supervisor of a church cafeteria, a twenty-two-year-old single male Mexican-American working in a meat-packing plant, and seven others. The fifty judges were all students but they were summer session students and so a more than ordinarily heterogeneous lot. The judging instruments included standardized objective personality inventories, word associations, sentence completions, and trait ratings. The interviewees had responded to all these instruments in private and the judges had to try to predict their responses.

The results suggest that accuracy in judging others is a general skill. The scores judges obtained for one set of five interviewees were correlated with the scores they obtained for the other set of five. These correlations ranged from .66 to .79 and they argue that judging skill is general across persons judged. The accuracy scores for each test were correlated with the scores for each other test and these correlations ranged from .30 to .65. They argue that skill is general across items to be judged.

Cline and Richards made various detailed analyses of their data, directed, in part, at the kinds of complications we have discussed. These analyses did not wash out the evidence for generality though one of them somewhat complicates the conclusion. Cline and Richards separated the judges' stereotype accuracy, their accuracy in predicting for persons in general, from their differential accuracy, their accuracy in predicting for individuals. They found, as had Bronfenbrenner and his associates (1958) that the two kinds of accuracy were independent. However, each kind of accuracy was general. The authors conclude that accuracy in perceiving others is a general ability, but a general ability that can be analyzed into two independent components: stereotype accuracy and differential or interpersonal accuracy.

Why should Cline and Richards have found more evidence of generality than most other investigators have done? At present the question cannot be answered with confidence because the Cline and Richards study differed from such others as that of Crow and Hammond (1957) in many respects. But we can try answering without confidence. There are three aspects of the Cline and Richards procedure that converge on a single explanation of the obtained generality. The first of these is the fact that the ten filmed interviews used as stimulus material were selected from a set of twenty such interviews. They were chosen because of their technical excellence but also because, on a pretest, the selected ten had been especially useful for distinguishing good judges from poor judges. It is legitimate to pretest in this way to find items that will establish generality. If someone were devising an intelligence test he would be free to drop those items which, on a trial run, did not predict his criterion or hang together with his other items. When we say that intelligence is a general characteristic we do not mean that it strongly affects every conceivable intellectual performance. Similarly, accuracy in judging others can be a general trait even if it does not affect every conceivable problem in person perception. However, in order to know the range and dimensions of the generality we need to know the difference between problems that are loaded with the general skill and those that are not. How did the retained ten interviews differ from the rejected ten? That is a critical question.

There are two other aspects of the Cline and Richards procedure that are suggestive. The content of the interviews seems to have had some relevance to the responses to be predicted though, of course, the interviews did not give away any specific responses. The interviewer probed personal values, personality strengths and weaknesses, hobbies, etc. Information in these areas should help one to make trait ratings and fill out personality inventories. The final feature of the Cline and Richards procedure that helps the outcome is the fact that judges were given a brief period in which to inspect the judging instruments they would have to fill out before they saw the film. Inspection of the instruments may have taught the judges what to look for in the interview; it may have "tuned" their perception. Jones and Thibaut (1958) have shown that tuning strongly influences what we perceive in another person.

The Cline and Richards procedure seems to have created conditions that made person perception into a reasonable intellectual problem; something it has not been in most experiments. In the information provided there must have been much that was relevant to the inferences required and judges had a chance to set themselves to pick out what they needed. A good score would seem to depend on ability to analyze out of the total interview the evidence that could be used, and on memory for this evidence, and on good rules of inference derived from past experience. It sounds like the kind of problem which depends on intelligence for its solution and intelligence is a general trait. Perhaps accuracy in making inferences about persons becomes a general trait when the problems are set up so as to respond to intelligent effort. The ten interviews that were rejected may have been interviews in which very little useful information about the interviewees' personalities happened to come to light; therefore interviews of which no intelligent use could be made; therefore interviews that would not discriminate the generally good judge from the generally poor judge.

QUALITIES OF A GOOD JUDGE

The second great question about accuracy in impression formation has always been: What are the qualities of a good judge and what are the qualities of a poor judge? The first question, the question of generality, has logical priority. Until we know whether judges are consistently good we cannot determine the qualities of people who are good judges. We can only discover the qualities of people who have been, in a particular experiment, good judges. But the qualities of people who have been good judges in a study that involved inferences to emotions from faces might be entirely different from the qualities of people who have been good judges in a study requiring members of a group to guess who likes whom. With the generality of accuracy not established and with judgment problems varying in a thousand dimensions it is to be expected that the evidence on qualities of good judges would be confused. It is.

Some of the personal characteristics that have, in one or more studies, distinguished those who were good judges from those who were not are: intelligence, similarity to the persons judged, experience, self-insight, cognitive complexity, social skill and adjustment, detachment, an aesthetic attitude, intraceptiveness (see Chapter 10), and taking a global or intuitive approach to the problem. However, where there are two or more studies involving the same variable the results are often contradictory or else statistically significant in one case and not in another. Two variables that hold up fairly well across studies are: 1) Similarity between the judge and the person judged; 2) Self-insight on the part of the judge as measured against the average ratings given him by others. These more consistent outcomes, however, can be generated by projection and the social desirability set and so it is not clear that they are characteristics of judges skilled at person perception as such. They may simply be characteristics of judges having certain habits in describing themselves or others which make for accuracy in certain kinds of experimental procedure. There are reviews of this literature by Taft (1955), Bruner and Tagiuri (1954) and Allport (1961).

The work of Bronfenbrenner and his associates (1958) is more critical and analytic than most; it separates stereotype accuracy from differential interpersonal accuracy and men's judgments from women's and, for each sex, judgments of the same sex from judgments of the other sex. The correlates of accuracy shift radically with the kind of accuracy. Men who were accurate about men had dominant characters; men accurate about women were timid. The correlates of general interpersonal accuracy were not correlates of stereotype accuracy. This complex pattern of data indicates that studies which do not distinguish varieties of accuracy but simply use global measures that combine various accuracies in unknown fashion cannot be expected to produce consistent results.

One outcome of the Bronfenbrenner work should be stressed because it contradicts a conventional assumption. The assumption is that accuracy in assessing others constitutes an unalloyed advantage in life. In the degree that one knows what others truly feel one should be effective in social interaction. Bronfenbrenner and his associates found evidence, however, that general interpersonal sensitivity is associated with passivity and withdrawal. The evidence, the authors stress, is not strong. However, it is important, because it jars us into recognizing that sensitivity need not be an advantage in all ways. Not everything that others feel and believe is agreeable to know. Knowledge, for the sensitive, can be bruising. The interests of others are often in conflict and having all the information may be paralyzing. Or cause and effect could work the other way. Someone who is by nature anxious in his personal contacts may acquire sensitivity because he feels an exceptionally strong need to know.

In sum, we do not know in what respects accurate person perception is a general characteristic and also do not know the qualities of an accurate judge. I would like to make the guess that the ability will be general in the degree that the problems set the judges are problems responsive to intelligence. This is not to say that accurate person perception is nothing but intelligence. Intelligence itself is factorially complex being made up of a large number of partially independent mental abilities. Ability in person perception probably is not the same as any one of these but it may be related to some or all of them.

One's Own Personality

Among the persons of whom one forms an impression in a lifetime there is one of peculiar interest—the self. The self is not the same as the human organism; the self is a cognitive construction of the organism which is, in certain ways, identified with the organism. The self is also not identical with the Freudian ego. For the most part Freud wrote about the ego as if it were a name for certain activities or processes of the organism, in particular the processes of perception and learning insofar as these are oriented to external reality. In this usage the ego is an aspect of the organism, a name for certain processes externally regarded. Sometimes, however, Freud's usage shifted and he wrote of the ego being judged or evaluated by some other agency such as the superego. Where Freud writes of the ego as an *object* rather than as an agent he is using the term *ego* in the sense in which we will use the term *self*.

William James (1890) has written, with unequaled sensitivity and wisdom, of the self as an object of knowledge, as a mental construction of the human organism. George Herbert Mead (1934) has very persuasively argued that the self is a derivative of social life. The human organism is able to conceive of its self, in Mead's opinion, only by participating in the minds of others. From the point of view of another, the organism is a person having certain traits, abilities, and motives. A man can perceive his own personality, Mead argues, only by reflection in the eyes of another. In recent years Gordon Allport (1961) has written a good summary of psychological knowledge concerning the development of the self in childhood and throughout a lifetime. Allport does not, by the way, think that Mead's version is the whole story.

In this chapter I would like to make just two points about the self. The first point, flatly stated, is that the self-conception is created by a process of impression formation much like the process by which conceptions of others are created. The second point is that the organism's conceptions of the self and of other persons are highly interdependent entities. Conceptions of the self and of salient others are joined together into what might call "the theory of one's life." If one entity in this construction is changed it is usually the case that others must also change. What now follows is an expansion of these points.

THE SELF AND IMPRESSION FORMATION

The persons a single organism is likely to conceive include a wife, a mother, a father, a son, a daughter, a few friends, and myriad acquaintances as well as a self. The self seems in various ways to be unique in this company. It is, to begin with, unique in an epistemological sense, unique, that is, from the point of view of the theory of knowledge. In forming an impression of the self the organism can draw upon certain classes of data that are not available to it when it forms impressions of others. These are such data as the visceroceptors and proprioceptors provide. The rest of the world may see a smile on the face of the organism but only the organism can feel the tension in the voluntary musculature that makes that smile a "forced" one.

Because the organism has privileged access to certain data it is sometimes assumed that the organism cannot be corrected on the subject of the self. It is sometimes even assumed that the organism, because of its privileged epistemological position, which puts it privy to inner speech and palpitations of the heart, has no reason to be interested in ordinary public data. For anyone thinking this way about the self it must seem bizarre to speak of the creation of the self as a process of "impression formation." The word "impression" with its connotations of sensory impress and of imperfect, always corrigible, knowledge may be an appropriate term for knowledge the organism has of others but it seems inappropriate for knowledge the organism has of its self. I believe that "impression formation" is an appropriate term in both cases.

We do not really behave as if we thought we had all the answers about the self. We behave as if we thought the private data simply a part of the total data, not invariably the more valid part. Data from the muscles and viscera are not necessarily more informative than is the continuing sight of the face. The organism that thinks it is the only one that knows its smile is forced should see the face the rest of us see.

Consider the ways in which an organism decides whether its self is "warm" or "cold," "mature" or "immature," "intelligent" or "unintelligent." Not only by attention to events within. The organism is quite likely to try to get an impression of its self by filling out a paper-and-pencil personality inventory or by taking an intelligence test. If all the answers were available from within would we bother to make behavioral records accessible to anyone's exteroceptors? And if our private knowledge were not subject to correction would we await the results of personality and intelligence tests with a certain suspense? It seems to me that on the subject of its self, as on the subject of another, the organism never has more than an opinion.

INTERDEPENDENCE OF THE SELF-CONCEPTION AND THE CONCEPTIONS OF OTHERS

A simple form of interdependence can be represented in terms of the principle of cognitive consistency (see Chapters 11 and 13). The representation could be made in terms of congruity or balance or dissonance. We will make it in terms of balance.

The characters involved are the self, which can be symbolized with the letter S, and some other person who can be symbolized with the letter O. Both S and O must be understood to have their existence within the mind of a single organism. The organism has value-laden conceptions of S and O and also some conception of the relation between the two. Let us suppose that the organism has a good impression of the moral nature, the "character" of S. We might represent that impression by a +. Let us further suppose that the organism recognizes a relation of close kinship between S and O. In fact let O be the wife of S. This "unit-forming" relation (see Chapter 11) can be represented by the letter p. The question then is whether the organism is free to have either a good ($+$) or a bad ($-$) opinion of the moral character of O. If our mapping into the terms of balance theory is correct then the answer to the question is that the organism is not free to have a bad opinion of O. If a negative value is assigned to O we have a bond of the form $+ p -$. This constitutes a state of cognitive imbalance and so, theoretically, an unstable state. If the organism thinks well of the self and has a positive unit-forming relation with the other then balance requires the organism to think well of the other. And so the conception of the self and conceptions of others to whom the self is related are interdependent.

If the organism must, for some reason, have a poor opinion of O then the balance formulation requires one or another adjustive change in the organism's conception of the self or of the bond. The organism can think badly of the other and preserve the positive bond if it will consent to think badly of the self. In short the following is a balanced proposition: That valueless woman is married to my valueless self ($- p -$). Alternatively the organism can think well of the self and badly of the woman if it will consent to a divorce of either the legal or psychological kind which means the creation of a negative bond (n) linking a positive object and a negative object ($+ n -$). The resultant bond constitutes a balanced state. In the balance formulation the interdependence of self and other is complete. Given the evaluation of one person and the nature of the bond, the evaluation of the other person is predictable.

With the certainty of being a little absurd let me describe a real situation, something like the abstract case represented above. In his later years the great Leo Tolstoy strove to live in literal accordance with Jesus' Sermon on the Mount. He wanted to sign over his royalties to the persecuted Dukhobors and open his home to the poor. Luxury, even comfort were a torture to him. He wanted above all to be free to seek God in his own life. His wife, the Countess Tolstoy, opposed these high aspirations. She was a shallow woman fond of fine gowns and of parties who could see no reason to give away money the Count had gained from his novels nor to share the property he had inherited. She frustrated his noblest intentions, and aggravated his soul with a thousand petty household affairs.

Ignoring ambivalences and other matters too complex for this model, we may say that in Leo Tolstoy's mind, in his later years, the self had assumed a positive value ($+$) and the other, his wife, a negative value ($-$). This had not always been so, of course. In earlier years he had respected her and a strong bond of sympathy (p) had existed between them. As their characters grew unlike they experienced a psychological separation, the relation between them became a negative (n) one. The marriage was balanced, toward the end of their lives, as a bond of the form $+ n -$.

There was no possibility of denying the characterological opposition of the Count and Countess Tolstoy and no possibility of denying the psychological gulf between them. The bond was unmistakably of the type $+ n -$. However, there was more than one way of assigning referents to the $+$ and $-$ of the bond. The Countess Tolstoy, and some of her children, favored the following version.

Countess Tolstoy was a loving, selfless wife who had had a hard and drab early life caring for her many children and managing a large country estate. Now that most of her children were grown and Tolstoy had become the most famous writer in Russia, she naturally wished for an easier life, for a little social gaiety. As for Count Tolstoy, he was an obsessed, self-indulgent ideologue. To conceal the fact that he did not love as well as he should those closest to him, he filled his life with an abstract passion for the remote poor.

This second theory of the Tolstoy family life was of course known to the Count and he was often urged to adopt it. He resisted doing so and this resistance is unaccountable from the point of view of cognitive balance alone. Both theories represent bonds of the form: $+ n -$. The only difference between them is in the identities of the $+$ and $-$. Of the two possibilities the Court preferred the one that identified his own self with the positive value. The Countess preferred the other theory which assigned the positive value to her self. In forming a theory of one's life the maintenance of self-esteem is probably at least as important as the maintenance of balance.

We have come upon one respect in which the self is unique among perceived persons. The organism is partial to it and prefers to assign to it a positive value. In fact a positively valued self is tacitly assumed in the various formulations of the principle of balance presented in Chapter 11.

The interdependence among conceptions of self and others extends beyond positive and negative evaluations. A particular trait in one often seems to require a particular trait in another. If Tolstoy was unloving and self-deceived then his wife was, not simply positively valued, but long-suffering and insightful. It would be a much harder job to model these detailed interdependencies than it has been to model the simple interdependence of evaluations.

Not all of the conceptions interdependent with the self are of family members. Neither are they necessarily of particular individuals. Conceptions of groups, even geographically remote groups, can affect the self. Consider the following rather common transformation in the thinking of a Negro who has grown up in the United States in recent years. We may suppose that, when he was a boy, African Negroes seemed to him to be the painted savages who chased a heroic white Tarzan in Saturday-after-noon movies and American Negroes the forever-inferior descendants of these savages and himself an average American Negro. When he grows older he learns that: 1) The art of African Negroes is as highly regarded by some intelligent people as is the art of Europeans; 2) African colonies can become African nations and produce their own leaders who are treated deferentially by European and American heads of state; 3) American Negroes, the descendants of Africans, sometimes go to college, enter professions, become famous artists or statesmen. All of this has implications for his self-concept. He comes to think of himself as a young person of some ability and good character who has been given no opportunities. Treatment by whites that once seemed reasonable enough and certainly inevitable now seems a wrong that must be righted. Obstreperous fellow Negroes who used to be considered stupid for inviting trouble now seem to be far-sighted leaders. Acquiescent fellow Negroes who once seemed to be the sensible ones now seem to be the cowardly ones. A change in a man's impression of certain geographically remote others—Africans—might in this way effect a transformation in his impression of himself and those nearest him.

Finally, it seems to me that the interdependence of self-conception and other conceptions can be demonstrated in one's own mind. Try the effect of a really radical change in your opinion of your father or your wife or your best friend, the sort of change that a quarrel can bring. The change will start a shock wave that alters the self-conception and it will initiate a reinterpretation of past events and of the people in them. Try the effect of a radical change in your opinion of yourself, the sort of change that can be produced by a frank negative opinion from the outside. *If you accept this evaluation* the other people in your mind must do flip-flops as a consequence. One of the interesting things about the effect of a force of this kind is that even when one knows that the force will seem unimportant tomorrow, that its effects will be short lived, the effects nevertheless temporarily occur. It is as though our theory of the life we are living must respond to salient new data, even when we know the significance of the data will dwindle with time. It is as though the human mind cannot suspend theoretical work of this kind.

Since, in life, conceptions of others are interdependent with the self-conception, the research literature on impression formation must be charged with unrepresentativeness. The faces from which emotions have been read, the hypothetical persons to whom traits have been attributed, the stooges feigning anger or high spirits have not stood in any *known* relation to the perceiver. We are sometimes concerned to form impressions of strangers and the study of this process is a legitimate one. But when the persons of whom impressions are formed stand in some definite relation to the perceiver, as in life they often do, the problem changes. We are not always free to conceive of persons as their expressive behavior alone would dictate. Neither are we always free to revise impressions in the light of new data. Impressions of others are hypothetical constructions in the organism's theory of its life and they must fit into the total pattern of that theory.

REFERENCES

Allport, G. W. *Pattern and growth in personality*. New York: Holt, Rinehart & Winston, 1961.

Asch, S. E. Forming impressions of personality. *J. abnorm. soc. Psychol.*, 1946, **41**, 258–290.

Ax, A. The physiological differentiation between fear and anger in humans. *Psychosom. Med.*, 1953, **15**, 433–442.

Bender, I. E., & Hastorf, A. H. On measuring generalized empathic ability (social sensitivity). *J. abnorm. soc. Psychol.*, 1953, **48**, 503–506.

Boring, E. G., & Titchener, E. B. A model for the demonstration of facial expression. *Amer. J. Psychol.*, 1923, **34**, 471–485.

Bronfenbrenner, U., Harding, J., & Gallwey, Mary. The measurement of skill in social perception. In D. C. McClelland, A. L. Baldwin, U. Bronfenbrenner, & F. L. Strodtbeck (Eds.), *Talent and society*. Princeton: D. Van Nostrand, 1958.

Bruner, J. S. Social psychology and perception. In Eleanor Maccoby, T. M. Newcomb, & E. L. Hartley (Eds.), *Readings in social psychology*. (3rd ed.) New York: Holt, 1958.

Bruner, J. S., Shapiro, D., & Tagiuri, R. The meaning of traits in isolation and in combination. In R. Tagiuri, & L. Petrullo (Eds.), *Person perception and interpersonal behavior*. Stanford: Stanford Univer. Press, 1958.

Bruner, J. S., & Tagiuri, R. The perception of people. In G. Lindzey (Ed.), *Handbook of social psychology*. Vol. 2. Cambridge: Addison-Wesley, 1954.

Cannon, W. B. *Bodily changes in pain, hunger, fear and rage*. (2nd ed.) New York: Appleton, 1929.

Cantril, H., & Hunt, W. A. Emotional effects produced by the injection of adrenalin. *Amer. J. Psychol.*, 1932, **44**, 300–307.

Carmichael, L., Roberts, S. O., & Wessel, N. Y. A study of the judgment of manual expression as presented in still and motion pictures. *J. soc. Psychol.*, 1937, **8**, 115–142.

Chowdhry, Kamla, & Newcomb, T. M. The relative abilities of leaders and non-leaders to estimate opinions of their own groups. *J. abnorm. soc. Psychol.*, 1952, **47**, 51–57.

Cline, V. B., & Richards, J. M., Jr. Accuracy of interpersonal perception—a general trait? *J. abnorm. soc. Psychol.*, 1960, **60**, 1–7.

Cottrell, L. S., Jr., & Dymond, Rosalind F. The empathic responses: a neglected field for research. *Psychiatry*, 1949, **12**, 355–359.

Cronbach, L. J. Processes affecting scores on "understanding of others" and "assumed similarity." *Psychol. Bull.*, 1955, **52**, 177–193.

Cronbach, L. J. Proposals leading to analytic treatment of social perception scores. In R. Tagiuri, & L. Petrullo (Eds.), *Person perception and interpersonal behavior*. Stanford: Stanford Univer. Press, 1958.

Crow, W. J., & Hammond, K. R. The generality of accuracy and response sets in interpersonal perception. *J. abnorm. soc. Psychol.*, 1957, **54**, 384–390.

Dubin, S. S., Burke, L. K., Neel, R. G., & Chesler, D. J. Characteristics of hard and easy raters. *U. S. A. Persona. Res. Br. Note*, 1954, No. 36.

Dusenberry, D. & Knowrer, F. H. Experimental studies of the symbolism of action and voice. II. A study of the specificity of meaning in abstract tonal symbols. *J. Speech*, 1939, **25**, 67–75.

Edwards, A. L. The relationship between the judged desirability of a trait and the probability that the trait will be endorsed. *J. appl. Psychol.*, 1953, **37**, 90–93.

Feleky, Antoinette M. The expression of the emotions. *Psychol. Rev.*, 1914, **21**, 33–41.

Feleky, Antoinette M. *Feelings and emotions*. New York: Pioneer, 1924.

Gage, N. L. Judging interests from expressive behavior. *Psychol. Monogr.*, 1952, **66**, No. 18 (Whole No. 350).

Gage, N. L., & Cronbach, L. Conceptual and methodological problems in interpersonal perception. *Psychol. Rev.*, 1955, **62**, 411–422.

Gates, Georgina S. An experimental study of the growth of social perception. *J. educ. Psychol.*, 1923, **14**, 449–462.

Guilford, J. P. An experiment in learning to read facial expression. *J. abnorm. soc. Psychol.*, 1929, **24**, 191–202.

Heider, F. *The psychology of interpersonal relations*. New York: Wiley, 1958.

Heider, F., & Simmel, Marianne. An experimental study of apparent behavior. *Amer. J. Psychol.*, 1944, **57**, 243–259.

Hulin, W. S., & Katz, D. The Frois-Wittman pictures of facial expression. *J. exp. Psychol.*, 1935, **18**, 482–498.

Hunt, J. McV., Cole, M. W., & Reis, Eva E. Situational cues distinguishing anger, fear and sorrow. *Amer. J. Psychol.*, 1958, **71**, 136–151.

James, W. What is an emotion? *Mind*, 1884, **9**, 188–205.

James, W. *The principles of psychology*. Vol. I. New York: Holt, 1890.

Johnson, Linda. Stereotypes and perceptual distortion. Unpublished honors thesis, Mary Washington College, 1955. Cited by P. Secord. Facial features and inference processes in interpersonal perception. In R. Tagiuri, & L. Petrullo (Eds.), *Person perception and interpersonal behavior*. Stanford: Stanford Univer. Press, 1958.

Jones, E. E., & Thibaut, J. W. Interaction goals as bases of inference in interpersonal perception. In R. Tagiuri, & L. Petrullo (Eds.), *Person perception and interpersonal behavior*. Stanford: Stanford Univer. Press, 1958.

Kanner, L. Judging emotions from facial expressions. *Psychol. Monogr.*, 1931, **41**, No. 3 (Whole No. 186).

Kelly, E. L., & Fiske, D. W. *The prediction of performance in clinical psychology*. Ann Arbor: Univer. of Michigan Press, 1951.

Landis, C. Studies of emotional reactions. II. General behavior and facial expression. *J. comp. Psychol.*, 1924, **4**, 447–509.

Landis, C., & Hunt, W. A. Adrenalin and emotion. *Psychol. Rev.*, 1932, **39**, 467–485.

Latané, B., & Schachter, S. Adrenalin and avoidance learning. *J. comp. physiol. Psychol.*, 1962, **55**, 369–372.

Lindsley, D. B. Emotion. In S. S. Stevens (Ed.), *Handbook of experimental psychology*. New York: Wiley, 1951.

Luchins, A. S. Experimental attempts to minimize the impact of first impressions. In C. I. Hovland, et al., *The order of presentation in persuasion*. New Haven: Yale Univer. Press, 1957. (a)

Luchins, A. S. Primacy-recency in impression formation. In C. I. Hovland, et al., *The order of presentation in persuasion.* New Haven: Yale Univer. Press, 1957. (b)

Mandler, G. Emotion. In R. Brown, E. Galanter, E. H. Hess, & G. Mandler (Eds.), *New directions in psychology.* New York: Holt, Rinehart & Winston, 1962.

Marañon, G. Contribution à l'étude de l'action émotive de l'adrenalin. *Rev. Franc. D'endocrinol.*, 1924, **2**, 301–325.

Mead, G. H. *Mind, self, and society.* C. W. Morris (Ed.). Chicago: Univer. of Chicago Press, 1934.

Michotte, A. *La perception de la causalité.* (2nd ed.) Louvain: Publications universitaires de Louvain, 1954.

Munn, N. L. The effect of the knowledge of the situation upon judgment of emotion from facial expressions. *J. abnorm. soc. Psychol.*, 1940, **35**, 324–338.

Piderit, T. *Mimik und physiognomik.* (1st ed., 1859). Detmold: Meyer, 1925.

Riecken, H. W., & Homans, G. C. Psychological aspects of social structure. In G. Lindzey (Ed.), *Handbook of social psychology.* Vol. 2. Cambridge: Addison-Wesley, 1954.

Ruckmick, C. A. A preliminary study of the emotions. *Psychol. Monogr.*, 1921, **30**, No. 3, 28–35.

Schachter, J. Pain, fear, and anger in hypertensives and normotensives: A psychophysiologic study. *Psychosom. Med.*, 1957, **19**, 17–29.

Schachter, S., & Singer, J. E. Cognitive, social and physiological determinants of emotional state. *Psychol. Rev.*, 1962, **69**, 379–399.

Schachter, S., & Wheeler, L. Epinephrine, chlorpromazine and amusement. *J. abnorm. soc. Psychol.*, 1962, **65**, 121–128.

Schlosberg, H. A scale for judgment of facial expressions. *J. exp. Psychol.*, 1941, **29**, 497–510.

Schlosberg, H. The description of facial expressions in terms of two dimensions. *J. exp. Psychol.*, 1952, **44**, 229–237.

Secord, P. F. Facial features and inference processes in interpersonal perception. In R. Tagiuri, & L. Petrullo (Eds.), *Person perception and interpersonal behavior.* Stanford: Stanford Univer. Press, 1958.

Sherman, M. The differentiation of emotional responses in infants: I. Judgments of emotional responses from motion picture views and from actual observations. *J. comp. Psychol.*, 1927, **7**, 265–284.

Singer, J. E. The effects of epinephrine, chlorpromazine and dibenzyline upon the fright responses of rats under stress and non-stress conditions. Unpublished doctoral dissertation, Univer. of Minn., 1961.

Skinner, B. F. The operational analysis of psychological terms. *Psychol. Rev.*, 1945, **52**, 270–277.

Taft, R. The ability to judge people. *Psychol. Bull.*, 1955, **52**, 1–23.

Tagiuri, R., Bruner, J. S., & Blake, R. R. On the relation between feelings and perception of feeling among members of small groups. In Eleanor E. Maccoby, T. M. Newcomb, & E. L. Hartley (Eds.), *Readings in social psychology.* (3rd ed.) New York: Holt, 1958.

Wishner, J. Reanalysis of "Impressions of personality." *Psychol. Rev.*, 1960, **67**, 96–112.

Wolf, S., & Wolff, H. G. Human gastric function. New York: Oxford Univer. Press, 1943.

Woodworth, R. S. *Experimental psychology.* New York: Holt, 1938.

Woodworth, R. S., & Schlosberg, H. *Experimental psychology.* (Rev. ed.) New York: Holt, 1954.

CHAPTER 13

Group Dynamics

It very often happens that individuals make private decisions concerning a problem and then meet together to arrive at a group decision concerning that same problem. In 1962 the information that there were Soviet missiles in Cuba led the United States to institute a blockade of Cuba. Probably President Kennedy's advisers made their individual decisions from a study of intelligence reports and a consideration of alternatives before meeting as a group to decide on a course of action. It is clearly of some importance to know how such group decisions following discussion differ from individual decisions and that is one of the problems to which research on group dynamics has been addressed.

There are many dimensions on which decisions can vary and therefore many dimensions on which group decisions might consistently differ from individual decisions. One such dimension, one that was important in the decision about Cuba, is *riskiness*. Committees and boards in business and government have been generally thought to favor the pussyfooting compromise rather than the bold action. Whyte (1956), for example, has argued that the team approach in business enterprises leads inexorably to an inhibition of daring and risk-taking, a preference for the conservative course when a choice must be made between more and less risky courses of action. The academic committees on which one has served, committees to decide on appointments, course offerings, and degree recommendations do not leave one breathless with their daring. Consequently a recent discovery that group decisions following discussion are consistently riskier than individual decisions has occasioned some surprise.

Stoner first reported the effect in a dissertation submitted to the School of Industrial Management at M.I.T. (1961). Stoner's advisers were Donald Marquis and Michael Wallach; both of these men have contributed to the later research history of the effect Stoner obtained. Stoner used problems that were devised by Wallach and Kogan (1959, 1961) and first used by them for the investigation of individual differences in risk-taking. Each problem describes a situation in which the central person is faced with a choice between two actions whose outcomes differ in their attractiveness and their probability. The respondent is to act as an adviser to the central person in the story and is asked to indicate the minimum probability of success that he would demand before recommending the alternative that might have the more desirable outcome. Here is an example of the problems used by Stoner:

1. Mr. A, an electrical engineer who is married and has one child, has been working for a large electronics corporation since graduating from college five years ago. He is assured of a lifetime job with a modest, though adequate, salary, and liberal pension benefits upon retirement. On the other hand, it is very unlikely that his salary will increase much before he retires. While attending a convention, Mr. A is offered a job with a small, newly founded company with a highly uncertain future. The new job would pay more to start and would offer the possibility of a share in the ownership if the company survived the competition of the larger firms.

Imagine that you are advising Mr. A. Listed below are several probabilities or odds of the new company's proving financially sound. Please check the *lowest* probability that you would consider acceptable to make it worthwhile for Mr. A to take the new job.

☐ The chances are 1 in 10 that the company will prove financially sound.

☐ The chances are 3 in 10 that the company will prove financially sound.

☐ The chances are 5 in 10 that the company will prove financially sound.

☐ The chances are 7 in 10 that the company will prove financially sound.

☐ The chances are 9 in 10 that the company will prove financially sound.

☐ Place a check here if you think Mr. A should *not* take the new job, no matter what the probabilities.

Brief résumés of several of the other problems, numbered as they were by Stoner, will suggest their range:

3. A man of moderate means may invest some money he recently inherited in secure "blue-chip" low-return securities or in more risky securities that offer the possibility of large gains.

4. A captain of a college football team, in the final seconds of a game with the college's traditional rival, may choose a play that is almost certain to produce a tie score, or a more risky play that would lead to sure victory if successful, sure defeat if not.

6. A college senior planning graduate work in chemistry may enter University X where, because of rigorous standards, only a fraction of the graduate students manage to receive the Ph.D., or he may enter University Y which has a poorer reputation but where almost every graduate student receives the Ph.D.

In this chapter I will call the problems Stoner used the "Stoner problems" even though they were originally written by Wallach and Kogan (1959). We shall be interested in the problems in connection with Stoner's experiment and the phenomenon uncovered in that experiment. For this reason it will be more helpful to identify the problems by the name of a man who used them rather than by the names of the men who invented them.

What is a "risky" decision and how is the amount of risk determined? A person in a state of risk must have something to lose, a stake. For Mr. A in the first story above it is an assured lifetime job with an adequate salary. To take a risk is voluntarily to endanger this stake. Presumably neither Mr. A nor anyone else would do such a thing unless there were also a prize; the prize in the present case is a superior job in a new firm. If the individual is to have a problem of decision-making the prize must exceed the value of the stake but be less certainly available than the stake. If the prize and stake were equally valuable and yet the probability of attaining the prize varied, as it does in problem 1 above, then Mr. A would not consider risking his stake. Would he give up his present job in order to take a new job exactly like the one he has in a company that might fail? Probably not.

If the prize and stake were equally available and the prize the more valuable then, too, there would be no problem. If Mr. A were offered the new job described above with perfect certainty that the company would succeed then he would unhesitatingly take the new job. A decision under risk involves choosing between a more certain less attractive alternative and a less certain more attractive alternative.

In the problems Stoner used a decision gets riskier as the probability of obtaining the prize decreases. However, riskiness could also have been varied in other ways. For example, it would be possible to maintain the probability of getting the prize at a fixed level, say five chances in ten, and to vary the size of the stake. A riskier decision would then have been one that endangered a larger stake for a fixed prize and a fixed chance of winning. Risk, in general, increases with the size of the stake and decreases as the probability of gaining the prize goes up. In the problems Stoner used, a greater risk is always a decision to accept a lower probability of success.

Stoner's subjects were graduate students of industrial management. They first studied the problems, twelve problems in all, and made individual decisions on each problem. Subsequently they were assembled in groups of six and instructed to discuss each problem and to arrive at a unanimous group decision. Twenty-three other subjects did not meet as groups but did study the problems a second time, after a lapse of a few weeks. Stoner put together thirteen groups and for twelve of these the predominant direction of shift on the problems between the means of the initial individual decisions and the later group decisions was toward greater risk. The twenty-three control subjects showed no systematic shift in either direction.

Stoner also asked his subjects to record their private judgments after the group decision had been made; it was understood that a man's private opinion might or might not agree with the group consensus. These private opinions, subsequent to discussion, were compared with the private opinions expressed in advance of discussion. About 45 per cent of the subjects did not change their private views; of the remainder, however, 39 per cent changed toward greater risk and only 16 per cent toward greater caution. Something in the group discussion appears to have influenced private opinions, as well as the group decision, in the direction of greater riskiness. We will call the change "the shift to risk."

Stoner's finding is not a one-time outcome; it has been replicated with several kinds of subject. Wallach, Kogan, and Bem (1962) repeated the procedure with more than two hundred undergraduate students in the liberal arts curriculum at the University of Colorado. Groups were either all male or all female. Fourteen out of fourteen male groups shifted in a risky direction and twelve out of fourteen female groups did the same. In this experiment, as in Stoner's, subjects were asked to record their individual decisions following the discussion, and while these decisions often did not agree with those reached by the group they ran to greater risk then the decisions made prior to the group discussion. Some subjects were given the problems again some two to six weeks later and asked to reconsider each situation, not simply to try to recall their earlier positions. These decisions, too, were riskier than those made originally.

Marquis (1962) used the problems with mature middle-level managers in the Sloan Executive Training Program at M.I.T. Marquis used six problems and he created seven groups; therefore there were forty-two opportunities for group decisions to shift. In seven of these cases the groups deadlocked on the problem and no decision was made. Nine shifts were in the direction of caution and twenty-four in the direction of increased risk. Individual decisions, made after the discussion, showed the same tendency toward risk. Nordhøy (1962), a student of Marquis's, used some of the Stoner problems with students from Northeastern University and again confirmed the familiar results.

The Stoner problems describe hypothetical persons and hypothetical situations and so one naturally thinks of the possibility that the shift to risk occurs because the advisers of Mr. A and Mr. B and Mr. C can take their responsibilities very lightly. Would such a shift occur if the payoffs were real rather than imaginary? There is some reason to think that they would. In contriving situations which involve real payoffs, it has, of course, been necessary to desert the Stoner problems. Wallach, Kogan, and Bem (1964) asked for decisions involving real financial prizes ranging from $.17 to $1.50 per decision. Group decisions following a discussion were consistently riskier than individual decisions in the absence of discussion. The same investigators, in a new order (Bem, Wallach, and Kogan, In press) described a "psycho-physiological experiment" for which subjects elected to risk such disagreeable side effects as headache, nausea, and stomach cramps. Subjects believed that the negative payoffs they risked were real, though in fact they were not. Group decisions following a discussion were, as usual, riskier than individual decisions. The private opinions of the members composing the groups had also shifted to greater risk.[1]

In experiments with several kinds of subjects and with payoffs both

1. Wallach, Kogan, and Bem (e.g., 1962; 1964) believe that the shift to risk occurs because of the diffusion of responsibility that occurs when a decision is made by a group. They believe that when one individual has complete responsibility he is afraid to risk bad consequences, whereas when several persons share the responsibility, they are less afraid. It does seem to be the case that organizations delegate to committees the responsibility for decisions that may entail disagreeable consequences. Marquis (1962) has made one sort of experimental test of the hypothesis that diffusion of responsibility is the cause of the shift to risk. In his experiment it was not. The evidence for diffusion of responsibility in the Wallach, Kogan, and Bem papers is largely negative evidence. Their experiments seek to establish the diffusion of responsibility explanation by excluding all reasonable alternatives. I do not believe that they have succeeded in excluding the two most reasonable alternative explanations of the shift on the Stoner problems, explanations in terms of the disclosure of relevant information and the realization of a cultural value. The problems they used in two of their experiments do not admit of the introduction of much relevant information. Their experimental conditions (Bem, Wallach, and Kogan, In press) designed to disprove the values explanation, do not allow for specification of the value and that is an essential part of the explanation. It is possible that diffusion of responsibility makes for risk on some problems, but I am not persuaded that it has been a main factor in the shift to risk on the Stoner problems. However, if you were to read the Wallach, Kogan, and Bem papers, you might agree with them that diffusion of responsibility is the answer.

actual and hypothetical, both positive and negative, groups have arrived at unanimous decisions that were riskier than the average of the decisions made by the individuals prior to discussion. In addition the individual opinions taken after discussion have been riskier than they were before discussion. What causes these effects? A large part of the research literature on group dynamics promises to help with this question: there is work examining the quality of group problem-solving in comparison with individual problem-solving, work analyzing the content of group discussions, work on the emergence of discussion leaders, and work showing the power of a majority to cause dissident members to conform. Somewhere in all this we may reasonably expect to find the reason why group decisions shift to risk. I have used the search for that reason to give direction to our inquiry into group dynamics. It is, you will see, an expository "device" in the sense that one could look for the answer to the question without being so longwinded about related matters along the way. But the related matters have an importance of their own and we will always come back from them to the problem of riskiness in group decisions.

A Sample Discussion

On one occasion when Marquis made a demonstration of the Stoner effect I was a volunteer subject and, incidentally, argued a very risky line. I have listened to two other groups discuss the problems and have read the transcripts of some of Stoner's original tapes. No single discussion brings out all or even most of the forceful arguments and so I have put together a composite discussion that includes speeches from four different groups. For this interchange that never occurred in just this form I have imagined a typical outcome.

The participants are six men whom we will identify by the letters A to F.

A. Let's see where we stand. I favor taking the job if the odds are one in ten.

B. Only if they are seven in ten.

C. Right, seven in ten.

D. I say nine in ten.

E. My judgment is three in ten.

F. Also three in ten.

A. (To D) Where do you get that nine in ten?

D. This guy is not on his own, he's not free to do whatever he———. He has a wife and child to support.

C. He will have the expense and trouble of moving and he will lose his retirement benefits which means something after all.

B. Why should he leave a sure thing, a perfectly secure job? Only greed could lead him to———.

A. What's the matter with you guys? Security! Retirement! What're you, half dead? Be dynamic! Go forward, have a spirit of adventure. Nothing ventured, nothing gained!

E. My reasoning is this: The man is out of school almost five years; he is a relatively young man, school-wise or experience-wise. I feel he has nothing to lose by taking the chance of going with a new, young company and possibly going much farther than he will as an organization man in some huge outfit.

C. You're all talking as if this is the only chance he's ever going to get to move. Just because he turns down this job doesn't mean he has to stay put the rest of his life. Within two years or so he will get another offer so why should he go with a company that only has one chance in ten of making it. Statistics on the failure and success of new businesses show that the large majority actually succeed.

F. Yes, but the most he can lose on this change is moving expenses. I read in *The New York Times* or somewhere that there is a big demand for electrical engineers. Even if this company should fall through he can always get a job, probably at the same salary. I figure even if the company goes broke, he can still claim valuable experience in looking for another job later on. That's why I'd say three in ten.

C. That's true, if the company fails, it isn't a personal failure. I'll shift to three in ten.

D. I guess I will too.

B. Ok.

A. Ok.

E. That's what I said in the first place.

The initial individual decisions of the persons comprising this group were: 1 in 10, 3 in 10, 3 in 10, 7 in 10, 7 in 10, and 9 in 10. The mean of these values is 5 in 10 and the unanimous group decision is represented to be 3 in 10. Let us imagine that the subjects were also asked to record their personal decisions following the discussion and that it was pointed out to them that these might not agree in every case with the group consensus. In Figure 13-1, we have an imaginary but typical set of final positions compared with the initial positions. The two effects common to all the experiments we have cited can be observed in these data: the unanimous group decision is riskier than the mean of initial individual decisions; the final individual positions are generally riskier than the initial positions.

These data of Figure 13-1 are in one additional respect typical. The final range of opinion is not so wide as the initial one. The data are convergent. When individual judgments converge following group discussion a social psychologist thinks at once of the emergence of a group standard or norm and the operation of conformity forces. We will look first then at the study of conformity to see how much it can explain of the riskiness of group decisions.

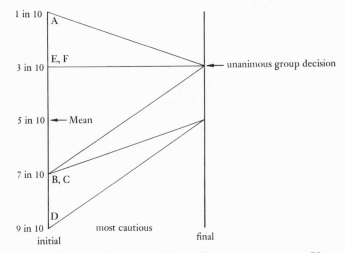

FIGURE 13-1. INITIAL POSITIONS, FINAL POSITIONS, AND THE UNANIMOUS GROUP DECISION ON A PROBLEM INVOLVING RISK

Conformity

It has occurred to more than one social psychologist that the convergence of opinion which develops when individuals become a group is a manifestation of the principle of balance (Heider, 1958). In Chapter 11 we discussed the principle of balance in connection with attitude change, giving close attention to the model formulated by Rosenberg and Abelson (1960) and briefly mentioning the related models of Cartwright and Harary (1956), Heider (1958), and Newcomb (1953). For the conformity problem it is convenient to symbolize elements and bonds as Newcomb (1953) has done, but our treatment is basically compatible with any of the models.

CONFORMITY AND THE BALANCE PRINCIPLE

The essential elements in a conformity or convergence situation are two persons (A and B) and some judgment or opinion or object of common concern (X). In addition to the elements there are relations among the elements. The relation between A and B can be positive (+), negative (−), or null. Positive relations include two sorts of things: a favorable sentiment such as liking, approval, admiration, etc., and a unit-forming relation of identification, of belonging together, ownership, or endorsement. Negative relations, correspondingly, either involve dislike or detachment. The null case is simply the absence of any relationship.

Consider subjects A and B in the group that discussed the proper advice to give an electrical engineer who was thinking of taking a job with a new company. Subject A, working individually, decided that the

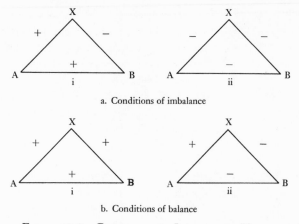

a. Conditions of imbalance

b. Conditions of balance

FIGURE 13-2.   BALANCED AND IMBALANCED TRIADS

engineer ought to take the job even if the chances that the new company would succeed were only 1 in 10. That decision may be designated "X" and the relation between A and X is initially positive since X was chosen by A; X belongs to A. Subject B, working individually, decided that the probabilities should be 7 in 10. By implication then, B has a negative relation with X since he has, in effect, rejected X. Of course, B is positively related to his own opinion which we could designate "Y" but Y can be disregarded for the present purposes. It only remains to say what relation exists between A and B. Perhaps there is a null relation, which is no relation at all, when they work individually. When A and B are brought together (with others) as a face-to-face group, with a common task, a positive relation of identification should be created between them. Perhaps there is also a positive relation of liking, since new acquaintances usually expect to like one another.

The three elements, A, B, and X are now related in the manner of Figure 13-2ai. Two persons who identify with one another and who perhaps like one another, disagree about a matter of common concern. This is a condition of imbalance. Triads of the A-B-X variety are considered to be balanced in either of two circumstances. They are balanced if all signs are positive which occurs when two people who like one another subscribe to the same opinion (Figure 2bi). Triads are also balanced when two signs are negative and one is positive, as, for instance, when two people who dislike one another have unlike opinions about the same X, one favoring a decision that the other opposes (Figure 2bii). The remaining possible pattern is a condition of imbalance. When all signs are negative, when two enemies oppose the same position or dislike the same object, the system is not balanced (Fig. 13-2aii).

The general conception of balance (developed at length in Chapter

11) is that people who like one another or who form a unit will expect to agree (to have similar opinions) and will wish to agree, whereas people who dislike one another will expect to disagree and will like it that way. Considerable evidence supporting this assumption is reported in Chapters 2 and 11. In Chapter 2 we reviewed work by Homans (1950) on the workmen in the Bank Wiring Room, work by Newcomb (1961) on undergraduate cliques at the University of Michigan, work by Hollingshead (1949) on high-school cliques at Elmtown, work by Kahl and Davis (1955) on "best friends" in Cambridge, Massachusetts, and more besides. From all of this work it appears that people who like one another or who are in some way identified with one another, tend to have similar values, interests, political convictions, occupations, and the like. In Chapter 11 there is a detailed description of the study we have called Fenwick's Art Display (Rosenberg, et al., 1960). This study shows among other things that if a store manager (A in our present model) likes modern art (X) and also likes Fenwick (B), then Fenwick is expected to like modern art. A departure from this pattern constitutes an imbalanced state and subjects in the experiment tended to put it right.

Newcomb (1953), in his discussion of the A-B-X treatment of balance, reports a demonstration of the principle that is particularly relevant to the conformity problem. In 1951 President Truman dismissed General MacArthur and public opinion in the United States was sharply divided over the President's action. Some college students were asked to guess whether their closest friends would be pro-Truman or pro-MacArthur. Of the forty-eight students who were themselves pro-Truman, forty-eight guessed that their friends would also be pro-Truman and none that their friends would be anti-Truman. Of the thirty-six students who were themselves anti-Truman, thirty-four guessed that their friends would be anti-Truman and two that their friends would be pro-Truman. In short, almost all the students predicted the opinions of their friends as if they were operating on the balance principle. If the principle is correct, we must believe that the two anti-Truman students whose friends did not agree with them felt some need to give up their friends or to convert them, or else to change their own minds about Truman.

Now we return to the A and B of the risk experiment, A and B who disagree about the odds the electrical engineer should accept. How can their imbalance be corrected? In many ways; if either one will change his mind to agree with the other that will do it, or if both will change a little so that they can agree on a compromise, that will do it. Alternatively they can both adhere to their decisions but then the principle of balance says they must reject one another. In fact, as you can see in Figure 13-1, each gave a little and they came to agreement on odds of 3 in 10.

Subjects A and B were not alone with their problem. There were four other subjects and some of these others were in disagreement with one another and with A and B. So the imbalance was a complex one but if all subjects felt positively toward one another, the forces for change on each one should have been toward the central tendency of the group. That was the general trend of the changes between the initial and final decisions. The members' opinions converged toward a central value. They seemed to be finding a norm that all members would support.

Newcomb (1953) has suggested that imbalance in a triad or a larger group provides the occasion for communicative acts. Members will talk to try to eliminate the imbalance. When a majority of a group agrees on a certain position and only one member deviates then a greatly disproportionate number of communications should be addressed to the deviant member. Persuasive talk should flow toward the member who is responsible for the imbalance. In a very important study Schachter (1951) has shown this to be the case. When stooges were planted in groups and played the role of deviant from the norm of the group they received a disproportionate number of communications, far more, for instance, than did stooges who subscribed to the most popular (the modal) position in the group. In the discussions of the Stoner problems that I have heard the flow of communications has, similarly, been toward the subjects who were "farthest out." In the Schachter experiment persistent deviants were eventually rejected by some of the other members, that is to say the rejecting members, after the meeting, said that they did not wish for any further association with the deviants. The interesting thing is that the communications addressed to deviants by rejecting members fell off very sharply whereas the communications to deviants from members who never did reject them never did fall off. It is as if some members attained balance by changing the sign of the relation between themselves and the deviant from positive to negative. Once that is done, a difference of opinion does not constitute imbalance and so there is no further need to communicate. Members who continued to accept the deviant had to seek balance by trying to change his views. The Schachter study has been substantially replicated in seven European nations so its findings appear not to be peculiarly American (Schachter, et al., 1954).

Newcomb (1953) has argued that the pressure to agree between two persons or in a group is a function of the strength of the interpersonal attraction and there is substantial research support for this generalization. Back (1951), for instance, found that subjects who started with different interpretations of the same material and who were given an opportunity to discuss the matter were influenced by one another as a direct function of attraction. Festinger, Schachter, and Back (1950) in their study of a housing project found a high correlation between a measure of attraction and a measure of "conformity in attitude." In the groups of strangers convened to discuss the Stoner problems it seems likely that attraction was very slight. Indeed one might reasonably question whether the relation between A and B was positive at all. In none of these experiments on risk was there any independent objective evidence of liking or attraction among the members. There are other factors that can cause convergence of opinion.

In Schachter's experiment and in the group discussions of the Stoner problems participants were free to argue, to cite evidence and authority, to give one another explicit signs of approval and disapproval. The groups discussing the risk problems had even been instructed to reach unanimity. Probably the opportunity to communicate freely and the direction to achieve unanimity contributed to the tendency toward convergence but there is reason to believe that the tendency exists even when these features are absent.

MINIMAL CONDITIONS FOR CONFORMITY

Since the groups that discussed the risk problems were directed to reach unanimous decisions the convergence of the initial opinions upon the group decision is fully accounted for by the experimental task. However, there was always also a convergence of the final individual, privately expressed, opinions. The six participants were more nearly of the same opinion after they had convened as a group than they were beforehand. This convergence was not explicitly requested by the experimenter. It is possible, however, that convergence of individual opinion would not have occurred had there not been an obligation to attain a public consensus. Pennington, Harary, and Bass (1958) have shown that individual opinion change is greater when subjects are instructed to discuss a question in order to arrive at a group consensus than when groups are simply asked to have a discussion without being required to make a group decision.

Marquis (1962) has done a variation of the Stoner experiment which shows that convergence toward a position of greater risk occurs even when there is no requirement to reach a unanimous decision. In each group he designated one person to be the leader; this man was to listen to the discussion and then, himself, to make the final decision. The members other than the leader were a set of advisers who could say what they thought but the decision itself and the responsibility for the decision belonged to one man. In these circumstances, with no necessity of reaching consensus, the final private opinions nevertheless converged—and on a position of greater risk. The groups Marquis created that were not required to reach group decisions did, however, permit free argument and expression. Subjects did try to persuade one another. No one as yet has created groups in which the members do not argue the risk problems but simply state their positions. There are other experiments in group dynamics which suggest that even in this much reduced situation some convergence would occur.

The classical study is that of Sherif (1947). Sherif set his subjects the task of estimating the extent of movement of a single point of light in a completely dark room. A light of this kind cannot be definitely localized because there is nothing in reference to which one can locate it. Such a light, though it is in fact perfectly stationary, will seem to move and these movements are likely to appear erratic in direction and extent. This effect, called the autokinetic effect, was discovered by astronomers staring at a single star in the night sky, before psychology began. Sherif used it to explore the emergence of group standards.

The subject was told: "When the room is completely dark, I shall give you the signal *Ready* and then show you a point of light. After a short time the light will start to move. A few seconds later the light will disappear. Then tell me the distance it moved" (Sherif, 1947, p. 79). The light was exposed to the subject by a small shutter controlled by the experimenter. Any subject's first judgments were likely to range rather widely but in the course of one hundred trials Sherif found that each subject settled down to a rather narrow range with a consistent central value. These ranges and standard values were quite different from one subject to another but very consistent for a given subject, even across several series of judgments made on different days. These individual judgments are analogous to the personal decisions made on the risk problems in advance of any group discussion.

What happened when individuals who had established individual ranges in private sessions were combined into groups of two or three and asked to report their judgments aloud? Their judgments converged. In one group of three, individual A started by guessing that the light moved about seven inches; B guessed that it moved two inches and C that it moved less than one inch. After several sessions together all three subjects were consistently guessing in the range between two and 4 inches. Sometimes judgments converged on a value nearer the larger extreme and sometimes on a value nearer the smaller extreme but the general outcome was convergence toward the central tendency of the group. In these groups there was no request for unanimity, no argument, no effort to persuade, no clear sanctions for disagreement and often no awareness of any social influence. Nevertheless the individuals were much closer together in their judgments after they had been convened as groups than before.

In the groups created by Sherif there is only the expression of individual judgment to produce convergence and this would seem to be a minimal condition. How can individuals converge unless they know one another's position?

Sherif's situation, however, is not the simplest social condition imaginable. The simplest condition would seem to be one in which individuals work in one another's presence but without any explicit communication, the coworking group. The empirical study of group processes began with the coworking group, with comparisons between the performance of individuals working alone and working side by side. In one of these F. H. Allport (1924) had subjects judge the degree of pleasantness of odors in a series and the heaviness of a series of weights. He obtained a result which suggests that the wish to agree, to establish a norm, exists even in the coworking group. Subjects made fewer extreme judgments, that is judgments toward the ends of the scale, in the "together" condition than they did when working alone. It is as if they were trying to avoid deviation from a *presumed* central tendency of the group.

In other researches F. H. Allport (1924) compared the work of individuals alone with individuals together on a variety of tasks: problems in multiplication, verbal reasoning, perceptual judgments, etc. Generally in situations in which speed and quantity of work were measured more effort was expended by individuals together than by individuals alone. Allport called this phenomenon "social facilitation." Quite recently (1962) he has said that social facilitation, like the avoidance of extreme judgments, strikes him as an effort to "belong with" those around us. The subjects in these experiments did not communicate and they knew that no comparisons whatever were to be made of their productions. Still it seems to Allport that each one felt a concern not to fall behind the others, not to "fail to measure up," to be at one with those around him.

The initial individual judgments for the experiments on risk have all been made in coworking situations and so we can make no comparison with judgments made in solitude. Since the judgments were made on a scale, subjects may have felt some need to avoid the extremes and the danger of deviation from a presumed central opinion. If this were the case there would be a convergence of opinion between initial solitary judgments and judgments obtained after discussion still more striking than the convergence that appears in the data so far reported.

There seems to be an almost ineradicable tendency for members of a group to move toward agreement. It occurs when there is no instruction to reach a consensus. It occurs when there is no opportunity to argue. It even occurs, incipiently, when the members do not know one another's opinions but can only guess at them. It occurs when the positive relations among the members are very weak. Festinger and Thibaut

(1951) varied "pressure toward uniformity" in groups but found some change toward uniformity following a discussion in all groups under all conditions. Sherif's subjects and the subjects in the risk experiments, introduced to one another on the occasion of the experiment, must have had minimally strong positive bonds.

The autokinetic effect and the Stoner problems and Allport's aesthetic judgments do not have objectively correct answers and that may be the reason why opinions converged. I say that the problems do not have objectively correct answers because individuals, who understand them and who possess the relevant allowable information, if they work in isolation will not necessarily arrive at the same answer. On matters of this kind a consensus may be essential because the consensus is the only reality (Festinger, 1954; Schachter, 1959). Asch, in a vastly influential series of experiments (1956), has studied conformity effects with problems that do have objective answers.

THE ASCH EXPERIMENT

If you were a subject for Asch you would have been recruited for an experiment in visual perception. On arriving at the designated room you find Dr. Asch already there and also some other subjects like yourself. Subjects are to be seated in a row and you take the position next to the far left (actually you have been jockeyed into that position). Dr. Asch says that the experiment will involve the discrimination of length of lines. Before you, in the front of the room, is a single vertical line and just to the right of it, on cards, are three lines differing in length and numbered 1, 2, and 3. The cards will change but one of the three lines at the right will always be equal to a standard line on the left and it will be your job to select the correct line and report it by number. Judgments are to be spoken aloud, which seems to you a rather poor experimental procedure, but then that is the way with these pseudo-sciences. The order of reporting is from right to left down the row of subjects so you will be next to the last.

The first lines appear and the match is an obvious one. In fact the standard is 10 inches tall and the comparison lines are: Number 1 = 8¾ inches; Number 2 = 10 inches; Number 3 = 8 inches. It is quite easy to see that Number 2 is the correct answer, and apparently it is easy for everyone since the judges all report that number and so, when your turn comes, do you. The second trial is equally easy and the judgments are equally consistent and you begin to wonder whether the experimenter has not made some mistake and selected stimuli that are too obvious. The third set of lines appears and the match is as easily made as on the first two trials; it is Number 3 this time. The first subject in order calls out his answer. He says, "Number one." Number 1 is *obviously* longer than the standard; in fact it is three-quarters of an inch longer. But the second subject says "Number one" and so does the third and so do they all and now it is your turn. On subsequent trials a unanimous majority very frequently reports an answer you know to be incorrect. This happened, you will later learn, because all the "subjects" other than yourself were confederates of the experimenter reporting falsely on a prearranged schedule.

The situation is an epistemological nightmare. The judgments involved concern the nature of physical reality and they are not the sort of near-threshold difficult judgment on which some variation is to be expected. The equivalence between the standard line and the line you perceive to be of the same length is an objective fact. The proof of its objectivity is a set of comparison data Asch collected for the case in which subjects judged the same lines but each subject worked all alone. They almost invariably reported correctly; of thirty-seven subjects one made one error and one made two errors. These are judgments on which one expects a unanimous opinion. Sherif's subjects, working alone, did not all make the same judgments of the extent of movement in a pinpoint of light and had F. H. Allport's subjects made their asethetic judgments in isolation we can be sure that they would not have perfectly agreed with one another. To separate unanimity and the clear evidence of one's senses is to set in opposition the two means by which we recognize reality. It is a powerful situation.

One can see the power of the Asch situation in the distress of subjects who are in the presence of a false majority. Bogdonoff and his associates (1961) working at the Duke University Medical Center, have obtained evidence that there are physiological effects consequent upon deviance. While the subjects were working at the perceptual-judgment task sequential physiological measures were taken of the increase in plasma-free fatty acid level which is an index of central nervous system arousal. When a naïve subject was confronted with the majority opposition the level of the fatty acids went up. For those who yielded to the majority the level was reduced, but for those who resisted the group the level remained high.

About one-third of the reports made by subjects in the Asch situation are not correct but are in accordance with the group judgment. Subjects can be characterized as largely independent or as largely conforming though the greater number by far conform on some trials and are independent on others.

The Asch method is a slow one for accumulating data since there is only one subject to a group and Crutchfield has invented a more economical procedure (see Krech, Crutchfield, and Ballachey, 1962 for a comprehensive report). All participants are real subjects; groups work simultaneously but not face-to-face. Each subject is in a booth which screens him from the others. The lines to be judged are projected on a wall visible to all subjects. Each one has in his booth a set of switches he uses to signal his judgment. And each one sees lights that are purported to reveal the decisions of the other subjects. Decisions are made one at a time and in a fixed order. In fact the lights are not responsive to the judgments actually made by others but are controlled by the experimenter in such a way as to confront each subject with cases of unanimously incorrect response. Furthermore, each subject believes himself to be the last in the order of report and so all are exposed to the same conformity pressure. Crutchfield's procedure speeds things up.

With the Crutchfield technique more than six hundred people have been exposed to contrary group opinions and substantial amounts of conformity obtained with a wide variety of tasks (see Krech, Crutchfield, and Ballachey, 1962). One problem that stays close to the original, in that it is a problem for visual perception, presents side by side a star and a circle and subjects are asked which has the larger area. When the circle was a full one-third larger, 46 per cent of a sample of subjects subscribed to a contrary majority opinion. Many individuals have even yielded on opinion and attitude items where one would think that deviation would be bearable. Sometimes these opinions have been the sort of thing on which a subject might reasonably regard himself as the best authority. Military officers, when they were questioned privately, all rejected the statement, "I doubt whether I would make a good leader," but, with a majority against them, 37 per cent accepted it. Majority pressures have brought individuals to accept such manifestly absurd statements as: "The United States is largely populated by old people, 60 to 70 per cent being over sixty-five years of age." Positions that were ideologically repugnant to subjects questioned individually have been adopted under pressure. Of a sample of college students 58 per cent agreed: "Free speech being a privilege rather than a right, it is proper for a society to suspend free speech when it feels itself threatened."

The differences of length presented by Asch are real and sizeable. A subject working all alone at these judgments can feel greater confidence in his decisions than can a subject who is all alone with the autokinetic phenomenon. Because Sherif's subjects could not be quite sure what they saw one would expect the opinions of others to be more influential with them than with Asch's subjects. However, the Asch case balances the objectivity of the judgment by increasing the power of the majority. In Sherif's groups of three there was no majority opinion but simply three opinions. Subjects were not confronted with a norm; they were given the occasion to forge a norm, and this could be done by converging on a central tendency since judgments were free to assume any value on the continuum of distance. Asch's subjects had only three discontinuous alternatives and usually there was no compromise position available. Sherif's is a study of the emergence of norms and Asch's is a study of the impact of norms with absolute conformity the only alternative to deviance on a particular trial.

The Sherif subject in the group situation found himself with only one or two others whereas Asch has sometimes arrayed majorities as large as fifteen against one subject. However, Asch has tried the effects of majorities of different sizes. The case most comparable to that of Sherif's subject is that in which a single confederate disagrees with a single naïve subject. Here there is no norm or majority opinion but simply, as in Sherif's studies, a single other opinion. It is very interesting to find that the one opposing opinion produces a few more false responses in the subject than occur when he is all alone. The result suggests again, as do F. H. Allport's findings with coworking individuals, that the impulse to agree is coincident with the creation of interpersonal bonds. Even when the task in no sense requires agreement this is so and even when agreement means the assertion of manifest falsehoods.

Asch's inquiries into the importance of the size of the majority resulted in an interesting discovery. The strength of the conformity effect increases as the number of confederates increases only up to a majority of three. Beyond that value, increasing the size of the majority results in no further significant increments in conformity. This fact gives some guidance to anyone interested in mapping the conformity situation into the terms of a balance model. So long as only two or three persons are opposed on an issue it may be best to represent each one individually, together with his stand on the issue and his bonds with each other person (Figure 13-3a). But when three or more are joined together in a common opinion it may be possible simply to map the totality as "Group" and represent the Group's position on the issue and the Group's relation with the remaining individual (Figure 13-3b). Three-agreed is, it would appear, the clotting point.

THE ASCH EXPERIMENT AND THE BALANCE PRINCIPLE

The Asch situation can be mapped into the A-B-X form of the balance model and the result is prediction of the gross outcomes but not of the finer ones. The failures of the model point to the places where it needs to be repaired or elaborated. The naïve subject shall be A and, in place of B, we had better use G for the group. The X of the model is any one of the judgments which the group reports (thereby establishing a positive G to X relation) and which A sees to be false (thereby establishing a negative A to X relation). Between A and G there is a positive relation since they find themselves engaged in the same task at the same time and, furthermore, have agreed with one another on the first two judgments. The triad is not in balance since there are two positive relations and one negative; A and G though positively bonded find themselves in disagreement.

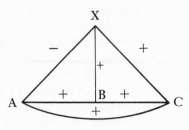
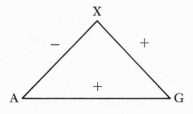

a. Members of the majority
separately represented

b. The majority represented as
a single group

FIGURE 13-3.   MAPPINGS OF THE ASCH CONFORMITY SITUATION IN TERMS
OF BALANCE

The resultant state of imbalance cannot long be comfortably endured if balance theory is correct. Presumably the subject is in distress what with fatty acids in his blood and all. What is it that the balance model says cannot happen? The subject cannot settle on the view that he himself understands Asch's instructions and is a good judge of visual extent while also taking the view that the members of the majority are a bunch of fine fellows, as good at perceptual problems as himself and having an equally good understanding of the task while also recognizing that the group believes X whereas he himself believes not-X. These ideas are supposed to constitute an unendurable combination and it is, in fact, a rare subject who asserts anything like the combination above. However, with some judgments that are conspicuously matters of opinion an occasional subject will say that he just reconciled himself to a difference of opinion. Not without discomfort in most cases, however. Newcomb (1953) has hypothesized that when the attraction between A and B is not very strong the need to agree is not general but is restricted to matters on which one must reckon with the position of the other. Perhaps the weakness of the bond between A and G makes it possible for an occasional person to endure imbalance with respect to some X.

Imbalance predicts change but not necessarily a change to agreement about X. In about 30 per cent of the cases it is agreement that produces balance and that agreement is produced by the conforming response of A. In the remaining cases, the larger number after all, conformity does not occur and agreement is not reached. However, the situation is not usually left imbalanced. When subjects maintain their independence they commonly give an account of their mental processes which suggests severance of the positive bond with the group. Either there is a null bond between A and G or the bond has become negative. In either case the triad is balanced since one positive relation and one negative relation (the disagreement about X) are consistent either with a third negative relation or with a null relation.

What do the independent subjects say? One will have decided that the group has not understood the instructions; another that the group is subject to an optical illusion from which A himself is immune. Another subject will find the fault in himself; he is poor at numbers or at spatial imagery or he has poor eyesight. Another will explain the disagreement by differentiating his own circumstances from those of the group without enshrining either judgment as the correct one. They view the lines from different angles. These thoughts break down the unity of A and G, segregating one from another. Thinking can also take a more affective line and A can decide that the group is stupid or that most of them are, like sheep, copying the man who speaks first.

Balance is most commonly restored by severing the positive bond between A and G and next most commonly by a change in A's judgment to accord with the judgment of G. How else could balance be obtained? There is only a single relation remaining to be considered: the positive bond of endorsement between G and X. If that would assume a negative value then A and G would agree. However, the group G never does change the judgments it reports and that is because they are the confederates of the experimenter. But the principle of balance is a model of cognition, not of objective reality. Perhaps A can "think away" the positive bond between G and X even though it will not change on the level of verbal report. And an occasional subject does so, by seeing through the deception, by realizing that the members of G are confederates, reporting falsely for hire or for the fun of it. It follows that they privately see the lines as A does and that their true judgmental relation with X is negative. There is no imbalance left and A smiles with amusement at the whole charade. However, this is a rare outcome. The deception is cleverly contrived and is not often discovered.

There are three simple alternatives, any one of which will restore balance to the triad that includes one naïve subject and an opposed majority. What determines the selection of one alternative rather than another? It is reasonable to expect the strength of a relation between two elements to be inversely related to the likelihood of that relation being changed. Asch varied the objective discrepancy between the standard line and the line the majority called equal to the standard and found that, as the discrepancy increased, the number of subjects who yielded to the majority grew smaller. In other words, as the judgments made by the majority became increasingly grotesque, subjects became less willing to go along, though Asch notes that even a discrepancy of six inches did not produce independence in all. As the discrepancy grows greater in the perceptual judgment problem the correct answer becomes more obvious and the problem easier. The easier the judgment, then, the smaller the number of conformers. Coleman, Blake, and Mouton (1958) have found a high correlation between the difficulty of general information items and the tendency to conform. Krech, Crutchfield, and Ballachey (1962) subscribe to the general proposition that conformity declines as the task grows easier and increases with difficulty. This proposition is easily translated into the terms of the balance model. With an easier task A will feel more confident of his judgment that X is incorrect and so the negative relation between A and X will be strong. The subject A will then be less likely to yield in this case than he will be when the task is difficult and he feels confident of his judgment.

When the relation between A and G is strong A should be unlikely to restore balance by rejecting G and likely to restore it by the major alternative method—conforming to G. Gerard (1954) and also Jackson and Saltzstein (1958) found that conformity increased with the attractiveness of a group to the subject and greater attractiveness perhaps implies a stronger positive relation. In one of Crutchfield's studies (Krech, Crutchfield, and Ballachey, 1962) a very real positive bond was deliberately created between A and G. All the members together were competing for a fifty-dollar prize which was to be shared equally among them if they should win. This common fate ought to have strengthened the positive bond between A and G and, in these groups of Crutchfield's, conformity was more frequent than in groups of the usual kind.

The remaining positive relation is the one between G and the false judgment X. Apparently no group of confederates has as yet foresworn X and decided to tell the truth. The objective bond has never given way and the cognitive bond, the belief that G supports judgment X, has very seldom given way. For the most part, balance has been restored by altering one of the other two relations, by yielding or by rejecting G.

The balance model easily *accommodates* the findings which suggest that relations are less likely to change when they are more confidently maintained or more extremely polarized. In its present form, however, the explicit model provides only for three sorts of relation: the positive, the negative, and the null. It makes no provision for degrees of positiveness and negativeness or for variations in the firmness or intensity of bonds.

The model does not even tell us whether degree of polarization and intensity are one dimension or two.

There are some findings which the balance model cannot gracefully accomodate. Numerous investigators have found that the large individual differences in amount of conforming behavior show some consistency across different kinds of tasks. (See, for example, Blake, Helson, and Mouton [1957]; Tuddenham [1957]; Rosner [1957].) Conformity is then something of a personal characteristic and it is related to other personal characteristics. The most interesting of these relationships is the finding (Krech, Crutchfield, and Ballachey, 1962) that a strong conformity bent is associated with pronounced feelings of personal inadequacy and inferiority. A result easily understood. The man who feels inferior will set the group's judgment above his own and do what the group does. But this is common sense rather than the balance model we are using.

The only way that I can see to represent the distinction A makes between his own poor quality as a judge and the good quality of the group is with a negative relation of disassociation between A and G. But if there is a negative relation at this point the triad is balanced; A is a poor judge and G a good judge and so the two judges disagree. Things are as they should be. In the balance representation low self-esteem should be an alternative to conformity not a cause of conformity. These are ways to alter the balance model so as to bring it into line with the facts but alterations are required.

The balance model also predicts some conformity outcomes that do not seem likely ever to be obtained. Consider the case above in which A has a poor opinion of himself and a good opinion of the group. The negative relation between A and G required disagreement about X for a state of balance. But now what if the group were to answer truly instead of falsely. A ought to be motivated to report falsely in order to put himself in disagreement with G. Would that happen? A negative bond between A and G would also exist if A thought very well of himself and very ill of the group. What if a detested or despised group reported truly; would A be motivated to report falsely in order not to agree with them? He might if his rejection of the group were founded in a bad opinion of their ability to make perceptual judgments. He probably would not disagree if his rejection of the group were founded on a dislike of their politics. The simple A-B-X triad does not even make this distinction. On the other hand the hypotheses probably would not come to mind without the aid of the theory.

One experiment (Gerard, 1961) has been done which shows that a balance-type theory can lead to the discovery of unexpected phenomena in connection with conformity. It was Festinger's dissonance theory that suggested the experiment. Some subjects were given reason to believe that they were very good at making perceptual judgments and other subjects were convinced that they were poor at it. All subjects then participated in an Asch-type procedure but with a difference. The subject had electrodes attached to his arm and these electrodes, he was told, would pick up his impulse, whether it was to go along with the group or to answer correctly. Some subjects who thought themselves good judges and some who thought themselves poor judges were then given to believe that it was their consistent inclination to conform. Afterwards all subjects were asked to rate the attractiveness of the group.

The subject who thought himself a good judge ought to have experienced strong dissonance on learning that he was disposed to conform. The only way to reduce this dissonance, to account for his unaccountable behavior, would be to rate the group as extremely attractive and so perhaps explain his impulse to please them. The subject who thought himself a poor judge would have no difficulty accounting for his supposed tendency to follow the lead of the others. He would therefore experience little dissonance and so have no need to rate the group as very attractive. And that is the way the results went.

CONFORMITY AND THE SHIFT TO RISK

What can conformity account for in the behavior of the groups with which we started, the groups discussing Stoner's problems? It can account for the convergence of individual judgments toward a central value. That is in fact exactly what happened to the judgments of Sherif's subjects. Probably the impulse to agree is coincidental with the creation of a group. However new the acquaintance, however temporary the aggregation, however restricted their common concerns, there seems always to be enough of a positive bond among the members to motivate a balancing convergence of opinion.

However, the novelty in Stoner's research is the fact that the final decision was not the mean of the initial positions but a position somewhat riskier than the mean. Stoner found convergence toward a central value in the final judgments but the striking finding is that the more conservative initial opinions converged more sharply than the riskier initial positions. Both the unanimous group decision and the mean of the final individual decisions fell, not on the exact center of the original opinions but on a position riskier than the center.

The experiments of Asch and of Crutchfield do not yield data converging on a mean position; a shift to a particular judgment is the outcome for their "yielders." However, the forces producing this shift cannot explain the shift to risk that Stoner found. A subject of Asch's changes his judgment because the norm is located elsewhere; there is a consensus on a different judgment. In Stoner's groups there are no such norms, no majorities, no confederates, to draw the judgments of subjects. But something there must be, beyond conformity, to bring these judgments to a position that is consistently on one side of the mean.

A Leadership that Favors Risk

The decision of a group will settle on a position that is not the mean of the group if some members are disproportionately influential. When one member is notably more influential than the others he is a leader. Like the leader of a group of nomadic anthropoids he is the one "out front," the one who seems to select the way that all will go. Perhaps the shift to risk in group decisions on the Stoner problems is a phenomenon of leadership. The group decisions depart from the mean of the individual decisions in a consistent direction. If this departure is to be explained by leadership it must be shown that those who are outstandingly influential, those who assume leadership, are for some reason inclined to take greater risks than are the less influential.

LEADERSHIP RESULTING FROM OFFICE, STATUS, OR POSITION IN A COMMUNICATION NET

There are many factors that can cause influence to be unequally divided among the members of a group. A small group that belongs to a larger organization, a committee of a club or a faculty or a corporation, is likely to have an official leader, the chairman, either appointed or elected. Such a formal or official leader is often called the *head* in social psychology to distinguish him from an informal leader. The head of a group is likely to be disproportionately influential but he is not invariably so; *headship* can be rejected. In any case the Stoner groups were headless, they had no formal leadership. Like the majority of the small groups created for the purposes of social psychological study the Stoner groups began existence with no official distinctions of status among the members.

If the members of a group are selected randomly from a population in which sex and occupational status vary then, even though no distinctions are officially recognized in the face-to-face situation, the familiar differences of external status can affect interaction. In large metropolitan centers of the United States jurors are selected by a random process from voter registration lists and so a particular jury is likely to include both men and women and may include professional men, business proprietors, and unskilled laborers. However, the requirement in our legal system that jury decisions be unanimous creates an official equality of power and the general presumption is that jurors will treat one another as equals. Strodtbeck and his associates (1958) at the University of Chicago have shown that jurors do not, in fact, function as equals.

The deliberations of a real jury are private and so may not be studied by social scientists. The Chicago researchers drew subjects by lot from the regular jury pools of the Chicago and St. Louis courts and created mock juries which listened to recordings of real trials and then deliberated and returned verdicts in the manner of real juries. The findings are derived from ninety-one such juries and it seems very probable that they may be generalized to the deliberations of real juries. The foreman of a jury is a "head" elected by the membership. Men were much more often elected to this position of potential influence than were women, and persons of higher occupational status were elected foremen in greatly disproportionate numbers compared to persons of lower occupational status.

In group interaction, participation is often very unequal, a few people may do most of the talking, and the participation level of a member is generally related to his influentiality. In the Chicago mock juries, males and persons of high occupational status were outstandingly active participators, were disproportionately powerful in shaping the final jury decision and seemed to the jury members to have special competence for the jury task. In deliberations lasting only an hour or two and governed by a strong value on equality, differences of external status were nevertheless powerfully influential.

The groups that have discussed the Stoner problems have been either all male or all female and so sexual status cannot account for any inequality of influence that may have existed. Furthermore these groups have been occupationally uniform—all undergraduates, all graduate students of industrial management, or all senior business executives. External status did not determine whatever leadership arose and so the shift to risk cannot be explained in terms of the possibly risk-prone character of men, in contrast with women, or of business managers, in contrast with unskilled workers.

It is certain that mixing the sexes or occupations would affect what happens in a discussion of the Stoner problems though no one knows what systematic changes would occur. I once put together a group of three men and three women to work out advice for the electrical engineer of the first Stoner problem. They talked for thirty-five minutes, the usual group takes five or ten, and then only concluded because I asked them to. By coincidence the three men had all made the same individual decision, a more conservative decision than any of the women made. The males solidified into a determined subgroup and pulled sexual status on the females. Witness the remark: "Don't you think this really is a decision for a man to make?" The girls, protestingly and with mental reservations, went conservative. However, the results in the literature are founded on uniform groups and cannot be explained by either sex or occupational status.

In addition to official headship and external status a privileged position in the communication network of a group can create leadership. By isolating the members of a group from one another, an experimenter can control the channels of communication among them. Leavitt (1951), for example, seated five persons around a table with vertical partitions separating one from another, and assigned them a problem-solving task. The subjects were allowed to communicate with one another only by passing notes through slots in the partitions. By changing the slots that were open any desired network of communications could be created. In what is called a "circle net" each person can communicate with those on his immediate right and left but with no others. In what is called a "wheel net" there is a central person with whom all others can exchange messages but they are prohibited from communicating with one another. The peripheral persons connect with the central person like spokes to the center of a wheel but these human spokes are not connected with one another; it is a wheel without a perimeter. Experimental arrangements of this kind capture one abstract feature of many organizations: the formal "channels of communication" in the church, the army, the government, or a business. Anyone would guess that the person in a "central" position in a communication network, a position connected with many others, has a superior opportunity to be influential.

Numerous studies have compared the efficiency of network patterns for the solution of problems of different kinds and also for the satisfaction they give to the membership (for example, Leavitt [1951]; Christie, Luce, and Macy [1952]; Shaw [1954]; Gilchrist, Shaw, and Walker [1955]; Shaw, Rothschild, and Strickland [1957]). In many of these studies the all-channel net, in which each person can communicate with each other, produced a solution in shorter time and with fewer errors than did any other net. The all-channel net has usually also been associated with a higher level of group satisfaction than has any other net. The satisfaction of the individual member has proved to be related to his centrality in the net. And the likelihood of emerging as leader of the group is also, as one would anticipate related to centrality. Berkowitz (1956) has even found that subjects with the personality trait of "low ascendance" when they are repeatedly placed centrally in a net come to behave like leaders in the group task.

Centrality can produce leadership but centrality like headship and external status will not account for the leadership that appears in Stoner's groups. Communication was completely open in the discussion of these groups and the position of one member as good as that of any other. With structural positions and external status both equated we might wonder whether any leadership, any differential influence, would arise. It does arise and indeed the emergence of leadership in groups of this general kind, made up of college students who are unacquainted with one another or very slightly acquainted, has been much studied.

EMERGENT LEADERSHIP

One of the first laboratories for the study of interaction in small groups was founded at Harvard University in 1947 by Robert F. Bales (1950). The physical facility is simply a large room for the group under study and an adjoining room for observers who listen to the proceedings and watch through windows with one-way vision. The windows, which look like mirrors from inside the main room, are not there to deceive subjects but simply to minimize interaction with the observers; subjects in a group are usually told that they are under observation. Typically the subjects have been Harvard undergraduates, randomly composed into groups, and unacquainted with one another. There is a rather standard task and it has some resemblance to the Stoner problems. Each subject has a five-page summary of facts about a problem of human relations which faces an administrator. A group is given forty minutes in which to discuss the case and arrive at a recommendation for action, to be made to the administrator.

For the members of a Bales group or a Stoner group there is no initial differentiation of roles. A role (see Chapter 4) is a set of expectancies applied to individuals in a given category and role performance is the behavior covered by the expectancies. An institutionalized role, such as the role of student or physician, exists as a stable set of expectancies awaiting new recruits and shaping their performance. In the Bales group there is initially only one rather vague role for everybody—to work on the problems, listen when not talking, forego personal abuse, and the like. All members are likely to meet these expectancies but in other dimensions, not specified by the initial common roles, performances will vary. One subject will have a great many ideas and will do more than his share of talking. Another one will say almost nothing. A third may chiefly make himself agreeable by reacting favorably to the ideas of others, and a fourth may elect to be disagreeable. If the same group meets a number of times (Slater, 1955) their individual interpretations of the group-member role may be consistently maintained. When that happens, of course, the expectancies the members have of one another will become appropriately differentiated. You know that this has occurred by the reactions to uncharacteristic performance: "What's wrong with Bill today that he has so little to say?" In these informal groups, which must create their own structure, differential role performance is prior to differential expectancy. What if a group, which had reason to go on meeting for a long time, suffered the loss of a member whose characteristic contributions were valued—perhaps Bill who always had the best ideas and who kept everyone from talking at once? One can imagine that Bill's characteristic performance would be named and assume reality as a slot needing to be filled. "We need a new 'chairman.' " And so a true role might be created out of a characteristic interpretation of a very generic role.

What are the dimensions of variation in individual performance? They can be discovered in the direct observation of the interaction process or in reports members of the group make about one another's performances. Bales first began to develop a systematic procedure for analyzing social interaction when he became interested in accounting for the success of Alcoholics Anonymous. He would attend meetings and try to take notes on who spoke to whom and what kind of thing was said. In his Harvard laboratory this scheme (Bales, 1950) became the method of "interaction process analysis" by which the observers behind the one-way window keep a chronological record of the source and addressee of each expressive act and sort the acts by content into twelve categories. These categories have such designations as "Asks for information," "Gives opinion," "Shows antagonism," etc. The complete list appears as Figure 13-4. Using these categories, interaction process analysis is able to describe the activities of each person in a group as a twelve-dimensional profile.

After a meeting, group members can be asked questions which will reveal the differences they have detected in one another's performances. "Who contributed the best ideas for solving the problem?" "How well did you personally like each of the other members?" "Which member of the group would you say stood out most definitely as a leader in the discussion?" Answers can be made comparable by asking for rankings of all members or ratings on some numerical scale.

The direct study of interaction and the analysis of ratings and rankings converge on a single conclusion (Bales, 1958; Carter, 1954). There are three principal dimensions in which individual performances differ. One of these is "activity"; how much does a man talk? Activity ranks are directly obtainable from the interaction records. A second dimension is "task ability," and this is revealed by members' ratings of one another. It is also reflected, in the interaction record, in the number of problem-solving attempts each person makes. The third dimension is "likeability" which is obtained from members' ratings and, in interaction, is reflected

Social-emotional area: positive	A	1. *shows solidarity*, raises other's status, gives help, reward
		2. *shows tension release*, jokes, laughs, shows satisfaction
		3. *agrees*, shows passive acceptance, understands, concurs, complies
Task area: neutral	B	4. *gives suggestion*, direction, implying autonomy for other
		5. *gives opinion*, evaluation, analysis, expresses feeling, wish
		6. *gives orientation*, information, repeats, clarifies, confirms
	C	7. *asks for orientation*, information, repetition, confirmation
		8. *asks for opinion*, evaluation, analysis, expression of feeling
		9. *asks for suggestion*, direction, possible ways of action
Social-emotional area negative	D	10. *disagrees*, shows passive rejection, formality, withholds help
		11. *shows tension*, asks for help, withdraws out of field
		12. *shows antagonism*, deflates other's status, defends or asserts self

KEY

A Positive Reactions   C Questions
B Attempted Answers   D Negative Reactions

FIGURE 13-4. THE SYSTEM OF CATEGORIES USED IN INTERACTION PROCESS ANALYSIS

by the frequency with which a member reacts positively to the contributions of others.

All three of the dimensions of individual variation are somewhat related to popular conceptions of leadership. After the first session of a group it often happens that members' positions on one dimension are closely related to their positions on the other dimensions (Bales, 1958).

The man credited with the best ideas is likely to be the one who has had the highest rate of participation. The man credited with the best ideas is also often the best-liked. In later sessions Slater (1955) has shown that these dimensions become increasingly independent, and Bales (1958) holds that over a large range of members, meetings, and groups the dimensions tend to be uncorrelated with one another.

From the three major dimensions of individual performance, Bales (1958) has constructed a typology of common varieties of leadership. A member who is high on activity and on task-ability ratings but less high on likeability may be called the "task specialist." A member who is high on likeability but less high on activity and on task ability may be called the "social specialist," Thibaut and Kelley (1959) call him a "maintenance specialist." It is a common thing to see the leadership of a group divided between two persons filling these two complementary roles.

Any group or organization has two principal problems to solve: the achievement of the purposes for which it exists, the business of the group; and the provision of personal satisfactions to individual members sufficient to keep them together, to maintain their interdependence. There is an inherent difficulty, that Bales has emphasized, in one member attempting to meet both of these needs simultaneously. Consider the case of a college seminar. Its business is to come as near as possible to the truth about questions raised. If several arguments are offered, arguments that oppose one another, the relentless pursuit of truth requires that one identify those ideas that are better and those that are worse. But ideas have sponsors and the evaluation of the idea reflects back upon the sponsor. Those who are shown to be wrong suffer some loss of self-esteem and may wish to withdraw from the group that gave them this unpleasant experience. The relentless pursuit of social welfare on the other hand requires that all ideas, of whatever quality, be received with enthusiasm and then it is truth that must suffer. It is hard for one man to work steadily at the task and also work steadily at group maintenance and so it often happens that one member keeps his eye on the task while another devotes himself to emotional repairs.

However, social and task leadership are not always kept apart; there is also the kind of leader whom Bales and his associates call the "Great Man." This is the leader who is high on all three dimensions: task ability, activity, and likeability. Since the three dimensions tend to be uncorrelated over groups, Great Men cannot be very numerous. However, there is some evidence that whoever is "Great" in one of these headless groups is likely to be "Great" in others. Borgatta, Couch, and Bales (1954) identified eleven men who, in their respective groups, ranked high on all three leadership dimensions. These men were then placed in new groups, not once but three times, and seven of them placed at the tops of all the groups in which they participated.

Persistent leadership suggests a personality with a need or a talent or a potential for leadership. The notion that leadership is a trait of personality, something that some possess and some do not or, at any rate, that some possess in higher degree and some in lesser degree is popular with military men and headmasters. Properly qualified it is true. If leadership were a completely general trait then a person who emerged as leader in one group would emerge as leader in all groups and that is clearly not true. Alexander Woollcott was a "star" among those who met at the Algonquin Hotel but he might not have been a star among the New York Yankees. It is equally obvious that leadership is not perfectly specific, that Woollcott would have been influential in almost any group that valued acidulous wit.

The study by Borgatta, et al. testifies that extreme leadership in a certain kind of discussion group is somewhat general. During World War II the Assessment Staff of the Office of Strategic Services used the "headless" group discussion as a test for measuring leadership potential among candidates for the OSS. Bass (1960) has reviewed the many studies relating leadership in this kind of situation to real-life situations. The (relatively) real-life situations included ratings on leadership potential while serving as NROTC cadets on a summer cruise, ratings by superiors on success as foremen in shipyards, ratings by supervisors on success as Civil Service administrators. The correlations between emergence as a leader in the headless group and leadership evaluation in real situations are all positive and this is evidence that leadership is somewhat general. On the other hand the correlations are all low and that is evidence that leadership is somewhat specific. Gibb is the author of a very sensible discussion (1947) of the issue of generality and specificity in leadership.

R. Mann (1959) has reviewed studies of group leadership carried out from 1900 to 1957 in an attempt to discover the personality characteristics that are most generally related to leadership. Mann was ingenious in finding ways to combine the results of all these studies. He found slight tendencies for leaders to be more dominant than rank-and-file members and more masculine and better adjusted and the like. However the one personality characteristic that was associated in impressively consistent degree with leadership was superior intelligence. This is a reasonable result since general intelligence should make for superior task ability on many kinds of task. Still it is not clear that intelligence of a very high order will make for leadership in every sort of group. Hollingworth (1942) found that, among children, the leader was likely to be more intelligent but not too much so. When there was a difference of more than 30 IQ points a leader-follower relation either did not develop or, if it developed, did not last very long.

It is clear then that leadership, of one kind or another, usually does develop in "headless" groups. We must, therefore, expect it to have developed in the groups that discussed the Stoner problems. If there should be some reason for this leadership to be regularly associated with risk-taking, in the way that leadership generally is related to intelligence, we will have the explanation of the shift to risk.

EMERGENT LEADERSHIP IN THE STONER GROUPS

For his original group Stoner checked to see whether the members who initially took riskier positions did more talking than members who took conservative positions. Level of participation is a dimension of leadership, one that in initial meetings is often related to rated task ability. However, Stoner did not find any relation between level of participation and the riskiness of the individual's position. Wallach, Kogan, and Bem (1962) inquired about leadership or influentiality in a different way. After the group discussions each subject was asked to rank everyone in the group (except himself) in terms of how much each had influenced the group decision. These ranks were significantly correlated with the riskiness of the initial individual decisions, though the correlations were very small (.32 for males and .22 for females). Marquis (1962) also asked his subjects about the influence exerted by the members and also found that those thought to have been more influential were initially riskier.

What does the relation between risk and perceived influence mean? It is of course an accurate perception. The groups have in fact taken up positions riskier than their central tendency and so the risk-prone members have indeed been more influential. But is it the members who were responsible for the influence or is it the position they assumed, the arguments they used? Is this a sensible question? Are the members separable from their views? In principle, yes.

Suppose we were to alter the procedure a bit. Ask each subject to make his own decisions—as usual. Then take those who have adopted the riskier positions apart from the others and advise them that they are to set aside their real views and argue instead for a conservative position. Now if it is a quality of the risk-prone person to be influential in these discussions, regardless of the views he adopts, if it is a *charisma* of the person, then the groups should go conservative. This experiment has not been done.

What could it be, other than the qualities of the person, that causes perceived influentiality to be related to initial riskiness? It could be something about the risky position itself. Some susceptibility in the group to the rhetoric of risk; some disposition to be persuaded by arguments favoring greater risk. By this view the risky members would seem to be influential only because they have happened to hold views or values to which the group is already disposed. They seem to influence because they are representative of what the group in any case wishes to do. They are in the vanguard only because they are going the way the herd is already headed.

We have come upon a central paradox of social leadership. Riecken and Homans (1954) have summarized the outcomes of very many studies with the assertion that the leader of a group is the member who most fully lives up to the norms of the group. Krech, Crutchfield, and Ballachey (1962) have more recently come to the same conclusion. The leader accepts the central values of the group and realizes them better than anyone else. And so one must ask, about leadership in general, the question we have asked about the risky influentials. Is a man a leader because he realizes the values of a certain group or has he perhaps, by means of personal persuasiveness, imposed his values on the group? The question is related to the question of generality in leadership. For if the leader imposes his values he can lead in many kinds of group, whereas if the man is a leader because he has the values of a certain group then his leadership will not export.

There are a few studies that ask whether a group follows its leader or shapes its leader. Merei did one with children (1949). He formed twelve groups from children who tended to be "followers" rather than leaders. The groups met in separate rooms for thirty to forty minutes each day and after several sessions each group had formed its own distinctive culture governing the way the members played together. After the group had formed such a culture a "leader" was introduced, a leader being a child who was judged by nursery school teachers to show high initiative and directing power. The responses of groups to twenty-six such leaders were observed and in all but one case the leader was forced to accept the rules of the group.

In every case, however, the dominant child found a way to play a leader's part. Sometimes the newcomer would start out giving orders to the other children, orders that ran strongly counter to their established ways. When he did so he was avoided and ignored. Some children then abruptly changed the content of their orders to accord with the group customs. These children assumed leadership by ordering their followers to do exactly what they would, in any case have done. Sometimes a leader who began in this way later introduced small changes in the group's games and by successive approximations brought them nearer his own inclinations.

We do not know whether adults who favored risky decisions on the

Stoner problems had personal qualities that enabled them to influence the group and so cause the shift to risk. The evidence for this interpretation is equivocal. Risk-prone persons may have seemed influential because they happened to adopt the right position. It can be argued that their advice is good advice, that their position is the correct position.

Risk and the Right Answer

"Are groups superior to their average individual member?" This was one of the earliest questions asked and has been one of the most persistent questions asked in group dynamics research (Kelley and Thibaut, 1954). When solutions to problems are attained through group discussion is the quality of those solutions higher than the quality of solutions reached by individuals? The question has been put to the experimental test many times since Münsterberg, in 1914, reported the first relevant data. Of course the question in its first unqualified form has no answer; there are several answers to several more restricted questions (see Kelley and Thibaut, 1954).

Suppose a problem has an objectively correct answer that is not known to all the subjects available for group discussions but is known to some of them. Here is such a question: "If you were to go due south from Detroit, Michigan what would be the first foreign country you would reach? Brazil? Cuba? Mexico?" The answer is Canada; the city of Windsor, Ontario because of a twist in the United States-Canadian border lies south of Detroit. If each member of a population of subjects answered independently, then those who knew the correct answer would give it and the rest would not. If the subjects were then convened as small groups to discuss the question there would be some groups in which one or two members knew the answer and the rest did not. The correct answer would prevail more often than the various incorrect answers. This answer—Canada—would usually not represent the most common prior response of the members and so its victory could not be attributed to majority pressures. Neither is "Canada" the mean or central tendency of the initial opinions and so the simple impulse to converge will not account for the agreement on "Canada." "Canada" is a minority answer, on one side of the mean, which happens to be correct. If the decision to take a high risk on the Stoner problems could be considered objectively correct then the shift to risk would be explained.

R. L. Thorndike (1938) compared individual and group answers to True-False information items on geography, economics, politics, and the like. Thorndike used almost 1200 subjects to create 222 groups of four, five, or six members and he found that the answers provided by groups, after discussion, were more often correct than the answers of individuals, made prior to any discussion. An especially instructive comparison occurs in those groups of four where opinion was initially divided evenly between the True and False alternatives and so there was no "majority" to influence the outcome. The final group decision was correct about twice as often as it was incorrect.

Surely it is pointless to compare the Stoner problems with questions of fact concerning geography, economics and the like. Where is the encyclopedia in which we can look up the answer to the problem of the electrical engineer in the way that we can look up the answer to the question about Detroit? Of course there is none, but what of that since neither Thorndike's subjects nor Stoner's was permitted to look at any books? Thorndike's subjects had to recognize the correctness of an answer without recourse to outside authority.

Thorndike had each individual rate the confidence with which he made each of his private prior decisions and a confident tone in the discussion seems to have been a cue to correctness for the group. In those groups where the persons having the wrong answers were more confident than those having the right answers the group decision tended to go wrong. Usually, however, those who were right were the more confident and then the group decisions went right in the great majority of cases. One source of confidence of course is acquaintance with an outside authority, and the persons favoring riskier alternatives on the Stoner problems could not have derived confidence in this way. Evidently outside authority is not the only source of confidence, however, since subjects with wrong answers in Thorndike's experiments were often very confident. It is just possible that there is some ground for greater confidence in the riskier answers to the Stoner problems, some ground other than the authority of the encyclopedia.

A confident champion is not the only mark of a correct answer. If a problem is logical or mathematical the rightness of an answer can be determined by intellectual operations without recourse to authority. The rightness of the Canada answer, on the other hand, is suggested by its paradoxical quality. Since Canada, in general, lies north of the United States and everyone knows that, then anyone who asserts that a part of Canada lies south of a part of the United States must have good reason for doing so. The surprise in the answer also suggests its rightness. We have learned that dull and obvious questions are not ordinarily asked unless the answer is improbable. There are many qualities that can cause an argument to be perceived as sound, an answer as correct, even when objective correctness does not exist.

In the sample discussion of the problem of the electrical engineer that appears early in this chapter we find the following speech made by Subject F: "Yes, but the most he can lose on this change is moving expenses. I read in *The New York Times* or somewhere that there is a big demand for electrical engineers. Even if this company should fall through he can always get a job, probably at the same salary." What is the logical structure of this argument and the many others like it that are offered in support of a risky decision? An authority is quoted but the authority has made no statement about the specific problem of the engineer. However, the assertion attributed to the authority somehow bears on the problem of the engineer.

A decision under risk involves choosing between a more certain, less attractive alternative (the "stake") and a less certain, more attractive alternative (the "prize"). Mr. A., the electrical engineer of Stoner's problem, must put up the stake of his present secure job in order to try for the prize of a better professional future. In essence he is offered a bet in which he must chance losing a smaller sum of money in the hope of winning a larger sum. With the stake fixed and the prize fixed the riskiness of the bet varies with the probability of gaining the prize.

Suppose we invent a set of money bets having the abstract properties of the Stoner problems: a fixed stake and a fixed prize having a value greater than the stake with a varied set of probabilities that the prize will be won. "Your friend, Mr. A, must say which of the bets listed below he would be willing to make. What is the minimal probability of winning that you would advise him to take?

Stake	Probability	Prize
$.70	.1	$3.50
$.70	.2	$3.50
$.70	.3	$3.50
$.70	.4	$3.50

Do you see why the probability of .3 might be defended as the rational answer? If someone bet $.70 ten times and won three times as the probability says he should, then his total take would be 3 × $3.50 or $10.50 whereas his total losses would be 10 × $.70 or $7.00. With a probability of .2 he should expect to win twice in ten times and so his total take would be 2 × $3.50 or $7.00, the same as his losses. With a lower probability he must expect to win less than he will lose. This relationship can be expressed by calculating the "expected value" of a single bet; it will be the value of the prize times the probability of gaining the prize (e.g., $3.50 × .2 = $.70). It can be argued that a rational man would not accept any bet whose "expected value" did not exceed the value of the stake. However, you will realize that there are reasonable answers to this argument.

The problem of the electrical engineer cannot be settled in terms of expected values because no dollar values are set on the stake and the prize. In fact while the stake and prize are fixed, insofar as the wording of the question can fix them, the discussions that take place show that these values are actually subject to interpretation. When Subject F said: "Yes, but the most he can lose on this change is moving expenses," Subject F was arguing about the value of the stake. *The New York Times* is cited to support the contention that the dollar value of the stake is really much smaller than one may have thought, no more in fact, than the cost of moving.

How should this argument affect the others in the group? It does not after all, establish any particular probability as the correct answer. Suppose, however, that the information from the *Times* is new to the other members. Each of them has made a prior decision without this information. The information argues that the stake is smaller than they had imagined. It follows that they should be willing to accept a lower probability, a greater risk, than before—whatever the probability originally accepted. It is exactly as if one settled on a probability of .3 as the lowest acceptable probability justifying the money bet described above and then learned that one had misread the stake; it was not to be $.70 at all but only $.35. In such a case a lower probability is acceptable. Even a probability of .1 gives an expected value of $.35, the value of the stake.

Information such as Subject F provided does not identify the single correct answer but it does identify a "correction" that should be made by any subject to whom the information is new. Whatever that subject's prior individual decision was, it ought now to be made riskier.

A subject discussing Stoner's problems cannot cite authorities for particular decisions and also cannot prove that any particular decision is the most rational decision. However authority and reason can be supplied for arguments concerning the true value of the stake and the prize and a change in these values usually has implications for the decision. But such arguments do not all favor increased risk. Subject C, in our sample discussion, pointed out that the engineer would lose his accumulated retirement benefits in leaving his present job. For anyone who had not thought of that consideration the value of the stake must now seem greater than it had formerly seemed and so his decision ought to be less risky.

If the shift to risk is caused by the flow of information objectively relevant to the decision then there must be, in the discussions of Stoner's problems, more information that argues for risk than information that argues for conservatism. To learn whether that is the case we would have to find a way of analyzing the *content* of the discussion so as to compare the amounts of information arguing both ways. That is not an easy thing to do.

ANALYSIS OF VERBAL CONTENT

The most famous scheme for analyzing the content of discussion is the system of "interaction process analysis" developed by Bales (1950) which was mentioned in the preceding section of this chapter. The twelve categories of the system are named and defined in Figure 13-4. Discussions of the Stoner problems have not been analyzed by this method but it is perfectly clear that the method would not provide the data we require. Information concerning the value of the prize and of the stake would probably be categorized as either *Gives opinion* or as *Gives orientation*. The categorization would be the same whether the information argued for risk or for caution and so would not yield comparative data. The system of interaction process analysis does not make the distinction our problem requires.

Stone and Bales and their coworkers (1962) have recently devised a system of generalized content analysis that makes very much finer distinctions than the old twelve-category system. By utilizing a computer the General Inquirer system codes verbal interaction into 164 categories. This is a very promising new research technique, so let me take a little space to describe it even though it is not going to give us the data we require on the Stoner discussions.

For a General Inquirer analysis the total verbal output in a group discussion is punched on IBM cards and what the computer does, essentially, is to score the words that occur for 164 different kinds of content. The scoring manual for McClelland's Achievement Motive (Atkinson, 1958), you may recall from Chapter 9, also suggests that the appearance of certain words in a story means that certain content categories ought to be scored. Words like *good, better,* and *best* applied to the quality of a performance suggest that Achievement Imagery in general should be scored. Words like *want* and *hope* used with reference to an achievement goal suggest that the subcategory N (or Need) should be scored. However, in this manual, and the manuals like it developed for other motives, no content category is completely specified by word lists. The subject is expected to use his judgment, to register the meaning a word has in its particular context, to register the meanings of total sentences and the relations among sentences in a story. The rules for doing these things have not been made perfectly specific and so a machine could not do the scoring. A human coder can, from some approximate rules, from many examples, and a certain amount of practice with correction, learn to score for the strength of achievement motivation. If we were to specify each content category of the Achievement Motive scoring by a list of words, requiring that the category be scored whenever a word on

TABLE 13–1. TAGS FOR THE CONTENT CATEGORIES OF THE GENERAL INQUIRER

1. Persons
    person, male, female
        baby, child, youth, father, mother, sib, spouse
        friend, enemy, writer (of case or reading),
        guest, member (of group), leader, follower,
        alone
    group, family, minority

2. Behavioral processes
        react, iao (is aware of, is conscious of), see,
        hear, smell, taste, touch, icw (is concerned with,
        is important), think, defend, decide, try, act,
        come, go, work, use, keep, tie, get, own, lose,
        joke, play, dream, escape, rest
    specific to information transmission
        ask
        tell (veridical transmission)
        slant (distorted transmission)
    specific to interpersonal action
        direct, give, pos, depend, obey, resist, neg, reject

3. Qualities
        big-little, strong-weak, able-unable, hard-easy, open-secret, full-empty,
        noisy-quiet, high-low, far-near
        good-bad, well-sick, just-unjust, warm-cold, light-dark, clean-dirty
        oral, anal, genital
        slow-quick, old-new, plain-fancy, general-unique

4. Things
    natural environment
        place, time, chance, object, earth, air, fluid, life, plant, animal, body,
        food, building, death, chaos
    cultural environment
        a. God, art, beauty, ethos, sign, form
        b. status, money, cover, count
    psychological states
        psy, need, sex, anger, anx (for anxiety), pain, gratif (for gratifica-
        tion)
    psychological representations
        safety danger, block, target, means, goal, achiev, fail
    special environment
        school, course, exper (for experiment), c (for case), r (for reading)

5. Abstract relations
    equal
    not (all forms of possible negation)
    if (conditional)
    ought (words implying the desirability of a condition or event)
    belong, include, margin, alike

6. Abstract processes
    begin, create, cause, grow, exist, order, move,
    shrink, recur, ruin, end

its list occurred in a story, we should be dealing with this material in the manner of the General Inquirer.

The 164 categories of the General Inquirer are listed in Table 13-1, arranged under six major headings. The words listed in this table are the names of the content categories or as the authors say the category tags. Each such category is exhaustively defined by a list of words; the appearance of any of the words in the text is the occasion for scoring the content categories for which the word is listed. One content category, for example, is named (or tagged) "Dirty." This category is scored whenever any of the words of Table 13-2 occurs in a text; words ranging from *ash* through *decay*, *incest*, and *mud*, to *worm* and *wound*. The insensitivity of the computer program appears in that fact that *ash* in the context *ash tree* would be scored "Dirty." The great advantage of the computer program appears in the fact that it has made it possible to obtain, in rather short time, a 164-dimension profile of the content of verbal interaction.

TABLE 13-2. WORDS FOR THE TAG CONCEPT "DIRTY"

ash	devil	mill	smoke
awful	dig	mine	soil
bitter	dirty	mouse	spit
black	discharge	mud	spot
bothersome	disgust	murder	tobacco
bottom	dull	murderer	train
cellar	dust	naked	trick
chimney	evil	pick	ugliness
cities	floor	pig	ugly
city	fly	pigeon	vice
clay	hell	poison	war
coal	herd	politic	waste
commercial	hole	powder	worker
cruel	horror	rat	worm
curse	incest	rear	worse
damage	industrial	scheme	worst
darkness	industry	shame	wound
decay	labor	slave	
deceive	mass	slop	

The computer proceeds, in what is called a "tagging run," by taking each word of the verbal proceedings and looking it up in the 164 lists corresponding to the 164 categories. The text word is then tagged for all the categories under which it is subsumed and in the General Inquirer a word can appear on more than one list. The word *acid*, for example, would be tagged for "Danger," "Fluid," "Means," "Quick," and "Reject." The computer would find *acid* on these five lists and fail to find it on 159 others. This "tagging run" sounds a laborious business, the sort of thing

that would take ten clerks ten years to accomplish. The computer processes about 1,000 text words per minute.

The next step is the Tag Tally in which the computer examines the
previously tagged text and counts up the frequencies with which each
concept (or tag) is scored. It is this run that will yield a profile of interaction showing the frequencies with which 164 kinds of content have
occurred. The Tag Tally proceeds at the rate of about 5000 tagged words
per minute.

The Tag Tally, with all its 164 categories, would not tell us whether
discussions of the Stoner problems bring out more information lowering
the apparent value of the stake (hence arguing for increased risk) or more
information raising its apparent value (hence arguing for greater caution).
There are not two lists of words in the General Inquirer corresponding to
the two kinds of information. The Inquirer is a system of generalized
content analysis; it will analyze any verbal material in terms of 164
categories, categories that are frequently important. But the human mind
operates with more categories than 164 and we have the bad luck to
be concerned with a couple that lie outside the scope of the Inquirer.

However, the Inquirer can do more than tag and tally. It enables us,
for instance, to direct the computer to retrieve all sentences containing
some particular word or combination of words. If we have punched the
original text using a code to mark certain gross syntactic features we can
issue a more precise directive. The computer will retrieve, for instance,
all the sentences in which a particular word is used as subject. In short
the Inquirer would call up the relevant sentences from tagged discussions
of the Stoner problem if we could tell it what words to look for. What
will the words be that are associated with information lowering the
apparent value? It is impossible to say without making a close study of
actual discussions. If that is to be done one might as well make the content analysis by hand, as it were. However, if many discussions were to
be analyzed we should want to tell the computer what we learned from
the first analysis and let it do the later ones.

VERBAL CONTENT IN STONER'S GROUPS

Nordhøy, for the thesis he wrote under Marquis's direction, analyzed
discussion of the Stoner problems in terms of a set of specific content
categories tailored to the requirements of the present problem. Nordhøy
(1962) had listened to the tapes of Stoner's original groups and had
formed the impression that the weight of the information brought out in
each discussion generally favored the change that occurred. Again and
again he found that a problem elicited certain arguments and these seemed

to cause a shift in the decisions. Arguments for risk either attempted to show that the prize was greater than had been imagined or that the stake was smaller and arguments for caution did the converse. For a sample of twelve discussions, representing all twelve problems but from different Stoner groups, Nordhøy categorized arguments into those favoring risk and those favoring caution, those directed at conceptions of the prize and those directed at conceptions of the stake. Any segment of speech that could be categorized by this scheme was tallied. In all twelve discussions there were more arguments favoring the direction in which the decision shifted than there were arguments favoring the other direction. The shift to risk follows a discussion about the value of the stake and the prize, a discussion that contains more information favoring risk than it does information favoring caution.

The other direct evidence in favor of the view that it is the information produced in discussion that causes the shift to risk derives from another thesis directed by Marquis. Hinds (1962) devised sets of betting problems for which the stakes, prizes, and probabilities were all made explicit. For each set of bets the subject was to select the one bet he would most like to make. Here are a few bets from one set:

Stake	Probability of Winning	Prize
$.60	.1	$6.00
.55	.2	2.75
.50	.3	1.60
.45	.4	1.13
etc.		

Notice that, in the above set, the expected value of the bet (Probability of Winning X Prize) always equals the value of the stake. In the long run with any of these bets one must expect to come out even. On a single bet, however, a person favoring risk will elect to chance a larger stake (perhaps $.60) to try for a larger prize ($6.00) even though the probability of winning is very low (.1). Such problems do not invite nearly as much discussion of the value of the prize and stake as do the Stoner story problems. And with such problems Hinds found that group decisions after discussion were not consistently riskier than individual decisions before discussion.

There is direct evidence, then, that the information brought out in group discussions causes the shift to risk on the Stoner problems. Although these problems do not have objective answers they are able to bring out objective information which exerts a force toward increased risk. The theory is a good one but it does not give complete satisfaction.

Why should it be the case that a whole set of story problems unfolds in the same way to disclose more information favoring risk than caution. How does it happen that there is always more latent information of one kind than another? And is there really? One can think of very powerful arguments favoring caution that for some reason are not usually elicited. One of these was made by Subject C in the sample discussion concerning the electrical engineer: "Just because he turns down this job doesn't mean he has to stay put the rest of his life. Within two years or so he will get another offer so why should he go with a company that has only one chance in ten of making it? Statistics on the failure and success of new businesses show that the large majority actually succeed."

Perhaps the latent information for the Stoner problems is really about evenly balanced between caution and risk. The fact is, however, that it is chiefly risky information that discussion brings forward when the decision shifts to risk and the content of the discussion seems to affect the group decisions; Nordhøy's subjects thought it did so. But there may be a cause behind this cause. There may be something directing the subjects' minds toward information supporting risk, something distracting them from or suppressing information that supports caution.

Risk as a Value

Stoner's subjects were graduate students in the School of Industrial Management at M.I.T. and when members of the school first heard about the outcome of Stoner's experiment they argued that it could be explained by the fact that the field of industrial management sets a positive value on the ability to take risks. It is a part of the role of an industrial management student to favor risky decisions, they held. The assertion may be true but it will not of itself account for Stoner's result. The subject is equally a student of industrial management when he answers the questions individually and when he agrees to a group decision following discussion. The effect is an increase of riskiness in the same subjects. One must argue, therefore, that the value or the role is more salient, more firmly engaged, when the management student is talking with his peers. That seems reasonable enough. The student alone would be less concerned to manifest ideal role behavior than would the student in the presence of other students. In the group each one has an audience to play to and that audience values riskiness.

The value theory had to be modified when results came in demonstrating the Stoner effect with undergraduates in a liberal arts curriculum and with mature business executives. If Wallach, Kogan, and Bem (1962) had not created all-female groups and found the effect strongly present in such groups one might have argued that risk is a value for the male role, whatever the male's occupation. As it is, however, the generality of the effect compels a value theory to argue in terms of cultural values rather than values peculiar to certain roles. Is it perhaps an American value to be risky?

There is a certain kind of rhetoric regularly produced in discussions of the Stoner problems. "Life is not static; it's dynamic. You have to go forward, have a spirit of adventure. Nothing ventured, nothing gained." Sometimes it takes a threatening line. "Don't be such a stick-in-the-mud. It's so stodgy, so dull to stay in a job just because it is secure." This talk is almost purely evaluative and it often seems to have a strong effect.

Do Americans value risk? There are a number of ways one could find out. Suppose we constructed for the Stoner problems two patterns of response, two profiles in risk for a hypothetical Mr. A and Mr. B. Mr. A would be represented as one who consistently accepted low probabilities of success and Mr. B as one who consistently held out for high probabilities. A sample of Americans could be shown these two profiles and asked to guess at certain further characteristics of A and B. One of the two, we might say, is twenty-nine years old and one is fifty-two; which one is Mr. A and which one B? One man drives a red Sting Ray automobile and one drives a black Plymouth. Which is which? One man is an accountant and one man is a motion picture director; which is A and which is B? Our subjects might find it rather insulting to be asked to guess such things from the decision profiles, but if they were willing to answer probably they would flesh out the risk-taker with more glamorous attributes than the cautious Mr. B. Of course one could not take the value for granted. It would remain to ask. Which man would you yourself rather be?

This process of inferring one trait from another is something people readily do. The work of Asch (1946), of Wishner (1960), and others on the perception of persons demonstrates that (see Chapter 12). There is sometimes even some truth in these inferences. The problems Stoner used were devised, you may remember, by Wallach and Kogan for the study of individual differences in risk-taking. One of the things those investigators did (1961) was present the problems to a sample of aged persons for comparison with younger subjects and the older people answered more cautiously. The fact that caution increases with age is easily observed on a superhighway; the people who pass you are generally younger than you, while the people you pass are generally older. Perhaps the elderly are cautious because they need to be so in order to compensate for the decline of their physical powers. Perhaps the reason is different. The young have a wonderful sense of invulnerability. Because nothing very bad has happened to them they somehow feel nothing bad can happen. Do they even realize that they are mortal? On a verbal level of course they do, but a full sense of one's vulnerability and mortality is a lesson that develops with the rude shocks which accumulate in time. The elderly lady driving her car so slowly and deliberately has a head full of catastrophes known to be possible which the teenager has not . . . yet. In any case there is truth in the notion that riskiness is a concomitant of youth and since Americans like to appear youthful perhaps they also like to appear risky.

The problem of determining whether riskiness is indeed an American value could be approached more directly. One could present a sample of Americans with decisions involving alternatives that varied in risk and ask them to mark the best alternative in each case. If Americans value risk they ought to agree in preferring the riskier alternatives. But this is a curious paradox. Are not the Stoner problems themselves just such a set of decisions? The Americans so far tested do not, when answering individually, agree in preferring the riskier decisions. The data for individuals do not present a cultural consensus, they present a distribution, a set of answers dispersed as widely as the alternatives permit. How then can one argue that risk is a value?

There is an empirical finding that fits here. Hinds, in the thesis he wrote under Marquis's direction (1962), asked subjects to try to guess for some of the Stoner problems what alternative would be chosen by two hundred "other people like you." They might reasonably have answered that "people like me will choose what I choose" but they seem to have assumed that these two hundred people were not exactly like them, only similar. The important thing is that the subjects very consistently guessed that others would choose more cautiously than did they themselves. I have asked one undergraduate class of thirty and one graduate seminar of sixteen to answer a Stoner problem for themselves and then to guess the mean answers of, respectively, "other Harvard undergraduates" and "other Harvard graduate students." Not one subject guessed that these others would answer more riskily than themselves; they guessed the others to be the same as themselves or more conservative. It looks as if each person answering as an individual conceives himself to be at least as risky as the average of a reference group.

One of the groups I watched did not begin discussion by asking each member to state his preference. They started arguing without knowing one another's position on the scale of probabilities. One man made great use of the rhetoric that exhorts others to take a chance. He urged them to courage and confidence; he even used the phrase "nothing ventured, nothing gained." When the group was ready for a decision they finally thought to take a poll of initial opinions. The rhetorician who had led the forces favoring risk turned out to have selected odds of 7 to 10, the second most conservative position in the group. He had conceived of that decision as a daring one but in terms of the actual scores it was a very cautious one.

Now the pieces can be put together. Perhaps riskiness is indeed an American value and each individual answering the Stoner problems means to be at least as risky as people like himself. The guesses they make about other people's scores show this. However, the individual who has not talked with anyone about the problems cannot know how to be truly risky because risk is relative to a group norm and the location of the norm on the scale of probabilities is not known. Each man, on his own, guesses the norm to be at or below his own selection. When individuals talk together and disclose their decisions the actual distribution is made known. Those who find themselves below the mean of the six members of the group discover that they are failing to realize the ideal of riskiness that they may have thought they were realizing. Consequently they feel impelled to move in a risky direction both in accepting the decision of the group and in changing their private opinions. Subjects at or above the group mean feel no such impulsion, they are relatively risky just as they meant to be. The result would be, of course, a shift in the group decision toward greater risk than the mean of the individual decisions.

If risk is a value and subjects mean to be risky, why do they not all select the one answer that maximizes the chances of being riskier than the average? That answer would be the absolutely riskiest answer—the lowest probability of gaining the prize. Probably subjects do not regularly select it because it is not limitless risk-taking that is valued, but moderate risk-taking. Decisions somewhat riskier than the average may suggest a "venturesome" or "audacious" character, but decisions much riskier than the average probably suggest a "foolhardy" or "harebrained" character. If limitless risk-taking were valued, the individual subject who wished to appear risky could choose his answer without information about the answers of other subjects. Because the value is probably attached to moderate risk-taking which is defined as a position somewhat, but not too much, riskier than the norm, individual subjects do need the information that a group discussion can provide.

Bem, Wallach, and Kogan (In press) have done an experiment which was designed to test the value explanation (as well as some other explanations) of the shift to risk. They did not use the Stoner problems but rather asked subjects, who were to participate in a psycho-physiological experiment, to select the experimental treatment they would endure where the various treatments were more or less likely to involve disagreeable physical side effects. The investigators reasoned that in this situation risk-taking would connote the valued qualities of courage and boldness. In one condition subjects making individual decisions thought that these decisions would remain private, whereas in another condition they were given to believe that their decisions would be made public. If risk is a cultural value, this latter condition should provide an opportunity to play the hero. However, the decisions in the latter condition were not significantly more risky than in the former condition. The authors conclude that the shift to risk in group decisions is not attributable to a social value on greater risk-taking. We note, however, that the subjects who thought their decisions would be made public were not actually informed of one another's decisions and so would not have known what levels to select in order to appear brave or bold without appearing foolhardy. Each subject may have thought himself bold already because he imagined that the average decision would be more cautious than his own.

Our theory holds that riskiness is indeed a cultural value but that cultural values cannot be realized in concrete situations until they are "specified" (to use Talcott Parsons' term [1964]). The function of the group discussion, this theory says, is chiefly informative. It teaches the individuals how to be risky in the present concrete task; it gives specificity to the value. The content of the discussion, the arguments pro and con are of no importance by this theory. It is the information about other people's answers that makes individuals move toward greater risk after group discussion.

A Dash of Dissonance and the Grand Conclusion

The trouble with writing about something on the frontiers of knowledge is that the frontier is likely to move while you are writing. I had worked out much of what you have read when I made a light-hearted call to Dr. Marquis to ask whether there was anything new on the "shift to risk phenomenon." "Yes," he said. "It turns out not to be a shift to risk. Nordhøy has written some problems for which the decision after discussion is more cautious than the mean of the individual decisions. Isn't that interesting?"

Before I made that phone call it had seemed to me that we were near to an answer. The impulse to converge or conform accounted for an important feature of the decisions after discussion, the reduction in the range of the initial decisions, but conformity could not account for the characteristic effect—the shift to risk. Leadership by the risk-prone remained a possible explanation but a doubtful one since the subjects who had favored risk must necessarily seem to have been influential in a group that shifted to a greater risk. The explanation in terms of the disclosure of objectively relevant information about the value of the stake and the prize looked stronger to me. The shortcoming of this explanation was the fact that it did not explain why a whole series of problems should have the power to elicit more information that argued for risk than information arguing for caution. The cultural value explanation seemed the best of the lot. It accounted for the finding that subjects guessing the decisions favored by people like themselves guessed a more cautious decision than the one they themselves chose. The value hypothesis, in addition, could incorporate the theory of relevant information. Probably there was as much latent information arguing one way as another on these problems but the value on risk favored the elicitation of this kind of information. The cultural value theory was a good theory. But it was conceived to explain a shift to risk. And now it seemed there was also a shift to conservatism. The consequence was a thunderous dissonance.

After some weeks of not-thinking, denial, somatic conversion, and derogation of the source I felt well enough to learn the details of Nordhøy's interesting results. Making a close study of Stoner's findings Nordhøy noticed that one of the twelve problems had usually generated group decisions that were more cautious than the individual decisions. When he followed this eccentric problem through subsequent researches Nordhøy found that it had preserved its eccentricity. The decision after discussion had usually become more conservative though not always significantly so. Here, without the probability options, is this peculiar twelfth problem.

> Mr. M is contemplating marriage to Miss T, a girl whom he has known for a little more than a year. Recently, however, a number of arguments have occurred between them, suggesting some sharp differences of opinion in the way each views certain matters. Indeed, they decide to seek professional advice from a marriage counselor as to whether it would be wise for them to marry. On the basis of these meetings with a marriage counselor, they realize that a happy marriage, while possible, could not be assured. Imagine that you are advising Mr. M and Miss T. Listed below are several probabilities or odds that their marriage could prove to be a happy and successful one. PLEASE CHECK THE LOWEST PROBABILITY THAT YOU WOULD CONSIDER ACCEPTABLE FOR MR. M AND MISS T TO GET MARRIED.

What do you think subjects say about this problem in the group discussions? Here it is in colloquial English: "If anybody goes to marriage counselor before they are married, it is not love, they should never, they should just say to hell—." Nordhøy took instruction from this sort of comment and made two small changes in problem twelve. He added a statement that the quarreling man and woman were very much in love and made the consultation incidental rather than deliberate. They ran into a psychiatrist-friend at a party and asked his advice. In this version problem 12 produced the shift to risk after group discussion. "All for love" seemed to displace "If they are already going to a marriage counselor then—"

Nordhøy wrote some other problems that produced a shift to caution after group discussion. In one of these a forty-five-year-old dentist with two children in high school, is told by his physician that he has a plugged artery (sclerosis) in his right arm. This condition is a continuous source of pain but it does not prevent the dentist from working and does not even reduce his skill. It seems that there is an operation which, if successful, would completely relieve the condition but, if unsuccessful, would leave the hand useless and the dentist would be unable to carry on with his work. What is the minimal probability of the operation being successful that will justify having the operation? The other problem concerns a man with children and a modest income who is thinking of raising money on his life insurance in order to buy a stock that may triple in value. What is the minimal probability of the stock tripling in value that will justify risking the insurance? In both cases the group decision became more cautious after discussion. These two problems produced the consequence that Nordhøy intended, but some others did not. Several problems intended to produce a shift to caution produced no significant changes at all.

Apparently group decisions on problems involving risk are sometimes riskier than the mean of prior individual decisions, sometimes more cautious, and sometimes not significantly different from the mean. This sounds as if group decisions are related to individual decisions in the three ways that are logically possible; in fact as if no law exists and the relation is unpredictable. But that is not right. The decisions are highly consistent for particular problems. A problem that shows the shift to risk does so consistently and a problem that shows the shift to caution does so consistently. There is no regularity on the level where we thought it existed. It is not true that all problems involving risk show a shift to greater risk after discussion; neither is it true that they show a shift to greater caution.

How well do the four principles explored in this chapter serve to explain the contingent regularities that do exist in group decisions on problems involving risk? Conformity works, as before, to explain the reduced range but not the shift to either risk or caution. The hypothesis that risk-prone persons are generally influential may be discarded thanks to one of Nordhøy's findings. When groups that shifted to caution were asked to name their more influential members they tended to name those who had, in their initial decisions, been relatively cautious. It seems to be true, then, that this sort of perceived leadership falls to him who is disposed to go the way the group is going. If risk-prone persons were "Great Men" they ought always to seem so.

We are left with the relevant-information theory and the value theory and they will still work. The value theory seems the more fundamental.

But now we cannot invoke a general American value on risk, an idea that might have been checked. But did that idea really make sense? Can one say that Americans think it is a good idea to take risks—always? Do we praise the father of twelve who scoffs at life insurance and takes mountain climbing for his favorite sport? I think not. We value both risk and caution, according to the circumstances.

At present we can only say that a story-problem involving risk may engage either the value on caution or the value on risk. The group decision will be more extreme than the individual decision—in the direction of the value engaged, whichever that direction may be. Why should this be so since the value ought also to be engaged by each subject answering individually? For two reasons. The value engaged will influence the flow of information so that more relevant information will be elicited supporting the value than opposing it. A story that makes Americans in general feel like taking a chance, such as the story of the two young people who are very much in love, will draw from these Americans supporting information. No single member of a group is likely to possess all the information that objectively bears on the decision and so the discussion will give each one some new reasons for moving toward the value.

There is a second reason why decisions after discussion should move in the direction of the value engaged. Values are not specified, in advance, in terms of particular probabilities on the story problems. On problems involving the value of risk we know that each individual before the discussion thinks himself at least as risky as the average person. We argued that the discussion served to make known the actual distribution and all those who were below the group average could no longer think of themselves as living up to the value on risk. So—we have suggested—they change to riskier decisions. Now we must predict in addition that for problems engaging the value on caution individuals will initially guess that "others like themselves" would adopt somewhat less cautious and so less ideal decisions. When the true distribution has been disclosed in discussion the subjects who find themselves riskier than the average of the group ought to shift to greater caution—the direction of the value.

While research support for the combined information and value theory is incomplete, it is reasonably clear how to obtain it. However, the theory is deficient in another respect that is not so easily corrected. Problems have been written that engage the caution value and problems have been written that engage the risk value. It is not too difficult to think one up either way. But we have no general prescription for doing so and no general rule for identifying in advance those problems that will cause a shift to risk and those problems that will cause a shift to caution. If we had such a rule that rule would formulate the contingencies governing the two values and so it would be a general statement about American culture. How would it read? The caution problems that Nordhøy wrote suggest it might go like this: One should be cautious in making a decision such that the stake involves the vital interests of others. Any others or only one's children? Must the interests be vital? What if the interests are not vital and the others would share in the prize? Until we can accurately formulate such generalizations and write problems by rule to go either way, the nature of group decisions on problems involving risk will not be fully understood.

REFERENCES

Allport, F. H. *Social psychology.* Boston: Houghton Mifflin, 1924.

Allport, F. H. A structuronomic conception of behavior: Individual and collective. I. Structural theory and the master problem of social psychology. *J. abnorm. soc. Psychol.,* 1962, **64,** 3–30.

Asch, S. E. Forming impressions of personality. *J. soc. Psychol.,* 1946, **41,** 258–290.

Asch, S. E. Studies of independence and conformity. A minority of one against a unanimous majority. *Psychol. Monogr.,* 1956, **70,** No. 9 (Whole No. 416).

Back, K. The exertion of influence through social communication. *J. abnorm. soc. Psychol.,* 1951, **46,** 9–23.

Bales, R. F. *Interaction process analysis: A method for the study of small groups.* Cambridge: Addison-Wesley, 1950.

Bales, R. F. Task roles and social roles in problem-solving groups. In Eleanor E. Maccoby, T. M. Newcomb, & E. L. Hartley (Eds.), *Readings in social psychology.* (3rd ed.) New York: Holt, 1958.

Bass, B. M. *Leadership, psychology, and organizational behavior.* New York: Harper, 1960.

Bem, D. J., Wallach, M. A., & Kogan, N. Group decision-making under risk of aversive consequences *J. abnorm. soc. Psychol.* In press.

Berkowitz, L. Personality and group position. *Sociometry,* 1956, **19,** 210–222.

Blake, R. R., Helson, H., & Mouton, Jane S. The generality of conformity behavior as a function of factual anchorage, difficulty of task, and amount of social pressure. *J. Pers.,* 1957, **25,** 294–305.

Bogdonoff, M. D., Klein, R. F., Estes, E. H., Jr., Shaw, D. M., & Back, K. W. The modifying effect of conforming behavior upon lipid responses accompanying CNS arousal. *Clin. Res.,* 1961, **9,** 135.

Borgatta, E. F., Couch, A. S., & Bales, R. F. Some findings relevant to the great man theory of leadership. *Amer. sociol. Rev.,* 1954, **19,** 755–759.

Carter, L. F. Recording and evaluating the performance of individuals as members of small groups. *Personnel Psychol.,* 1954, **VII,** 477–484.

Cartwright, D., & Harary, F. Structural balance: A generalization of Heider's theory. *Psychol. Rev.,* 1956, **63,** 277–293.

Christie, L. S., Luce, R. D., & Macy, J., Jr. *Communication and learning in task-oriented groups.* Cambridge: Research Laboratory of Electronics, 1952.

Coleman, J. F., Blake, R. R., & Mouton, Jane S. Task difficulty and conformity pressure. *J. abnorm. soc. Psychol.,* 1958, **57,** 120–122.

Festinger, L. A theory of social comparison processes. *Hum. Relat.,* 1954, **7,** 117–140.

Festinger, L., Schachter, S., & Back, K. *Social pressures in informal groups: A study of human factors in housing.* New York: Harper, 1950.

Festinger, L., & Thibaut, J. Interpersonal communication in small groups. *J. abnorm. soc. Psychol.*, 1951, **46**, 92–99.

Gerard, H. B. The anchorage of opinions in face-to-face groups. *Hum. Relat.*, 1954, **7**, 313–325.

Gerard, H. B. Inconsistency of beliefs and their implications. Paper read at American Psychological Association, New York, September 1961. Cited by J. W. Brehm, & A. R. Cohen, *Explorations in cognitive dissonance*. New York: Wiley, 1962.

Gibb, C. A. The principles and traits of leadership. *J. abnorm. soc. Psychol.*, 1947, **42**, 267–284.

Gilchrist, J. C., Shaw, M. E., & Walker, L. C. Some effects of unequal distribution of information in a wheel group structure. *J. abnorm. soc. Psychol.*, 1955, **51**, 119–122.

Heider, F. *The psychology of interpersonal relations*. New York: Wiley, 1958.

Hinds, W. C. Individual and group decisions in gambling situations. Unpublished Master's thesis, School of Industrial Management, M.I.T., 1962.

Hollingshead, A. B. *Elmtown's youth*. (1st ed. 1949) New York: Wiley (Science ed.), 1961.

Hollingworth, L. S. *Children above 180 I.Q. Stanford-Binet; Origin and development*. Yonkers-on-Hudson: World Book, 1942.

Homans, G. C. *The human group*. New York: Harcourt, Brace & World, 1950.

Jackson, J. M., & Saltzstein, H. D. The effect of person-group relationships on conformity processes. *J. abnorm. soc. Psychol.*, 1958, **57**, 17–24.

Kahl, J. A., & Davis, J. A. A comparison of indexes of socio-economic status. *Amer. sociol Rev.*, 1955, **20**, 317–325.

Kelley, H. H., & Thibaut, J. W. Experimental studies of group problem solving and process. In G. Lindzey (Ed.), *Handbook of social psychology*. Vol. II. Cambridge: Addison-Wesley, 1954.

Krech, D., Crutchfield, R. S., & Ballachey, E. L. *Individual in society*. New York: McGraw-Hill, 1962.

Leavitt, H. J. Some effects of certain communication patterns on group performance. *J. abnorm. soc. Psychol.*, 1951, **46**, 38–50.

Mann, R. D. A review of the relationships between personality and performance in small groups. *Psychol. Bull.*, 1959, **56**, 241–270.

Marquis, D. G. Individual responsibility and group decisions involving risk. *Industr. Mgmt. Rev.*, 1962, **3**, 8–23.

Merei, F. Group leadership and institutionalization. *Human Relat.*, 1949, **2**, 23–39.

Münsterberg, H. *Psychology and social sanity*. Garden City: Doubleday-Page, 1914.

Newcomb, T. M. An approach to the study of communicative acts. *Psychol. Rev.*, 1953, **60**, 393–404.

Newcomb, T. M. *The acquaintance process*. New York: Holt, Rinehart & Winston, 1961.

Nordhøy, F. Group interaction in decision-making under risk. Unpublished master's thesis, School of Industrial Management, M.I.T., 1962.

Parsons, T. The American value system. Unpublished manuscript. 1964.

Pennington, D. F., Harary, F., & Bass, B. M. Some effects of decision and discussion on coalescence, change, and effectiveness. *J. appl. Psychol.*, 1958, **42**, 404–408.

Riecken, H. W., & Homans, G. C. Psychological aspects of social structure.

In G. Lindzey (Ed.), *Handbook of social psychology.* Vol. II. Cambridge: Addison-Wesley, 1954.

Rosenberg, M. J., Hovland, C. I., McGuire, W. J., Abelson, R. P., & Brehm, J. W. *Attitude organization and change.* New Haven: Yale Univer. Press, 1960.

Rosner, S. Consistency of response to group pressures. *J. abnorm. soc. Psychol.,* 1957, **55**, 145–146.

Schachter, S. Deviation, rejection, and communication. *J. abnorm. soc. Psychol.,* 1951, **46**, 190–207.

Schachter, S. *The psychology of affiliation.* Palo Alto, California: Stanford Univer. Press, 1959.

Schachter, S., Nuttin, J., De Monchaux, Cecily, Maucorps, P. H., Osmer, D., Duijker, H., Rommetveit, R., & Israel, J. Cross-cultural experiments on threat and rejection. *Hum. Relat.,* 1954, **7**, 403–439.

Shaw, M. E. Some effects of problem complexity upon problem solution efficiency in different communication nets. *J. exp. Psychol.,* 1954, **48**, 211–217.

Shaw, M. E., Rothschild, S. H., & Strickland, J. F. Decision processes in communications nets. *J. abnorm. soc. Psychol.,* 1957, **54**, 323–330.

Sherif, M. Group influences upon the formation of norms and attitudes. In Newcomb, T. M., & Hartley, E. L. (Eds.), *Readings in social psychology.* (1st ed.) New York: Holt, 1947.

Slater, P. E. Role differentiation in small groups. *Amer. sociol. Rev.,* 1955, **20**, 300–310.

Stone, P. J., Bales, R. F., Namenwirth, J. Z., & Ogilvie, D. M. The General Inquirer: A computer system for content analysis and retrieval based on the sentence as a unit of information. *Behav. Sci.,* 1962, **7**, 484–498.

Stoner, J. A. F. A comparison of individual and group decisions including risk. Unpublished master's thesis, School of Industrial Management, M.I.T., 1961.

Strodtbeck, F. L., James, Rita M., & Hawkins, C. Social status in jury deliberations. In Eleanor E. Maccoby, T. M. Newcomb, & E. L. Hartley (Eds.), *Readings in social psychology.* (3rd ed.) New York: Holt, 1958.

Thibaut, J. W., & Kelley, H. H. *The social psychology of groups.* New York: Wiley, 1959.

Thorndike, R. L. The effect of discussion upon the correctness of group decisions, when the factor of majority influence is allowed for. *J. soc. Psychol.,* 1938, **9**, 343–362.

Tuddenham, R. D. The influence upon judgment of a grossly distorted norm. *Tech. Rep.* No. 2. Contract Nr. 170–159. Berkeley: Univer. of California, 1957.

Wallach, M. A., & Kogan, N. Sex differences and judgment processes. *J. Pers.,* 1959, **27**, 555–564.

Wallach, M. A., & Kogan, N. Aspects of judgment and decision making: Interrelationships and changes with age. *Behav. Sci.,* 1961, **6**, 23–36.

Wallach, M. A., Kogan, N., & Bem, D. J. Group influence on individual risk-taking. *J. abnorm. soc. Psychol.,* 1962, **65**, 75–86.

Wallach, M. A., Kogan, N., & Bem, D. J. Diffusion of responsibility and level of risk-taking in groups. *J. abnorm. soc. Psychol.,* 1964, **68**, 263–274.

Whyte, W. H., Jr. *The organization man.* New York: Simon & Schuster, 1956.

Wishner, J. Reanalysis of "Impressions of personality." *Psychol. Rev.,* 1960, **67**, 96–112.

CHAPTER 14

Collective Behavior and the

Psychology of the Crowd

Collective behavior includes riots, crazes, lynchings, panics, and revolutions. Collective behavior is extraordinary behavior, dramatic behavior, and so while it is likely to be foolish, disgusting, or evil it will always also be something of an entertainment. H. L. Mencken (1924) put both the truth and its cruel irony in a quip about lynchings in the rural South; he said that they "often take the place of the merry-go-round, the theater, the symphony, and other diversions common to larger communities."

When a collective manifestation occurs, one or another newspaper reporter in any large city is likely to put in a call to a social psychologist at the university to "get his interpretation." In Boston these calls go first, of course, to Gordon W. Allport and he passes them on to one or another colleague, occasionally to me. The question will be: "How do you account for these prison riots?" Or, it may concern popularity of the twist, the craze for hula hoops, the occurrence of pantie raids, a worldwide swastika epidemic, or the rise of the Black Muslim movement. I never can account for anything but it does not matter because the reporter has a theory of his own. "Don't you feel, doctor, that there is a mob psychology at work here? Aren't these people giving in to their primitive nature, to their animal impulses?" "Yes," I say, "that must be right, what you said."

The ultimate source of the reporter's theory is Gustave Le Bon, whose book *La Foule* (1895) appeared in English in 1896 as *The Crowd*. The crowds Le Bon had chiefly in mind were those of the French Revolution and of the Third Republic and he did not admire them: ". . . the crowd is always intellectually inferior to the isolated individual . . ." (1960, p. 33). The mob man is "fickle," "credulous," and "intolerant," Le Bon held. The mob man shows the violence and ferocity of "primitive beings." "Primitive beings" in Le Bon's listing were women, children, savages, and the lower classes. These inferior forms of life, in Le Bon's view, regularly manifested the emotionality and irrationality to which civilized man might give way when he was in a crowd. Le Bon even offered a neurological theory of the mob mind and the primitive minds it resembled; the lot of them were operating "under the influence of the spinal cord." Though writing in a relatively comfortable time, the end of the nineteenth century, Le Bon managed to sound like a French aristocrat, breathless from the mob's pursuit, dashing off an indictment of the Revolution before it should be his turn to meet the guillotine. *The Crowd* has all the color and extravagance of its subject and for that reason it has always seemed closer to that subject than more dispassionate analyses.

There have been many dispassionate analyses however; each of the great men in the early days of social psychology contributed one. For Tarde (1903), Freud (1922), McDougall (1920), and F. H. Allport (1924) the crowd was a major topic. In the university today, classicists and others remote from social psychology are likely still to think of social psychology as "the study of mobs and that kind of thing." In fact, however, crowd behavior has not been a leading topic in social psychology for many years and there are contemporary textbooks that do not mention the subject. In the late 1920's social psychology turned from discussion to empiricism and tried to make the empiricism reliable and quantitative and, whenever possible, experimental. Crowd behavior is not easily studied in an experimental way.

There was not much empiricism of any kind in the early days. Indeed, one has the impression that Le Bon's heated descriptions of the crowd were as near as many scholars cared to come to the "beast with many heads." These scholars were, however, very keen on detecting unclarities in one another's concepts and vicious circularity in one another's reasoning. Sometimes the discussion, perhaps needing some new facts to refresh it, grew testy. Freud, writing about the mental unity of the crowd in *Group Psychology and the Analysis of the Ego* contended that: ". . . what we are offered as an explanation by authorities upon Sociology and Group Psychology is always the same, even though it is given various names, and that is the magic word 'suggestion'" (1922, p. 34). About McDougall's concept of "primitive sympathy," Freud wrote: "McDougall for a moment gives us an impression that his principle of primitive induction of emotion might enable us to do without the assumption of suggestion. But on further consideration we are forced to perceive that this principle says no more than the familiar assertion about 'imitation' or 'contagion' except for a decided stress on the emotional factor" (1922, pp. 34–35). McDougall, in turn, had something to say in evaluation of Freud's theories of crowd and group behavior: "Not proven and wildly improbable" (1925, p. 27).

There were some attempts between 1930 and 1950 to adapt the empirical methods of psychology to the study of the crowd and descriptions of two of these will show why the topic languished. Meier, Mennenga, and Stoltz (1941) attempted to discover what kinds of persons are disposed to participate in mob action. A brutal kidnapping was realistically reported to students in the form of news dispatches said to have been received just that moment from a local newspaper office. The dispatches reported a mob of three thousand persons to be storming the local jail. At the height of the students' excitement (one imagines them about ready to rush down to the jail) they were handed questionnaires and asked to indicate the kind of action they were prepared to take. In these circumstances it was only the less intelligent students who reported themselves ready to join a mob. Is it true when a real mob forms that only the less intelligent are prepared to join? We cannot be sure. Real mobs do not respond to mock dispatches and they do not pause at excitement's peak to fill out questionnaires.

French (1944) wanted to compare the behavior of organized and unorganized groups in a fear-provoking situation. The unorganized groups were composed of Harvard students who had not met one another before, and the organized groups were Harvard athletic teams and clubs from a neighborhood house in East Boston. The experimental group worked for nearly an hour trying to solve some intellectual and motor skill problems. Then the experimenter handed out questionnaires for them to complete and left the room. The lock on the door had been so fixed as to lock automatically when the door was shut; it could only be opened from the outside. A few minutes later a technician switched on a smoke apparatus and in a short time smoke was curling under the door into the experimental room. When the smoke was thick a fire engine siren was sounded from a remote part of the building. The reactions to all this inventive staging were disappointingly calm. In one group a man said: "I smell smoke, is there a fire?" but another detachedly responded: "They probably want to test our psychological reactions." In a second group the first man to notice the smoke gave a push to the door, the door gave way easily and knocked over the smoke machine.

Although experimental manipulations and rating scales are not easily adapted to the study of collective behavior it is not, on that account, necessary to forego all empiricism. There remain the methods of the journalist, the content analyst, the anthropologist, the detective, the clinician, the opinion analyst, and the demographer. Since collective behavior is extraordinary behavior it is "news" and newspaper stories are data. Ginzburg (1962) has gone over local papers in the South to obtain detail about lynchings over the past one hundred years and this detail gives us some guidance in trying to figure out the causes of lynching. Sometimes a good social scientist has been on the scene when a mob developed and has written a report more useful than any provided by a newspaper. The sociologists Lee and Humphrey were in Detroit at the time of the 1943 race riot and their excellent little book (1943) provides information about the tensions preliminary to the riot, about the precipitating event, the character of the rioters, the behavior of the police, etc.

Often there is no social scientist on the scene when a collective outburst occurs but one may get there soon afterwards. In 1930 there were twenty-one lynchings in the United States and as each one became known the Southern Commission on the Study of Lynchings (1931) dispatched an investigator to the scene. The resultant data (Raper, 1933) teach us a great deal about who participated in lynchings and why. In the years since World War II the Committee on Disaster Studies of the National Academy of Science has sponsored field studies of the social and psychological effects of fires, floods, tornados, and explosions wherever these have occurred.

There are many kinds of data other than the experimental. There are naturalistic data, anecdotes, documents, and lists of mass phenomena. Bogardus (1942), for instance, had a panel of 150 persons identify the five major fads of the year for many years and he classified them and kept track of the distribution of types over time. They are as colorful as a collection of jungle butterflies. For the great follies and explosions of the past there are histories: Melville on *The South Sea Bubble* (1921); Rudé on *The Crowd in the French Revolution (1959)*; Ruppelt's *The Report on Unidentified Flying Objects* (1956). There have even been a few opinion survey studies. On Hallowe'en in 1938 Orson Welles broadcast a play called *The War of the Worlds* which was mistaken for a series of news reports by something like one million people and so caused widespread terror. The Columbia Broadcasting System and several survey research organizations afterwards interviewed people who had heard the broadcast and Cantril used the results in his book *The Invasion from Mars* (1940) to explain what happened.

There is much more information available today on collective behavior than was available to Le Bon, Freud, and McDougall. These data have begun to revive the subject and have somewhat changed it. The crowd or the mob is only one topic now in the large domain of collective behavior which includes also fads, crazes, panics, and social movements. We will, in the section that immediately follows, sample the phenomena included within this domain describing examples of each major type.

Recent advances in the study of collective behavior have come from the sociological end of social psychology rather than from the psychological. The most important study, Smelser's *Theory of Collective Behavior* (1963) attempts to account for the occurrence of each kind of collective behavior in almost purely sociological terms. Using a method he calls "systematic comparative illustration," Smelser has tried to identify the necessary and sufficient conditions producing each kind of collective outburst. He has compared published accounts of such occurrences with accounts of situations in which such outbursts have nearly occurred but not occurred. This method of comparing and contrasting naturalistic accounts has many shortcomings but Smelser's use of it has yielded a more systematic account of collective behavior than any psychological account. In the second section that follows we will review the main line of Smelser's theory and argue that there is some implicit psychology along with the explicit sociology.

In the third and final section of the chapter we will come back to Le Bon and a problem he posed. Why do people in a crowd behave as they do not behave in more ordinary circumstances? Why do violence and selfishness and folly and extravagance, in general, emerge in the crowd? This seemed to Le Bon to be the central problem about crowd behavior and later theorists agreed with him.

The Field of Collective Behavior

Let us not begin with a definition but rather end with one. If you read, first, descriptions of some of the phenomena that the definition must encompass you may be able to anticipate the definition or to improve upon it. The negative cases to keep in mind, the behavior from which collective behavior is to be distinguished, include all those social actions that are organized or institutionalized. Students listening to a lecture are not engaged in collective behavior, neither is a committee operating under Roberts Rules of Order nor a Presbyterian congregation joined in a Responsive Reading nor an Army squad doing its "about faces" and "right obliques."

The first examples will be of panics of escape and panics and crazes of acquisition. These phenomena seem to have the same dynamics and to be fundamentally different from the hostile and expressive outbursts that are described next. Finally there is a short account of a contemporary social movement which is a more organized and enduring kind of collective behavior.

PANICS OF ESCAPE

Eugene O'Neill's *Long Day's Journey into Night* opened in Boston several years ago with Florence Eldridge and Frederic March. The play is a harrowing one and the audience was properly filled with pity and terror the night we were there. Suddenly the first row of the audience was on its feet and then the second and with a smooth motion each successive row went up. The wave reached us in the balcony in a few seconds and swept us to our feet in our turn. The actors cut off their speeches; the audience strained forward. We stood so for half a minute. I heard someone say "Fire" and I looked around to check the exits. An elderly man started to move out to the aisle and when he stumbled over my feet I remember that I felt a kind of rage at him for blocking my path.

Frederic March stepped to the footlights and calmly said. "Please be seated, ladies and gentlemen, nothing serious has happened. Just a little accident with a cigarette." Then for the first time we saw a curl of smoke, an innocuous curl it seemed, since March was saying: "The fire is out now and if you will sit down again we can resume." He walked off the stage looking like Frederic March and came immediately out again, totally in character, and speaking his entrance lines. The audience laughed and sat down.

The outcome was quite different in Chicago's Iroquois Theater on a December afternoon of 1903. Eddie Foy, the famous comedian, was on stage and here follows his account* of what happened:

> As I ran around back of the rear drop, I could hear the murmur of excitement growing in the audience. Somebody had of course yelled "Fire!"—there is almost always a fool of that species in an audience; and there are always hundreds of people who go crazy the moment they hear the word. The crowd was beginning to surge toward the doors and already showing signs of a stampede. Those on the lower floor were not so badly frightened as those in the more dangerous balcony and gallery. Up there they were falling into panic.

* From the book *Clowning Through Life* by Eddie Foy and Alvin F. Harlow. Copyright, 1928, by E. P. Dutton & Co., Inc. Renewal, ©, 1956 by Alvin F. Harlow. Reprinted by permission of the publishers.

I began shouting at the top of my voice, "Don't get excited. There's no danger. Take it easy!" And to Dillea, the orchestra leader, "Play, start an overture—anything! But play!" Some of his musicians were fleeing, but a few, and especially a fat little violinist, stuck nobly.

I stood perfectly still, hoping my apparent calm would have an equally calming effect on the crowd. Those on the lower floor heard me and seemed somewhat reassured. But up above, and especially in the gallery, they had gone mad.

As I left the stage the last of the ropes holding up the drops burned through, and with them the whole loft collapsed with a terrifying crash, bringing down tons of burning material. With that, all the lights in the house went out and another great balloon of flame leaped out into the auditorium, licking even the ceiling and killing scores who had not yet succeeded in escaping from the gallery.

The horror in the auditorium was beyond all description. There were thirty exits, but few of them were marked by lights; some had heavy portières over the doors, and some of the doors were locked or fastened with levers which no one knew how to work.

It was said that some of the exit doors leading from the upper tiers onto the fire escapes on the alley between Randolph and Lake Streets were either rusted or frozen. They were finally burst open, but precious moments had been lost—moments which meant death for many behind those doors. The fire-escape ladders could not accommodate the crowd, and many fell or jumped to death on the pavement below. Some were not killed only because they landed on the cushion of bodies of those who had gone before.

But it was inside the house that the greatest loss of life occurred, especially on the stairways leading down from the second balcony. Here most of the dead were trampled or smothered, though many jumped or fell over the balustrade to the floor of the foyer. In places on the stairways, particularly where a turn caused a jam, bodies were piled seven or eight feet deep. Firemen and police confronted a sickening task in disentangling them. An occasional living person was found in the heaps, but most of these were terribly injured. The heel prints on the dead faces mutely testified to the cruel fact that human animals stricken by terror are as mad and ruthless as stampeding cattle. Many bodies had the clothes torn from them, and some had the flesh trodden from their bones.

Never elsewhere had a great fire disaster occurred so quickly. From the start of the fire until all in the audience either escaped, died, or lay maimed in the halls and alleys, took just eight minutes. In that eight minutes more than 500 perished.

The fire department arrived quickly after the alarm and extinguished the flames in the auditorium so promptly that no more than the plush upholstery was burned off the seats. But when a fire chief thrust his head through a side exit and shouted, 'Is anybody alive in here?' no one answered. The few who were not dead were insensible or dying. Within ten minutes from the beginning of the fire, bodies were being laid in rows on the sidewalks, and all the ambulances and dead-wagons in the city could not keep up with the ghastly harvest. Within twenty-four hours Chicago knew that at least 587 were dead and many more injured. Subsequent deaths among the injured brought the list up to 602.

ACQUISITIVE PANIC AND NEAR PANIC

Panics involve a competition for something in short supply: exits in the case of the Iroquois Theater fire, land or gold or food in the case of acquisitive panics. I picked up some understanding of the acquisitive panic from participation in what might be called The Great Florida Food Rush.

The hotels in Miami Beach offer a modified American Plan by which one enjoys two meals a day for only a few dollars more than the cost of a room alone. The two meals are breakfast and dinner and for bargain vacationers determined to subsist on these two "included" meals the interval between them seems a long one. Dinner is served in two sittings, the first sitting at 6:00 P.M. and the second at 8:00 P.M. If you have been "holding out" since breakfast it is a matter of some urgency to make that first sitting. The difficulty is that the dining room will only seat about half of the hotel's guests at one time and at the hotel where we were staying more than half of the guests were making do with two meals a day.

This talk of economizing and "making do" may suggest that the hotel in question was a pretty common sort of place but that was not the case. The hotels in Miami Beach are all "luxury hotels"; the concept of a vacation in Miami Beach requires them to be. They have names like Fontainebleau and Versailles and Deauville, the ladies wear mink stoles to dinner, the dining-rooms have silk hangings and great chandeliers. All the hotels glitter and the main difference is that some have steak and chops on the menu every night whereas others have steak *or* chops every other night. Ours was a steak *or* chops hotel and a breakfast-and-dinner-but-no-lunch hotel. Nevertheless we were having a Miami Beach vacation and that inspired us all to comport ourselves with grace and style.

Along about 5:30 P.M. elegantly clad guests began to stroll down to the lobby. We promenaded in circles which, as the hour advanced, strayed less and less far from the dining-room door. About 5:45 one couple stopped just in front of the door for all the world as if they were queuing up. The rest of us looked away from this *gaucherie*. The couple endured the exposure and the chill for a few minutes and then walked off with a great show of having accidentally paused just there.

By five minutes of six there were more people in the lobby than could be seated in the dining room. Promenading was no longer possible and each guest took up a stationary position dictated by an implicit social contract. There was no line but there was an order and it was a just order. Without standing one behind another the guests could calculate their beeline distances from the door and the guests who had been longer in the lobby were nearer the door whereas those who had come down more recently were farther from the door. When the door should be opened, if each guest would walk, not run, to the door the probability that he would be admitted would be proportionate to the length of his wait. Exactly as if the guests had formed a line. But a line was forbidden by the requirements of high-style vacationing. An outsider would have thought the guests were haphazardly scattered about the lobby.

The implicit order threatened to become explicit whenever a recent arrival undertook to move a bit closer. People in apparently casual postures proved surprisingly unwilling to step aside. Openings one had seen just ahead closed as one approached. Eyes hardened, chins squared and you stayed where you were.

Exactly on the hour the maitre d'hotel moved to the dining-room door and slowly drew it open. He turned to greet the first guest and just missed being trampled to death. In some of the bank runs that occurred during the Depression, in a few hoarding panics during the War, and in hunger riots throughout history the dynamics have been the same but the stakes higher and so true panics occasionally occurred.

Banks are not ordinarily prepared to pay out all accounts; they rely on their depositors not to appear simultaneously and demand payment. If depositors should come to fear that a bank is not sound, that it cannot pay off all its depositors, then that fear might cause all the depositors to appear on the same day. If they did so the fear would be confirmed because it would not be possible to pay all accounts. However, if they did not all appear at once then there would always be funds to pay those who wanted them when they wanted them.

In a short, interesting article Mrs. Elsie Vaught (1928) has given us an account of a bank run that became a panic. One day in December of 1925 several small banks failed to open in the city where Mrs. Vaught lived. The other banks anticipated a run the next day and so the bank where Mrs. Vaught worked as a teller had enough funds on hand to pay off as many depositors as might apply. The tellers were simply instructed to pay on demand. Next morning a crowd gathered in the bank and on the sidewalk outside. The length of the line convinced many that the bank could not possibly pay off everyone. People began to push and then to fight for places nearer the teller's windows. Clothing was torn and women fainted but the jam continued for hours. The power of the panic atmosphere is evident in the fact that two tellers, though they knew that the bank was sound and could pay out all deposits, nevertheless asked for their own balances. Mrs. Vaught says that she had difficulty restraining herself from doing the same.

THE TULIPOMANIA CRAZE.

Fads and fashions and crazes have to do with actions or artifacts which enjoy a rapid use in popularity followed by an abrupt decline. L. S. Penrose (1952) thinks that the typical curve for these cultural phenomena resembles that for an epidemic disease: a latent period during which the idea is present in the minds of a few but shows little sign of spreading; an explosion period in which the number of people adopting the idea mounts at an accelerating rate; a final period in which immunity to further infection develops. Because the ideas and actions and artifacts involved sharply decline in value, even in some cases to the point of being valueless or positively disliked, the popularity they briefly enjoy seems "faddish" or "crazy"; a mad exaggeration of intrinsic worth. The general lines of the distinctions among the three kinds of contagious follies are obvious enough: fads are trifling and crazes more serious, economic booms and busts in which large sums of money are lost are crazes. Fashions, of course, have chiefly to do with clothing and are more highly institutionalized than are fads or crazes (Hurlock, 1929).

A list of fads makes melancholy reading. The magic has gone out of so many things: Mary Pickford curls, Chaplin moustaches, rolled stockings, "Knock Knock Who's There?", Monopoly, hula hoops, even fifty-mile hikes (Nystrom, 1928; Bogardus, 1942). It is particularly difficult to imagine what made certain language forms faddish; those words or phrases that are, for a season, used in the widest imaginable range of circumstances and always received as an exquisitely clever sally. No one today employs the word "quoz" and I suppose if someone did, the rest of us would not break into hilarious laughter—but all London did so at one time (Mackay, 1841). The expression "flare up" was first applied in England to the flames of Bristol when that city was half burned in a series of riots. The phrase absolutely captivated the masses and Mackay in his book *Extraordinary Popular Delusions and the Madness of Crowds* offers an entertaining paragraph illustrating the ways in which the phrase was used. "The drunkard reeling home showed that he was still a man and a citizen by calling 'Flare up' in the pauses of his hiccough. . . . When, in due time afterwards, the policeman stumbled upon him as he lay, the guardian of the peace turned the full light of his lantern on his face and exclaimed, 'Here's a poor devil who has been flaring up!' Then came the stretcher, on which the victim of deep potation was carried to the watch house and pitched into a dirty cell, among a score of wretches about as far gone as himself, who saluted their new comrade by a loud, long, shout of 'Flare up!' (Mackay, 1962, p. 624)

Fashions and fads are often status symbols (see Chapter 3) and they have a very rapid turnover in our society. This condition is the result of a set of related historical processes. Flugel (1930) observes that for many centuries in Europe there was a "fixed" costume associated with each social grade. As social mobility increased, there developed the impulse to imitate the dress of those belonging to higher strata. The contemporary emphasis on geographical mobility and on mass education has reduced differences of speech and education which can be among the more inflexible of status symbols (Smelser, 1963). At the same time, laws regulating extravagance of food or dress on moral grounds have declined; new techniques of manufacturing and transportation have made it possible to produce cheap imitations of valuable objects; mass communications can make large populations aware of the availability of the imitations. The result is a perpetual restless shuffling of symbols.

Crazes involve larger sums of money than fads and fashions and that makes them more serious; good examples are the Florida land boom of the 1920's (Vanderblue, 1927), the South Sea Bubble of eighteenth century England (Melville, 1921) but the maddest folly was the tulip mania of seventeenth century Holland (Mackay, 1841, 1962; Posthumus, 1928). The tulip is a nice enough flower, the range of color is excellent, and the association with spring is pleasant. Most gardeners like to have some tulip bulbs, but none would value a single bulb at six thousand florins, which was the price for one bulb of the variety called *Semper Augustus* in Holland in 1636. Six thousand florins was approximately the cost of a house and grounds. The account that follows is based on Mackay (1962).

The tulip was introduced into Europe from Constantinople in the middle of the sixteenth century. For unknown reasons the flower became especially popular in Holland, at first with the rich and eventually with the middle classes. It was deemed a proof of poor taste for a man of any fortune to be without a collection of tulips and even people of very modest means began to vie with one another in the rarity of their blooms and in the proportionately preposterous prices they paid for them.

By 1634 the rage for tulips was so great that ordinary industry was being neglected and the larger part of the population of Holland was engaged in the tulip trade. People who had been absent from Holland and who returned at the height of the mania sometimes made awkward mistakes. A sailor is said to have mistaken a bulb worth several thousand florins for an onion and to have cut it up to eat with his herring.

For a time it seemed that the demand for tulips would hold forever; wealthy people the world over were expected to find the flowers irresistible and so to be willing to pay any price for them to the merchants of Holland. Eventually, however, the Dutch could not fail to see that the appeal was largely limited to Holland and in Holland most people were buying bulbs only to sell them again. Even the rich were not planting the rarer bulbs but seemed only to be interested in selling at a profit. As in the game of musical chairs somebody must eventually be left standing so it began to appear that someone was going to be left holding tulips that nobody else wanted anymore. To recognize this outcome as inevitable was, of course, to bring it about. And so the panic came and the price of tulips fell to a reasonable sort of value and very many people were very much poorer.

THE LEEVILLE LYNCHING

This is the story of one of the twenty-one lynchings that occurred in 1930. The Southern Commission on the Study of Lynching (1931) investigated all twenty-one and the Leeville lynching is one of only eight in which the Southern Commission thought it fairly likely that the lynching victim had been actually guilty of the crime of which he was accused. The description that follows is based on an account by Cantril (1941).

One Saturday morning in the spring of 1930 a Negro laborer on a white man's farm near Leeville, Texas, dropped by the farmer's house to pick up the week's wages due him. The farmer's wife told him that her husband was away from the house and had not left the money. The Negro, feeling disgruntled, left the house but came back a short time later with a shotgun and demanded his money. The farmer's wife ordered him out of the house but he backed her into the bedroom and assaulted her sexually several times. Then he fled the house. The woman ran to a neighbor who phoned the sheriff. The Negro was soon captured; he confessed, agreed to plead guilty, and for safekeeping was taken to jail some miles from Leeville.

The above is the version that was commonly accepted by the white population of Leeville, but investigators listening to gossip heard other versions. Negroes in the area, for the most part, believed that the whole story was a frame-up to permit cheating the Negro laborer of his wages. Some of the white farmers said, in private, that they suspected the farmer's wife had invited the Negro to have intercourse with her and then had been frightened into a lie, possibly because her five-year-old child had interrupted the pair. A medical record showed only that intercourse had occurred; it was possible that the Negro was guilty of rape and possible that he was not. In others of the twenty-one lynchings of 1930 it was much less likely that the victim had been guilty.

In spite of the threatening mood of the Leeville community the judge insisted on holding the trial in that town, but he had four Texas Rangers detailed to preserve order. The Rangers brought the Negro into the courtroom early in the morning before any crowd had gathered. That day a large number of people came into Leeville from the farms outside of town. During the morning a crowd gathered in the courtyard and the crowd grew increasingly belligerent. At this critical juncture a rumor developed that the governor of the state had ordered the Rangers not to fire on the crowd in their efforts to protect the accused. The rumor was not true, but it was believed and it lifted the major restraint on the crowd.

About one o'clock the farmer's wife, the presumed rapist's victim, was brought from the hospital by ambulance to give testimony at the trial. When the presumably assaulted woman was carried in on a stretcher the crowd went wild. At first the Rangers kept them back with tear gas and the Negro was taken from the courtroom to a fireproof vault room. Later in the afternoon the mob burned down the courthouse and that night they used an acetylene torch to make a hole in the vault. They inserted dynamite and blew a large enough hole to permit one man to crawl into the vault. A few minutes after disappearing he tossed out the dead body of the Negro.

The corpse was raised with a rope to an elm tree in the courthouse yard so that every one might see it. Then it was tied to a Ford car and dragged through the town; five thousand howling people paraded behind. Finally the body was chained to a tree in the Negro section of Leeville and burned. Some say that the mob leader unsexed the Negro's body just before lighting the fire. Some say that, on this occasion, that was not done. The Leeville lynching turned into prolonged terrorization of the Negro population and it took several hundred members of the National Guard to restore order.

THE 1943 DETROIT RACE RIOT

I can remember the build-up of tensions preliminary to this outburst because I was a high-school student in Detroit at that time; the statistics are from Lee and Humphrey's book (1943) about the riot.

In 1940 there were about 160,000 Negroes in Detroit; in 1943 there were 222,000. Large numbers had migrated from the South, bringing with them a tradition of Negro-white antagonism. Many of these people earned the best wages of their lives in Detroit but they were nearly all crowded into the city's Negro ghetto—the Paradise Valley section—which was and is a substandard, overcrowded, high rental area near the center of the city. Negroes were prevented from finding better housing by restrictive practices and the recreational facilities that were open to them were extremely limited and unsatisfactory.

Negro resentment was probably deepened in 1943 by certain segregation practices which arose nationally during the war. The Red Cross, for instance, separated white blood from Negro. Jim Crow transportation facilities were fairly common in the army. Negroes in the Navy were almost entirely limited to messboy ratings. The Air Force was practically closed to the Negro. There were racial clashes in a number of Army camps. Many of these resentments were probably given aggressive focus by Negro publications.

In the three years 1940–43, Detroit added some 490,000 whites to its population. Many of them came from the South—refugees from a sharecropper system of peonage. They brought with them a set of ideas concerning the proper treatment of Negroes; ideas bred in a land of stunted opportunities where the Negro had been an economic competitor. These Southern whites were greatly irritated by the necessity of coming in close contact with the Negro at work, in vehicles of public transportation, and in public facilities of all kinds. Some of these Southern whites joined the Detroit police force.

Inflaming prejudices in Detroit in 1943 were a number of demagogues, including Father Charles Coughlin, Gerald L. K. Smith, and the Rev. Frank J. Norris. Detroit was unique in the North in having its own unit of the KKK and was a center of operations for the Black Legion.

The exact nature of the incident that precipitated the riot is not known. It occurred on a humid Sunday evening—June 20, 1943—on the bridge leading to Belle Isle which is a large recreational area in the Detroit River. The newspapers reported a fight between a Negro and a white man. There were frequent popular rumors that a Negro baby was thrown from the bridge by white hoodlums. The same rumor was popular in other quarters, with the racial roles reversed. The fighting spread from the bridge to a nearby park and into the city itself. In a very short time five thousand persons were estimated to have become involved. All police precincts sent reserves to the scene. Looting and destruction broke out in Paradise Valley. On Monday, white mobs hunted Negroes, turning the downtown area into a battleground. By midnight Monday the governor had finally taken the necessary steps to obtain Federal troops and the soldiers established a truce. Thirty-four persons had been killed (twenty-five Negroes, nine whites), hundreds were hurt, and there had been thousands of dollars worth of property damage.

COLLECTIVE EXPRESSION IN A REVIVAL MEETING

One way of classifying crowds is by mode of behavior. The important types are the aggressive crowd, the escaping crowd, and the acquisitive crowd. These three kinds of behavior all have external objects or goals: aggression seeks a target; escape seeks an exit or means of removal; acquisition seeks some economic good. Behavior in an expressive crowd has no such clear external goal. The behavior itself seems to be the only end. Pantie raids and spring riots at colleges are usually revelrous as are celebrations of victory at war or in football and some of the things done in Rio de Janeiro at Carnival time. Collective behavior is never institutionalized behavior; it is behavior that is not clearly governed by cultural norms. Much revelrous behavior is institutionalized including many of the extravagances of Mardi Gras and New Year's Eve. Not all group revelry, therefore, counts as a collective or crowd expression.

Revival meetings in which conversion experiences occur and miracle cures and confessions and "speaking with tongues" are classified as expressive crowds unless these manifestations are clearly governed by norms. Davenport's book *Primitive Traits in Religious Revivals* (1905) sets forth an analysis in the style of Le Bon and a point of view that is offensively racist. Boisen (1939) has made a more sympathetic study of the "holy roller" religious sects that prospered in the United States during the Great Depression. He includes such organizations as the Assemblies of God and the Pentecostal Assemblies of Jesus. These were essentially laymen's movements, fundamentalist in doctrine, with no interest in social betterment. Their concern was to save people out of a sinful world; their hopes focused on the after-life. Although austerity was usually practiced —no card-playing, dancing, or theater-going—it was the mystical experience of salvation, the union with a Greater-than-Self that was most important.

Boisen quotes extensively from a pamphlet called *My Baptism* which was written by a middle-aged white man, a one-time Sunday School superintendent who was converted to a Negro mission. At his first meeting this man stood apart and thought supercilious thoughts. This is the way the proceedings looked to him at that point.

> They came forward at once, some twenty of them (in response to the altar call) and kneeled about the altar and then began the strangest prayer I have ever experienced. Someone began singing "Savior lead me lest I stray"; others joined in and the song seemed finally to dissolve in a prayer of many voices, mingled with groans, moans, shouts, and cryings and the fantastic musical wail so peculiar to the colored race. This prayer lasted about twenty minutes. It was brought to a close by an ardent prayer from the black man on the platform. When they arose their faces were beaming with joy. Some one then started singing, "Who shall abide in thy tabernacle? he that walketh uprightly and speaketh the truth in his heart." It was begun by a voice a bit out of tune, but taken up by the others it soon improved in form and tone and with the staccato of clapping hands and the even tinkling of tambourines it became rythmically irresistible. Again and again they sang it with swaying bodies and beating feet, gaining in power amid the shouts of glory. Suddenly a woman on my right shouted, "Praise Him! Praise Him!" Jumping up she began to dance, seemingly without thought as to any one's opinion as to the propriety of the act (Boisen, 1939, p. 188).
>
> [After some months of attendance the Congregational Sunday School superintendent experienced conversion and lost his concern for propriety.] Then I said, "So this is it—well, praise God!—Holy, holy, holy, Lord God almighty!" Then I began to have intervals of liberty—for waves of glory swept over me and when they came I praised God with a loud voice and in the spirit I clapped my hands and rejoiced. (Boisen, 1939, pp. 188–189).

THE BLACK MUSLIM MOVEMENT

A social movement is an effort to change the social order; a social movement is in some degree subversive. Movements that seek a limited change, movement like the Townsend Plan or Technocracy or the desegregation movement, are usually called *reform* movements (Blumer, 1951). Movements that seek to change fundamental beliefs and values, movements like the Protestant Reformation, the Russian Revolution, the American Revolution, and the Black Muslim movement are usually called revolutionary movements.

Smelser (1963) makes a distinction essentially the same as that between the reform and the revolution but he calls the former a norm-oriented movement and the latter a value-oriented movement. A norm-oriented movement, such as the effort of the NAACP to advance desegregation in the United States, is critical of certain practices in the society but not of its fundamental values. Indeed the reform movement always justifies its efforts by an appeal to the society's values. Negroes should not be segregated because Americans value equality of opportunity; the reform proposed is represented as a more adequate realization of basic values than is provided by present practices. A value-oriented movement, on the other hand, criticizes values, and the Black Muslim movement is value oriented. In some societies almost any effort to change the social order will constitute an attack on values. This will happen for instance in a theocratic society where many specific norms are integrated into the religious system. Any criticism in such a society becomes a heresy and may be punished with ultimate sanctions. In a totalitarian society, too, criticism or opposition or deviance may constitute disloyalty. In such a society a movement for change must, of necessity, be revolutionary. The United States offers a contrasting case in which many kinds of reform movements are possible.

The Black Muslim movement is revolutionary because it advocates change at society's core. Not norms but values and basic tenets are the target, beginning with a tenet that we had not realized we held until its contrary was pronounced by the Muslims. "God is black," say the Muslims. What makes this pronouncement so startling is the realization it brings that we had dared to suppose He was white.

The best study of the Black Muslims is a book by C. Eric Lincoln (1961). Lincoln is a professor of social philosophy at Clark College in Atlanta. He is a Negro and so was able to attend Muslim meetings from which whites are barred. Lincoln also had the cooperation of Mr. Malcolm X who was at the time minister of Muslim Temple No. 7 in Harlem and Muhammed's first plenipotentiary. The "X," by the way, is adopted by every Muslim to replace the family name he took from his white owner, the name that marked him as a chattel. Muhammed himself has been interviewed a number of times and the reports of these interviews are good sources of information on the Black Muslim movement. I particularly like Robert S. Bird's article in the *New York Herald Tribune* of April 30, 1963, because it quotes Muhammed at length. James Baldwin's (1963) account of a visit to Muhammed is interesting because of Baldwin's own qualities and because Muhammed seems to have hoped to convert Baldwin.

The Black Muslim movement was started in Detroit in the early 1930's by a man named W. D. Fard who mysteriously disappeared about June of 1934. The leadership passed to Fard's disciple, Elijah Muhammed, who was born in Georgia and originally had the name of Elijah Poole. There is a legend that Elijah Poole as a boy of six or so witnessed the lynching of his own father and that we owe his ministry to this experience.

The headquarters of the Muslim movement is in Chicago, though Muhammed, who suffers from asthma, spends much of his time in Phoenix, Arizona. From Harlem the movement publishes a newspaper called *Mr. Muhammed Speaks.* That newspaper can be bought on Saturdays in Harvard Square and I first became aware of the movement when I noticed a Negro, who was selling the paper, try to give one to a Negro Harvard student. The student, streaming Harvard's long crimson scarf, was on his way to the Dartmouth game and had no time for Mr. Muhammed. However, other Negroes do have time. No one knows how many, but Bird (1963) estimates that there are about 150,000 adherents and some much larger number who are seriously interested.

Muslim doctrine is a figure-ground reversal of familiar theology; it transforms the European and his God into so much white space. God or Allah is black and the first men were black. The white man was not part of the original creation but is the outcome of certain infernal experiments which Allah permitted the devil to make. The devil produced white men whose nature is evil. The parallel is striking with the white segregationists' story that the Negro is the son of the accursed Ham. Allah decreed that the white devils should rule the earth for a few thousand years but their time is now nearly over. The white man will be destroyed and Allah will restore the rule of peace for the sons of Islam—the world's colored population.

The Muslim movement is antagonistic to Christianity because the colored peoples of the world have been enslaved and oppressed by Christian powers and because the Christian ministry has bolstered oppression by counseling the colored people to "turn the other cheek." In effect, Christian America has preached to the Negro: "Do not hate us for hating you." The Muslims prefer the Mosaic *lex talionis:* "An eye for an eye, a tooth for a tooth." Malcolm X put their position in words in a speech at Boston University on May 24, 1960: "We will not attack *anyone*. We strive for peaceful relationships with everyone. BUT—[we teach our people that] if anyone attacks you, *lay down your life!*" (Lincoln, 1961, p. 4)

The Black Muslims teach Arabic in their schools and face toward Mecca when they pray; they are seriously Islamic. The great strength of the religion of Islam is, of course, in Africa and Asia where there are something like 400 million Moslems. It is a Muslim teaching that the "so-called American Negro" derives from these Islamic peoples. The spelling *Muslim* (a perfectly correct dictionary alternative) serves chiefly to separate the Negro sect from the small orthodox Moslem groups in the United States. These orthodox groups in America do not recognize the Muslims as a legitimate Islamic sect. However, Moslems abroad have been more hospitable. Both Malcolm X and Muhammed have travelled in Egypt and other Moslem lands and been welcomed as brothers. Malcolm X wrote back to those at home: "The people of Arabia are just like our people in America . . . ranging from regal black to ash brown. But none are white. It is safe to say that 99 per cent of them would be jim-crowed in the United States of America" (Lincoln, 1961, p. 225). The orthodox international religion of Islam is not racist but rather believes in the all-embracing brotherhood of man. Even so it seems that the Black Muslims are acceptable as a somewhat deviant sect.

The Muslim program follows from their theology: to hold themselves aloof, to sanctify themselves, against their Great Day which is imminent. The Muslims do not gamble, smoke, drink liquor, or eat pork. Muhammed has set his face against conspicuous consumption. There is no vulgar display, no "flash." They live simply and dress conservatively. The movement seems to have been extraordinarily successful in reforming criminals and delinquents as well as in curing alcoholism and drug addiction. The Muslims teach that all of these evils have befallen the black man because he did not know who he was. What he has learned from Muhammed enables him to overcome his sins and weaknesses.

The Muslims scorn Negro leaders like Ralph Bunche and Martin Luther King who seem to them to beg "crumbs from the white man's table." They do not believe in passive resistance or lunch counter sit-ins or in the legal maneuvers of the NAACP. Malcolm X has said of the executive secretary of the NAACP: "Every time I've seen Roy Wilkins he's been at the Waldorf or in the vicinity of the Waldorf. I have never seen him with black people unless they were looking for white people" (Lincoln, 1961, p. 151).

The moderate norm-reforming Negro, in his turn, is likely to be appalled by the Muslims. Thurgood Marshall, the chief legal counsel for the NAACP, said in a speech at Princeton that the Muslims are "run by a bunch of thugs organized from prisons and jails and financed, I am sure, by Nasser or some other Arab group" (Lincoln, 1961, p. 148).

The Muslims believe in segregation, not integration. Muhammed said to Bird (1963): "What do we want to marry a white woman for when we are black men? That is going to ruin our family. We will spotty up our family. What does she want a black man for? Or what does the black man want the white one for? (p. 10)" Economically too, they are segregationists. Muhammed now urges his following to "buy black" as far as possible so that they may enrich one another rather than the white man. The Muslims want a territory to themselves, and it will have to be a large one since they believe that by 1970 all or nearly all of the 20 million Negroes in the United States will believe in Islam. Malcolm X has suggested that nine or ten states would do. Muhammed has sometimes seemed to have United States territory in mind and sometimes territory abroad.

How do the Muslims plan to obtain their territory? They do not make themselves clear on this point. Muhammed has predicted the imminent downfall of the white race. There is frequent talk of the coming Battle of Armageddon. Within the movement there is an elite military group called the Fruit of Islam. But then the Muslims insist they will not attack anyone and the Sons of Islam do not bear arms. Still the Federal Bureau of Investigation watches the Muslims closely. What may be planned by the Muslims remains mysterious. Malcolm X as usual has said it better than anyone else: "Those who say don't know, and those who know aren't saying" (Lincoln, 1961, p. 94). Muhammed insisted to Bird (1963) that he does not preach violence and has never preached violence. He does not even preach Negro supremacy; that is an unwarranted inference from Muhammed's disclosure that the Negro was the first man on earth.

Muhammed does preach that the white man is a devil. "We are tired of suffering, brutality, beatings, killings, just because you don't like us, and just hate us, and absolutely knowing that we are powerless to resist because you have every odd against us" (Bird, 1963, p. 10). Muhammed further declares: "You are our worst enemy. We have no other people who is an enemy to us but you, because we don't live in the country of other people" (Bird, 1963, p. 10). And finally Muhammed says: "If you tell me, I don't want you here, that's sufficient. I'm gone" (Bird, 1963, p. 10).

Why do we not answer: "We do want you here. Not just because you have a lawful right to be here but because we like you. Life would be worse here without you, life would be duller and colder and uglier"? Why do we not answer in that way the Black Muslims and all the American Negroes?

A GENERAL CHARACTERIZATION OF
COLLECTIVE BEHAVIOR

The Black Muslim movement, the Tulip mania, the run at Mrs. Vaught's bank, the Iroquois Theater panic, the Leeville lynching, the Detroit race riot: these are instances of "collective behavior." Now we must attempt to characterize collective behavior in general. It is, in the first place, behavior involving a number of interacting persons. The interaction need not be face-to-face, the persons need not be assembled in one place, but they must influence one another. The many seventeenth-century Dutchmen who were speculating in tulips did not gather together but they were reacting to one another.

Collective behavior is not institutionalized behavior; it is not governed by established norms. There were leaders in the Leeville lynching but they were not selected in accordance with any accepted procedures; they just emerged. It is possible to speak of membership in the rioting crowds in Detroit but there were no pre-established membership criteria. Norms do sometimes develop in collective behavior, especially in collective behavior that endures for a while. There come to be regularities of action and shared ideas about what will be done and ought to be done. But, as Turner and Killian put it in their book *Collective Behavior* (1957), the norms in collective behavior are emergent or spontaneous rather than formalized. A social movement like the Black Muslim is much more formalized and organized than is a crowd and there is some doubt in my mind whether such movements should be considered collective behavior.

On the characterization of collective behavior as interaction that is not institutionalized there is rather good consensus (Blumer, 1951; Brown, 1954; Turner and Killian, 1957; Smelser, 1963). Beyond this point various authors diverge and their definitions become involved with their theories of collective behavior. Smelser, for example, holds that collective behavior is behavior dominated by certain kinds of beliefs, beliefs in extraordinary forces at work in the world, beliefs in great dangers, in conspiracies, in golden wish-fulfilling prospects. We will leave the definitional problem at the level of the rough characterization above since it marks out what sociologists and social psychologists mean by collective behavior. We will, however, follow one theory a little further because it provides a good model for the causation of collective phenomena.

Smelser's "Value-Added" Theory

Smelser begins his book, *Theory of Collective Behavior* (1963), by defining the field, marking out the external boundaries of collective behavior which set it apart from other kinds of social behavior. His definition includes what has been said above and adds several additional qualifications. Smelser then subdivides the field of collective behavior, marks out its internal divisions, which are, for him, the panic, the craze, the hostile outburst, the norm-oriented social movement and the value-oriented movement. All of this is done in terms of a more general theory of social action, the theory closely associated with the name of Talcott Parsons (Parsons, 1951; Parsons and Shils, 1953). Smelser's theory is, in the highest degree, systematic and its complexity is such as to discourage a general summary. However, the most original part of the theory, its treatment of the determinants or causes of collective behavior, can be discussed in isolation from the rest.

Smelser is an economist as well as a sociologist and he takes his conception of the determinants of collective behavior from economics, from the notion of "value-added," which you will find described in Samuelson's famous textbook, *Economics: An Introductory Analysis* (1958, pp. 187–188). Consider the stages by which iron ore is converted into finished automobiles. There must be mining, smelting, tempering, shaping, the combining of steel parts with other components, painting, delivery to a retailer, and selling. Each stage in the process adds its value to the final cost of the product. Outbursts of collective behavior seem to Smelser to be like automobiles in that they are produced by an elaborate sequence of determinants.

The determinants of collective behavior are, in Smelser's theory: *Structural conduciveness, structural strain, growth and spread of a generalized belief, precipitating factors, mobilization of participants for action, operation of social control.* Each of these six conditions is said to be a necessary condition for the production of collective behavior and all six together are said to be sufficient. While the same six kinds of determinant are said to be necessary and sufficient for the production of every sort of collective behavior each determinant comes in many varieties and the combinations of varieties determine what kind of collective behavior will occur—a craze, a panic, a hostile outburst, or a social movement.

We can acquire some understanding of the six determinants of collective behavior by trying to identify them in one familiar case, the Detroit race riot of 1943. You have read most of the facts but it remains to sort them into Smelser's six categories. Consider first *structural conduciveness.*

Structural conduciveness refers to social conditions that are permissive of a given sort of collective behavior. A race riot is a battle between two groups; in the United States, race riots have usually been battles between a white majority and a Negro minority. If a minority simply submits to aggression as did the Negroes in Leeville then that is a terrorization rather than a riot. To make a riot the minority must fight back and for that to happen there probably must be a large compact minority population. Such populations exist only in cities and so the race riot is an urban phenomenon. The presence in Detroit of a large residentially segregated Negro population was a structural feature conducive to or permissive of a race riot. Clearly this determinant is necessary but very far from sufficient; the population is still there in Detroit, larger than it was, but, as of September, 1964, there have been no recent race riots.

Structural strain, the second determinant, is a matter of conflict among values or norms. The present inequality of Negroes and whites in the United States is a source of structural strain because we also believe that all citizens should have equal opportunities. In the two world wars this strain was exacerbated since the American Negro was required to fulfill the sternest obligation of citizenship, service in the armed forces, but was not granted the full privileges of citizenship. Equality of opportunity to die without equality of opportunity to live is a source of strain and probably accounts for the fact that race riots have tended to cluster around the world wars. There were strains for the white population too, especially for the Southern whites who had come to Detroit for war work and were not accustomed to the degree of equality that prevailed there, to unsegregated public transportation and partially unsegregated recreational facilities. Strains of this kind are not enough to produce a race riot; they might equally well have led to passive protest by the Negro or to withdrawal into a new religion.

As the value-added sequence that begins with the mining of iron moves along there is a progressive narrowing of the range of possible final outcomes and this is also true of the determinants of collective behavior. The mining and smelting of iron ore are necessary to the manufacture of many kinds of things, including steel girders, stoves, and locomotives, in addition to automobiles. In the field of social behavior a large, compact ethnic minority and a set of majority-minority strains can lead to legislation, segregation, passive resistance, terrorization, peaceful coexistence, and many other outcomes. In both value-added sequences as each successive determinant is added the outcome becomes more certain.

The growth and spread of a generalized belief is the third determinant. The belief identifies the source of the strain, attributes certain characteristics to this source and recommends that certain actions be taken to relieve the strain. The beliefs in Detroit in 1943 were hostile and fearful on both sides. Among the whites it was something like: "The damn niggers are pushing us off the sidewalks, running down the value of property, and threatening our women. We ought to get rid of them." Among the Negroes it was something like: "The damn ofays hate us and will never give us our rights. We ought to do something about it." There were plenty of racist demagogues to formulate these beliefs and spread them abroad.

The major *precipitating factor* in 1943 was an incident on the Belle

Isle bridge. It was rumored, you remember, that a white baby had been thrown off the bridge and also rumored that a Negro baby had been thrown off. It may be that neither of these things actually happened. But evidently there was some kind of racial "incident" on the bridge on a humid Sunday afternoon when crowds of both Negroes and whites were nearby. The precipitating factor is close in time to the riot and, more than the other determinants, it looks like a sufficient condition unto itself. But it is not. A fight between a black man and a white man is not inevitably a "racial incident." What makes it a racial incident is its interpretation in terms of the hostile beliefs and its occurrence in a situation of structural conduciveness and strain. But it takes more than all these to make a genuine riot.

There must be a fifth determinant, *the mobilization of participants for action.* This is a matter of leadership and communication. In Detroit on the evening of June 20 one Leo Tipton, a Negro, is said to have grabbed a microphone in a Negro night club and urged some five hundred patrons "to take care of a bunch of whites who killed a colored woman and her baby at Belle Isle Park" (Lee and Humphrey, 1943, p. 27). There must have been many such mobilizing communications though most would not have reached a large audience all at once and would not have become part of the historical record.

The operation of social control, the sixth determinant, is not like the others. Social control is really a counter-determinant and it is its relative weakness or absence that makes collective behavior possible. In Detroit in 1943 the social controls were poor. The police, many of them Southern whites, often acted like members of the white mob. The whites were more violent by far than the Negroes but the police arrested 310 Negroes and only thirty whites. In addition the local authorities took some time to decide to request Federal troops and were even not quite clear how to go about it. Consequently the city was a battleground for more than twenty-four hours. There was a race riot in Harlem in the same year as the Detroit riot but the violence was more rapidly quelled and there was much less personal injury. The principal difference lay in the operation of social controls. In the Harlem case, Negro police were used to quell Negro rioters and so the conflict between the mob and the law could not be construed as a part of the battle between the races.

Smelser's theory appears to be almost completely sociological; there is no talk of minds or personalities. His six determinants are not psychological characteristics but are rather variables descriptive of social systems: *structural conduciveness, structural strain, growth and spread of a generalized belief, precipitating factors, mobilization of participants for action,* and *operation of social control.* To be sure, *belief* is a psychological term but notice that the determinant is *growth and spread of belief* which is something that occurs in a social system. Nevertheless it seems to me that the theory is as psychological as it is sociological and to make that case we must return briefly to the value-added model.

The statement that mining, smelting, tempering, shaping, assembling, and painting are all stages in the manufacture of automobiles is acceptable only because we make certain implicit assumptions. The main assumption is that there is a continuity of substance across processes. It is one mass of iron that is mined, melted, tempered, shaped, assembled, and painted. It is this assumption that makes the several distinct processes parts of, or stages in, some single larger process. Perhaps this seemed to Smelser too obvious to say, but not saying it has helped to obscure the psychological dimension of his theory.

There is an assumption of continuity of substance which is implicitly made when we accept Smelser's six determinants of collective behavior as parts of one process, as multiple determinants of some single outcome like the 1943 riot. The independent occurrence of the several determinants will not add up to a race riot or any other kind of collective behavior. A large compact Negro population in Detroit, structured strain in South Africa, a precipitating event on board an ocean liner, will not result in a riot anywhere. Obviously Smelser intends us to understand that the six determinants must all exist in the same nation, or even as in the case of the 1943 riot, the same city. The continuity involved is perhaps better described as a continuity of locus rather than of substance and the locus is simply the relevant social unit.

I think however that a social unit will not do the job. The locus involved (perhaps it is a substance) must really be the human mind. Consider the precipitating event on the Belle Isle Bridge, whatever it was; probably some kind of altercation between a Negro and a white man. Suppose that the persons involved in the altercation and also those witnessing it had been Detroiters who did not feel the strain put on racial ralations by wartime living, and who had not adopted hostile beliefs about the other race. In these circumstances the event would not have precipitated a race riot. The presence in one city, Detroit, of structurally conducive conditions and of structured strain and of a potentially precipitating factor would not have sufficed to make these conditions determinants of a race riot. Smelser's six determinants will only generate collective behavior if they are at work in the same mind. It is continuity of mind that fills the role of continuity of substance. Even as one mass of iron must be successively mined, smelted, shaped and slapped with paint so one mind must successively apprehend conducive circumstances and strain, adopt a generalized belief, interpret an incident in the light of that belief and thereby make of it a precipitating factor.

While Smelser does not explicitly distinguish the mere occurrence of his six determinants from their combination in one mind he does make a distinction between the mere existence of a condition and its "activation as a determinant." The two distinctions may come to the same thing. Here are quotations from Smelser (1963) which suggest that they do. "In the value-added process, then, we must distinguish between the *occurrence* or *existence* of an event or situation, and the *activation* of this event or situation as a determinant" (p. 19). "A loud explosion may have occurred some time in the past without causing any particular alarm. Once certain determinants of panic have accumulated, however, this explosion may be remembered and reinterpreted (i.e., activated as a determinant) in the light of the new situation" (p. 20). Finally, the quotation that comes nearest to saying that the determinants must be psychologically combined. "For instance, a racial incident between a Negro and a white may spark a race riot. But unless this incident occurs in the context of a structurally conducive atmosphere (i.e., an atmosphere in which people perceive violence to be a possible means of expression) and in an atmosphere of strain (i.e., an atmosphere in which people perceive the incident as symbolic of a troubled state of affairs), the incident will pass without becoming a determinant in a racial outburst" (p. 269).

The determinants, as a set of external conditions are not, then, really sufficient to produce collective behavior. Even as conditions apprehended by the same mind the determinants are not sufficient. The way in which they are apprehended or combined is critical. In the next section we will try to characterize the kinds of psychological pattern or combination that belong to the sufficient conditions for some kinds of collective behavior. Social movements will not be treated but only crowds.

The position will be taken that crowds indulge in panics of escape or acquisition, in outbursts that are hostile or expressive when certain patterns of impulse, restraint, and preference are present in a large number of people. For the most part these psychological variables of impulse, restraint, and preference are Smelser's determinants reconceptualized and located in minds. Structural conduciveness and structured strains and social controls and the rest are reinterpreted as mental forces in an effort to find the critical pattern of combination that activates them as determinants.

Psychology of the Crowd

Le Bon's characterization of crowds and his formulation of the problems they pose for scientific explanation dominated the literature on the subject for several generations. The characterization has two parts. Crowds are, in the first place, held to be homogeneous in action and thought. "Whoever be the individuals that compose it, however like or unlike be their mode of life, their occupations, their character, or their intelligence, the fact that they have been transformed into a crowd puts them in possession of a sort of collective mind" (1895, 1960, p. 27).

The actions and mental states which are held to be the same in all members of a crowd are also held to have a particular character; they are highly emotional and irrational. The emotionality and irrationality of crowd behavior seemed to Le Bon to exceed anything in the private life of the individuals composing the crowd. He was much impressed by the fact that ". . . among the most savage members of the French Convention were to be found inoffensive citizens who, under ordinary circumstances, would have been peaceable notaries or virtuous magistrates" (1960, p. 25). He generalized this observation as follows:

> Contrary to an opinion which one is astonished to find coming from the pen of so acute a philosopher as Herbert Spencer, in the aggregate which constitutes a crowd there is in no sort a summing up of or an average struck between its elements. What really takes place is a combination followed by the creation of new characteristics just as in chemistry certain elements when brought into contact—bases and acids for example—combine to form a new body possessing properties quite different from those of the bodies that have served to form it. [1960, p. 27].

The character of the mob, Le Bon held, is more brutish than the average of the private characters of the persons composing it.

THE PROBLEMS OF EMERGENCE AND CONTAGION

What are the chief problems which crowd behavior poses for scientific explanation? Le Bon's conception of the problems follows from his characterization of the phenomenon. Science must explain the two aspects of this characterization; it must explain the emergence in crowds of primitive emotional behavior and must account for the way in which that behavior sweeps through the crowd to produce a homogeneity of thought and action. Le Bon not only set the problems but also set the general character of the answers.

The wildness and folly of the crowd are not created *de novo* in the crowd. The impulses are always there in all of us but crowd behavior seems to be inconsistent with private character because impulses are acted out in the crowd which are ordinarily controlled and even kept unconscious by social considerations. More primitive humans, Le Bon's odd list that included "savages" and children and women, do sometimes express their unsocialized natures outside of the crowd but it takes membership in a crowd to release stupidity and ferocity in a civilized man. The crowd lifts the lid on pre-existent primitive urges. It is not altogether clear in

Le Bon how the crowd is able to have this effect but he makes one plausible suggestion. The anonymity that comes with large numbers causes a loss of responsibility. Authors immediately after Le Bon departed from his theory chiefly by expanding the list of factors that might cause extraordinary behavior to be released in a crowd.

How does it happen that emotionality and irresponsibility, once they arise in a crowd, prove so powerfully contagious as to produce a kind of "mental unity." Le Bon referred vaguely to suggestion and hypnotic effects. McDougall suggested that a kind of "primitive sympathy" operates. "The principle is that, in men and in the gregarious animals generally, each instinct with its characteristic primary emotion and specific impulse is capable of being excited in one individual by the expressions of the same emotion in another by virtue of a special congenital adaptation of the instinct on its cognitive or perceptual side" (1920, p. 25). F. H. Allport (1924) wrote of "social facilitation," Park and Burgess (1921) of "rapport," Miller and Dollard (1941) and Blumer (1951) of "circular reactions." These concepts are largely equivalent to one another and to Le Bon's "contagion."

Turner and Killian (1957), though holding that Le Bon's description of the behavior of crowds was "graphic and highly accurate," point out that Le Bon and others somewhat exaggerated the homogeneity of behavior in a crowd. There is almost always some division of labor. In a lynching there are some who bring ropes, some who threaten the sheriff, some who light fires, and some who only stand by and watch. Turner and Killian also take exception to Le Bon's characterization of crowd behavior as "irrational" and "emotional." What he ought to have said is that crowd behavior, like collective behavior in general, is spontaneous and uninstitutionalized.

> Emotion and reason are not today regarded as irreconcilables. Emotion may accompany the execution of a well-reasoned plan, and the inadequately-reasoned plan may be accompanied by no arousal of emotions. The rational-irrational dichotomy seems to have two distinct kinds of meanings. Based on external criteria, behavior can be called rational when it is an efficient way of achieving some goal. By this definition much institutional behavior is irrational and much collective behavior is rational. Who can say that the occasional lynching was not for several decades a fairly efficient way of keeping the Negro in a subordinate place? Using internal criteria, behavior is irrational when the individual does not weigh all possible alternatives of which he can be aware in deciding his course of action. By this definition most institutional behavior is irrational, since social norms narrow the range of alternatives which the individual can consider. While each of the major types of collective behavior has its own characteristic ways of so restricting attention within the range of potential alternatives, collective behavior is not different from other types of behavior in this respect. [Turner and Killian, 1957, p. 17].

The root of the confusion is that behavior conforming to norms is behavior we are used to and can predict. Behavior we can predict seems reasonable or rational and unpredictable behavior seems irrational. "Irrational," in Le Bon's day, implied "emotional" and so collective behavior was characterized as irrational and emotional.

While there are these various criticisms of Le Bon's descriptions and his concepts most of us think that he caught something important when he observed that individuals combined into a crowd manifest "new characteristics." Turner and Killian reformulate the point in these terms: ". . . there is a decision-making process which takes place on a group basis, reaching conclusions which would not have eventuated from individual decision-making" (p. 15). The new "characteristics" or "conclusions" are not necessarily emotional and irrational but they are non-normative and are generally in clear opposition to norms. We will address ourselves to the problems of emergence and contagion of non-normative behavior.

CONSTITUTION OF A CROWD

The general circumstances necessary for the emergence and contagion of behavior that is counter to the norms seem to be:

1. There must be a large number of people in communication with one another. How large the number must be is a question to which we will return.

2. These people must have two opposing impulses, the same two impulses for everyone. One of the impulses, the one initially dominant, is in conformity with a recognized norm or value, the other is not. The opposed impulses are such things as: To rush an exit in a theater, to take one's turn in reaching the exit; to attempt to lynch someone, to let the law take its course; to try to push ones way to the teller's cage in a bank run, to take one's turn; to make a confession and be converted at a revival meeting, to remain a quiet member of the audience.

3. The situation must be such that it is physically possible to take the non-normative action; i.e., there must be a theater exit or a person to be lynched or a teller's cage or a revival meeting.

This is the setting for mob psychology: a large number of people with a common conflict of impulse, in communication with one another, and having the physical possibility of acting out the impulse they would not ordinarily act out.

What causes the non-normative behavior to occur and prove contagious? We will begin with the case of escape panic, try to show that it is essentially the same as the acquisitive panic and that both of these are fundamentally different from hostile and expressive outbursts (lynchings, riots, revival meetings) which are themselves fundamentally alike.

PANICS OF ESCAPE AND ACQUISITION

The word *panic* has never been used to designate orderly escape behavior. However great the danger, however high the emotion, if the escape effort observes social norms it is not called panic. The term is reserved for cases like the Iroquois Theater fire and the Cocoanut Grove fire in Boston when the social contract is thrown away and each man single-mindedly attempts to save his own life at whatever cost to others. When people are pushed and trampled and exits are jammed one speaks of panic. When people are ruthless and selfish beyond the ordinary and beyond what the culture approves one speaks of panic.

What causes the emergence of escape efforts that violate the norms? It cannot be danger alone nor the fear it causes since most air raids, including even the atomic bombing of Hiroshima (Janis, 1951) have not produced panic and the Committee on Disaster Studies has found that such natural disasters as tornados, floods, and explosions almost never produce panic. Smelser (1963) argues that there is a factor of structural conduciveness that is necessary to panic. There must be the possibility of escape and also the possibility of entrapment. When escape routes are completely closed as in mine disasters and submarine accidents no panic occurs. When escape routes are completely open panic also does not occur. Quarantelli puts it: "The flight of panic arises only when being trapped is sensed or thought of as a possibility . . ." (1954, p. 273).

A Paradigm of Panic. Alexander Mintz in 1951 pointed out that in a situation such as we have described the utility of taking one's turn or of rushing the exit is dependent on what other people decide to do. If all will be orderly then all may escape or perhaps all but those in the last rows of the balcony. You can safely take your turn if you are not in those rows. But if people behind you attempt to thrust ahead you may be last in line or the exit may become obstructed. If others bolt then your only chance is to bolt. Mintz believed that this "unstable reward structure," as he called it, was the essential condition for the occurrence of panic. He suspected that the threat to life and the extreme fear that are occasioned by a theater fire might not be necessary to panic and he contrived a laboratory paradigm, or model experiment, which is superficially very remote from panic but which preserves the essence as Mintz conceived it.

Aluminum cones with attached strings were put in a large bottle, the bottle having a narrow neck such that only one cone at a time could be withdrawn. If two cones arrived together they would jam the neck of the bottle. Experimental subjects held the ends of the strings. In one condition water was gradually admitted to the bottle from below and each subject was told that he would be given twenty-five cents if he removed his cone from the bottle while it was still dry. As the wet area of his cone increased he would be expected to pay increasingly large fines. The water is Mintz's fire, the neck of the bottle his exit, and the cones are people. In these conditions, intended to duplicate the conditions of panic, traffic jams invariably occurred. Some groups of subjects were allowed to hold preliminary discussions and to make a plan of cooperation. Even when such plans were made, however, serious traffic jams usually occurred. On the other hand when the water and the rewards and fines were removed and the subjects were simply told to draw the cones from the bottle no serious jams occurred even though Mintz instructed some subjects to make noise and do their best to "panic" the others.

Escape Panic as the Outcome of a Game. The abstract form of the panic, as Mintz has described it, resembles certain problems treated by Von Neumann and Morgenstern in their *Theory of Games and Economic Behavior* (1944). It resembles, in particular, the famous problem called "The Prisoners' Dilemma." However, the resemblance is not so strong that we can consider "The Prisoners' Dilemma" a model of panic. There is an analogy, nothing more. And the other games we will be describing are also only analogous with, not models for, crowd behavior. Here is "The Prisoners' Dilemma" adapted from a version used by Luce and Raiffa (1957).

Two men suspected of a crime have been taken into custody and separated. The district attorney is confident that the two together have committed the crime but he does not have evidence that is adequate to convict them. He points out to each prisoner alone that each has two alternatives: to confess to the crime the police are sure they have committed or not to confess. If they both do not confess the district attorney states that he will book them on some minor charge such as illegal possession of weapons and each will get one year in the penitentiary. If both confess they will be prosecuted but the district attorney will recommend less than the most severe sentence; both will get eight years in the penitentiary. However, if one confesses and the other does not then the one who confesses will receive lenient treatment for turning state's evidence while the other will get the maximum penalty. The lenient treatment might mean six months in jail and the maximum might be twenty years.

The essentials of the Prisoners' Dilemma are diagrammed in Table 14-1 as a payoff matrix, representing what will happen to each prisoner as a consequence of the four possible combinations of confessing and not confessing. Prisoner A's two options, "Confess" and "Not confess," are represented as the two rows and the same two options for Prisoner B appear as the columns. The four cells created by the intersections of the rows and columns are the four possible combinations of decisions by A and B. Both may "Not confess," A may "Not confess" and B "Confess,"

A may "Confess" and B "Not confess," both may "Confess." The entries in the cells represent the payoffs to A and B with the payoffs to A being listed first in each case.

Each prisoner knows that the other has the same options and knowledge as himself. Each can make a personal preferential order of the four outcomes and each can guess the other's order. Mutual non-confession would produce a reasonably agreeable outcome for both; in fact it would be their second choice of the four outcomes. However, the outcome that A would most prefer (six months for himself and twenty years for B) is necessarily the outcome that B would least prefer and vice-versa. Both would select mutual confession (eight years each) as their third choice among the outcomes. Because the preferences of the two prisoners are somewhat opposed (the outcome one likes best the other likes least) the two prisoners are somewhat competitive. Because their preferences are not completely opposed (they agree on their second and third choices) the prisoners are not completely competitive. These two properties make the problem an instance of what is called in game theory a "non-zero-sum game."

TABLE 14-1. PAYOFF MATRIX FOR THE PRISONERS' DILEMMA

		PRISONER B	
		Not confess	Confess
	Not confess	1 year for A; 1 year for B	20 years for A; 6 months for B
PRISONER A	Confess	6 months for A; 20 years for B	8 years for A; 8 years for B

What must be the state of mind of each prisoner? Will not each elect "Not confess" so that both can get off with just one year? But does A feel that he can trust B to choose "Not confess?" Suppose that A does so and B doublecrosses him and confesses. And B will be tempted to do just that since if he succeeds he will get off with just six months and A will get twenty years. Probably A will reluctantly decide that he dare not take the risk of getting twenty years, he must confess and hope that B will not confess. At worst A will get eight years. Probably B will decide the same and both will get eight years.

What is the analogy with panic? The differences are obvious and numerous. For instance, there are not two players but many in the panic. However, certain essentials can be captured by thinking of the problem from the point of view of one person at a time and representing the participants as P (person) and as G (for the group of persons nearby P).

The two possible actions available to both P and G are: 1) to rush the exit or the neck of the bottle and; 2) to take one's turn. We can set up these alternatives as a fourfold table in the manner of Table 14-1 but an appropriate representation of the payoffs is not easy to imagine.

If both P and G take their turns it may be the case that both P and G can expect to escape with minor burns or with aluminum cones only slightly wet and they will have behaved in the socially approved normative manner. This outcome we will assign the value +. If both P and G rush the exit it may be that they can expect more severe injuries, perhaps they run some risk of losing their lives; and they will have behaved in a ruthless antisocial manner. This outcome we will assign the value −. If, however, P should decide to take his turn while everyone near him rushes the exit then the others may be sure to escape without injury and he may be sure to lose his life or to get his cone completely wet. If it is P who rushes the exit while G does not, then the payoffs would be reversed. We will represent the most favorable outcome (certain escape without injury) as ++ and the most unfavorable outcome (certain entrapment) as −−. The result is the payoff matrix of Table 14-2.

TABLE 14-2. PAYOFF MATRIX FOR A PERSON (P) AND A GROUP (G)
IN AN ENTRAPMENT SITUATION

		G	
		Take turns	Rush exit
P	Take turns	+ for P; + for G	−− for P; ++ for G
	Rush exit	++ for P; −− for G	− for P, − for G

In many ways this model matrix is unrealistic. For example the payoffs would not be the same for each person in a theater when a fire breaks out. Those nearest the exit can count on escaping without injury (++) whether they rush or take their turns. Those farthest from the exit may have no chance of escaping, if they take their turns, no matter what the others do. The actual perceived prospects would depend on how bad the fire looked in any given case. But in all cases the prospects of taking your turn must look worse the farther P is from the exit. Recall Eddie Foy's words about the Iroquois Theater fire: "Those on the lower floor were not so badly frightened as those in the more dangerous balcony and gallery. Up there they were falling into panic" (p. 104). For those farthest from the exit in a bad fire there would be no dilemma, no conflict of impulse. For them there would be only the simple imperative to save one's life at any cost.

The matrix of Table 14-2 is unrealistic in other ways. For example, the consequence to P of a rush by G would not be the same as the consequences to G of a rush by P since P is but one and G is a group. In spite of its many arbitrary and unrealistic features the matrix of Table 14-2 seems to capture the essence of the escape dilemma. If everyone can be counted on to take his turn everyone can escape. But does P dare to trust G and does G dare to trust P? To be sure they are not in quite the situation of prisoners A and B since the members of the theater audience can watch one another for signs of bolting. However, this difference is probably not important since the decisions must be made quickly and in the smoke and confusion it would be hard to tell what anyone else is up to.

The Prisoners' Dilemma has a rational solution. It is clear what A and B ought to do. In Table 14-1 look at the row representing "Confess" for A. His payoffs in that row are better than his payoffs in the other row whatever B may do; six months instead of one year if B does not confess and eight years instead of twenty years if B does confess. A rational A, not knowing what B will do, should choose to confess. Look now at the column representing "Confess" for B. His payoffs in that column are better than his payoffs in the other column whatever A may do: six months instead of one year if A does not confess and eight years instead of twenty years if A does confess. A rational B, then, must also confess. Two rational players will confess and will thereby earn eight years apiece. This is a much less desirable outcome than the one year they could get if both would choose not to confess. Nevertheless confession is the rational choice for each prisoner since neither can know what the other will do. The peculiar irony of the Prisoners' Dilemma is the fact that rationality in both players produces a far from optimal outcome for both.

The Entrapment Dilemma represented in Table 14-2 contains the same irony. Everyone must choose to rush the exit for reasons exactly parallel to those that lead the prisoners to confess. The row marked "Rush exit" contains the better outcomes for P and the column marked "Rush exit" the better outcomes for G. But if both should choose rationally the result, for both, would be severe injuries and total blockage of the exit. It is this irony about escape behavior that is always worked over by newspaper editorialists after a panic occurs. "If only everyone had stayed calm and taken his turn, then. . . ."

Since the non-normative, socially disapproved action of rushing the exits is the rational solution of the entrapment problem one wonders why it does not occur always and immediately. The first answer is that rushing is not the rational solution unless the payoff matrix looks like the one in Table 14-2. A small fire that made enough smoke to force evacuation of a theater but which never seemed a serious threat would not cause panic because the payoff for pushing others and being discourteous would be worse than enduring a delay and inhaling a little smoke. When the payoff matrix is like the one in Table 14-2 there might still be a period of hesitation before panic. This could be the time that it takes for the values in the matrix to become clear to everyone in the house. It could be an interval produced by many practice fire drills which cause everyone to start out by being orderly.

What should a fire drill or an entrapment drill be like if it is to immunize people to panic? The fire drill, at present, constitutes practice of the approved gross muscle movements: stand in your row and file quickly out. This might be the right thing to do but there is another conceivable approach. We might practice playing games having the payoffs of the entrapment matrix; Mintz's little paradigm with cones and the bottle is such a game. Could one learn the necessity of behaving normatively and trusting others to do the same and would this lesson transfer to entrapment problems in life?

Both the Prisoners' Dilemma and the Entrapment Dilemma admit of a solution that would be fairly agreeable to all participants, much more agreeable than the outcome of mutual "rationality." If both prisoners will not confess then both will get just one year which is their second choice among the outcomes. If both P and G will take their turns they will escape without minor injuries and that is their second choice. Clearly, therefore, these are problems that call for cooperative behavior. If the participants could get together beforehand and make a pact to cooperate then they could guarantee a relatively favorable outcome. Let us imagine that prisoners A and B have a moment together and both swear they will not confess. Then they separate to two rooms and the district attorney interrogates one at a time; he begins with A and A is about to deny the crime. But hold on. It occurs to A that if B is going to keep the agreement and not confess then he, A, can break the agreement, turn state's evidence and get off with six months. That poor sap B, what a sucker! Except . . . B can have these same thoughts and try to leave A hung up on their cooperative pact. The payoff matrix is unchanged by the pact and it destroys confidence in the pact. Neither man will dare not to confess.

There is reason to think that agreements to cooperate will not work in either the Prisoners' Dilemma or the Entrapment Dilemma. Mintz, you may remember, allowed some of his groups of subjects to confer together before the water was introduced into the bottle and so to work out an order of evacuation. But when the entrapment started they almost invariably deserted the plan and jammed the neck of the bottle. Fire drills are really a general compact to behave well in entrapment situations but fire drills have not prevented all panics. We can only echo Luce and Raiffa's remark about the Prisoners' Dilemma: "There ought to be a law against such games!" (1957, p. 97)

Since the essence of panic seems to be a certain payoff matrix that need not involve more than two persons, why should panic be considered a form of crowd behavior? Why in the case of panic should it be necessary to have a *large number* of persons with the same conflict of impulse? The game theory analysis shows that the role of numbers in panic is almost incidental. The numbers must be great enough so that the exits are not completely adequate, so that there is a possibility of entrapment. If there had only been ten people in the Iroquois Theater there would have been no panic. This is not because ten people are too few to make a group mind or to generate hysteria or to activate "primitive sympathy" but because ten people, given the number of exits and their size, are not enough to create a competition. Mintz created the essence of panic with even fewer people by reducing the number of exits to one and the size to the narrow neck of a bottle. The game-theory analysis of panic provides a precise answer to the question: "How large a crowd does it take to make panic possible?" The answer is precise but it is not the kind of answer we might have expected; it is not a fixed number. The answer is: "It takes a crowd big enough to produce the Entrapment Dilemma in the given situation." Le Bon believed that the essential crowd mentality might be found in groups of any size. He had a strong intuition that the dynamic involved was essentially independent of numbers. We can agree completely with his statement: "At certain moments half a dozen men might constitute a psychological crowd . . ." (1960, p. 27).

Acquisitive Panic as the Outcome of a Game. The payoff matrix of Table 14-2 describes certain crazes, financial booms, bank runs, food riots, and wartime hoarding as accurately as it describes escape panic. All of these social processes involve competition. When the competition is for a scarce good we will speak of a panic of acquisition and when the competition is for a means of egress we will speak of a panic of escape.

TABLE 14-3. A PAYOFF MATRIX FOR TULIPOMANIA

	G	
	Buy bulbs	Sell bulbs
Buy bulbs	+ for P, + for G	— — for P, ++ for G
P		
Sell bulbs	++ for P, — — for G	— for P, — for G

We will try to imagine a payoff matrix to fit the Tulipomania. The participants must again be reduced to P and G. The two alternative actions that may be taken are: 1) To buy more tulip bulbs than one sells; 2) to sell more bulbs than one buys. What should the payoffs be? If both P and G are chiefly interested in buying, prices will tend to rise and P and G can buy cheap and sell dear and so make a profit. This outcome we will designate +. If both P and G are more interested in selling than in buying prices will go down, the first sales may be at fairly good figures but later sales will be at low figures. We will designate this outcome —. If P should continue chiefly to buy when everyone else is selling then he is going to get caught with a large collection of worthless bulbs; an outcome we will designate — —. G in this case will have unloaded his stock when prices were .gh and made good his profits; an outcome we will designate $++$. The unrealistic aspects of this mapping are numerous but it does account for the role of trust in crazes and booms and banking and the feelings of fear and urgency that arise when the trust fails.

Since there is a rational solution for the matrix of Table 14-3 as for the previous matrices and that solution is for both P and G to sell, the question arises as to how a craze or boom ever gets started. The answer is that the imperative to sell does not arise until the matrix takes on the form of Table 14-3 and for that to happen the price of tulips must be considerably inflated. In the beginning when prices are low there is no danger in buying while others sell and no great advantage in selling while others buy. If one values tulips for their own sake one is glad to own a large number permanently. With the inflation of the price it begins to be evident that most people cannot afford to plant tulips in the garden but must count on selling them and that means that someone is going to lose fearfully. Only the first to sell can keep his gains. And the panic is on.

The significance of the number of participants in a craze or a boom is the same as in a panic: there must be enough people involved to create a competition for the good in question. Sometimes the number is small and the good a trifling one. Consider the dynamics of a smorgasbord dinner at a restaurant for which one pays a flat fee but which includes a very desirable dish in limited quantity; perhaps some choice Swedish meatballs. If everyone takes a reasonable number, one or two, there will be enough for all and the possibility of a second run. But if people start loading their plates with all they want, then some must do without and he who took but one will be unable to eat what he has for fear that he will be too late to get more. Proprietors of smorgasbord restaurants know the vital importance of appearing to have an inexhaustible supply of the choice dishes. It is necessary for the same reason that it is necessary for banks to appear always able to pay out all accounts in full. Any sign of a shortage will create an artificial demand. The well-laden table will be knocked over and guests will pelt one another with bits of raw herring.

HOSTILE CROWDS AND EXPRESSIVE CROWDS

The conflict of impulse that operates in an escape panic is created in an instant. One impulse arises out of danger, like fire or flood, and a supply of exits inadequate to the demand. It is an impulse that will be the same for all human beings, it requires no special preparation. The other impulse, the impulse to take one's turn and to be considerate of others, is a cultural norm that comes into play whenever the members of a collectivity cannot all simultaneously escape from a danger. The conflict of impulse that dominates a lynching or riot is rather different. There is, to be sure, a normative restraining impulse, a very strong one, the legal and religious proscription of murder. The conflicting non-normative impulse, however, is not an aspect of universal human nature. While everyone can be counted on to want to escape a fire not everyone will want to injure or kill a Negro. The qualifications for membership in a lynching or race riot are more particular than the qualifications for participation in a panic of escape. The nature of those qualifications, the source of the non-normative impulse, is the important problem here as it is not in panics. We will consider that problem with respect to lynchings.

Reliable records of lynching date from 1882 when the *Chicago Tribune* began to publish at the end of each year an itemized summary of disasters and crimes in the United States. More than three thousand Negroes have been lynched since 1882 with the number declining in each successive decade. In the most recent complete decade, 1951–59, there were none except in 1955 when there were three. Still more recently, lynchings or something very like them, have been resumed. For example, the murder of the three civil rights workers, James Chaney, Michael Schwerner, and Andrew Goodman in Neshoba County, Mississippi, may have been a lynching.

Almost all lynchings in this century have occurred in the Southern states. The question is: Why have some Southern whites wanted to lynch Negroes? We will consider, first, explanations that the lyncher himself might have offered or, at any rate, found comprehensible and then, as the facts force us to do so, we will consider motives the lyncher would not have been prepared to acknowledge.

Lynching as Social Control. Lynching, an apologist might tell us, began as a form of frontier justice and, in the South, has been an adjunct of the law essential for controlling the excessive criminality of the Negro. Lynching does seem to have originated as a rather scrupulous and respectable, though extra-legal, procedure. There are conflicting accounts but J. E. Cutler in his *Lynch-law* (1905) accepts as best-authenticated its origin in connection with Colonel Charles Lynch, a Revolutionary War patriot who organized leading citizens in his region of Virginia to punish Tories who were harassing the Continental forces and otherwise impeding the cause. Since the nearest court was some two hundred miles distant, it had become necessary to institute some local authority. Lynch's court seems to have taken great care to act justly and it never invoked the death penalty. In its origin, then, lynch law was relatively mild extra-legal justice administered by community leaders to repair the inadequacies of the civil courts.

Lynching followed the frontier westward. Until 1830 the usual sentences were whipping, tarring and feathering, and banishment from the community. After that date such serious frontier crimes as horse stealing and cattle rustling were punished by death; usually hanging. As Abolitionist strength grew, lynch law was increasingly used to keep down that sentiment. Until 1890, however, lynching victims were mainly white. With the Reconstruction, the lynch became a bloody method for the control of the newly free Negro populations of the South. Walter F. White has suggested in his book *Rope and Faggot* (1929) that until the Negro was emancipated his cash value to his owner helped preserve him from attack but when he was freed he ceased to be anybody's property.

Why did lynching continue in this century? The Negro had been legally free for a generation by 1900; both he and the Southern white man had had an opportunity to get used to the new state of things. Why did lynchings continue? The answer might be given that lynching continued because the extreme criminality of the Negro race made it necessary. And in fact Negroes in America have contributed disproportionately to some crime rates and still do so. But is that criminality racial? And was lynching needed to supplement the law?

The *Uniform Crime Reports* for 1960–61 published by the Federal Bureau of Investigation (1961–62) show that the over-all crime rates for American Negroes ran two-and-a-half to three times the rates for whites. The reference is not to raw frequencies but to frequencies in relation to population size (or rates). In certain categories Negro rates in 1960–61, as in many prior years, were five to seven times as great as white rates. The categories are crimes of aggression, such as aggravated assault and homicide and crimes of escape, such as drunkenness, gambling, drug addiction. This general pattern appears also in statistics for the specific regions, years, and crimes most directly relevant to lynching. In 1921–22, for instance, the homicide rates in Atlanta, Birmingham, Memphis, and New Orleans per 100,000 Negro population were 103.2, 97.2, 116.9, and 46.7 while the corresponding rates for the white population were 15.0, 28.0, 29.6, and 8.4 (Southern Commission on the Study of Lynching, 1931).

From the fact that Negro Americans have high rates for certain crimes it does not necessarily follow that the rates are high because the Americans are Negro. A contrast between Negroes in general and whites in general is always a contrast that involves more than race. The Negroes are more likely to be unemployed, will have a lower average income and less education, will be more likely to live in slums and to belong to disorganized families (Pettigrew, 1964). All these "incidental" correlates of race are also correlates of crime independently of race, and plausible causes of crimes. There really is no evidence that the Negro is disposed to crime because of his race.

In the first place Negro populations do not always have high crime rates. Bohannan and his associates (1960) showed that 71 per cent of forty-one East African tribal groups had lower homicide rates than whites of either South Carolina or Texas in 1949–51. In that same period the homicide rate for Negroes in Texas and Florida was four times as great as the rate for Negroes in Massachusetts (Pettigrew and Spier, 1962). Apparently, then, the condition of being Negro is not sufficient to produce disposition to crime.

In the second place the incidental correlates of being Negro are, in the absence of the racial condition, sufficient to produce high crime rates. While white-collar crime does exist in the United States the great bulk of recorded crime in this country occurs in the lower socio-economic groups—of whatever race (London and Myers, 1961; Schmid, 1960). In Philadelphia, for example, over 90 per cent of the homicides are perpetrated either by the unemployed or by those in the least skilled occupations (Wolfgang, 1958). There is good reason to suspect, therefore, that the Negro crime rates are high because of the many kinds of disadvantage that Negroes suffer in the United States in general and in the Southern states in particular.

The crucial test of the racial disposition theory ought to be a comparison of Negro and white populations equated for socio-economic status. In such equated populations the Negro-white crime rate differential generally turns out to be much reduced but it does not altogether disappear (Blue, 1948; Moses, 1947; Wolfgang, 1958). The residual difference could be a consequence of racial dispositions but it probably is not. It probably is not because the equating is never perfect. Negro privation is more extreme than white privation. It probably is not possible to find white groups as destitute as are the Negro populations that have the highest crime rates (Pettigrew, 1964).

An apologist for lynching might respond to all these statistics by saying that it really does not matter *why* the Negro is prone to crime. The fact that the Negro *is* prone to crime justifies extraordinary measures —such as lynching. We might take the line that the lyncher ought, in strict consistency, to take the same extraordinary measures against those underprivileged white populations that are crime-prone, but I guess we do not really want to persuade him of this.

Granting the high crime rate (though not the racial disposition) it remains to ask whether the legal measures for controlling Negro crime require to be supplemented by lynching. Is there some danger that the police and courts will be unduly lenient with accused Negroes? In the

South? Here is a representative statistic (Federal Bureau of Prisons, 1962). Between 1930–61 some 442 rapists were legally executed in the United States. Ninety per cent of them were Negroes and all but two were executed in either a Southern or a border state. Was this because almost all convicted rapists in the United States were Negroes? No, more than half of them were white. The general picture is that Negroes convicted of any given charge are likely to receive more severe sentences than are whites (Federal Bureau of Prisons, 1955, 1957; Wolfgang, 1958). Negroes are also less likely to be parolled (Von Hentig, 1940). They are probably more likely to be arrested and charged for any given illegal action than are whites. This last possibility is an important one because it means that Negro crime rates may be inflated by discrimination, for the reason that crime rates are really rates of arrest, charge, or conviction. We do not know true rates of crimes committed.

There has never been any danger that law enforcement agencies in the South would be more lenient with the Negro than with the white. Why then should lynching have been necessary to control Negro crime if it was not necessary to control white crime? There is an answer that the lyncher might have accepted though he would have found it less agreeable than the answer he himself proposed. The chief shortcoming in the law was not leniency but the fact that it could only punish things that were unlawful. There were many ways in which the Negro could offend a lyncher that were not unlawful. Lynching was needed to take care of impertinence and assertiveness, to teach Negroes not to insist on being paid for their labor, not to press for their legal rights, not to speak familiarly to a white woman. It was needed, in sum, to buttress white supremacy.

The desire to maintain white supremacy is a desire the lyncher would have acknowledged, even though he might have been less proud of it than of a desire to control Negro crime. We must suggest, however, that it was not the only source of the impulse to lunch. There were still less honorable and much less "rational" desires involved.

Lynching as a Means to Selfish Economic Ends. Lynchings were not a uniform phenomenon and one variety, the "Bourbon" (Cantril, 1941) or "vigilante" (Myrdal, 1944) lynching, was a semi-institutionalized instrument of white supremacy. The Bourbon lynching was often engineered by leading citizens with the knowledge of law enforcement officers. The object was usually to punish a specific crime, there was at least some interest in establishing the guilt of the accused, and innocent Negroes were protected (Cantril, 1941). The Bourbon lynching was planned and orderly and so nearly institutionalized that it perhaps does not belong in a discussion of collective behavior. Its orderliness and social support link it to the lynch law of Revolutionary and frontier days.

There remains, however, an important distinction: Bourbon lynchings were not an adjunct of the law. They pursued the extra-legal aim of intimidation and suppression of a minority.

The contrast to the Bourbon lynching was the "mob lynching" (Myrdal, 1944) in which there was little concern with the guilt of the victim, the innocent were not protected, and the leaders were not "respectable" citizens. This is the kind of lynching that took place in Leeville. Such lynchings cannot be explained by the desire to control Negro crime or even entirely by the desire to preserve white supremacy. Negroes have sometimes been lynched because it suited the selfish interest of whites to be rid of them. In particular cases it is quite clear that this kind of motive operated. John Dollard reports in *Caste and Class in a Southern Town* (1937) a case in which a Negro was brutally whipped for the alleged "crime" of winking at a white woman. The husband of the woman led the mob in its defense of her virtue. He was a cabinetmaker and so was the Negro victim. After it was all over, folks recollected that the Negro's business had recently done very well, while the white man's had declined.

Raper reports of another case that: ". . . opinion was expressed in Scooba, Mississippi, that the two Negroes lynched there, on accusations of robbery, may have been the victims of an artful scheme on the part of their accusers to get money from the community to continue an interrupted motor trip" (1933, p. 35). The Leeville lynching, you may remember, turned into a general terrorization; the slogan of the destructive mob became, "run all the niggers out of Leeville." The Negroes in Leeville in 1930 were in competition with the whites for the very meager living available.

Lynchings in the South have usually occurred in poor rural counties where the Negro population was greatly outnumbered by the white population. These facts suggest that economic competition helped to create the wish to lynch. The Southern Commission on the Study of Lynchings (1931) studied in detail the twenty-one lynchings that took place in 1930. The counties in which the lynchings occurred were, by comparison with other counties in the same states, far below the economic average. In tax valuation, bank deposits, per capita income, farm and automobile ownership the lynching counties were strikingly inferior. Raper (1933) working on the Southern Commission, discovered that from 1900–30 the lynching rate per one thousand Negroes varied significantly with the white-Negro ratio of dwellers in a county. In "Black Belt" counties, which were at least one-half Negro, the rate was 1.64 while in counties with one-fourth Negro inhabitants the rate was 1.71, and in counties with less than one-fourth Negroes it was 2.44. Raper points out that, since the Black Belt counties were run on the plantation systems, Negro tenants and wage hands were practically indispensable. In the impoverished counties where the Negroes were a small minority they were also economic competitors with the poor whites and it was the poor whites who were the usual lynchers.

Lynching as Displaced Aggression. County by county statistics on lynching suggest a kind of motivation that is less rational than the desire to be rid of a competitor; they suggest an aggression that has been "displaced." When an animal or a human being is moving toward a goal, anything that impedes progress toward the goal is said to be a cause of frustration and frustration very often produces aggression (Dollard, et al., 1939). In poor rural Southern counties one would estimate the level of human frustration to have been high. It would have been high for economic reasons but also perhaps because of isolation and because the Protestant fundamentalist religion that prevailed in these counties forbade card-playing, dancing and theater attendance. When aggression is directed against the source of frustration in such a way as to relieve frustration then aggression is a "rational" act in the minimal sense of being instrumental. Driving the Negroes out of Leeville in order to improve employment opportunities for whites would have been this kind of direct aggression. But aggression can be displaced from actual sources of frustration to targets that are recommended by nothing but their defenselessness. It seems probable that the Negro because of his second-class citizenhip has often been the recipient of aggression generated by frustrations of which he was in no sense the cause.

Freud wrote about the displacement of aggression as it appeared in his patients and there have been some efforts to demonstrate the phenomenon in controlled circumstances (Dollard, et al., 1939). Freud was not the first to recognize displacement of aggression. The phenomenon is illustrated and the principle formulated in Sheridan's play *The Rivals* (1775). Sheridan causes the aggressive impulse to be inspired by a superior in each case and then displaced to an inferior; the antagonism bumps downhill from Sir Anthony Absolute to his son, Captain Absolute, to an adult servant, Fag, to a serving boy. We can trace its course with a few short excerpts, omitting some speeches that separate them in the play.

> SIR ANTHONY TO CAPTAIN ABSOLUTE: "—I'll disown you, I'll disinherit you, I'll unget you! and—d—n me, if ever I call you Jack again!"
> CAPTAIN ABSOLUTE TO FAG: "Cease your impertinence sir, at present.— Did you come in for nothing more?—Stand out of the way!" *Pushes him aside, and exit.*
> Boy. "Mr. Fag! Mr. Fag! Your master calls you."
> FAG. "Well, you little dirty puppy, you need not bawl so!" (Sheridan, in Nettleton and Case, 1939, p. 815).

A production I once saw at Wellesley College tacked on an exchange not written by Sheridan. The boy was asked where he was going and he answered: "Below stairs, sir, to kick cat." Sheridan puts the principle of this scene very neatly: "When one is vexed by one person, to revenge one's self on another who comes in the way—is the vilest injustice!" (p. 815). Probably the Negro has often been the victim of this vilest injustice.

Lynching and the Miscegenation Tabu. The motives we have invoked to account for lynching leave an unexplained residue, the residue of sexual sadism. It was almost routine in the mob lynching to unsex the victim. At Moultrie, Georgia, in 1921 the man's chopped-off parts were forced into his mouth (Ginzburg, 1962). At a lynching in Nodena, Arkansas, when a man was roasted alive, efforts were repeatedly made to revive him and prolong his suffering. Burning and mutilation played no part in the lynchings of frontier days but they have usually occurred in mob lynchings of Negroes. The motives we have listed are not able to explain these horrors. These effects do not inhabit the same universe with the causes we have discovered. There must be some additional need in the lyncher.

In the American South and also in South Africa there is a miscegenation tabu set in a pattern of evidence something like the pattern Freud exposed for the incest tabu. Freud suggested that we consider the implications of three facts: 1) Human beings express revulsion at incest; 2) Incest is forbidden and the most severe punishments await anyone who commits incest; 3) Incest does sometimes happen. What does this pattern suggest about human nature? That there is an instinctive horror of incest? If so, why should there be prohibitions and punishments to prevent its occurrence? The instinctive in man does not require legal reinforcement. And why should incest occur? Is the instinct fitfully suspended? Freud judged that the pattern of evidence forced the conclusion that human beings had both a great desire for incest and a great horror of it. The legal sanctions express the horror but they also witness to the desire which is not invariably contained.

With regard to miscegenation the patterns for the white man and woman differ. Some white men in all circumstances would deny any sexual interest in Negro women and would say that the idea disgusted them. More white men would say this in some, relatively proper, circumstances. But many among themselves and feeling relaxed would talk in a notably salacious way about Negro women. The attraction felt sometimes exceeds that felt for white women. Why should that be so? Perhaps because helplessness is stimulating or perhaps because respect is inhibiting. From the earliest history of this country laws were passed against racial intermarriage. Many laws went so far as to prohibit such casual contacts as sitting together on the same bench. In South Africa too there are such laws. Nevertheless it has been estimated that between 70 and 80 per cent of American Negroes have at least one white forebear (Herskovits, 1930; Wirth and Goldhamer, 1944). In South Africa there are millions of "coloreds" or persons of mixed ancestry.

White men copulate with Negro women but do not marry them. Slaveowners sometimes bred themselves a larger slave population by the women they owned. Southern white boys, too young to marry, were often encouraged to use Negro women to take the edge off their desires. The men did not, of course, marry the girls; that would have been ruinous. Probably there has been and is some guilt about this sexual exploitation and that guilt is somewhat relieved by imagining the Negro woman to be a hot-blooded creature who seduces the white man. The stereotype makes a comfortable rationalization. But the human mind seeks always the broader generalization and the broader generalization in this case is not so comfortable. If the Negro woman is hot-blooded and abandoned, what should the Negro man be like? As Myrdal (1944) and Baldwin (1964) and others have observed, the Negro man is presumed to be a sexual athlete, superior in this regard to the white man.

Southern white women do not say much on the subject of the sexual attractiveness of Negro men. But their husbands and brothers will say it for them. The ladies find the Negro brutes revolting. But the mind just cannot stop entertaining generalizations. If a white man can find colored girls so titillating why then may not a white woman find the Negro men exciting? And if Negro men are especially accomplished copulators the women may like them especially well. This must be a very distasteful line of thought for the white man who likes his colored girls dirty but his white women pure, for the man who would believe that wives, mothers, and sisters are women who know the meaning of love but not of sex. "How would you like your sister to marry one?" has been the archetypal question in both North and South for generations. No one worries much about his brother marrying one.

What do the women feel about all this? Probably most of them, in the past, found it agreeable to seem a purer creation than the male, as far as sex is concerned a less "appetitive" creation. And certainly they averred that the Negro man did not attract them. If, sometimes, they felt attracted or behaved familiarly it must have been very important to them to deny the attraction and to blame the familiarity on the Negro. And it must have been important to their menfolk to agree with them.

Approximately 25 per cent of lynchings of Negroes have been for alleged rape or alleged attempted rape (Guzman, 1952). Walter White, a past president of the National Association for the Advancement of Colored People, once wrote a novel (1929) in which a character holds that not once in all the lynchings where rape was alleged had such a crime occurred. While this is probably not true it is true that in the cases that have been closely studied there was always some doubt about the truth of the charge. But then that is the nature of the crime. It is not easily proved. The woman accuses and the man denies. In the South the presumption has been that the community must act as if the woman had told the truth. It would be too strong to say that the presumption has been that the woman has in fact told the truth. The presumption is rather that all must act as if she had. Of course an outsider does not feel the force of this norm and so Dollard could write: "In relation to this idea I cannot refrain from guessing that the accusations of the Negro man by the white woman may often times be a denial of her own excitation directed toward the Negro" (1937, p. 333).

An important motive behind many lynchings has been denial of the possibility that a white woman could be attracted to a Negro man. The alleged "crime" in many lynchings has been trifling—writing a note to a white woman or winking at a white woman. These were not economic threats or threats to white supremacy but they were sexual threats, they were intimacies that must not seem to have been desired by the woman. Even when it was clear that the woman made no claim to innocence and was herself clearly responsible for what had happened the Negro was punished. A Negro who operated a brothel for Negroes had two white girls there for a time and of course he had to be lynched (Ginzburg, 1962). If the woman did not cooperate in sustaining the rape fiction, as sometimes happened when a white girl had taken a Negro lover, the girl herself went in danger of lynching. Sexual mutilation of lynched Negroes could have been a symbolic rite to exorcise fear of what may have been in the white woman's mind. A Black Muslim speaking of Southern poor whites has described the role of sex in lynchings much more succinctly than we have done: "They can't keep out of the Black Man's bed, and they have to keep lynching to keep it covered up" (Lincoln, 1961, p. 124).

The complicated problem in the case of lynchings (and also of race riots) is to account for the existence of the non-normative aggressive impulse. It takes more than a conducive occasion to make a person commit murder; it takes a certain kind of life history. The non-normative impulses acted out in expressive crowds, such as revival meetings also have complex origins. Not everyone is prepared to "wrestle with the spirit" and "speak in tongues." By contrast the impulse to escape from a burning theater or from a sinking ship seems to depend on something as simple and general as the wish to survive.

Hostility and Expression as Outcomes of Games. Given the counter-normative impulse and also the norms of restraint there remains a problem of mob psychology. Ordinarily, people who have some latent desire to lynch or riot, some need to experience conversion, do not do so. But when large numbers of such people are gathered together in one place with the physical possibility of acting out the counter-normative impulse they will often do it. Why should congregation and communication change the balance of forces?

The payoff matrix that I imagine for such mobs as the one that gathered before the Leeville courthouse is fundamentally different from the matrix for panics. Again let us represent the participants as a person, P, and a group, G. The two actions that might be taken, the actions following from the conflicting impulses, may be represented as taking part in a lynching ("Lynch") or refraining from doing so ("Not lynch"). The options for P and G are the same. What should the outcome be?

There were several thousand people in the mob at Leeville and only four Texas Rangers to protect the prisoner. The local police were busy directing traffic. It must have seemed to the mob that if everyone would participate in the lynching then no one could be punished for it and no one would be criticized for it. If everyone would help to lynch the prisoner then everyone could enjoy the prisoner's agony without fear of punishment and perhaps even with some sense of having helped to uphold an ideal. For both P and G to choose to lynch then would produce the most preferred outcome ($++$) for both of them. If neither P nor G attempted to lynch the Negro then all would have had a hot day in the sun with little entertainment or satisfaction and that would seem to be a less preferred outcome for both, though not a clearly disagreeable outcome. It can be represented as 0.

While the payoff matrix is not yet complete we are already in a position to understand the importance of numbers in a lynching or riot, to understand why there must be many people of like mind gathered together. For an escape panic or an acquisitive panic there must be enough people to create a competition for a scarce good and the number will be relative to the supply of the good. For an unlawful hostile outburst there must be enough people to overwhelm the police, and enough people all together so that each one can feel anonymous and therefore secure against legal reprisals. In addition, numbers help to create a temporary belief that the unlawful action is a morally right action. F. H. Allport (1924) used the phrase "impression of universality" to refer to the sense one sometimes has in a crowd that everyone approves of an unlawful action and that the action must therefore be right.

There exist odd bits of evidence for the reality of the "impression of universality." Raper (1933) tells of a lynching crowd that only numbered about seventy people. Members wanted at least one hundred because they had some idea that one hundred would make the whole thing "legal." After the Detroit race riot some participants accounted for their own activities in terms that suggest an impression of universality: "We were about 15 feet from the men when Aldo pulled up, almost stopped, and shot. He wasn't bothering us. But other people were fighting and killing and we felt like it too" (Lee and Humphrey, 1943, p. 38). The "impression of universality" is temporary. When the crowd is dispelled, after the riot or lynching, the usual norms reassert themselves and some participants at least suffer a moral hangover.

If general participation in an unlawful aggressive action is to be the most preferred outcome for the members of a crowd, that crowd must exceed some minimal size. No single number can be specified since it must depend upon such factors as the size and determination of the police force. However, the significance of numbers seems to be generally the same for riots, lynchings, and expressive behavior and different from the significance of numbers for panics. In a panic, numbers are important because they create competition for a good. In hostile and expressive outbursts numbers are important because they make for anonymity and an impression of universality.

The most-preferred outcomes in the matrix of Table 14-4 are the same for both P and G and so there is not yet any conflict of interests or competition in the matrix. If this were the whole story the game would be a trivial one since everyone would without hesitation act so as to produce the desired outcome. However, we have yet to fill in the outcomes to be expected when P and G take different actions.

Suppose P elects to lynch and rushes the courthouse with a gun whereas the crowd, as a whole, decides to refrain. P would run a serious risk. He might be shot or arrested; a least preferred outcome for P $(--)$. For G this outcome would be a shade more entertaining than just going home without any action at all and so it can be represented as $+$. If G were to lynch and P to hold back the outcomes would not simply be reversed for the reason that G is a crowd and P only one person. This is one of the limitations of treating the situation as a two-person problem instead of as the many-person problem it really is. Notice, however, that if G is thought of as any person other than P the outcomes would be reversed. For G who acted to lynch there would be the risk of arrest $(--)$ and for P who refrained there would be some small entertainment. The full matrix appears as Table 14-4.

The outcomes following from different actions by P and G introduce a conflict of interest but a conflict quite unlike the conflict that lies behind panic. In the case of panic one participant's most preferred outcome corresponds with another participant's least preferred outcome and so each must be suspicious that the other will sacrifice him. In the present case the participants disagree on their second and fourth choices but they

TABLE 14-4. PAYOFF MATRIX FOR A LYNCHING MOB

	G	
	Lynch	Not lynch
P Lynch	++ for P; ++ for G	-- for P; + for G
Not lynch	+ for P; -- for G	0 for P; 0 for G

agree on their first and third choices. In the games to which game theory applies each participant must know the preferences of the other participants. If the condition held for the present case, P would know that G prefers the outcome in which everyone takes part in a lynching, and so P would confidently choose to lynch, knowing that G would do the same.

In real crowds, with some potential for lynching or rioting or for outlandish expressive behavior members are not ordinarily certain of one another's preferences. They are especially uncertain when they first congregate. Do the others really want, above all, to have a lynching, or to let themselves go in religious frenzy? One cannot be sure; not at least as sure as one can be in a fire that each other person wants, most of all, to escape without injury.

The Leeville crowd began gathering in the early morning but did not take action until the afternoon. In the interval they "milled" about. The term "milling" was originally applied to the slow, circular, aimless movement of cattle. Some such movement often occurs in crowds before they become actively aggressive or expressive and some students of collective behavior have considered "milling" to be an essential prerequisite to mob action. What is it that milling accomplishes? It seems to be primarily a process of informal communication, a process by which members learn that they are of one mind, that they are individually eager to lynch, riot, or otherwise "let go." It is a process of acquainting one another with their preferences and when those preferences correspond with the matrix of Table 14-4 the crowd members are ready for action.

The Role of Rumor. In the milling process rumors are likely to be transmitted which help to establish and communicate the matrix. In Leeville there was a very telling rumor: the governor, it was said, had telegraphed the Rangers not to shoot anyone, no matter what the crowd did to the Negro. The rumor was untrue but it helped to establish the most preferred outcome—general participation in a lynching. Without the assurance that no one would be shot each participant might have had as first choice the outcome in which others attempt to lynch and get shot while he refrains and watches.

Allport and Postman (1947) have used a laboratory method to simulate certain aspects of rumor transmission. One subject looks at a picture of some occurrence; in a famous example the occurrence is an altercation in a subway train. The picture contains a wealth of detail: one quarreling man is a Negro and one is white, the white man wields a razor; other passengers watch from the sidelines; there are street names visible and newspapers and the like. The first subject, while looking at the picture, describes it in great detail to a second subject who is not able to see the picture. The second subject relays the story as best he can remember it to a third subject who has not heard the first version. And the chain of successive communications goes on, through as many links as may be desired. The interest is in the transformations of content that occur across transmissions.

In the laboratory problem certain effects are quite reliably obtained. There is, of course, a great loss of detail between the first and second versions and some further loss in the next few versions with a leveling-off thereafter. Details are sometimes retained but altered so as to bring them into conformity with conventional expectation; a result that Allport and Postman call "assimilation." In the case of the fight in a subway the razor which was actually in the white man's hand sometimes comes to be reported in the Negro's hand.

In some respects the laboratory problem is unlike the transmission of real rumors and so certain laboratory effects do not appear in field studies (Peterson and Gist, 1951). Outside the laboratory it does not often happen that one person describes an event, while watching it, to someone who is not watching it. It does often happen that one person who has seen an event recounts it from memory to someone who has not seen it but the account from memory cannot have the circumstantial detail of the account that is produced while watching the event. Consequently the drastic loss of detail, or "leveling," that Allport and Postman obtained is not usual in the transmission of real rumors.

Assimiliation effects such as the one obtained with the razor do occur outside the laboratory. The two rumors that helped to precipitate the Detroit rumor may have originated in the same real event and assumed unlike forms congruent with the expectations of the persons composing the two transmission chains. However, more than conventional expectation is involved when rumors circulate through a crowd. The transmitters possess a common conflict of impulse and the rumor is likely to be shaped by those impulses so as to support a certain conception of the common situation, a conception that will support action (Turner and Killian, 1957).

Milling and rumor and mutual assurance are seldom sufficient to create the matrix of Table 14-4. The consequences of a general violation of the norms cannot be foreseen with perfect confidence. It is always possible that the Rangers will fire, that the National Guard will appear. In a revival meeting it is always possible that the first extravagant confession will be laughed at; in a riot the police may decide to enforce the law after all. All these uncertainties and hesitations will vanish if someone acts and is not arrested or laughed at or condemned. The perfect releaser in this situation is the action of another. In short the explosive charge must be "triggered."

The Leader as "Trigger." Triggering mob action is a kind of leadership in the sense that the trigger does first what others do subsequently. Leadership, we saw in Chapter 13, is in large degree a function of the group led. Conventional leadership falls to those who best realize the conventional norms; it falls to people having high status. Leadership in a mob that violates conventional norms falls to those in whom the norms are weakest, to persons of low status. Some field work and experimentation on behavioral contagion among children carried out by Grosser, Polansky, and Lippitt (1951) is relevant here. These investigators found that behavior on which there is no serious restraint is imitatively picked up from individuals having high group prestige. When, however, there is a strong desire to act and also strong social restraint against acting, it is certain "impulsive" children who lead the way, children not having high prestige in the group.

Who are the impulsive triggers in a hostile mob outburst? The acknowledged leader of the Leeville mob was Hank Smith, a man who had no regular occupation, could neither read nor write, drank heavily, and had been before the courts for bootlegging. A few years after the events at Leeville he was killed in a drunken brawl on a South Texas sheep ranch. At least eleven other active participants had previous police records (Cantril, 1941). Following the 1943 riot in Detroit many leaders were identified as members of criminal gangs. Akers and Fox (1944) found that 74 per cent of the rioters who were arrested had police records. The *New York Herald Tribune* of February 9, 1936, carried a story about one Carl "Cowboy" Fisher, a young man who had led a mob in the lynching of a Negro three years earlier. The Negro had been lynched for the alleged crime of rape. The *Tribune* reported that Cowboy Fisher had just been sentenced to two years in prison for attempted rape (Ginzburg, 1962).

The people who trigger mob action are not always undersocialized, at least not permanently so. Alcohol can render someone temporarily unrestrained and so qualified to function as a trigger. In revival meetings the triggering problem is often solved by hired collaborators who are the first to come forward, make confessions and experience conversions. Sometimes revivalists start things off with a staged "miracle cure." When some have behaved in an undignified and abandoned way others feel free to do the same.

Expressive outbursts are usually harmless but hostile outbursts are not harmless and we should like to prevent their occurrence. What, in view of the present analysis, should be the most effective means of doing so? Elimination of the hostile impulse is the most fundamental answer but it is a remote answer and an answer to many problems other than collective behavior. Given the hostile impulse and also the inhibiting norm how can collective acting out of the impulse be prevented?

If the payoff matrix of Table 14-4 represents a collective state of mind in which collective outbursts will occur then either the matrix itself or knowledge of its existence must be prevented. The most effective way to destroy the matrix is to guarantee arrest and punishment for crowd participants. Chadbourne reported in 1933 that since 1900 only .8 of one per cent of the lynchings in the United States had been followed by conviction of the lynchers. Since the 1930's, however, both local and federal efforts to convict lynchers have been more strenuous and this is probably the chief reason why lynchings have been less common in recent years. However in 1964 it is still difficult to obtain convictions in such cases in many Southern courts. If individuals in a crowd could be as sure of punishment as are individuals by themselves then the crowd would lose its power to release evil.

If arrest is not certain or does not seem certain and a large crowd of persons gathers who are disposed to lynch or riot, providing only that others will do the same, then one must interfere with communication. The members must not be allowed to discover how like-minded they are. In short, police must interfere with the milling and rumor process; the crowd must be dispersed. If dispersal is not accomplished and the crowd stands on the brink of action, needing only a leader who will initiate unlawful action and so demonstrate the general readiness to take such action, the police may still save the situation by spotting potential leaders and picking them off for arrest. These recommendations correspond quite well with advice given by Joseph D. Lohman in his manual for the Chicago Park District called *The Police and Minority Groups* (1947). But neither Lohman's book nor this chapter can tell what to do when the police are in sympathy with the mob and this has often been the case.

CONCLUSION

In panics and riots and lynchings and expressive revelry man acts out impulses that he usually does not act out. Le Bon thought it important to explain why this should be so, why inoffensive citizens who, under ordinary circumstances, would have been "peaceable notaries or virtuous magistrates" should turn savage in a Revolutionary mob. It seemed to Le Bon that when individuals are formed into a crowd there is created "a new body possessing properties quite different from those of the bodies that have served to form it." It seems to me, too, that something new is created. To describe this new thing, this "emergent," as a "group mind" does not seem to be seriously misleading. It may be a degree more illuminating to say that what emerges in the crowd is a payoff matrix that does not exist for the members when they do not compose a crowd.

The basic situation is one of communication among persons having a similar conflict of mind, between an impulse that is socialized and one that is not, with the physical possibility of acting out the unsocialized impulse. This is the common set of circumstances prerequisite to every sort of acting-out crowd. Where the conflict is between the wish to escape or acquire, at whatever cost, and the requirement to respect the rights of others and where the number of persons is great enough in relation to the supply of exits or goods, to create a competition, panic will occur. It will occur because the total set of conditions produces a payoff matrix such that each person must choose to act in an unsocialized way. When the conflict concerns aggression and restraint, or expression and restraint, and the numbers are sufficient to produce anonymity and the impression of universality, either a hostile outburst or an expressive outburst will occur. The outburst will occur because the total set of conditions produces a payoff matrix such that each person can act on his unsocialized impulse and be free of punishment or guilt. Potential participants in an aggressive or hostile outburst can never be as sure of the nature of the payoff matrix, as sure of what others will do as can potential participants in a panic. For this reason hostile and expressive outbursts usually require to be triggered. Someone must initiate action so that others can believe in the action-readiness of the mass.

REFERENCES

Akers, E. R., & Fox, V. The Detroit rioters and looters committed to prison. *J. crim. Law Criminol.*, 1944, **35**, 105–110.

Allport, F. H. *Social psychology*. Cambridge: Houghton Mifflin, 1924.

Allport, G. W., & Postman, L. *The psychology of rumor*. New York: Holt, 1947.

Baldwin, J. Down at the cross: Letter from a region in my mind. In J. Baldwin, *The fire next time*. New York: Dial, 1963.

Baldwin, J. *Blues for Mister Charlie*. New York: Dial, 1964.

Bird, R. S. Ten Negroes. *New York Herald Tribune*, April 30, 1963.

Blue, J. T. The relationship of juvenile delinquency, race and economic status. *J. Negro Educ.*, 1948, **17**, 469–477.

Blumer, H. Collective behavior. In A. McC. Lee (Ed.), *New outline of the principles of sociology*. New York: Barnes & Noble, 1951.

Bogardus, E. S. *Fundamentals of social psychology*. New York: Appleton-Century, 1942.

Bohannan, P. (Ed.), *African homicide and suicide*. Princeton: Princeton University. Press, 1960.

Boisen, A. T. Economic distress and religious experience. A study of the Holy Rollers. *Psychiatry*, 1939, **2**, 185–194.

Brown, R. W. Mass phenomena. In G. Lindzey (Ed.), *Handbook of social psychology*. Vol. II. Cambridge: Addison-Wesley, 1954.

Cantril, H. *The invasion from Mars*. Princeton: Princeton Univer. Press, 1940.

Cantril, H. *The psychology of social movements*. New York: Wiley, 1941.

Chadbourne, J. H. *Lynching and the law*. Chapel Hill: Univer. of North Carolina Press, 1933.

Cutler, J. E. *Lynch-law*. London: Longmans Green, 1905.

Davenport, F. M. *Primitive traits in religious revivals*. New York: Macmillan, 1905.

Dollard, J. *Caste and class in a Southern town*. New Haven: Yale Univer. Press, 1937.

Dollard, J., Doob, L. W., Miller, N. E., Mowrer, O. H., & Sears, R. R. *Frustration and aggression*. New Haven: Yale Univer. Press, 1939.

Federal Bureau of Investigation, *Uniform Crime Reports*, 1960–61. Washington, D.C.: U.S. Government Printing Office, 1961–62.

Federal Bureau of Prisons. Executions, 1961. *National Prisoner Statistics*, April, 1962, **28**.

Federal Bureau of Prisons, *National prisoner statistics: Prisoners released from state and federal institutions, 1951*. Atlanta, Ga.: United States Penitentiary, 1955.

Federal Bureau of Prisons, *National prisoner statistics: Prisoners released from state and federal institutions, 1952 and 1953*. Atlanta, Ga.: United States Penitentiary, 1957.

Flugel, J. C. *The psychology of clothes*. London: Hogarth, 1930.

French, J. R. P. Organized and unorganized groups under fear and frustration. *University of Iowa studies: Studies in child welfare*. Iowa City: Univer. of Iowa Press, 1944.

Freud, S. *Group psychology and the analysis of the ego*. London: Hogarth, 1922.

Ginzburg, R. *100 years of lynching*. New York: Lancer Books, 1962.

Grosser, C., Polansky, N., & Lippitt, R. A laboratory study of behavioral contagion. *Hum. Relat.*, 1951, **4**, 115–142.

Guzman, J. P. (Ed.) *Negro Year Book, 1952*. Tuskegee: Tuskegee Institute, 1952.

Herskovits, M. J. *The anthropometry of the American Negro*. New York: Columbia Univer. Press, 1930.

Hurlock, E. B. *The psychology of dress: An analysis of fashion and its motive*. New York: Ronald, 1929.

Janis, I. L. *Air war and emotional stress*. New York: McGraw-Hill, 1951.

Le Bon, G. *The crowd*. (1st ed., 1895) New York: Viking, 1960.

Lee, A. McC., & Humphrey, N. D. *Race riot*. New York: Dryden, 1943.

Lincoln, C. E. *The Black Muslims in America*. Boston: Beacon, 1961.

Lohman, J. D. *The police and minority groups*. Chicago: Chicago Park District, 1947.

London, N. J., & Myers, J. K. Young offenders: Psychopathology and social factors. *Arch. gen. Psychiat.*, 1961, **4**, 274–282.

Luce, R. D., & Raiffa, H. *Games and decisions*. New York: Wiley, 1957.

Mackay, C. *Extraordinary popular delusions and the madness of crowds.* (1st ed., 1841) New York: Farrar, Straus & Cudahy, 1962.

McDougall, W. *The group mind.* Cambridge, Eng.: Cambridge Univer. Press, 1920.

McDougall, W. Professor Freud's group psychology and his theory of suggestion. *Brit. J. med. Psychol.*, 1925, **5**, 14–28.

Meier, N. C., Mennenga, G. H., & Stoltz, H. Z. An experimental approach to the study of mob behavior. *J. abnorm. soc. Psychol.*, 1941, **36**, 506–524.

Melville, L. *The south sea bubble.* London: Daniel O'Connor, 1921.

Mencken, H. L. Clinical notes. *The American Mercury*, 1924, **3**, 194–195.

Miller, N. E., & Dollard, J. *Social learning and imitation.* New Haven: Yale Univer. Press, 1941.

Mintz, A. Non-adaptive group behavior. *J. abnorm. soc. Psychol.*, 1951, **46**, 150–159.

Moses, E. R. Differentials in crime rates between Negroes and whites, based on comparisons of four socio-economically equated areas. *Amer. sociol. Rev.*, 1947, **12**, 411–420.

Myrdal, G. *An American dilemma.* Vol. I. New York: Harper, 1944.

Nystrom, P. H. *Economics of fashion.* New York: Ronald Press, 1928.

Park, R. E., & Burgess, E. W. *Introduction to the science of sociology.* Chicago: Univer. of Chicago Press, 1921.

Parsons, T. *The social system.* New York: Free Press, 1951.

Parsons, T., & Shils, E. A. *Toward a general theory of action.* Cambridge: Harvard Univer. Press, 1953.

Penrose, L. S. *On the objective study of crowd behaviour.* London: H. K. Lewis, 1952.

Peterson, W. A., & Gist, N. P. Rumor and public opinion. *Amer. J. Sociol.*, 1951, **57**, 159–167.

Pettigrew, T. *A profile of the Negro American.* Princeton: D. Van Nostrand, 1964.

Pettigrew, T. F., & Rosalind B. Spier. The ecological structure of Negro homicide. *Amer. J. Sociol.*, 1962, **67**, 621–629.

Posthumus, N. W. The tulip mania in Holland in the years 1636 and 1637. *J. econ. business History*, 1928, **1**, 434–466.

Quarantelli, E. L. The nature and conditions of panic. *Amer. J. Sociol.*, 1954, **60**, 267–275.

Raper, A. *The tragedy of lynching.* U.S. No. 614.35. Chapel Hill: Univer. of North Carolina Press, 1933.

Rudé, G. *The crowd in the French Revolution.* Oxford: Clarendon Press, 1959.

Ruppelt, E. J. *The report on unidentified flying objects.* Garden City: Doubleday, 1956.

Samuelson, P. A. *Economics: An introductory analysis.* (4th ed.) New York: McGraw-Hill, 1958.

Schmid, C. F. Urban crime areas: Parts I and II. *Amer. sociol. Rev.*, 1960, **25**, 527–642, 655–678.

Sheridan, R. B. The rivals. (1st ed., 1775) In G. H. Nettleton & A. E. Case, (Eds.), *British dramatists from Dryden to Sheridan.* Cambridge, Mass.: Houghton Mifflin, 1939.

Smelser, N. J. *Theory of collective behavior.* New York: Free Press, 1963.

Southern Commission on the Study of Lynching. *Lynchings and what they mean.* U.S. 614.20. Atlanta, Ga., 1931.

Tarde, G. *The laws of imitation*. Transl. by Elsie Parsons. New York: Holt, 1903.

Turner, R. H., & Killian, L. M. *Collective behavior*. Englewood Cliffs: Prentice-Hall, 1957.

Vanderblue, H. B. The Florida land boom. *J. Land Pub. Utility Econ.*, 1927, 3, 113–131, 252–269.

Vaught, Elsie. The release and heightening of individual reactions in crowds. *J. abnorm. soc. Psychol.*, 1928, 22, 404–405.

Von Hentig, H. Criminality of the Negro. *J. crim. Law Crim.*, 1940, 30, 662–680.

Von Neumann, J., & Morgenstern, O. *Theory of games and economic behavior*. Princeton: Princeton Univer. Press, 1944.

White, W. *Rope and faggot*. New York: Knopf, 1929.

Wirth, L., & Goldhamer, H. Passing. In O. Klineberg (Ed.), *Characteristics of the American Negro*. New York: Harper, 1944.

Wolfgang, M. E. *Patterns in criminal homicide*. Philadelphia: Univer. of Penn. Press, 1958.

List of Journal Abbreviations

Amer. Anthropologist	American Anthropologist
Amer. J. Psychol.	American Journal of Psychology
Amer. J. Sociol.	American Journal of Sociology
Amer. midl. Nat.	American Midland Naturalist
Amer. Psychologist	American Psychologist
Amer. sociol. Rev.	American Sociological Review
Ann. Amer. Acad. polit. so-cial Sci.	Annals of American Academy of Political and Social Science
Ann. N. Y. Acad. Sci.	Annals of the New York Academy of Sciences
Arch. gen. Psychiat.	Archives of General Psychiatry
Arch. Psychol., Geneva	Archives de Psychologie
Arch. Psychol.	Archives of Psychology
Arch. néerl. Zool.	Archives néerlandaises de zoologie
Aust. J. Psychol.	Australian Journal of Psychology
Aust. J. Zool.	Australian Journal of Zoology
Behav. Sci.	Behavioral Science
Beitr, fortpfl. Biol. Vögel	Beitraege zur fortpflanzungs Biologie der Vögel
Brit. J. Anim. Behav.	British Journal of Animal Behaviour
Brit. J. educ. Psychol.	British Journal of Educational Psychology

Brit. J. med. Psychol.	British Journal of Medical Psychology
Brit. J. Psychol.	British Journal of Psychology
Brit. J. Sociol.	British Journal of Sociology
Canad. J. Psychol.	Canadian Journal of Psychology
Child Develpm.	Child Development
Clin. Res.	Clinical Research
Comp. Psychol. Monogr.	Comparative Psychology Monographs
Ecol. Monogr.	Ecological Monographs
Educ. psychol. Measmt	Educational and Psychological Measurement
Fed. Probation	Federal Probation
Genet. Psychol. Monogr.	Genetic Psychology Monographs
Hum. Relat.	Human Relations
Industr. Mgmt Rev.	Industrial Management Review
Int. J. Amer. Ling.	International Journal of American Linguistics
J. abnorm. soc. Psychol.	Journal of Abnormal and Social Psychology
J. Acoust. Soc. Amer.	Journal of the Acoustical Society of America
J. appl. Psychol.	Journal of Applied Psychology
J. comp. physiol. Psychol.	Journal of Comparative and Physiological Psychology
J. comp. Psychol.	Journal of Comparative Psychology
J. conflict Resolut.	Journal of Conflict Resolution
J. crim. Law Criminol.	Journal of Criminal Law and Criminology
J. econ. business History	Journal of Economic and Business History
J. educ. Psychol.	Journal of Educational Psychology
J. exp. Psychol.	Journal of Experimental Psychology
J. Ornithol.	Journal für Ornithologie
J. gen. Psychol.	Journal of General Psychology
J. genet. Psychol.	Journal of Genetic Psychology
J. land pub. utility Econ.	Journal of Land and Public Utility Economics
J. Negro Educ.	Journal of Negro Education
J. Pers.	Journal of Personality
J. Psychol.	Journal of Psychology
J. Relig.	Journal of Religion
J. soc. Psychol.	Journal of Social Psychology
J. Speech	Journal of Speech
J. speech Disord.	Journal of Speech Disorders
J. speech hear. Disord.	Journal of Speech and Hearing Disorders
J. verbal Learn. verbal Behav.	Journal of Verbal Learning and Verbal Behavior
Lang. Speech	Language and Speech
Mankind Quart.	Mankind Quarterly
Monogr. Soc. Res. Child Develpm.	Monographs of the Society for Research in Child Development

Opin. News	Opinion News
Pediatrics Sem.	Pediatrics Seminar
Psychoanal. Quart.	Psychoanalytic Quarterly
Psychol. Bull.	Psychological Bulletin
Psychol. Clin.	Psychological Clinic
Psychol. Monogr.	Psychological Monographs: General and Applied
Psychol. Rep.	Psychological Reports
Psychol. Rev.	Psychological Review
Psychometr. Monogr.	Psychometric Monographs
Psychosom. Med.	Psychosomatic Medicine
Publ. Opin. Quart.	Public Opinion Quarterly
Rev. Franc. d'Endocrinol.	Revue Française d'Endocrinologie
Scand. J. Psychol., Stockholm	Scandinavian Journal of Psychology
Scient. American	Scientific American
Scient. Mon.	Scientific Monthly
Soc. Forces	Social Forces
Soc. Probl.	Social Problems
U. S. Fish Wildlife fishing Bull.	U. S. Fish & Wildlife Fishing Bulletin
Vita hum., Basel	Vita Humana
Verhl. V. Int. Orn. Kongr. 1910	Verhandlungen 5th Internationaler Ornithologisch Kongress
Z. Psychol.	Zeitschrift für Psychologie
Z. Säugetierkunde	Zeitschrift für Säugetierkunde
Z. Tierpsychol.	Zeitschrift für Tierpsychologie
Zool. Anz. Supp.	Zoologischer Anzeiger, Supplement

INDEXES

Author Index

7 7 1

Subject Index